ULNERABILITY TO

VULNERABILITY TO DRUG abuse

EDITED BY

MEYER GLANTZ

AND

ROY PICKENS

AMERICAN PSYCHOLOGICAL ASSOCIATION   WASHINGTON, DC

First printing January 1992
Second printing July 1993
Third printing November 1996

Published by the
American Psychological Association
750 First Street, NE
Washington, DC 20002

Copies may be ordered from
American Psychological Association
Order Department
P.O. Box 92984
Washington, DC 20090-2984

In the U.K. and Europe, copies may be ordered from the American Psychological Association, 3 Henrietta Street, Covent Garden, London WC2E 8LU, England

Designed by Grafik Communications Ltd.
Typeset by Harper Graphics, Waldorf, MD
Printed by BookCrafters, Inc., Chelsea, MI
Technical editing and production by Olin J. Nettles

Library of Congress Cataloging-in-Publication Data
Vulnerability to drug abuse / edited by Meyer Glantz and Roy Pickens.
    p.   cm.
    Based in part on material presented at a conference held Nov.
13–14, 1989, co-sponsored by the American Psychological Association
Science Directorate and the National Institute of Drug Abuse.
    Includes index.
    ISBN 1-55798-142-6 (acid-free paper)
    1. Drug abuse—Etiology—Congresses. I. Glantz, Meyer D.
II. Pickens, Roy W. III. American Psychological Association.
Science Directorate. IV. National Institute on Drug Abuse.
    [DNLM: 1. Substance Abuse—etiology—congresses. 2. Substance
Abuse—psychology—congresses.   WM 270 V991 1989]
RC563.2.V85   1991
616.86′071—dc20
DNLM/DLC
for Library of Congress   91-35242
                                                                      CIP

Printed in the United States of America

For Benjamin and for Marks

Contents

Contributors

Arthur Alterman, University of Pennsylvania and Philadelphia Veterans Affairs Medical Center

Thomas F. Babor, University of Connecticut School of Medicine

Judith Brook, New York Medical College

Ann F. Brunswick, Columbia University

Remi J. Cadoret, University of Iowa

Richard R. Clayton, University of Kentucky

Patricia Cohen, Columbia University

Deborah Curtis, Stanford University

Mark Davies, New York State Psychiatric Institute

Meyer D. Glantz, National Institute on Drug Abuse

Ann S. Gordon, New York Medical College

Robert J. Johnson, Kent State University

Valerie Johnson, Rutgers University

Howard B. Kaplan, Texas A&M University

Denise B. Kandel, Columbia University and New York State Psychiatric Institute

Roy King, Stanford University

Guenther Knoblich, Stanford University

Erich W. Labouvie, Rutgers University

Joan McCord, Temple University

Kathleen R. Merikangas, Yale University

Peter A. Messeri, Columbia University

Ada C. Mezzich, University of Pittsburgh

Michael D. Newcomb, University of Southern California

Robert J. Pandina, Rutgers University

Roy W. Pickens, National Institute on Drug Abuse

Brigitte A. Prusoff, Yale University

Bruce J. Rounsaville, Yale University

Charles R. Schuster, National Institute on Drug Abuse

Ralph E. Tarter, University of Pittsburgh

Stephen P. Titus, Columbia University

Roger Weiss, Harvard University

Martin Whiteman, Columbia University

George E. Woody, University of Pennsylvania and Philadelphia Veterans Affairs Medical Center

Harold C. Urschel III, University of Pennsylvania and Philadelphia Veterans Affairs Medical Center

Acknowledgments

The efforts and support of many people were required to make the Vulnerability Conference and this book possible. We wish to express our great appreciation to Charles R. Schuster, Zili Amsel, and Catherine Bell-Bolek of the National Institute on Drug Abuse, and Gary VandenBos, Julia Frank-McNeil, and Barbara Calkins of the American Psychological Association. The technical assistance of Theodore Baroody and Olin J. Nettles was indispensable. We are very grateful to the authors who contributed not only their considerable expertise, but also their valuable time and support.

Forewords

D rug abuse affects everyone. Even those who do not use illegal drugs themselves may be directly affected through family or friends, and everyone is indirectly affected by the accidents, crimes, and public health expenditures that are the inevitable consequence of drug abuse. In addition, the public risk for the spread of hepatitis, AIDS, and possibly other diseases is also a consequence of drug abuse. Despite the significant gains made in the last 5 years in combating drug abuse, the necessity for improving the efficacy of the available preventive interventions is clear.

A better understanding of the interactions of genetic, psychiatric, environmental, and pharmacological factors leading to abuse would make more effective prevention possible, and this is a major priority of the National Institute on Drug Abuse (NIDA). NIDA supports a variety of research programs exploring the risk factors for drug involvement and escalation of drug use to abuse and dependence. From this research has come information that suggests that patterns of abuse and dependence have a different etiology than do other patterns of use. If this is the case, and if the factors specific to increased vulnerability to drug abuse were identified, then powerful prevention programs for higher risk individuals could be developed. With the goal of determining what research information is available on the vulnerability to drug abuse, NIDA, in collaboration with the American Psychological Association (APA), sponsored a conference on the "Transition from Drug Use to Abuse/Dependence."

The meeting, held in November 1989, drew together a multidisciplinary group of leading drug abuse etiology researchers. The participants presented original data and reviewed and synthesized the literature; both the meeting and the collaboration with APA were successful. That conference laid the groundwork for this volume. The original group of presenters revised and expanded their papers into chapters, and several additional research and review chapters were added to make this book a comprehensive state-of-the-art presentation of the latest research and theory on drug abuse vulnerability.

The research and reviews presented here indicate that those users who make the transition to higher levels of abuse have different predrug involvement characteristics than those who do not. Additionally, it appears that there is not a single critical vulnerability characteristic, but rather a complex of factors involving multiple domains ranging from the biological to the psychological and the social. Escalation to the higher levels of drug abuse seems to involve predominantly biological and psychiatric processes. Furthermore, there is more than one possible etiological path leading to drug abuse. Lastly, the findings imply that there is great potential benefit from identifying individuals who are at particularly high risk for drug abuse and dependence and using interventions that target their vulnerability characteristics. These conclusions and the others presented in this volume represent an important new perspective on the understanding of the etiology of and transition to drug abuse. They provide a preliminary basis for the development of new interventions and a direction for future research.

Charles R. Schuster, Director
National Institute on Drug Abuse

D rug abuse in the United States is a major health issue, a law enforcement problem, and a public policy issue. Psychoactive substance abuse is an integral part of American culture, studies of the lifetime prevalence of use of alcohol and illegal drugs have shown that a majority of Americans have had experience with at least one of these substances. During any given month in the past 20 years, at least 14 million individuals in the United States consumed some type of illicit drug. Each of these individuals had a specific history of drug experience and unique physiological and psychological circumstances, resulting in different patterns of risks and consequences.

The Committee for the Substance Abuse Coverage Study of the Institute of Medicine (IOM; *Treating Drug Problems*, 1990, Volume 1) reported that its combined estimate of the point-in-time need for treatment on a typical day in 1987–1988 was approximately 5.5 million individuals. This number includes about 1 in 50 household residents older than 12 years of age, more than one third of all prison and jail inmates, and more than one fourth of all parolees and probationers. The total estimate is about 2.7% of the population of the United States 12 years or older. Initial experimental drug use occurs predominantly during the teenage years. Recent research findings indicate that most new users of any drug do not progress very far, but if progression occurs (from use to abuse), it generally takes a few years following the first experimental use of any drug—usually in the teens or early 20s. The IOM further reported that progression seems to be more rapid with stimulants like cocaine and amphetamines than with other types of drugs.

The treatment and rehabilitation of addicted individuals is a costly enterprise. Major financial impact follows for both the abuser (and for his or her family) and for the community at large. From the perspective of the affected individual and his or her family, there are lost jobs, family disruption, money wasted on drugs, and physical and psychological abuse. On the part of society, there are the direct costs of law enforcement, court expenses, medical care, and rehabilitation. The financial burdens of drug abuse to individuals and society further escalate when the costs of drug-related accidents, fatalities, and crime figure in the equation. Most drug treatment and prevention services are government supported, although there is also significant private support. Expenditures for drug treatment were about $1.3 billion in 1987; prevention activities for drugs and alcohol abuse cost $212 million in 1987. Some 25% of all AIDS cases have a history of intravenous drug use; drug-abuse related AIDS costs in 1985 were about $967 million.

Thus, from a humanitarian perspective as drug abuse relates to the affected individual, and from the perspective of maximizing the cost benefit of governmental dollars, the prevention of drug abuse would be very beneficial for society. To build a maximally effective drug abuse preventive program, information is needed about individuals' specific vulnerabilities to drug abuse. The literature on drug abuse vulnerability reported in this volume represents a major effort to integrate current knowledge both in sharpening future research and in facilitating current applications.

With considerable enthusiasm, the American Psychological Association, through the APA Science Directorate, agreed to cosponsor a conference in collaboration with the National Institute on Drug Abuse (NIDA) on the "Transition from Drug Use to Abuse/Dependence." The conference was held on November 13–14, 1989. The present scholarly volume on the vulnerability to drug abuse is based, in part, on material presented at the conference. The APA is particularly proud to publish this volume, joining with NIDA in furthering research on the origins and causal factors and patterns leading to the abuse of drugs, and in creating a better understanding of the factors that predispose an individual to, or protect a person from, drug abuse. Such research is essential to the successful prevention of drug abuse.

This volume provides current information on the etiology of drug abuse, focusing on the factors that differentially affect individual behavioral outcomes (i.e., vulnerability) to drugs and on the factors that contribute to the progression from drug use to abuse. Of particular value to the drug abuse literature is a new perspective presented by the articles in this volume showing that the etiology of drug abuse is commonly very different from the etiology of nonescalating drug use and that individuals who make the transition from user to abuser have significantly different psychological and behavioral characteristics from those who do not become abusers. Understanding the factors that determine an individual's vulnerability to drug abuse is a crucial element in developing intervention strategies for prevention and treatment. We hope that this volume will give researchers and practitioners an appreciation of the heterogeneity of drug abuse patterns and of the diverse etiologies of such patterns, and thereby promote further insights for future research. This will facilitate the translation of scientific knowledge into sound clinical application.

Lewis P. Lipsitt
Executive Director for Science

Gary R. VandenBos
Executive Director, Publications
and Communications

Vulnerability to Drug Abuse: Introduction and Overview

Meyer D. Glantz and Roy W. Pickens

P eople differ in their use of illicit drugs. Some people never experiment with them. Of those who do, some discontinue use after a few experiences and never use them again. Others continue to use them on an irregular basis or become regular and consistent users. Finally, some develop pathological patterns of drug use that may terminate in addiction. Thus, not everyone uses illicit drugs, not all of those who do become regular users, and not all regular users become drug addicted. This difference in behavioral outcome is attributable to differences in "vulnerability" to drug involvement. Attempting to better understand the factors that determine vulnerability is a focus of this book. Attempting to better understand the factors that contribute to the progression from drug use to abuse is another focus of this volume.

Although particular abusable substances wax and wane in popularity over time, larger population trends demonstrate that at least some level of involvement with alcohol or drugs is very common in our society. Despite great strides in attempting to limit substance use and abuse, studies of the lifetime prevalence of consumption of alcohol and/or illegal drugs find that the vast majority of adults have had some experience with at least one psychoactive substance during their lifetime (National Institute on Drug Abuse, 1990). Vulnerability to drug problems is greater the earlier drug involvement begins; it is especially unfortunate that some degree of involvement with illegal psychoactive substances (including underage alcohol use) is currently prevalent among adolescents in our society because this early exposure increases the potential for substance abuse problems for this population.

The National Household Survey on Drug Abuse conducted by the National Institute on Drug Abuse (NIDA) found that in 1990, lifetime prevalence of illegal drug use for youth age 12 to 17 was 22.7%, use in the year prior to the survey was 15.9%, and use in the prior month was 8.1%. Comparable figures for young adults age 18 to 25 are 55.8%, 28.7%, and 14.9% respectively. Lifetime prevalence of use of alcohol for 12-to-17-year-olds was 48%, past-year use was 41%, and past month use was 24.5%. Comparable figures for young adults age 18 to 25 were 88.2%, 80.2%, and 63.3% (NIDA, 1990). Because this survey was limited by factors related to household participation and self-reports, the findings may be conservative in their estimations.

According to NIDA's 1990 National High School Senior Drug Use Survey (NIDA, 1991), 47.9% of the participating seniors reported having at least some experience with an illicit drug at least once in their life. In the year prior to the survey, 5.3% used cocaine, 27% used marijuana, 9% used an illicit prescription-type stimulant, and 80.6% used alcohol; overall, 32.5% had used some illicit drug in the previous year. Daily alcohol consumption among reporting seniors was 4%, and 32.2% reported having five or more drinks during a single drinking occasion within the previous 2 weeks. School dropouts and absentees, a more heavily drug- and alcohol-involved group, were not included in the survey. If the substance-use rates for school dropouts were included, the percentages reported above would be expected to be much higher; estimates are that drug involvement among dropouts is at least 63% higher (NIDA, 1990).

The 1987 National Adolescent Student Health Survey (American School Health Association, Association for the Advancement of Health Education, & Society for Public Health Education, 1989) reported that 20.4% of eighth graders and 24.6% of tenth graders consumed some alcohol in the previous month; 12.5% of eighth graders and 15.8% of tenth graders had a minimum of five or more drinks on at least one occasion in the previous 2 weeks. In the previous month, 3.7% of eighth graders and 8.1% of tenth graders reported having used or abused an illicit drug. Although the data from all three of these national surveys clearly demonstrate declines in drug involvement over the past decade, they also demonstrate that there is a general prevalence of exposure to, and experience with, psychoactive substances, typically before adulthood.

Federal, state, community, and private agencies have, over the pst decade, launched a host of intensive anti-drug-and-alcohol-abuse efforts. Partly as a consequence, there appears to have been a societal shift in attitudes toward tolerance of illicit drug and alcohol abuse. These efforts have had a positive effect. There are indications that the "drugs of choice" have changed in the past decade and that the level and type of use and abuse by many segments of the population have significantly diminished; however, overall levels of illicit drug and alcohol use and abuse remain at unacceptably high levels. Unfortunately, in some segments of the population, including adolescents, the level of combined illicit-drug and alcohol involvement has not changed significantly.

Transition From Use to Abuse

While any illicit drug use may be viewed as abuse, in the present volume the term *use* will refer to experimentation with or low-frequency irregular use of illicit drugs, whereas *abuse* will refer to regular or compulsive use of illicit drugs. Although such a distinction may seem artificial to some, it serves to distinguish people on the basis of whether illicit drug use has or has not become a regular feature of their life-style.

Fortunately, the majority of those who engage in the use of an illegal drug or of a restricted legal psychoactive substance (e.g., alcohol, which is prohibited for adolescents) do not escalate their involvement to drug abuse (Johnston, O'Malley, & Bachman, 1986; Kandel & Yamaguchi, 1985); unfortunately, far too many do. The factors that determine an individual's low level of drug use may not be the same as those that determine an individual's vulnerability to drug abuse. *Vulnerability* refers to the observation that individuals are differentially at risk for engaging in drug use and, in particular, for making the transition from drug use to drug abuse. We believe that individuals are premorbidly differentially at risk for drug abuse and that vulnerability to drug abuse is a critical issue.

Many clinicians and others have long believed that those users who make the transition to drug abuse have fundamentally different pre-exposure characteristics compared with users who do not make the transition. Clearly, some factors or characteristics other than vulnerability to use are involved; use is a necessary but not sufficient condition for escalation to abuse. In fact, one of the most frightening future possibilities is the development of a drug for which use is a sufficient condition for escalation to abuse.

Understanding what determines an individual's vulnerability to drug abuse is crucial to effective preventive intervention. Although there has been a fair amount of etiologically oriented drug-abuse research, the basic questions about the etiology of drug abuse remain unanswered. Much of the early research that attempted to determine the risk factors for drug abuse was plagued by serious conceptual limitations and methodological problems. For example, many early studies were based on retrospective self-reports of long-established abusers, with minimal independent verification of the collected information. Control samples were often poorly matched or not employed at all. Numerous other studies adopted a correlational design that could not discriminate causes from consequences, could not identify the nature of the correlational association, and could not determine whether the correlated behaviors were themselves the products of more fundamental and causative factors. Furthermore, these studies frequently assessed only one or perhaps a few characteristics, contributing to the impression that drug abuse was a simply determined behavior. Various patterns of drug abuse were commonly not discriminated. For example, users were sometimes grouped together regardless of which drug or drugs they used and regardless of the frequency and level of their drug involvement; infrequent "experimental" or "recreational" users were often categorized with high frequency users and abusers. Early studies often relied on convenience or other atypical samples, which produced results with questionable generalizability.

Another limitation of this early research was the failure to view drug abuse in terms of the social context in which it occurs. The same behavior will have vastly different significance and be associated with different causal factors at different points in time and for different populations. This affects the generalizability of the etiological information, a fact often not considered. For example, the factors predictive of teenage pregnancy during the 1920s might have little applicability to understanding, predicting, and preventing teen pregnancy in the 1990s. The earliest research on risk factors for drug abuse studied a highly deviant population engaged in a very exotic and rare behavior for the time. The next wave of research in the 1960s and 1970s focused on a generation in which the large majority of young individuals had some degree of involvement in illicit drug use. This risk factors for drug involvement when the behavior is extremely rare and deviant are quite different from those when at least some drug-use experience is highly prevalent. Furthermore, neither of these patterns from the past necessarily informs us about the risk factors for contemporary drug involvement. Additionally, the factors predictive of drug abuse for one segment of the population may be different from those predictive of abuse in another. Considering that early researchers used simplistic correlational models, made few of the necessary discriminations among their samples, and drew their conclusions without the perspective of the social context in which they occurred, it is not surprising that the usefulness of the early research is often questioned. Although more recent studies have typically been much more sophisticated and powerful in concept and design, they have not generally focused on the etiology of abuse as distinct from the etiology of use.

The Vulnerability Conference and This Publication

Under the cosponsorship of the National Institute on Drug Abuse and the American Psychological Association, leading drug-abuse researchers were invited to participate in a multidisciplinary conference whose purpose was to explore vulnerability to drug abuse, focusing specifically on those factors and patterns associated with the transition from drug use to abuse. Although some of the papers presented dealt with more conceptual issues, many reported original data on some aspects of the transition from drug use to abuse; all included some synthesis of research and new ideas.

The conference was held in November 1989 in Washington, D.C. The meeting was a very fruitful one and the discussions of the presented papers were both stimulating and encouraging about the potential of the questions being addressed. Drawing on the discussions held at the conference and on other input, the authors took the opportunity over the following year to revise and expand their papers. These works, joined by several additional invited chapters, are presented in this book. We think that these chapters represent the foremost contemporary thought on the etiology of drug abuse. The reader should note that the opinions expressed by the authors do not necessarily represent those of the American Psychological Association, the National Institute on Drug Abuse, or the federal government.

Editorial Assumptions

We believe that drug abuse is not a homogeneous phenomenon. Drug abusers are a heterogeneous group, and there are multiple patterns of abuse, each potentially having multiple etiologies. The contributing and prodromal factors and systems of factors that may predispose an individual to or protect from initiation, escalation, and maintenance of drug abuse may be a combination of biomedical (including genetic), psychological, psychiatric, social, familial, and environmental factors.

Abusers use a wide variety of different drugs and engage in many different patterns of use. Different high abuse liability drugs have different pharmacologic and psychoactive effects, and a given drug may be abused in different fashions. A commonly observed example is the contrasting use patterns of the alcoholic who drinks himself to unconsciousness versus the alcoholic who uses alcohol to disinhibit himself and permit a radical behavior shift to unconstrained behavior. Comparable contrasting use patterns have been noted in abusers of heroin, marijuana, and other drugs. The class of "drug abuse" includes many different patterns and degrees of abuse ranging from relatively moderate frequency and low-quantity use to high-frequency, high-quantity use of a drug or, more commonly, drugs. Drug abuse is also extremely diverse in terms of its concomitants and its consequences. The heterogeneity of drug abuse and of its etiology have complicated research and theory.

Obviously, any group that is considering the issue of the transition from use to abuse must have some consensually acceptable notion of what *abuse* is. The concept of *abuse*, however, involves a host of vital conceptual, as well as major methodological (measurement), issues. Although the questions of what constitutes abuse and in what ways it can accurately be identified and measured are critical ones, the entangled issues and conflicting opinions are so enormous and complex that we felt that an attempt at a resolution as part of this project would preclude the consideration of the designated topic. Certainly, abuse is qualitatively different than simply an elevated prolonged magnitude of use. We have assumed that there is no clear demarcation in the spectrum of use to abuse but that the extreme poles of the dimension can be consensually recognized. Although a few of the chapters address some diagnostic and nosological aspects of this matter, no final resolution or consensus was expected, and authors were asked to focus on the contrast and to minimize their consideration of the transition threshold.

A second necessary editorial decision was whether to include research and papers focusing on alcohol abuse. Our primary concern in this project is with drug abuse, and the relationship of alcohol abuse to drug abuse is not clear. Not only are the substances involved pharmacologically different, but their differing legal statuses further distinguish the two. We believe that there is some overlap between alcohol and drug abuse and that in all likelihood, alcohol abuse is a subset of the larger set of psychoactive substance abuses. For this reason, we have included some work on alcohol abuse, although most of the chapters focus on the abuse of illegal drugs. We assume that the information from the alcohol studies will be instructive but not necessarily completely generalizable to the broader category of drug abuse.

Summary of Findings

In reading the chapters presented here, a number of major points seem to emerge. It was generally agreed that consistent behaviorally based diagnostic criteria and conceptually founded but behaviorally defined nosological categories are necessary not only for conducting sound research but also for understanding the phenomenon of drug abuse and the complex associated factors and patterns. The revised third edition of the *Diagnostic and Statistical Manual of Mental Disorders* (as well as the forthcoming fourth edition), developed by the American Psychiatric Association (1987), and the generally comparable ninth edition of the *International Classification of Diseases* (and the forthcoming tenth edition), developed by the World Health Organization (1980), both of which are problem-oriented systems, are the diagnostic standards. Contemporary researchers have generally relied on these nosological systems to identify drug abusers, or have used strongly behaviorally based classifications (such as a frequency-of-use measure).

Drug use and abuse are not independent, discrete phenomena; although they have observable qualitative differences, they define the contrasting points of a continuum. An analogy might be a continuum with severe clinical depression at one endpoint and a generally normal mood with some depressed periods at the other endpoint. However, despite the irrefutable relation of use to abuse, the etiology of drug use does not appear to be identical with the etiology of drug abuse. That is, the factors that constitute risk for use do not in themselves necessarily predict the transition from use to abuse; vulnerability to use seems to be largely distinct from vulnerability to abuse.

This implies that there are significant differences between those who make the transition from use to abuse and those who do not. Relatedly, individuals are differentially at risk for drug abuse; only some users will be at high risk for making the transition to drug abuse. Most of the consensually identified escalation influences seem to be such that they would exist and perhaps be detectable prior to the individual's involvement with drugs. This implies that effective drug-abuse prevention is possible through early identification of and appropriate intervention with high-risk individuals.

No single factor "causes" drug abuse; instead, drug abuse develops from the interaction of multiple influences including biological, psychological, and social/environmental factors. Furthermore, there is no single path or combination of factors that lead to drug abuse; rather, there are numerous possible etiological patterns. Neither single-factor explanations of drug abuse nor simple models of etiology are likely to be highly valid or predictive.

Protective factors also play a role, and their involvement is as complex as that of the risk factors. Protective factors appear to work in opposition to risk factors and, if sufficient in magnitude, may nullify the predispositional influence of even potent risk factors. At least in some cases, the bipolar contrasts of the risk factors may serve as protective factors; for example, poor academic achievement is a risk factor, whereas strong school achievement seems to have protective influences.

Some, if not most, etiological patterns are likely to be developmental in nature. As used here, this contention indicates that etiologic factors are not merely antecedent. Rather, at a given stage, the extant determinative influences interact to produce new factors that, in turn, will have further determinative effects in subsequent interactions in subsequent stages. To illustrate with a simplified example, an infant with a more difficult temperament may get less affection from his parents, may therefore be more subject to their rejection and even aggression, and as a result may have a weaker bond with his parents and an impaired social development and orientation. Later, the weaker parental bond may diminish the extent to which the parents can serve as positive role models to avoid drugs. Furthermore, the child's poor social skills may contribute to his association with other alienated, deviant children, who are more likely to be engaged in and promote drug abuse.

Although some individuals may be particularly biologically susceptible or responsive to certain substances, preinvolvement risk for abuse does not generally appear to be highly drug-specific. For some, risk may be related to drugs with a particular type of effect, such as vulnerability to stimulants. At least in terms of some etiologic patterns, the risk may not even be specifically for substance abuse, but rather for a cluster of behaviors that are considered deviant or antisocial and that include substance abuse. The manifestation of substance abuse and the particular drug used may be related to a more general behavioral disposition that is heavily influenced by environmental factors including drug exposure/availability variables and behavior norms of referent deviant subgroups.

To some extent, different risk factors are likely to be associated with different substances. This appears to be particularly true for alcohol, perhaps because of its legal availability and its general cultural acceptance. Because of these factors, an alcohol abuser need not commit an illegal act or associate with others engaging in illegal acts to gain access to alcohol. Compared with drug abuse, a greater number of etiological patterns related to alcohol abuse may not involve more extreme deviant or antisocial characters. Therefore, although alcohol abuse or alcoholism is not a distinct phenomenon from drug abuse, findings from alcohol-abuse research cannot automatically be assumed to relate to the abuse of illegal drugs.

Just as certain individuals have an exacerbated vulnerability to drug abuse, so may certain subgroups of the population. In some cases, this greater vulnerability may be based on the influence of extreme social–environmental stresses and constraints on goals and role fulfillment. Social-role deprivation and the absence of bonding to institutions supportive of traditional norms and values were of greatest importance in predicting drug abuse among African-Americans. Observed ethnic-group differences may be largely if not entirely attributable to these legal, sociocultural, and economic factors. Although probably to a lesser extent, observed gender differences may also be influenced by these factors.

Substance use and abuse does not exist in a social or environmental vacuum. Social attitudes and perceptions, policies, economic circumstances, and law-enforcement patterns all contribute to abuse behaviors, sometimes in unexpected ways. An examination of the history of prohibition shows that a well-intentioned set of laws had, in some groups, the paradoxical effect of increasing alcohol abuse and antisocial behavior. This suggests that a simple, straightforward interdiction approach to controlling substance abuse may ultimately have limited potential in reaching its goals; other social and individual/psychiatric factors must also be taken into account.

In general, drug use appears to be more a function of social and peer factors, whereas abuse appears to be more a function of biological and psychological processes. Risk factors for use include "bad" friends, friends using drugs, peer influences on use, drug availability, bad conduct, unconventionality, low involvement with traditional value-oriented institutions (i.e., family, religious institutions, school), poor academic achievement, poor-quality relations with (and attachment to) parents, and having parents with problems.

There is also a fair degree of consensus on the risk factors for drug abuse. Interestingly, one identified vulnerability risk is not tied to any specific factor, but rather to the number of factors. The greater the number of drug-abuse risk factors, the greater the risk for drug abuse. This lends credence to a more systemic view of drug-abuse etiology.

Although drug use cannot be said to "cause" drug abuse, use of drugs and the nature of that use contributes strongly to escalation to the abuse of drugs. Two use characteristics in particular have been identified in this respect: Early age of onset of use and high-frequency use of drugs presage greater involvement with drugs, including involvement with other drugs that have more immediate dangers and greater abuse liability.

Family factors include parental substance abuse and antisocial behavior, a family history of psychopathology, and family disruption, including divorce. Alcoholism, and possibly drug abuse, demonstrate some degree of heritability, indicating a genetic contribution. This genetic influence does not seem to be sufficient by itself, but rather seems to interact with other influences to lead to substance abuse. Neurobiologic dysfunction related factors seem likely to be involved in at least some etiological patterns of drug abuse, although their exact nature and mechanism are only beginning to be identified.

At least some psychopathologies seem to have an etiological influence. Antisocial personality, conduct disorder, and criminal behavior are clear vulnerability factors. Childhood conduct/behavior problems, aggressivity, acting out, and a high childhood activity level are also risk factors for abuse. There is a risk-factor cluster associated with emotional/behavioral arousal, self-regulation difficulties (possibly including sensation seeking), impulsivity, and hyperactivity/attention deficit disorder. Other factors include generally poor function, difficulties in coping, social isolation, interpersonal difficulties, traumatic experiences, including childhood physical and sexual abuse, and not having good school achievement.

Certain other risk factors were implicated, but either there was no clear distinction as to their differential involvement in use versus abuse or there was some disagreement. These factors include aggression, arousability, emotional distress and problems (negative affectivity), other deviant behaviors and unconventionality, including the related aspects and self-labeling consequences, and poor school achievement. Role asynchrony/deprivation may also have some etiological influence. There may be some factors whose etiological contributions are neither necessarily clear nor consistent, but that may at least function as excellent risk indicators; the best example of this would be sibling drug abuse.

Finally, there is a clear consensus that these findings have strong implications for prevention programming and point to the need for further research. Although the research described in this volume is not an exhaustive consideration of all possible factors or domains, it does provide a sound research-based foundation for beginning to understand the etiology of drug abuse and for developing future research and interventions.

Other Relevant Research

The researchers whose work is presented in this volume have been responsible for most of the primary drug-abuse etiology research. However, despite the best intentions and efforts of the editors, it was not possible to arrange for all of the researchers who have conducted major work in the area to participate in the conference or this publication.

The reader is strongly encouraged to consult the research literature, particularly including the work of Robins (Robins, 1974; Robins & McEvoy, 1990), Jessor and Jessor (Donovan & Jessor, 1985; Jessor & Jessor, 1977, 1978), Kellam and Ensminger (Kellam, Brown, Rubin, & Ensminger, 1983; Kellam, Ensminger, & Simon, 1980; Kellam, Simon, & Ensminger, 1982), Block (Block, Block, & Keyes, 1988; Shedler & Block, 1990), Oetting (Swaim, Oetting, Edwards, & Beauvais, 1989), Baumrind (Baumrind, 1985), Bry (Bry, 1983; Bry, McKeon, & Pandina, 1982), Lykken (Grove et al., 1990), Zinberg (Zinberg & Jacobson, 1976), Shiffman (Shiffman, 1989; Shiffman, Fisher, Zettler-Segal, & Benowitz, 1990), and Hawkins (Hawkins, Lishner, Catalano, & Howard, 1985). Also recommended are related areas of etiological research, such as those relevant to alcoholism (Cloninger, 1987; Cloninger, Sigvardsson, & Bohman, 1988; Knorring, Cloninger, Bohman, & Sigvardsson, 1983; Shuckit, 1987, 1988; Schuckit, Goodwin, & Winokur, 1972; Tarter, 1988; Tarter, Alterman, & Edwards, 1985; Tarter & Edwards, 1987; Vaillant, 1983), delinquency (Elliot, Huizinga, & Ageton, 1985; Loeber, 1988, 1990; McCord & McCord, 1959; Olweus, Block, & Radke-Yarrow, 1986; Robins, 1966, 1978; Robins & Rutter, 1990; Rutter & Giller, 1983), and psychopathology and behavior disorders (Chess & Thomas, 1984, 1989; Garmezy, 1974, 1981; Werner, 1989).

This book is not expected to answer all of the questions about the etiology of drug abuse. However, it presents what is currently known and demonstrates the fruitfulness of focusing on drug-*abuse* etiology and on the application of more sophisticated, multifactorial, multidisciplinary longitudinal research approaches. Although we hope that researchers and intervention-program developers will find the present work to be useful, we also hope that it will encourage more research along these lines of thought.

References

American Psychiatric Association. (1987). *Diagnostic and statistical manual of mental disorders* (3rd ed. rev.). Washington, DC: Author.

American School Health Association, Association for the Advancement of Health Education, & Society for Public Health Education. (1989). *The national adolescent health survey: A report on the health of America's youth.* Oakland, CA: Third Party.

Baumrind, D. (1985). Familial antecedents of adolescent drug use: A developmental perspective. In C. L. Jones & R. Battjes (Eds.), *Etiology of drug abuse: Implications for prevention* (pp. 13–44). Rockville, MD: National Institute on Drug Abuse.

Block, J., Block J., & Keyes, S. (1988). Longitudinally foretelling drug usage in adolescence: Early childhood personality and environmental precursors. *Child Development, 59*, 336–355.

Bry, B. (1983). Predicting drug abuse: Review and reformulation. *International Journal of the Addictions, 18*, 223–233.

Bry, B., McKeon, P., & Pandina, R. (1982). Extent of drug use as a function of number of risk factors. *Journal of Abnormal Psychology, 91*, 273–279.

Chess, S., & Thomas, A. (1984). *Origins and evolution of behavioral disorders: From infancy to early adult life.* Cambridge, MA: Harvard University Press.

Chess, S., & Thomas, A. (1989). Temperament and its functional significance. In S. Greenspan & G. Pollock (Eds.), *The course of life: Vol. II. Early childhood* (pp 163–227). Madison, CT: International Universities Press.

Cloninger, C. (1987). Neurogenetic adaptive mechanisms in alcoholism. *Science, 236*, 410–416.

Cloninger, C. R., Sigvardsson, S., & Bohman, M. (1988). Childhood personality predicts alcohol abuse in young adults. *Alcoholism: Clinical and experimental research, 12*, 494–505.

Donovan, J., & Jessor, R. (1985). Structure of problem behavior in adolescence and young adulthood. *Journal of Consulting and Clinical Psychology, 53*, 890–904.

Elliot, D., Huizinga, D., & Ageton, S. (1985). *Explaining delinquency and drug use.* Beverly Hills, CA: Sage.

Garmezy, N. (1974). Children at risk: The search for the antecedents of schizophrenia. *Schizophrenia Bulletin, 9*, 55–125.

Garmezy, N. (1981). Children under stress: Perspectives on antecedents and correlates of vulnerability and resistance to psychopathology. In A. Rubin, J. Aronoff, A. Barclay, & R. Zucker (Eds.), *Further explorations in personality* (pp. 196–269). New York: Wiley.

Grove, W., Eckert, E., Heston, L., Bouchard, T., Segal, N., & Lykken, D. (1990). Heritability of substance abuse and antisocial behavior: A study of monozygotic twins reared apart. *Biological Psychiatry, 27*, 1293–1304.

Hawkins, J. D., Lishner, D., Catalano, R., & Howard, M. (1985). Childhood predictors of adolescent substance abuse: Toward an empirically grounded theory. *Journal of Children in Contemporary Society, 18*, 11–48.

Jessor, R., & Jessor, S. (1977). *Problem behavior and psychosocial development: A longitudinal study of youth.* San Diego, CA: Academic Press.

Jessor, R., & Jessor, S. (1978). Theory testing in longitudinal research on marijuana use. In D. Kandel (Ed.), *Longitudinal research on drug use: Empirical findings and methodological issues* (pp. 41–71). Washington DC: Hemisphere–Wiley.

Johnston, L., O'Malley, P., & Bachman, J. (1986). *Drug use among American high school students, college students, and other young adults: National trends through 1985.* Ann Arbor, MI: University of Michigan, Institute for Social Research.

Kandel, D., & Yamaguchi, K. (1985). Developmental patterns of the use of legal, illegal, and medically prescribed psychotropic drugs from adolescence to young adulthood. In C. L. Jones & R. Battjes (Eds.), *Etiology of drug abuse: Implications for prevention* (pp. 193–235). Rockville, MD: National Institute on Drug Abuse.

Kellam, S., Brown, C., Rubin, B., & Ensminger, M. (1983). Paths leading to teenage psychiatric symptoms and substance use: Developmental epidemiological studies in Woodlawn. In S. Guze, F. Earls, & J. Barrett (Eds.), *Childhood psychopathology and development* (pp. 17–51). New York: Raven Press.

Kellam, S., Ensminger, M., & Simon, M. (1980). Mental health in first grade and teenage drug, alcohol, and cigarette use. *Drug and Alcohol Dependence, 5,* 273–304.

Kellam, S., Simon, M., & Ensminger, M. (1982). Antecedents in first grade of teenage drug use and psychological well-being: A ten-year community-wide prospective study. In D. Ricks & B. Dohrenwend (Eds.), *Origins of psychopathology: Research and public policy.* New York: Cambridge University Press.

Knorring, A., Cloninger, C. R., Bohman, M., & Sigvardsson, S. (1983). An adoption study of depressive disorders and substance abuse. *Archives of General Psychiatry, 40,* 943–950.

Loeber, R. (1988). The natural history of juvenile conduct problems, delinquency, and associated substance use: Evidence for developmental progressions. In B. Lahey & A. Kazden (Eds.), *Advances in clinical child psychology* (Vol. 11, pp. 73–124). New York: Plenum Press.

Loeber, R. (1990). Development and risk factors of juvenile antisocial behavior and delinquency. *Clinical Psychology Review, 10,* 1–41.

McCord, W., & McCord, J. (1959). *Origins of crime: A new evaluation of the Cambridge–Somerville study.* New York: Columbia University Press.

National Institute on Drug Abuse. (1990). *National Household Survey on Drug Abuse, 1990.* Rockville, MD: National Institute on Drug Abuse, Division of Epidemiology and Prevention Research.

National Institute on Drug Abuse. (1991). *Monitoring the future, 1990: National High School Senior Drug Abuse Survey, 1990.* Rockville, MD: National Institute on Drug Abuse, Division of Epidemiology and Prevention Research.

Olweus, D., Block, J., & Radke-Yarrow, M. (Eds.). (1986). *Development of antisocial and prosocial behavior: Research, theories and issues.* San Diego, CA: Academic Press.

Robins, L. (1966). *Deviant children grown up: A sociological and psychiatric study of sociopathic personality.* Baltimore: Williams & Wilkins.

Robins, L. (1974). *The Vietnam drug user returns.* Washington, DC: Special Action Office Monograph.

Robins, L. (1978). Sturdy childhood predictors of adult antisocial behavior: Replications from longitudinal studies. *Psychological Medicine, 8,* 611–622.

Robins, L., & McEvoy, L. (1990). Conduct problems as predictors of substance abuse. In L. Robins & M. Rutter (Eds.), *Straight and devious pathways from childhood to adulthood* (pp. 182–204). Cambridge, MA: Cambridge University Press.

Robins, L., & Rutter, M. (Eds.). (1990). *Straight and devious pathways from childhood to adulthood.* Cambridge, MA: Cambridge University Press.

Rutter, M., & Giller, H. (1983). *Juvenile delinquency: Trends and perspectives.* New York: Guilford Press.

Schuckit, M. (1987). Biological vulnerability to alcoholism. *Journal of Consulting and Clinical Psychology, 55,* 301–309.

Schuckit, M. (1988). A search for biological markers in alcoholism: Application to psychiatric research. In R. Rose & J. Barrett (Eds.), *Alcoholism: Origins and outcome.* New York: Raven Press.

Schuckit, M., Goodwin, D., & Winokur, G. (1972). Study of alcoholism in half-siblings. *American Journal of Psychiatry, 128,* 1132–1136.

Shedler, J., & Block, J. (1990). Adolescent drug use and psychological health: A longitudinal inquiry. *American Psychologist, 45,* 612–630.

Shiffman, S. (1989). Tobacco "chippers": Individual differences in tobacco dependence. *Psychopharmacology, 97,* 539–547.

Shiffman, S., Fisher, L., Zettler-Segal, M., & Benowitz, N. (1990). Nicotine exposure among non-dependent smokers. *Archives of General Psychiatry, 47,* 333–336.

Swaim, R., Oetting, E., Edwards, R., & Beauvais, F. (1989). Links from emotional distress to adolescent drug use: A path model. *Journal of Consulting and Clinical Psychology, 57,* 227–231.

Tarter, R. (1988). Are there inherited behavioral traits that predispose to substance abuse? *Journal of Consulting and Clinical Psychology, 56,* 189–196.

Tarter, R., Alterman, A., & Edwards, K. (1985). Vulnerablity to alcoholism in men: A behavioral–genetic perspective. *Journal of Studies on Alcohol, 46,* 329–356.

Tarter, R., & Edwards, K. (1987). Vulnerability to alcohol and drug abuse: A behavior–genetic view. *Journal of Drug Issues,* 67–81.

Vaillant, G. (1983). *The Natural history of alcoholism: Causes, patterns, and paths to recovery.* Cambridge, MA: Harvard University Press.

Werner, E. (1989). High-risk children in young adulthood: A longitudinal study from birth to 32 years. *American Journal of Orthopsychiatry, 59,* 72–81.

World Health Organization. (1980). *International classification of diseases* (9th ed.). Geneva: Author.

Zinberg, N., & Jacobson, R. (1976). The natural history of "chipping." *American Journal of Psychiatry, 133,* 37–40.

CHAPTER 1

Transitions in Drug Use: Risk and Protective Factors

Richard R. Clayton

Risk and Protective Factors for Drug Abuse

A number of chapters in this volume are data-based. This chapter is designed to be more introductory and conceptually based. The main thrust of this chapter will be to examine the "risk factor" literature. An incredible amount of attention has been devoted in recent years to understanding the predictors of drug *use*; less attention has been directed to the risk factors for drug *abuse*. Although there are differences among the so-called experts concerning exactly what constitutes the dividing line between use and abuse, virtually everyone agrees that there is a continuum that goes from use to abuse to dependence. In this chapter, an attempt will be made to focus more on the abuse part of the continuum, although it will be necessary in some instances to extrapolate from the literature on risk factors for use to risk factors for abuse.

Risk and Protective Factors Defined

A *risk factor* is an individual attribute, individual characteristic, situational condition, or environmental context that increases the probability of drug use or abuse or a transition in level of involvement with drugs.

Work on this paper supported by Grant DA-05312 from the National Institute on Drug Abuse.

A *protective factor* is an individual attribute, individual characteristic, situational condition, or environmental context that inhibits, reduces, or buffers the probability of drug use or abuse or a transition in level of involvement with drugs.

There are at least two ways that risk and protective factors have been dealt with in the literature. The simplest approach has been to identify "types of people" who, because of their individual attributes or characteristics, are thought to be higher at risk for drug abuse than others. The second and more complex approach is based on a more dynamic, multidimensional, and multivariate orientation, often fusing individual-level variables with more situational and macro-level contextual variables.

Individual Attributes as Risk Factors

The 1986 Anti-Drug Abuse Act defined high-risk youth as those "children and teenagers under age 18 who, because of the presence of certain characteristics and conditions, are especially likely to use illegal drugs and/or alcohol."

There are two elements of this definition that are important to note. First, factors that may encourage drug use (e.g., its initiation, continuation, or progression) may be "characteristics" that exist "within" the individual. Second, drug use and abuse may be related to the "conditions" in which an individual lives. Therefore, at the very least, high-risk youth may be differentiated from those not at high risk for drug abuse by their personal characteristics or the conditions that influence how they lead their lives. The risk factors in the 1986 Act are as follows: (a) the economically disadvantaged; (b) children of substance-abusing parents; (c) victims of physical, sexual, or psychological abuse; (d) runaways or homeless youth; (e) school dropouts; (f) youth who are pregnant; (g) youth involved in violent or delinquent acts; (h) youth with mental health problems; and (i) youth who have attempted suicide. For the most part, these are the "types" of individuals toward whom services are directed in communities.

The first two of these risk factors describe attributes or conditions that may increase the likelihood of drug abuse. It is unlikely that a young person's use of drugs "causes" his or her poverty or his or her parents' patterns of drug abuse. However, it is possible that a person's drug abuse may make him or her more vulnerable to victimization. The last six of the above risk factors could serve as both "causes" and "effects" of drug abuse. This highlights an important issue in research on risk and protective factors and drug abuse: the temporal ordering and direction of the relationship.Some relationships are clearly asymmetrical, whereas others are clearly reciprocal.

The following are assumptions about risk and protective factors:

1. A single risk or protective factor can have multiple outcomes.
2. Several risk or protective factors can have an impact on a single outcome.
3. Drug abuse itself may have important effects on risk and protective factors.
4. The relationship of risk and protective factors to each other and to transitions in drug abuse may be influenced significantly by age-graded norms.

Characteristics and Conditions as Risk Factors

Some researchers have moved beyond the simple attributes and "types" of persons to identify some of the individual characteristics and conditions that may "predict" risk for drug abuse. Although this is a rapidly growing literature, it should be noted that systematic and credible research on risk factors for drug abuse is a relatively recent phenomenon.

Three teams of reserchers (Bry, McKeon, & Pandina, 1982; Labouvie, Pandina, White, & Johnson, 1986; Newcomb, Maddahian, & Bentler, 1986) have produced similar lists of potential risk factors (see Table 1.1). In fact, Newcomb and his colleagues (1986) merely accepted six (grade point average, lack of religiosity, psychopathology, poor relationship with parents, early alcohol use, and low self-esteem) of the risk factors identified by Bry et al. (1982) and added four others (lack of conformity, sensation seeking, perception of availability, and perception of norms concerning drug use). Labouvie and his colleagues (1986) organized the 12 specific risk factors under four general domains: (a) psychological risk; (b) parent risk; (c) school risk; and (d) peer risk.

As shown in Table 1.1, there are two risk factors identified by Bry et al. (1982) that are not covered by Labouvie et al. (1986): lack of religiosity and early alcohol use. Likewise, there are two risk factors identified by Newcomb et al. (1986) that are not picked up by Labouvie et al. (1986): lack of conformity and perceived availability.

It appears that Labouvie and his colleagues (1986) attempted to get multiple indicators of most of their basic domains. Instead of just low self-esteem, they have broken the self-esteem construct into self-esteem, self-derogation, and self-confidence. Instead of just poor relationship with parents, they have divided this construct into two dimensions: parental warmth and parental hostile control.

Hawkins and Catalano (1989) made perhaps the most ambitious attempt thus far to organize the known risk factors specifically for adolescent drug use and, by assumption, for drug abuse. As shown in Table 1.1, most of these specific risk factors coincide or at

TABLE 1.1

Typologies of Risk Factors for Adolescent Drug Use

Bry et al. (1982)	Newcomb et al. (1986)	Labouvie et al. (1986)	Hawkins & Catalano (1989)
Low grade point average	Low grade point average	Low academic performance Low educational aspirations Low achievement orientation	Low commitment to school Cognitive impairment Intelligence
Lack of religiosity	Lack of religiosity		Low religious involvement
Early alcohol use	Early alcohol use		Early persistent problem behaviors Early onset high-risk behavior
Low self-esteem	Low self-esteem	Low self-esteem Self-derogation	
Psychopathology	Psychopathology	Emotional outbursts	
Poor relationship with parents	Poor relationship with parents	Low parental warmth Parental hostile control	Poor, inconsistent family management practices Family conflict Low bonding to family Alienation/ rebelliousness
	Lack of conformity		Attitudes favorable to drug use
	Sensation seeking	Impulsivity	Sensation seeking Attention deficit/ hyperactivity Low autonomic and central nervous system arousal Hormonal factors

(continued)

TABLE 1.1 *(Continued)*

Bry et al. (1982)	Newcomb et al. (1986)	Labouvie et al. (1986)	Hawkins & Catalano (1989)
	Perceived peer drug use	Friends' deviance Negative activities with friends	Peer rejection in elementary school Association with drug-using peers
	Perceived adult drug use		
			Laws/norms Availability Extreme economic deprivation Neighborhood disorganization School organization factors
			Intergenerational transmission

least overlap with those identified earlier by Bry, Newcomb, Labouvie, and their respective colleagues. However, there are three additional and very important domains introduced by Hawkins and Catalano that deserve further examination: (a) contextual and environmental factors (laws and norms, availability of drugs, extreme economic deprivation, neighborhood disorganization, school organizational factors; (b) neurophysiological factors (attention deficit hyperactivity disorder, cognitive impairment from damage, intelligence, hormonal imbalances); and (c) intergenerational transmission (living with parents and siblings who abuse alcohol and/or other drugs).

Risk and Protective Factors: General Principles

The alternative approaches to understanding the "predictors" of drug abuse represented by Bry, Newcomb, Labouvie and their colleagues, by Hawkins and Catalano, and by the listing included in the 1986 Anti-Drug Abuse Act provide "different" but important windows on a very complex problem. The difference in these approaches can be reconciled by considering the following principles:

1. Risk factors (individual characteristics or environmental conditions) are either present or not. When a risk factor is present, the person is more likely to use or abuse drugs than when the risk factor is not present.

2. Mere presence of a risk factor is not a guarantee that drug abuse will occur. Absence of a risk factor(s) is no guarantee that drug abuse will not occur. The same is true for protective factors. Drug abuse results from many factors and occurs on the basis of probability, not certainty.

3. The number of risk factors present is directly related to the likelihood of drug abuse, although this additive effect may be buffered by the nature, content, and number of protective factors present.

4. Most risk and protective factors have multiple measurable dimensions, each of which has independent influence, all of which may have a composite influence on drug abuse.

5. Direct intervention is possible with some risk factors and can lead to an elimination or reduction of the risk factor and a lessening of the likelihood of drug abuse. For some risk factors, direct intervention is simply not possible. The principal hope is to "buffer" the influence of the risk factor and thus reduce the likelihood it will lead to drug abuse.

Number of Risk Factors Present

A study of 994 adolescents in grades 10–12 by Newcomb et al. (1986) illustrates one of the principles above, the importance of number of risk factors present. These students were first studied when they were in grades 7–9 in 11 schools in Los Angeles.

Although 51% of the sample had used marijuana at some time in their life, only 22% with none of the risk factors measured by Newcomb et al. had used marijuana, compared with 94% of those with seven or more risk factors present. Similar differences were also observed for the other drugs studied, with the exception of over-the-counter drugs that do not require a prescription.

For the total sample, 14% reported "heavy" use of cigarettes, 2% "heavy" use of alcohol, 8% "heavy" use of marijuana, and 3% "heavy" use of other illicit drugs. The percentage of heavy users was directly related to the number of risk factors present. For example, only 1% of the students with no risk factors reported daily use of marijuana, compared with 56% of those with seven or more risk factors. Similar linear-type effects were apparent for all of the other drugs except over-the-counter medications.

It is important to note that Newcomb et al. (1986) used individual characteristics rather than environmental or contextual conditions as risk factors. However, Newcomb et al., as well as Labouvie et al. (1986), have consistently attempted to measure the multiple dimensions of most constructs, as opposed to just single measured variables.

Multiple Dimensions of Risk Factors

Each of the risk and protective factors for transitions in drug abuse is anchored in some substantive content, whether it be intraindividual, interpersonal, or contextual and external to the individual. Perhaps a construct such as religiosity would provide a good example.

Religiosity is a multidimensional phenomenon (see Clayton & Gladden, 1975). From a "content" perspective, religiosity can be measured on the ideological or belief dimension, the intellectual or knowledge dimension, the ritualistic dimension (i.e., frequency of church attendance, etc.), the experiential dimension (i.e., "personal" experiences of deeply religious connotation), and the consequential dimension (i.e., application of religious principles to situations). It is one thing, for example, to believe intellectually that the Bible is a book "inspired" by God. It is quite another to believe intensively and emotionally that this is so (the "intensity" component or degree to which the belief or attitude is held). The degree to which the various dimensions of religiosity are integrated into a comprehensive and personal model for decision making reflects closure.

Religiosity is a risk/protective factor for drug use (Bachman, Schulenberg, O'Malley, & Johnston, 1990). However, use of very simple measures of religiosity that do not reflect its multidimensional nature may produce spurious interpretations of the relationship of this risk/protective factor to drug use. The relationship of the multiple dimensions of religiosity to drug abuse is not clear. However, the relevance of complex multidimensional constructs such as religiosity in the cessation of drug abuse cannot be overstated. A key element of 12-step, self-help treatment programs is religiosity in all of its dimensions.

Transitions in Drug Use: the Dependent Variables

In any examination of the etiology of a phenomenon, it is essential that some consensus be reached about the appropriate outcome variables. As is well known, there are multiple outcome variables in the fields of alcohol and drug abuse, as well as multiple substances that are relevant. These substances have different degrees of embeddedness within our society, different meanings, and different reinforcement schedules for the development of dependence.

Kandel (1975) and her colleagues (Kandel & Logan, 1984; Yamaguchi & Kandel, 1984a, 1984b), as well as others (Clayton, Voss, & LoSciuto, 1987; Huba, Wingard, & Bentler, 1981; O'Donnell & Clayton, 1982) have tested models accounting for the "initiation of use" of various drugs. However, it should be noted that the models focus almost entirely on "first" events and thus ignore, for the most part, the frequency, quantity, and volume dimensions of drug abuse, as well as the complexity of abuse of multiple drugs.

Thus, our etiological models of transitions must begin to focus on the following types of transitions, which reflect different dimensions of drug use and abuse: (a) initiation; (b) continuation; (c) maintenance and progression within drug classes; (d) progression across drug classes; (e) regression, cessation, and relapse cycles.

Initiation

In a sense, the key transition in drug abuse is initiation; movement from being a nonuser to being a user. In the risk-factor literature and in the drug-abuse field in general, there is a clear and strong emphasis on adolescents. Therefore, many of the attempts to identify risk or protective factors for drug involvement focus on initiation, first use, or simply ever using a drug, and fail to consider abuse or dependence on drugs. More attention is paid to modal versus nonmodal patterns of use and to the circumstances and context of initiation than to the factors that lead to compulsive abuse of drugs. In this chapter, although some discussion will be given to risk/protective factors for initiation, the central concern will be with transitions that reflect more intensive, extensive, and excessive use of drugs.

Continuation

The second transition in drug abuse involves a decision concerning continuation. Why is it that some people try a drug and never use it again, whereas others try the same drug and seem propelled to use it again and again? It is not unusual in groups of drug abusers to hear someone say, "I knew from the first time I used that drug that it was for me!" In contrast, others may say, "That drug just didn't do anything for me so I never used it again." Very little work has been conducted on risk factors for the transition between experimentation and continuation of use. One potentially important measure concerns the elapsed time between first use and subsequent use. The shorter the hiatus, the greater the likelihood of eventual abuse of that substance. There is a need to understand whether an aversive first experience with a drug reduces, increases, or has little or no effect on continuation of use of a particular drug. Again, continuation as a transition in drug use exists at the less severe end of the continuum and will not be given much additional attention in this chapter.

Maintenance and Progression Within a Class of Drugs

The third transition in drug abuse is maintenance and progression within a class of drugs. Maintenance has a number of important dimensions. One is simply conformity with age-graded norms of consumption. Maintenance may include commonly understood norms about what to drink/use, the appropriate frequency and severity of excessive use episodes, and appropriate and inappropriate behavior while under the influence. During this particular stage of drug involvement, it is not unusual for a person to self-identify as a "heavy" user, but this is usually within the context of significant others in the peer group. The rationale for individuals is that their behavior is not inconsistent with the behavior of their friends. The relevant measurement criteria regarding alcoholic beverages would be frequency, quantity, and volume. The ability to consume larger amounts of the drug(s) may very well be evidence of increasing tolerance to the substance. A relevant measurement criterion with regard to drugs such as cocaine may be transition from snorting to smoking or to injection. In a purely developmental sense, college students are particularly at high risk for excessive drug consumption, yet very little research has been conducted on this age group concerning risk factors for maintenance of high levels of use, or progression within drug classes to excessive use of a substance.

Progression Across Drug Classes

A fourth transition is progression across drug classes. It is not unusual for persons in this particular stage of drug involvement to begin experimenting with simultaneous use of multiple drugs in a pharmacologically functional manner. Thus, a person will use the anti-emetic properties of THC in cannabis to facilitate greater use of alcohol, or use alcohol and marijuana to take the edge off of the cocaine high. However, the explanation for simultaneous multiple abuse of drugs may vary by culture. In Colombia, middle-class cocaine abusers report that they use the stimulant properties of cocaine to offset the stupor that results from excessive alcohol consumption so that they can drink more. It is clear that progression across drug classes constitutes a transition in drug involvement that is closer to the "abuse" end of the continuum. The risk factors for this transition are not well understood, and much of the research has focused only on predicting abuse of alcohol. An important question to ask is the following: How appropriate is it to extrapolate from the literature on alcohol abuse to drug abuse?

Regression, Cessation, and Relapse Cycles

The fifth transition in drug abuse is regression, cessation, and relapse cycles. The goal of treatment is to facilitate the movement from active abuse of drugs to a reduction and complete cessation of drug abuse. This is an important transition and may occur a number of times during a person's career as a drug abuser. The scientific literature focusing on regression, cessation, and relapse cycles is growing. A systematic paradigm of the risk factors for these transitions in drug abuse is emerging but still needs considerable work to determine if the risk factors are similar across substances.

It is not possible to review thoroughly the extensive literature dealing with each of these categories of transitions, or the separate items under each general transition. Suffice it to say that etiological research may discover that different risk factors or different configurations of risk factors are important for each of the transitions. If this sounds complex, it is. To make matters even more complex, these transitions are appropriate for each substance. If drug use is conceived of as a career, and those who use drugs to excess are often multiple drug users/abusers (see Clayton, 1986; Skinner et al., 1989), then etiological research must take into account the different stages of transitions being experienced for each drug used by a person.

Therefore, *use* and *abuse* as well as *dependence* are important terms to be considered. Although no consensus exists on the meaning of these terms, use and abuse are often used interchangeably for adolescents but not for adults. It is clear that adolescents and adults make different distinctions among various drugs with regard to perceived harmfulness (see Johnston, O'Malley, & Bachman, 1989; National Institute on Drug Abuse, 1988). Although there is considerable variability concerning the perceived harmfulness of experimentation, occasional use, and even regular use of marijuana, virtually everyone believes that there is great risk in any use of PCP.

The most consistent solution to this conceptual dilemma from a public health perspective would be to label any use as abuse. However, there are some who believe that experimentation with drugs is statistically normative in our society and that the proper focus should be on "excessive" use (defined in terms of frequency, quantity, and loss of control), which is probably close to a consensual meaning of "abuse."

Most researchers seem to prefer defining use and abuse as a continuum ranging from first ingestion to regular and excessive ingestion to the point of impairment. Dependence is generally thought to occur after a period of sustained and life-organizing drug-abusing episodes and periods. Strictly speaking, dependence should not occur until tolerance has developed and withdrawal appears when the drug is reduced or stopped. However, strong psychological symptoms of withdrawal may occur even when tolerance and physical dependence are not present.

The Reality of Multiple Drugs

The drug abuse field seems to have been driven by what can cynically be called the "drug of the month" club. So-called "licit" drugs have been separated from the so-called "illicit" drugs. Federal policies and pronouncements of public policy leaders in the drug abuse field have created an artificial and unrealistic demarcation among drugs available, used, and abused in this country. Our rhetoric is driven by outmoded stereotypes of "addicts." The reality today is that most who use and abuse drugs, particularly those who account for the lion's share of drug consumption in this country, are abusing multiple drugs (Clayton, 1986).

To illustrate this point, a measure of multiple drug abuse was constructed from reports of "past year" use of alcohol and illicit drugs and reports of "simultaneous" use of alcohol and/or illicit drugs. The data were taken from the 1985 National Household Survey on Drug Abuse gathered through personal interviews with a stratified random probability sample of 8,038 people living in households in the continental United States. The response rate was 83%. Oversampling provided approximately 2,000 interviews with both Blacks and Hispanics and 4,000 with Whites. The resulting sample was representative of all persons 12 years old and older living in households in the continental United States.

The measure included five categories: (a) no use of alcohol or drugs in the previous 12 months; (b) only alcohol use reported in the previous 12 months; (c) use of illicit drugs in the previous year with or without alcohol use but with no simultaneous use of drugs or alcohol; (d) use of alcohol and illicit drugs simultaneously at some time in the previous 12 months; (e) use of two or more illicit drugs simultaneously with or without alcohol use.

As the data shown in Table 1.2 reveal, the majority of people had not used illicit drugs in the previous year, although for White males 18–25 years old, it is a bare majority. For the total sample, about a quarter had used no alcohol or drugs in the previous year, and about 20% had used illicit drugs either alone or simultaneously with alcohol or other drugs. Within the demographic subgroups, these percentages vary considerably. For example, it is apparent that men more than women use substances simultaneously, although the differences are somewhat less pronounced in the youngest age group.

The differences among the race/ethnicity groups are not large. Across all groups, simultaneous use peaks in the 18–25 age group, falls off somewhat in the 26–34-year-old group and falls precipitously in the group 35 years old and older to levels actually below those observed for youth.

It should be noted that these data are for the general population; they do not include those parts considered more deviant with regard to drug abuse (e.g., treatment populations, prisoners, transients, etc.). Therefore, if the purpose is to develop an etiological map of drug abuse patterns and transitions in drug abuse, it is imperative that our focus begin to shift from drug-specific models to multiple-drug models.

The Dilemma of Chipping

An important issue concerning the etiology of drug abuse is "chippers," people who do not seem to develop tolerance, who do not seem to become physically, psychologically, or socially dependent on the drugs, who use drugs sporadically, and who can seemingly quit using anytime they wish. How do we explain chippers? They are clearly "at risk" to make a transition to greater or more regular use, but manage somehow to maintain an episodic contact with the substance (see Shiffman, 1989; Surgeon General of the United States, 1988; Zinberg & Jacobson, 1976).

As Shiffman (1989) notes, "chippers are of interest, not because they are common, but because their behavior is inconsistent with theory.... While classical notions of dependence suggest that chronic exposure to an addictive drug leads inexorably and inevitably to dependence, chippers have smoked for years, yet show no evidence of dependence." Careful study of this group that defies some of the most enduring assumptions about drug abuse and dependence may be an important way to better understand the etiology of transitions in drug use and abuse.

The Dilemma of Precocious Drug Use

Developmental psychologists have studied stages of language acquisition, cognition, affect, moral development, and so on. These phenomena are often studied independently of

TABLE 1.2

Percent Distribution of Level of Multiple Drug Use in Previous Year by Demographic Characteristics: 1985

Group	Level of Multiple Drug Use in Previous Year				
	No alcohol or drug use	Alcohol use only	Illicit drug use	Simultaneous alcohol and illicit drug use	Simultaneous use of two or more illicit drugs
Total sample	25.7	54.6	6.4	8.4	4.9
All men	20.5	55.8	6.7	10.3	6.6
White men	18.8	57.8	6.2	10.3	6.8
12–17 years	39.9	35.8	9.0	8.9	6.5
18–25 years	6.7	44.5	10.6	23.6	14.6
26–34 years	10.0	49.4	7.9	18.3	14.3
35+ years	21.5	70.2	3.4	3.3	1.6
Black men	32.8	40.0	8.8	12.3	6.2
12–17 years	59.7	18.8	12.5	7.1	2.0
18–25 years	21.4	33.6	13.6	20.2	11.2
26–34 years	16.0	47.6	8.1	17.2	11.0
35+ years	35.2	48.0	5.4	8.2	3.2
Hispanic men	23.5	54.4	8.9	9.8	3.3
12–17 years	51.4	25.4	12.8	6.5	3.9
18–25 years	14.4	45.9	14.8	18.0	7.0
26–34 years	11.1	59.8	7.2	17.1	4.8
35+ years	24.4	67.1	5.2	2.8	*
All women	30.5	53.6	6.1	6.6	3.3
White women	27.0	56.8	5.9	6.9	3.5
12–17 years	39.9	34.8	12.1	9.4	3.9
18–25 years	10.1	49.2	10.1	21.5	9.2
26–34 years	15.9	56.3	8.9	11.1	7.8
35+ years	32.9	62.9	2.6	1.0	0.5
Black women	45.5	37.2	7.8	6.8	2.7
12–17 years	67.2	16.7	9.3	4.9	1.9
18–25 years	25.9	41.4	13.3	14.4	5.0
26–34 years	24.9	49.3	12.5	8.1	5.2
35+ years	55.6	36.5	3.2	3.6	1.0
Hispanic women	45.0	42.7	6.8	3.6	1.8
12–17 years	59.4	21.0	12.3	3.9	3.3
18–25 years	30.0	45.8	9.2	10.2	4.5
26–34 years	30.3	56.8	6.4	4.2	2.3
35+ years	53.2	42.1	4.2	0.5	*

Note. Because of rounding, row percentages may not total 100.0.

From National Institute on Drug Abuse, 1988 (*National Household Survey on Drug Abuse*, 1985).

* Less than one half of one percent.

external forces such as drug use and abuse that may hinder or suppress such development. For example, Inciardi & Pottieger (1991) studied 254 youth between the ages of 12 and 17 (average age 14.7 years) involved in the crack distribution business in Miami. First regular use of alcohol was at age 9 (61.4% of sample), first regular use of marijuana was at age 11 (100% of sample), and first regular use of cocaine was at age 12 (100% of sample). Slightly over half were crack dealers involved directly in the retail sale of crack. Another 18% were also involved in the manufacture, smuggling, or wholesaling of the drug. Those adolescents identified as "dealers" spent an estimated average of $2,000 or more on crack during the previous 90 days.

What does such heavy involvement in drug abuse at such an early age do to "regular" psychosocial development? Surely early onset of experimentation and especially of multiple drug abuse must interfere with learning and performing other developmental tasks. From an etiological perspective, it is essential that attention be focused on those who become excessive drug users early on, to see how this affects development in other spheres of life.

Development and Drug Use Transitions

The intersection and interaction of normal developmental stages of growth and transitions in drug use and abuse is a topic requiring significantly more attention. This is true not only for youth but for adults as well. Kandel and her colleagues (e.g., Yamaguchi & Kandel, 1984a, 1984b) have focused on the relationship of adult role transitions to drug use (i.e., marijuana use). A central concept in Kandel's work is role incompatibility, which is used to examine the ways in which adoption of adult roles (work, marriage, parenthood) discourages either initiation or continuation of drug use, and the ways that drug use disrupts the normative transition to adult roles. Yamaguchi and Kandel found that marijuana users in young adulthood have lower rates of participation in adult roles and experience greater instability in conventional roles as measured by job changes and marital disruption (see Kandel, 1984).

The effects (of roles on drug abuse and of drug abuse on roles) are reciprocal and are explained by two concepts: role selection (marijuana users postpone the transition to marriage and parenthood) and anticipatory socialization (drug use tends to cease shortly before entry into adult roles).

Using data from the 1985 National Household Survey on Drug Abuse, Robbins (1989) examined racial/ethnic differences in drug use and transitions into adult roles, using social bonding theory and Kandel's concept of role incompatibility. She found that

Black youths and young adults had lower levels of drug use than would be expected given their school, work, and family experiences. Older blacks had relatively high levels of drug use that were not accounted for by marital status, employment, or educational attainment.

Considerably more research is needed on the correlational or causal nexus between role transitions (marriage, parenthood, work, religious and civic organizational involvement, education, military service, etc.) and transitions to drug use and abuse.

Selected Risk Factor Domains

As noted above, the concept of transitions in life and in drug use and abuse are complex phenomena. Even more complex are the presumed links between these types of transitions. Even so, there is a reasonable consensus about the key stages in these transitions, and research is beginning to explore how best to study these links. Ultimately, the goal in etiologic research should be to carefully examine the paths between the risk/protective factors and transitions in drug use specified or conditioned by life-course transitions.

The risk-factors approach to drug abuse is similar to risk-factor models for other problems. For example, negative risk factors for cardiovascular disease are known to consist of individual "characteristics" (e.g., family history of heart disease, weight, eating habits, cholesterol, smoking status, marital and ethnic status) and "conditions" (e.g., degree of stress in life, worksite conditions, place of residence, degree of crowding in home and neighborhood). No one of these risk factors is sufficient to account for disease; the greater the number of risk factors, the greater the likelihood the disease will appear.

In the sections that follow, I will attempt to organize some of the risk factors for drug abuse identified by Bry, Labouvie, Newcomb, Hawkins, and their respective colleagues, along with the types of people at high risk for drug abuse, as found in the 1986 Anti-Drug Abuse Act. In the process, I will attempt to elaborate on some potential risk factors not covered by any of these groups.

Genetic–Biological Risk Factors

Researchers in the field of alcohol abuse have been searching for the gene(s) responsible for the development of alcoholism for at least two decades. The impetus for the search is at least threefold. First, the common ideology concerning the "causes" of alcoholism emphasizes that it is genetic and inborn and that victims are "predisposed" from birth to abuse alcohol. If we could just locate the gene(s) responsible, it might be possible to eliminate the problem before it appears in behavioral form. Second, there are new discoveries reported almost daily as progress is made toward understanding the genetic bases for a host of disorders such as schizophrenia, depression, and so on. Thus, hope increases that the genetic basis for alcoholism may be discovered as well. Third, there is the clinical and research-based observation that alcoholism seems to "run in families." It is this observation that serves as a foundation for a discussion of genetic and biological risk factors for drug abuse.

Cloninger, Bohman, & Sigvardsson (1981) and others have found that identical (monozygotic) twins are about twice as likely as fraternal (dizygotic) twins of the same sex to be concordant for alcoholism. Furthermore, children adopted away from alcoholic biological parents and raised in nonalcoholic adopted families develop many more problems with alcohol as adults than adoptees whose natural parents were not alcoholic. The possible genetic basis for alcoholism is also supported by production of strains of mice who differ significantly in their probability of drinking excessive amounts of alcohol when given a choice between alcohol and water. Finally, there is considerable research on physiological markers that are correlated with alcoholism or the risk for it.

Recently, Blum, Noble, Sheridan, and their colleagues (Blum et al., 1990) identified as a candidate for the gene involved the dopamine D2 receptor, and compared the brains of a group of deceased alcoholics with those of a group of deceased nonalcoholics. They controlled statistically for sex and race without any change in the strong relationship between the A1 allele, which was present in 24 (69%) of the brain samples of alcoholics and absent in 28 (80%) of the 35 nonalcoholics.

In reaction to the Blum et al. (1990) findings, Gordis, Tabakoff, Goldman, and Berg (1990) put the entire research agenda on the genetic bases of alcoholism in perspective:

> Since alcoholism appears to be at least clinically heterogeneous, it is highly unlikely that the same gene or genes confer vulnerability in all families. What the function of such genes might be or whether these genes are going to be specific for alcoholism or be of more general influence on affect, appetite, personality, or behavior is also unknown. The analysis is complex, not only because alcoholism is probably heterogeneous and polygenic but because genes for alcoholism may display incomplete penetrance, and, in addition, there may be phenocopies (alcoholism of a nongenetic type that is clinically identical to genetically influenced variants) mixed into the same families as the genetically influenced alcoholism. (p. 2094)

In their conclusion, Gordis et al. (1990) stated that "genetics accounts for only part of the vulnerability to alcoholism. Understanding how genes and environment interact to produce alcoholism in any individual is the larger challenge to both genetic and psycho-social research" (p. 2095). A key concept here is vulnerability. For any one person, vulnerability is genetic, biological, and environmental in nature. There are probably multilateral relationships among the various domains of variables. The behavioral manifestations of genetic vulnerability to drug abuse (assuming it exists) may be inhibited, enhanced, or altered by environmental conditions. The behavioral manifestations of environmental vulnerability to drug abuse (assuming it exists) may be shaped significantly by genetic predispositions.

In social science research, a positive family history for alcoholism is often a rough proxy for genetic transmission of the tendency to become an alcoholic. In fact, this variable is often measured simply as a dummy: zero or one. However, in their prospective, longitudinal study of a representative sample of 12-, 15-, and 18-year-olds in New Jersey, Pandina and Johnson (1989) included several levels of risk. The highest risk group was positive for family history, defined as "history of alcoholism and/or past treatment for alcoholism and/or alcoholism as a factor in divorce" (p. 251). The next highest risk group contained parents who consumed relatively large quantities of alcohol, consumed alcohol frequently, or both. Some of the parents in this group were probably well on their way to becoming alcoholics but were not alcoholic at the time of the study. It is clear that the parents in this category were modeling excessive use of alcohol to their children. The third group of parents demonstrated no evidence of excessive drinking or alcoholism but did have a history of ulcers or a family history of nervous breakdown or of treatment for depression. The last and lowest risk group was free of the symptoms identified in the other three groups.

An important question to ask of each risk and protective factor is whether it has some kind of biological basis. To the extent that the answer is yes, the risk factor is truly a "PRE-disposition" and distal in origin as opposed to being more proximate to the behavior under study (i.e., transitions in drug use).

However, as Tarter, Alterman, and Edwards (1988) note, there are many levels between genetics, on one end of the continuum, and the behavioral manifestations of alcoholism and/or drug abuse (e.g., the neuroanatomical substrate, intervening biological mechanisms, and the developmental acquisition of diverse psychological processes encompassing cognition, emotion, motivation, and organismic arousal regulation). The excavation process required to separate the biological and other internal causal factors for alcohol and drug abuse from the intrapsychic, interpersonal, and social environmental factors is or should be a key goal of truly interdisciplinary research efforts. No one discipline or theoretical orientation can account for "most" of the variance in the various transitions in drug abuse. Therefore, "us versus them" types of discussions deflect and postpone recognition of the inevitable; a comprehensive understanding of the etiology of transitions in drug abuse requires collaboration and synergistic research and theory.

The genetic and biologic bases of alcoholism have been a clear target of research for a number of years. Ethanol is essentially only one substance, and there is still substantial disagreement among researchers about whether alcoholism is genetically based. How much more difficult will it be to discover the genetic and biologic bases of the vast menu of drugs now being abused, drugs that have different abuse liabilities, different actions on brain receptors, and different psychological effects?

Psychological Risk Factors

A hallmark of American society is the belief in the concept of individualism: the notion that each individual can create for himself or herself a future of his or her own choosing. A common perception is that "the" causal factors in explaining human behavior, any human behavior, lie somewhere "inside" the individual, at the psychological level.

There is an intuitive ring of truth to this orientation. Certainly, our ability to interpret and organize past experiences and current situations and then to implement rational decision making, to "cope" with the stresses and strains of modern life, requires a "stable" and reasonably integrated personality. People who "have their act together" are described as functioning well psychologically. People who do not have their act together are said to be psychologically impaired or disturbed. In this orientation, which is pervasive in our society, people who use and abuse drugs are assumed to have psychological deficits.

Self-Esteem, Self-Derogation

These psychological risk factors or indicators of poor psychological functioning have many names. Many of these names focus attention on the self-concept, the assumption being that poor self-esteem or self-derogation (see Kaplan, Martin, Johnson, and Robbins, 1986) leads a person to use drugs in order to increase self-esteem. In fact, changing self-esteem is at the heart of many programs designed to prevent drug use, delinquency, or some other problem behavior.

Because of the demands for "reliable" and thus "replicable" measurement scales and instruments, there is a tendency to use existing scales rather than raising questions about the conceptual underpinnings and the actual measurement procedures used to establish scales. Perhaps the best example is the scale developed by Rosenberg (1965) to measure self-esteem among adolescents. It contains only a small number of items, and its zero-order correlation of self-esteem with drug use is low (see Kaplan, Martin, & Robbins, 1984; White, Johnson, & Horwitz, 1986). However, it would be inappropriate to conclude that the relationship does not exist. The answer may be that self-esteem has been inadequately measured, perhaps inadequately conceptualized. Self-esteem among adolescents may be situationally anchored and extremely variable because of constantly changing interactions with peers and adults. If the items designed to measure self-esteem are not temporally anchored and contextualized, a score on such a scale may reflect randomness of time and measurement as much as it measures the actual construct of self-esteem.

Sensation Seeking

One of the most attractive aspects of the construct of sensation seeking is the assumption (see Zuckerman, 1979) that it has a biological and biochemical basis in monoamine oxidase. If this is true, the genesis of sensation seeking is at the biochemical level and is not solely cognitive, emotional, or social.

Sensation seeking is defined by Zuckerman (1979) as "the need for varied, novel, and complex sensations and experiences and the willingness to take physical and social risks for the sake of such experiences" (p. 17). The general construct is described as having four dimensions: (a) experience seeking, (b) thrill or adventure seeking, (c) disinhibition, and (d) boredom susceptibility.

The empirical relationship among these dimensions is not clear at this point. They are presumed not to be orthogonal to each other, but the relative strength of the associations among them could vary depending on the age of the respondent (developmental stage) and on the particular stresses and strains (role transitions) being faced. Maturation, whether measured on social, psychological, physical, emotional, or cognitive terms, may be an important concern. Piaget suggested that thinking/reasoning "develops." Therefore, if a person (a) has not achieved the formal or at least concrete operations stage of cognitive development or (b) has not reached "closure" on either the entire construct or the relative importance of each element of the construct, then something that is multidimensional like sensation seeking may not be a coherent predictor of drug use. In addition, it is possible that specific drugs that facilitate "disinhibition" may have a "causal" effect on various elements of sensation seeking. The presumption that the relationship between sensation seeking and drug use is asymmetrical focuses on "initiation" and may not be accurate for the other transitions in drug use such as progression, regression, cessation, or relapse.

Sensation seeking, both as a total construct and as separate dimensions (e.g., experience seeking, thrill or adventure seeking, disinhibition, boredom susceptibility), has been related to a number of behaviors, such as drug use, alcohol use, and criminality (see Bates, Labouvie, & White, 1986; Huba, Newcomb, & Bentler, 1986), primarily in adolescent or young adult populations.

Pandina (this volume, chapter 9) has incorporated some of the dimensions of sensation seeking into a construct labeled *arousability* and has examined this construct along with constructs of positive and negative affectivity regarding drug use and abuse in the longitudinal Rutgers sample. He notes that positive affectivity has much smaller effects on drug use than arousability and negative affectivity and that the latter two constructs have both independent and synergistic effects on drug use.

Newcomb and McGee (1989) hypothesized that sensation seeking might be a "general" factor or underlying need or predisposition, to help explain the connection between alcohol use and delinquency. Thus, sensation seeking was included as a control for a possible common cause of spuriousness in this relationship. The hypothesis was not supported. Sensation seeking did seem to have an influence on alcohol use, but not on delinquency. Overall, the results for sensation seeking were more complex than expected and were different for men and women.

Depression

There have been major improvements in diagnostic techniques for mental illness and in the standardization of diagnoses. However, evidence linking specific mental health problems with drug use patterns is not as robust or consistent as desirable. For example, Kaplan (1985) and Huba, Newcomb, and Bentler (1986) indicate that drug use is often preceded by some type of emotional distress. However, it appears that the effect is often short-lived. Labouvie (1986) found that drugs are sometimes used to relieve emotional distress. Aneshensel and Huba (1983) found that drugs are often used to relieve depression. Drugs may in fact have that effect in the short term, but the long-term effects of drug use may be to increase depression.

Newcomb and Bentler (1988) found that alcohol produced some decrease in depression in a normal sample of adolescents followed up over time. However, teenage use of drugs other than alcohol was essentially unrelated to affective disorders such as emotional distress, purpose in life, and depression.

Does this mean that drug use is not related to mental health problems in adolescents? The answer is simple: of course not. Drug use may be strongly related to mental health problems among youth with other high risk factors present. For example, Elliott and Huizinga (1984) used two measures of mental health problems, a social isolation or loneliness scale and an emotional-problems scale, in their study of a national sample of youth. Those classified as having emotional problems and being socially isolated reported higher levels of use of alcohol, marijuana, and other illicit drugs. Multiple illicit drug users had the highest scores on these two measures of mental health problems. However, this study was somewhat limited by the relatively small percentage of youths in the extreme categories on the drug use and the mental health problems scales.

Using a sample of detainees in a juvenile detention center, Dembo et al. (1987) found that drug use is moderately related to emotional and psychological functioning.

Self-destructive behavior

One indicator of psychological malfunctioning among youth is suicide, the second leading cause of death among adolescents in the United States. Youth who consider suicide are characterized by a sense of being overwhelmed by circumstances, a pervasive feeling of hopelessness, and an inability to see beyond the present. Adolescence is generally a time when expectations run high, when every event is earth-shaking, and when the heights of the peaks are equalled by the depths of the valleys.

Newcomb and Bentler (1988) report the following from their long-term study of adolescents who were followed into young adulthood:

> Drug use during adolescence was related to increased psychotic thinking in young adulthood, and thus could be seen as interfering with important cognitive processes, perhaps to the detriment of other life arenas.... Drug use decreased deliberateness.... This suggests that early drug use has a long-term impact on planning, organization, and directed behavior as reflected in a decrease in deliberateness. Adolescent hard drug use was associated with increased suicide ideation in young adulthood, beyond levels of emotional distress already experienced in adolescence. (p. 180)

It is clear from even the small body of existing research that much more needs to be done concerning the complex role that drug use may play in various indices of psychological functioning such as depression, as well as its relationship to excessive thinking about death, attempts at suicide, and completed suicide among adolescents.

Stability of Predictors

Brook, Whiteman, Gordon, and Cohen (1989) studied a sample of over 600 adolescents and their mothers at three different points in time. The study examined the direct and mediated influences of childhood and adolescent personality factors on drug use initiation and escalation. Brook et al. (1989) concluded as follows:

> A number of complex personality traits tapping unconventionality, poor control of emotions, interpersonal difficulty, and intrapsychic distress were related to drug escalation. It was

also shown that childhood vulnerabilities could be mitigated by protective adolescent personality traits leading to a decrease in drug escalation, suggesting that childhood vulnerability need not invariably result in greater adolescent drug involvement. (p. 724)

This study is consistent with the work of Kellam et al. (1990), which emphasized the predictive power of personality traits such as shyness, aggressivity, and depression in the first grade regarding later drug use.

Family Risk Factors

We are all influenced by our families: biologically through genetics, psychologically and socially through the socialization process, and culturally through the traditions, customs, and values passed on to us from our parents and their parents before them. The family consists of a structure, functions that are related to the roles that exist within and are enacted by family members, and the process by which the family gives the children in it the skills and values to make decisions about various issues, including drug use and abuse.

Family Structure

We all have a stereotypical or ideal image of *the* American family. It usually resembles the Cleaver Family: Ward, June, Wally, and the Beaver—husband, wife, two children, house in the suburbs, and rock-solid stability. Television is not reality; the reality is that there is incredible diversity in families.

In the annual (since 1975) *Monitoring the Future* studies of drug abuse among high school seniors (Johnston, O'Malley, & Bachman, 1989), there is a question that asks, "Which of the following people live in the same household with you?" There are nine response alternatives: *father, mother, brothers and/or sisters, grandparents, my husband/ wife, my children, other relatives, non-relatives,* or *I live alone.* The 17,000 or so high school seniors who complete this questionnaire each year can check as many answers as apply. There were 64 different family structures that emerged: 64 different combinations of these types of household composition, 64 different "families" for the students in this survey. If family factors are thought to be "risk/protective" factors for drug abuse, then it may be necessary to specify what is meant by the term *family.*

In the mid-1960s, Kellam, Simon, and Ensminger (1983) conducted a study of first graders and their mothers in the Woodlawn neighborhood, a poor, predominantly Black area near the University of Chicago. They found that there were 76 different family structures by identifying the different types of people living with these first graders. In long-term followup studies of these youths, Kellam and his associates discovered that, counter to common belief, it was not the absence of the father that was predictive of later drug use, but rather the aloneness of the mother. If the mother had another adult present, regardless of the specific role played by that adult, the likelihood of subsequent drug use and delinquency was close to that found for children growing up in homes where both the mother and father were present.

One of the most common causes of a change in family structure is divorce and remarriage. Needle, Su, and Doherty (1990) conducted a 5-year, prospective, longitudinal study of a group of youths and their families. Of the 508 families involved, 67 (13%) experienced a divorce prior to the study (1975–82) or during the course of the study (1982–87). The youths were classified according to whether their parents were continuously married, divorced when they were a child, or divorced with they were an adolescent.

Needle et al. (1990) found that there were differential effects by sex. Parental divorce during the adolescent years was a significant predictor of overall drug involvement for boys and had an effect as well on reported consequences from drug abuse. Parental divorce that occurred during adolescence had a larger effect on overall drug involvement and consequences of that drug abuse for boys than did divorce that occurred when the boys were children. Overall, drug involvement or substance use consequences among girls did not appear to be affected by parental divorce, even when family environment, peer influences, and personal adjustment variables at the beginning of the study were statistically controlled.

Remarriage of the custodial parent produces another "intact" family from a structural perspective and does not seem to significantly influence overall drug involvement of boys, but does have a moderate predictive effect on reports of consequences of substance use. However, among girls, remarriage of the custodial parent is predictive of a significant increase in overall drug involvement but not in reported consequences.

This study underscores that families are complex and that family disruption is not a discrete event, but an on-going process that requires substantial changes from all involved. *When* this occurs in the life of a young person, particularly boys, is a risk factor for drug abuse. This is consistent with research on other effects of divorce (see Block, Block, & Gjerde, 1986; Guidubaldi & Perry, 1985; Wallerstein, 1987). In addition, boys derive greater benefit than girls from the remarriage of the custodial parent, specifically with regard to drug abuse. This is consistent with research on other effects of divorce (Emery, 1988; Hetherington, Cox, & Cox, 1985; Peterson & Zill, 1986).

Family Process

Each individual inherits from parents and generations of family members before them a unique and complex genetic map that affects their growth and development in numerous ways, many of which are still not understood. Some of the family-history impact is biological and may involve genetic transmission of the potential for alcohol and substance abuse (see Lester, 1988). Some of the impact of the family occurs because the child sees and incorporates into his or her life the response and behavioral styles of the parents (Wilson, 1988). Imitation is perhaps the first, and an enduring, way in which humans develop a repertoire of behaviors to apply in the proper situation. Some of the impact of the family is due to the specific ways that parents socialize and treat the child (Baumrind, 1983). Regardless of *how*, it is clear that the family exerts an extremely powerful influence on its members.

Parenting behavior is generally classified into two broad categories: closeness or parental warmth (affectionate, nurturing, accepting of child) on the positive side and control or monitoring (parental involvement in child's life, close supervision of activities, firmness in setting controls and limits) on the negative side. Kandel, Kessler, and Margulies (1978) found that lack of closeness to parents increased the risk that adolescents who experimented with marijuana would use other illicit drugs.

Drug Abuse Within the Family

The "availability" of alcohol and other substances in the home, the presence of adult role models who alter their consciousness by using drugs, and the inadequate family management techniques exhibited by drug-impaired parents all have an impact on the likelihood that children in these circumstances will themselves use and abuse drugs (Baumrind, 1983). A substantial proportion of clients in treatment for alcohol and drug abuse have had chemically dependent parents, relatives, or siblings.

Some researchers attribute much of the likelihood of intergenerational transmission of drug abuse to genetic or biochemical factors (Cloninger, Bohman, & Sigvardsson, 1981), whereas others argue that the major risk factors involve psychosocial and environmental conditions in addition to biological vulnerability (DeMarsh & Kumpfer, 1986). Glantz (this volume) suggests that many of the familial influences on the likelihood that a child will use drugs during adolescence occur quite early in life and are risk factors that can be reduced or entirely eliminated.

Unfortunately, being the child of a substance abuser is one type of high risk about which knowledge is insufficient to justify strong conclusions. Much of what is known is now limited to children of alcoholic parents. However, given estimates of the magnitude of the problem, youth who are in homes where alcohol and other substances are abused should be given high priority, from both a research and an intervention perspective.

Physical, Sexual, or Psychological Abuse

In 1980, Straus, Gelles, and Steinmetz reported the results of a nationwide study of domestic violence conducted in 1976. The study was limited because only intact families were included. The levels of of parent–child, husband–wife, wife–husband, and sibling–sibling violence were substantial. Because of its limitations, that study should be viewed as setting low boundaries on the prevalence of the phenomenon. Even so, 20% of the youths reported being hit by their parents with something, and 4% had been beaten up by their parents.

Dembo et al. (1987) examined similar types of interpersonal violence in a sample of detainees in a juvenile detention center: 43% had been beaten or really hurt by being hit; 21% had been beaten or hit with something hard like a club or stick; and 17% had been hurt badly enough to need a doctor, bandages, or medical treatment. Some 61% of the girls and 25% of the boys in this sample reported sexual victimization. Rates of drug abuse were substantial in this sample. Dembo et al. concluded, "Our results support the proposition that child abuse, either sexual or physical, is positively related to high rates of illicit drug use" (p. 30).

The influence of the family on drug abuse among youth is multifaceted, not unidirectional or monolithic. There will always be children who grow up in "bad" conditions or "bad" families but who overcome those deficits to become leading citizens. By the same token, there will be some children who, despite the quality of their family life, become "rotten" kids. The risk-factor approach to drug abuse is based on probability. When the family is not functioning well, the likelihood of drug abuse is higher than it might be otherwise. Poor functioning may result from an inadequate structure, from family management techniques and performance of roles that are inconsistent, or from socialization that is on balance destructive rather than constructive.

School Risk Factors

Other than the home, young people spend more time in school than anywhere else. Even more than being a son or daughter, being a student determines the age-graded norms that set the boundaries for appropriate and inappropriate behavior.

A young person's sense of self-worth is often fragile; it is certainly variable in terms of perceived competence. There are many opportunities within the school context for one's self-worth and sense of competence to be threatened. Acceptance or rejection at school, whether by teacher or peer, is often seen by the young person as almost a life-or-death situation. Thus, Hawkins and Catalano (1989) specifically identify peer rejection in elementary school as an important risk factor in the probability of subsequent drug abuse. A low grade point average or poor performance in school is also listed as an important risk factor. How well one is doing in the student role can affect every other aspect of life. Teachers and one's same-age peers can be cruel, even vicious, in the labels they apply. In the youth culture that exists within the school context, being labeled a hood or a druggie or a nerd carries strong meaning and often requires certain specific patterns of behavior.

Dropping Out of School

Dropping out of school is a "process," not just a discrete event. The school system necessarily collects data relevant to the etiology of dropping out, drug abuse, and other forms of "deviant" behavior. Transitions in the student role are probably related to transitions in drug abuse.

We do not know for certain what the dropout rate is, but the estimates are not encouraging. For example, census statistics indicate that among 25-to-29-year-olds nationally, 14% of White men and 13% of White women did not complete high school. The respective rate for Black men and women are similar, 15% and 18%, respectively. However, among Hispanic men and women 25 to 29 years old, 41% and 39%, respectively, did not complete high school. These are "national" figures about dropping out. In some inner cities, as well as in depressed rural counties, the dropout rates may be considerably higher.

The relationship between dropping out of high school and drug abuse was explored using a national longitudinal sample of people who were 19 to 27 years old in 1984. Mensch and Kandel (1988a) found that 22.3% had dropped out (24.2% of the men and 20.4% of the women). However, only 14.8% (16.1% of the men and 13.4% of the women) had no high school credentials. Of those who had dropped out, 5.1% of the men and 7.3% of the women obtained a high school diploma, and 28.6% and 28.9%, respectively, obtained a GED. Therefore, about two thirds of those who had dropped out at some point in their school career never obtained a high school diploma or its equivalent.

Mensch and Kandel (1988a) found that dropouts were more likely to abuse drugs. Those who eventually received a GED were highest on every measure. Mensch and Kandel state that "prior use of cigarettes, marijuana, and other illicit drugs at any age increases the propensity of both sexes to drop out. In addition, the younger the initiation into alcohol, marijuana, and other illicit drugs for men, and cigarettes and marijuana for women, the greater the likelihood of leaving school without a diploma" (p. 111). Dropping out of school is not a phenomenon of interest just for high school: Dropping out is also related to drug abuse when the focus is on college dropouts (see O'Donnell, Voss, Clayton, Slatin, & Room, 1976).

It is important to note that the risk factors for drug abuse are also significant risk factors for dropping out of school (see Barro & Kolstad, 1987). Thus, dropouts are at high risk for drug abuse, and drug abuse puts one at higher risk for dropping out of school: high school and college. The above quote from Mensch and Kandel (1988a) points out the significance of "early onset" of drug use.

Youth who are doing well in school and feel strong bonds to school are less likely to feel alienated from this system. Those who are bored and those who find themselves so far behind that catching up seems impossible are the most likely candidates for dropping out or for coming to school drugged. They do not feel they are an integral part of the process; they feel left out and unwanted. Kellam et al. (1990) focused attention on early problems with concentration, early achievement-test scores, and self-reports of depression as predictors of later drug use. Important questions need to be asked. Can communities use risk factors related to academic progress and success as a way of reducing the dropout rate? Are there early markers in the school system that can effectively predict who will drop out, so that intervention is possible before the die is cast? Can the same be done for drug abuse?

Sexual Activity, Pregnancy, and Dropping Out

Becoming pregnant is a major transition in life. It is tough to be a parent, even when one has the education, maturity, and economic resources and sincerely wants the responsibility. It is clearly much more difficult when none of these factors are present. As many as 4 out of every 10 girls in the United States will become pregnant at some time during their teen years, and more than half who become pregnant will leave school.

As Mensch and Kandel (1988b) found for the women 19 to 27 years old in their longitudinal survey, 69% who had first intercourse at age 12 or earlier dropped out of school, compared with 60% for those whose first intercourse occurred at age 13 or 14. When first intercourse occurred at age 15 or 16, the dropout rate was 44%, and it was 20% for those for whom intercourse first occurred at age 17 or 18. The dropout rate was 10% for those who waited until age 19 or later and 6% for those who had never had intercourse. Although the rates were somewhat different, age at first intercourse was linearly related to dropout status for men as well. As noted earlier, dropout status is related to drug abuse.

In analyses based on a national longitudinal study of youths 11 to 17 years old in 1976 and 15 to 21 years old in 1980, Elliott and Morse (1987) examined the interrelationship of drug use, delinquency, sexual activity, and pregnancy. Their conclusion is important from the standpoint of risk factors for drug abuse among high-risk youth: "Sexual activity and even pregnancy, particularly at an early age, is not an isolated phenomenon but occurs within the larger context of deviant behaviors" (p. 26). For example, in 1976, when the sample was 11 to 17 years old, 71% of the boys and 52% of the girls who were using multiple illicit drugs were sexually active, in comparison with 10% of the boys and only 3% of the girls who were not using any drugs.

Teenage pregnancy is a major problem in the United States. However, it is neither an isolated problem nor one limited only to the girls involved. It is a problem that is seriously intermeshed with drug abuse and other forms of deviance, including dropping out. One thing common to all youth is their presence in and progress through a system controlled by adults who are committed to laying the foundation for helping them become mature and productive citizens. Multiple-problem youths are visible and identifiable in this system early on. The challenge is to move beyond being fearful of labeling these youth to recognizing the opportunity to intervene early and effectively to neutralize the risk factors known to be predictive of "failure" in achieving productive adult status.

Environmental Context Risk Factors

Environmental context is a very broad concept that can contain a number of different kinds of specific risk factors. The most common such risk factor would be living in a "culture of poverty." In this case, being poor would be an individual characteristic and living in a poor neighborhood would be the context. Another such risk factor would be involvement in delinquent behavior. Much of the research on delinquency has focused on the delinquent person, but that delinquent more often than not lives in an environment where many of his or her associates are also involved in delinquent behavior. This is sometimes referred to as a subculture of delinquency.

Risk Factors External to the Individual

In the late 1960s, Brunswick (1979, 1988) began a study of health and health-compromising behavior in a sample of youths drawn to be representative of all youths growing up in Central Harlem. By the mid-1970s, when they were 18 to 23 years old, 18% of the Black males had used heroin and 42% had used cocaine, figures considerably in excess of those reported for 18-to-25-year-olds from the National Household Survey, suggesting a contextual effect.

In 1974–75, O'Donnell and his colleagues conducted two studies; one consisted of a nationwide sample of 2,510 men 20 to 30 years old (see O'Donnell et al., 1976), and the other was a representative sample of 20-to-30-year-old men selected from areas of Manhattan known to be high in drug abuse, including Central Harlem (see Clayton & Voss, 1981). In the nationwide sample, 14% of the Black men had used heroin and 24% had used cocaine. In the Manhattan sample, 39% of the Black men had used heroin and 50% cocaine. For these two drugs, the rates were considerably higher in places where drug abuse was rampant. Where a person grows up and lives influences the probability that he or she will have an opportunity to use drugs and will, in fact use them.

Poverty at the Individual Level, Poor Neighborhood at Macro Level

Among all children under the age of 18, approximately 1 in 5 live in families classified as poor. However, poverty is far from being equally distributed. Imagine visiting a school and having the principal show you three lines of children. In one line, all are White. The other two lines consist of children who are Black and Hispanic. Each line contains 100 children. The poor children are asked to step forward. Sixteen of the White children step forward. However, 43 of the Black and 38 of the Hispanic children step forward. But what is "poor"? It is densely crowded living conditions, being hungry, living in substandard housing, and having drugs, drug addicts, and drug dealers as a "normal" part of the neighborhood environment.

As Brunswick (1988) noted from her long-term study of youths from Central Harlem,

> An often overlooked cornerstone of hard drug use among urban young black males is that it is not only, and perhaps even not primarily a consumption and/or recreational behavior. It also serves economic functions of occupation and career for this group (Johnson, Goldstein, Preble, Schmeidler, Lipton, Spunt, & Miller, 1985; Preble & Casey, 1969; Williams & Kornblum, 1985). In a population subgroup where employment opportunities are severely constrained, and at a life stage when economic independence is expected and required, the drug economy is one of the relatively few options open. (p. 168)

Although hard, cold numbers that differentiate the truly poor from the nearly poor exist, poverty itself is relative. There are many people living in the "rich" ghettos who are characterized by a poverty of affluence. They have all of the material possessions that the kids in the "poor" ghettos want, but few of the nonmaterial things that make life more worthwhile. Extreme economic deprivation is not the only end of the rich-poor continuum where people are at risk for drug abuse, but it is simply more likely there than at the rich end. A detailed understanding of the relationship of economic resources and economic context to drug abuse is still incomplete. An important issue is the relationship of the flow of drug-trafficking money into impoverished neighborhoods and the increased reliance of the residents on that money.

Delinquency/Criminality at the Individual Level, Deviant Subcultures at the Macro Level

The relationship between delinquency and drug abuse is a strong and complex one. From just a temporal-order perspective alone, first involvement in delinquency usually occurs prior to first illicit drug use (i.e., marijuana, cocaine, etc.). Some researchers (e.g., Elliott, Huizinga, & Ageton, 1985) see drug abuse and delinquency as a part of a general pattern of rebellion and nonconformity (White, 1990). This has been labeled a "deviance syndrome" (Jessor & Jessor, 1977) or evidence of an "antisocial personality."

Among juveniles processed through the juvenile justice system for violent crimes, one half reported that they used alcohol or other drugs prior to their involvement in violence; 40% reported using drugs immediately prior to committing the offense for which they were adjudicated (Harstone & Hansen, 1984).

One of the principal reasons for concern about the relationship of drug abuse during adolescence to delinquency, violent or otherwise, is the possibility that both behaviors may persist. Of even greater concern is that, together, both drug abuse and delinquency may get worse and, feeding on each other, lead to a criminal career. Research indicates that this will happen to only a small minority of youths, but they will be very active in terms of both drug abuse and crime. For example, in a long-term study of people born in 1945, 6% of the cohort was responsible for 52% of the recorded offenses (Wolfgang & Tracy, 1982).

Chronic offenders constituted only 7.5% of the 1958 birth cohort in Philadelphia, but accounted for 69% of all index offenses, including 61% of the homicides, 76% of the rapes, 73% of the robberies, and 65% of the aggravated assaults (Wolfgang & Tracy, 1982). In a nationwide study, Johnson, Wish, and Huizinga (1983) divided youths into several drug-abusing categories (no use, use of alcohol, use of marijuana, use of pills, and use of cocaine). Those who had used cocaine were, in fact, the most serious multiple-drug users. Although those who used cocaine and committed multiple index offenses constituted only 1.3% of all youths studied, they accounted for 40% of all index crimes committed by the entire sample.

Most of these items reflect "conditions" that put some youth at high risk for drug abuse and other forms of deviance. It is important to note that economic deprivation and family disorganization and less-than-adequate functioning within the family are present. Perhaps most important, most of these are conditions that can be observed and counted. They are risk factors that could be used to target these and similar youth for specialized interventions that may go beyond the kinds of generic interventions that occur in schools and communities.

There are two very important and related questions that are usually raised with data like these. First, how early do the risk factors appear? Second, how accurate are our predictions of future problems based on early behavioral characteristics? These high-risk multiple-problem youths constitute a relatively small percentage of each cohort. What are the chances that false positive labeling of youth as "heading for trouble" will be more harmful than waiting to see if they mature out of the problem behaviors or waiting for more evidence to appear before an intervention is attempted?

Discussion

The scientific study of a phenomenon, any phenomenon, requires a recognition of the evolutionary and inductive nature of research. In fact, a useful way to view the study of transitions in drug abuse is from a career or life-history perspective. The study, with this orientation, of drug abuse and transitions in drug abuse is developmentally in its early infancy, in spite of the fact that it has been a topic of research for a number of years.

In this chapter, a principal goal was to identify and discuss the "appropriate" dependent variables. More than a little attention has been devoted to discussions about what differentiates drug use from drug abuse. Such a gross categorization probably limits the field for researchers as well as for treatment and prevention specialists. A more robust conceptualization of "the" dependent variables focuses on "transitions" (e.g., initiation, continuation, maintenance, progression within and across drug classes, regression, and cessation and relapse cycles). This approach would allow for different configurations of risk and protective factors at each transition in drug use status and would also tend to focus attention on stability and instability in the risk and protective factors.

Although movement toward transitions in drug abuse as the "appropriate" dependent variables constitutes progress, a great deal of work is still required. For example, little is known about who gets involved in drug use at a very early age and who moves through the transitions rapidly toward heavy involvement in abusing multiple drugs. Furthermore, very little is known about the epidemiology and etiology of multiple drug use. Even less is known about how to measure and characterize this phenomenon. How these drug-consumption behaviors are related to the ease or difficulty of making "other" transitions in life is relatively uncharted. Finally, a focus on transitions in drug abuse will allow for greater attention to problems and consequences associated with drug use.

Another principal goal of this chapter was to review existing taxonomies of risk and protective factors and to discuss research findings that might clarify factors that are still relatively unexplored. A review of the elements in Table 1.1 reveals an emergent consensus on the most important risk factors for drug use and abuse. However, there are probably a number of other risk factors missing from the table that need examination. Furthermore, there is a strong need for research on the dimensionality of some of these risk and protective factors. Efforts to explore the dimensionality of risk factors should enhance efforts to improve the measurement of risk factors. This would include searching for the possible biological bases as well as untangling the temporal ordering of the risk factors in their influence on each other and on drug abuse transitions.

Finally, a principal goal of this chapter was to reiterate the importance of environmental contextual factors in drug abuse. This is not to deny the importance of biological or psychological factors. However, the social and cultural contexts within which people live exert a strong influence on their opportunities to use drugs and on the normative pressures and values to continue or progress. Macro-level or ecological approaches to understanding and intervening in the problem of drug abuse may be as effective or even more effective than attacking risk factors that are operative primarily at the individual level.

At the individual level, very little is known about how people get involved in the drug distribution system and about the relationship of their role in dealing with transitions in drug abuse. At the macro level, a potentially important line of research might be the role of drug trafficking in the economic stability or instability of communities and their institutional settings (e.g., families, churches, businesses, etc.). In reviewing the literature on risk factors for transitions in drug abuse, I was struck by the dearth of serious research on risk factors "external" to the individual, suggesting the need for greater involvement of ethnographers and sociologists in studying drug use.

In conclusion, a significant amount of high-quality research has been completed on the risk and protective factors for transitions in drug use, most of it in the 1980s. In the 1990s, the goal should be the development of comprehensive conceptual and theoretical models explaining who will use drugs (make transitions in drug use), who will not, and under what circumstances the probability of transition is greater or less. Special attention must be given to improvements in the measurement of both the dependent and the independent etiological variables for transitions in drug abuse. This will require a far greater commitment to longitudinal studies in which tracking the stability, instability, and relative efficacy of variables in predicting drug use transitions is a major focus. This may require a greater use of collaborative agreements in research so that the enhanced etiological map can be subdivided across investigative teams for special focus on certain domains of variables.

Further progress in unraveling the mystery of transitions in drug abuse will require a new commitment to rigorous research designs, innovative research efforts, collection of quality data, and close attention to the pitfalls that surround "chains of inference" and "rules of evidence" in research.

Any examination of the etiological factors associated with transitions in drug abuse should have as its goal the "application" of knowledge to address the problem. However, the driving force behind application and interventions should or must be innovative and comprehensive examinations of a wide range of risk and protective factors and the development of advanced theory to guide the interventions. Failure to engage in developmental work at the conceptual, theoretical, and empirical research levels will be fruitless. Untangling the "causes" of drug abuse is absolutely essential. It requires a long-range view and a commitment to programmatic research that is interdisciplinary. It requires a long-term commitment to longitudinal studies. It also requires more exploratory research.

References

Aneshensel, C. S., & Huba, G. J. (1983). Depression, alcohol use, and smoking over one year: A four-wave longitudinal causal model. *Journal of Abnormal Psychology, 92,* 134–150.

Bachman, J. G., Schulenberg, J. E., O'Malley, P. M., & Johnston, L. D. (1990, March). *Short-term and longer-term effects of educational commitment and success on the use of cigarettes, alcohol, and illicit drugs.* Paper presented at the Third Biennial Meeting of the Society for Research on Adolescence, Atlanta.

Barro, S. M., & Kolstad, A. (1987). *Who drops out of high school? Findings from high school and beyond.* Washington, DC: U.S. Government Printing Office.

Bates, M. E., Labouvie, E. W., & White, H. R. (1986). The effect of sensation seeking needs on alcohol and marijuana use in adolescence. *Bulletin of the Society of Psychologists in Addictive Behaviors, 5,* 29–36.

Baumrind, D. (1983). Specious causal attributions in the social sciences: The reformulated steppingstone theory of heroin use, an exemplar. *Journal of Personality and Social Psychology, 45,* 1289–1298.

Block, J. H., Block, J., & Gjerde, P. F. (1986). The personality of children prior to divorce: A prospective study. *Child Development, 57,* 827–840.

Blum, K., Noble, E. P., Sheridan, P. J., Montgomery, A., Ritchie, T., Jagadeeswaran, T., Gagami, H., Briggs, A., & Cohn, J. (1990). Alcoholic association of human dopamine D_2 receptor gene in alcoholism. *Journal of the American Medical Association, 263,* 2055–2060.

Brook, J. S., Whiteman, M., Gordon, A. S., & Cohen, P. (1989). Changes in drug involvement : A longitudinal study of childhood and adolescent determinants. *Psychological Reports, 65,* 707–726.

Brunswick, A. F., (1979). Black youths and drug use behavior. In G. Beschner, & A. Friedman (Eds.), *Youth and drug abuse: Problems, issues, and treatment.* Lexington, MA: Lexington Books.

Brunswick, A. F., (1988). Drug use and affective distress: A longitudinal study of urban Black youth. *Advances in Adolescent Mental Health, 3,* 101–125.

Bry, B. H., McKeon, P., & Pandina, R. J. (1982). Extent of drug use as a function of the number of risk factors. *Journal of Abnormal Psychology, 91,* 273–279.

Clayton, R. R., & Gladden, J. W. (1975). The five dimensions of religiosity: Toward demythologizing a sacred artifact. *Journal for the Scientific Study of Religion, 13,* 135–143.

Clayton, R. R. (1986). Multiple drug use: Epidemiology, correlates, and consequences. In M. Galanter (Ed.), *Recent developments in alcoholism* (Vol. 4, pp. 7–38). New York: Plenum Press.

Clayton, R. R., & Voss, H. L. (1981). *Young men and drugs in Manhattan: A causal analysis.* Rockville, MD: National Institute on Drug Abuse.

Clayton, R. R., Voss, H. L., & LoSciuto, L. A. (1987). Gateway drugs: What are the stages people go thru in becoming drug abusers? *Pharmacy Times, 53,* 28–35.

Cloninger, C. R., Bohman, M., & Sigvardsson, S. (1981). Inheritance of alcohol abuse: Cross fostering analysis of adopted men. *Archives of General Psychiatry, 38,* 861–868.

DeMarsh, J., & Kumpfer, K. L. (1986). Family oriented interventions for the prevention of chemical dependency in children and adolescents. In S. Griswold, S. Ezekoye, K. L. Kumpfer, & W. J. Bukoski (Eds.), *Childhood and chemical abuse: Prevention and intervention.* New York: Haworth.

Dembo, R., Dertke, M., La Voie, L., Border, S., Washburn, M., & Schmeidler, J. (1987). Physical abuse, sexual victimization and illicit drug use: A structural analysis among high risk adolescents. *Journal of Adolescence, 10,* 13–33.

Elliott, D. S., & Huizinga, D. H. (1984). *The relationship between delinquent behavior and ADM problems.* Unpublished manuscript.

Elliott, D. S., Huizinga, D., & Ageton, S. S. (1985). *Explaining delinquency and drug use.* Beverly Hills, CA: Sage.

Elliott, D. S., & Morse, B. J. (1987). *Drug use, delinquency, and sexual activity.* Unpublished manuscript.

Emery, R. E. (1988). *Marriage, divorce, and children's adjustment.* Beverly Hills, CA: Sage.

Gordis, E., Tabakoff, B., Goldman, D., & Berg, K. (1990). Finding the gene(s) for alcoholism. *Journal of the American Medical Association, 263,* 2094–2095.

Guidubaldi, J., & Perry, J. D. (1985). Divorce and mental health sequalae for children: A two-year follow-up of a national sample. *Journal of the American Academy of Child Psychiatry, 24,* 531–537.

Harstone, E., & Hansen, K. V. (1984). The violent juvenile offender. In R. Mathias, P. DeMuro, & R. S. Allinson (Eds.), *An anthology on violent juvenile offenders.* Newark, NJ: National Council of Crime and Delinquency.

Hawkins, J. D., & Catalano, R. F. (1989). *Risk and protective factors for alcohol and other drug problems: Implications for substance abuse prevention.* Unpublished manuscript.

Hetherington, E. M., Cox, M., & Cox, R. (1985). Long-term effects of divorce and remarriage on the adjustment of children. *Journal of the American Academy of Child Psychiatry, 24,* 518–530.

Huba, G. J., Newcomb, M. D., & Bentler, P. M. (1986). Adverse drug experiences and drug use behaviors: A one-year longitudinal study of adolescents. *Journal of Pediatric Psychology, 11,* 203–219.

Huba, G. J., Wingard, J. A., & Bentler, P. M. (1981). A comparison of two latent variable causal models for adolescent drug use. *Journal of Personality and Social Psychology, 40,* 180–193.

Inciardi, J. A., & Pottieger, A. E. (1991). Kids, crack and crime. *Journal of Drug Issues, 21,* 257–270.

Jessor, R., & Jessor, S. L. (1977). *Problem behavior and psychosocial development: A longitudinal study of youth.* San Diego, CA: Academic Press.

Johnson, B. D., Goldstein, P. J., Preble, E., Schmeidler, J., Lipton, D., Spunt, B., & Miller, T. (1985). *Taking care of business: The economics of crime by heroin abusers.* Lexington, MA: Lexington Books.

Johnson, B. D., Wish, E., & Huizinga, D. (1983). *The concentration of delinquent offending: The contribution of serious drug involvement to high-rate delinquency.* Unpublished manuscript.

Johnston, L. D., O'Malley, P. M., & Bachman, J. G. (1989). *Drug use, drinking, and smoking: National survey results from high school, college, and young adult populations 1975–1988.* Rockville, MD: National Institute on Drug Abuse.

Kandel, D. B. (1975). Stages in adolescent involvement in drug use. *Science, 190,* 912–914.

Kandel, D. B. (1984). Marijuana users in young adulthood. *Archives of General Psychiatry, 41,* 200–209.

Kandel, D. B., Kessler, R. C., & Margulies, R. Z. (1978). Antecedents of adolescent initiation into stages of drug use: A developmental analysis. *Journal of Youth and Adolescence, 7,* (1) 13–40.

Kandel, D. B., & Logan, J. A. (1984). Patterns of drug use from adolescence to young adulthood: I. Periods of risk for initiation, continued use, and discontinuation. *American Journal of Public Health, 74,* 660–667.

Kaplan, H. B. (1985). Testing a general theory of drug abuse and other deviant adaptations. *Journal of Drug Issues, 15,* 477–492.

Kaplan, H. J., Martin, S. S., Johnson, R. J., & Robbins, C. A. (1986). Escalation of marijuana use: Application of a general theory of deviant behavior. *Journal of Health and Social Behavior, 27,* 44–61.

Kaplan, H. J., Martin, S. S., & Robbins, C. (1984). Pathways to adolescent drug use: Self-derogation, peer influence, weakening of social controls, and early substance use. *Journal of Health and Social Behavior, 25,* 270–289.

Kellam, S. G., Simon, M. B., & Ensminger, M. E. (1983). Antecedent of teenage drug use and psychological well-being: A ten-year community wide prospective study. In D. Ricks, & B. S. Dohrenwend (Eds.), *Origins of psychopathology: Research and public policy* (pp. 17–42). Cambridge, MA: Cambridge University Press.

Kellam, S. G., Werthamer-Larsson, L., Dolan, L., Brown, C. H., Laudolff, J., Anthony, J., Wilson, R., Edelsohn, G., & Spencer, P. (1990). *Developmental epidemiologically-based preventive trials: Baseline modeling of early target behaviors and depressive symptoms.* Unpublished manuscript.

Labouvie, E. W. (1986). The coping function of adolescent alcohol and drug use. In R. K. Silbereisen, K. Eyferth, & G. Rudinger (Eds.), *Development as action in context* (pp. 229–240). New York: Springer.

Labouvie, E. W., Pandina, R. J., White, H. R., & Johnson, V. (1986). *Risk factors of adolescent drug use: A cross-sequential study.* Unpublished manuscript.

Lester, D. (1988). Genetic theory: An assessment of the heritability of alcoholism. In C. D. Chaudron & D. A. Wilkinson (Eds.), *Theories on alcoholism* (pp. 1–28). Toronto: Addiction Research Foundation.

Mensch, B. S., & Kandel, D. B. (1988a). Do job conditions influence the use of drugs? *Journal of Health and Social Behavior, 29,* 169–184.

Mensch, B. S., & Kandel, D. B. (1988b). Dropping out of high school and drug involvement. *Sociology of Education, 61,* 95–113.

National Institute on Drug Abuse. (1988). *National Household Survey on Drug Abuse: Main findings, 1985.* Rockville, MD: Author.

Needle, R. H., Su, S., & Doherty, W. J. (1990). Divorce, remarriage, and adolescent substance use: A prospective longitudinal study. *Journal of Marriage and the Family, 52,* 157–169.

Newcomb, M. D., & Bentler, P. M. (1988). *Consequences of adolescent drug use: Impact on the lives of young adults.* Beverly Hills, CA: Sage.

Newcomb, M. D., Maddahian, E., & Bentler, P. M. (1986). Risk factors for drug use among adolescents: Concurrent and longitudinal analyses. *American Journal of Pubic Health, 76,* 625–630.

Newcomb, M. D., & McGee, L. (1989). Adolescent alcohol use and other delinquent behaviors: A one-year longitudinal analysis controlling for sensation seeking. *Criminal Justice Behavior, 16,* 345–369.

O'Donnell, J. A., & Clayton, R. R. (1982). The stepping-stone hypothesis: Marijuana, heroin, and causality. *Chemical Dependencies, 4,* 229–241.

O'Donnell, J. A., Voss, H. L., Clayton, R. R., Slatin, G. T., & Room, R. G. W. (1976). *Young men and drugs: A nationwide survey.* Rockville, MD: National Institute on Drug Abuse.

Pandina, R. J., & Johnson, V. (1989). Familial history as a predictor of alcohol and drug consumption among adolescent children. *Journal of Studies on Alcohol, 50,* 245–253.

Peterson, J. L., & Zill, N. (1986). Marital disruption and behavior problems in children. *Journal of Marriage and the Family, 48,* 295–308.

Preble, E. A., & Casey, J. J., Jr. (1969). Taking care of business: The heroin user's life on the street. *The International Journal of the Addictions, 4,* 1–24.

Robbins, C. A. (1989). Sex differences in psychosocial consequences of alcohol and drug abuse. *Journal of Health and Social Behavior, 30,* 117–130.

Rosenberg, M. (1965). *Society and the adolescent self-image.* Princeton, NJ: Princeton University Press.

Shiffman, S. (1989). Tobacco "chippers": Individual differences in tobacco dependence. *Psychopharmacology, 97,* 539–547.

Skinner, W. F., Clayton, R. R., LoSciuto, L. A., Martin, S. S., Robbins, C., & Voss, H. L. (1989). *The epidemiology of multiple drug use in the 1985 National Household Survey.* Rockville, MD: National Institute on Drug Abuse.

Straus, M. A., Gelles, R. J., & Steinmetz, S. K. (1980). *Behind closed doors: Violence in the American family.* New York: Anchor/Doubleday.

Surgeon General of the United States. (1988). *The health consequences of smoking: Nicotine addiction.* Washington, DC: U.S. Government Printing Office.

Tarter, R. W., Alterman, A. I., & Edwards, K. L. (1988). Neurobehavioral theory of alcoholism etiology. In C. D. Chaudron & D. A. Wilkinson (Eds.), *Theories on Alcoholism* (pp. 73–102). Toronto: Addiction Research Foundation.

Wallerstein, J. S. (1987). Children of divorce: Stress and developmental tasks. In N. Garmezy & M. Rutter (Eds.), *Stress, coping, and development in children* (p. 265–302). New York: McGraw-Hill.

White, H. R. (1990). The drug-use delinquency nexus in adolescence. In R. Weisheit (Ed.), *Drugs, crime and the criminal justice system* (pp. 215–256). Champaign, Illinois: Anderson.

White, H. R., Johnson, V., & Horwitz, A. (1986). An application of three deviance theories to adolescent substance use. *International Journal of the Addictions, 21,* 347–366.

Williams, T. M., & Kornblum, W. (1985). *Growing up poor.* Lexington, MA: Lexington Books.

Wilson, G. T. (1988). Alcohol use and abuse: A social learning analysis. In C. D. Chaudron & D. A. Wilkinson (Eds.), *Theories on alcoholism* (pp. 239–288). Toronto: Addiction Research Foundation.

Wolfgang, M. E., & Tracy, P. E. (1982). *The 1945 and 1958 birth cohorts: A comparison of the prevalence, incidence, and severity of delinquent behavior.* Unpublished manuscript.

Yamaguchi, K., & Kandel, D. B. (1984a). Patterns of drug use from adolescence to young adulthood: II. Sequences of progression. *American Journal of Public Health, 74,* 668–672.

Yamaguchi, K., & Kandel, D. B. (1984b). Patterns of drug use from adolescence to young adulthood: III. Predictors of progression. *American Journal of Public Health, 74,* 673–681.

Zinberg, N. E., & Jacobson, R. C. (1976). The natural history of "chipping." *American Journal of Psychiatry, 33,* 37–40.

Zuckerman, M. (1979). *Sensation seeking: Beyond the optimal level of arousal.* Hillsdale, NJ: Erlbaum.

CHAPTER 2

Nosological Considerations in the Diagnosis of Substance Use Disorders

Thomas F. Babor

R ecent developments in the conceptualization of substance use disorders are consistent with a multidimensional model that considers individual vulnerabilities, harmful consequences, and dependence symptomatology as independent but potentially interrelated components of a comprehensive nosological system. Although most psychoactive substances are potent pharmacological reinforcers that exert profound effects on biological systems and behavior, the consequences of even chronic substance use cannot properly be diagnosed or predicted without taking into account a variety of contributing factors. To the extent that individual differences in substance-abuse vulnerability, as well as social and pharmacological modifying variables, can be specified, a more complete diagnosis of a specific substance use disorder can be made. As the remainder of this chapter will illustrate, individual differences among persons who abuse psychoactive substances are likely to affect natural history, presenting symptoms, severity of dependence, and treatment response.

The writing of this chapter was supported in part by grants from the National Institute on Alcohol Abuse and Alcoholism (AA03510) and the National Institute on Drug Abuse (DA05592).

A conceptual scheme is illustrated in Figure 2.1 to show a set of hypothetical relationships among vulnerability, exposure, modifying factors, and consequences. These are mapped above three diagnostic categories (hazardous use, dependence, and harmful use) that represent different degrees of behavioral involvement with psychoactive substances.

In Figure 2.1, the differential risks of developing substance use disorders and experiencing adverse effects from them are divided into two elements, vulnerability and exposure. Vulnerability refers to the physiological, psychological, or social characteristics of individuals that make them more likely to develop dependence and adverse consequences. Vulnerability may be expressed in terms of personality and biological characteristics that predispose some substance users to develop rapid tolerance to a substance, act more impaired when intoxicated, or respond less vigorously to treatment interventions.

For example, certain population groups (e.g., people who are older, female, and low in body mass) are more vulnerable to the acute effects of alcohol intoxication than are other population groups (e.g., younger men who are overweight). The risk of alcohol and other drug problems may be greater among individuals having attention deficit disorder, childhood conduct disorder, aggressive tendencies, and family histories of alcoholism (Alterman, Petrarulo, Tarter, & McGowan, 1982; Kellam & Werthamer-Larsson, 1986; Loney, 1988; Tarter, McBride, Buonpane, & Schneider, 1977; Tsuang, Simpson, & Kronfol, 1982). Social antecedents may also contribute to vulnerability. Socially learned attitudes

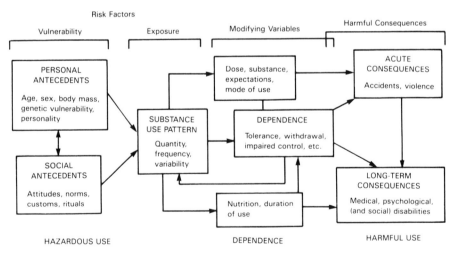

FIGURE 2.1 Conceptual framework of risks associated with psychoactive substance use.

may lead drug users to expect that cocaine will "cause" the release of aggression or sexual inhibitions. These expectations may do more to guide behavior during intoxication than the pharmacological effects of the substance. Social norms that tolerate opium smoking, as in Laos, or that call for punishing drunkenness, as in Islamic societies, may result in drastically different consequences for the substance user, and therefore represent different social vulnerabilities. Socially learned drinking customs, like buying rounds, may predispose large segments of the male population in a country like France to drink intensively in response to social pressures.

In general, it can be hypothesized that the greater the number of personal and social vulnerability factors, the greater the exposure to substance use patterns that entail risk. For example, Jellinek (1960) suggested that because frequent consumption of large amounts of alcohol is a prerequisite to addiction, those most prone to heavy consumption, such as members of cultural groups that accept high alcohol intake, would be at greater risk of developing subsequent problems. The risks of exposure also depend on different aspects of the substance use pattern. The acute consequences of a given drug dose are affected by how fast it is metabolized, mode of administration, and the social context of the occasion. The long-term consequences of substance use are modified by such life-style factors as the duration of exposure to harmful substances and the substance user's diet and nutritional status.

In Figure 2.1, dependence is characterized both as a modifying variable and as a risk factor that may intensify drinking or drug use. The greater the tolerance, for example, the lower the likelihood that psychomotor performance will be affected at a given dose of a substance. Tolerance, however, may lead to increased consumption, which could increase the risk of long-term medical consequences. Dependence itself can be considered a health consequence to the extent that it disrupts sleep patterns, mood states, and the substance user's control over drug ingestion.

As suggested in Figure 2.1, a number of variables may color the clinical picture in complex ways. Polysubstance use makes it more difficult to classify substance use disorders according to individual drugs. Other mental and physical disorders, which may be either primary or secondary to substance use, further complicate the diagnostic task. Diagnostic evaluation along multiple dimensions of a multiaxial schema can provide valuable insights into the underlying dynamics of substance use disorders, primarily because personality factors, developmental disorders, and psychosocial stressors all affect natural history and prognosis.

New Developments in Diagnostic Classification

Alcoholism and drug addiction have been variously defined as medical diseases, mental disorders, social problems, behavioral conditions and, in some cases, the symptom of an underlying mental disorder (Babor, 1990). The intent of many of these definitions is to permit the classification of alcoholism and drug dependence within standard nomenclatures such as the World Health Organization's (1990) *International Classification of Diseases (ICD–10)* and the third revised edition of the *Diagnostic and Statistical Manual of Mental Disorders (DSM–III–R)* of the American Psychiatric Association (1987). Recent work on the revision of these influential diagnostic systems has resulted in a high degree of compatibility between the classification criteria used in the United States and those used internationally. Both systems now define dependence according to the elements first proposed by Edwards and Gross (1976), and they also include a residual category (harmful alcohol use *[ICD–10]*; alcohol abuse *[DSM-III–R]*) that allows classification of psychological, social, and medical consequences directly related to substance use. In addition, initial versions of *ICD–10* included the category of hazardous alcohol use, designed to alert health workers to the early identification of substance use patterns that carry a high risk of future harm. Although this concept was not incorporated into the final draft of *ICD–10* , it did raise some important nosological and public health questions that are important to consider. For example, are there different types of substance users who differ in their vulnerability profiles, natural histories, problem severity, and treatment response? To what extent is the same substance use pattern more hazardous for one individual than another because of different vulnerability profiles? Are there identifiable doses of alcohol and other drugs that constitute a threshold above which the risk of acute and long-term consequences are increased significantly (Babor, Kranzler & Lauerman, 1986)?

The World Health Organization and *ICD–10*

The *International Classification of Diseases (ICD)* is the official classification system of the World Health Organization (WHO). The international dimensions of psychoactive substance use have created a need for a common frame of reference for communication and statistical reporting. Recent developments in the revision of the *ICD* section on psychoactive substance use are designed to satisfy this need. Continuing a programmatic effort to join expert opinion with diagnostic research and cross-cultural clinical experience, the Mental Health Division of WHO has refined the concept of alcohol and drug dependence in a way that permits classification of different substances according to an identical set of criteria (WHO, 1990).

Central to the WHO approach to the classification of substance use disorders is the concept of a dependence syndrome that is distinguished from disabilities caused by substance use (Edwards, Arif, & Hodgson, 1981). The dependence syndrome is seen as an interrelated cluster of cognitive, behavioral, and physiological symptoms. A diagnosis of dependence in the *ICD–10* system is made if three or more of the eight criteria listed in the appendix have been experienced or exhibited at some time in the previous 12 months. The criteria include psychological symptoms (e.g., a strong desire [craving] to take the substance), physiological signs (e.g., tolerance and withdrawal), and behavioral symptoms (e.g., use of substance to relieve withdrawal discomfort).

The dependence syndrome in *ICD–10* may be present for a specific substance (e.g., tobacco, alcohol, or diazepam), for a class of substances (e.g., opioid drugs), or for a wider range of pharmacologically different substances. As suggested in Figure 2.1, a diagnosis of dependence does not necessarily imply the presence of physical, psychological, or social consequences, although some form of harm is usually present.

Many patients with a dependence syndrome give a history of rapid reinstatement of features of the syndrome following resumption of substance use after a period of abstinence. Such a history is a powerful diagnostic indicator of dependence because it points to the presence of progressive impairment of control over substance use, the rapid development of tolerance, and, frequently, physical withdrawal symptoms.

It should be noted that patients who receive opiates or other drugs for pain relief following surgery (or for malignant disease) may show signs of a withdrawal state when drugs are not given. The great majority have no desire to continue taking drugs and would not fulfill the criteria for dependence. The presence of a physical withdrawal syndrome does not *ipso facto* indicate dependence, but rather a state of neuroadaptation to the drug that was being administered.

The American Psychiatric Association and *DSM–III–R*

The second major approach to the development of formal diagnostic criteria was initiated during the 1970s by researchers affiliated with the Washington University School of Medicine (Feighner et al., 1972). This "research diagnostic" approach strongly influenced the classification of substance use disorders adopted by the American Psychiatric Association (1980) in the third edition of its *Diagnostic and Statistical Manual* (*DSM–III*).

In contrast with previous editions of the *DSM*, *alcoholism* and *drug dependence* in *DSM–III* were included within the separate category of *substance use disorders*, rather than as a subcategory of *personality disorder*. Reflecting a trend toward greater semantic precision, the term *dependence* was used in preference to the more generic terms, *alcoholism* or *addiction*. Separate categories of *alcohol abuse* and *drug abuse* were added to permit greater differentiation. *Dependence* was distinguished from *abuse* by the presence of tolerance or withdrawal symptoms.

As part of the American Psychiatric Association's ongoing program of work on nomenclature and classification, a set of changes has recently been made to the entire Substance Use Disorders section of the *DSM–III* (American Psychiatric Association, 1987; Rounsaville, Spitzer, & Williams, 1986). The most important change involves the adoption of a dimensional model of dependence that closely resembles the WHO dependence syndrome concept (Edwards et al., 1981). Significantly, the medical and social consequences of both acute and chronic intoxication are not among the primary diagnostic criteria of dependence in the *DSM–III–R*. These consequences do, however, play a prominent role in the definition of a residual category termed *substance abuse.*

Abuse and Harmful Use in the *DSM–III–R* and the *ICD–10*

In the *ICD–10*, harmful use is a pattern of using one or more psychoactive substances that cause damage to health. The damage may be: (a) physical (physiological), such as fatty liver, pancreatitis from alcohol, or hepatitis from needle-injected drugs, or (b) mental (psychological), such as depression related to heavy drinking or drug use. Adverse social consequences often accompany substance use but are not in themselves sufficient to result in a diagnosis of "harmful use".

Harmful patterns of use are often criticized by others and sometimes legally prohibited by governments. The fact that a pattern of use or a particular drug is disapproved by another person or by the culture is not in itself evidence of harmful use unless socially negative consequences have actually occurred at dosage levels that also result in psychological and physical consequences. This is a major difference that distinguishes the *ICD–10's* "harmful use" from the *DSM–III–R's* "substance abuse": The latter category permits the use of social consequences in the diagnosis of abuse.

An important diagnostic issue is the extent to which dependence is sufficiently distinct from abuse or harmful use to be considered a separate condition. In the *DSM–III–R*, substance abuse is a residual category that allows the clinician to classify clinically meaningful aspects of a patient's behavior when that behavior is not clearly associated with a dependence syndrome (Rounsaville et al., 1986). In the *ICD–10*, harmful substance use implies identifiable substance-induced medical or psychiatric consequences that occur in the absence of a dependence syndrome. In both classification systems, dependence is conceived of as an underlying condition that has much greater clinical significance be-cause of its implications for understanding etiology, predicting course, and planning treat-ment. This will become clear in the following discussion of the assumptions behind the dependence syndrome concept.

The Dependence Syndrome Concept as a Theory of Alcoholism and Addiction

The syndrome concept implicit in the diagnosis of alcohol and drug dependence in the *ICD–10* and the *DSM–III–R* can be considered as an organizing principle for a general theory of addiction (Edwards, 1986; Edwards et al., 1981). The core syndrome elements include the cognitive, behavioral, and physiological symptoms summarized in the *ICD–10* and the *DSM–III–R* and elaborated further in a dynamic biobehavioral model illustrated in Figure 2.2. Although this model is based in part on the work of Edwards and others (Edwards et al., 1981; Edwards & Gross, 1976; Edwards, Gross, Keller, & Moser, 1976), it represents my attempt to link the clinical symptomatology proposed in the *ICD–10* and the *DSM–III–R* with a more comprehensive set of postulates and explanatory mecha-nisms. What ties together the elements of the syndrome and helps to account for their interrelationships is an often-unstated set of assumptions about the learning mechanisms

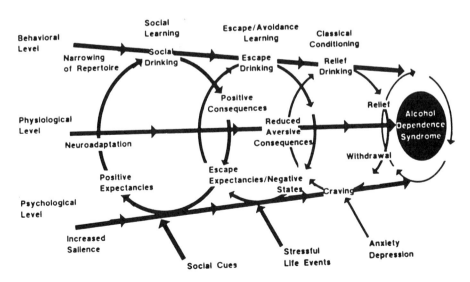

FIGURE 2.2   Theoretical model of alcohol dependence syndrome.

and neurobiological processes behind the acquisition and maintenance of alcohol and drug dependence. The learning processes include social learning, operant conditioning, and classical conditioning. At a more basic level of analysis, these processes may be linked to the brain mechanisms that mediate positive and negative reinforcement (Wise, 1988).

The essential postulates of the syndrome concept of dependence include the following: (a) the clustering of cognitive, behavioral, and physiological elements that are related to a common psychobiological process; (b) the distribution of these elements along a continuum of severity; (c) recognition of individual differences in the patterning of elements according to such influences as culture and personality; (d) substance-specific manifestations of the syndrome, particularly with respect to tolerance and withdrawal phenomena; and (e) conceptual as well as statistical independence of dependence from substance-related disabilities. Although no assumptions are made with respect to the progressiveness of the syndrome or its irreversibility, it has been suggested (Babor, Cooney, & Lauerman, 1987; Edwards and Gross, 1976) that severe alcohol dependence is not reversible, as indicated by rapid reinstatement of dependence when substance use is resumed after a period of detoxification.

Syndrome Elements

Figure 2.2 illustrates the development of alcohol dependence along three converging axes that represent behavioral, physiological, and psychological levels of analysis. At the behavioral level, narrowing of the behavioral repertoire refers to the tendency for alcohol use to become progressively stereotyped around a prescribed routine of customs and rituals, and characterized by increased facility of performance. Examples include the use of accustomed beverages and doses and lack of variation in time, place, or manner of drinking. Narrowing of the repertoire also implies that the individual's substance use has become functionally autonomous.

Tolerance and withdrawal phenomena constitute the physiological level of dependence. Tolerance is defined as a decrease in response to a psychoactive substance that occurs with continued use. For example, increased doses of alcohol are required to achieve effects originally produced by lower doses. Tolerance may be physical, behavioral, or psychological. Physiological tolerance is a change in receptor cells such that the effects of alcohol are reduced, even though the receptor cells are subjected to the same concentration. Tolerance may also develop at the psychological and behavioral levels of analysis, quite independently of the biological adaptation that takes place (Babor, Mendelson, Greenberg, & Kuehnle, 1975). Behavioral tolerance is a change in the effect of a substance because of the alteration of environmental constraints.

A withdrawal state is a group of symptoms occurring upon cessation of substance use after repeated, and usually prolonged, drinking or drug use. Onset and course of the withdrawal state are time-limited and are related to type of substance and dose being used immediately prior to abstinence.

Tolerance and withdrawal can exist in the absence of the behavioral and cognitive elements. When this occurs, the term "neuroadaptation" is used to suggest that tolerance and withdrawal are not identical to the broader phenomenon of a biobehavioral dependence syndrome.

Beyond the biological changes associated with both physical tolerance and withdrawal is the psychological element of increased salience. Salience means that drinking or drug use is given a higher priority than other activities in spite of its negative consequences. This is often reflected in the emergence of substance use as the preferred activity from a set of available alternative activities, and in diminished responsiveness of the individual to the normal processes of informal social control. For example, when drinking contravenes tacit social rules governing the time, place, or amount typically expected by the user's reference group, this may indicate increased salience.

Another psychological element, craving, is defined as the overwhelming desire for a psychoactive substance or for its intoxicating effects. Considered a central feature of dependence, craving is thought to develop as a result of conditioned associations that evoke conditioned withdrawal responses (Ludwig & Wikler, 1974). It may also be induced by the provocation of any physiological arousal state resembling an alcohol or drug withdrawal syndrome (Wikler, 1965). Both salience and narrowing of the repertoire describe gross, macro-level phenomena that represent much more complicated levels of analysis than do the elements of withdrawal and tolerance.

Learning Mechanisms

The assumptions behind the dependence syndrome concept are a synthesis of both general learning theory and more specific conditioning models of dependence. The theoretical underpinnings of the model described in Figure 2.2 can best be explained by reference to recent applications of social learning, escape/avoidance learning, and classical conditioning to the study of alcohol and drug use in animals and humans. When these learning mechanisms are applied to a syndrome model, one can portray the transition from substance use to abuse and dependence along a progressive continuum in terms of increasingly concentrated cycles of reciprocal reinforcement. These cycles cut across the behavioral, physiological, and psychological levels of analysis, suggesting that as dependence develops, drinking *behavior* is influenced simultaneously by psychological and physiological processes. To emphasize that dependence does not arise *sui generis,* and that the cycles leading to the syndrome are not self-contained systems, the model includes a number of social, environmental, and psychological inputs that may exacerbate each of the cycles.

Learning theories of alcohol and drug abuse suggest that dependence is a complex phenomenon with multiple determinants. Although many theories have been developed to explain use and abuse of a single drug (e.g., alcohol, opiates), the following learning principles may be applicable to dependence on any psychoactive substance: (a) social reinforcement of the initiation and maintenance of substance use, (b) operant reinforcement of drug- or alcohol- seeking behavior, (c) cognitive mediation of conditioned responses, and (d) classical conditioning of substance-related cues. As discussed later, different concepts from psychological learning and motivational theory apply to different elements of the dependence syndrome. To the extent that these theories complement one another, they provide a powerful framework for understanding the nature of dependence and how to diagnose it.

As suggested in Figure 2.2, the initial cycle of alcohol dependence is best explained according to cognitive social learning theory (Bandura, 1977). Theories of alcohol abuse derived from social learning theory incorporate a wide variety of explanatory constructs. In general, these constructs include social modeling; secondary reinforcement of drinking; cognitive expectancies that, once learned, lead the drinker to anticipate rewarding effects from drinking; and confirmation of those expectancies some or most of the time (positive consequences). For many drinkers, this cycle of social cues that set the stage for drinking, positive expectancies in response to these cues, and positive consequences during or after drinking is rarely associated with excessive alcohol use or intoxication. Some individuals, however, begin to develop different expectancies that represent a personal belief in the power of alcohol to serve as an escape from problems or a culturally sanctioned excuse for avoiding responsibility. When these expectations are reinforced from time to time by the temporary relief of negative feeling states or by society's forgiveness of drunken comportment as "time out" from conventional rules, the drinker enters into a new and more insidious cycle.

This formulation of the initial stages of alcohol dependence is consistent with a theory of opiate addiction proposed by McAuliffe and Gordon (1980). According to their combination of effects theory, it is the potential for enjoying opiate euphoria, in combination with the relative permanence of acquired reinforcers, that plays a crucial role in initiating and maintaining drug use and precipitating relapse. In this model, long-term abstinence by addicts is facilitated by successful reintegration into society, which provides an alternative system of rewards. Zinberg (1980) has emphasized the influence of social settings that, operating through such mechanisms as social sanctions and rituals, play an active role in controlling substance use, even for those who at one time have been severely dependent. In related cognitive theories, it has been suggested that the strength of an individual's expectation regarding coping, called *perceived self-efficacy,* influences the probability of controlling substance use. Individuals who are severely alcohol dependent may believe that they are unable to cope with temptation after a first drink. Rapid relapse in dependent individuals may be mediated by their low perceived self-efficacy (Rollnick & Heather, 1982; Wilson, 1978). In this view, the belief that one will lose control after a single drink becomes a self-fulfilling prophecy.

Behavioral theories of choice (Vuchinich & Tucker, 1988) are another learning-based approach to the explanation of drinking behavior that has implications for the explanation of the dependence syndrome. The salience of substance-seeking behavior, a central element of dependence, is explained as a choice between valued alternatives, on the basis of the relative reinforcement value of the substance, the constraints on its use, and the constraints on competing activities. The probability of drinking, for example, increases under circumstances where alcohol is readily available, alternative activities (e.g., reading a book) have less reinforcement value, and the alternative activities are under greater environmental constraint (e.g., movies are less available than drinking establishments). Consistent with Skinnerian theory, the cost-decisional model of Vuchinich and Tucker (1988) eschews mentalistic concepts like cognitions or expectations in favor of probabilistic statements linking environmental events (e.g., lower costs of alcohol relative to other beverages) to observable behaviors (e.g., choice of alcohol as preferred beverage) that have been previously reinforced.

Other varieties of learning theory, particularly cognitive behavioral approaches, may also be useful in explaining how salience develops. The cognitive–behavioral explanation of salience suggests that response outcome expectancies are responsible for directing the ongoing behavioral stream in the direction of drinking (Goldman, 1989). A response outcome expectancy is the anticipation of a systematic relationship among events or objects in some imminent situation. For example, once alcohol is considered to be available (e.g., the time for afternoon cocktail hour approaches), the recognition of this anticipated event signals that a particular desired outcome is achievable (e.g., euphoria, sociability, stimulation) by means of a particular response (e.g., having one or two drinks).

Like other habitual behaviors, once drinking has been repeated with sufficient regularity in a variety of situations and contexts, it requires less effort, is less demanding of active attention, and tends to follow a ritualized pattern upon initiation of the behavioral sequence. Expectancy theory thus provides a useful way of explaining what is meant by narrowing of the behavioral repertoire. According to Goldman (1989),

> With sufficient repetition of actual drinking, the ongoing behavioral repertoire becomes automatic. That is, rather than being guided by choices based upon competition of expectancies, a stereotyped cognitive and motor sequence develops. It begins with the seeking of circumstances in which alcohol can be consumed, followed by the consumption of alcohol, and the performance of behaviors which are consequences of alcohol consumption. Once begun, this sequence plays itself out from beginning to end without much variation. At this point, the expectancy sequence can be regarded as automatic and residing in part in the procedural memory store. Moving through this sequence is not consciously considered, is not processed at a verbal level, and is not even completely verbalizable. (p. 20)

As illustrated in Figure 2.2, the third stage of dependence is explained best by respondent or Pavlovian conditioning principles. In a chronic drinker, certain environmental stimuli, such as people, places, or things (e.g., the sight of a bar or the smell of liquor) are repeatedly paired with withdrawal symptoms arising from periods of acute abstinence between drinking episodes. These previously neutral stimuli acquire the ability to produce conditioned withdrawal reactions long after cessation of alcohol use (Ludwig & Wikler, 1974). These conditioned withdrawal reactions are interpreted as "craving" by the alcoholic, and prompt the individual to seek relief through alcohol use (Ludwig, 1988).

In Siegel's (1979) model of opiate tolerance, the environmental stimuli that reliably anticipate drug ingestion enable the addict to make adaptive, compensatory, physiological responses in preparation for the drug's effects. These conditioned responses are opposite to the acute drug effects, thus serving to maintain homeostatic balance. This process explains in part the development of tolerance. Furthermore, when these conditioned responses are not followed by drug ingestion, they result in conditioned withdrawal or craving. Thus, Siegel uses respondent conditioning to link drug craving, tolerance, withdrawal, and drug self-administration. This model is consistent with the cycle of interoceptive stimuli (anxiety, craving, withdrawal symptoms), cognitive mediation (craving), and behavior (relief drinking) that links operant and respondent conditioning in the final cycle portrayed in Figure 2.2.

Impaired control can also be explained by conditioning theory. The most common cues for substance use are those associated with the act of alcohol or drug self-administration. The process of "cooking up" heroin, gulping a first drink, or puffing on a cigarette provides a basis for developing strong conditioned stimuli that in turn produce conditioned craving or withdrawal responses. Such responses may dramatically increase motivation for substance use and lead to a perception of impaired control. A slightly different process underlying loss of control in alcoholics was proposed by Ludwig and Wikler (1974). They hypothesized that loss of control represents an inability to accurately use information from interoceptive cues (e.g., perceived intoxication), which are considered necessary to regulate the rate or quantity of alcohol consumed. Although Wikler (1965) and Siegel (1979) based their classical conditioning models on opiate dependence, these concepts have been adapted to explain alcohol dependence (e.g., Ludwig, 1988; Ludwig & Wikler 1974) and nicotine dependence (Pomerleau, 1981).

Brain Mechanisms

The dependence syndrome concept (Edwards et al., 1981) suggests that positive and negative reinforcements are strongly involved in the initiation and maintenance of alcohol and drug dependence. Moreover, the biopsychological scope of the concept implies that reinforcement processes, although linked to cognitive and social learning, are basically related to brain mechanisms. According to Wise's psychomotor stimulant theory of addiction (Wise, 1988; Wise & Bozarth, 1987), a common brain mechanism of psychomotor activation is stimulated by all positive reinforcers. This mechanism mediates the positive reinforcing effects of a wide variety of addictive substances, including amphetamine, cocaine, opiates, barbiturates, alcohol, nicotine, caffeine, and cannabis. Amphetamine and cocaine, like most psychoactive substances, increase synaptic dopamine levels, which is the primary basis for their addiction liability. Despite the fact that other substances, like opiates and alcohol, induce sedation and relaxation, they too have strong stimulant properties that result from their ability to activate dopaminergic cells.

The theory proposes that the positive reinforcing effects of drug stimulation occur within the medial forebrain bundle. These effects are remembered for long periods of time and depend on the activation of brain dopamine systems. The theory holds that a different mechanism mediates the negative reinforcing effects of these substances (i.e., the increase in substance use that occurs when a drug terminates distress or disphoria). The negative reinforcing effects depend on after-effects of stimulation that temporarily enhance the reinforcing potency of stimulation. These effects decay quickly and do not depend on dopaminergic activation.

Because different drug classes produce different physical dependence symptoms and relieve different withdrawal syndromes, it is believed that different negative reinforcement mechanisms are involved. According to Wise (1988),

> Negative reinforcement effects are not necessarily restricted to physical dependence phenomena: Drug-induced negative reinforcement—and the cravings that are associated with it—could result from analgesic, anxiolytic, sedative, or other drug actions that need not be linked to physical dependence. The multiple mechanisms of negative reinforcement are each, however, viewed as independent of the common mechanism of positive reinforcement. (p. 119)

Alcohol, barbiturates, opiates, and benzodiazepines are associated with physical dependence symptoms that are similar but not identical. They tend to relieve psychological distress as well as physical pain. The mechanisms for these sources of negative reinforcement may be mediated some distance away from the medial forebrain bundle mechanisms of positive reinforcement. Cannabis and cocaine produce different and substantially weaker withdrawal syndromes, suggesting that their abuse liability is related to positive reinforcement mechanisms alone.

Research on the neurobiology of drug reinforcement suggests that drug and alcohol cravings may result from more than one source, one derived from a previous history of positive reinforcement and the other from a current condition (physical dependence) that confers negative reinforcing potential on a particular substance. This perspective also calls attention to the likelihood that there is a biological basis for "psychological" dependence and drug craving that is not rooted in withdrawal distress or other sources of negative affect. Finally, this perspective explains why psychoactive substances are capable of achieving such a high degree of salience in the behavioral hiearchy. According to Wise (1988), "If drugs of abuse activate positive reinforcement mechanisms directly and centrally, they may do so with much greater intensity than can ever be summoned by environmental stimuli like food, water, or the reinforcing beauty of nature, art, or music ..." (p. 127), which must depend on sensory transducers and the propagation of nerve impulses across axons and synaptic junctions.

Nosology and the Distinction Among Use, Abuse, and Dependence

Like any good theory, the dependence syndrome concept should help to explain, predict, and control the development of substance use disorders. As suggested in Figure 2.1, dependence itself is only one part of a broader network of variables that are responsible for the initiation, maintenance, and control of psychoactive substance use. These variables include the type of psychoactive substance, the dose taken, the response costs involved, the route of administration, the schedule of access, the organism's prior history and functioning, and the environmental context of substance use (Carroll, Stitzer, Strain, & Meisch, 1990). Psychological learning theory has shown that nearly all dependence-producing drugs have the ability to serve as positive reinforcers, a phenomenon that goes beyond their connection with the relief of withdrawal symptoms. It also shows that the mechanisms of acquisition involved in drug self-administration may be quite different from those that maintain the behavior.

Although learning models provide valuable insights into the mechanisms of acquisition, maintenance, and extinction of drug-seeking behaviors, psychiatric and personality research has emerged as an important source of information about individual differences in susceptibility to dependence following initial use and subsequent abuse. For example, Hesselbrock, Meyer, & Keener (1985) found that alcoholics with a family history of alcoholism had an earlier onset and greater severity of alcohol-related problems and that these relationships were closely linked with the simultaneous presence of antisocial personality disorder. Alterman et al. (1982) identified a consistent relationship between hyperactivity and alcoholism and suggested that this relationship is probably coincidental to the conjoint presence of aggressive and antisocial behaviors in the same individuals. Penick et al. (1987) proposed that certain kinds of childhood vulnerabilities, such as those identified by Tarter et al. (1977), are associated with specific kinds of co-occurring psychiatric disorders that emerge later in the adult life of alcoholics and subsequently influence the course and consequences of problem drinking. Familial psychopathology, early childhood vulnerabilities, and psychiatric comorbidity may increase the probability of an earlier onset of problem drinking, a more rapid course, and a more severe dependence syndrome.

For individuals with these vulnerability factors, alcohol and drug intoxication may be particularly reinforcing because of the low salience of alternative reinforcers and the unique ability of psychoactive substances to provide immediate mood alteration, personality change, and psychological stimulation. Once substance use is initiated, vulnerable individuals may be less responsive to environmental contingencies. These considerations suggest that individual differences in vulnerability may hasten the transition from abuse to dependence, and should be taken into account in diagnosis and treatment planning.

Implications for Diagnostic Research and Practice

The adoption of a generic dependence syndrome concept as the basis for national and international classifications of psychoactive substance use disorders is an invitation to conduct research that will evaluate the major assumptions of this model. That research should determine the independence of substance-related problems from the dependence elements themselves, the actual coherence of dependence symptoms as a clinical syndrome, and the generalizability of the dependence concept across drugs and across cultural groups. To the extent that consistency is found across disparate samples of alcoholics and users of other substances in different cultures, the case for a universal dependence syndrome would be strengthened. An organizing principle that has cross-cultural applicability is desirable, especially in the context of the *ICD*. The present review suggests that the syndrome concept may have merit as a theory of drug and alcohol dependence but should be subjected to a more rigorous program of research aimed at better operational measures and more intensive hypothesis testing, especially in samples of drug users.

The syndrome concept provides the basis for a relatively unambiguous set of hypotheses about the conditions under which alcoholics and opiate addicts re-acquire dependence after a period of abstinence. Instead of conceiving relapse as a symptom of some underlying personality problem, it focuses attention on the patient's maladaptive habit patterns and learning history and the environmental as well as interoceptive stimuli that precipitate reinstatement of dependence. When considered in this way, reinstatement becomes a hypothesis to be tested under specific conditions, such as when a "slip" occurs for an abstinent alcoholic.

The concept of *dependence* has had a long history, with different scientific disciplines, theoretical approaches, and methodological procedures all contributing to a diversity of definitions. Is dependence a biological condition, a personality disorder, a form of psychopathology, a learned behavior, a social construction of reality, or a culturally conditioned form of social imitation? Despite the difficulty that psychiatrists, psychologists, pharmacologists, biologists, sociologists, and anthropologists have experienced in communicating with each other about the nature of alcohol and drug dependence, there has been substantial progress in the past decade in the development of concepts that can be used to diagnose substance use disorders reliably, to conduct research, and to guide further theory development.

References

Alterman, A. I., Petrarulo, E., Tarter, R. & McGowan, J. R. (1982). Hyperactivity and alcoholism: Familial and behavioral correlates. *Addictive Behaviors, 7,* 413–421.

American Psychiatric Association. (1980). *Diagnostic and statistical manual of mental disorders* (3rd ed.). Washington, DC: Author.

American Psychiatric Association. (1987). *Diagnostic and statistical manual of mental disorders* (3rd ed., rev.). Washington, DC: Author.

Babor, T. F. (1990). Social, scientific, and medical issues in the definition of alcohol and drug dependence. In G. Edwards & M. Lader (Eds.), *The nature of drug dependence* (pp. 19–36). Oxford, England: Oxford University Press.

Babor, T. F., Cooney, N. L., and Lauerman, R. J. (1987). The drug dependence syndrome concept as a psychological theory of relapse behavior: An empirical evaluation. *British Journal of Addiction, 82,* 393–405.

Babor, T. F., Kranzler, H. R., & Lauerman, R. J. (1986). Social drinking as a health and psychosocial risk factor: Anstie's limit revisited. In M. Galanter (Ed.), *Recent developments in alcoholism* (Vol. 5, pp. 373–402). New York: Plenum Press.

Babor, T. F., Mendelson, J. H., Greenberg, I., & Kuehnle, J. C. (1975). Marihuana consumption and tolerance to physiological and subjective effects. *Archives of General Psychiatry, 32,* 1548–1552.

Bandura, A. (1977). Self-efficacy: Toward a unifying theory of behavioral change. *Psychological Review, 84,* 191–215.

Carroll, M. E., Stitzer, M. L., Strain, E., & Meisch, R. A. (1990). The behavioral pharmacology of alcohol and other drugs: Emerging issues. *Recent Developments in Alcoholism, 8,* 5–34.

Edwards, G. (1986). The alcohol dependence syndrome: A concept as stimulus to enquiry. *British Journal of Addiction, 81,* 171–183.

Edwards, G., Arif, A., & Hodgson, R. (1981). Nomenclature and classification of drug- and alcohol-related problems: A WHO memorandum. *Bulletin of the World Health Organization, 59,* 225–242.

Edwards, G., & Gross, M. M. (1976). Alcohol dependence: Provisional description of a clinical syndrome. *British Medical Journal, 1,* 1058–1061.

Edwards, G., Gross, M. M., Keller, M., & Moser, J. (1976). Alcohol-related problems in the disability perspective. *Journal of Studies on Alcohol, 37,* 1360–1382.

Feighner, J., Robins, E., Guze, S., Woodruff, R., Winokur, G., and Munoz, R. (1972). Diagnostic criteria for use in psychiatric research. *Archives of General Psychiatry, 26,* 57–63.

Goldman, M. S. (1989). Alcohol expectancies as cognitive–behavioral psychology: Theory and practice. In T. Loberg, W. R. Miller, P. E. Nathan, & G. A. Marlatt (Eds.), *Addictive behaviors: Prevention and early intervention* (pp. 11–30). Swets & Zeitlinger.

Hesselbrock, M. N., Meyer, R. E., Keener, J. J. (1985). Psychopathology in hospitalized alcoholics. *Archives of General Psychiatry, 42,* 1050–1055.

Jellinek, E. M. (1960). *The disease concept of alcoholism.* New Brunswick, NJ: Hillhouse Press.

Kellam, S. G., & Werthamer-Larsson, L. (1986). Developmental epidemiology: A basis for prevention. In M. Kessler & S. E. Goldston (Eds.), *A decade of progress in primary prevention* (pp. 154–180). Hanover, NH: University Press of New England.

Loney, J. (1988). *Substance abuse in adolescents: Diagnostic issues derived from studies of attention deficit disorder with hyperactivity* (NIDA Research Monograph 77, DDHS Publication No. ADM 88–1523). Washington, DC: U.S. Government Printing Office.

Ludwig, A. M. (1988). *Understanding the alcoholic's mind: The nature of craving and how to control it.* London: Oxford University Press.

Ludwig, A. M., & Wikler, A. (1974). "Craving" and relapse to drink. *Quarterly Journal of Studies on Alcohol, 35,* 108–130.

McAuliffe, W. E., & Gordon, R. A. (1980). Reinforcement and the combination of effects: Summary of a theory of opiate addiction. In D. J. Lettieri, M. Sayers, & H. W. Pearson, (Eds.), *Theories on drug abuse: Selected contemporary perspectives* (NIDA Research Monograph 30, DHHS Publication No. ADM 80–967). Washington, DC: U.S. Government Printing Office.

Penick, E. C., Powell, B. J., Bingham, S. F., Liskow, B. I., Miller, N. S., & Read, M. R. (1987). A comparative study of familial alcoholism. *Journal of Studies on Alcohol, 48,* 136–146.

Pomerleau, O. (1981). Underlying mechanisms in substance abuse: Examples from research on smoking. *Addictive Behaviors, 6,* 87–196.

Rollnick, S., & Heather, N. (1982). The application of Bandura's self-efficacy theory to abstinence-oriented alcoholism treatment. *Addictive Behaviors, 7,* 243–250.

Rounsaville, B. J., Spitzer, R. L., & Williams, J. B. W. (1986). Proposed changes in the *DSM–III* substance use disorders: Description and rationale. *American Journal of Psychiatry, 143,* 463–468.

Siegel, S. (1979). The role of conditioning in drug tolerance and addiction. In J. D. Keehn (Ed.), *Psychopathology in animals: Research and clinical applications* (pp. 143–168). San Diego, CA: Academic Press.

Tarter, R. E., McBride, H., Buonpane, N., & Schneider, D. V. (1977). Differentiation of alcoholics: Childhood history of minimal brain dysfunction, family history, and drinking pattern. *Archives of General Psychiatry, 34,* 761–768.

Tsuang, M. T., Simpson, J. C., & Kronfol, Z. (1982). Subtypes of drug abuse with psychosis. *Archives of General Psychiatry, 39,* 141–147.

Vuchinich, R. E., Tucker, J. A. (1988). Contributions from behavioral theories of choice to an analysis of alcohol abuse. *Journal of Abnormal Psychology, 97,* 181–195.

Wikler, A. (1965). Conditioning factors in opiate addiction and relapse. In D. Wilner & G. Kassenbaum, (Eds.), *Narcotics* (pp. 85–100). New York: McGraw-Hill.

Wilson, G. T. (1978). Booze, beliefs, and behavior: Cognitive processes in alcohol use and abuse. In P. E. Nathan, G. A. Marlatt, & T. Loberg, (Eds.), *Alcoholism: New directions in behavioral research and treatment* (pp. 315–339). New York: Plenum Press.

Wise, R. A. (1988). The neurobiology of craving: Implications for the understanding and treatment of addiction. *Journal of Abnormal Psychology, 97,* 118–132.

Wise, R. A., & Bozarth, M. A. (1987). A psychomotor stimulant theory of addiction. *Psychological Review, 94,* 469–492.

World Health Organization. (1990). *Mental, behavioral and developmental disorders: Clinical descriptions and diagnostic guidelines (International Classification of Diseases,* 10th ed., draft of Chapter 5, Categories F00–F99). Geneva: World Health Organization.

Zinberg, N. E. (1980). The social setting as a control mechanism in intoxicant use. In D. J. Lettieri, M. Sayers, & H. W. Pearson (Eds.), *Theories on drug abuse: Selected contemporary perspectives* (NIDA Research Monograph 30, DHHS Publication No. ADM 80–967). Washington, DC: U.S. Government Printing Office.

DEPENDENCE CRITERIA PROPOSED IN THE 10TH EDITION OF THE *INTERNATIONAL CLASSIFICATION OF DISEASES* (WORLD HEALTH ORGANIZATION, 1990) FOR SUBSTANCE USE DISORDERS

(i) A strong (sometimes overpowering) desire to take alcohol or drugs. This is seen shortly after a session of drug taking has begun (when the initial dose can be said to have had a "priming effect") or during attempts to stop or control substance use.

(ii) Evidence of an impaired capacity to control the onset of substance use, its level or termination.

(iii) A progressively stereotyped pattern of substance use, in terms of the type of drug (or alcohol) taken, the mode of administration and the quantity over a given period of time. Substance use becomes less responsive to external influences and more to internal ones (e.g., mood states or the presence of physical withdrawal syndrome).

(iv) Progressive neglect of alternative pleasures or interests in favor of substance use, or failure to fulfill major role obligations.

(v) Evidence of tolerance such that increased doses of the substance are required to achieve effects originally produced by lower doses.

(vi) A physical withdrawal state.

(vii)   Use of substance to relieve or avoid withdrawal symptoms, and with awareness that this strategy is effective.

(viii)   Persistance with substance use despite clear evidence of overtly harmful consequences. Adverse consequences may be physical (medical), psychological or social.

CHAPTER 3

Familial Factors in Vulnerability to Substance Abuse

Kathleen R. Merikangas, Bruce J. Rounsaville, and Brigitte A. Prusoff

Family Studies

The family study is an important method for identifying whether a disorder, or vulnerability for a particular disorder, is transmitted in families. Family studies may also be used to validate diagnostic categories and to examine whether subtypes of disorders breed true. Family studies can distinguish between transmissible factors that result from shared etiologic factors among relatives, and nontransmissible factors that result from nonshared environmental factors that are unique to individual family members. However, because both shared genes, shared environmental factors, including culture, diet, life events, and biologic factors, and their interaction, may contribute to the etiology of a particular condition in families, it is generally not possible to discriminate among the possible sources of

This work was supported by the following grants from the Administration of Drug Abuse, Alcoholism, and Mental Health: K02-MH0499, R01-AA07080, and R01-DA50348 to Kathleen R. Merikangas and R01-DA04029 and R01-DA05592 to Bruce J. Rounsaville.

familial aggregation. To identify the role of genes in the etiology of a disorder, it is necessary to use design studies that can discriminate shared genes from shared environment among relatives.

The traditional study paradigms that have been used to identify the role of genetic factors in the etiology of a trait or disorder are twin studies, which compare the prevalence of a disorder among twin pairs who possess identical genes (i.e., monozygotic twins) with twin pairs who have only half of their genes in common (i.e., dizygotic twins). Even more powerful are hybrid designs such as adoption studies of twins, which enable discrimination of the roles of genetic and environmental factors in the etiology of a condition.

The observation that familial factors are involved in the etiology of psychiatric disorders including schizophrenia, the major affective disorders, and the anxiety disorders has been well established. Moreover, evidence from twin and adoption studies has demonstrated that a significant proportion of the familial aggregation of these conditions can be attributed to genetic factors. However, the specific role of genes, the degree of heritability (i.e., the proportion of the variance that can be attributed to genetic factors), and the mode(s) of transmission of most of these conditions have not been elucidated. The inconsistent results of linkage studies of these disorders underscore the complexity of the phenotypic definitions and the patterns of transmission of these conditions.

Family Studies of Substance Abuse

Familial transmission of alcoholism has also been confirmed consistently, with approximately 30% of the variance being attributable to genetic factors (Merikangas, 1990). In contrast with other psychiatric disorders, however, the manifestation of alcoholism requires voluntary exposure to the substance ethanol. Studies of nonalcoholic individuals have attempted to examine which components of the complex behavior involved in drinking, including frequency, quantity, and consequences of consumption of ethanol, are attributable to heritable factors. Moreover, studies of alcoholic twins have shown that genetic factors are more important in alcohol dependence than alcohol abuse (Pickens et al., 1991). Nevertheless, it is not known whether the genetic vulnerability to alcoholism results from factors related to initiation or maintenance of alcohol use, such as the reinforcing properties of the substance or its effect on normalization of a negative baseline state.

There is much less evidence regarding the familial transmission of abuse of substances other than alcohol, particularly illegal substances such as cannabis, cocaine, and opiods. Numerous studies have examined the role of genetic factors in the etiology of use of substances including caffeine, tobacco, and prescription drugs. Gurling, Murray, & Clifford (1981) and Pedersen (1981) have shown that there is substantial heritability for tobacco use and coffee use in large samples of twins. The general findings across studies of substance use are as follows: There are substantial biologic–genetic factors that influence both the initiation and persistence of the use of these substances; common family environment has a negligible effect on the initiation or use of these substances; and the "unique environment" such as the network of peer relationships is strongly related to these behaviors, particularly if there is also a biologic–genetic background (Gurling et al., 1981).

In the only twin study of drug abuse, Pickens et al. (1991) found that although the concordance rates for drug abuse were greater for monozygotic than for dizygotic twins, the differences were not statistically significant. Furthermore, there was stronger evidence for the role of genetic factors in men than in women. However, it is unlikely that the same etiologic factors are involved in the use and abuse of all substances. It is therefore important to discriminate between the factors that contribute to the initiation to and maintenance of use of specific substances and those that may be associated with substance abuse in general.

Comorbidity

There has been a recent resurgence in interest in the co-occurrence of substance abuse and psychiatric disorders, often referred to as *dual diagnosis.* However, because this term implies the presence of two independent diagnoses, it is preferable to consider the two conditions as *comorbid,* as described below.

The term *comorbidity,* introduced by Feinstein (1970), refers to the presence of any additional coexisting ailment in a patient with a particular index disease. Failure to classify and analyze comorbid diseases can create misleading medical statistics and may cause spurious comparisons during the planning and evaluation of treatment for patients. Comorbidity can alter the clinical course of patients with the same diagnosis by affecting the time of detection, prognostic anticipations, therapeutic selection, and post-therapeutic outcome of an index diagnosis (Kaplan & Feinstein, 1974).

In psychiatry, comorbidity appears to be the rule rather than the exception. Numerous studies of clinical samples of inpatients and outpatients have demonstrated the large proportion of patients who simultaneously meet diagnostic criteria for more than a single disorder, both within Axis I and between Axes I and II of the third edition of the *Diagnostic and Statistical Manual of Mental Disorders* (*DMS–III*; American Psychiatric Association, 1980; Pfohl, Coryell, & Zimmerman, 1986; Roth, Gurney, Garside, & Kerr, 1972). Similarly, multiple diagnoses within individual subjects appear to be quite frequent in epidemiologic surveys of the general population in the United States (Boyd et al., 1984) and Europe (Angst, Vollrath, Merikangas, & Ernst, 1990).

Two major approaches have been applied to classify multiple diagnoses within a single individual: assignment of a primary and secondary diagnosis on the basis of order of onset; and application of a hierarchical diagnostic system in which one condition is inferred to supersede the other. Examples of these two approaches would be the co-occurence of a phobic disorder with onset at age 8, and alcoholism with onset at age 23, respectively. With the former approach, phobia would be considered primary, because the age of onset of phobia preceded that of alcoholism. Application of the latter approach would lead to the diagnosis of alcoholism only, because alcoholism would be presumed to be higher on the hierarchy than phobia.

The former approach is preferable because no preconceived etiologic assumptions regarding the relationships between disorders are necessary. However, the primary–secondary distinction may be difficult to apply to the assignment of retrospectively ascertained lifetime diagnoses, which require accurate determination of the age of onset of disorders that often emerge in an insidious manner (Woodruff, Murphy, & Herjanic, 1967).

The latter approach has not been applied consistently across studies because of differences in the assumptions regarding the hierarchical structure of the diagnostic systems used. The elimination of hierarchical relationships among many of the disorders in the revised *DSM–III* criteria (American Psychiatric Association, 1987) will facilitate the assessment of relationships between two or more disorders. Methods for assessing associations between disorders are described below.

Explanations for Associations Between Disorders

Before concluding that there is a true association between two or more disorders, the following methodologic biases that may lead to spurious associations between disorders should be ruled out: (a) *treatment-seeking bias,* known as "Berkson's Bias," in which persons with two conditions are more likely to be hospitalized or treated (Berkson, 1946), and (b) *assessment bias,* which may include investigator bias, the lack of discrete diagnostic definitions in which a large degree of symptom overlap exists between two diagnostic categories, or the application of diagnostic hierarchies that may mask an association. Spurious associations between disorders may also occur because of the lack of an appropriate comparison or control group, or the failure to adjust for confounding factors such as sex or age. For example, population stratification may lead to artifactual associations between diseases; if the sample includes a subpopulation in which there is an increased frequency of two unrelated disorders, the disorders may appear to be associated.

If a true association exists between two disorders, there are two possible explanations for this association. First, it could be etiologic in that one disorder causes or leads to the second disorder. The presence of one disorder is a necessary precondition for the expression of the other. For example, alcoholism may cause depression, or vice versa.

A second possible explanation for an association is that the two disorders are manifestations of the same underlying etiologic factors. For example, this model would propose that alcoholism and depression result from the same etiologic factors. Pleiotropic effects of the same genes could lead to alcoholism, depression or a combination of the two, depending on background genes and the intrinsic and extrinsic environment in which they are expressed.

Use of Familial Transmission Data to Assess Mechanisms for Associations

Data on familial transmission of disorders can be used to study the validity of diagnostic categories and subtypes thereof. If the association between two disorders were attributable to a causal model (as described earlier), the two disorders would be expected to breed true in families. That is, it would be expected that relatives of probands with one disorder would have an elevated risk of that disorder and not the other disorder. If relatives did exhibit an increased risk of the other disorder, it would occur only in the presence of the disorder expressed by the proband. For example, if alcoholism caused depression, one would expect an elevation of depression among the relatives of alcoholic probands, but only in combination with alcoholism.

The predictions of the family data for the second possible mechanism for an association between two disorders, that each disorder is a manifestation of similar underlying factors (i.e., genetic or intrinsic vs. extrinsic environment or a combination thereof), are as follows: Relatives of probands with pure forms of either disorder should have elevated rates of pure forms of the other disorder, as compared with expected population rates. With alcoholism once again as an example, shared etiologic factors between depression and alcoholism would be demonstrated by both an increase in the prevalence of alcoholism alone among the relatives of probands with depression alone, and an increased prevalence of depression alone among the relatives of probands with alcoholism without depression.

Associations Between Substance Abuse and Psychiatric Disorders

The association between substance abuse and psychiatric conditions has long been of interest to clinicians (Boyd et al., 1984; Helzer & Pryzbeck, 1988). However, the specific mechanisms for the relationship have been controversial. On the one hand, it has been proposed that the psychiatric disorders lead to substance abuse either because they constitute different manifestations of an underlying biologic relationship or because the symptoms of psychiatic conditions lead indirectly to the development of substance abuse through self-medication (Lader, 1972). Alternately, psychiatric symptoms or syndromes, such as major depression, could also be consequences of substance abuse (Bernadt & Murray, 1986). In recent reviews of the evidence for the association between alcoholism and depression, both Schuckit (1986) and Merikangas and Gelernter (1990) concluded that depression and alcoholism do not result from the same underlying etiologic factors. Rather, the data suggest that depression is more likely to be a consequence than a cause of alcoholism. Moreover, the latter review found that bipolar depression was also etiologically rather than causally related to alcoholism, with alcoholism resulting from bipolar disorder.

There is also a substantial degree of co-occurrence of alcoholism and drug abuse and dependence. In a review of 40 studies conducted between 1925 and 1972, Freed (1973) found an association between alcoholism and drug abuse in approximately 20% of the subjects. In a review of susequent studies that examined the overlap between alcohol and drug use or abuse, Grande, Wolf, Schubert, Patterson, & Brocco (1984) confirmed the positive association cited above in the majority of studies. More recently, Boyd et al. (1984) and Helzer and Pryzbeck (1988) have shown that the association between alcohol abuse/dependence and drug abuse/dependence also exists in a probability sample of the U.S. population (odds ratio = 10.7, $p < .001$). An exception to this generally strong association between drug abuse and alcoholism was shown by Weller and Halikas (1985), who found that the prevalence of alcoholism was not significantly greater among chronic marijuana abusers than among nonabusers.

Most of the family, twin, and adoption studies have focused on the transmission of a single disorder, rather than studying simultaneous manifestation of two or more conditions. Thus, there are no family or genetic studies that have examined the mechanisms for the associations between alcohol and drug abuse. However, the family study is an excellent method for studying the mechanisms for associations between two or more conditions.

Nonrandom Mating

Assortative mating, the tendency for mated pairs to be more similar for a particular trait than persons selected at random from the population, has been shown to occur for most of the major psychiatric conditions (Merikangas, 1982). Cross-mating, the tendency for persons with one disorder to marry persons with another disorder more frequently than would be expected if they were chosen at random from the population, is another important mating pattern that should also be studied. In a review of the literature, Jacob and Bremer (1986) found a strong tendency toward assortative mating for alcoholism. Moreover, assortative mating for psychiatric disorders has been shown to be associated with a dramatic increase in the risk of psychopathology among offspring.

In a family study of depression, we investigated the occurrence and effects of nonrandom mating, both assortative and cross-mating, on familial transmission of affective disorders and alcoholism (Merikangas, Prusoff, & Weissman, 1988). Cross-mating between parents could lead to transmissible associations between the disorders in offspring when the two disorders are actually distinctly transmitted (Weissman, Myers, & Harding, 1978).

In our previous family studies of depression and alcoholism, we found that the most common type of cross-mating involved alcoholic fathers with depressed or anxious (nonalcoholic) mothers (13%). Indeed, this mating type was almost as common as assortative mating for depression or anxiety. The alcoholic man – depressed/anxious woman mating type was sex-specific: None of the women with alcoholism in the study were married to men who did not also have alcoholism. Thus, in addition to the effects of assortative mating on rates of illness among offspring, cross-mating may also be involved in the association among the disorders observed in the offspring of such matings (Merikangas, Weissman, Prusoff, & John, 1988).

In an evaluation of the effects of parental concordance for alcoholism and drug abuse on the risk of illness among offspring, we found a strong linear trend in the relationship of rates of alcohol and drug dependence among offspring to the number of parents with alcoholism (Merikangas, Weissman, & Prusoff, 1990). Offspring had a twofold risk of alcoholism when one parent had alcoholism compared with the offspring of couples in which neither parent had alcoholism. Offspring of couples concordant for alcoholism had a three-fold increase in risk compared with offspring having only one affected parent. Similarly, for antisocial personality and conduct disorder, there was a strong significant linear trend according to the number of parents with alcoholism. However, rates of major depression and anxiety disorders were not significantly increased among offspring of alcoholic parents.

Because the offspring in our previous family study of depression (Merikangas, Weissman, Prusoff, & John, 1988) were generally older than 20, we were able to examine the rates of disorders in the offspring of the probands and their siblings. Of all the disorders examined, the strongest effect of parental assortative mating was seen for alcoholism. Offspring had a three-fold increase in risk of alcoholism compared with the offspring of couples in which only one member had alcoholism. When the offspring over age 18 were examined separately, it was found that nearly 50% of the offspring of those couples concordant for alcoholism had alcoholism themselves, compared with 11% when neither parent had alcoholism. The effect of assortative mating for alcoholism was also seen in the increased risk of antisocial personality in the offspring over age 18, where 30% had antisocial personality compared with 2% of the offspring of couples without alcoholism. There was a 1.7-fold increase in the risk of conduct disorder in the younger offspring and of antisocial personality in the older offspring of parents who were concordant for alcoholism.

Regardless of the mechanism or specific traits involved in the observed concordance for alcoholism, the data suggested that such concordance was a potent risk factor for the development of alcoholism and either conduct disorder or antisocial personality in offspring. Whether the increased manifestation of disorders results from increased genetic loading, detrimental environmental factors, or both could not be determined from the family study data. Nevertheless, the role of the presence of alcoholism in both parents should be considered in both research and treatment involving these children.

This chapter examines the role of familial factors in the abuse of alcohol, cocaine, and opioids. In addition to the complexity described earlier in studying the exposure to and maintenance of alcohol abuse, the assessment of the role of familial and genetic factors in the etiology of substance abuse is further complicated by the phenomenon of cohort-dependent exposure to specific drugs. Because of differences in patterns of availability of drugs across generations, one cannot assess the vertical transmission of patterns of drug use and abuse. It is therefore necessary to limit analyses of familial aggregation of substance abuse to persons within the same cohort, where one can assume similarity in exposure to particular substances.

In this chapter, we use family study data to address some of the issues described earlier. We first examine rates and patterns of drug abuse and psychiatric disorders in the siblings of the three groups of probands with opioid abuse with and without comorbid psychiatric disorders (as described in Probands below). We then investigate intergenerational patterns of substance abuse and psychiatric disorders among the parents and siblings of the probands. In the evaluation of intergenerational patterns, the role of parental concordance for substance abuse in the development of substance disorders among their offspring is also examined. Data from our previous family studies of substance abuse and psychiatric disorders are also presented to illustrate the methods for assessing the effects of these phenomena (Merikangas, Leckman, Prusoff, Pauls, & Weissman, 1985; Merikangas et al., 1988a, 1988b).

Method

Probands

The methods of this study are described in detail by Rounsaville et al. (1991). The probands (i.e., index cases) for this study were 201 White adult (over age 18), opioid-dependent patients admitted to the Substance Abuse Treatment Unit of the Connecticut Mental Health Center between 1983 and 1985. The mean age of the probands was 28 (range = 18–35). All probands were interviewed directly. The diagnostic criteria for opioid dependence were derived from the Research Diagnostic Criteria (RDC) (Spitzer, Endicott, & Robins, 1978). More stringent criteria were applied by requiring that all probands also meet entry criteria for treatment with methadone maintenance, which involves regular opioid use for at least two years. Three groups of opioid-addicted probands were group-matched by age and sex and classified according to the co-occurrence of the lifetime history of opioid dependence and major depression or antisocial personality as defined according to the RDC. The three groups of probands were as follows: (a) opioid dependence only; (b) opioid dependence plus major depression; and (c) opioid dependence plus antisocial personality. To identify probands in these groups, all adult nonadopted patients who were seeking treatment for opioid dependence were screened for psychiatric diagnosis using the Lifetime Version of the Schedule for Affective Disorders and Schizophrenia (SADS–L), which assesses all of the major disorders included in the RDC. Patients meeting criteria for the three subgroups were then invited to participate as probands in this study.

Relatives

The purpose of this study was to obtain comprehensive diagnostic estimates of probands with opioid abuse with and without comorbid antisocial personality and/or major depression, and of their first-degree relatives. The 1,030 adult first-degree relatives and spouses were examined systematically with direct interviews, using a modification of the SADS–L RDC (Spitzer et al., 1978), family history from multiple informants, and available medical records to make diagnoses. Children of the probands were not assessed systematically because they were generally quite young because of the youthful age of the proband sample.

Procedure

Diagnostic assessments were made for all living and deceased first-degree relatives and spouses. Relatives were enumerated systematically and were interviewed independently with limited knowledge of the clinical status of the proband. Interviewers of family members were aware that the proband was an opioid abuser, but unaware of the coexistent diagnosis.

A structured interview form, modified from the Schedule for Affective Disorders and Schizophrenia—Lifetime Version (SADS–L; Endicott & Spitzer, 1978), was used to obtain family history information from each interviewed person about his or her own first-degree relatives. Permission to contact relatives for direct interview was obtained from the proband. Probands were not excluded if they refused permission to have their relatives interviewed, but relatives could not be contacted if permission was denied. Hence, in some families information was obtained only from the proband (i.e., 43%).

For opioid-dependent probands and their families, a best-estimate diagnosis was based on a review of all available information by two experienced clinicians using the diagnostic system. The full details of the reliability and procedure for the final best-estimate diagnoses are described in Rounsaville et al. (1991).

Familial Factors in the Transition From Substance Use to Abuse

Use of a substance is an obvious precondition for the development of its abuse. In the general population, initiation to most substances leads to abuse in only a minority of users. In this analysis, we apply the family study design to examine the proportion of siblings with a history of drug abuse in general and of use of specific substances. This analysis is limited to siblings who were directly interviewed, to enhance the reliability of reporting.

Table 3.1 presents the rates of use of a variety of substances according to the presence or absence of abuse of any drug among interviewed siblings. Sixty-nine percent of the total sample of interviewed siblings reported using at least one class of illicit substances at least one time. Only a minority (14.6%) of the siblings who did not meet criteria for abuse of any substance had used any other illicit substance. In contrast, the majority of siblings with drug abuse reported using a variety of substances (range =

TABLE 3.1

Interviewed Siblings of Opioid Abusers with *Use* of Specific Substances by Presence or Absence of Substance *Abuse*

Substance used	No drug abuse (N = 48; 37%)	Drug abuse (N = 85; 63%)
Cocaine	6.3	70.6
Amphetamines	6.3	70.6
Hallucinogens	6.3	57.6
Marijuana	14.6	92.9
Narcotics	2.1	49.4
Sedatives	2.1	58.8
Solvents	4.2	32.9
Any of the above	14.6	100.0

Note. *N* = 133. Figures are percentages.

32.9–92.9%). Thus, polysubstance use appears to be the rule rather than the exception once a sibling has developed abuse of any single substance.

Table 3.2, presents the proportion of siblings who proceeded from experimentation to abuse of particular substances. Ninety-two percent of the siblings who tried even a single class of substances proceeded to develop abuse of that substance. For all substances, over 90% who tried the substance eventually proceeded to develop abuse. The rate of transition was greatest for narcotics and sedatives. Nearly 100% of those who tried narcotics proceeded to abuse them as well.

There was also a strong tendency toward polydrug abuse among the siblings of opioid addicts who became drug abusers. That is, if the siblings abused any substance, they were likely to develop polysubstance abuse. Only 15% reported using only one type of illicit substance, and 65% reported using three or more types of illicit substances. Thus, 90% of the sibling of opioid addicts who reported using any illicit substances proceeded to develop substance abuse.

These findings suggest that the siblings of opioid addicts are indeed a very high-risk group for the development of substance abuse. Moreover, this finding has important implications for planning of treatment and intervention. The data suggest that siblings of drug abusers represent a target group to whom powerful attempts for interventions should be directed. Although factors such as selective reporting by the non-drug-abusing siblings may account for some of the difference between the two groups, it is unlikely to

TABLE 3.2

Abuse of Specific Substances Among Interviewed Siblings of Opioid Abusers With a History of Use of that Substance

Drug	Use (%)	Abuse (%)
Cocaine	47	95
Amphetamines	47	95
Hallucinogens	39	94
Marijuana	65	92
Narcotics	32	98
Sedatives	38	98
Solvents	23	93
Any combination of the above	69	92

Note. $N = 133$.

account for the major finding. These data have been examined in greater detail to investigate the age of onset and patterns of use and transition to abuse among the siblings of the opioid abusers.

Comorbidity of Substance Abuse and Psychiatric Disorders in Probands and Siblings

A major potential risk factor for development of drug abuse is the presence of a preexisting psychiatric disorder. Persons with major psychiatric disorders may have increased vulnerability to drug abuse resulting from self-medication of the underlying psychiatric condition. The likelihood that psychiatric disorders would enhance vulnerability to drug abuse among the siblings would be demonstrated by the tendency for the onset of the psychiatric symptoms to precede that of the substance abuse.

In Table 3.3, we present the rates of the most frequent comorbid disorders among siblings with drug abuse according to comorbid diagnoses among the probands. Because of the low sensitivity of the family history method in detecting comorbid disorders, data are presented only for siblings who were interviewed directly. Although the entire range of psychiatric disorders covered by the SADS–L was assessed, only major depression, antisocial personality, alcoholism, and anxiety disorders (i.e., panic, phobia, general anxiety) were sufficiently common to permit statistical analyses.

The rates of comorbid disorders were dramatically elevated among siblings with drug abuse contrasted with those without drug abuse. That is, significantly elevated rates of alcoholism, antisocial personality, and major depression were found among the siblings with drug abuse, irrespective of the presence of comorbid disorders in the probands. However, the rates of anxiety disorders were not different for the siblings with and without drug abuse.

However, there appeared to be little specificity of transmission of the comorbid disorders among probands and their siblings. The rates of antisocial personality were similar among the siblings of probands with antisocial personality, depression, and neither (i.e., 46%, 48%, and 38%, respectively). Likewise, rates of antisocial personality were nearly identical among siblings of the three groups of probands (i.e., 29%, 24%, and 24%, respectively). This indicates that comorbid psychiatric symptoms, which were severe enough to warrant a diagnosis, are strongly associated with drug abuse. However, it appears that these disorders are associated with drug abuse rather than representing manifestations of

TABLE 3.3

Psychiatric Disorders in Drug-Abusing and Non-Drug-Abusing Siblings of Probands

	Probands											
	Drug use only				Depression				Antisocial personality			
	DA		NDA		DA		NDA		DA		NDA	
Sibling disorders	N	%	N	%	N	%	N	%	N	%	N	%
Alcoholism	10	58.8	1	8.3	21	67.7	1	6.7	22	59.5	5	23.8
Antisocial personality	7	41.2	0	0	10	32.3	1	6.7	16	43.2	1	4.8
Any anxiety	4	23.5	3	25.0	9	20.0	3	20.0	10	27.0	9	42.9
Major depression	10	58.8	0	0	11	35.5	4	26.7	17	46.0	4	19.1
Total N	17		12		31		15		37		21	

Note. N = 133. DA = Drug abuse; NDA = No drug abuse.

shared underlying etiologic factors in these families. Therefore, the comorbid disorders are likely to be either consequences of or antecedent factors for drug abuse. If these results are taken together with the findings of previous studies on alcoholism, it is likely that depression is a consequence of substance abuse, whereas antisocial personality is likely to lead to drug and alcohol abuse.

In either case, our data are consistent with a causal mechanism rather than with shared etiologic factors involved in the association between substance abuse and psychiatric disorders. If shared etiologic factors contributed to both disorders, rates of the comorbid disorder would have been similar among relatives of probands with and without the comorbid disorder. Instead, the data show that psychiatric disorders are elevated among siblings with a history of drug abuse compared with those with no history of drug abuse.

Parental Psychiatric Disorders as a Risk Factor

The association between parental psychiatric disorders or substance abuse and psychiatric disorders in their offspring (i.e., the siblings of opioid addicts) was examined to assess the intergenerational patterns and specificity of transmission of comorbid disorders in the families of opioid addicts. If the risk for disorders is specific, we would expect the siblings of opioid addicts to have higher rates of those disorders manifested by their parents than would siblings of parents without the comorbid disorder. For example, children of depressed parents would be expected to have higher rates of depression than would children of nondepressed parents, and so forth. Because of the differences in patterns of exposure to illicit drugs, the intergenerational patterns of drug abuse could not be examined.

In Table 3.4, we present the rates of alcoholism, drug abuse, anxiety disorders or depression, and antisocial personality in siblings according to the presence of these disorders in their mothers and fathers. Similar to the findings for the probands and siblings in Table 3.3, these results show that offspring of mothers or fathers with a disorder generally had higher rates of all disorders, suggesting a more general conveyance of risk for disorder from parents to opioid addicts' siblings.

To assess the role of such confounding variables as sex of relative, age of relative, or interview status (i.e., whether the relative was directly interviewed) in the association between parental and sibling diagnoses, a logistic regression analysis was performed. Table 3.5 presents the significance of the findings for the rates presented in Table 3.4. The following findings emerged for maternal disorders: Alcohol abuse was significantly related

TABLE 3.4

Disorders in Siblings of Probands by Diagnoses in Mothers and Fathers

		Disorders in siblings							
	N	Alcoholism		Drug abuse		Anxiety and/or depression		Antisocial personality	
Parent diagnosis	siblings	%	*N*	%	*N*	%	*N*	%	*N*
Mother									
Alcoholism									
with	65	33.9	22	52.3	34	24.6	16	16.9	11
without	411	24.3	100	30.4	125	19.7	81	10.0	41
Drug abuse									
with	9	44.4	4	66.7	6	44.4	4	44.4	4
without	467	25.3	118	32.8	153	19.9	93	10.3	48
Anxiety and/or depression									
with	150	36.7	55	49.3	74	33.3	50	17.3	26
without	326	20.6	67	26.1	85	14.4	47	8.0	26
Father									
Alcoholism									
with	192	35.9	69	40.1	77	23.9	46	10.9	21
without	283	18.4	52	28.6	81	18.0	51	10.6	30
Drug abuse									
with	18	38.9	7	55.6	10	22.2	4	22.2	4
without	457	25.0	114	32.4	148	20.4	93	10.3	47
Anxiety and/or depression									
with	84	35.7	30	47.6	40	32.1	27	17.9	15
without	391	23.3	91	30.2	118	17.9	70	9.2	36
Antisocial personality									
with	8	12.5	1	25.0	2	50.0	4	25.0	2
without	467	25.7	120	33.4	156	19.9	93	10.5	49
Total *N* of siblings	475	121		158		97		51	

to sibling drug abuse; and anxiety or depression was associated with higher rates of alcoholism, drug abuse, and anxiety or depression in siblings. After controlling for the effects of sex, age, maternal diagnoses and interview status, these associations between paternal disorders and those among their offspring remained significant. That is, paternal alcohol abuse was associated with alcohol abuse in the siblings; paternal drug abuse was associated with drug abuse in the siblings; and paternal antisocial personality was associated with higher rates of depression or anxiety disorders in the siblings. Taken together, these

TABLE 3.5

Significance of Effects of Logistic Regression Analyses of Parents on Disorders in Their Nonproband Children

	Siblings of probands (N = 476)			
Variable	Alcohol abuse (N = 121)	Drug abuse (N = 158)	Anxiety and/or depression (N = 97)	Antisocial personality (N = 51)
Main effects				
Mother				
Alcohol abuse				
Drug abuse		**		
Anxiety and/or depression	**	***	**	
Father				
Alcohol abuse	***			
Drug abuse		*		
Anxiety and/or depression				
Antisocial personality			*	
Sibling characteristics				
Sex	*	**		***
Age				**
Interview status (interviewed or not)	***	**	***	***

*p < .05. **p < .01. ***p < .001.

findings appear to provide limited support for greater specificity of transmission of risk for disorders between opioid addicts' fathers and their offspring than for their mothers. Although no consistent effects of specificity were found for either maternal or paternal disorders on elevation of risk to the siblings of the addicts, maternal drug abuse appeared to have a more pervasive association with substance abuse or psychopathology in general among the siblings. These interpretations are discussed more fully by Merikangas, Weissman, Prusoff, & John (1988).

Nonrandom Mating and Risk Factors

In Tables 3.6 and 3.7, we examine parental and spouse concordance for substance abuse and psychiatric disorders. Table 3.6 displays the rates of alcoholism, drug abuse, antisocial personality, and anxiety or depression in the siblings of opioid addicts by the presence of the same disorder in their mothers, fathers, or both. The only disorder for which there was a direct relationship between the number of parents ill and the prevalence of that disorder in their offspring was drug abuse. The risk of drug abuse among offspring of couples in which one parent was a drug abuser was 1.5 times greater than among offspring of couples in which neither member had a history of drug abuse. There was an additional twofold increase in the risk of drug abuse among offspring whose parents both had a history of drug abuse. However, there were no differences in the rates of disorders in the offspring according to the sex of the affected parent.

However, although approximately 44% of opioid addicts had a parent with alcoholism and 38% had a parent with anxiety or depression, only 5% had a parent with drug

TABLE 3.6

Disorders in Siblings of Opiod Addicts by the Presence of Same Disorders in Parents ($N = 475$)

	Disorders in parents			
Disorders	Neither	Mother	Father	Both
Alcoholism	17.1	25.9	35.9	37.5
Drug abuse	26.2	40.7	37.2	57.5
Anxiety and/or depression	19.1	3.7	20.5	40.0
Antisocial personality	9.5	11.1	10.9	17.5

Note. Figures are percentages.

abuse and 2% had a parent with antisocial personality. Hence, the number of subjects at risk is quite low, and the estimates are likely to be highly unreliable.

Finally, we investigated the occurrence of spouse concordance among the probands with opioid abuse. Table 3.7 shows that there were exceedingly high rates of psychiatric disorders, most notably drug abuse, among both the male and female spouses of the opioid abusers. Both the male and female spouses reported an average fivefold greater prevalence of alcoholism, antisocial personality, and drug abuse than population expectations. This finding demonstrates the clustering of these conditions in these families and the strong environmental instability that characterizes the offspring of such marriages (Merikangas, Weissman, Prusoff, & John, 1988).

Discussion and Summary

Investigation of the familial factors associated with substance abuse yielded significant findings in all three of the areas examined in this chapter.

Patterns of Substance Use and Abuse Among Siblings

There was a dramatically high lifetime prevalence of substance abuse among the interviewed siblings of substance abusers. Nearly two thirds of the siblings of substance-dependent probands had a history of substance abuse themselves. This rate is five times greater than the lifetime rates of drug abuse in a comparable age group in the general population of the United States (Robins et al., 1984). There was also a striking increase in

TABLE 3.7

Lifetime Disorders in Spouses (*N* = 153) of Probands with Opioid Abuse

	All spouses		Interviewed only	
	Female **(*N* = 47)**	**Male** **(*N* = 106)**	**Female** **(*N* = 13)**	**Male** **(*N* = 26)**
Alcoholism	14.9	40.6	23.1	76.9
Antisocial personality	10.6	37.7	30.8	69.2
Drug abuse	38.3	69.8	92.3	96.2
Anxiety and/or depression	21.3	13.2	46.2	42.3

Note. Figures are percentages.

the proportion of siblings with transition from use to abuse of substances. The vast majority of siblings who reported ever using a particular substance proceeded to develop abuse of that substance. Moreover, polysubstance abuse was clearly the rule rather than the exception. This suggests that there was little evidence of specificity of drug preference between drug abusers and their siblings. If specific drug preference were familial, it would be expected that there would be an elevation of abuse of particular substances between sibships, rather than an elevation of rates of abuse of all substances. We are investigating this finding in depth to determine whether familial factors are involved in drug preference.

Intergenerational Patterns of Substance Abuse and Comorbid Disorders
The assessment of intergenerational patterns of transmission of substance abuse also yielded several important findings. Most notable was the association between parental and sibling substance abuse. Offspring of parents (i.e., siblings of substance abusers) with substance abuse were twice as likely to develop substance abuse. Moreover, there was a tendency for specificity of transmission of paternal alcoholism and drug abuse. That is, offspring of fathers with alcoholism were twice as likely to develop alcoholism as offspring of fathers without alcoholism; similarly, paternal drug abuse was directly associated with drug abuse in siblings. Specificity of maternal drug abuse could not be assessed because of the low frequency of drug abuse among mothers. This illustrates the limitations of investigation of intergenerational patterns of substance abuse, because of the strong cohort effects for availability and exposure to illicit substances. However, maternal alcohol abuse was associated with increased rates of drug abuse in the offspring.

Interesting findings emerged with respect to the intergenerational patterns of comorbid psychiatric disorders as well. Maternal anxiety disorders and major depression were associated with an increased risk of both substance abuse and anxiety and major depression among the offspring. In contrast, paternal anxiety disorders and depression were not associated with elevated risks of any disorders among the offspring. The lack of specificity of comorbid psychiatric disorders, taken together with the absence of a paternal effect, suggests that the comorbid conditions may be secondary to parental substance abuse or may result from the disrupted environment that characterizes the homes of substance abusers. In any event, it does not appear that these conditions comprise underlying etiologic factors in substance abuse.

Nonrandom Mating

Examination of parental concordance for substance abuse revealed that there was a direct relationship between the number of parents with substance abuse and drug abuse in their offspring (i.e., the siblings of the probands). It was particularly interesting that this relationship was unique to substance abuse; there was no monotonic relationship between the number of parents with alcoholism, anxiety disorders and/or major depression, or antisocial personality and these same disorders in their offspring.

The most remarkable finding from the analysis of nonrandom mating among the substance abusers was that nearly 100% of both the male and female spouses of drug abusers were drug abusers themselves. The finding of high frequencies of antisocial personality and alcoholism in the male spouses of drug abusers was notable. Although this is not surprising to clinicians involved in the treatment of substance abuse, if one considers the effect of drug abuse in both parents on the environment in which they rear children, this finding is disturbing. Moreover, any attempt to investigate the role of genetic factors in the transmission of drug abuse would be severely limited by the high frequency of couples in which both members have drug abuse.

In summary, these results show that the following factors may accelerate the transition from drug use to abuse: history of drug abuse in a parent or sibling, the presence of antisocial personality disorder, and concordance for substance abuse in parents. The specific mechanisms associated with these factors need to be identified to gain an understanding of how such factors may exert their effects (Fisher, Harder, & Kokes, 1980). We are currently evaluating the children of parents with alcoholism, cocaine abuse, heroin abuse, marijuana abuse, depression, anxiety, and no substance abuse or psychiatric disorder, to study specific risk factors associated with these conditions. Nevertheless, persons with the risk factors described above should be identified as targets for prevention prior to their exposure to any use of illicit substances.

References

American Psychiatric Association. (1980). *Diagnostic and statistical manual of mental disorders* (3rd ed.) Washington, DC: Author.

American Psychiatric Association. (1987). *Diagnostic and statistical manual of mental disorders* (3rd ed., rev.). Washington, DC: Author.

Angst, J., Vollrath, M., Merikangas, K. R., & Ernst, C. (1990). Comorbidity of anxiety and depression in the Zurich cohort study of young adults. In J. D. Maser & C. R. Cloninger (Eds.), *Comorbidity of mood and anxiety disorders* (pp. 123–138). Washington, DC: American Psychiatric Press.

Berkson, J. (1946). Limitation of the application of the 4-fold table analysis to hospital data. *Biometrics, 2,* 47–53.

Bernadt, M. W., & Murray, R. M. (1986). Psychiatric disorder, drinking and alcoholism: What are the links? *British Journal of Psychiatry, 148,* 393–400.

Boyd, J. H., Burke, J. D., Gruenberg, E., Holzer, C. E. III, Rae, D. S., George, L. K., Karno, M., Stoltzman, R., McEvoy, L., & Nestadt, G. (1984). Exclusion criteria of DSM–III: A study of co-occurrence of hierarchy-free syndromes. *Archives of General Psychiatry, 41,* 983–989.

Endicott, J., & Spitzer, R. L. (1978). A diagnostic interview: The Schedule for Affective Disorders and Schizophrenia—Lifetime Version (modified for the study of anxiety disorders). *Archives of General Psychiatry, 35,* 837–844.

Feinstein, A. R. (1970). The pre-therapeutic classification of co-morbidity in chronic disease. *Journal of Chronic Disease, 23,* 455–468.

Fisher, L., Harder, D. W., & Kokes, R. F. (1980). Child competence and psychiatric risk: III. Comparisons based on diagnosis of hospitalized parent. *Journal of Nervous Mental Disease, 168,* 338–342.

Freed, E. (1973). Drug abuse by alcoholics. *International Journal of Addiction, 8,* 451–473.

Grande, T. P., Wolf, A. H., Schubert, D. S. P., Patterson, M. B., & Brocco, K. (1984). Associations among alcoholism, drug abuse and antisocial personality: A review of the literature. *Psychological Reports, 55,* 455–474.

Gurling, H. M. D., Murray, R. M., & Clifford, C. A. (1981). *Investigations into the genetics of alcohol dependence and into its effects on brain function: Twin Research 3. Epidemiologic clinical studies.* New York: Liss.

Helzer, J. E., & Pryzbeck, T. R. (1988). The co-occurrence of alcoholism with other psychiatric disorders in the general population and its impact on treatment. *Journal of Studies of Alcohol, 49,* 219–224.

Jacob, T., & Bremer, D. A. (1986). Assortative mating among men and women alcoholics. *Journal of Studies of Alcohol, 47,* 219–222.

Kaplan, M. H., & Feinstein, A. R. (1974). The importance of classifying initial co-morbidity in evaluating the outcome of diabetes mellitus. *Journal of Chronic Disease, 27,* 387–404.

Lader, M. (1972). The nature of anxiety. *British Journal of Psychiatry, 121,* 481–491.

Merikangas, K. R. (1982). Assortative mating for psychiatric disorders and psychological traits. *Archives of General Psychiatry, 39,* 1173–1180.

Merikangas, K. R. (1990). The genetic epidemiology of alcoholism. *Psychological Medicine, 20,* 11–22.

Merikangas, K. R., & Gelernter, C. S. (1990). Co-morbidity for alcoholism and depression, *The Psychiatric Clinics of North America, 13,* 423–442.

Merikangas, K. R., Leckman, J. F., Prusoff, B. A., Pauls, D. L., & Weissman, M. M. (1985). Familial transmission of depression and alcoholism. *Archives of General Psychiatry, 42,* 367–372.

Merikangas, K. R., Prusoff, B. A., & Weissman, M. M. (1988). Parental concordance for psychiatric disorders: Psychopathology in offspring. *Journal of Affective Disorders, 15,* 279–290.

Merikangas, K. R., Weissman, M. M., & Prusoff, B. A. (1990). Depression and families: Impact and treatment. In I. Keitner (Ed.), (pp. 85–100). Washington, DC: American Psychiatric Press.

Merikangas, K. R., Weissman, M. M., Prusoff, B. A., & John, K. (1988). Assortative mating and affective disorders: Psychopathology in offspring. In S. Kellam (Ed.), *The family and psychopathology* (pp. 48–57). New Brunswick, NJ: Rutgers University Press.

Pedersen, N. (1981). Twin similarity for usage of common drugs. In L. Gredda, P. Paris, & W. Nance (Eds.), *Twin research 3: Epidemiological and clinical studies* (pp. 53–59). New York: Liss.

Pfohl, B., Coryell, W., & Zimmerman, M. (1986). DSM–III personality disorders: Diagnostic overlap and internal consistency of individual DSM–III criteria. *Comparative Psychiatry, 27,* 21–34.

Pickens, R., Svikis, D., McGue, M., Lykken, D., Heston, M., & Clayton, P. (1991). Heterogeneity in the inheritance of alcoholism: A study of male and female twins. *Archives of General Psychiatry, 48,* 19–28.

Robins, L. N., Helzer, J. E., Weissman, M. M., Orvaschel, H., Gruenberg, E., Burke, J. D., & Regier, D. A. (1984). Lifetime prevalence of specific psychiatric disorders in three sites. *Archives of General Psychiatry, 41,* 949–958.

Roth, M., Gurney, C., Garside, R., & Kerr, T. A. (1972). Studies in the classification of affective disorders: The relationship between anxiety and depressive illness. *British Journal of Psychiatry, 121,* 147–161.

Rounsaville, B. J., Kosten, T. R., Weissman, M. M., Prusoff, B. A., Pauls, D., Foley, S., & Merikangas, K. R. (1991). Psychiatric disorders in the relatives of probands with opioid addiction. *Archives of General Psychiatry, 48,* 33–42.

Schuckit, M. A. (1986). Genetic and clinical implications of alcoholism and affective disorder. *American Journal of Psychiatry, 143,* 140–147.

Spitzer, R. L., Endicott, J., & Robins, E. (1978). Research diagnostic criteria: Rationale and reliability. *Archives of General Psychiatry, 35,* 773–779.

Weissman, M. M., Myers, J. K., & Harding, P. S. (1978). Psychiatric disorders in a United States urban community: 1975–76. *American Journal of Psychiatry, 135,* 459–462.

Weller, R. A., & Halikas, J. A. (1985). Marijuana use and psychiatric illness: A follow-up study. *American Journal of Psychiatry, 142,* 848–850.

Woodruff, R. A., Murphy, G. E., & Herjanic, M. (1967). The natural history of affective disorders: 1. Symptoms of 72 patients at the time of index hospital admission. *Journal of Psychiatric Research 5,* 255–263.

CHAPTER 4

Genetic and Environmental Factors in Initiation of Drug Use and the Transition to Abuse

Remi J. Cadoret

T here have been many studies pointing to factors that lead to substance use or abuse. In practically every study, whether based on a clinical sample or a population sample, it is impossible to separate genetic or biologic factors leading to predisposition to drug use or abuse from environmental factors such as peer pressures, drug exposure, family stresses, and other important psychosocial conditions. Separation of genetic–constitutional inheritable factors that would predispose to substance use or abuse would be of considerable importance in directing the focus of etiologic research to the molecular genetic area. The obverse of the etiologic coin, the environmental aspect, could then be examined and factors could be discovered that in themselves could lead to use or abuse or that could affect the manifestation of the genetic predisposition through gene–environment interaction.

One approach to disentangling genetic from environmental factors is the adoption or separation paradigm, which has already met with success in demonstrating genetic causes for a variety of psychopathologic conditions such as depression, schizophrenia, antisocial personality, and alcoholism (reviewed in Cadoret, 1986). In addition, adoptees are usually not picked as subjects because they have sought treatment for their ills, with the result that adoption designs should select a sample of adoptees that is more representative of comorbid conditions found in the general population than are samples derived from clinical populations where there is the ever-present chance that disease comorbidity itself or psychosocial pressures based on comorbidity affect the decision to seek treatment.

The use of an adoption paradigm could contribute the following types of information to the question of factors differentiating abusers from occasional users:

1. What genetic factors are involved in use or abuse?
2. What environmental factors are involved in use or abuse?
3. Does gene–environment interaction play a role in use or abuse? For example, does a genetic predisposition manifest itself more strongly in the presence of certain environmental conditions, or do certain environmental conditions protect an individual from a genetic predisposition?
4. Which factors (both genetic and environmental) are responsible for the clinical comorbidity seen in substance abuse (Bukstein, Brent, & Kaminer, 1989; Cadoret, Troughton, O'Gorman, & Heywood, 1986; Clayton, 1981; Helzer & Pryzbeck, 1988; Hesselbrock, Hesselbrock, & Stabenau, 1985). For example, to what extent are conditions that appear to be important in substance abuse, such as conduct disorder, adult antisocial personality, attention deficit hyperactivity disorder, affective disorder, and alcohol abuse, influenced by genetic and environmental factors?

In this chapter, we will analyze data from two completed adoption studies that demonstrate the points made above. Data from these studies have been analyzed for the effects of several genetic and environmental factors on the occurrence in adoptees of drug abuse (Cadoret et al., 1986). Evidence was found that having a biologic parent with an alcohol problem (defined as psychosocial problems including treatment relating to alcohol use) increased the risk for drug abuse in adult offspring adopted away at birth who as adults did not meet criteria for antisocial personality. Furthermore, an environmental effect of having a disturbed adoptive parent was also associated with increased adult adoptee drug abuse, although the direction of effect was not clear. A disturbed adoptive parent is one with a psychiatric or antisocial problem or with a marital problem leading to separation or divorce. In this chapter, will use the same data set to examine the question of what genetic and environmental factors predispose these adoptees to make the transition from drug use to abuse or to initiate the use of drugs without making the transition to abuse.

Method

This study uses two samples of male adoptees who had been separated at birth and placed with nonrelatives. One sample of 158 men was from the Iowa Children's and Family Services (ICFS) of Des Moines; the second, of 125, was from Lutheran Social Services (LSS) of Des Moines. This total of 283 men was reduced to 238 for this study because we selected only interviewed adoptees for whom there was adequate information to diagnose drug use and abuse. Adoptees had been placed statewide by both agencies. Both samples consisted of two groups of adoptees: Group 1, of those adoptees whose biologic parents showed evidence from the adoption agency records of a psychiatric problem or behavior disturbance; Group 2, of those adoptees whose biologic parents showed no behavior problems. The groups were matched on the adoptee's age and sex and on age of the biologic mother at the time of the adoptee's birth. The criteria for selecting and diagnosing the biologic parents from adoption agency records have been presented previously (Cadoret, 1978; Cadoret & Cain, 1980; Cadoret, Cain, & Grove, 1980; Cadoret & Gath, 1978, 1980). In the present study, two biologic-parent conditions turned out to be important: (a) alcohol problems, defined as the presence of one or more recorded social or medical problems due to drinking, and (b) criminality/delinquency, defined as adjudication of delinquency as an adolescent or conviction of a felony as an adult. The adoptees in the present study ranged in age between 18 and 40 years. Their average age was 24.8 ± 6.2 ($M \pm SD$) and there was a strong correlation between current age and drug abuse: 15.1% of the 152 men under 26 years of age were abusers, whereas only 5.6% of the 89 men 26 years and older were abusers. This type of age difference is part of the phenomenon of increased drug abuse in younger cohorts (Christie et al., 1988). To control for this cohort effect, we used age as an independent variable in later logistic regressions. Information on the adoptees was gathered through a structured psychiatric interview given by telephone to the ICFS sample. In the LSS sample, both the Diagnostic Interview Schedule (DIS; Robins, Helzer, Croughan, & Radcliff, 1981) and the Lifetime Version of the Schedule for Affective Disorders and Schizophrenia (SADS–L; Spitzer & Endicott, 1979) were used, and interviews were carried out in person by a research assistant. All interviews were done blind to the status of the biologic parent. Further information on the adoptees' early life was gathered through a structured interview administered to the adoptive parents. The adoptive-parent interview also enquired about the adoptive family's circumstances and was the chief source of information relating to the adoptees' environment. The criteria for diagnosis of the family environment are given in Cadoret, O'Gorman, Troughton, & Heywood (1985).

The adoptive-parent interview was the main source of information about behaviors that occurred during the infancy, childhood, and adolescence of the adoptees. This includes behaviors contributing to diagnoses of temperament, attention-deficit/hyperactivity, aggressivity, and childhood and early adolescent conduct disorders. Definitions of agression, attention-deficit/hyperactivity, and impulsivity conditions are detailed in Cadoret and Stewart (1989). Temperament was defined using Chess-Thomas descriptors as described in Mauer, Cadoret, and Cain (1980).

Analyses of these data have involved formulating hypotheses about genetic and environmental factors and using appropriate multivariate statistics such as log-linear analyses or logistic regression to test these hypotheses. For the present chapter, we used a different approach. We did not have specific hypotheses about what genetic and environmental factors might be involved in the initiation of drug use and the transition from use to abuse. Therefore, we divided the adoptees, on the basis of their drug use as reported on the DIS or the SADS–L, into three groups that characterized three types of drug behavior in the male sample: (a) a group of 103 who reported no drug use; (b) a group of 107 who reported having used one or more drugs at some time in their life but whose use never met the criteria of the third edition of the *Diagnostic and Statistical Manual of Mental Disorders (DSM–III;* American Psychiatric Association, 1980) for abuse; and (c) a group of 28 who met *DSM–III* criteria for drug abuse at some time in their life. In the sample studied, use was defined in such a way as to exclude those who abused, although it is possible that a number of "users" could, over time, develop into abusers and that nonusers could move into use or even into abuse.

The experimental plan was to use differences in genetic and environmental variables between Group 1, (nonusers) and Group 2 (drug users only) to define etiologic factors leading to initiation of drug use. Differences between Group 2 (drug users) and Group 3 (drug abusers) were examined to define factors involved in the transition from drug use to abuse–dependency. To uncover these etiologic factors, preliminary analyses were done by looking at values for each of the various genetic and environmental factors in the three groups, using analysis of variance for continuous variables or 2×3 chi-square tables for nominal data. Significant genetic and environmental variables were selected for further multivariate analyses such as logistic regression.

Table 4.1 shows some characteristics of the drug abuse reported by the 28 abusers/dependents in Group 3 and the 107 drug users in Group 2. Table 4.2 shows the length of time that the use or abuse occurred in both user and abuser groups. It is evident that abusers were much more involved with drugs both in number of drug types used (Table 4.1) and in length of time that drugs were taken (Table 4.2).

TABLE 4.1
Number of Drug Types Used by Drug Users and Abusers

Number of drug types	% Users—no abuse (N = 107)	% Abuse (N = 28)	% Total users and abusers (N = 135)
1	73	11	60
2	19	18	19
3	5	18	8
4	3	46	12
5	0	7	1

TABLE 4.2
Duration of Drug Use and Drug Abuse/Dependence

Drug type	Users—no abuse (N = 107)		Abuse/dependency (N = 28)	
	Range (years)	Median (years)	Range (years)	Median (years)
Cannabinoids	<1–7	2	2–10	6
Stimulants (includes cocaine)	<1–7	1	<1–17	4
Hypnotics	<1–1	0.5	<1–7	2
Opioids	—		<1–1	1
Hallucinogens	<1–<1	0.5	<1–8	2

Results

Table 4.3 shows adult adoptee outcome divided by reported type of drug experience for the 238 men. The table shows the dramatic increase in the conditions of alcohol abuse and antisocial personality in those reporting drug abuse. The other significant adult outcome is the lower educational level achieved by the drug abusers. These outcome variables were not selected for analysis as etiologic factors because in most cases the drug-taking behavior, whether use or abuse, could well have led to antisocial behavior or to drinking, as well as to leaving school early. However, early childhood behaviors or early adolescent behavior occurring prior to drug abuse or use were screened as potential etiologic factors. These items are shown in Table 4.4 and comprise several types of temperament, an attention-deficit/hyperactivity syndrome, an aggression variable, and a measure of impulsivity. The number of conduct-disorder behaviors occurring throughout adolescence is also shown, although this variable could well have been influenced by drug-taking behavior. Four items were selected from this table for future analysis as etiologic factors because of significant or near-significant correlations with type of drug use: attention-deficit syndrome, aggressivity count, the number of impulsive behavior items, and having "bad" friends.

Genetic variables and their relationship to drug-taking behavior is shown in Table 4.5, and only one factor is significant: biologic parent with an alcohol problem. Accordingly, this genetic variable was selected for further analysis as an etiologic factor. Criminality/delinquency in a parent was also selected for further analysis, although it was significant at only the 20% level.

TABLE 4.3

Adoptee Adult Outcome Divided by Type of Drug Experience

Outcome	No drug use ($N = 103$)	Drug use only ($N = 107$)	Drug abuse/ dependence ($N = 28$)	p difference
Age (years)	25.4	24.6	22.6	ns
Education (grade)	13.8	13.7	12.3	<.05
Alcohol abuse	8.7%	29.9%	71.4%	<.001
Antisocial personality	2.9%	9.4%	75.0%	<.001
Major depression	2.9%	10.3%	10.7%	.09

Note. Probabilities for continuous variables are based on analysis of variance and on $2 \times 3 \; \chi^2$ analysis for nominal data.

Environmental factors are shown in Table 4.6. Parental divorce appears to be the most significant predictor and was selected as a possible etiologic factor. Two remaining items, antisocial problem and sibling with problem, turned out to be correlated to drug

TABLE 4.4
Adoptee Childhood and Adolescent Outcome Divided by Type of Adult Drug Experience

Outcome	No drug use (N = 103)	Drug use only (N = 107)	Drug abuse/ dependence (N = 28)	Significance
Difficult temperament	17.5%	25.2%	28.6%	ns
Slow-to-warm-up temperament	20.4%	28.0%	25.0%	ns
Easy temperament	30.1%	29.9%	14.3%	ns
Attention-deficit/hyperactivity syndrome	13.6%	15.0%	28.6%	.15
"Bad" friends	14.6%	30.8%	53.6%	.001
Number of aggressive behavior items (average)	1.1	1.7	2.6	<.01
Number of impulsive behavior items (average)	1.9	2.1	3.4	<.05
Number of adolescent conduct disorder symptoms (average)	1.3	2.1	4.5	<.01

Note. Probabilities for continuous variables are based on analysis of variance and on 2×3 χ^2 analysis for nominal data.

TABLE 4.5
Biologic Parent Genetic Variables Divided by Type of Proband Drug Use

Variable	% No drug use (N = 103)	% Drug use only (N = 107)	Drug abuse/ dependence (N = 28)	Significance[a]
Parent with alcohol problem (N = 22)	4.9	8.4	28.6	.001
Parent with criminality/delinquency (N = 35)	14.6	15.9	28.6	.20
Parent with mental retardation (N = 10)	3.9	5.6	0.0	ns
Parent with psychiatric problem (N = 23)	10.7	10.3	3.6	ns

[a]Significance determined by 2×3 χ^2 analysis.

TABLE 4.6

Adoptive Home Environmental Variables Divided by Type of Proband Drug Use

Variable	% No drug use (N = 103)	% Drug use only (N = 107)	% Drug abuse/ dependence (N = 28)	Significance[a]
Alcohol problem (N = 47)	17.5	21.5	21.4	ns
Antisocial problem (N = 20)	2.9	12.2	14.3	.03
Psychiatric problem (N = 43)	14.6	19.6	25.0	ns
Sibling with problem (N = 44)	10.7	25.2	21.4	.02
Parental death (N = 15)	5.8	8.4	0.0	ns
Parental divorce (N = 11)	1.9	3.7	17.9	.002
High socioeconomic status (N = 86)	35.0	37.4	35.7	ns
Urban home (N = 164)	68.0	71.0	64.3	ns

[a]Significance determined by 2×3 χ^2 analysis.

behavior almost entirely because of adopted siblings who had antisocial behavior. Accordingly, another variable, antisocial sibling, was used in the further analyses and consisted of siblings who manifested antisocial behaviors while living in the adoptive home.

To determine possible etiologic factors, selected variables from Tables 4.4, 4.5, and 4.6 were used in two logistic models. In one model, the variables were entered to predict no-drug versus drug-use-only outcomes; in the second model, these variables were entered to predict the drug-use-only and abuse outcomes. All selected variables were entered, and a backward solution found in which variables had to maintain a probability level of 5% to stay in the model. Adoptee age was forced into each model to control for the correlation found between age and drug abuse outcome reported in the Method section.

Table 4.7 shows the variables predicting the use of drugs only, and Table 4.8 shows the variables that predict the change from drug use to abuse. Figure 4.1 shows the significant factors from both of these analyses, divided into social, genetic, and individual categories. In the analysis leading to the results in Table 4.8, criminality/delinquency in a biologic parent achieved the 5% level of significance but was displaced finally by the biologic-parent-alcohol-problem variable. Thus, criminality/delinquency appears as a possibility in Figure 4.1. One other variable that started at a less than 5% significance level in the analysis leading to Table 4.8 was adoptive parent divorce. It, like criminality, was not retained in the analysis, but its final probability value just prior to its removal from the model was .06. The variable of adoptee age was forced into both models shown in Tables 4.7 and 4.8. In neither case did it show an independent correlation with the dependent variable, and its presence served to control for the age effect that appeared to be present in these data.

Discussion

This exploratory study found evidence that different factors contribute to initiation of drug use and to the transition from use to abuse. The analyses showed that environmental factors such as "bad" friends (i.e., friends not approved of by the adoptive parents) and the presence of a sibling with antisocial behavior in the adoptive home were associated with the initiation of drug use. The factor of "bad" friends could also measure

TABLE 4.7
Logistic Regression, Variables Predicting Use of Drugs Only (Backward Solution)

Variable	β	SE	χ^2	p
Intercept	−0.34	0.63	0.30	.59
Antisocial sibling	1.50	0.68	4.93	.03
"Bad" friends	0.74	0.37	4.04	.04
Aggression	0.33	0.12	6.93	.009
Adoptee age	−0.01	0.02	0.34	.56

TABLE 4.8
Logistic Regression: Variables Predicting Change From Drug Use to Abuse/Dependency (Backward Solution)

Variable	β	SE	χ^2	p
Intercept	−1.11	1.23	0.81	.37
Aggression	0.43	0.17	6.45	.01
Alcohol problem in parent	1.41	0.60	5.56	.02
Adoptee age	−0.06	0.05	1.79	.18

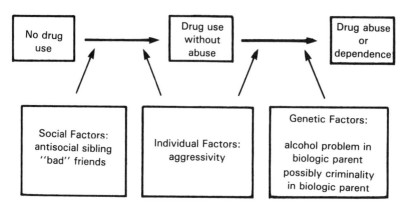

FIGURE 4.1 Factors involved in change in drug use.

an adoptee personality type or temperament (possibly itself genetically determined) that leads the individual to seek such disapproved-of company. In this case, the "bad" friend environmental factor might represent a gene–environment correlation. "Bad" friends could also be a product of drug use, reflecting, for example, the need to cultivate drug dealers to assure a ready supply. One obvious way to sort out these different interpretations would be a study of where "bad" friends entered chronologically into adoptees' experience; "bad" friends in kindergarten would carry a different weight than "bad" friends in high school. On the other hand the antisocial sibling probably is more representative of an environmental factor. In almost all cases, the antisocial sibling was adopted and was present in the household during the childhood and adolescence of the adoptee proband, and so was in a position to influence the other members of his or her family by antisocial behavior (e.g., early substance abuse, association with drug users, etc.).

A genetic factor, having a biologic parent with an alcohol problem, appeared to be more important in determining the transition from use to abuse. Because of the incompleteness of adoption agency records, we cannot know how many of these biologic parents had alcohol abuse or dependency as currently defined by *DSM–III* criteria. Furthermore, the agency records say next to nothing about use of illegal drugs by biologic parents, so we cannot draw conclusions about specificity of type of inheritance, whether alcoholism, drug abuse, or even polysubstance abuse is the factor.

An individual's aggressivity appears to be important in both the initiating use and in the transition from use to abuse. The behavioral items making up the aggressivity factor were bullying, defiance, insolence, fighting, and rebelliousness. These items came from the

adoptive parent interview and represented behavior present during childhood and early adolescence. To what extent early drug use influenced the aggressive behavior cannot be determined. Aggressivity has been significantly positively correlated both with adoptee police
contact and with adoptees' adult diagnosis of antisocial personality (Cadoret & Stewart,
1989), but in the present study, it did not correlate with any genetic factor.

Although the present study found some predictive variables, limitations of the findings include the small sample size, which makes Type II errors likely and leads to over-
looking the importance of certain variables. Small numbers of adoptive families
undergoing divorce could well be the reason that this variable dropped out of the logistic
regression analysis shown in Table 4.8. Families disturbed by divorce have been reported
as an etiologic factor in drug abuse in earlier analyses of these data that included female
as well as male abusers (Cadoret et al., 1986). Other limitations would be the failure to
include in the present study certain variables known to be associated with drug use and
abuse, such as availability of drugs, peer pressures, attitudes toward substance use,
(adoptive) parental drug-taking behavior, and so on. (Kandel, 1981).

Efforts to find evidence of gene–environment interaction in the genesis of drug-use
initiation or in the transition to abuse failed with the variables used in Tables 4.5 and 4.6.
However, interaction analyses are difficult to do with the small number of observations
used here, especially when accompanied by colinearity, which appeared to complicate the
situation with some of the variables.

The variables found in these analyses to be predictive of both drug use and abuse
have for the most part been previously described in the literature. For example, the factor
of aggressivity has been described in a number of other studies as predictive of substance use or abuse. Kellam, Ensminger, and Simon (1980) reported that boys who were
seen as aggressive at the end of the first grade in school had much higher rates of alcohol and drug use when compared with their less aggressive peers. Block, Block, & Keyes
(1988) described a correlation of .38 between expressing hostility and hard drug use at
age 14. Johnston, O'Malley, & Eveland (1978) reported significant increases in drug abuse
in those with more interpersonal aggression. Muntaner et al. (1989) reported that early
childhood aggression not only predicted later antisocial personality and criminality, but
also predicted the incidence and severity of substance abuse. Not all studies have found
an involvement of aggression with later use of drugs or alcohol. Sieber, Stahli & Angst
(1985) reported that aggressiveness measured at age 19 did not predict alcohol or cannabis use at age 31 in a birth cohort of 1,577 men in Switzerland. There are a number of

potential reasons for this failure to find a correlation. It is possible that the measures of aggression made at 19 do not define the kind of aggressiveness measured at an earlier age. Also, there could be a correlation with use of drugs such as cocaine and opioids, which was not reported. With reference to factors predicting a switch from drug use to abuse, Brook and colleagues (this volume, Chapter 12) describe acting out and aggression during childhood as potent predictors of abuse of alcohol. In that study, acting out, but not aggression, during childhood predicted a switch from moderate use to heavy use of marijuana.

Childhood aggressivity is correlated significantly in our data with the adult diagnosis of antisocial personality (Cadoret & Stewart, 1989) but is not correlated with any of the biologic background factors. The adult diagnosis of antisocial personality correlated very highly with the move from use to abuse (Table 4.3), but not with the initiation of the use of drugs. Antisocial personality or conduct disorder is strongly associated with drug abuse in both clinical samples (Bukstein et al., 1989; DeMilio, 1989; Ross, Glaser, & Germanson, 1988) and population surveys (Robins, Helzer, Pryzbeck, & Regier, 1988). Whether antisocial personality and aggression act as independent predictors of the transition from use to abuse was tested in the present data by putting both of these variables into a logistic regression as predictors of drug abuse. The result showed that with antisocial personality diagnosis added to the regression model shown in Table 4.8, the significance of the aggression factor drops to .22; whereas the added antisocial personality factor is highly significant at less than the .01% level. The genetic factor of an alcohol problem in the biologic parent remains significant at the .05 level even with antisocial personality in the model.

These results suggest that antisocial personality is an important element in the change from drug use to drug abuse. Aggressivity, it would appear, is important in the transition from use to abuse only insofar as it is correlated with antisocial personality. However, aggressivity remains a factor in the transition from no use to use because antisocial personality does not appear to enter into this transition as a significant variable. In this case, aggressivity could be correlated with other behaviors, such as socially deviant conduct disorders, that do not necessarily lead to antisocial personality. Such conduct problems and their correlation with substance use and abuse were documented by Robins and McEvoy (1990), who showed that fighting, for example, by itself increased the relative risk of abuse threefold. Hyperactivity/attention deficit did not predict changes in drug use (Table 4.4), although its significance was close to the 10% level. This could represent a Type II error because these are population-based and clinical-based samples indicating a correlation between hyperactivity and drug use. For example, Block, Block, & Keyes (1988) reported a .31 Spearman correlation between hard drug use at age 14 and restlessness and fidgetiness in nursery school; DeMilio (1989) reported in a clinical sample of adolescent substance abusers that 21% had an attention deficit or hyperactive diagnosis. Again, as with antisocial personality, one etiologic factor of hyperactivity is genetic, with its roots in parental criminality or delinquency (Cadoret and Stewart, 1989).

In summary, these data suggest the importance of both genetic and environmental factors in drug abuse. The study did not detect the presence of gene–environment interaction as a factor in initiating drug use or abuse. However, the numbers involved are small and gene–environment interaction might not have been detected. The condition of antisocial personality and its attendant aggressivity is highly predictive of the transition from drug use to abuse. Because antisocial personality has in its etiology a genetic factor of criminality or delinquency in the biologic parent (Cadoret, Troughton, Bagford, & Woodworth, 1990), there are additional genetic factors relevant to substance abuse. This explains the borderline correlation seen in Table 4.5 of criminal or delinquent parent with drug abuse.

These results indicate the importance of considering genetic and environmental factors that affect conditions comorbid with drug abuse. The results also point to the fact that drug abuse is a product of many factors, social as well as genetic.

References

American Psychiatric Association. (1980). *Diagnostic and statistical manual of mental disorders* (3rd ed.), Washington, DC: Author.

Block, J., Block, J. H., & Keyes, S. (1988). Longitudinally foretelling drug usage in adolescence: Early childhood personality and environmental precursors. *Child Development, 59,* 336–355.

Bukstein, O. G., Brent, D. A., & Kaminer, Y. (1989). Comorbidity of substance abuse and other psychiatric disorders in adolescents. *American Journal of Psychiatry, 146,* 1131–1141.

Cadoret, R. J. (1978). Psychopathology in adopted-away offspring of biologic parents with antisocial behavior. *Archives of General Psychiatry, 35,* 176–184.

Cadoret, R. J. (1986). Adoption studies: Historical and methodological critique. *Psychiatric Developments, 1,* 45–64.

Cadoret, R. J., & Cain, C. (1980). Sex differences in predictors of antisocial behavior in adoptees. *Archives of General Psychiatry, 37,* 1171–1175.

Cadoret, R. J., Cain, C. A., & Grove, W. M. (1980). Development of alcoholism in adoptees raised apart from alcoholic biologic relatives. *Archives of General Psychiatry, 37,* 561–563.

Cadoret, R. J., & Gath, A. (1978). Inheritance of alcoholism in adoptees. *British Journal of Psychiatry, 132,* 252–258.

Cadoret, R. J., & Gath, A. (1980). Biologic correlates of hyperactivity: Evidence for a genetic factor. In S. B. Sells, R. Crandall, M. Roff, J. S. Strauss, & W. Pollin (Eds.), *Human functioning in longitudinal perspective* (pp. 103–114). Baltimore: Williams & Wilkins.

Cadoret, R. J., O'Gorman, T., Troughton, E., & Heywood, E. (1985). Alcoholism and antisocial personality: Interrelationships, genetic and environmental factors. *Archives of General Psychiatry, 42,* 161–167.

Cadoret, R. J., & Stewart, M. A. (1989). *Genetic and environmental factors in hyperactivity attention deficit disorder.* Unpublished manuscript.

Cadoret, R. J., Troughton, E., Bagford, J., & Woodworth, G. (1990). Genetic and environmental factors in adoptee antisocial personality. *European Archives Psychiatric and Neurological Sciences, 239,* 231–240.

Cadoret, R. J., Troughton, E., O'Gorman, T. W., & Heywood, E. (1986). An adoption study of genetic and environmental factors in drug abuse. *Archives of General Psychiatry, 43,* 1131–1136.

Christie, K. A., Burke, J. D., Regier, D. A., Rae, D. S., Boyd, J. H., & Loche, B. Z. (1988). Epidemiologic evidence for early onset of mental disorders and increased risk of drug abuse in young adults. *American Journal of Psychiatry, 145,* 971–975.

Clayton, R. R. (1981). The delinquency and drug use relationship among adolescents: A critical review. In D. J. Lettieri & J. Ludford (Eds.), *Drug abuse and the American adolescent* (NIDA Research Monograph No. 38). Washington, DC: U.S. Department of Health and Human Services.

DeMilio, L. (1989). Psychiatric syndromes in adolescent substance abusers. *American Journal of Psychiatry, 146,* 1212–1214.

Helzer, J., & Pryzbeck, T. (1988). The cooccurrence of alcoholism with other psychiatric disorders in the general population and its treatment. *Journal of Studies on Alcohol, 49,* 219–224.

Hesselbrock, V. M., Hesselbrock, M. N., & Stabenau, J. R. (1985). Alcoholism in men patients subtyped by family history and antisocial personality: *Journal of Studies on Alcohol, 46,* 59–64.

Johnston, L. D., O'Malley, P. M., & Eveland, L. K. (1978). Drugs and delinquency: A search for causal connections. In D. B. Kandel (Ed.), *Longitudinal research on drug use.* New York: Wiley.

Kandel, D. B. (1981). Drug use by youth: An overview. In D. J. Lettieri & J. R. Ludford (Eds.), *Drug abuse and the American Adolescent* (pp. 1–24; NIDA Research Monograph No. 38). Washington, DC: Department of Health and Human Services.

Kellam, S. G., Ensminger, M. B., & Simon, M. B. (1980). Mental health in first grade and teenage drug, alcohol, and cigarette use. *Drug and Alcohol Dependence, 5,* 273–304.

Mauer, R., Cadoret, R. J., & Cain, C. (1980). Cluster analysis of childhood temperament data on adoptees. *American Journal of Orthopsychiatry, 50,* 522–534.

Muntaner, C., Nagoshi, C., Jaffe, J., Walte, D., Haertzen, C., & Fishbern, D. (1989). Correlates of self-reported early childhood aggression in subjects volunteering for drug studies. *American Journal of Drug and Alcohol Abuse, 15,* 383–402.

Robins, L. N., Helzer, J. E., Croughan, J., Radcliff, K. S. (1981). National Institute of Mental Health Diagnostic Interview Schedule: Its history, characteristics and validity. *Archives of General Psychiatry, 38,* 381–389.

Robins, L. N., Helzer, J. E., Pryzbeck, T. R., & Regier, D. A. (1988). Alcohol disorders in the community: A report from the epidemiologic catchment area. In R. M. Rose & J. Barret (Eds.), *Alcoholism: Origins and outcome.* New York: Raven Press.

Robins, L. N., & McEvoy, L. (1990). Conduct problems as predictors of substance abuse. In L. Robins & M. Rutter (Eds.), *Straight and devious pathways from childhood to adulthood* (pp. 182–204). Cambridge, England: Cambridge University Press.

Ross, H. E., Glaser, F., & Germanson, T. (1988). The prevalence of psychiatric disorders in patients with alcohol and other drug problems. *Archives of General Psychiatry, 45,* 1012–1031.

Sieber, M., Stahli, R., & Angst, J. (1985). Entwicklung des Alkohol-Tabak-und Medicamentenkonsums bei 19 jahrigen Mannern: Ein Querschnittvergleich 1971–1978–1982 [Development of alcohol, tobacco, and medication use in 19-year-old men: A cross-sectional comparison 1971–1978–1982]. *Schweitzerisch Medicinisch Wochenschrift, 115,* 865–870.

Spitzer, R. L., & Endicott, J. (1979). *Schedule for affective disorders and schizophrenia: Life-time version (SADS–L).* (3rd ed.). New York: New York State Psychiatric Institute.

CHAPTER 5

Biological Factors in Sociopathy: Relationships to Drug Abuse Behaviors

Roy King, Deborah Curtis, and Guenther Knoblich

T he search for the biological underpinnings of human behavior has a long history. The classical opposition between strict biological determination of action and social learning models governing behavior is clearly an overly reductive argument. Most would agree that constitutional factors interact with environmental constraints to determine manifest behavior. However, such a truism lacks specificity, and although now widely accepted, it gives little guidance to an interpretation of individual behaviors. Indeed, the problem may be semantic in nature in that any description of phenomena from a psychological perspective may be in incommensurable with the language of biological sciences such as neuroscience and neuropharmacology. Clearly, it is difficult to translate moment-to-moment decisions such as the use of psychoactive drugs into the vicissitudes of receptor ligand binding or gene expression. However, a more modest approach, such as analysis of more encompassing systems that allow for interaction among various levels of description, may prove to be of use in understanding addictive disorders.

The development of experimental paradigms and theoretical formulations for specialized behavior patterns is worthy of examination. Because the use and abuse of substances definitely involves both neurochemical systems and the pharmacological effects of the psychotropics on these systems, it would seem that the exploration of models of substance dependence would form an ideal field for distinguishing the relative contributions of biological and psychosocial factors invoved in this behavior. In this chapter, we consider a series of three overall structures; one component of each includes specific neuromodulatory systems, and another component of each includes patterns, observed behaviors, cognition, and affect. We assume a reciprocal interaction between these two components for drug abuse and related behaviors. We hypothesize a neurochemical trait model of risk for these abuse behaviors; that is, individuals differing in their tonic activity of certain neuromodulatory systems will be more prone to display personality traits that in themselves predispose individuals to specific observed behaviors. In line with this model, consumption of drugs would be a response to the existence of these individual temperamental variables and would hence be self-medication for those specific traits. Given that the literature on this idea, self-medication, is mostly psychoanalytic and psychodynamic in nature (Khantzian, 1985; Schiffer, 1988), we hope that this research into the biological mechanisms of such behavior can augment current understanding of drug use. This chapter will examine the relationship among neuromodulatory systems, personality, and substance abuse by focusing on three conceptual models: aversive arousal, incentive motivation, and aggression.

The aversive arousal system mediates the behavioral and autonomic responses of an organism to either the expectation or delivery of aversive stimuli (M. Davis, 1989). The second separate system, incentive motivation (Klinger, 1975), is one in which the behavioral activity of an animal is guided in response to incentives in the environment. It prepares the individual, through motivational excitement, for the consumption of anticipated reward. The third system to be discussed is aggression (Blanchard & Blanchard, 1988), a more complex mechanism than either aversive arousal or incentive motivation because it involves a multitude of behaviors that are situationally determined. For example, there may be pronounced differences between what is known as social aggression and the other type, known as defensive or irritable aggression. These two types of aggression, furthermore, may vary among individuals and may even involve differences in their underlying neurobiological systems. Before embarking on a review of each of these constructs, it would be useful to present a causal diagram of how we see these system interactive with behavior.

Figure 5.1 illustrates a three-tiered feedback model of the interactions among neurochemical systems, temperament, and manifest behavior. This is a modification of a classical interactionist model with environmental variables and individual difference variables

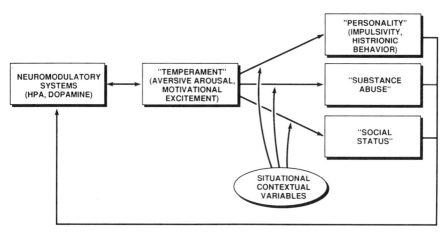

FIGURE 5.1   A three-tiered feedback model of the interactions among neurochemical systems, temperament, and manifest behavior.

contributing to observed behaviors. The present model is unique, however, because overt behavior per se can, through feedback interactions, influence both short-term and long-term functioning of neuromodulatory systems. More specifically, we propose that basal differences in the activity of certain neurochemical systems are integrally related to individual differences in temperament; in this work, the three systems of interest are aversive arousal, incentive motivation, and aggression. Because in the absence of external cues or of an environmental context, behaviors linked to these systems are infrequently present, situational variables (i.e., developmental, experiential, cognitive) will elicit differences in behavior in any given paradigm. The behaviors of interest include, but are not limited to, substance abuse and associated drug-seeking activities. These behaviors, in turn, profoundly influence neuromodulatory tone in a variety of manners, from the direct release of neurotransmitters by the ingested substance to the indirect effects of stress on neuroendocrine systems. As would be expected in such feedback systems that depend on such a dynamics of the system, the feedback can lead to an ever-increasing amplification or act to dampen the behavior. We will now consider each of the three systems in detail and review the work with humans and animals contributing to the aforementioned systems in terms of this conceptual model.

Aversive Arousal: Cortisol and Impulsivity

Animal models of anxiety indicate that certain neuroendocrine and autonomic indicators of arousal are acutely elevated during the presence of both physical and psychological stressors. Such signals include increased levels of glucocorticoids, reflecting the activity of the hypothalamic–pituitary–adrenal (HPA) axis, as well as more classically measured levels of autonomically released catecholamines. Work by Levine and his colleagues over the past 20 years has focused on the HPA axis as a sensitive indicator of not only acute stress, but also the anticipation of stress (e.g., Hennessy & Levine, 1979). Elevated baseline levels of corticosterone can, across individuals, correlate with avoidance responding (Wertheim, Conner, & Levine, 1969). Furthermore, low levels of basal plasma corticosterone are associated with heightened aggressive behavior in individually housed mice (Politch and Leshner, 1977). It has also been suggested that the expectation of stressful events may be reflected in an elevation of glucocorticoids, whereas the anticipation of reward or the ability to cope with stressors causes a lowering of plasma levels of this steroid hormone (Coover, 1983). This is supported by studies showing that the consumption of rewarding solutions by thirsty rats result in lower levels of corticosterone; moreover, coping with a stressful schedule-induced activation leads to a decrease of corticosterone in those rats who engage in adjunctive behaviors, such as polydipsia (Brett and Levine, 1979). To the extent that individuals are constitutionally predisposed to active coping or discover such coping mechanism, the HPA axis will be dampened during stressful events.

Not only is the literature supportive of the notion that the HPA axis may reflect tonic levels of aversive arousal in animals, but there are similar, although less controlled, studies of humans suggesting such a relationship. Developmental work has found that behaviorally inhibited, shy children have high levels of salivary cortisol taken at baseline (Kagan, Resnick, & Snidman, 1988), suggesting that shyness may indeed be a state of high arousal, with its characteristic high vigilance and overcontrolled behavior. This is especially important because such behaviors appear to be somewhat stable over time of development, from infancy to young childhood. In adults, it has been found that, in a series of normal control subjects, plasma cortisol is negatively correlated with scores on the hypomania scale of the Minnesota Multiphasic Personality Inventory (Ballenger, Post, & Goodwin, 1983). Indeed, hypomanic acting-out behavior may reflect a form of active coping with stressful psychosocial events. Another study using an inmate population demonstrated that habitually violent sociopaths have lower levels of urinary cortisol than other nonsociopathic criminals (Virkkunen, 1985). This finding is supported by the animal studies mentioned earlier that found that individual differences in plasma corticosterone in isolated mice are associated with aggressive behavior. Thus, low levels of glucocorticoids in both animals and humans seem to reflect a temperamental variable predisposing one to display disinhibited, aggressive, and impulsive behavior.

With this background data in mind, we (King, Jones, Scheuer, Curtis, & Zarcone, 1990) recently studied a sample of male substance abusers, comparing levels of baseline cortisol to that of a group of age-matched normal controls. The subjects with a diagnosis of substance abuse/dependence were inpatients in a long-term milieu-oriented treatment program. There was a total of 53 volunteers, of whom approximately 20% were cocaine abusers, 15% alcoholics, 10% heroin abusers, 38% abusers of both alcohol and other drugs, and 13% polysubstance abusers. In addition to their diagnosis of substance abuse, about 50% of this population fit the diagnosis of antisocial personality and 50% fit the diagnosis of borderline, with an overlap of 25% of the population satisfying the criteria for both diagnoses, as evaluated by criteria from the third revised edition of the *Diagnostic and Statistical Manual of Mental Disorders* (*DSM–III–R*; American Psychiatric Association, 1987). Normal controls were recruited through advertisements and were instructed to abstain from taking psychoactive medications for 2 weeks before the experiment. On average, the comparison group of substance abusers was free from psychotropic medication for 10 weeks. In the protocol, blood samples were drawn from between 7:30 and 8:30 A.M. after an overnight fast, and plasma levels of cortisol were assayed using a radioimmunoassay. In addition to the clinical diagnosis of substance abuse, all subjects were given the Eysenck Personality Inventory (Eysenck and Eysenck, 1964) to assess traits relevant to aversive arousal. More particularly, the inventory was scored for impulsivity and sociability subscales in addition to the neuroticism and lie subscales. Log cortisol levels were calculated to test the hypothesis that substance abusers had lower levels of this steroid, and a *t* test was performed comparing the substance abusers to the normal control sample. As a group, the abusing population was much less sociable, more impulsive, and more neurotic than the control group as measured by the above psychiatric tools. As predicted, the plasma cortisol levels were significantly lower in the 53 substance abusers than in the 20 controls. Moreover, within the group of normals, impulsivity was associated with lower baseline cortisol. Thus, we find statistically independent but conceptually related results. First, the abusing group, which is more impulsive than the controls, have reduced activity of HPA axis functioning. Second, even in the group of nonabusing normals, a self-report measure of impulsivity was also linked to lower levels of plasma cortisol. One could speculate that cortisol reflects specifically the trait of impulsivity rather than specific deviant drug-using behavior and that the relationship between this impulsivity and drug-use behaviors is a separate system, with higher impulsivity related to increased drug use behaviors. This idea of the duality of these two systems is supported by the fact that indices of lifetime use of the specific abused substances, as measured by the

Addiction Severity Index (McLellan, Luborsky, & O'Brien, 1980), were not significantly related to the cortisol levels. Figure 5.2 graphically represents this correlation of impulsivity and HPA activity. Again, low levels of the HPA system seem to be associated with impulsivity. In turn, impulsivity may be a risk factor of drug use and abuse behaviors; observation would, indeed, indicate this possibility. Furthermore, the act of engaging in drug-seeking and consumptive behaviors may in itself affect the HPA axis. That is, the risk inherent in these activities may acutely raise aversive arousal, leading to immediate changes in HPA activity. Over time, these changes may result in an adapted state of reduced HPA activity . This, we assume, may be reflected in the reduced HPA activity seen in our group of substance abusers. It should be noted that the drug-abusing population in this study differed from the control group not only in trait impulsivity, but also in its level of personality psychopathology. A majority of the sample satisfied the critieria for antisocial or borderline personality disorder. Given the familial clustering and longitudinal consistency of these severe personality disorders, it is possible that personality psychopathology is an additional moderating factor leading to drug abuse rather than limited drug use (Shedler and Block, 1990)

Incentive Motivation System: The Cocaine–Dopamine–Histrionic Triad

The second system to be considered involves reward-related behavior rather than aversive behavior. Recent theoretical work on reward dynamics center on the notion of *incentive motivation*. Such a concept postulates that a central motivation state is initiated in an organism in response to cues that predict reward (Klinger, 1975). Thus, the presentation of food-related cues to a hungry animal or novelty signals to an animal in an open field will elicit "motivational excitement." Such an animal will exhibit a range of motor behaviors (e.g., locomotion, exploration, and oral behaviors). In the past decade, there has been

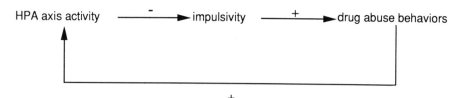

FIGURE 5.2   Cortisol and impulsivity.

increasing interest in the idea that an essential element mediating this motivational excitement is the central dopaminergic system (Wise, 1988). Specifically, this effect of dopamine may be neuroanatomically selective; it appears to involve predominantly the dopaminergic projections from the ventral tegmental area to the "limbic" striatum. This limbic area of the basal ganglia, which receives input from limbic regions of the cortex, the hippocampus, and the amygdala, is ideally situtated to process complex, emotionally laden stimuli. Dopamine may gate the activity of neurons within the limbic striatum, thereby biasing the behavioral responsiveness of the organism to emotional signals (Morgenson & Neilsen, 1984). Thus, increasing dopamine activity in the limbic striatum may lower the threshold for responding actively to incentives, whereas decreasing dopamine activity may raise the apparent threshold for responding (King, 1986).

However, given our feedback model of system interactions, there exist other plausible interpretations of these observations. The presence of incentive per se may induce dopamine release and thereby, through its gating function, faciltitate the motor output needed to acquire that incentive. This aspect of dopaminergic function forms the basis of the hypothesis that dopamine release may be a proximal signal for reward (Wise, 1988). That is, because both brain-stimulation reward and natural reinforcers release mesolimbic dopamine, one must assume that reward itself is closely linked to dopaminergic activity. Thus, a model emerges in which incentives release dopamine, which then facilitates approach or investigative behaviors, which in turn lead potentially to a further enhancement of incentive value (see Figure 5.3). This would be particularly evident for very complex incentives such as those associated with social rewards (i.e., affiliation).

Because various drugs of abuse, particularly psychostimulants, directly lead to enhanced dopamine activity (Deminiere, Piazza, LeMoal, & Simon, 1989; Koob & Bloom, 1988), this model may be pertinent to understanding the etiology of stimulant abuse. In fact, theories exist postulating that cocaine "craving" may be the result of dopaminergic depletion and its consequent anhedonia (Dackis and Gold, 1985; Gawin & Ellinwood, 1988). However, the effects of stimuli on neurochemical systems is, in fact, more complex

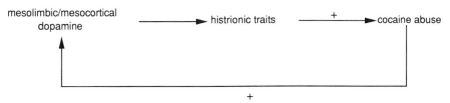

FIGURE 5.3   Dopamine and cocaine abuse.

than this idea implies. Cocaine, for example, has effects on multiple monoaminergic systems, such as the blockage of the re-uptake of serotonin and norepinephrine, as well as of dopamine, in the nerve terminals. Therefore, a causal explanation of cocaine withdrawal and craving behavior implicating only one neurochemical may, indeed, be overly reductive and simplistic. Nevertheless, there seems to be some intimate relationship among dopamine, reward, and reinforcement-type behaviors.

For example, the relationship between the dopaminergic system and incentive motivation in animal models has lead to a variety of hypotheses concerning the effect of dopaminergic activity on temperament in humans. Because social incentives are the preeminent rewards for primates, such models have oriented themselves toward the interpersonal modes of behavior. Both Cloninger (1987) and King (1986) have hypothesized that histrionic personality traits may be associated with variations in dopaminergic activity, and have proposed that low basal dopaminergic activity might be a correlate of histrionic and antisocial personality traits with their craving for excitement and emotional expressiveness. Release of dopamine in response to incentives would lead to an exaggerated dopamine response because of supersensitive postsynaptic dopaminergic function (Cloninger, 1987). It has also been hypothesized that histrionic personality may be associated with high levels of basal dopaminergic activity (King, 1986; King, Bayon, Clark, & Taylor, 1988). Such a hypothesis has been supported by studies in which cerebrospinal (CSF) dopamine levels were measured in a group of depressives (King et al., 1986). In that study, extroversion, as measured by the Eysenck Personality Inventory, was significantly correlated with high levels of CSF dopamine. Thus, some theoretical work, as well as experimental data, suggests a relationship among locomotion, dopaminergic activity, and histrionic, extroverted, or emotionally expressive traits.

Let us now turn to some experimental work done by us that has shown relationships between histrionic traits and cocaine use. Using the structured interview for assessing personality disorder traits according to the *DSM–III–R*, a group of 200 male subjects, including 40 community controls, 70 patients in a long-term drug rehabilitation program, and approximately 90 other male psychiatric controls were rated according to the severity of their *DSM–III–R* Axis II disorder traits using the Personality Disorders Examination (Loranger, Sussman, Oldham, & Rossakoff, 1987). A principal component of analysis was performed on these 11 dimensions of Axis II traits, which demonstrated the presence of two unrotated components with eigenvalues greater than 1.

Table 5.1 demonstrates the factor loadings for each of the Axis II personality traits on these two factors. Clearly, Factor 1 is a general psychopathology factor involving a

TABLE 5.1

Personality Disorders Examination: Principal-Components Analysis ($N = 200$ men)

Diagnosis	Factor 1	Factor 2
Paranoid	0.86	0.10
Schizoid	0.46	0.80
Schizotypal	0.79	0.37
Compulsive	0.66	0.11
Histrionic	0.65	−0.50
Dependent	0.69	−0.26
Antisocial	0.67	−0.13
Narcissistic	0.83	−0.32
Avoidant	0.79	0.27
Borderline	0.89	−0.05
Passive–aggressive	0.70	−0.20

multitude of interpersonal and affective problems; it is highly loaded for borderline, paranoid, and narcissistic personality disorder traits. Factor 2 is bipolar, loaded at one extreme on histrionic personality traits and in the other direction on schizoid personality traits. Table 5.2 shows the correlation of these two factor scores with our measures of lifetime abuse, using the Addiction Severity Index; lifetime abuse of cocaine was strongly associated with the histrionic versus schizoid factor ($r = -0.52$, $p < .0001$). Specifically, on the basis of post hoc correlations of individual traits, those who are histrionic appear to have a longer use of cocaine ($r = 0.41$, $p < .0004$). Moreover, these observations are in accordance with our proposed model of the interaction of abused drugs with personality and neurochemistry. That is, individual differences in mesolimbic dopamine activity, which may be temperamentally based, could lead to differences in histrionic, prosocial, and emotionally expressive behavior. Those who are readily excited by social cues, (i.e., histrionic characters), might be more sensitive to the rewarding aspects of cocaine consumption, specifically the dopaminergically mediated activating effects, such as increased activity, talkativeness, and emotionality. Because of this increased sensitivity, such individuals might be more likely to continue long-term cocaine use. Furthermore, the acute effects of cocaine ingestion could release dopamine in humans, as has been shown in animals, thereby exaggerating those very personality traits presumed to be at risk for cocaine use (i.e., histrionic behaviors).

TABLE 5.2

Correlations of Lifetime Medications Usage (Addiction Severity Index) With Personality Disorders Examination Factors

Lifetime use (years; $N = 72$)	Factor 1	Factor 2
Ethanol	−0.10	−0.02
Ethanol intoxication	0.07	0.04
Heroin	−0.17	0.07
Methadone	−0.12	0.05
Other opiates	0.09	0.11
Barbiturates	−0.03	0.01
Other sedatives/hypnotics	−0.03	−0.09
Cocaine	−0.02	−0.52*
Amphetamines	−0.17	−0.03
Cannabis	0.00	0.01
Hallucinogens	0.08	−0.12
Inhalants	0.12	−0.14
Polydrug	−0.14	−0.08

*$p < 0.0001$.

This idea of cocaine use modulating dopamine levels is especially enlightening in terms of the current "dopamine depletion" hypothesis of chronic cocaine use. That is, chronic cocaine use seems to deplete central levels of dopamine, which would presumably lead to a blunting of the histrionic/social behaviors; indeed, observations of social withdrawal have been documented in naturalistic studies of the cocaine withdrawal process (Gawin & Kleber, 1986).

An alternative explanation of the data is that the prolonged use of cocaine leads individuals to modify their self-concept. Because cocaine appears to block the re-uptake of dopamine at the nerve terminal, frequent or prolonged use might lead to enhanced histrionic behavior under the influence of the drug. Thus, individuals may, over a period of time, begin to acquire the self-concept of being social or histrionic under chronic use. However, our basic notion of the etiology of cocaine abuse is, again, that individuals who are histrionic prior to using cocaine might be predisposed by abnormal sensitivity to its reinforcing effects. The possible causal reasons for this include higher levels of basal dopamine, more easily released dopamine, or more potentiated receptors. Hence, one may find the self-administration of cocaine rewarding enough to overcome the dysphoric effects of the drug. As a result of this, one would be particularly prone to developing cocaine abuse. Only a longitudinal study could distinguish these three distinct explanations of the relationships hypothesized here. Much work has been done and is continuing on the relationship between cocaine and its proposed cell receptor (Woolverton & Kleven, 1988) and on the possibility of these receptors becoming supersensitized by the drug. We are currently investigating the other possibility by studying a group of chronic cocaine abusers to determine whether basal levels of CSF dopamine are elevated. In any case, there appears to be an intimate relationship among the motivation and reward systems, certain temperamental variables, the dopaminergic system, and the prolonged use of cocaine. Much more research into this area can be expected.

Phenylacetic Acid and Aggressiveness

The third system to be considered is that of aggression. As mentioned earlier, aggression is a very complex construct with multiple, contextually constrained types of behavior. Defensive behavior is frequently exhibited when an animal is threatened by an overwhelming external attack without the possibility of escape. Social aggression invoves dominance hierarchies in a variety of mammalian species and is associated with very species-specific behaviors. Often, defensive and social aggression are mutually exclusive affective expressions and depend on separate neuroanatomical, neurochemical, and neuroendocrine processes.

Much of the neurochemical work on aggression has centered on the monoamine serotonin; this work is consistent and exemplary in the domain of biological psychiatry. Low levels of CSF 5-hydroxyindoleacetic acid (5-HIAA), the primary metabolite of serotonin, have been linked to impulsive aggression in psychiatric patients and violent criminals and to hostility in normal subjects (Coccaro, 1989). The focus of our review will be on a more readily obtained measurement, plasma phenylacetic acid, which also has been correlated with aggressive behavior, and with social status in animals.

The trace amine phenylethylamine and its metabolite phenylacetic acid (PAA) have been the focus of considerable research in the past decade because of their possible relationship with several psychiatric disorders such as schizophrenia (Karoum & Wyatt, 1984) and depression (Sabelli & Jefferies, 1983a, 1983b; Sabelli & Mosnaim, 1974; Sandler, Ruthven, Goodwin, & Coppen, 1979) as well as with violent behavior (Boulton, Davis, Yu, Wormith, and Addington, 1983; Davis, Yu, Boulton, Wormith, and Addington, 1983). A clear elucidation of the function of these neuropharmacologic substances and of any role they may play in human behavior has not been reached. Levels of PPA have also been implicated in differentiating various temperaments. Low levels of PAA have been observed in isolated aggressive mice (Dourish, Davis, Dyck, Jones, & Boulton, 1982) and are probably a mediator of the greater "isolation syndrome" (Valzelli, 1973) seen in mice. This link between levels of PAA and aggression has also been shown in human studies, with prisoners incarcerated for violent crimes having lower levels of PAA (Davis et al., 1983) and higher monoamine oxidase levels (Boulton et al., 1983; Yu, Davis, & Boulton, 1985) than those convicted of nonviolent crimes. Other studies have shown increased CSF PAA levels in aggressive psychopaths (Sandler, Ruthven, & Goodwin, 1978), and our own studies using an observer-rated scoring system have shown that low levels of plasma PAA correlated strongly with antagonistic, borderline behavior. Thus, there seems to be a viable association between low levels of this neurometabolite and what we would generally call "aggressive behavior." It has also been shown that minor tranquilizers such as the benzodiazepines act as "antiaggression" agents (Blanchard, Hori, Rodgers, Hendrie, & Blanchard, 1989; Ueki & Kawamoto, 1987) and that, in our group of polysubstance abusers, lifetime abuse of sedatives correlated strongly with low levels of PAA ($p < .001$; $r = -0.43$).

It is when these findings are viewed together that a unique model of motivation behavior emerges. (see Figure 5.4, top). That is, low PAA has been associated with both aggressiveness and violent behavior, as well as with the abuse of sedatives, which in turn act to reduce the underlying aggressive behavior. Furthermore, one would presume that this reduction is effected through a pharmacologic mechanism. Phenylacetic acid, with its associations with aggresion and violent behavior, would be one probable mediator of this reduction. Again, we observe the pattern of a drug's being used to achieve an effect that is specific to an individual's psychological and psychopharmacologic composition, and the effect that the drug produces in turn regulates the pharmacology of the temperament itself. In this case, tranquilizers are used to reduce the dysphoria of excessive aggressiveness, and this use in turn down regulates levels of PAA, a probable causitive psychoactive substance.

Phenylacetic Acid and Dominant–Submissive Behavior

There may be, however, another effect that is produced by sedatives and that would also be marked by low levels of PAA. That is, PAA has been shown to be a key modulator of

Phenylacetic Acid and Aggressiveness

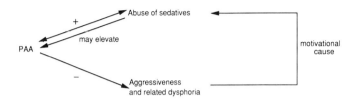

Phenylacetic Acid and Dominant/Submissive Behavior

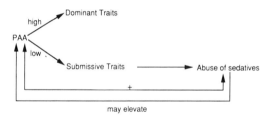

Vigilance as an Axis of Temperament

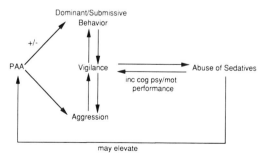

FIGURE 5.4 Theoretical models of the relationship between phenylacetic acid and sedative abuse.

submissive and dominant behavior (Elsworth, Redmond, Ruthven, & Sandler, 1985), and this association is state dependent, with levels of PAA varying consistently with the differing status of the individual at any point in time (Greene, 1989). Dominance was characterized in these simian studies by offensive behavior such as approaching, grabbing, or relative victory in competition tests for water or females. Submissiveness was characterized by essentially the opposite behaviors, with the animal allowing approach and grab behavior as well as loss in competition. This behavior presumably translates into a wide range of psychosocial attributes in higher primates such as humans. Therefore, we could assume PAA to be low in people where social rank is consistently submissive in their interpersonal relationships. We assume that the substance is used to effect a desired state and that the transition is mediated through a pharmacologic mechanism. That is, the individual may abuse sedatives to achieve a dominant state in social interactions. We can theorize that the abuse of sedatives may effect this rank change by elevating levels of PAA (see Figure 5.4, middle). Again, this would be an example of the abuse of a substance to achieve a state through the change in the levels of a neuropharmacologic agent. People with low PAA, itself associated with submissive behavior, tend to abuse sedatives, which, in turn, may raise the levels of PAA itself. The effect that is desired, we can then speculate, is one of dominance in interpersonal actions.

This idea of submissive individuals using sedatives in the face of feelings caused by repeated defeat fits observations of populations of sedative abusers in rehabilitation who "must deal with the diffuse hostility, expectations of failure and defeat ... that they display" (Spotts & Shontz, 1984). Thus, we see that the concept of dominance and submission would fit our model of effect-motivated behavior of sedative abuse: submissive, defeated individuals experiencing the anxiety and dysphoria of their social situation or rank and using sedatives to reverse these subjective effects. Furthermore, the use of the drug may regulate the pharmacogenic cause of the social rank itself.

Vigilance as an Underlying Axis of Temperament

Thus, sedative abuse behavior may be regulated by feelings of aggression and the dysphoria of such hostility or may be modulated by submissive status and the desire for cessation of the dysphoria that is involved in the repeated defeat associated with such status. In both cases, low plasma levels of PAA would be a marker for such abusers. Although these may seem to be two distinct theories of motivational behavior, there may indeed be an underlying axis explaining both observations (see Figure 5.4, bottom). This axis would be one of vigilance. The axis ranges from low levels of PAA, corresponding to low-vigilant states, to high levels, associated with hypervigilant states. We could theorize, then, that individuals with low PAA, hence submissive, may be in such a social status because of their relative inadequacy in the cognitive–psychomotor performance one associates with vigilance and that dominance is actually a display of the possession of such abilities. This is substantiated by findings that low-dose tranquilizers actually increase vigilance and related performance (Gerhard, 1984), although they decrease such parameters at higher doses.

Thus, the state dependent increase seen in the plasma PAA levels of dominant monkeys may actually be a reflection of increased cognitive–psychomotor vigilance. Further elucidation of the exact metabolic function would be needed to resolve the cause-and-effect relationship of these two factors, but the idea of a vigilance axis is further supported by studies of agoraphobic individuals, who are in what would be called a hypervigilant state and who have been shown to have abnormally high levels of monoamine oxidase, the enzyme responsible for the conversion of phenethylamine (PEA) to PAA (Yu, 1983).

These findings showing tranquilizers to be associated with increased levels of vigilance and dominant behavior while reducing levels of aggression raise some interesting questions about dominance and our perceptions of it, and studies into both the neurochemistry and behavioral aspects of these temperaments will be needed to explain their etiology.

Summary

The understanding of the biological basis of behavior is only starting to take form. However, it is clear that differences in neurochemistry can be associated with various behavioral traits. Furthermore, it appears that these neuropharmacologic agents and their metabolites may be linked to personality traits and behavioral variables in classical feedback systems, with either up-regulation or down-regulation of biological parameters by psychobehavioral actions. The knowledge of such modulatory systems is especially useful when examining our ideas concerning the compulsive behavior of drug abuse. In terms of the general hypothesis in this chapter, we propose that individuals having different extremes of temperament will, under the appropriate developmental and social influences, use illicit drugs either to restore an internal disequilibrium in mood or to amplify a current mood state. Some of the various mood states discussed in this paper include the ennui of low arousal, which leads to impulsive acts, the emotional excitement of behavioral activation in the face of incentives, and moment-to-moment changes in perceived aggressive feelings. However, the actual use of these medications or the concomitant behaviors associated with the acquisition of them may have profound effects on both mood and neurochemistry. This can lead to more chronic adaptational responses of neurochemical systems that may be manifested in changes in personality or temperament. For a long-term drug abusers, it is nearly impossible to disentangle the effects of drugs on their current personality from their personality prior to the drug-using period. However, longitudinal studies looking at the transition from use to abuse behaviors may be useful for providing data on temperamental risk factors associated with various substances of abuse.

As specifically presented in this chapter, Table 5.3 summarizes the interrelationships among neurochemistry, temperament, and drug abuse. The first system considered is the hypothalamic–pituitary–adrenal axis. Here, low plasma cortisol appears to be a biological marker for impulsivity, as well as a possible marker for drug abuse. It may also be a marker for many other risk-seeking behaviors besides drug use. The axis is clearly responsive to environmental events, and even early environment can have effects on HPA functioning into adulthood. The next system is the incentive motivation system. High mesolimbic dopamine activity is reflected in traits such as motivational excitement and activity. Here, associations were found with personality variables such as extraversion and histrionic traits in long-term cocaine users. Again, the actual use of cocaine acutely affects dopaminergic functioning, and it is possible that long-term use affects tonic levels of dopaminergic activity, production, and turnover. Finally, the third and most complex system is that of aggression, in which monoaminergic measures such as low levels of the serotonin metabolite 5-HIAA in the CSF and measures of the putative PEA metabolite PAA in the plasma have been associated with aggressive behavior in humans and animals. In the population studied here, plasma PAA is correlated with sedative abuse and borderline personality traits, implying that such individuals may use sedatives to cope with an underlying state of aggressive dysphoria.

These models lead to several cross-sectional predictions of neurochemistry and drug abuse. For instance, measures of CSF dopamine would be postulated to be elevated in cocaine abusers either prior to first-time usage of the drug or after a time of detoxification suitable to return dopamine to the normal nonmedical level. In addition, because some of the differences in cortisol may be due to reactivity to the stress inherent in venipuncture, elaboration of experimental protocol will be needed before more predictions can be made. Long-term monitoring of cortisol, as with an indwelling catheter, would be

TABLE 5.3

Summary of Interrelationships Among Temperament, Neurobiology, and Drugs of Abuse

Neurobiological system	Biological marker	Temperament	Personality traits and behavioral manifestations	Environmental feedback
Hypothalamic–pituitary–adrenal (HPA) axis	Low plasma cortisol	Impulsivity	General propensity for risk-seeking behavior, including drug use	Environmental exposure to stress can have persistent effects on HPS function.
Incentive motivation system	High mesolimbic dopamine	Motivational excitement, activity	Extraversion, emotional expressiveness, histrionic personality traits, long-term cocaine use	Cocaine enhances dopamine function.
Aggression	CSF 5-HIAA plasma PAA	?	Defensive and offensive behaviors, dominant social status, sedative abuse, borderline personality traits	Change in social status influences plasma PAA. Drug influence on PAA is unclear.

Note. CSF = cerebrospinal; 5-HIAA = 5-hydroxyindoleacetic acid; PAA = phenylacetic acid.

optimal in delineating its role in the prospensity for impulsive behavior compared with its role in the stress response. Finally, because little is known about the effects of drugs on plasma PAA, studies looking at plasma PAA response to sedatives would be useful. An elevation in PAA after sedative use would further indicate an association between the abuse of such medications and submissive and aggressive behaviors, and also would confirm the neurochemical mediation of such behaviors. Further studies in this area will need to address these associations not only in a cross-sectional manner but also longitudinally, so that the development of abuse behavior can be investigated. It is in studying this development that we may begin to truly elucidate the interplay among neurochemistry, personality, and drug abuse.

References

American Psychiatric Association. (1987). *Diagnostic and statistical manual of mental disorders* (3rd ed., rev.). Washington, DC: Author.

Ballenger, J. C., Post, R. M., and Goodwin, F. K. (1983). Neurochemistry of cerebrospinal fluid in normal individuals. In J. Wood (Ed.), *Neurobiology of cerebrospinal fluid* (Vol. 2, pp. 143–152). New York: Plenum Press.

Blanchard, D. C., and Blanchard, R. J. (1988). Ethoexperimental approaches to the biology of emotion. *Annual Review of Psychology, 39,* 43–68.

Blanchard, D. C., Hori, K., Rodgers, R., Hendrie, C., & Blanchard, R. J. (1989). Attenuation of defensive threat and attack in wild rats (Rattus rattus) by benzodiazepines. *Psychopharmacology, 97,* 392–401.

Boulton, A. A., Davis, B. A., Yu, P. H., Wormith, J. S., & Addington, D. (1983). Trace acid levels in the plasma and MAO activity in the platelets of violent offenders. *Psychiatry Research, 8,* 19–23.

Brett, L. P., & Levine, S. (1979). Schedule-induced polydipsia suppresses pituitary-adrenal activity in rats. *Journal of Comparative and Physiological Psychology, 93,* 946–950.

Cloninger, C. R. (1987). A systematic method for clinical description and classification of personality variants. *Archives of General Psychiatry, 44,* 573–589.

Coccaro, E. F. (1989). Central serotonin and impulsive aggression. *British Journal of Psychiatry, 155,* 52–62.

Coover, G. D. (1983). Positive and negative expectancies: The rat's reward environment and pituitary-adrenal activity. In H. Ursin and R. Murison (Eds.), *Biological and psychological basis of psychosomatic disease.* New York, Pergamon Press.

Dackis, C., & Gold, M. S. (1985). New concepts in cocaine addiction: The dopamine depletion hypothesis. *Neuroscience and Biobehavioral Reviews, 9,* 469–477.

Davis, B. A., Yu, P. H., Boulton, A. A., Wormith, J. S., & Addington, D. (1983). Correlative relationship between biochemical activity and aggressive behavior. *Progress in Neuropsychopharmacology and Biological Psychiatry, 7,* 529–535.

Davis, M. (1989). The role of the amygdala and its efferent projections in fear and anxiety. In P. Tyrer (Ed.), *Psychopharmacology of anxiety* (pp. 53–77). London: Oxford University Press.

Deminiere, J. M., Piazza, P. V., LeMoal, M., & Simon, H. (1989). Experimental approach to individual vulnerability to psychostimulant addiction. *Neuroscience and Biobehavioral Reviews, 13,* 141–147.

Dourish, C. T., Davis, B. A., Dyck, L. E., Jones, R. S. G., & Boulton, A. A. (1982). Alterations in trace amine and trace acid concentrations in isolated aggressive mice. *Pharmacology, Biochemistry, and Behavior, 17,* 1291–1924.

Elsworth, J. D., Redmond, D. E., Ruthven, C. R. J., & Sandler, M. (1985). Phenylacetic acid production in dominant and nondominant vervet monkeys. *Life Science, 37,* 727–730.

Eysenck, H. J., & Eysenck, S. B. G. (1964). *Manual for the Eysenck Personality Inventory.* London: University of London Press.

Gawin, F. H., & Ellinwood, E. H. (1988). Cocaine and other stimulants: Actions, abuse and treatment. *New England Journal of Medicine, 318,* 1173–1182.

Gawin, F. H., & Kleber, H. D. (1986). Abstinence symptomatology and psychiatric diagnosis in chronic cocaine abusers. *Archives of General Psychiatry, 41,* 903–910.

Gerhard, U. (1984). Cognitive psychomotor functions with regard to fitness for driving in psychotic patients treated with neuroleptics and antidepressants. *Neuropsychobiology, 12,* 39–47.

Greene, K. A. (1989). *The involvement of monoamine neurotransmitters in dominance behaviors in male squirrel monkey dyads.* Unpublished doctoral dissertation, Stanford Medical School.

Hennessy, J., & Levine, S. (1979). Stress, arousal and the pituitary-adrenal system: A psychoendocrine model. In J. Sprague & A. Epstein (Eds.), *Progress in psychobiology and physiological psychology* (Vol. 8, pp. 133–178). San Diego, CA: Academic Press.

Kagan, J., Resnick, J. S., & Snidman, N. (1988). Biological basis of childhood shyness. *Science, 240,* 167–171.

Karoum, F., & Wyatt, R. J. (1984). Phenylacetic acid excretion in schizophrenia and depression: The origins of PAA in man. *Biological Psychiatry, 19,* 165–78.

Khantzian, E. J. (1985). The self-medication hypothesis of addictive disorders: Focus on heroin and cocaine dependence. *American Journal of Psychiatry, 142,* 1259–1264.

King, R. J. (1986). Motivational diversity and mesolimbic dopamine: A hypothesis concerning temperament. In R. Platchik & H. Kellerman (Eds.), *Biological Foundations of Emotion.* San Diego, CA: Academic Press.

King, R. J., Bayon, E. P., Clark, D. B., & Taylor, C. B. (1988). Tonic arousal and activity: Relationships to personality and personality disorder traits in panic patients. *Psychiatry Research, 25,* 65–72.

King, R. J., Jones, J., Scheuer, J. W., Curtis, D., & Zarcone, V. P. (1990). Plasma cortisol correlates of impulsivity and substance abuse. *Personality and Individual Differences, 2,* 287–291.

King, R. J., Mefford, I. N., Wand, C., Murchison, A., Claigari, E. J., & Berger, P. A. (1986). CSF dopamine levels correlate with extraversion in depressed patients. *Psychiatry Research, 19,* 305–310.

Klinger, E. (1975). Consequences of commitment of and disengagement from incentives. *Psychological Review, 82,* 1–25.

Koob, G. F., & Bloom, F. E. (1988). Cellular and molecular mechanisms of drug dependence. *Science, 242,* 715–723.

Loranger, A. W., Sussman, V. L., Oldham, J. M., & Rossakoff, L. M. (1987). The personality disorder examination: A preliminary report. *Journal of Personality Disorders, 1,* 1–13.

McLellan, A. T., Luborsky, L., & O'Brien, C. P. (1980). An improved evaluation instrument for substance abuse patients: The Addiction Severity Index. *Journal of Nervous and Mental Disorders, 168,* 26–33.

Morgenson, G. J., & Neilsen, M. (1984). A study of the contribution of hippocampal accumbensubpallidal projections to locomotor activity. *Behavioral and Neural Biology, 42,* 38–51.

Politch, J. A., & Leshner, A. I. (1977). Relationship betwen plasma corticosterone levels and levels of aggressiveness in mice. *Physiology and Behavior, 19,* 775–780.

Sabelli, H. C., & Jefferies, H. (1983a). Urinary phenylacetate: A diagnostic test for depression? *Science, 220,* 1187–1188.

Sabelli, H. C., & Jefferies, H. (1983b). Phenylacetic acid as an indicator in bipolar affective disorders [letter]. *Journal of Clinical Psychopharmacology,* Vol. 3.

Sabelli, H. C., & Mosnaim, A. D. (1974). Phenylethylamine hypothesis of affective behavior. *American Journal of Psychiatry, 131,* 695–699.

Sandler, M., Ruthven, C. R. J., & Goodwin, B. L. (1978). Phenylethylamine overproduction in aggressive psychopaths. *Lancet, 2,* 1269–1270.

Sandler, M., Ruthven, C. R. J., Goodwin, B. L., & Coppen, A. (1979). Decreased cerebrospinal fluid concentration of free phenylacetic acid in depressive illness. *Clinica Chemica Acta, 93,* 169–171.

Schiffer, F. (1988). Psychotherapy of nine successfully treated cocaine abusers: Techniques and dynamics. *Journal of Substance Abuse Treatment, 5,* 131–137.

Shedler, J., & Block, J. (1990). Adolescent drug use and psychological health: A longitudinal inquiry. *American Psychologist, 45,* 612–630.

Spotts, J. V., & Shontz, F.C. (1984). The phenomenological structure of drug induced ego states: Barbiturates and sedative-hypnotics: Phenomenology and implications. *International Journal of the Addictions, 19,* 295–326.

Ueki, S., & Kawamoto, H. (1987). Behavioral and electroencephalographic effects of zopi-clone, a cyclopyrrolone derivative. *Japanese Journal of Pharmacology, 43,* 309–326.

Valzelli, L. (1973). The "isolation syndrome" in mice. *Psychopharmacologia, 31,* 305–20.

Virkkunen, M. (1985). Urinary free cortisol secretion in habitually violent offenders. *Acta Psychiatrica Scandinavica, 72,* 40–44.

Wertheim, G. A., Conner, R. L., & Levine, S. (1969). Avoidance conditioning and adrenocortical function in the rat. *Physiology and Behavior, 4,* 41–44.

Wise, R. A. (1988). The neurobiology of craving: Implications for the understanding of treatment of addiction. *Journal of Abnormal Psychology, 97,* 118–132.

Woolverton, W. L., & Kleven, M. S. (1988). Multiple dopamine receptors and the behavioral effects of cocaine. *NIDA Research Monograph Series, 88,* 160–184.

Yu, P. H. (1983). Platelet monoamine oxidase activity and trace acid levels in plasma of agoraphobic patients. *Acta Psychiatrica Scandinavica, 67,* 188–194.

Yu, P. H., Davis, B. A., & Boulton, A. A. (1985). Further studies on platelet monamine oxidase and phenosulfotransferase and plasma levels of acid metabolites in aggressive and non-aggressive prisoners and children with attention deficit disorders. In A. A. Boulton (Ed.), *Neuropharmacology of the trace amines* (pp. 329–342). Clifton, NJ: Humana Press.

CHAPTER 6

The Role of Psychopathology in the Transition From Drug Use to Abuse and Dependence

Roger D. Weiss

I n recent years, there has been a burgeoning clinical and research interest in the relation between substance abuse and psychopathology. This increased attention has been stimulated by several factors: A number of reports have shown a high incidence of substance use disorders in psychiatric patients (Caton, Gralnick, Bender & Simon, 1989; Drake & Wallach, 1989; Galanter & Castaneda, 1988; Miller & Busch, & Tanenbaum, 1989); conversely, numerous studies have shown that many patients entering primary substance abuse treatment facilities suffer from coexisting psychiatric illness (Khantzian and Treece, 1985; Ross, Glaser, & Germanson, 1988; Rounsaville and Kleber, 1986; Weiss, Mirin, Griffin, & Michael, 1988). The development of effective pharmacological and psychological therapies for some of these disorders (in particular, mood disorder, panic disorder, and attention deficit disorder), coupled with evidence supporting the importance of matching subgroups of drug-dependent patients with specific treatment modalities (Gawin et al.,

This paper was supported in whole or in part by Grant 1 R29 DA05944-01 from the National Institute on Drug Abuse, by BRSG Grant RR05484 awarded by the Biomedical Research Support Program, Division of Research Resources, National Institutes of Health, and by a grant from the Engelhard Foundation.
The author would like to thank Marjorie Maxwell for her help in manuscript preparation.

1989; McLellan, Luborsky, Woody, O'Brien, & Druley, 1983; Weiss, Pope, & Mirin, 1985), has continued to promote further investigation in this area.

Meyer (1986) has described six potential relationships between psychopathology and substance abuse: (a) Axis I or Axis II disorders may serve as risk factors for substance use disorders; (b) psychopathology may modify the course of a substance use disorder; (c) psychiatric symptoms may occur in the course of chronic intoxication; (d) psychiatric disorders may develop as a result of drug use and persist despite remission of the substance abuse; (e) substance use and psychiatric symptoms may become meaningfully linked over time; or (f) a psychiatric disorder and a substance use disorder may occur in the same individual but not be related. When considering the transition from drug use to abuse and dependence, two of these relationships are critical: psychopathology as a risk factor and psychopathology as a modifier of course. Indeed, these are indistinguishable in the early stages of drug use, because we are trying to understand how psychopathology may alter the course of drug use by increasing the likelihood of subsequent abuse or dependence.

Evidence for the Link Between Drug Abuse and Psychopathology

Numerous studies of patients entering drug abuse treatment have shown that the prevalence of other psychiatric disorders in this population is substantially higher than one would expect to find in the general population. For example, Ross et al. (1988) found that 78% of their sample of 501 patients at the Clinical Institute of the Addiction Research Foundation of Toronto met criteria of the third edition of the *Diagnostic and Statistical Manual of Mental Disorders (DSM–III,* American Psychiatric Association, 1980) for a lifetime psychiatric disorder in addition to substance abuse, with 65% suffering from a current psychiatric disorder. The most common disorders diagnosed were antisocial personality disorder, phobias, psychosexual dysfunctions, major depression, and dysthymia. Severity of substance abuse was highly correlated with additional psychopathology, with the presence of each increasing the likelihood of the coexistence of the other. Rounsaville and Kleber (1986) also demonstrated a high rate of psychiatric illness in a sample of 533 opioid addicts entering treatment; 87% of their sample met diagnostic criteria for one or more lifetime disorders other than drug abuse, and 70% suffered from a current psychiatric illness. The most common coexisting disorder in this group was major depression, with 24% currently depressed and 54% having met criteria for a lifetime diagnosis of depression. Antisocial personality disorder was present in 27% of the sample population.

Khantzian and Treece (1985) also found that a majority of their sample of 133 opioid addicts met *DSM–III* criteria for another psychiatric disorder, with 77% meeting criteria for an Axis I disorder and 65% receiving a personality disorder diagnosis. Affective disorder and antisocial personality disorder were diagnosed most commonly. Weiss et al. (1988) found that a substantial minority of their sample of hospitalized drug dependent patients suffered from another psychiatric illness, with affective disorder particularly common in cocaine abusers, panic and anxiety disorders most common in sedative–hypnotic abusers, and antisocial personality disorder most prevalent in opioid addicts.

Studies of substance abusers in the community have also shown a high rate of coexisting psychiatric disorders, thus arguing against the possibility that the psychiatric comorbidity found in the aforementioned treatment populations of substance abusers was due primarily to sampling bias. Helzer and Pryzbeck (1988), reporting data from the Epidemiologic Catchment Area Survey, showed a high prevalence rate of psychiatric illness in alcoholics. A study by Rounsaville & Kleber (1985) also showed substantial psychiatric comorbidity in untreated opioid addicts; the only significant difference between that population group and a treatment sample of opioid addicts was a higher prevalence rate of major depression in the latter group.

Despite the overall agreement among the aforementioned studies, none of them has clearly elucidated the nature of the relationship between psychiatric disorders and drug dependence. Ross et al. (1988) found that, although the majority of patients with coexisting Axis I disorders and most patients with antisocial personality disorder began abusing substances after the development of their other disorders, a substantial minority of patients developed their coexisting disorders after becoming drug dependent. The criteria used by Rounsaville & Kleber (1986) and Weiss et al. (1988) did not clearly distinguish between "primary" and "secondary" psychiatric illness according to chronology of onset. However, a comparable study of alcoholics by Hesselbrock, Meyer, & Keener (1985) did examine this issue and found that, with some exceptions (notably antisocial personality disorder, which almost always preceded the onset of alcohol abuse), more women than men had psychopathology that preceded alcohol abuse, whereas most men (with the exception of patients with antisocial personality disorder and panic disorder) became alcoholic prior to the onset of coexisting psychiatric illness. Thus, psychopathology may exert a different role as a risk factor in men and women.

Studies of patients entering treatment for primary psychiatric illnesses have also shown a higher rate of substance abuse than one would expect to observe in the general population. Specifically, a number of researchers have reported a rate of substance abuse ranging from 20% to 50% among patients with bipolar disorder (Miller et al., 1989), schizophrenia (Caton et al., 1989; Drake & Wallach, 1989; Miller et al., 1989), eating disorders (Henzel, 1984), antisocial personality disorder (Lewis, Rice, & Helzer, 1983), and major depression (McLellan & Druley, 1977). Although alcohol is the usual drug of choice among primary psychiatric patients, illicit drug use and polysubstance abuse are not uncommon.

In addition to the high prevalence rate of combined substance abuse and psychiatric illness, a number of studies have shown that this "dually diagnosed" population has a particularly poor prognosis (McLellan, 1986; Safer, 1987). We have also found that in at least one group of dual-diagnosis patients, cocaine abusers with affective disorder, the progression from initial use to drug dependence was more rapid than that of cocaine abusers without coexisting affective disorder (Weiss et al., 1988). This suggests that comorbid psychopathology may, indeed, hasten the transition from drug use to addiction. Because the coexistence of substance use disorders and major psychiatric illness is associated with an increased rate of hospitalization (Safer, 1987), poor medication compliance (Drake et al., 1989), homelessness (Benda and Dattalo, 1988), criminality (Safer, 1987), and suicidal behavior (Caton, 1981), it is important to evaluate carefully both substance abusers and psychiatric patients for the presence of comorbidity.

Psychopathology as a Risk Factor for Drug Abuse

Even if it is known that a psychiatric disorder has preceded the onset of substance abuse, the mere coexistence of the two disorders does not explain the mechanism by which a psychiatric disorder predisposes an experimental drug user to subsequent abuse or dependence. I posit that there are several different ways in which this risk factor can manifest itself.

Patients with certain psychiatric disorders may find particular drugs to be especially reinforcing, perhaps because they relieve their psychiatric symptoms. This explanation of drug abuse, sometimes termed the *self-medication theory* (Khantzian, 1985), emphasizes the importance of "drug of choice" as a specific modifier of particular symptoms. Post, Kotin, & Goodwin (1974) investigated one aspect of this hypothesis by studying the potential antidepressant effects of cocaine. They found that approximately one third of a sample of severely depressed patients experienced mood elevation after being given low to moderate doses of cocaine; administration of higher doses generally resulted in an exacerbation of depressive symptoms. Despite the latter finding, however, it is nevertheless possible that a subgroup of significantly depressed patients will initially experience powerful reinforcement from cocaine use as a result of rapid symptom improvement; this may lead to repetitive use and, ultimately, abuse of the drug in this population. Indeed, we (Weiss et al., 1988), as well as Gawin and Kleber (1986), have found a high rate of affective illness in patients seeking treatment for cocaine abuse. The fact that cocaine may later worsen the original symptoms does not necessarily reverse this pattern of drug use, because many substance abusers continue using drugs or alcohol despite their long-term adverse effects on mood and psychiatric symptomatology (Mendelson & Mello, 1966; Mirin, Meyer, & McNamee, 1976).

Weiss et al. (1988) and Gawin and Kleber (1986) also found that approximately 5% of cocaine-dependent patients suffer from attention deficit disorder, residual type. These patients usually report experiencing an early calming effect from cocaine and an initial improvement in their attention span. Like the depressed patients, this effect is generally present only initially and is followed over time by a general worsening of the overall symptoms. However, this early symptom relief (in addition to the typical euphoriant properties of cocaine) may be sufficiently reinforcing in some of these patients to predispose them to further use and, ultimately, to abuse or dependence.

Patients with bipolar or cyclothymic disorder may be at increased risk for substance abuse for several reasons. When depressed, some of these patients may attempt to self-medicate (as described above). When manic, the use of certain drugs may either modify unwanted symptoms of mania (e.g., insomnia, irritability, agitation) or enhance other, more desirable manifestations (e.g., euphoria, grandiosity, hypersexuality). Thus, for example, there have been reports of increased marijuana use among some manic patients (Harding & Knight, 1973), which may represent an attempt to decrease symptoms of irritability and insomnia. Conversely, we and others (Gawin & Kleber, 1986; Weiss et al., 1988) have found a high prevalence rate of bipolar disorder and cyclothymia among cocaine abusers, most of whom use the drug primarily when endogenously "high," in order to enhance their underlying mood. One could posit that patients with euphoric mania prefer stimulant drugs, whereas patients with primarily dysphoric mania use alcohol, sedative–hypnotics, marijuana, or opioids in an attempt to reduce unwanted symptoms. Although it is known that patients with dysphoric mania have a worse overall prognosis (Post et al., 1989), no studies examining drug choice in subgroups of manic patients have been undertaken.

Patients with panic or anxiety disorders may be at increased risk for benzodiazepine abuse because of the ability of these agents to relieve the symptoms of these disorders. Although the relative rate of benzodiazepine abuse among these patients is relatively low (Garvey & Tollefson, 1986), one could hypothesize that a partial response to benzodiazepines could lead to dose escalation and abuse. Although de Wit, Uhlenhuth, Hedeker, McCracken, & Johanson (1986) showed no difference between anxious and nonanxious volunteers in drug preference when offered diazepam or a placebo, it is possible that some subgroups of anxious patients may be at increased risk to abuse certain benzodiazepines. For example, Ciraulo, Barnhill, Ciraulo, Greenblatt, & Shader (1989) recently reported a different response to alprazolam among sons of alcoholics when compared with sons of controls, whereas this result was not found by M. A. Schuckit (personal communication, 1989) in a similar study that used diazepam. Thus, it is possible that certain subpopulations may be at increased risk to abuse different specific benzodiazepines.

The use of opioids to control symptoms of severe rage has been described by Khantzian (1985), who cites the antiaggression effects of opioids as one of the major reasons for their appeal. Although he has not linked the use of these drugs to any discrete psychiatric disorder, it is possible that these drugs may be particularly reinforcing for patients with impulse control disorders or certain personality disorders that are characterized by frequent angry outbursts.

Some patients with eating disorders may find cocaine to be particularly reinforcing because of its ability to diminish appetite and induce weight loss. Thus, for these patients, one of the side effects of the drug may be a primary reason to continue its use. Several researchers (Bulik, 1987; Hatsukami, Eckert, Mitchell, & Pyle, 1984; Henzel, 1984) have reported a high prevalence rate of substance abuse among patients with eating disorders; Jonas, Gold, Sweeney, & Pottash (1987) have also described the converse, with a relatively high rate of eating disorders among callers to the 800-COCAINE telephone hotline.

A final disorder that may represent a risk factor for substance abuse is schizophrenia. Castaneda, Galanter, & Franco (1989) have reported that among patients diagnosed with both schizophrenia and substance abuse, the majority of heroin addicts and alcoholics reported drug-induced improvement of their primary psychiatric symptoms, although cocaine addicts reported an exacerbation of symptoms after drug use. R. E. Drake (personal communication, 1989) also reported some decreased symptomatology among schizophrenics who drank alcohol, although he noted a reduction in anxiety caused by the primary symptoms (i.e., hallucinations), rather than a decrease in the schizophrenic symptoms themselves. Thus, it is possible that certain types of substance use within a subgroup of the schizophrenic population may increase the likelihood of repeated use, abuse, and dependence.

A second mechanism by which psychopathology may predispose an individual to make the transition from drug use to abuse or dependence may be related to a person's failure to appreciate the consequences of further drug use. Schuckit (1989) reported that up to one third of individuals in their early 20s experience temporary alcohol related problems. However, most of these people then modify their drinking habits so as not to reexperience these problems. Those who eventually become alcoholics do not, of course, modify their drinking, and, indeed, frequently increase their intake of alcohol. What, then, characterizes those who recognize early drug-related problems and modify their behavior accordingly? Conversely, why do some people fail to recognize that a problem is drug related, or continue to use drugs that they realize are harmful?

One explanation is that accompanying psychopathology may interfere with a person's ability or willingness to understand or alter his behavior. This impairment may reflect a "trait" predisposition (e.g., antisocial personality disorder) or a "state" disorder (e.g., an Axis I disorder such as severe depression, mania, or severe anxiety). For example, antisocial personality disorder, which has clearly been shown to increase the risk of substance abuse, is characterized by "failure to ... plan ahead, and reckless behavior without regard to personal safety" (American Psychiatric Association, 1987, p. 342).

Patients with mood disorders may also have a difficult time foregoing the potential immediate euphoriant effects associated with intoxication in order to avoid potential long-term adverse consequences. Depending on the particular disorder present, the process by which this decision is influenced may vary. For example, a severely depressed patient may feel so hopeless about his or her future that the patient may not care whether he or she will later experience drug related problems. Indeed, some addicts may use a drug even if they anticipate immediate problems as a result of this action. This behavior is consistent with the hypothesis that in some cases, a change in affective state is more important than the direction of that change. Evidence supporting this theory includes research showing that regular phencyclidine users continue to use this drug despite the fact that they generally experience negative consequences when intoxicated (Mello, 1978). Khantzian (1989) has discussed the reinforcing aspects of mood change, albeit mood worsening, in patients with affective instability. These individuals may turn to drugs despite their attendant adverse effects as a means of gaining control over their moods despite the fact that this may only give them control over the ability to worsen mood.

Hypomanic patients may be unable to appreciate the consequences of their substance use because of their recklessness, poor judgment, distractibility, and grandiosity. Indeed, one of the nine *DSM–III–R* criteria for mania is "excessive involvement in pleasurable activities which have a high potential for painful consequences" (American Psychiatric Association, 1987, p. 217). Patients with panic attacks may abuse drugs during a period of high anxiety or panic because their severe anxiety, and perhaps even a fear of impending death, may weaken judgment and impair the ability to engage in future oriented thinking.

A third mechanism by which psychopathology may increase the risk of drug dependence is the possibility that patients with underlying psychiatric vulnerability may experience more dysphoria from chronic substance use or more severe withdrawal symptoms upon cessation of drug use. Although this is an area that has received little research attention, Gawin & Kleber (1986) did report more severe abstinence symptoms in cocaine abusers with major depression when compared with nondepressed or dysthymic patients. Although this does not answer the question of whether these individuals experienced more severe withdrawal symptoms during the early phases of their cocaine use, this possibility should be explored.

A fourth hypothesis is linking psychopathology and increased risk for drug abuse may be related to social as well as pharmacological factors. For example, it is possible that some patients with chronic mental illness are attracted to a drug using subculture because of the appeal of a new identity, a peer group, and clear behavioral expectations and norms. Drake et al. (1989) reported that patients with chronic schizophrenia who drink alcohol describe improved socialization despite their increased likelihood of relapse to psychosis. This finding raises the possibility that the appeal of drinking is great enough in some schizophrenic patients to outweigh their concerns regarding the general course of their illness. The fact that these researchers found a high rate of schizophrenic patients who drink alone argues against this hypothesis to some extent. However, the importance of the social context of drug abuse should not be minimized (Gorsuch, 1980).

Conclusion

Numerous studies have shown a statistical association between substance abuse and psychopathology. In some drug dependent patients, the presence of a psychiatric disorder has undoubtedly increased their vulnerability to progress from drug use to abuse or dependence. For many individuals, it is likely that the following factors are involved: increased reinforcement from drug use, a reduced ability to appreciate the adverse consequences of continued drug use or change one's behavior accordingly, the possibility of accelerated addiction as the result of more severe abstinence symptoms, and the reinforcement of the social context of drug use. Some research questions that remain include whether specific diagnoses or the severity of illness affects the response to drugs. Work by McLellan (1986) suggested that overall psychiatric severity worsens prognosis in patients who are already drug dependent. However, the impact of psychiatric severity on the development of drug dependence would be an important topic for future research. Similarly, research on the interaction between specific psychiatric disorders and drug response (reinforcing properties, abstinence syndromes, changes in level of socialization) would be very useful in helping to explain the interaction of psychopathology, drug effects, and social context. As we and others have written, drug dependence, like many other disorders, can be seen as an interaction among host, agent, and environment (Goodwin, 1980; Weiss & Mirin, 1984; Zinberg, 1981). Further research on the longitudinal history of the interaction of these three variables will be critical in advancing our understanding of the development of drug dependence.

References

American Psychiatric Association. (1980). *Diagnostic and statistical manual of mental disorders* (3rd ed.). Washington, DC: Author.

American Psychiatric Association. (1987). *Diagnostic and statistical manual of mental disorders* (3rd ed., rev.). Washington, DC: Author.

Benda, B. B., & Dattalo, P. (1988). Homelessness: Consequence of a crisis or a long-term process? *Hospital and Community Psychiatry, 39,* 884–886.

Bulik, C. M. (1987). Drug and alcohol abuse by bulimic women and their families. *American Journal of Psychiatry, 144,* 1604–1606.

Castaneda, R., Galanter, M., & Franco, H. (1989). Self-medication among addicts with primary psychiatric disorders. *Comprehensive Psychiatry, 30,* 80–83.

Caton, C. (1981). The new chronic patient and the system of community care. *Hospital and Community Psychiatry, 32,* 475–478.

Caton, C. L. M., Gralnick, A., Bender, S., & Simon, R. (1989). Young chronic patients and substance abuse. *Hospital and Community Psychiatry, 40,* 1037–1040.

Ciraulo, D. A., Barnhill, J. G., Ciraulo, A. M., Greenblatt, D. J., & Shader, R. I. (1989). Parental alcoholism as a risk factor in benzodiazepine abuse: A pilot study. *American Journal of Psychiatry, 146,* 1333–1335.

de Wit, H., Uhlenhuth, E. H., Hedeker, D., McCracken, S. G., & Johanson, C. E. (1986). Lack of preference for diazepam in anxious volunteers. *Archives of General Psychiatry, 43,* 533–541.

Drake, R. E., Osher, F. C., & Wallach, M. A. (1989). Alcohol use and abuse in schizophrenia: A prospective community study. *Journal of Nervous and Mental Disease, 177,* 408–414.

Drake, R. E., & Wallach, M. A. (1989). Substance abuse among the chronic mentally ill. *Hospital and Community Psychiatry, 40,* 1041–1046.

Galanter, M., & Castaneda, R. (1988). Substance abuse among general psychiatric patients: Place of presentation, diagnosis, and treatment. *American Journal of Drug and Alcohol Abuse, 14,* 211–235.

Garvey, M. J., & Tollefson, G. D. (1986). Prevalence of misuse of prescribed benzodiazepines in patients with primary anxiety disorder or major depression. *American Journal of Psychiatry, 143,* 1601–1603.

Gawin, F. H., & Kleber, H. D. (1986). Abstinence symptomatology and psychiatric diagnoses in cocaine abusers: Clinical observations. *Archives of General Psychiatry, 43,* 107–113.

Gawin, F. H., Kleber, H. D., Byck, R., Rounsaville, B. J., Kosten, T. R., Jatlow, P. I., & Morgan, C. (1989). Desipramine facilitation of initial cocaine abstinence. *Archives of General Psychiatry, 46,* 117–121.

Goodwin, D. W. (1980). The bad-habit theory of drug abuse. In D. J. Lettieri, M. Sayers, & H. W. Pearson (Eds.), *Theories on drug abuse: Selected contemporary perspectives* (National Institute on Drug Abuse Research Monograph 30; DHHA Publication No. ADM 80-967; pp. 12–17). Washington, DC: U.S. Government Printing Office.

Gorsuch, R. L. (1980). Interactive models of nonmedical drug use. In D. J. Lettieri, M. Sayers, & H. W. Pearson (Eds.), *Theories on drug abuse: Selected contemporary perspectives* (National Institute on Drug Abuse Research Monograph 30; DHHA Publication No. ADM 80-967; pp. 18–23). Washington, DC: U.S. Government Printing Office.

Harding, T., & Knight, F. (1973). Marihuana-modified mania. *Archives of General Psychiatry, 29,* 635–637.

Hatsukami, D., Eckert, E., Mitchell, J. E., & Pyle, R. (1984). Affective disorder and substance abuse in women with bulimia. *Psychological Medicine, 14,* 701–704.

Helzer, J. E., & Pryzbeck, T. R. (1988). The co-occurrence of alcoholism with other psychiatric disorders in the general population and its impact on treatment. *Journal of Studies on Alcohol, 49,* 219–224.

Henzel, H. A. (1984). Diagnosing alcoholism in patients with anorexia nervosa. *American Journal of Drug and Alcohol Abuse, 10,* 461–466.

Hesselbrock, M. N., Meyer, R. E., & Keener, J. J. (1985). Psychopathology in hospitalized alcoholics. *Archives of General Psychiatry, 42,* 1050–1055.

Jonas, J. M., Gold, M. S., Sweeney, D., & Pottash, A. L. C. (1987). Eating disorders and cocaine abuse: A survey of 259 cocaine abusers. *Journal of Clinical Psychiatry, 48,* 47–50.

Khantzian, E. J. (1985). The self-medication hypothesis of addictive disorders: Focus on heroin and cocaine dependence. *American Journal of Psychiatry, 142,* 1259–1264.

Khantzian, E. J. (1989). Addiction: Self-destruction or self-repair? *Journal of Substance Abuse Treatment, 6,* 75.

Khantzian, E. J., & Treece, C. (1985). *DSM–III* psychiatric diagnosis of narcotic addicts. *Archives of General Psychiatry, 42,* 1067–1071.

Lewis, C. E., Rice, J., & Helzer, J. E. (1983). Diagnostic interactions: Alcoholism and antisocial personality. *Journal of Nervous and Mental Disease, 171,* 105–113.

McLellan, A. T. (1986). "Psychiatric severity" as a predictor of outcome from substance abuse treatments. In R. E. Meyer (Ed.), *Psychopathology and addictive disorders* (pp. 97–139). New York: Guilford Press.

McLellan, A. T., & Druley, K. A. (1977). Non-random relation between drugs of abuse and psychiatric diagnosis. *Journal of Psychiatric Research, 13,* 179–184.

McLellan, A. T., Luborsky, L., Woody, G. E., O'Brien, C. P., & Druley, K. A. (1983). Predicting response to alcohol and drug abuse treatments. *Archives of General Psychiatry, 40,* 620–625.

Mello, N. K. (1978). Control of drug self-administration: The role of aversive consequences. In R. C. Petersen & R. C. Stillman (Eds.), *Phencyclidine (PCP) abuse: An appraisal* (National Institute on Drug Abuse Research Monograph 21; DHHS Publication No. ADM 79-728; pp. 289–308). Washington, DC: U.S. Government Printing Office.

Mendelson, J. H., & Mello, N. K. (1966). Experimental analysis of drinking behavior of chronic alcoholics. *Annals of the New York Academy of Sciences, 133,* 828–845.

Meyer, R. E. (1986). How to understand the relationship between psychopathology and addictive disorders: Another example of the chicken and the egg. In R. E. Meyer (Ed.), *Psychopathology and addictive disorders* (pp. 3–16). New York: Guilford Press.

Miller, F. T., Busch, F., & Tanenbaum, J. H. (1989). Drug abuse in schizophrenia and bipolar disorder. *American Journal of Drug and Alcohol Abuse, 15,* 291–295.

Mirin, S. M., Meyer, R. E., & McNamee, H. B. (1976). Psychopathology and mood during heroin use. *Archives of General Psychiatry, 33,* 1503–1508.

Post, R. M., Kotin, J., & Goodwin, F. R. (1974). The effects of cocaine on depressed patients. *American Journal of Psychiatry, 131,* 511–517.

Post, R. M., Rubinow, D. R., Uhde, T. W., Roy-Byrne, P. P., Linnoila, M., Rosoff, A., & Cowdry, R. (1989). Dysphoric mania: Clinical and biological correlates. *Archives of General Psychiatry, 46,* 353–358.

Ross, H. E., Glaser, F. B., & Germanson, T. (1988). The prevalence of psychiatric disorders in patients with alcohol and other drug problems. *Archives of General Psychiatry, 45,* 1023–1032.

Rounsaville, B. J., & Kleber, H. D. (1985). Untreated opiate addicts. *Archives of General Psychiatry, 42,* 1072–1077.

Rounsaville, B. J., & Kleber, H. D. (1986). Psychiatric disorders in opiate addicts: Preliminary findings on the course and interaction with program type. In R. E. Meyer (Ed.), *Psychopathology and addictive disorders* (pp. 140–168). New York: Guilford Press.

Safer, D. (1987). Substance abuse by young adult chronic patients. *Hospital and Community Psychiatry, 38,* 511–514.

Schuckit, M. A. (1989). *Drug and alcohol abuse* (3rd ed.). New York: Plenum Press.

Weiss, R. D., Mirin, S. M., Griffin, M. L., & Michael, M. L. (1988). Psychopathology in cocaine abusers: Changing trends. *Journal of Nervous and Mental Disease, 176,* 719–725.

Weiss, R. D., & Mirin, S. M. (1984). Drug, host and environmental factors in the development of chronic cocaine abuse. In S. M. Mirin (Ed.), *Substance abuse and psychopathology* (pp. 41–55). Washington, DC: American Psychiatric Press.

Weiss, R. D., Pope, H. G., Jr., & Mirin, S. M. (1985). Treatment of chronic cocaine abuse and attention deficit disorder, residual type, with magnesium pemoline. *Drug and Alcohol Dependence, 15,* 69–72.

Zinberg, N. E. (1981). Social interactions, drug use, and drug research. In J. H. Lowinson (Ed.), *Substance abuse: Clinical problems and perspectives* (pp. 91–108). Baltimore: Williams & Wilkins.

CHAPTER 7

Ontogeny of Substance Abuse: Perspectives and Findings

Ralph E. Tarter and Ada C. Mezzich

T he consumption of psychoactive drugs and alcohol in the United States is omnipresent; the lifetime prevalence rate approaches 100% for at least a single experience. For some, but not all, the consumption of drugs having abuse liability is problematic to the degree that health and psychosocial adjustment in the individual are severely compromised and the costs to society from law enforcement, health service delivery, job absenteeism, and accidental injury are economically burdensome and alienating. The sudden and dramatic increase in drug use and the response to the problem by government agencies have been compared to the Black Plague of the 13th century (Tarter & Edwards, 1988).

There is a dizzying assortment of drugs having addictive liability. They all, however, share the fundamental characteristic of requiring the user to consume increasing amounts to achieve the desired effects (tolerance), and, upon cessation of consumption, the individual experiences an adverse physiological and psychological reaction (withdrawal). Addictive drugs include psychotropic medications prescribed by physicians to relieve negative mood states, as well as anesthetics and analgesics. Numerous proprietary drugs have addictive potential, and nicotine, the most addictive such substance, can simply be

Research for this chapter was supported by Grant DA05605.

purchased as tobacco from vending machines. Drugs having addictive liability are thus easily available. Furthermore, the multiple routes of administration of such drugs (e.g., swallowing, chewing, sniffing, injecting, etc.) and the multifaceted motivations for use (e.g., recreation, religious ritual, medication, performance enhancement, etc.) clearly underscore the central position that drugs having addictive liability occupy in contemporary Western society. The smorgasbord of accessible psychoactive drugs notwithstanding, it is important to note that alcohol and tobacco contribute to more deaths, crime, and chronic disease than does the use of all other psychoactive drugs combined.

Given such endemic drug use, several important questions need to be raised, each of which has substantial ramifications for devising rational regulatory policies, as well as for the prevention of substance abuse and the treatment of persons already dependent on drugs:

1. What criteria distinguish drug *use* from drug *abuse*? For instance, nicotine has greater addictive liability than heroin. Does nicotine use thus necessarily imply abuse despite its legality and widespread consumption? Also, what factors differentiate drug abuse from drug dependence? Terminology has changed substantially throughout the past few decades, with labels such as *addiction, physiological dependence, abuse,* and *psychological dependence* often used interchangeably. It is thus important to determine whether current taxonomic descriptions of abuse and dependence are based on empirical objective findings or instead merely sustain diagnostic ambiguity. Moreover, it is essential to ascertain whether specific factors predict or differentiate the age at which a diagnosis can be assigned (i.e., whether they influence the rate of transition from drug use to a threshold diagnosis of abuse or dependence; American Psychiatric Association, 1987).

2. Are all individuals in the population at equal risk for becoming addicted to drugs? If not, what are the characteristics that distinguish individuals at high risk from those at low risk?

3. How do organismic and environmental factors interact to influence the transition from drug initiation to habitual drug use without accompanying health or psychosocial problems to, finally, a threshold diagnostic disorder of drug abuse or dependence in which the condition is of such severity so as to jeopardize health and mitigate social adjustment?

4. Does the risk for substance abuse in a given individual extend to all drugs having addictive liability, or is the risk specific to a particular drug or class of drugs?

The following discussion examines each of these questions, with the intention of developing a conceptual foundation for conducting research into the etiology of drug abuse, as well as for promoting a methodology for such research.

Criteria for Substance Abuse

In a democratic society, where individual rights, especially the right to privacy, are constitutionally protected, individuals who deviate from normative standards of behavior are ordinarily of no special concern to government. The court-mandated deinstitutionalization of chronic patients who were housed in long-term facilities aptly illustrates the protection of individual freedom, even in many instances where such individuals are arguably not fully capable of caring for themselves. Behavioral deviation, that is characterized by behavior that can be considered excessive in some people and uncommon according to prevailing normative standards, but posing no threat to the safety or health of the individual or to society, is also explicitly protected by the U.S. constitution. There are numerous "excessive behaviors" in which the judicial or professional institutions of society have no interest (e.g., great amounts of time spent watching television, playing video games, sunbathing, jogging, eating, or having sexual activity). Thus, excessive behavior, as defined by prevailing, ambiguous, and changeable normative standards, does not by itself imply the presence of a clinical disorder. Commonly, however, behavioral excess can result in significant disruption in social role performance (e.g., employee, parent, etc.), health (e.g., obesity, heart disease, etc.), or psychological distress (e.g., depression, anxiety). When the consequences of excess are not innocuous, a clinical disorder can be implicated.

Figure 7.1 delineates the distinction between simple individual differences or variations of behavior in the general population and the presence of a clinical problem. As can be seen, behavior contributing to disease or psychological disturbance lies within the purview of society's health professionals and institutions. Authority to protect, as well as to promote, health is granted through legislative action and regulated through state licensing or certification boards. Hence, physicians, psychologists, and chiropractors, as well as certain other professionals, exercise a stewardship role in promoting health in society. An important point is that health professionals have a circumscribed role that does not extend to an interest in all behavior. It is under circumscribed conditions in which the deviancy takes on certain properties so that the person is dysfunctional or is unable to control or regulate behavior to satisfy multiple role requirements that a clinical disorder

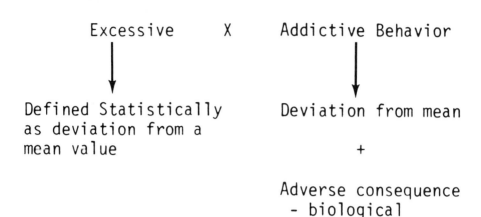

FIGURE 7.1   Distinction between variation of behavior in the population and a clinical disorder.

is defined. Whereas atypical behavior may be of intellectual interest (i.e., because research will enhance the understanding of human behavior), its manifestation cannot be simply construed to necessarily reflect the presence of a clinical problem.

Having thus defined the boundaries of professional involvement, we face the rather difficult problem of defining drug abuse. The term *abuse*, as used herein, denotes current or potential adverse psychological or physical consequences. In attempting to devise systematic diagnostic criteria, it is thus important to be aware of the fact that *use* and *abuse* as defined herein are situationally specific. For example, several drinks of an alcoholic beverage at a party simply characterizes *use;* however, to then drive a car would be considered *abuse* because there is immediate health endangerment to the person.

In attempting to define this terminology precisely, it is important to review its confusing history. Because the words that are used to denote events or objects shape our interpretation and understanding of the world, it is relevant to briefly illustrate the current ambiguity of terminology. Perhaps the earliest scientific terms used were *dipsomania* and *narcomania*; these labels were applied respectively to alcoholics and users of illegal drugs. Subsequently, the term *addiction* was invoked, whose precise meaning derives from the Latin for "given over," as in one person awarded to another as a slave. Thus, the perception of the drug user transformed from that of a person engaging in excess ("mania") to that of a person held in bondage to the substance; indeed, the locus of causality also changed from that of an internal to that of an external cause of the person's problem. Along with a diminution of responsibility ascribed to the individual, there has also been a parallel dilution of the definition of the disorder; originally, *addiction* or *dependence* specified an individual who needed the drug to prevent adverse and possibly life-threatening consequences from withdrawal. Contemporary use of the term *dependence* is more broadly applied to mean a psychological need without necessarily a physiological need (American Psychiatric Association, 1987).

The most commonly used and widely accepted taxonomic system is based on criteria advanced by the American Psychiatric Association. These criteria have undergone several dramatic revisions, perhaps reflecting the most fundamental problem with this system: It is based more on consensual decision making than on empirical research. Currently, the third revised edition of the *Diagnostic and Statistical Manual of Mental Disorders* (*DSM–III–R*; American Psychiatric Association, 1987) is standard; however, the *DSM–IV* looms on the horizon. The *DSM–IV*, although still largely based on consensus, will be more refined than the *DSM–III–R* because of empirical research findings obtained in the past decade. The criteria for a diagnosis of substance abuse in all of the editions of the American Psychiatric Association criteria encompass an assortment of adverse social, physiological, psychological, and medical sequelae that have occurred singly and together within a specific time frame. From the standpoint of the present discussion, these criteria extend beyond the scope of health concerns in classifying individuals as having a "drug abuse" disorder, thus arguably exceeding the limits of medical authority and expertise. Therefore, in attempting to comprehensively characterize the disorder "drug abuse", we must draw upon the resources and skills of multiple professional disciplines, especially those of the behavioral sciences. Moreover, there is no single condition in the *DSM* that must be present to specify the disorder. There is also no underlying principle that relates in logical fashion substance abuse disorders to other psychiatric disturbances. Most important, however, as a medical diagnostic system, the *DSM* contains criteria that are irrelevant to health. These criticisms aside, as a prototypical classification system, it serves the important purpose of setting a threshold level of disturbance for advancing a diagnosis, recognizing that the diagnosis is an admixture of medical, psychological, and social criteria.

The importance of establishing a diagnostic threshold cannot be overemphasized. First, it explicitly prevents arbitrarily labeling a user of a substance as an abuser. Even a casual review of the literature reveals how commonly the terms *use* and *abuse* have been used interchangeably, thereby sustaining confusion and ambiguity with respect to terminology and contributing to persisting uncertainty about the characteristics of substance abusers. Furthermore, setting a threshold for "abuse" allows the delineation of specific consequences with respect to health status, measurable in terms of severity. This would be consistent with the focus of a medical diagnostic system. Unfortunately, this aspect of comprehensive diagnosis has been relatively ignored. For example, severity of "alcohol abuse" or "marijuana abuse" could be objectively determined by explicitly incorporating the magnitude of liver injury or bronchial-pulmonary injury as a component of the medical diagnosis, rather than using nonmedical criteria (e.g., work adjustment, family adjustment, etc.). Furthermore, although there is presumed to be a progression from use to abuse to dependence, this pathway is highly variable in the population and is typically nonlinear. That is, there is usually an unequal period of elapsed time between use and abuse and between abuse and dependence. For some individuals, and depending on the particular drug, a pattern of use may or may not progress further to a diagnosis of abuse. For other individuals, a very long period of use may occur, following which, rather late in life, a diagnosis of abuse can be applied. The most obvious case in point is the population of social drinkers, of whom a subset will increase their alcohol consumption so as to qualify for a diagnosis of abuse soon after retirement or widowhood. For other individuals, especially those for whom there is a familial history of alcoholism, the progression from alcohol use to a disorder of abuse occurs early in life and is much more rapid. Less is documented about the consumption patterns associated with other drugs (e.g., cocaine, heroin, etc.); however, it is a common clinical observation that many individuals use these substances without harmful consequence, whereas others progress to a threshold disorder of abuse, and of these, some progress further to a disorder of dependence. The transition from use to abuse to dependence, reflecting a progression of severity, is actually highly individualized and is invariably not a linear process.

Age of Drug Use Onset and Psychiatric Disorder

The initiation of psychoactive drug consumption may or may not lead to a criterion disorder of abuse. Public concern about both drug use and abuse has been primarily confined to drug use among youth. This is not surprising because adolescence is the time of disengaging from parental authority, and, under the increasing influence of peers, the youngster initiates "adult" behaviors, including sexual relationships, work, driving a car, and alcohol and tobacco use. For this reason, the adolescent period of development is particularly critical for ultimately shaping outcome in adulthood.

Age of drinking onset has been shown to be an important variable influencing the natural history of alcoholism. Although an extensive examination of this issue lies outside the purview of this discussion, the findings generally indicate that early onset of alcoholism is frequently associated with antisocial propensities and possibly also with a higher prevalence of childhood disturbances such as hyperactivity and neurotic behaviors (Alterman, Tarter, Baughman, Bober, & Fabian, 1985; Gomberg, 1982; Rosenberg & Buttsworth, 1969).

Less is known about drug abuse; however, some of the behavior traits linked to vulnerability to alcohol abuse have also been implicated in other substance abuse. Neurotic propensities, emotional instability, high behavioral activity level, and social deviance, for example, have been linked to an increased risk for substance abuse (Jessor & Jessor, 1977; Loney, 1988; Rathus, Fox, & Ortins, 1980). Significantly, virtually no systematic longitudinal research has been conducted to clarify the association between age of drug use onset and progression to a threshold psychiatric disorder of substance abuse.

In a series of 99 adults admitted for substance-abuse treatment at Western Psychiatric Institute and Clinic, we found that there were only modest differences between individuals who developed their substance abuse disorder before age 18 and those whose problem was first diagnosed after age 18. This age was used to dichotomize the sample because it classified the subjects according to whether drug abuse began in high school or later. All of the subjects were between 22 and 25 years old at the time of entry into the study.

Each subject was administered the Initial Evaluation Form (IEF; Mezzich, Dow, Munetz, & Zittler-Segal, 1986) to document the type and aggregation of psychiatric symptoms and to formulate a psychiatric diagnosis according to *DSM–III* criteria. The IEF is a semistructured interview that identifies and aggregates psychiatric symptoms, evaluates neurodevelopmental history, indexes social adjustment, and delineates health or medical problems that could contribute to or otherwise exacerbate emotional disturbances. As can be seen in Table 7.1, the early onset group had more school and legal problems. Table 7.2 presents the percentage of individuals in each group who manifested specific psychiatric symptoms. Only 3 of 64 variables discriminated the groups. Although the possibility remains that these differences are due to chance, it is also consistent with current understanding that the weight and appetite decrease in the older-onset group reflects concomitant psychopathology, particularly features of an affective disorder. The higher prevalence of acquired intellectual impairment is consistent with the higher injury risk concomitant with a developmentally based socialization disorder in the younger age onset

TABLE 7.1

Percentage of Subjects in Each Group With Personal and Social History Problems

Personal and social history	Age of onset of substance abuse		X^2
	Before 18 years (N = 55)	After 18 years (N = 44)	
Perinatal problems	5.4	0.0	2.47
Developmental delays	5.4	0.0	2.47
Broken family	64.0	55.0	0.83
Difficulties at school*	51.0	32.0	3.64
Behavioral problems in school***	76.3	32.0	19.74
Military difficulties	5.4	14.0	1.98
Unemployment	60.0	55.0	0.29
Marital disharmony	24.0	25.0	0.02
Arrests with convictions**	44.0	20.4	5.91
Lack of confidence**	38.0	16.0	5.97
Social isolation	35.0	32.0	0.002

$*p < .05.$ $**p < .01.$ $***p < .001.$

group. Overall, however, it is noteworthy that robust or striking group differences were not observed.

As shown in Table 7.3, age of onset was not associated with a differential prevalence of physical symptoms. Nor was there an association between ratings of levels of psychosocial stress and of adaptive functioning and age of onset of substance abuse. These findings suggest that associations between health status, stress, or quality of psychosocial adjustment and age at which a person is likely to qualify for a diagnosis of substance abuse, if these associations exist at all, are probably complex and mediated by a variety of other factors.

Thus, using objective criterion-level diagnoses to characterize substance abusers, it appears that there are greater psychosocial problems in individuals who have an early-age onset (i.e., a diagnosis that could be assigned for the first time before age 18). These problems appear to be related to behavioral adjustment, such as conforming to the law and performance in school, rather than to acute psychiatric disturbance per se. These preliminary findings point to the need for more systematic investigation using standard diagnostic criteria. From such study, *outcomes*, defined in terms of criterion-level diagnoses, can be classified with respect to their developmental antecedents in combination

TABLE 7.2

Percentage of Cases Reporting Symptoms According to Age of Onset of Drug Abuse

Psychiatric symptoms	Age of onset of substance abuse		X^2
	Before 18 years ($N = 55$)	After 18 years ($N = 44$)	
Hyposomnia	53.0	61.3	0.74
Hypersomnia	20.0	11.3	1.34
Appetite decreased*	38.1	64.0	6.33
Appetite increased	15.0	16.0	0.03
Weight decreased*	31.0	52.2	4.63
Weight increased	16.3	16.0	0.003
Libido decreased	11.0	16.0	0.53
Libido increased	4.0	5.0	0.05
Disturbed sexual performance	4.0	2.2	0.15
Abnormal sexual object	0.0	0.0	—
Sexual identity problem	7.2	5.0	0.31
Alcohol abuse	60.0	77.2	3.33
Other central nervous system depressant abuse	16.3	18.1	0.05
Use of other drugs	60.0	61.3	0.01
Violent behavior	20.0	30.0	1.21
Impulsivity	38.1	35.0	0.25
Other antisocial behavior	33.0	32.0	0.009
Hypersensitivity to criticism	31.40	32.0	0.009
Emotional distance	35.0	41.0	3.30
Eccentricity	13.0	2.2	3.59
Overly dramatic behavior	31.0	25.0	0.42
Self-centeredness	22.0	11.3	1.87
Instability in relations	42.0	39.0	0.10
Undue dependence on others	33.0	20.4	1.85
Intentional ineffectiveness	20.0	9.0	2.26
Undue perfectionism	5.4	11.3	1.14
Increased motor activity	31.0	36.0	0.32
Decreased motor activity	27.2	34.0	0.53
Social withdrawal	44.0	27.0	2.82
Self-neglect	31.0	30.0	0.02
Bizarre behavior	4.0	0.0	1.63
Hostility	27.2	20.4	0.61
Dissociative symptoms	2.0	0.0	0.80
Conversion symptoms	0.0	0.0	—
Thought disorganization	11.0	5.0	1.33
Slow speech thought	20.0	13.6	0.69
Speech pressure	9.0	11.3	0.13

(continued)

TABLE 7.2 *(Continued)*

Psychiatric symptoms	Age of onset of substance abuse		X²
	Before 18 years (*N* = 55)	After 18 years (*N* = 44)	
General anxiety	29.0	30.0	0.002
Panic attack	0.0	5.0	2.55
Situational anxiety	7.2	7.0	0.007
Depressed mood	69.0	68.0	0.009
Low self-esteem	60.0	66.0	0.36
Lability of mood	15.0	18.0	0.23
Elated mood	7.2	5.0	0.31
Incongruous affect	22.0	25.0	0.13
Suspiciousness	27.2	20.4	0.61
Somatic preoccupation	0.0	2.2	1.2
Suicidal indicators	51.0	59.0	0.66
Homicidal ideation	9.0	18.0	1.77
Homicidal behavior	7.2	7.0	0.007
Obsessive-compulsive behavior	5.4	5.0	0.04
Depersonalization	11.0	9.0	0.08
Schneiderian symptoms	9.0	2.2	1.99
Other auditory hallucinations	9.0	23.0	3.53
Visual hallucinations	9.0	7.0	0.16
Other hallucinations	2.0	2.2	0.02
Delusions of reference	9.0	5.0	0.76
Depressive delusions or hallucinations	5.4	2.2	0.63
Other delusions	4.0	5.0	0.05
Impaired sensory orientation	5.4	2.2	0.63
Acquired intellectual deficit	27.2	11.3	3.83
Developmental intellectual deficit	4.0	5.0	0.05
Poor concentration	45.4	48.0	0.05
Lack of insight	45.4	43.1	0.05

*$p < .05$.

with the patterning and change of psychiatric disorder across the life span. In this way, the natural history of substance abuse can be better comprehensively characterized.

In summary, in lieu of an empirically derived system of classification, the term *abuse* should be confined to cases in which a threshold diagnosis of psychoactive substance use disorder can be made according to *DSM–III–R* criteria. With the advent and

TABLE 7.3

Percentage of Cases Reporting Physical Symptoms in Early Onset and Late Substance-Abuse Groups

| Symptom | Age of onset | | X^2 |
	Before 18 years ($N = 55$)	After 18 years ($N = 44$)	
Respiratory	9.0	20.4	2.59
Cardiovascular	15.0	7.0	1.47
Gastro-intestinal	31.0	43.1	1.59
Genito-urinary	4.0	11.3	2.22
Endocrine	0.0	0.0	0.00
Neurological-muscular	11.0	18.1	1.06
Miscellaneous (joint, back or muscle pain, arthritis, anemia, bruising)	9.0	22.7	3.5

widespread adoption of structured interviews, such a diagnosis can be made reliably. Failure to adopt a uniform system of taxonomy invariably results in the inconsistent, arbitrary, and potentially capricious use of emotionally charged terms like *drug abuse*, thereby obscuring their meaning. Advancing criteria that are circumscribed by health injury created a reference point for involvement by both health service professionals and researchers. Hence, even though the current diagnostic system is beset with many problems, some of which were noted earlier, it is nonetheless the most consensually accepted method for diagnosing substance abuse.

Risk for Substance Abuse

Evidence accumulated during the past two decades indicates strongly that the risk for developing alcoholism is not the same for everyone in the population. Individuals who have a family history of alcoholism are at especially high risk for becoming alcoholic themselves (Cloninger, Bohman, & Sigvardsson, 1981). Behavioral problems such as a conduct disorder in childhood also augment the risk for subsequent development of alcoholism (McCord, McCord, & Gudeman, 1960; Robins, 1966). Less is known about the factors that predispose to drug abuse; however, recent findings suggest that both family history and childhood behavior problems are potent risk factors (Baumrind, 1985; Grove et al., 1990).

The observation that not all individuals are equally susceptible to a substance abuse disorder has led to an intensive search for vulnerability characteristics. A genetic predisposition appears important, although the biological mechanisms of gene expression remain unknown. At least with regard to alcoholism, the evidence suggests that the mode of inheritance is complex and that the susceptibility may be expressed phenotypically as numerous characteristics, involving neurochemical, neurophysiological, and behavioral processes (Tarter, Alterman, & Edwards, 1985). The vulnerability factors that may be associated with other types of drug abuse have not as yet received systematic study.

Figure 7.2 depicts a conceptual model for researching the etiology of and developmental pathways to a substance abuse outcome. A genetic predisposition, ranging from low to high, is hypothesized to be normally distributed in the population. Substance abuse, as a complex behavioral disorder, probably has its genetic basis rooted in the additive effects of many genes located on at least several chromosomes (Plomin, 1990). We emphasize that genetic susceptibility is neither a necessary nor a sufficient condition to

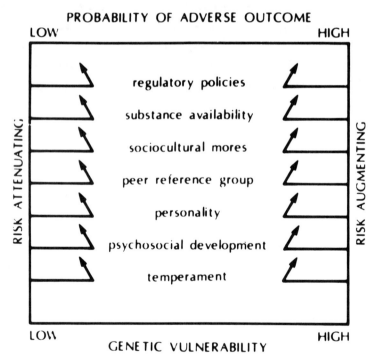

FIGURE 7.2   Dynamic lifetime interplay among risk-enhancing and risk-attenuating factors interacting with genetic predisposition for substance abuse outcome.

induce an adverse outcome. An individual with high genetic vulnerability (having many of the genes) can potentially be protected from a drug abuse outcome by a protective environment (e.g., low drug availability, cultural sanctions, strong social support, etc.), whereas a person with low genetic susceptibility may succumb to such an outcome where drug exposure is high, access to drugs is easy, and the social environment is facilitative. As can be seen in Figure 7.2, a drug-abuse outcome can theoretically occur at any stage in life, contingent on the dynamic interplay among genetic and environmental factors. Genetic factors should not be viewed as operating only between conception and birth. For example, depressive disorders commonly (although not always) have their onset in adulthood. Because depression often precedes the use of drugs and alcohol, and has a genetic contribution, the onset of psychoactive drug use may reflect genetic factors operating in adulthood. In the same vein, environmental challenges that the person can surmount at one stage of life may be inordinately stressful at another. Thus, the risks for a drug-abuse outcome must be considered in the specific framework of unique and specific factors occurring throughout life.

Furthermore, not only does the individual predisposed to drug abuse react to environmental contingencies, but such persons seek out specific environmental circumstances (e.g., high stimulus intensity, non-normative peers, etc.). The quality of these interactions additionally determines outcome throughout the life span. Therefore, there is some degree of risk for an adverse outcome at any stage in life. Depending on the changing contingencies involved in gene–environment interactions, the triggering of a drug abuse disorder at one stage in the life span (e.g., adolescence) may be different from the precipitating factors at another stage (e.g., late adulthood). Similarly, the factors that trigger drug-use initiation differ during the course of the life span; this consideration has important ramifications for the design of effective primary prevention programs.

Investigations directed toward elucidating the characteristics associated with the vulnerability to substance abuse have yielded an emerging body of intriguing but somewhat disparate findings. The strongest evidence characterizing the nature of the vulnerability derives from behavioral research; to date, no convincing evidence has been presented identifying a genetic or biological marker for alcoholism or substance abuse. For example, a conduct disorder in childhood is a well-established predisposing risk factor for subsequent substance abuse in men (Cadoret, Cain, & Grove, 1980; Lund & Landesman-Dwyer, 1978). Less is known about women; however, an affective disorder appears to be an especially prominent vulnerability characteristic for women (Turnbull &

Gomberg, 1988). A detailed review of the literature on substance abuse vulnerability lies outside of the scope of this discussion; however, it is important to emphasize that there are numerous predisposing behavioral features, although no single personality type characterizes children who subsequently become substance abusers.

Of the plethora of psychological characteristics that have been implicated as being associated with alcoholism vulnerability, high behavioral activity level probably merits the most interest. Among alcoholics, a stronger euphoric reinforcing effect concomitant with the first drinking experience is found where there is a large number of retrospectively reported childhood hyperactivity symptoms (Tarter, McBride, Buonpane, & Schneider, 1977). It was also found by Tarter (1982) that alcoholics who report hyperactivity in childhood have a higher prevalence of alcoholism in the family than do other alcoholics, and they also begin problem drinking earlier in life. High behavioral activity level has also been reported to be associated with substance abuse (Gittelman, Manuzza, Shenker, & Bonagura, 1985), although these results are less definitive than with alcoholism. These findings suggest that high behavioral activity level in childhood may be one vulnerability feature of alcoholism and substance abuse, particularly where there is a familial history of such a disorder. Among alcoholics, the number of childhood hyperactivity characteristics, combined with a score measuring severity of psychosocial immaturity, accounts for almost half of the variance on a scale measuring alcoholism severity (Tarter, 1982). These findings raise two important research issues. First, they raise the specter that alcoholism and other forms of substance abuse may have a common vulnerability. (There is mounting evidence that this may be the case, as will be discussed in the section Generalizibility of Substance Abuse.) Understanding drug abuse may be advanced more by learning about person–environment interactions than about person–type-of-drug (e.g., crack, marijuana) associations. Second, in addressing the issue of behavioral activity level, it is presumed that this is a trait that is normally distributed in the population. In its extreme manifestation, the person may qualify for a diagnostic disorder such as attention deficit disorder, but the trait need not be viewed as a dichotomous variable (e.g., normal–hyperactive), and, as discussed later, even subthreshold levels of elevated behavioral activity level, consisting of the components of high vigor and tempo, are relevant to elucidating the vulnerability to substance abuse.

Hyperactive boys are also more likely than other children to have a biological father who is alcoholic (Cantwell, 1972). An association between childhood hyperactivity and paternal alcoholism has been observed even when the child is reared by adoptive nonbiological parents (Morrison & Stewart, 1973).

Other lines of research further support an association between high behavioral activity level in childhood and subsequent alcohol abuse. Adolescents who were diagnosed as hyperactive as children are more likely to be problematically involved with alcohol (Mendelson, Johnson & Stewart, 1971); this association appears to be unrelated to academic performance or a learning disability (Blowin, Bornstein, & Trites, 1978). It appears, however, that the alcohol-abuse outcome, as noted previously, may be mediated by a conduct disorder in childhood. Also, fast behavioral tempo (Vaillant, 1983) has been reported to augment the risk for alcoholism in adulthood. Up to 20% of the population of hyperactive children may be at risk for developing alcoholism, indicating that this trait may be the single best biobehavioral predictor of an adverse outcome (Wood, Reimherr, Wender, & Johnson, 1976).

Children of alcoholics, who are at known increased risk to develop alcoholism score higher on scales of behavioral activity than do children of nonalcoholics (Tarter, Kabene, Escallier, Laird, & Jacob, 1990). However, at least in the conduct-disordered population, no significant differences in the number of hyperactivity features are found between those with familial alcoholism and those without such a family disorder (Tarter, Hegedus, & Gavaler, 1985). Both groups exhibit an equally high number of hyperactivity features. From the limited available prospective research, it appears that where an alcoholism outcome is manifest, the high activity level in childhood is often, but not necessarily, encompassed within a conduct disorder (Alterman & Tarter, 1986). Evidence from a variety of sources also indicates a particularly important role of high activity level in childhood as a risk factor for substance abuse, besides alcoholism (Loney, 1988).

Interestingly, youthful substance abusers in treatment also report high behavioral activity level (Tarter, Laird, Kabene, Bukstein, & Kaminer, 1990). As shown in Table 7.4, substance-abusing and normal control adolescents differ on most trait dimensions measured by the revised Dimensions of Temperament Scale (DOTS–R). Upon aggregating the DOTS–R scales using factor analysis, and correlating the factor scores with the scales of the Drug Use Screening Inventory (DUSI; Tarter, 1990), it is noteworthy that only Factor 3, behavioral activity regulation (consisting of the general activity, sleep activity, and flexibility–rigidity scales) correlates with drug-use severity and associated psychosocial problems. These correlations, summarized in Table 7.5, indicate that activity level explains 34% of the variance of the overall problem density index of the DUSI. In addition, severity of behavior disturbance, impaired health status, psychiatric disorder, work maladjustment, and disturbed peer relationships correlated significantly with behavioral dysregulation.

TABLE 7.4

Dimensions of Temperament (Revised) Scale Scores of Substance-Abusing Adolescents and Normal Controls

	Substance abusers		Controls		
	M	SD	M	SD	F
General activity**	20.13	5.11	16.33	4.82	11.08
Sleep activity	10.40	3.58	10.24	3.64	0.03
Approach/Withdrawal	18.43	4.54	19.43	3.34	1.25
Flexibility/Rigidity**	13.47	3.18	15.86	2.30	14.95
Mood*	20.83	5.16	23.88	3.70	9.29
Sleep rhythm	13.50	3.40	14.65	3.61	1.98
Eating rhythm*	12.47	4.29	14.47	3.67	4.87
Daily rhythm**	10.77	3.47	12.84	2.87	8.23
Task orientation**	17.63	5.74	20.86	4.12	8.40

$*p < .05.$ $**p < .01.$

TABLE 7.5

Association Between Dimensions of Temperament (Revised) Factor Scores and Absolute Problem Density Scores of the Drug Use Screening Inventory (DUSI)

DUSI scales	Factor 1 (Rhythms)	Factor 2 (Motivation)	Factor 3 (Behavioral dysregulation)
Substance use	.09	−.11	.55**
Behavior disturbance	.23	−.25	.54**
Health status	.17	−.16	−.40**
Psychiatric disorder	.24	−.30	.63***
Social skills	−.01	−.48**	.35
Family adjustment	−.08	.16	.26
School adjustment	−.15	.03	.33
Work adjustment	.19	−.06	.48**
Peer relationships	.02	.05	.50**
Leisure and recreation	−.19	−.09	.36*
Overall problem index	.07	−.16	.58**

$*p < 05.$ $**p < 01.$ $***p < .001.$

Whereas high behavioral activity has received increasing support as an important vulnerability trait underlying alcoholism risk, especially in men, there is also mounting evidence implicating an important role for other temperament traits. Tarter, Alterman, and Edwards (1985), in a comprehensive review of the literature, concluded that the temperament traits of high emotionality, low attention span and persistence, low sociability, and slow return to homeostasis (soothability) after stress are also features of alcoholism vulnerability. Specifically, these latter temperament traits are hypothesized to be characteristic of the Type 2 alcoholic, for whom drinking typically begins early in life, with accompanying antisocial behavior.

Clarifying the vulnerability to alcoholism and other types of psychoactive substance abuse from the perspective of temperament trait deviations has several heuristic implications. These include the following:

Gene–Environment Interaction

Temperament traits are highly heritable and their study thus affords the opportunity to elucidate vulnerability from a behavior–genetic perspective (Tarter, 1988). Behavior genetics is the study of individual variation of behavior in the population that is influenced by genetic factors; this perspective thus allows the integration of genetic methods and findings into the investigation of the psychological processes underlying substance abuse.

Developmental Sequencing

Temperament traits are detectable and measurable soon after birth. Hence, they are manifested by behaviors that are initially largely unconfounded by the social environment. Temperament traits can thus be viewed as the "building blocks" from which the complex behavioral repertoire consisting of personality traits and habits ultimately develops. These acquired behaviors can, in turn, be viewed as *emergent traits,* which themselves make up vulnerability features. An emergent trait is one in which the properties of the product are qualitatively different from its constituents (e.g., the water molecule has properties that are uniquely different from and not predicted by its constituent hydrogen and oxygen atoms). One developmental scenario of how substance vulnerability develops as a succession of emergent traits is as follows: Children whose temperament is characterized by high activity level are more likely to experience punitive rearing practices from their parents (Webster-Stratton & Eyberg, 1982); this inculcates and legitimizes aggressivity. Not surprisingly, aggressivity and, in the larger context, conduct disorder and delinquency have been frequently observed to presage alcoholism and are concomitant with and, indeed in many cases, are the cardinal feature of substance abusers. Another potential pathway is that children with high behavioral activity level, because of the interpersonal problems this behavior generates, are at risk not to have their emotional needs satisfied. By the combined influence of acquired negative affects and being "pushed" to the outer limits of normative social interaction, the stage is set for deviancy as an adaptive style or psychopathology to predispose to psychoactive drug use. Thus, complex behaviors that predispose to drug abuse can be understood as having their origins as temperament traits that, through the course of maturation, evolve into increasingly complex behavior patterns which in turn either promote or protect the person from adverse outcomes.

Prodromal to Psychopathology

Certain temperament traits, especially those of the "difficult child syndrome," presage psychopathology manifested by early adolescence (Thomas & Chess, 1984). Because adolescence is the time when drug use is typically initiated, it is potentially useful to clarify whether particular configurations of temperament traits are associated with early-age onset of drug abuse. Most important, however, the risk for maladjustment is dependent not only on temperament traits or on environmental conditions, but also on the interaction between these two sets of factors. As pointed out by Thomas and Chess (1984), the degree of "goodness of fit" is the primary determinant of the quality of adjustment in adolescence. Thus, another major advantage of investigating substance-abuse vulnerability from the standpoint of temperament is that it enables (as shown in Figure 7.2) the elucidation of the pathways to either a positive or a negative outcome in the context of the developmental process.

In summary, certain behavioral characteristics, particularly high activity level, appear to be associated with a heightened risk for substance abuse. In its most extreme manifestation, this trait may, but not necessarily, present as the clinical disorder of behavioral hyperactivity. These characteristics can be most parsimoniously understood at the outset in the perspective of a temperament trait that is normally distributed in the population. Although high activity is a lifelong trait, its manifestations do, however, change over time as it becomes embedded in an increasingly more complex behavior repertoire with maturation. There are several other important reasons that investigating substance abuse vulnerability from a temperament perspective is heuristic. Temperament traits arguably make up the fundamental units of behavioral analysis from which complex behaviors, including alcohol and drug use, develop. Interestingly, an analysis of temperament deviations in high-risk individuals, considered in conjunction with neuropsychological findings, suggests tentatively that the vulnerability may involve a dysfunction of neural systems lying along the frontal–midbrain neuroaxis (Tarter, Alterman, & Edwards, 1989). Although the data supporting this conclusion are far from definitive at this time, they are nonetheless quite intriguing because they accommodate the diversity of results accrued from studies of the cognitive, emotional, and motivational characteristics concomitant with substance-abuse vulnerability. In this regard, the investigation of temperament traits offers the additional advantage of accommodating behavior–genetic methods into a broad neurobehavioral paradigm.

Organism–Environment Interactions

Alcohol and drug use are not necessarily stable behaviors. On the basis of epidemiological research, it appears that the population of consumers of large quantities of alcohol is quite transitory. It also appears that substance use is to a great extent under environmental control. For example, a study by Robins, Helzer, and Davis (1975) demonstrated that most heroin users among servicemen in Vietnam returned to the United States without a need to sustain drug-use behavior. Although there was a higher prevalence of psychopathology in this population, substance use need not invariably imply a chronic, progressive, and irreversible condition. This conclusion is buttressed by numerous epidemiologic studies of alcohol-consumption patterns in the general population (Cahalan & Room, 1972). Nor is there a priori reason to assume that a pattern of use leads inevitably to a disorder of abuse, although such is obviously the case for a significant minority of individuals.

Little formal research has been conducted to elucidate the factors contributing to the initiation and cessation of substance use. Environmental influences, especially laws and regulatory policies, social mores, and peer-affiliation patterns, are well-known important factors influencing the level and pattern of drug consumption. The complex array of factors contributing to the cessation of substance use in people who qualify for a threshold diagnosis is, unfortunately, poorly understood. It appears, however, that changing either the individual or the environment may be effective in modifying substance-use behavior. As illustrated by Vaillant (1983), even mundane activities such as chewing candy or meditation can serve as replacement behaviors or alternative coping strategies for alcohol consumption in individuals who voluntarily terminate problem drinking. It is also well established that changing peer affiliation patterns can reduce alcohol or drug consumption. Whether the focus of inquiry is on clarifying the factors influencing drug-use initiation or on discontinuation, the model presented in Figure 7.2 provides a heuristic framework for analysis: The outcome status (e.g., use, abuse, abstinence) at any time in the life span depends on the dynamic interplay between organismic vulnerability and environmental contingencies. As discussed earlier, a geneticly influenced liability, expressed as temperament, is hypothesized to be normally distributed in the population. Individuals in the population with strong deviations in these traits, of which high behavioral activity level is perhaps the most important, are especially susceptible to an adverse outcome such as alcohol or drug abuse. This outcome depends, however, as depicted in Figure 7.2, on the cumulative developmental experiences of the child such that, through continued interaction with environmental contingencies, the behavioral repertoire becomes increasingly complex and dispositionally stable. As a youngster and later on as an adult, the behavioral disposition defines the magnitude of vulnerability, which, depending on risks in the environment, determines the likelihood of an adverse outcome.

Conceptualizing outcome, either drug abuse or sobriety, within the perspective of a dynamic and lifetime interaction between organismic and environmental factors has several important ramifications:

1. The model explicitly asserts that the genetic (as well as nongenetic) predisposition changes over time. For example, certain genes may be activated at different phases during the life span; hence, how the organism reacts to a stimulus (e.g., a stressor) may be different at various times in life.

2. The model provides a basis for understanding the differential rate of progression from drug initiation to drug abuse among individuals in the population. Conversely, the model affords a framework for understanding why most users never qualify for a diagnosis of abuse.

3. The model is compatible with emerging findings indicating that there is no invariant pattern of progression from substance use to abuse. Rather, there are myriad pathways to this outcome, with each route reflecting genetic individuality, an idiosyncratic developmental history, and the person's unique micro- and macroenvironments. Thus, it is not surprising that attempts to identify subtypes of alcohol or drug abusers have been largely unsuccessful, as aptly illustrated by the substantial heterogeneity within each putative subtype reported and by the lack of consistent replication of reported subtypes across studies.

4. The model implies that every individual in the population is theoretically at risk for an adverse outcome. Risk status is, however, changeable contingent on changes in either the organism the environment.

In summary, the complexity of variables notwithstanding, the etiology of drug abuse is amenable to empirical analysis. Whereas the multifactorial basis of drug abuse is universally recognized, it is nonetheless an unfortunate state of affairs that current research is mostly restricted to characterizing either the nature of the organismic vulnerability or the characteristics of the environment. Research focusing on the interactions between the organismic susceptibility (diathesis) and environmental stressors is urgently needed to advance our understanding of the initiation of drug-use behavior and the development of a threshold diagnosis of drug abuse.

Generalizability of Substance Abuse

With the advent and widespread acceptance of disease models of addiction, there has been the implicit assumption that each disease (i.e., type of addiction) has a specific etiology. This belief ultimately hinges on the assumption that a specific neuronal receptor for each drug determines the eventual addiction. However, various substance-abuse disorders aggregate within families, and polydrug abuse is increasingly typical of the substance-using population. Thus, it is reasonable to conjecture that drug abuse may merely be the ramification of a generalized behavioral disposition. Substantial research has shown that alcohol and substance abuse can also be comorbid with virtually any psychiatric disorder.

It is also not uncommon to observe individuals who, after terminating longstanding use of one drug, initiate the use of another. Furthermore, in the current polypharmacy era, exclusive use of only one drug is the exception rather than the rule. Moreover, no vulnerability features have been identified that specifically portend the eventual use of any particular drug. Finally, there is no substantive support for the notion that heroin, cocaine, alcohol or marijuana "breeds true" across generations. Instead, the available evidence suggests that the liability is not to a specific type of drug abuse but, rather, to a predisposition to any type of drug abuse, with the particular addictive substance being determined by availability, cost, social acceptability, symbolic meaning, and expected effects.

Extending this line of discussion, it is also intriguing to speculate whether the vulnerability to substance abuse is distinctive from other behaviors of excess that have potentially harmful health consequences. For example, there is the question of the extent to which the temperament trait deviations described earlier also make up the vulnerability to other adverse outcomes that are, in certain circumstances, also distinguished by poor behavioral self-regulation, as indicated by their compulsivity and all-encompassing personal involvement. Examples of such behaviors include gambling, bulimia, sunbathing, and sex with multiple partners. In effect, these types of behaviors may reflect a common vulnerability and may be topologically different only because of unique socialization experience, exposure to the opportunity for the particular outcome, and unique environmental contingencies. Insofar as these other disorders of behavioral dysregulation aggregate with alcohol and drug abuse, it is plausible to hypothesize a common diathesis or predisposition. The common clinical observation that individuals exhibiting one type of excessive behavior acquire other such disorders, and do so in a rapidly progressive fashion, suggests that there may be a common underlying vulnerability (Mule, 1981; Orford, 1985; Peele, 1985).

The notion that a disorder of behavioral self-regulation denotes a common vulnerability for a variety of outcomes, all sharing the cardinal features of behavioral excess and health disturbance, has several interesting ramifications:

1. In the organism–environment interaction model described in Figure 7.2, certain topologically dissimilar behaviors (or psychopathology) may be fundamentally interconnected. This observation could yield a taxonomy of disorder that has an empirical basis and a systematic framework; this is in contrast with the array of disparate categories in contemporary psychiatric classification systems such as *DSM–III–R* or the World Health Organization *International Classification of Diseases.*
2. Behavioral self-regulation has been extensively studied from both psychophysiological and neuropsychological perspectives. These perspectives emphasize the roles of arousal and cognition, respectively. From the neuropsychological perspective, self-regulation is subserved by the executive cognitive functions that are anatomically represented in the anterior region of the frontal lobes. The processes encompassed by the executive function include the abilities to plan strategies of goal-directed behavior, to sustain, through ongoing monitoring, goal persistence, and to flexibly respond to changing demands through the use of feedback information in modifying the behavioral course to its termination. Importantly, these integrated cognitive–motivational processes also entail matching organismic activation to meet environmental conditions or demands. A failure to exercise these capacities

results in a variety of cognitive, motivational, and emotional disturbances. It is note-worthy that a dysfunction of neural systems lying along an axis connecting the anterior and midbrain regions has been implicated as underlying the vulnerability to substance abuse (Tarter et al., 1989).

3. Because of the maladaptive behavioral consequences of an incapacity for self-regulation, the individual is hypothesized to be motivated to attempt strategies that can potentially optimize behavior. By manipulating arousal, either pharmacologically or through control of stimulus input, the person may achieve the reinforcing effects of homeostasis. Hence, drugs may not be consumed merely to stimulate or to tranquilize but rather to achieve a stable optimal arousal state. That is to say, the fundamental disorder is hypothesized to consist of a variable and suddenly changing arousal state; hence, psychoactive drugs afford the opportunity to achieve stability or homeostasis. Perhaps for this reason, such drugs may have far greater reinforcing properties for such individuals. Support for this notion is derived from the observation that alcohol is stress dampening in high-risk individuals (Levenson, Oyama, & Merk, 1987; Sher and Levenson, 1982). Moreover, the observation that amphetamines, as well as other stimulants (e.g., nicotine, caffeine), are quite commonly used to excess by alcoholics suggests that the desired effect is not simply to achieve activation or sedation, but rather is directed to achieve a physiological state that is stable or optimal to the environmental context. Furthermore, certain behavioral manipulations are especially capable of optimizing arousal level as well. For example, sensation-seeking behavior which is common among substance abusers has the effect of bolstering activation. Thus, augmenting and attenuating activation, either pharmacologically or behaviorally, is especially reinforcing if stability in activation level is achieved.

In summary, there is mounting evidence indicating that the different types of substance abuse do not represent specific or discrete taxonomic entities. Although the differential neuropharmacological properties of drugs having addictive liability are important determinants of the rate at which dependence may occur, there is no definitive evidence indicating that individuals who habitually and preferentially use one substance are fundamentally different from those who use another. The addictive liability of drugs most likely depends most on their concentration and the speed by which they can be transported to the brain to exercise their reinforcing effects. Not surprisingly, nicotine and crack cocaine are highly addictive, whereas caffeine and alcohol are less addictive. In terms of this discussion, however, these disorders of excess do not appear to differ from each other beyond their superficial behavioral topology. It is plausible, therefore, to conjecture that there is a common vulnerability underlying these outcomes, of which the cardinal feature is a disorder of behavioral self-regulation. Reviews of the evidence supporting the hypothesis of such a disorder have been published elsewhere (Tarter, Alterman, & Edwards, 1985; Tarter & Edwards, 1988). For now, suffice it to say that, although not conclusive, this interpretation of the available evidence can most parsimoniously account for the variety of empirical findings reported to date. Thus, although the evidence favors a generalized vulnerability, the factors that determine specific drug preference, although important, are probably best understood in the framework of social learning, sociocultural influence, and prevailing regulatory policies. Orford (1985), in a very thoughtful analysis of this issue, identified a number of key psychological factors that characterize the individual's involvement with all drugs having abuse liability: These factors are a strong inclination to repetitive use, low restraint, and strong attachment to the substance. Beyond these general shared features, and recognizing both biological individuality and pharmacological specificity, there appears to be little, if any, evidence suggesting that abusers of one substance are uniquely different from abusers of other substances.

Implications for Research and Practice

Several conclusions are worth reiterating from the previous discussion. First, there is substantial interindividual variability in the population with respect to the susceptibility to developing a drug-abuse disorder. Second, for both practical and theoretical reasons, it is essential that a criterion threshold be established to define a substance-abuse disorder. For reasons of convenience and in light of its consensus use, we propose *DSM–III–R* criteria as a basis for characterizing the population of individuals labeled as substance abusers. Third, there is emerging evidence indicating that a substance-abuse disorder is only one of a number of possible outcomes that are highly intercorrelated and that often aggregate in the same individual, as well as in families. These disorders share the common characteristic of behavioral excessivity; however, the extent to which they have shared and differing vulnerability features, ranging from genetic predisposition to biochemical and behavioral predispositions, is unclear. And fourth, there is emerging evidence indicating that temperament traits may serve as a very useful vehicle for understanding the basis of both biological and behavioral individuality that predisposes to a substance-abuse outcome. As discussed earlier, individuals who are at high risk, as well as already-affected young substance abusers, demonstrate marked deviations on certain specific temperament dimensions.

Against this background, it is intriguing to note that a number of as yet untried but nonetheless heuristic prevention and treatment interventions merit consideration. With respect to prevention, these efforts have not yet been directed to selected individuals at known high risk. Rather, preventions are invariably directed to the population at large despite the fact that only a small number of individuals will ever go on to develop a substance abuse disorder. It would appear that a more cost-efficient approach would be to target preventions to those individuals who are at known high risk. Also with respect to prevention, as well as to treatment intervention, procedures have not been applied that are specifically targeted to the known aspects of drug abuse etiology. Interventions tend to be primarily confined to values clarification and typically contained within an educational program aimed at major life-style changes, such as the traditional 12-step Alcoholics Anonymous programs. Although we do not wish to minimize these latter approaches, it is important to emphasize that they are not integrally linked to an understanding of the etiology of substance abuse. It would appear that the application of procedures that address the courses of substance abuse would be effective, at least as adjuncts to traditional modes of intervention. In this regard, even though they are considered as an anathema to present clinical practice in most institutions, pharmacotherapeutic procedures should not be dismissed. As a case in point, because high activity level was discussed in this chapter as a precursor to drug abuse, it is interesting to note that hyperactive boys who are unmedicated report more instances of drunken driving, as well as more severe legal involvement, as a result of their drug use (Loney, 1988). The point is that both the prevention and the treatment of drug abuse may be substantially augmented through a better understanding of the etiological determinants considered from a biopsychological perspective and within a developmental framework.

There is substantial individuality with respect to the causes of substance abuse. This was discussed earlier with respect to the degree to which vulnerability interacts in highly idiosyncratic fashion with the plethora of environmental variables to culminate in the outcome of substance abuse. Individuals who qualify for a diagnosis of substance abuse make up an extraordinarily heterogeneous population with respect both to the pathway to this outcome and to their clinical presentation. Hence, it is not feasible to consider this population as a homogeneous entity or to even attempt to derive clear and mutually exclusive subgroups.

A great gap exists in our understanding of why some individuals can sustain a long-term pattern of drug use without qualifying for a diagnosis of abuse, whereas others rapidly progress to a diagnosable condition. Factors such as family history, magnitude of childhood disturbance, drug availability and offer rates, personality disturbance, and peer affiliation patterns, as well as a myriad of other factors, undoubtedly interact synergistically to promote or protect the person from developing a criterion-level substance abuse disorder. What factors separate those individuals who culminate in a threshold disorder from those who do not is a prime question in need of research. From such investigations it may be possible to identify the factors that place certain individuals at high risk, which in turn can enable the application of prevention and treatment strategies targeted to the specific risk characteristics.

In promoting a conceptual model for a better understanding of the development of substance abuse, we proposed a developmental framework. It is implicitly implied that a substance-abuse outcome does not merely happen suddenly but rather, as a process, is the culmination of an ongoing series of adaptational changes occurring in the individual throughout the life span. For example, prior to the onset of drug abuse, the most salient disturbance present, may be a conduct disorder or an affective disturbance. Following substance abuse, a variety of disorders can subsequently emerge and remain present, even if the drug abuse were to spontaneously abate. The point is that substance abuse is not an absolute end point but rather may be an intermediary outcome that, in addition to having shared characteristics with other outcomes, may simply precede or emerge after other disorders. Substance abuse is overrepresented in virtually every major psychiatric disorder, compared with the general population. Therefore, among children and adults who have a psychiatric disorder, it is important to recognize that a substance-abuse outcome may succeed their present disturbance even if it is effectively treated. Although this latter point is admittedly conjectural, there is a strong indication in the literature that a substance abuse disorder can occur in parallel, as well as successively, with other psychiatric disorders.

Finally, the discussion in this chapter has important ramifications for health and social policy. Drugs having addictive liability are omnipresent in society. For example, in 1986, over 81 million prescriptions for benzodiazepenes were issued. Considering all of the other types of drugs that are readily available through either legal or illegal means, it is an incontrovertible fact that contemporary society is saturated with drugs that have abuse potential. Given the fact that the lifetime prevalence of at least initial experimentation with such drugs is close to 100%, it would appear that prevention efforts directed to reducing this number is not as viable as efforts directed to identifying and helping individuals who are at known high risk for a diagnosable disorder of abuse or dependence. On the basis of familial history, behavioral pattern, and psychopathology, individuals who are at risk to develop a threshold-level substance abuse disorder can be identified. It would thus appear to be economically advantageous to develop health and behavioral intervention programs that are directed specifically to this high-risk population.

References

Alterman, A., Tarter, R., Baughman, T., Bober, R., & Fabian, S. (1985). Differentiation of alcoholics high and low in childhood hyperactivity. *Drug and Alcohol Dependence, 15*, 111–121.

Alterman, A., & Tarter, R. (1986). An examination of selected typologies: Hyperactivity, familial and antisocial alcoholism. In M. Galanter (Ed.), *Recent developments in alcoholism* (Vol. 4, pp. 169–189). New York: Plenum Press.

American Psychiatric Association. (1987). *Diagnostic and statistical manual of mental disorders* (3rd ed., rev.). Washington, DC: Author.

Baumrind, D. (1985). Familial antecedents of adolescent drug use: A developmental perspective. In C. Jones & R. Battjes (Eds.), *Etiology of drug abuse: Implications for prevention* (Research Monograph No. 56, pp. 13–44). Rockville, MD: National Institute of Drug Abuse.

Blowin, A., Bornstein, R., & Trites, R. (1978). Teenage alcohol use among hyperactive children: A five year follow-up study. *Journal of Pediatric Psychology, 3*, 188–194.

Cadoret, R., Cain, C., & Grove, W. (1980). Development of alcoholism in adoptees raised apart from alcoholic biologic relations. *Archives of General Psychiatry, 37*, 561–563.

Cahalan, D., & Room R. (1972). Problem drinking among American men aged 21–59. *American Journal of Public Health, 62*, 1473–1482.

Cantwell, D. (1972). Psychiatric illness in the families of hyperactive children. *Archives of General Psychiatry, 27*, 414–417.

Cloninger, C., Bohman, M., & Sigvardsson, S. (1981). Inheritance of alcohol abuse: Cross fostering analyses of adopted men. *Archives of General Psychiatry, 38*, 861–868.

Gittelman, R., Manuzza, S., Shenker, R., & Bonagura, N. (1985). Hyperactive boys almost grown up. *Archives of General Psychiatry, 42*, 937–947.

Gomberg, E. (1982). The young male alcoholic: A pilot study. *Journal of Studies on Alcohol, 43*, 683–701.

Grove, W., Eckert, E., Heston, L., Bouchard, T., Segal, N., & Lykken, D. (1990). Heritability of substance abuse and antisocial behavior: A study of monozygotic twins reared apart. *Biological Pyschiatry, 27*, 1293–1304.

Jessor, R., & Jessor, S. (1977). *Problem behavior and psychosocial development: A longitudinal study of youth.* San Diego, CA: Academic Press.

Levenson, R., Oyama, O., & Merk, P. (1987). Greater reinforcement from alcohol for those at risk: Parental risk, personality risk, and sex. *Journal of Abnormal Psychology, 96,* 242–253.

Loney, J. (1988). Substance abuse in adolescents: Diagnostic issues derived from studies of attention deficit disorder with hyperactivity. In E. Rahdert & J. Grabowski (Eds.), *Adolescent drug abuse: Analyses of treatment research* (NIDA Research Monograph No. 77, pp. 19–26). Washington, DC: U.S. Department of Health and Human Services.

Lund, C., & Landesman-Dwyer, S. (1978). Pre-delinquent and disturbed adolescents: The role of parental alcoholism. In M. Galanter (Ed.), *Currents in alcoholism* (Vol. 5, pp. 339–345). New York: Grune & Stratton.

McCord, W., McCord, J., & Gudeman, J. (1960). *Origins of alcoholism.* Stanford, CA: Stanford University Press.

Mendelson, W., Johnson, N., & Stewart, M. (1971). Hyperactive children as teenagers: A follow-up study. *Journal of Nervous and Mental Disease, 15,* 273–279.

Mezzich, J., Dow, J., Munetz, M., & Zittler-Segal, M. (1986). Computerized initial and discharge evaluations. In J. Mezzich (Ed.), *Clinical care and information systems in psychiatry.* Washington, DC: American Psychiatric Press.

Morrison, J., & Stewart, M. (1973). The psychiatric status of the legal families of adopted hyperactive children. *Archives of General Psychiatry, 28,* 888–890.

Mule, S. (Ed.). (1981). *Behavior in excess: An examination of the volitional disorders.* New York: Free Press.

Orford, J. (1985). *Excessive appetites: A psychological view of the addictions.* New York: Wiley.

Peele, S. (1985). *The meaning of addiction: Compulsive experience and its interpretation* (pp. 1–203). Lexington, MA: Lexington Books.

Plomin, R. (1990). The role of inheritance in behavior. *Science, 248,* 183–188.

Rathus, S., Fox, J., & Ortins, J. (1980). MacAndrew scale as a measure of substance abuse and delinquency among adolescents. *Journal of Studies on Alcohol, 36,* 579–583.

Robins, L. (1966). *Deviant children grown up: A sociological and psychiatric study of sociopathic personality.* Baltimore: Williams & Wilkins.

Robins, L., Helzer, J., & Davis, D. (1975). Narcotic use in Southeast Asia and afterward. *Archives of General Psychiatry, 32,* 955–961.

Rosenberg, C., & Buttsworth, F. (1969). Anxiety in alcoholics. *Quarterly Journal of Studies on Alcohol, 30,* 729–732.

Sher, K., & Levenson, R. (1982). Risk for alcoholism and individual differences in the stress response dampening effect of alcohol. *Journal of Abnormal Psychology, 91,* 350–367.

Tarter, R. (1982). Psychosocial history, minimal brain dysfunction and differential drinking patterns of male alcoholics. *Journal of Clinical Psychology, 38,* 867–873.

Tarter, R. (1988). Are there inherited behavioral traits which predispose to substance abuse? *Journal of Consulting and Clinical Psychology, 56,* 189–196.

Tarter, R. (1990). Evaluation and treatment of adolescent substance abuse: A decision tree method. *American Journal of Drug and Alcohol Abuse, 16,* 1–46.

Tarter, R., Alterman, A., & Edwards, K. (1985). Vulnerability to alcoholism in men: A behavior–genetic perspective. *Journal of Studies on Alcohol, 46*, 329–356.

Tarter, R., Alterman, A., & Edwards, K. (1989). Neurobehavioral theory of alcoholism etiology. In C. Chaudron and D. Wilkinson (Eds.), *Theories of alcoholism.* Toronto: Addiction Research Foundation.

Tarter, R., & Edwards, K. (1988). Psychological factors associated with the risk for alcoholism. *Alcoholism: Clinical and Experimental Research, 12*, 471–480.

Tarter, R., Hegedus, A., & Gavaler, J. (1985). Hyperactivity in sons of alcoholics. *Journal of Studies on Alcohol, 46*, 259–261.

Tarter, R., Kabene, M., Escallier, E., Laird, S., & Jacob, T. (1990). Temperament deviations and risk for alcoholism. *Alcoholism: Clinical and Experimental Research, 14*, 380–382.

Tarter, R., Laird, S., Kabene, M., Bukstein, O., & Kaminer, Y. (1990). Drug abuse severity in adolescents is associated with magnitude of deviation in temperament traits. *British Journal of Addiction, 85*, 1501–1504.

Tarter, R., McBride, H., Buonpane, N., & Schneider, D. (1977). Differentiation of alcoholics: Childhood history of minimal brain dysfunction, family history, and drinking pattern. *Archives of General Psychiatry, 34*, 761–768.

Thomas, A., & Chess, S. (1984). Genesis and evolution of behavior disorder: From infancy to early adult life. *American Journal of Psychiatry, 140*, 1–9.

Turnbull, J., & Gomberg, E. (1988). Impact of depressive symptomatology and alcohol problems in women. *Alcoholism: Clinical and Experimental Research, 12*, 374–381.

Vaillant, G. (1983). *The natural history of alcoholism.* Cambridge, MA: Harvard University Press.

Webster-Stratton, C., & Eyberg, S. (1982). Child temperament: Relationship with child behavior problems and parent–child interactions. *Journal of Clinical Child Psychology, 11*, 123–129.

Wood, D., Reimherr, F., Wender, P., & Johnson, G. (1976). Diagnosis and treatment of minimal brain dysfunction in adults. *Archives of General Psychiatry, 33*, 453–460.

CHAPTER 8

Affectivity: A Central Mechanism in the Development of Drug Dependence

Robert J. Pandina, Valerie Johnson, and Erich W. Labouvie

R ecent advances in affectivity research have potentially special significance for theories of vulnerability to drug abuse. Specifically, it is our view that individuals who are subjected to biological, psychological, or socioenvironmental conditions conducive to the development of an emotional profile characterized by pervasive and persistent negative affectivity and energized by prolonged and heightened arousability are especially vulnerable to transit from minimal levels of drug use associated with "casual" or "experimental" use to more intensive and problematic use associated with "abuse." In this chapter, we examine the salience of two central constructs of affectivity—negative affectivity and arousability—for understanding vulnerability to problematic drug-using behaviors subsumed in the general construct of drug abuse. First, we briefly review the reemergence of affectivity as a key mechanism in the shaping and control of behavior, with an emphasis on those elements of special import for understanding the development of

This research was supported by grants from the National Institute on Drug Abuse (DA-03395) and the National Institute on Alcohol Abuse and Alcoholism (AA-05823).

drug abuse. Next, we explore the theoretical linkage among negative affectivity, arousability, and vulnerability to drug abuse. Finally, we present empirical evidence from our ongoing longitudinal study of drug-abuse vulnerability (Pandina, Labouvie, and White, 1984) that, we believe, demonstrates the importance and centrality of incorporating recent formulations regarding affectivity into etiological models of vulnerability.

Affectivity and Behavioral Control

The roles of feelings, emotions, and emotional regulation in the development and direction of human behavior has been a source of debate in psychology since its inception as a discipline (James, 1890; Lange & James, 1922). With the ascendence of functionalism and its logical extension, behaviorism, the centrality and salience of affectivity and related concepts in accounting for the direction and strength of human behavior were seriously challenged (Brown & Farber, 1951; Lazarus, 1968, 1982). In the face of such a strong challenge and in light of the hold that behaviorism gained on theoretical and applied psychology, the study of affectivity lost popularity as a subject of empirical psychological study (Lazarus, 1984). In fact, several influential learning theorists have not included the concept in their formulations (e.g., Bandura, 1977, 1989).

Recently, however, affectivity and its role in shaping and controlling behavior have again begun to receive serious consideration (Tomkins, 1962, 1982; Zajonc, 1984). Current investigations of affectivity have attempted to answer previously cited deficiencies by addressing central concerns such as the identification of possible physiological substrata (Blanchard & Blanchard, 1988; Heilman & Satz, 1983; Leventhal & Tomarken, 1986; Olds, 1962), the specification of potential structures for "emotional space" (i.e., the identification of basic emotions and their interrelationships; Frijda, 1986, 1988; Izard, 1977; Plutchik, 1980; Watson & Tellegen, 1985), the delineation of developmental processes and sequences in the emergence of emotions (Dodge, 1989; Ford & Ford, 1987), and the relationship between emotions and other fundamental psychological processes (e.g., cognitive abilities, social competencies; Blaney, 1986; Buck, 1985; Ford, 1987; Weiner, 1985). Included in the more recent investigations are studies of the impact of affect development on a wide range of behavioral processes and outcomes (Emmons, 1986; Higgins, 1987; Kopp, 1989; Levenson, Aldwin, Bosse, & Spiro, 1988; Watson & Clark, 1984).

It is worthwhile to briefly review research in the area of affect structure in humans, which is especially relevant for understanding drug-use behaviors, particularly those that are used to characterize drug abuse, a construct that is itself multidimensional, as we shall discuss later.

Watson and Clark (1984) and Watson and Tellegen (1985), in research aimed at achieving a consensus view of mood structure, suggested that affectivity may be partitioned into two independent dimensions, positive affectivity (PA) and negative affectivity (NA). These factors have been described as "descriptively bipolar but affectively unipolar dimensions" (Zevon & Tellegen, 1982, p. 112). Two weaker constructs, pleasantness–unpleasantness and strong engagement–disengagement (alternatively labeled as arousal) have also been identified but are viewed as less robust and as potentially embedded in the principal dimensions (Watson & Tellegen, 1985). Extensive empirical evidence, including a thorough meta-analysis by these investigators of a wide range of mood-related research, confirms the viability of their proposed structuring of mood space.

NA is seen as "a mood-dispositional dimension [that] reflects pervasive individual differences in negative emotionality and self-concept" (Watson & Clark, 1984, p. 465). Individuals high on the NA dimension tend to be distressed, upset, nervous, and tense even in the absence of overt external stressors. Such individuals tend to dwell on and amplify mistakes, frustrations, disappointments, threats, and, presumably, other conditions and circumstances that have the potential to evoke discrete uncomfortable emotional states such as fear, anger, disgust, and contempt. Watson and his colleagues have suggested that high-NA individuals are especially sensitive and hyperreactive to minor failures and the hassles of daily living. As a pervasive mood-dispositional dimension, it is likely that high NA is generalized to and carries across a wide range of life scenes and is relatively stable across life stages. This conceptualization of NA is consistent with, but broader than, other formulations of pervasive personality dimensions such as "neuroticism" or, more recently, "emotionality" (as proposed by Eysenck and Eysenck, 1975), as well as the even more narrowly defined construct of "trait anxiety" (Spielberger, Gorsuch, & Lushene, 1970).

Its character as a pervasive and stable mood-dispositional dimension of personal style suggests a potent role for NA as a mechanism that sets the tone for many, if not all, transactions of the individual, including those that are internal (either transient, e.g., thoughts, feelings, and urges, or more tonic, e.g., self-concept) and external (either transient, e.g., passing conversation, or more persistent, e.g., formal relationships such as marriage and occupation). In this regard, NA is a superordinate construct broader than a single personality trait in that it supercedes, interacts with, and provides a backdrop for many individual personality dimensions.

D. H. Ford (1987), like Watson and his colleagues, sees a central role for affect in directing human behavior. In his extensive living-systems analysis of human behavior, Ford (1987) views emotions as serving evaluative/regulatory and arousal functions. In its simplest form, the idea of the evaluative function posits that an internal or external event gains personal salience only if it is associated with some reasonably strong affect. Without affect, no event has personal relevance. Ford conceptualized arousal as a fundamental energizing principle in the living organism. In his view, somewhat in contrast with Watson's, arousal is a strong determinant of behavior. As a complex construct, arousal encompasses a variety of activation functions ranging from internally driven self-directed (i.e., "spontaneous") actions to those functions selectively responsive to the specific and time-limited demands of external environmental events.

We view arousability (AR) as a central but limited dimension of the broader arousal construct. AR is an enduring state of excitatory potential that may be evoked by internal (i.e., "spontaneous") and external (i.e., "reactive") cues. Consistent with Ford's theories, AR serves an essential energizing function for all emotions. Thus, AR is a pervasive behavioral disposition characterizing activation tendency generalized across a variety of circumstances and persisting over relatively long developmental periods. In this regard, AR exhibits properties similar to the mood-dispositional character of NA. In contrast with NA, AR is a bipolar construct in which descriptors such as "impulsive," "sensation seeking," "action prone," and "disinhibited" characterize the high-arousability pole. However, the nature of "arousal space" has not been as well studied as that of mood. As indicated earlier, Watson and his colleagues have identified an AR-like factor that is described as strong engagement–disengagement. This factor, they argue, may be reasonably subsumed under the broader PA–NA structure. In keeping with D. H. Ford (1987), we would suggest that this is an independent factor conceptually orthogonal to both PA and NA and of somewhat different character in that AR characterizes activation potential and is bipolar, whereas NA and PA characterize chiefly valence states and are unipolar. The orthogonal structure that we propose is compatible with the views of both Watson and Ford.

The origins of NA, PA, and arousal (and its critical subdimension, AR) are not fully specified in mood-structure formulations such as Watson's, summarized above. D. H. Ford (1987), however, did provide a speculative but thoughtful and well-documented account of the biological, psychological, and socioenvironmental conditions that could interact to generate, incorporate, and sustain any affectivity profile of a given individual. Consistent with Ford's notions, we believe that the NA–AR profile becomes established at the biological level, although the agency that incorporates and fixes this profile need not be solely biologic. Once established, it is reasonable to expect that a particular NA and AR profile would be manifested in a broad range of behaviors and would influence the development of functioning across many life domains throughout the life span. This would be in part due to the central role that affectivity plays in energizing and setting valences for behaviors of the organism. The influence and consequences of the persistently high NA–AR profile would be reflected in a wide range of probes that could be used to assess individual functioning.

Negative Affect, Arousability, and Drug Abuse

Interestingly, and importantly for theories of drug-abuse vulnerability, several of the key elements in the proposed structure of affectivity dovetail reasonably well with formulations regarding central-nervous-system (CNS) circuitry associated with the appreciation of positive and negative reinforcement, punishment, and, in the mechanisms that control approach, avoidance and escape behaviors. This critical CNS circuitry is the same "wetware" that is the target for many drugs with high abuse liability.

The careful delineation of CNS sites and mechanisms of actions of drugs of abuse is a major thrust in current psychopharmacological research. A significant portion of these findings suggests that at least loci, and perhaps mechanisms, of drug action are congruent with loci and potential mechanisms postulated to mediate more naturally occurring (that is, ecologically valid) affective experiences.[1] At the conceptual level, it has become commonplace to view drugs of abuse as potent inducers of positive, and reducers of negative, affect states through direct modulation of neural circuits that inherently subserve these natural functions.

Empirical validation of the exact CNS pathways and mechanisms that are affected by specific drugs has been more difficult. In an intriguing review, Wise and Bozarth (1987) suggest that a common CNS mechanism mediates the reinforcing potential of many psychotropic drugs with high addiction potential and that this is the same mechanism which mediates reinforcements derived from a wide range of ecologically relevant environmental stimuli. Neural units within the mesocortical dopaminergic fiber system

---

[1] *A second and complimentary focus of this research is the delineation of drug effects on cognitive functioning. This thrust has a longer history and, in that regard, is better established as a line of research. The interaction between drug-induced alterations in cognition and affect has begun to receive attention, although the research to date is limited. These two lines of research will not receive extensive treatment here.*

are suggested as the putative critical substrata. Wise and Bozarth (1987) suggested that this circuitry is particularly sensitive to the psychomotor stimulant action of drugs of abuse. Such action is homologous with approach behavior, which they view as the key benchmark of reinforcement. Furthermore, drugs as pharmacologically different as marijuana, alcohol, cocaine, and opiates have common properties of stimulation induction and promote approach behavior. Thus, drugs with high addiction potential may have the dual properties of general stimulation of neural circuits typically associated with approach (the arousal function of affectivity) and more specific stimulation of circuits associated with positive and negative reinforcement and, by extension, punishment (the evaluative–regulatory function of affectivity). Note that this formulation assumes that reinforcing and punishing events give rise to internal affective states encoded as neural events of at least transient (and potentially longer) duration.

Wise and Bozarth's (1987) observations show the power of drugs to induce affective change acutely. More speculative and controversial but equally intriguing is the possibility that drug-induced affective states and functioning change (especially when use is intensive and chronic) may persist for relatively long periods after detoxification (for example, cocaine: Chitwood, 1985; Post, 1975; alcohol: Schuckit, 1986; marijuana: Mendelson, 1983).

Given the nature of drug action as postulated here, we would expect that those individuals most likely to find drug intoxication attractive and desirable are those who are chronically in need of heightened levels of activation (or, alternatively, who are especially responsive to stimulation resulting from activation) and who can be characterized as chronically deprived of positive reinforcement. Furthermore, we would expect those who are positive-reinforcement deprived to be dominated by persistent and pervasive negative mood states. In our formulation, individuals whose reinforcement repertoire is dominated by negative reinforcement or punishments are viewed as reinforcement deprived. Note that the response repertoire of these individuals is dominated by avoidance and escape responses. This description is consistent with the high-AR–high-NA profile.

We speculate that such chronic "needy" states and accompanying negative mood states may be induced, maintained, and enhanced by a variety of biological, psychological, and environmental factors but, ultimately, are encoded and sustained at the biologic level. Furthermore, satisfaction of these needs and relief from negative mood states may, at least temporarily, be achieved by drug ingestion and the consequent intoxication, which serves to activate, at least temporarily, neural circuits associated with positive reinforcement and approach. Of course, there are other CNS circuits that may be affected, with less desirable results, from the view of the individual. However, these competing undesirable consequences may be viewed as minor side effects in the context of the high NA–AR affectivity profile.

Given the satisfying, albeit temporary, outcome of drug intoxication for the high-NA–AR-profiled individual, it is expected that use, once initiated, will persist across time, increase in intensity, and result in extensive consequences. In short, the high-NA–AR individual would be vulnerable to make the transition from casual or experimental use to drug abuse. This proposition assumes, of course, reasonably favorable conditions exposing the individual to use, such as drug availability, social supports for use, and so on.

Although the terms *intensive use, problem use*, and *drug abuse* have been used somewhat interchangeably in this chapter, we see the drug-abuse construct itself as multidimensional. No single benchmark can capture the complexity of the construct, especially when attempting to trace abuse patterns across the life span in the same individual or to compare individuals from markedly differing developmental periods. This complexity has been, and continues to be, a major study focus in the field of addictions (see Pandina, White, & Yorke, 1981; White, 1989; White & Labouvie, 1989, for more detailed discussion). For this reason, we typically use several indicators to characterize major components of the drug-abuse construct. It is expected that the high-NA–AR-profile vulnerability will be expressed across a range of drug-abuse indicators.

An Empirical Demonstration of the NA, AR, and Drug-Abuse Nexus

Elements of NA and AR are explicitly incorporated, or implicitly embedded, in a variety of important etiological perspectives of drug use, abuse, and dependency (e.g., see Lettieri, 1985; Lettieri, Sayers, & Pearson, 1980). These include, but are not limited to, theories emphasizing personal and social competence (e.g., Kandel, Davies, Karus, & Yamaguchi, 1986; Pandina, Labouvie, Johnson, & White, 1988, 1990); those using a coping-perspective framework in which affect-based regulation of behavior is especially important (e.g., Labouvie, 1986, 1987; Wills & Shiffman, 1985); those emphasizing more cognitive components of functioning, such as intentions, motivations and expectancies (e.g., Cox & Klinger, 1988; Marlatt, 1987); and those using more traditional personality-trait explanations (e.g., Cox, 1987) or general deviance theories (e.g., Jessor & Jessor, 1977; Kaplan, 1985). However, most theories have not reflected the magnitude of influence over the development of drug abuse that is implied in considering the potential influence of such pervasive dimensions as negative affectivity, as outlined in the conceptualization of Watson and his colleagues, and arousability, as we have proposed to extend D. H. Ford's (1987) use of the arousal construct.

The more limited role of emotionality in most theories is reflected, in part, by the limited indicators chosen to characterize affectivity and the limited role of affectivity as a mediating factor in drug-abuse vulnerability. Nevertheless, for these reasons, we propose that affectivity plays a central role in many of the mechanisms and constructs linked to drug-abuse vulnerability. Given that the high NA–AR profile may influence a wide range of developmental processes, it is reasonable that this profile may be embedded in a wide range of relevant constructs and that it may be expressed in many assessment measures.

In the empirical investigation detailed in the following sections, we intended to accomplish three objectives. First, we wanted to determine if an NA dimension (as well as other affectivity dimensions), as suggested by the work of Watson and his colleagues, and AR, as we have characterized it by extending the framework of Ford (1987), can be reliably identified across a wide range of theoretically relevant constructs representing several major life-functioning domains across relatively long developmental periods. The analysis will also permit an examination of the contributions of the NA, AR, and other affectivity dimensions to critical developmental processes purportedly related to various aspects of drug abuse. Second, we wished to examine the stability of affectivity dimensions across time. Recall that it is expected that persistence in the high NA–AR profile is an important determinant of vulnerability. In a sense, the persistent dimension represents a dynamic quality in the construct. Third, we wished to determine the relationship between affectivity and several key indicators of drug abuse, including use intensity, use motivations, and use-related problems and consequences. The use of multiple indicators is in keeping with the view that drug abuse is complexly dimensioned. In addition, we wanted to examine the possiblity that affectivity profiles may be related differentially to specific aspects of the drug-abuse construct.

Method

Design

The population from which this sample was initially drawn consisted of New Jersey households. However, subjects from five rural counties far from the test site were excluded because of difficulty in transporting participants to the test site and because fewer than 2% of the target population was believed to reside in these areas. The final sampling frame included 95% or more of the total number of households in the specified geographical area. Telephone numbers were randomly generated by weighing telephone exchanges by population density. Telephone interviewers used initial calls to identify households with one or more eligible New Jersey adolescents and to gather sociodemographic information. Eligibility was based on year of birth and the absence of a serious physical or mental handicap or a language difficulty. About 83% of all eligible subjects agreed to be called back, and were assigned to a field interviewer. Of this group, 46% agreed to participate in the study. Enrollment in the study was closed once required Age × Sex cell frequencies were filled, yielding a quota sample of 1,380 subjects.

Procedure

Following the initial telephone recruitment, field interviewers went to the subjects' homes to (a) provide detailed information about the study, (b) schedule on-site appointments, and (c) obtain preliminary information (including medical histories of the extended family). In the period from 1979 to 1981, adolescents were initially tested at the ages of 12, 15, or 18 (Time 1; T1). Ninety-five percent of these subjects (1,380) returned 3 years (Time 2; T2) and 6 years (Time 3; T3) later. Data used in this study are from T1 and T2 only, when subjects ranged in age from 12 to 21. On all testing occasions, each subject was assigned to a trained interviewer who individually administered a wide range of self-report questionnaires, behavioral tasks, and physiological measures. Testing sessions were self-paced and lasted about 6 hours. Subjects were assured of complete confidentiality of all responses (including to their parents).

A comparison of T1 substance-use rates between those subjects who were retested and those who dropped out showed no significant differences. (For more extensive details of methodological and theoretical considerations of this study, see Pandina et al., 1984).

Sample

The sample was 90% White, a somewhat higher proportion than the 84% of Whites in New Jersey (U.S. Bureau of the Census, 1981). Half of the subjects were Catholic, 30% were Protestant, 9% were Jewish, and the remaining 11% had another or no religion. The median income of the sample at T1, between $20,000 and $29,000, was also comparable to that of the entire state at that time. With regard to family composition at T1, 80% of subjects lived with both natural parents, 10% with a single parent, and the rest in other arrangements. Overall, these data suggest that the sample of participants is representative of adolescents living in a suburban–urban working and middle-class environment.

Although participants were volunteers, self-selection does not appear to have threatened the representativeness of the sample. Participants were similar to nonparticipants in demographic characteristics and in selected use behaviors sampled during the original telephone survey. In addition, the data on the prevalence of alcohol and drug use in our sample are comparable to national surveys using other methods of data collection (Johnston, O'Malley, & Bachman, 1988).

Of the 1,308 subjects who were tested at both points in time, 439 (12-year-olds at T1) were excluded from the analyses because they were not administered Zuckerman's (1979) Sensation Seeking Scale at age 12 and also because they exhibited little or no use of alcohol, marijuana, or other drugs at that age. The remaining subjects were used in the use-intensity analyses. In the examination of problems related to, and motivations for, use, only alcohol users ($N = 836$) and marijuana users ($N = 670$) were analyzed, because an individual had to be classified as a user to complete sections regarding consequences of, and motivations for, use. Individuals who were not classified as users at T1 but who were users by T2 were included in all appropriate analyses.

Data Collection

To maximize the reliability and validity of the self-report data, questionnaires were administered individually by a trained interviewer assigned to a participant for the length of the testing day. Participants were instructed not to put their names on any questionnaire and were repeatedly assured of the complete confidentiality of all data. Self-reports have been generally accepted as a reliable indicator of use behaviors (Rouse, Kozel, & Richards, 1985).

Measures of Affectivity and Arousability

A list of measures used to tap affective constructs is presented in Table 8.1. The Symptom Check List (SCL-90; Derogatis, 1977) is a self-report symptom inventory. Levels of psychological distress were measured, and the four subscales of Depression, Anxiety, Interpersonal Sensitivity, and Hostility were used.

A factor analysis of responses to 32 items asking "When you have a problem, how often do you ... ?" (5-point scale from *never* to *always*), fashioned along the lines of the

TABLE 8.1

Measures of Affectivity and Arousal

Johns Hopkins Symptom Checklist (SCL-90) subscales
  interpersonal sensitivity
  depression
  anxiety
  hostility
Use of emotional outbursts to deal with problems
Self-derogation (dumb, mean)
Stress due to lack of
  personal competence
  social competence
  self-acceptance
Self-esteem (smart, good person)
Personality Research Form (PRF-E) subscales
  Achievement Orientation
  Impulsivity
Hardiness (active, competitive, self-confident)
Zuckerman Sensation Seeking subscales
  Disinhibition
  Experience Seeking

Response Profile of the Coping Assessment Battery (Wills, 1985; Wills & Shiffman, 1985), yielded a 4-item measure of *use of emotional outbursts* to cope with problems ($\alpha = .58$).

A factor analysis of responses to 13 items asking "How often do you feel ... ?" (5-point scale) yielded two scores: *Self-esteem* is the sum of 4 items (e.g., "I am an important person," $\alpha = .73$), and *self-derogation* is the sum of 4 items (e.g., "I am dumb," $\alpha = .59$). A factor analysis of 15 items fashioned along the lines of self-rated attributions (Spence, Hemreich, & Stapp, 1975) yielded a 7-item measure of *hardiness* (e.g., *active, self-confident,* $\alpha = .73$).

Respondents were asked how much each of 47 possible stressors bothered them (4-point scale). These items included stress due to (a) lack of personal competence (e.g., "I am not in control of my life"; Rotter, 1966), (b) lack of self acceptance (e.g., "I am not good-looking"), and (c) lack of social competence (e.g., "Classmates don't like me").

A shortened version of Jackson's (1974) Personality Research Form was administered to participants. The 17 subscales were subjected to a factor analysis, and two of the second-order factors were used. *Impulsivity* comprises (low) cognitive structure, (low) harm avoidance, impulsivity, and play ($\alpha = .65$), and *achievement orientation* comprises achievement, dominance, endurance, and understanding ($\alpha = .63$).

Disinhibition and *experience-seeking* were measured by the subscales of the same names from the Zuckerman's (1979) Sensation Seeking Scale.

Measures of Use

A list of variables used to measure aspects of alcohol, marijuana, cocaine, and other drug use at each measurement point are presented in Table 8.2. The use of alcohol, marijuana, and cocaine was measured independently by combining the frequency of use during the past year (9-point scale), the quantity consumed on a typical occasion (10-point scale), and subjects' estimated frequencies of getting intoxicated (6-point scale). Overall drug use was measured by the sum scores of alcohol, marijuana, and cocaine use.

Respondents were also asked to indicate if they had experienced any of a set of 23 possible negative events because of their alcohol or marijuana use. The events were summed into *problem scores* for alcohol and marijuana, respectively (White & Labouvie, 1989). In addition, subjects were asked to check off, from a list of 45 reasons, their motivations for use of alcohol or marijuana. The *negative motivations* score represents the sum of 8 items (e.g., "to escape," $\alpha = .79$), and the *positive motivations* score that of 18 items (e.g., "to have fun," $\alpha = .83$).

Results

To develop affectivity subscales, we conducted a principal components analysis (*SAS Users Guide*, 1985). This analysis resulted in the identification of three distinct domains.

TABLE 8.2

Measures of Use

AU	alcohol quantity, frequency, often intoxicated
MU	marijuana quantity, frequency, often intoxicated
CU	cocaine quantity, frequency, often intoxicated
DU	all drug-use quantity, frequency, often intoxicated
APU	number of problems experienced because of alcohol use
MPU	number of problems experienced because of marijuana use
NAM	number of negative motivations for alcohol use
PAM	number of positive motivations for alcohol use
NMM	number of negative motivations for marijuana use
PMM	number of positive motivations for marijuana use

The eigenvalues and loadings for each of these domains are shown in Table 8.3. The first component, NA, comprises nine variables including interpersonal sensitivity, depression, anxiety, hostility, emotional outbursts, self-derogation, and lack of social and personal competence. Component 2, PA, contains three variables: self-esteem, achievement orientation, and hardiness. The final component, AR, comprises impulsivity, disinhibition, and experience seeking. Variables loading within each domain were summed into overall scores for NA, PA, and AR, respectively.

The intercorrelations among the affectivity and arousability constructs for the middle and oldest age cohorts at both points in time are shown in Table 8.4. Generally speaking, PA and NA appear to be moderately negatively correlated (range $r = -.19$ to $-.35$), whereas PA and AR are only somewhat positively related (range $r = .16$ to $.24$), as are NA and AR (range $r = .13$ to $.23$). Stability coefficients appeared highest for the oldest age cohort, indicating that affective attributes may tend to stabilize by the end of

TABLE 8.3

Principal Component Loadings and Eigenvalues: Time 1 (T1) and Time 2 (T2)

Construct	Loadings		Eigenvalues	
	T1	T2	T1	T2
I. Negative affectivity			4.3	4.3
Interpersonal sensitivity	.35	.33		
Depression	.37	.37		
Anxiety	.35	.35		
Hostility	.34	.36		
Emotional outbursts	.23	.24		
Self-derogation	.24	.25		
Lack of personal competence	.29	.30		
Lack of social competence	.24	.21		
Lack of self-acceptance	.22	.20		
II. Positive affectivity			1.8	1.7
Self-esteem	.46	.44		
Achievement orientation	.40	.45		
Hardiness	.47	.46		
III. Arousability			2.2	2.3
Impulsivity	.42	.44		
Disinhibition	.37	.43		
Experience seeking	.28	.36		

TABLE 8.4

Correlations Among Affectivity Constructs at Time 1 (1) and Time 2 (2)

Construct	PA1	NA1	AR1	PA2	NA2	AR2
PA1	—	−.19*	.17*	.50*	−.17*	.02
NA1	−.28*	—	.18*	−.21*	.34*	.05
AR1	.16*	.20*	—	.06	.14*	.58*
PA2	.65*	−.18*	.11	— ,	−.28*	.18*
NA2	−.25*	.49*	.15	−.35*	—	.23*
AR2	.05	.14*	.72*	.24*	.13	—

Note. Fifteen-year-olds are above the diagonal; 18-year-olds are below the diagonal. PA = positive affectivity; NA = negative affectivity; AR = arousability.
*$p < .001$.

the teen years. AR exhibited the highest stability coefficients (.72 and .58), NA the lowest (.49 and .34).

Next, a series of hierarchical regression analyses were performed in an attempt to examine the contribution of each of the affective constructs to each of the use and use-related measures. (These findings are not presented here but are available from the authors.) For each point in time, three models were tested to predict each of the 10 use measures. PA was entered alone in Step 1. The results indicated that most of the models were nonsignificant and that no model explained more than 2% of the variance. In Step 2, both PA and NA were included. Increments in variance accounted for ranged from 2% to 11%, depending on the outcome measure. Finally, in Step 3, AR was added. There were additional increases in variance accounted for, ranging from 3% to 19%. Incremental F tests (Cohen & Cohen, 1983) were used to determine the significance of the increased variance from one model to the next. Comparison of the magnitude of, and p values for, the standardized beta weights indicated that AR was most important for the use-intensity measures, whereas a combination of NA and AR was important for problem scores. On the basis of these results, we decided to concentrate on the NA and AR domains and to eliminate the PA measure from further analysis.

Scores on NA and AR were recoded into dichotomies ($1 = low, 2 = high$) in reference to group means by age, sex, and time in order to achieve equal representation of gender and age in the various groups. Intraindividual stability and change in these dichotomized variables were used to assign each subject to one of 12 different groups (see Table 8.5). Subjects in Groups 1 through 4 maintained stability of both their NA and AR

TABLE 8.5
Classification Schema of Affectivity Groups

Affectivity group	N	NA		AR	
		T1	T2	T1	T2
Both NA and AR stable over time					
Group 1	157	L	L	L	L
Group 2	130	L	L	H	H
Group 3	55	H	H	L	L
Group 4	88	H	H	H	H
Stable AR; varying NA					
Group 5	39	L	H	L	L
Group 6	39	L	H	H	H
Group 7	43	H	L	L	L
Group 8	64	H	L	H	H
Stable NA; varying AR					
Group 9	43	L	L	L	H
Group 10	51	L	L	H	L
Group 11	36	H	H	L	H
Group 12	36	H	H	H	L

Note. NA = negative affectivity; AR = arousability; T1 = Time 1; T2 = Time 2; L = low; H = high.

classifications across time. Subjects in Groups 5 through 8 maintained a stable AR categorization but varied in their NA over time. In contrast, subjects in Groups 9 through 12 exhibited stable NA but varied in their AR over time. (Note that 88 subjects—about 10% of the study sample—were eliminated from further analysis because their NA and AR patterns could not be categorized within our framework.) Consistent with the previously reported stability coefficients, 49.5% of subjects fell into Groups 1–4.

Table 8.6 presents the percentage of subjects within each of the 12 groups who had initiated use of alcohol, marijuana, or another drug (at either point in time). Although the overwhelming majority of subjects had tried alcohol (range = 91%–100%), the highest percentage of marijuana and other drug initiators were found in Groups 4, 6, 8, and 11. In general, it appears that scoring high on AR (as well as on NA at least at one point in time) is associated with a greater probability of initiating marijuana or other drug use. Although scoring high on both NA and AR at both points in time greatly enhances the probability of marijuana and other drug initiation, it was the consistently high AR-only

TABLE 8.6

Percentage of Subjects in Each Affectivity Group Who Have Initiated Drug Use

	Affectivity group											
	1	2	3	4	5	6	7	8	9	10	11	12
Alcohol	91	99	96	100	90	100	88	100	95	96	97	97
Marijuana	61	81	71	95	54	90	74	88	70	82	92	69
Other drugs	25	54	35	73	28	64	44	61	35	43	58	50

group (as compared with the consistently high NA-only group) that exhibited the higher percentage of initiators. On the other hand, being consistently low in AR across time (Groups 1, 3, 5, 7) appears to somewhat reduce the likelihood of alcohol and other drug initiation.

To examine the possible unique and combined contributions of NA and AR on the various use measures, we conducted a series of repeated-measures (by time) analyses of variance (ANOVAs). We examined the main effects of NA, AR, age, sex, and time, as well as NA × AR interactions and interactions by age, sex, and time. Three separate comparisons were conducted: (a) Groups 1 through 4, (b) Groups 5 through 8, and (c) Groups 9 through 12. We wanted to examine the potential influence of stable versus changing affect status, as well as various affect subpatterns. As described in Table 8.5, these separate comparisons encompass NA–AR affect structure for about 90% of the sample. Results are presented in Table 8.7. An X indicates a significant main effect ($p < .05$), and any statistically significant interactions are indicated in the right column.

In comparisons of Groups 1–4 (that is, for individuals displaying a stable NA–AR profile), the main effect of NA was significant for all measures except cocaine use and the number of positive marijuana motivations. The main effect of AR was significant for all measures except marijuana problems and negative motivations of use. However, the interaction of NA × AR × Sex was significant for problem marijuana use and for positive motivations for use. Main effects of sex were evident for alcohol and marijuana use, for problems, and for positive motivations for which male subjects scored higher than girls. No sex differences were evident for cocaine or combined drug use or for negative motivations for use. Age differences were evident for all of the measures in that older subjects scored higher than did younger ones. In addition, main effects of time and Time

TABLE 8.7
Results of Repeated-Measures Analysis of Variance

Measure	Significant main effects*					Significant interactions*
	NA	AR	S	A	T	
			Groups 1–4 (stable NA and AR)			
AU	X	X	X	X	X	T × A
MU	X	X	X	X	X	T × A AR × A
CU		X		X	X	T × AR
DU	X	X		X	X	T × A
APU	X	X	X	X	X	T × A AR × S T × NA × A
MPU	X		X	X		T × A NA × AR × S T × NA NA × A
NAM	X			X	X	T × NA × AR
PAM	X	X	X	X	X	T × A T × S NA × AR × S
NMM	X			X		T × A
PMM		X	X	X	X	NA × AR × S T × AR × S
			Groups 5–8 (stable AR)			
AU	X	X	X	X	X	T × A
MU		X		X	X	T × A
CU		X		X	X	T × AR
DU	X	X		X	X	T × S T × A
APU		X				T × A
NAM		X				AR × S T × NA T × A
PAM	X	X		X		T × NA T × S T × A
			Groups 9–12 (stable NA)			
AU	X			X	X	T × AR T × A
DU	X			X	X	NA × AR T × A NA × AR × S
APU	X		X		X	T × NA T × AR T × AR × S
MPU	X					T × A T × S T × NA × S
NAM	X				X	
PAM	X			X	X	T × AR T × A
NMM	X					T × NA

Note. NA = negative affectivity; AR = arousability; S = sex; A = age; T = time. See Table 8.2 for explanation of abbreviations of measures.
* = $p < .05$.

× Age interactions generally exhibited significance (an overall greater use pattern existed at Time 2). These age trends and differences are consistent with what has previously been reported in other studies involving adolescents (e.g., Johnston et al., 1988).

In comparisons of Groups 5 through 8 (that is, subjects who displayed stable AR and variable NA), the main effect of NA was important only for alcohol and drug use and positive alcohol motivations, whereas the main effect of AR was important for all models. Main effects of age and test time were salient for all of the use categories, but sex differences did not exist except for alcohol use (males used more). The Time × Age interaction was significant for most measures.

In comparisons of Groups 9–12 (that is, subjects who displayed stable NA but variable AR), the main effect of NA was important in alcohol and drug use, problems related to use, motivations for alcohol use, and negative marijuana motivations. Although the main effect of AR was not significant for any variable, the NA × AR interaction was important for drug use.

To examine differences by affect group, we examined the means for each of the use-related variables at both measurement times. Table 8.8 presents results for Time 1, and Table 8.9 contains corresponding Time 2 data. From an analysis perspective, we consider these to be post hoc comparisons because they attempt to differentiate mean differences within affect groupings.

In the stable NA and AR comparisons, subjects in the low-AR categories exhibited lower mean scores regardless of their NA category, for all four drug-use measures. Those in the consistently high AR and NA group (Group 4) used alcohol and other drugs with the greatest intensity. These findings are similar for both test times. Also at both times, Group 4 exhibited a higher alcohol-problems score than did the other three groups, and Group 1 exhibited a lower marijuana-problems score than did the other groups. Subjects in the consistently high NA categories (Groups 3 and 4) reported a greater number of negative motivations for alcohol use, and members of Group 4 reported a greater number of positive motivations for alcohol use at both test times.

In the stable AR comparisons, results were similar for both test times. Membership in a low-AR category, regardless of the NA category, was found to be indicative of lower use of all drug types. This finding was also evident for the measures of alcohol problem use and positive motivations for alcohol use. Note that models for marijuana problems and motivations were not significant.

In the stable-NA comparisons, all models were nonsignificant at Time 1 except for combined drug use, in which Group 11 (consistent high NA and increasing AR) showed a

TABLE 8.8

Results of Analysis of Variance: Group Means for Time 1 Use Measures

Measure	Stable NA and AR				Stable AR				Stable NA			
	1	2	3	4	5	6	7	8	9	10	11	12
AU	2.4_a	3.4_b	2.6_a	4.1_c	1.8_a	3.7_b	2.6_a	4.0_b	2.5	3.6	3.4	3.1
MU	0.9_a	2.3_b	1.2_a	2.9_c	1.0_a	2.9_b	1.6_a	2.6_b	1.5	1.8	2.6	1.8
CU	0.1_a	0.4_b	$0.2_{a,b}$	0.4_b	0.1	0.4	0.2	0.3	0.1	0.2	0.4	0.1_a
DU	5.2_a	9.0_b	$7.0_{a,b}$	11.4_b	4.1_a	10.4_c	7.0_b	10.9_c	5.9_a	$7.8_{a,b}$	10.2_b	6.8_a
APU	4.0_a	5.9_a	6.6_a	11.9_b	3.8_a	$7.7_{a,b}$	6.8_a	11.2_b	4.0	6.8	6.1	6.9
MPU	5.3_a	6.9_b	7.7_b	8.8_b	3.7	6.1	7.1	7.5	3.5	5.1	9.9	11.2
NAM	0.6_a	0.6_a	1.3_b	1.7_b	0.7	1.0	1.1	1.6	0.4	0.8	1.0	1.2
PAM	2.3_a	3.1_b	3.1_b	4.1_c	1.8_a	3.2_b	3.2_b	4.3_c	2.4	3.0	3.2	3.2
NMM	0.4_a	0.9_b	1.4_c	1.5_c	0.5	1.0	0.9	1.3	0.8	0.8	0.9	0.7
PMM	1.8	3.2	3.0	3.3	1.6	3.1	3.2	3.3	2.6	2.6	2.7	2.2

Note. Means with different subscripts differ significantly ($p \leq .05$). NA = negative affectivity; AR = arousability. See Table 8.2 for explanation of abbreviations of measures.

TABLE 8.9

Results of Analysis of Variance: Group Means for Time 2 Use Measures

| | Group Comparisons | | | | | | | | | | | |
| | Stable NA and AR | | | | Stable AR | | | | Stable NA | | | |
	1	2	3	4	5	6	7	8	9	10	11	12
AU	3.2$_a$	4.4$_b$	3.8$_c$	5.4$_d$	2.6$_a$	5.1$_c$	3.3$_b$	4.9$_c$	4.1	4.0	4.8	4.2
MU	1.3$_a$	2.6$_b$	1.6$_a$	3.7$_c$	1.4$_a$	3.6$_b$	2.2$_a$	3.5$_b$	2.0	2.3	3.1	2.1
CU	0.3$_a$	1.2$_b$	0.4$_a$	1.4$_b$	0.4$_a$	1.3$_b$	0.3$_a$	1.0$_b$	0.4	0.6	0.8	0.5
DU	6.9$_a$	11.5$_b$	9.4$_c$	14.8$_d$	5.7$_a$	13.9$_c$	9.6$_b$	13.7$_c$	9.5$_a$	9.2$_a$	13.6$_b$	9.5$_a$
APU	4.2$_a$	7.5$_b$	7.5$_b$	13.1$_c$	4.8$_a$	10.5$_b$	7.8$_{a,b}$	11.6$_b$	6.0$_a$	4.8$_a$	12.1$_b$	10.5$_b$
MPU	3.2$_a$	7.3$_b$	7.6$_b$	9.4$_b$	3.6	11.0	10.5	8.0	2.3$_a$	4.1$_a$	10.5$_b$	10.7$_b$
NAM	0.6$_a$	1.0$_a$	1.8$_b$	1.7$_b$	0.9	1.5	0.9	1.1	0.8$_a$	0.8$_a$	1.8$_b$	1.5$_{a,b}$
PAM	3.1$_a$	4.0$_b$	4.4$_{b,c}$	4.9$_c$	2.6$_a$	4.4$_b$	3.5$_{a,b}$	4.0$_b$	4.0$_a$	3.4$_a$	5.3$_b$	4.1$_{a,b}$
NMM	0.7	0.9	1.1	1.3	1.0	1.7	1.1	1.2	0.6$_a$	0.6$_a$	1.5$_b$	1.6$_b$
PMM	3.7	4.5	4.5	4.7	4.7	5.0	3.8	4.2	4.5	3.9	4.9	4.4

Note. Means with different subscripts differ significantly ($p \leq .05$). NA = negative affectivity; AR = arousability. See Table 8.2 for explanation of abbreviations of measures.

significantly higher score. The results of Time 2 measures indicated that Group 11 scored statistically higher on drug use, whereas Groups 11 and 12 (consistently high NA) scored highest on both problems and negative motivations for alcohol and marijuana use.

Discussion

Affectivity Structural Dimensions

Three relatively robust dimensions of affectivity were identified: NA, AR, and PA. Unlike results of mood-structure research, which relies principally on adjective ratings of mood states (e.g., Watson & Clark, 1984; Watson & Tellegen, 1985), AR emerges as a major, as opposed to a weak, dimension of affectivity. The status of AR as a major dimension is consistent with D. H. Ford's (1987) view of arousal as a key energizing principle.

NA and PA dimensions in the present study do not appear to be totally independent; instead, they appear to be modestly, although negatively, related. This suggests a greater degree of obliqueness between dimensions when a broader sample of markers is used to probe affective space. However, NA and PA appear to be more independent from each other than from AR, which appears to be modestly, but significantly, related to both dimensions; in this latter regard, the present study confirms previous research suggesting similar oblique relationships. The positive association between AR and NA, and also between AR and PA, suggests that more intense affect, regardless of quality, is associated with heightened activation potential (i.e., "arousability", as we have defined it). Arousability would be reflected both in overt behavior tendencies and in internally experienced states.

All three dimensions appear to be relatively stable across time and across age-defined developmental stages. NA displays greater volatility than do other dimensions. The relationships between NA and PA dimensions appear to be relatively stable across time and across developmental stage. However, AR–NA and AR–PA relationships appear more labile. The stability of these dimensions and their interrelationships is somewhat remarkable given the number of markers used and functioning domains tapped. Note that the measurement interval is reasonably lengthy (approximately 3 years) and that the developmental stages of study participants (early to late adolescence) can be characterized as volatile (however, for a discussion of volatility in adolescent development and drug-use intensity, see Bates & Pandina, 1989). These observations support our suggestion that affectivity profiles may be represented or embedded in a variety of constructs demonstrated to have a significant relationship to drug-abuse vulnerability.

The stability of these factors and their dimensional relationships suggest that, taken together, they represent an important and major component of personal style. Thus, affectivity has a potentially determining, although far from exclusive, role in shaping behavior. This interpretation is consistent with the view that affect intensity is a stable personal characteristic that can be defined, in part, by an individual's typical response strength across a wide range of stimulating circumstances (Larsen & Diener, 1987). In a parallel vein, affectivity profile could influence response selection and strength across a range of situations. This view of affectivity is also congruent with the five-factor model of personality structure that is emerging as the consensus view in the area of personality theory (Digman, 1990). In that model, our characterization of affectivity would be embedded most clearly in Factor 4, labeled as Neuroticism/Emotional Stability (or Emotional Stability), but can also be seen in Factors 1, 3, and 5. However, we have progressed beyond the view that this construct is a simple linear dimension or trait. Affectivity appears to be a complex space, conceptually defined by three major obliquely related factors: NA, PA, and AR.

Interestingly, evidence is emerging from several lines of inquiry, suggesting potential CNS pathways that could subserve positive and negative emotions, as well as internal arousal and behavioral activation (Hellige, 1990; Sackeim et al., 1982; Tucker & Williamson, 1984). Of special interest for drug-abuse vulnerability is the fact that reasonably specific anatomical and biochemical pathways are associated with qualitatively distinct dimensions of affective experiences. Furthermore, critical subsets of these pathways are included in the neural networks suggested as critical in the development of addiction (Wise & Bozarth, 1987). These observations suggest a potentially significant degree of isomorphism between psychological constructs and physiological mechanisms of affective experience. By extension, these relationships provide a broad framework within which the interface between affective experience and drug abuse may be fruitfully explored. Although certainly speculative, this line of inquiry has the advantage of a supportive and growing empirical literature and convergent theoretical consistency.

Affectivity and Drug-Abuse Vulnerability

The results of this study indicate a strong role for the NA and AR but not the PA dimensions of affectivity in modulating various aspects of drug-abuse vulnerability, including use intensity, problematic consequences, and motivations for use, as well as risk for use initiation. The presence of high AR or NA alone appears to heighten risk for greater vulnerability, although combining high AR and NA has an apparent additive effect. Equally important is the persistence of AR and NA status. For example, individuals who display consistently heightened AR and NA, particularly in combination, appear to display the greatest use intensity over longer time intervals. Conversely, the fact that combined persistently low AR and NA were consistently related to lower rates of initiation to drug use (except for alcohol), lower use intensity, fewer problematic consequences, and reduced use motivation suggests a possible role for lowered levels of these dimensions as a protective factor against use initiation and transition to problematic outcomes more clearly indicative of abuse.

Although in this study we were more concerned with transition to more serious forms of drug use, it is of theoretical interest to note that use initiation was also related to the high NA–AR profile. This is significant because exposure is a necessary, although not sufficient, antecedent to abuse. More importantly, however, we would expect this profile to be predisposing to initiation and, by implication, to drug seeking. This finding suggests that all things being equal (or perhaps more accurately, random), high-NA–AR-profile individuals may be more sensitive to cues in our modern environment that prime or dispose to drug experimentation.

The effects of inconsistent (i.e., changing) affectivity status are more difficult to assess. Three prototypes of NA–AR changeability patterns were identified. Two dominant patterns were characterized by (a) stability in AR and change in NA status across the measurement interval (represented by Groups 5–8) and (b) stability in NA and change in AR status (represented by Groups 9–12). The third prototype—inconsistency in both NA and AR across time—characterized only 88 individuals (about 10% of the study sample) and was not included in the present data analysis. Examination of the two dominant patterns emphasized the importance of both stability and level of affective state.

For the most part, given stability in one affect dimension (either NA or AR) and instability in the other, level of affectivity in the stable dimension appeared to be the major determinant of vulnerability status for many use indicators. For example, stable high-AR (but variable-NA) individuals displayed heightened levels of alcohol, marijuana, and polydrug use. Stable high-NA (but variable-AR) individuals displayed heightened levels of polydrug use, as well as alcohol- and marijuana-related consequences.

Of particular interest is the impact of affectivity status on measures of use consequences. Assuming that use consequences are reasonably adequate indicators of "problem use" (and, perhaps, early signs of dependency risk), high NA, particularly in combination with high AR, appears to be related strongly to increased risk of experiencing problematic consequences of use. It appears that in the arena of problematic use, NA is an especially significant risk factor. Similar results supporting this interpretation have been obtained in the area of use motivations. Likewise, stable low-AR individuals displayed lower levels of drug use across time, even though NA increased across time. This point is illustrated by the results of ANOVA and post hoc comparisons in Table 8.9 (for Time 2 measures) for the DU variable for Groups 5–8; Group 5 represents individuals with stable low AR and increasing NA status. Note that persistently heightened NA is by itself often associated with heightened drug involvement.

Unfortunately for those wanting an elegantly balanced solution, the "affect dimension stability" rule does not hold perfectly across all possible NA–AR combinations and vulnerability indicators. For example, Group 7 (low stable AR and decreasing NA) individuals displayed alcohol and combined drug-use (excluding marijuana) levels intermediate to the invulnerable Group 5 and the heightened vulnerability Groups 6 and 8, across the measurement interval. It is tempting to speculate that this result indicates that early heightened NA in some way stimulates and sustains some degree of risk vulnerability. Drug-use levels for Group 10 (low stable NA, decreasing AR) represent an analogous exception to the "affect stability" rule. DU scores for Group 10 occupy an intermediate status between the highest levels displayed by the high-risk Group 11 and the low-risk Group 9. Again, one could speculate about the influence, however temporary, of heightened AR.

These exceptions to the "affect stability" rule, taken together with the observations regarding the general nature of relationships between NA and AR (and, for that matter, among NA, AR, and PA), raise the obvious question of potential interactive effects of NA–AR on drug vulnerability, in addition to the additive effects we have already discussed. We expected that the assessment of the main effects of NA and AR reported in Table 8.7 would yield a number of significant interactions, particularly between AR and NA. Such interactions, we speculated, would demonstrate a synergistic effect of heightened (or lowered) NA–AR on a number of vulnerability markers. Because, in our general framework of affectivity, we view AR as a potential energizer of heightened affect (irrespective of quality), we anticipated that intensified NA driven by intensified AR would yield greater than additive effects on at least use intensity. Surprisingly, few such interactions were found. Several factors may account for the lack of such interactions. In this first attempt to relate subdimensions of affectivity to use vulnerability, we partitioned the levels of NA and of AR into high and low levels on the basis of an individual subject's position relative to mean NA–AR level. Thus, actual position in the high or low NA–AR group may be variable among individuals at any point in time and may be variable for the same individual across time, even though group membership remains constant. Additionally, group membership (that is, high/low NA/AR) is determined by scores on several indicator variables. The net effect of these procedures may have been to obscure potential interactions that could be conceptually relevant. Certain features of our findings suggest the presence of interactive NA–AR effects. Also, significant (and expected) interactive effects (other than NA $\times$ AR) were found; for example; time $\times$ age and time $\times$ sex interactions were obtained for use intensity and use-related problems and motivations. These results are consistent with those typically found for such variables in cross-sectional and longitudinal samples (e.g., Johnston et al., 1988).

As indicated earlier, significant main effects of persistent levels of NA and AR were obtained across a wide range of indicators that were used to characterize drug-abuse vulnerability. However, our results suggest that some dimensions of the drug-abuse construct may be differentially sensitive to NA and AR states. This is of potential significance inasmuch as vulnerability itself is not a simple construct. Previous research, for example, has demonstrated a complex relationship between use intensity and other indicators of problem use (for example, see White, 1987, 1989; White & Labouvie, 1989).

If vulnerability is considered as a complex construct composed of several dimensional features, NA, AR, or both may contribute to different aspects of vulnerability; we believe that such is the case. AR appears to be most strongly related to use intensity and increased risk for initiation, whereas NA is a significant contributor to coping use and negative use outcomes. This assertion is suggested by the overall result pattern of our study. Of course, we do not mean to imply that NA or AR contributes only to one or another aspect of vulnerability. Rather, it is a question of blend or of relative contribution. Consider, for example, initiation into various drug stages. The stages outlined in Table 8.6 parallel the often-replicated stages-of-use model (Kandel, Kessler, & Margulies, 1978; Pandina, White, & Yorke, 1981). Greater proportions of subjects in our study transited to higher stages of use when AR was high (in the absence of high NA) than when AR was low (compare Groups 1, 2, and 3, Table 8.6); this appears true even when NA was high. Again, NA appears to play some role in initiation, but this is most apparent when AR is also heightened, as in Group 4. This latter observation points to the illusive interactive effects that were discussed earlier.

Use-rate results (Tables 8.8 and 8.9) also reflect AR's propensity to influence the intensity dimension of vulnerability. For example, Group 2 (high AR, low NA) displayed higher mean levels of alcohol, marijuana, and polydrug use than any low-AR groups, even when those groups exhibited high NA. Again, note that those with the highest mean use intensity are Group 4 individuals: high in both AR and NA.

On the other hand, in reviewing results for problem-use and use-motivations dimensions, it appears that NA is a prime contributor. For example, comparisons of Groups 9 through 12 (Table 8.9) indicate that high-NA individuals do not display, for the most part, differentially high use intensity, even when high AR is present. However, they do display higher scores for problem use and use motivation (a rough proxy for coping use). Again, some influence of heightened AR can be inferred in the case of problem use; for example, alcohol problem-use scores are highest for Group 4.

This study was not designed specifically to tease out differential effects of affectivity dimensions on various aspects of drug vulnerability. For example, we have not investigated the factor structure of vulnerability, using the various indicators included in this study. Nor did we investigate the relationship among vulnerability dimensions, although the selection of indicators was guided by such work. (We are pursuing these tasks elsewhere; e.g., White & Labouvie, 1989.) Nonetheless, we believe that the patterns of results obtained in the current study permit a qualified conclusion that distinctive aspects of affectivity, particularly NA and AR, differentially influence vulnerability to forms of drug use most clearly indicative of drug abuse. As might be expected, the nature of these influences is complex. Affectivity and drug-abuse vulnerability dimensional structures, the influence of dimensional persistence, the etiology of affective structure, and the possible recursive influence of drug use on affectivity structure and evolution are among key issues that remain to be resolved. We anticipate that clarification of these issues and greater specification of a model linking affectivity to vulnerabililty will also permit the application of analytical strategies more suited to the simultaneous consideration of the latent constructs that we believe will drive such a model.

Implications for Interventionists

The observations and conclusions of this study are interpretable as providing broad support for theories of vulnerability in which chronic heightened states of affectivity, particularly those that are subjectively expressed (and, presumably, experienced) as aversive or, in some cases, as extraordinarily reinforcing, as well as the accompanying pressure to regulate such states (through maintenance, enhancement, or diminishment), play key roles in stimulating and sustaining heightened levels of drug use and in the transition to "problem user" status—a stage arguably precursory to dependent and addictive use. The touchstone issue of factors that may generate or sustain negative affectivity and arousability, although informed, is still unresolved and invites future investigation. Biologic (e.g., CNS sensitivity), psychologic (e.g., temperament and self-view), and socioenvironmental (e.g., peer- or achievement-related opportunities) factors may each be viewed as potential substrata that shape or tone affective space either independently or cooperatively. We find it particularly encouraging that findings from studies that make use of clearly psychological concepts appear to have the potential to be reasonably reconciled with data and theory from physiologic and pharmacologic investigations and processes, as well as with speculations regarding drug influences on CNS functioning. Of course, we recognize that this reconciliation has just begun and will take considerable work and creativity to reach fruition. Furthermore, we recognize that we have taken advantage of the present forum to range into speculative territory in attempting to link theory and data from the sometimes disparate domains of physiology, psychology, and sociology.

We believe that there are also practical lessons to be gleaned from this line of study, which can be applied to intervention strategies. Given the persistent and pervasive nature of affectivity, as well as the real possibility that the experience of chronic states of arousal and affect may prime individuals for a range of undesirable drug-use outcomes, it seems imperative that we focus a reasonably significant portion of our intervention resources on the reduction of conditions and circumstances that promote and sustain such chronic states. This canon is simple to articulate, difficult to implement, and far-reaching in scope. It can be applied in both prevention and treatment environments. It lends itself more or less completely to psychological and socioenvironmental levels of analysis and probably has limited but significant application at the biological level. Application of this principle will require more than a particle of creativity. We will have to be especially adept because the elimination of transient arousal or negative feelings is no more feasible or desirable than the continual experience of euphoria. Learning, and instructing in, the management of affectivity may prove to be a major challenge to the management of drug abuse, dependency, and addiction.

References

Bandura, A. (1977). Self-efficacy: Toward a unifying theory of behavioral change. *Psychological Review, 84*, 191–215.

Bandura, A. (1989). Human agency in social cognitive theory. *American Psychologist, 44*, 1175–1184.

Bates, M. E., & Pandina, R. J. (1989). Individual differences in the stability of personality needs: Relations to stress and substance use during adolescence. *Personality and Individual Differences, 10*, 1151–1157.

Blanchard, D. C., & Blanchard, R. J. (1988). Ethoexperimental approaches to the biology of emotions. *Annual Review of Psychology, 39*, 43–68.

Blaney, P. H. (1986). Affect and memory: A review. *Psychological Bulletin, 99*, 229–246.

Brown, J., & Farber, I. E. (1951). Emotions conceptualized as intervening variables: With suggestions toward a theory of frustration. *Psychological Bulletin, 48*, 465–495.

Buck, R. (1985). Prime theory: An integrated view of motivation and emotion. *Psychological Review, 92*, 389–413.

Chitwood, D. (1985). Patterns and consequences of cocaine use. In N. J. Kozel & E. H. Adams (Eds.), *Cocaine use in America: Epidemiological and clinical perspectives* (pp. 111–129; NIDA Research Monograph No. 61). Rockville, MD: National Institute on Drug Abuse.

Cohen, J., & Cohen, P. (1983). *Applied multiple regression/correlation analysis for the behavioral sciences* (2nd ed.). New York: Erlbaum.

Cox, W. M. (1987). Personality theory and research. In H. T. Blane & K. E. Leonard (Eds.), *Psychological theories of drinking and alcoholism* (pp. 55–89). New York: Guilford Press.

Cox, W. M., & Klinger, E. (1988). A motivational model of alcohol use. *Journal of Abnormal Psychology, 97*, 168–180.

Derogatis, L. R. (1977). *SCL-90-R administration, scoring, and procedures manual* (Vol. 1). Baltimore: Johns Hopkins University, School of Medicine.

Digman, J. M. (1990). Personality structure: Emergence of the five-factor model. *Annual Review of Psychology, 41*, 417–440.

Dodge, K. A. (1989). Coordinating responses to aversive stimuli: Introduction to a special section on the development of emotional regulation. *Developmental Psychology, 25*, 339–342.

Emmons, R. A. (1986). Personal strivings: An approach to personality and subjective well-being. *Journal of Personality and Social Psychology, 51*, 1058–1068.

Eysenck, H. J., & Eysenck, S. B. (1975). *Eysenck personality questionnaire manual.* San Diego, CA: Educational & Industrial Testing Service.

Ford, D. H. (1987). *Humans as self-constructing living systems: A developmental perspective on behavior and personality.* Hillsdale, NJ: Erlbaum.

Ford, M. E., & Ford, D. H. (1987). *Humans as self-constructing living systems: Putting the framework to work.* Hillsdale, NJ: Erlbaum.

Frijda, N. H. (1986). *The emotions.* New York: Cambridge University Press.

Frijda, N. H. (1988). The laws of emotion. *American Psychologist. 43*, 349–358.

Heilman, K. M., & Satz, P. (Eds.). (1983). *Neuropsychology of human emotion.* New York: Guilford Press.

Hellige, J. B. (1990). Hemispheric asymmetry. *Annual Review of Psychology, 41*, 55–80.

Higgins, E. T. (1987). Self-discrepancy: A theory relating self and affect. *Psychological Review. 94*, 319–340.

Izard, C. E. (1977). *Human emotions.* New York: Plenum Press.

Jackson, D. N. (1974). *Personality research form manual.* Goshen, NY: Research Psychologists Press.

James, W. (1890). What is an emotion? *Mind, 9*, 188–205.

Jessor, R., & Jessor, S. (1977). *Problem behavior and psychosocial development.* San Diego, CA: Academic Press.

Johnston, L. D., O'Malley, P. M., & Bachman, J. R. (1988). *Drug use among American high school students, college students and other young adults* (DHHS Publication No. ADM 89-1602). Washington, DC: U.S. Government Printing Office.

Kandel, D. B., Davies, M., Karus, D., & Yamaguchi, K. (1986). The consequences in young adulthood of adolescent drug involvement. *Archives of General Psychiatry, 43*, 746–754.

Kandel, D., Kessler, R. C., & Margulies, R. S. (1978). Antecedents of adolescent initiation into stages of drug use: A developmental analysis. In D. Kandel (Ed.), *Longitudinal research in drug use: Empirical findings and methodological issues* (pp. 73–99). Washington, DC: Hemisphere – John Wiley.

Kaplan, H. B. (1985). Testing a general theory of drug abuse and other deviant adaptations. *Journal of Drug Issues, 15*, 477–492.

Kopp, C. B. (1989). Regulation of distress and negative emotions: A developmental view. *Developmental Psychology, 25*, 343–354.

Labouvie, E. W. (1986). The coping function of adolescent alcohol and drug use. In R. K. Silbereisen, K. Eyferth, & G. Rudinger (Eds.), *Development as action in context* (pp. 229–240). New York: Springer.

Labouvie, E. W. (1987). Relation of personality to adolescent alcohol and drug use: A coping perspective. *Pediatrician, 14*, 19–24.

Lange, C. G., & James, W. (1922). *The emotions* (I. A. Haupt, Trans.). Baltimore: Williams & Wilkins.

Larsen, R. J., & Diener, E. (1987). Affect intensity as an individual difference characteristic: A review. *Journal of Research in Personality, 21*, 1–39.

Lazarus, R. S. (1968). Emotions and adaptation: Conceptual and empirical relations. In W. J. Arnold (Ed.), *Nebraska symposium on motivation.* (pp. 175–266). Lincoln: University of Nebraska Press.

Lazarus, R. S. (1982). Thoughts on the relations between emotion and cognition. *American Psychologist, 37*, 1019–1024.

Lazarus, R. S. (1984). On the primacy of cognition. *American Psychologist, 39*, 124–129.

Lettieri, D. J. (1985). Drug abuse: A review of explanations and models of explanations. *Advances in Alcohol and Substance Abuse, 4*, 9–40.

Lettieri, D. J., Sayers, M., & Pearson, H. W. (1980). *Theories on drug abuse* (NIDA Research Monograph No. 30; DHHS Publication No. ADM 80-967). Washington, DC: U.S. Government Printing Office.

Levenson, M. R., Aldwin, C. M., Bosse, R., & Spiro, A. (1988). Emotionality and mental health: Longitudinal findings from the normative aging study. *Journal of Abnormal Psychology, 97*, 94–96.

Leventhal, H., & Tomarken, A. J. (1986). Emotion: Today's problems. *Annual Review of Psychology, 37*, 565–610.

Marlatt, G. A. (1987). Alcohol, the magic elixir: Stress, expectancy, and transformation of emotional states. In E. Gottheil, K. A. Druley, S. Pashko, & S. P. Weinstein (Eds.), *Stress and addiction* (pp. 302–322). New York: Brunner/Mazel.

Mendelson, J. H. (1983). Chronic effects of cannabis on human behavior and brain function. In K. O. Fehr & H. Kalant (Eds.), *Cannabis and health hazards* (pp. 475–500). Toronto: Addiction Research Foundation.

Olds, J. (1962). Hypothalamic substrates of reward. *Physiological Review, 42,* 554–604.

Pandina, R. J., Labouvie, E. W., Johnson, V., & White, H. R. (1988). The impact of prolonged marijuana use on personal and social competence in adolescence. In G. Chesher, P. Consroe, & R. Musty (Eds.), *Proceedings of the Melbourne Symposium on Cannabis* (pp. 183–200). Canberra: ANCADA, Australian Department of Health.

Pandina, R. J., Labouvie, E. W., Johnson, V., & White, H. R. (1990). The relationship between alcohol and marijuana use and competence in adolescence. *Journal of Health and Social Policy, 1*(3), 89–108.

Pandina, R. J., Labouvie, E. W., & White, H. R. (1984). Potential contributions of the life span developmental approach to the study of adolescent alcohol and drug use: The Rutgers Health and Human Development Project, a working model. *Drug Issues, 14,* 253–268.

Pandina, R. J., White, H. R., & Yorke, J. (1981). Estimation of substance use involvement: Theoretical consideration and empirical findings. *International Journal of the Addictions, 16,* 1–24.

Plutchik, R. (1980). *Emotion: A psychoevolutionary synthesis.* New York: Harper & Row.

Post, R. M. (1975). Cocaine psychoses: A continuum model. *American Journal of Psychiatry, 132,* 225–231.

Rotter, J. B. (1966). Generalized expectancies for internal versus external control of reinforcement. *Psychological Monographs, 80,* No. 1.

Rouse, B. A., Kozel, M. S., & Richards, L. G. (Eds.). (1985). *Self-report methods of estimating drug use* (NIDA Research Monograph No. 57). Rockville, MD: National Institute on Drug Abuse.

Sackeim, H. A., Greenberg, M. S., Weiman, A. L., Gur, R. C., Hungerbuhler, J. P., & Geschwind, N. (1982). Hemispheric asymmetry in the expression of positive and negative emotions. *Archives of Neurology, 39,* 210–219.

SAS Users Guide Version 5 Edition. (1985). Cary, NC: SAS Institute.

Schuckit, M. A. (1986). Genetic and clinical implications of alcoholism and affective disorder. *American Journal of Psychiatry, 143,* 140–147.

Spence, J. T., Hemreich, R., & Stapp, J. (1975). Ratings of self and peers on sex role attributions and their relation to self-esteem and conceptions of masculinity and femininity. *Journal of Personality and Social Psychology, 32,* 29–39.

Spielberger, C. D., Gorsuch, R. L., & Lushene, R. E. (1970). *Manual for the state-trait anxiety inventory.* Palo Alto, CA: Consulting Psychologists Press.

Tomkins, S. S. (1962). *Affect, imagery and consciousness: The negative affects* (Vol. 2). New York: Springer.

Tomkins, S. S. (1982). Affect theory. In P. Ekman (Ed.), *Emotion in the human face* (2nd ed., pp. 353–395). Cambridge, England: Cambridge University Press.

Tucker, D. M., & Williamson, P. A. (1984). Asymmetric neural control systems in human self-regulation. *Psychological Review, 91,* 185–215.

U.S. Bureau of the Census. (1981). *Current population survey: Money, income and poverty status of families and persons in the United States: 1980* (Current Population Reports, Series P-60, No. 127). Washington, DC: U.S. Government Printing Office.

Watson, D., & Clark, L. (1984). Negative affectivity: The disposition to experience aversive emotional states. *Psychological Bulletin, 96,* 465–490.

Watson, D., & Tellegen, A. (1985). Toward a consensual structure of mood. *Psychological Bulletin, 98*, 219–235.

Weiner, B. (1985). An attributional theory of achievement motivation and emotion. *Psychological Review, 92*, 548–573.

White, H. R. (1987). Longitudinal stability and dimensional structure of problem drinking in adolescence. *Journal of Studies on Alcohol, 48*, 541–550.

White, H. R. (1989). Relationship between heavy drug and alcohol use and problem use among adolescents. In S. Einstein (Ed.), *Drug and alcohol use: Issues and factors* (pp. 61–71). New York: Plenum Press.

White, H. R., & Labouvie, E. W. (1989). Towards the assessment of adolescent problem drinking. *Journal of Studies on Alcohol, 50*, 30–37.

Wills, T. A. (1985). Stress, coping and tobacco and alcohol use in early adolescence. In S. Shiffman and T. A. Wills (Eds.), *Coping and substance use* (pp. 67–94). San Diego, CA: Academic Press.

Wills, T. A., & Shiffman, S. (1985). Coping and substance use: A conceptual framework. In S. Shiffman & T. A. Wills (Eds.), *Coping and substance use* (pp. 3–24). San Diego, CA: Academic Press.

Wise, R. A., & Bozarth, M. A. (1987). A psychomotor stimulant theory of addiction. *Psychological Review, 94*, 469–492.

Zajonc, R. B. (1984). On the primacy of affect. *American Psychologist, 39*, 117–123.

Zevon, M. A., & Tellegen, A. (1982). The structure of mood change: An idiographic/nomothetic analysis. *Journal of Personality and Social Psychology, 43*, 111–122.

Zuckerman, M. (1979). *Sensation-seeking.* Hillsdale, NJ: Erlbaum.

CHAPTER 9

Progression to Regular Marijuana Involvement: Phenomenology and Risk Factors for Near-Daily Use

Denise B. Kandel and Mark Davies

A major contribution of the National Institute on Drug Abuse to the field of substance abuse has been the initiation and support of a number of longitudinal studies in the 1970s and early 1980s. These studies were designed to identify the psychosocial precursors of involvement in substance use. They relied on random samples of adolescents drawn mostly from schools or, more rarely, from the community, and used similar methods of data collection (for a review, see Kandel, 1978, 1980). These studies were well suited for examining the risk factors for initiation of drug use, because they were prospective and obtained baseline data, in most cases, prior to onset of drug use. Whether these studies are suited for examining vulnerability to more severe forms of substance use remains to be determined.

Onset of drug use is clearly defined and probably reliably measured (Single, Kandel, & Johnson, 1975). By contrast, the transition to drug dependence or abuse is gradual.

Work on this chapter has been supported by research grants DA00064, DA01097, DA03196, DA02867, and DA04866 and Research Scientist Award DA00081 from the National Institute on Drug Abuse to Denise Kandel. The research assistance of Christine Schaffran is gratefully acknowledged.

The definition of substance abuse and the timing of when it first occurs are matters of debate. As a result, the analysis of the risk factors for drug abuse is complex and faces issues similar to those raised by chronic disease epidemiology.

The specification of criteria defining psychiatric diagnoses, including substance abuse, and the development of structured interview schedules that incorporate these criteria have led to recent consensual agreement in psychiatric epidemiology. The diagnostic criteria, defined by the American Psychiatric Association (the third edition of the *Diagnostic and Statistical Manual of Mental Disorders* and its revision; *DSM–III* and *DSM–III–R*; 1980, 1987) and still in the process of being refined, contain a degree of arbitrariness, but they represent the collective judgment of a group of experts. The collection of data based on these criteria constitutes the hallmark of the Epidemiological Catchment Area (ECA) program of research (Robins et al., 1984), which has provided systematic information on the prevalence of substance abuse disorders in the general population according to *DSM-III* criteria. (These definitional issues are discussed in greater detail by other contributors to this volume, in particular Thomas Babor.)

If diagnostic criteria are not specifically assessed, indirect methods are not often used. These indirect methods for assessing abuse often lack calibration data with respect to *DSM-III* criteria and hence contain an additional degree of arbitrariness. As a result, pooling results across different studies is difficult, although common findings would presumably be robust.

In our analyses, we chose to focus on a frequency criteria for the assessment of substance abuse, in this case on the daily or near-daily use of marijuana. Near-daily use is a well-defined behavior that in most epidemiological surveys constitutes the highest degree of drug involvement that is generally measured. Furthermore, daily or nearly-daily use of marijuana is a source of concern because of the potentially negative consequences of such regular use.

The Concept of Daily Drug Use

To the best of our knowledge, empirical data on "daily" drug use were first presented by Johnston, Bachman, and O'Malley (1979) for national samples of high school seniors. Seniors who report using a drug 20 or more times in the past 30 days are classified as "daily" users. The proportions of daily users of specific drugs have been reported annually since 1975 to chart trends in patterns of heavy drug use by adolescents. Cigarettes, alcohol, and marijuana are the only drugs for which more than 1% of high school seniors report current daily patterns of use.

Young people who use marijuana on a daily or near-daily basis, whether in adolescence or young adulthood, have escalated to using other illicit drugs. At any particular time, they are much more heavily involved in other drugs than are other youths, and they perform at a lower level psychologically and socially than their peers who have not or do not use marijuana as regularly (Anthony, 1983; Johnston, 1980, 1981; Kandel, 1984; Kleinman, Wish, Deren, Rainone, & Morehouse, 1988). For instance, in the senior high school class of 1979 surveyed by *Monitoring the Future* (Johnston, 1980), 27% of the daily marijuana users drank alcohol daily, and 59% were daily cigarette smokers. Eighty-six percent of daily marijuana users in the senior high school class of 1980 had used illicit drugs other than marijuana in the preceding year, as well as cigarettes and alcohol (Clayton & Ritter, 1985). Kleinman et al. (1988) reported that, compared with other high school students who also participated in a school prevention program but did not use marijuana daily, the daily users were more likely to be using cigarettes heavily, to drink alcohol frequently, to have used illicit drugs for a long period of time, and to have initiated illicit drug use before the age of 13. Adolescents who are daily users are more likely to perform poorly in school, to be less religious, to be more delinquent, and to be friends with other adolescents who are using illicit drugs (Johnston, 1981; Kleinman et al., 1988).

In our own analyses of the characteristics of marijuana users at age 24–25, we found that those who reported using marijuana at least four to six times a week, a group whom we defined as near-daily users, were not only much more involved in drugs than were other young adults, but were performing at a much lower level in all areas of their lives (Kandel, 1984). The frequent marijuana users were much more likely to have used a variety of other licit and illicit drugs, to have used marijuana for a longer period of time, and to have started their use of marijuana at least one year earlier than any other group of marijuana users. The former exhibited a lower level of social achievement and psychological well-being and much more deviant life-styles. They had completed fewer years of schooling than their peers; they were more likely to be on public assistance, to have had discontinuous work histories and more periods of unemployment, and to have been divorced; and they were less likely to report themselves to be in good health. They were much more likely to have been involved in automobile accidents while high or drunk, to have participated in delinquent activities, to have been arrested by the police, and to have been convicted of a crime. A striking difference pertained to their histories of psychiatric hospitalization: Seven percent of the men and 8% of the women who used marijuana near-daily reported to have ever been hospitalized for psychiatric illness, compared with less than 1% of those who had stopped using marijuana or those who never used marijuana (Kandel, 1984). In the only other analysis of adult marijuana users known to us, Anthony (1983) reported that adults 18 to 34 years of age in Baltimore, Maryland, site of the ECA, who had used marijuana for 15 days in the month prior to the interview were also much more likely to have used alcohol that frequently.

Although multiple longitudinal studies exist that have examined the risk factors for onset of marijuana use, we are aware of only one study that has examined the risk factors for progression to daily or near-daily marijuana use: the study by Kaplan, Martin, Johnson, and Robbins (1986) of a sample of adolescents initially surveyed in seventh grade, 56% of whom were reinterviewed at age 22–23. Kaplan's general theory of deviant behavior provided the framework for the causal model tested in the analysis. Age of first marijuana experience had the strongest effect of any factor in the model. Rejection by peers in adolescence reduced the risk of escalation, whereas avoidant defenses increased the risk. Conditions at the time of the first marijuana experience, as reported retrospectively by subjects, also affected escalation: The experience of psychological distress and attenuation of ties to others inceased the risk; the experience of adverse consequences and conformity to peer norms reduced the risk.

Daily Use as a Criterion for Substance Abuse

Using frequency–duration criteria to classify substance abuse, and ignoring the criterion of functional impairment associated with drug use as in *DMS-III* nosology, most likely identifies a larger group of individuals than would be identified by using functional impairment criteria alone. Thus, the proportion of young adults age 28–29 (the age of respondents in the sample analyzed in the present study) in the five ECA sites who received a lifetime *DSM-III* diagnosis of any substance abuse is 11.5%; the proportion receiving a specific diagnosis of marijuana abuse is 7.8% (M. Weissman, personal communication, November 15, 1990). In comparison, the proportion of lifetime daily marijuana users in the general population is approximately 25%, according to various surveys. In the longitudinal cohort that we have been following up to their late twenties, 26.2% have ever used marijuana at least 4 to 6 times a week for more than a month. Similarly, Kaplan et al. (1986) reported that 24% of their sample had ever used marijuana "daily or nearly daily" for a period of at least one month by age 22–23. The same proportion of lifetime daily marijuana use was reported by Johnston, O'Malley, and Bachman (1984) for national samples of high school seniors followed to ages 25 to 29. Anthony (1983) reported that 9.5% of adults 18 to 34 years old had used marijuana for 15 days in the month preceding the interview. Because, as we will see later, the modal age for first spell of daily marijuana use is slightly over 19, the statistics from the various studies are based on individuals who have gone through the period of risk for transition to daily marijuana use. Because there is little or no right censoring of respondents, the prevalence of daily or near-daily use is unbiased.

The discrepancies in the number of individuals identified as substance abusers on the basis of different criteria can be explained by two assumptions: (a) lifetime prevalences of 12% for substance abuse defined on the basis of diagnostic criteria and 25% for substance abuse defined on the basis of frequency–duration and (b) a strong association between functional and frequency–quantity criteria (an odds ratio of 8.4). Under these assumptions, only 32% (positive predictive value) of individuals identified by frequency–duration criteria will also exhibit functional impairment by the time of assessment; on the other hand, 95% (negative predictive value) of individuals below the frequency–duration threshold for substance abuse will not exhibit functional impairment. There are more heavy users who are not dysfunctional than there are light users who are dysfunctional. Although the proportion of near-daily marijuana users may be more than three times higher than the proportion of cases of marijuana abuse and/or dependence, the evidence is strong that frequent or near-daily illicit drug use by young people represents a form of heavy drug involvement that is associated with a lower level of psychosocial performance. Near-daily use is the criterion of substance abuse used in our analyses.

Theoretical Framework

The theoretical framework underlying our investigation is that of socialization theory and focuses on the interpersonal nexus of parents and peers on developing adolescents. This framework makes use of concepts and processes derived from various theories, especially social learning and control.

The basic assumption is that the acquisition of behaviors and values is in large part determined by the matrix of social relationships in which individuals are embedded and that it is crucial to consider simultaneously the various members of this network in order to understand socialization processes. Drug use is one of the many behaviors that result from an interaction between individual characteristics and the competing influences of multiple social groups. The basic issue in adolescent socialization is the extent to which the behaviors of adolescents are dependent on the intragenerational influences of peers and the intergenerational influence of adults, especially parents. The values, attitudes, and behaviors of the parental and peer generations to which young people are exposed differ on many issues and are especailly divergent concerning the use of illicit drugs. In contrast with young people, most adults disapprove of the use of illegal drugs and do not themselves use these drugs. However, even such a clearly age-graded behavior as the use of illicit drugs could reflect adult influences, with adults who use drugs providing role models for their children in the use of mood-changing substances. For the parents of the subjects in our sample, the drugs would be licit or medically prescribed.

Two processes are posited to describe the influence of significant others on adolescents. The first is imitation, in which youths model their own behaviors or attitudes on others' behaviors by simply observing and replicating the behaviors or, in the case of parental drug behaviors, transposing them into forms more acceptable to the youths' lifestyle. Adolescents may be more likely to start using marijuana if their parents drink or use mood-changing drugs, such as alcohol or medically prescribed psychotropics. They may also be more likely to use illegal drugs if their friends use marijuana. The second process is social reinforcement, in which adolescents respond to what parents and peers define as appropriate behaviors and values concerning specific issues. For example, adolescents may be partially dissuaded from marijuana use if their parents express their views that the child should not be using the drug. Thus, behaviors and values are important components of interpersonal influence. An additional component derives from the notion of commitment in the control theory of delinquency and focuses on the parent–child relationship (Hirschi, 1969). The quality of the parent–child bond has been shown to have a restraining effect on involvement in deviant and delinquent activities, irrespective of parental behaviors and values (Hirschi, 1969; McCord & McCord, 1960).

The usefulness of this approach is supported by other investigators who have used similar or related conceptual frameworks for identifying risk factors for drug involvement (e.g., see Baumrind, 1985; Block, Keyes, & Block, 1986; Brook, Gordon, & Brook, 1980; Brook, Whiteman, Gordon, & Cohen, 1986a, 1986b; Brook, Whiteman, Nomura, Gordon, & Cohen, 1988; Coombs & Landsverk, 1988; Dishion & Loeber, 1985; Dishion, Patterson & Reid, 1988; Dishion, Reid, & Patterson, 1987; Elliott, Huizinga, & Ageton, 1985; Hawkins, Lishner & Catalano, 1985; Huba & Bentler, 1980; Hundleby & Mercer, 1987; Jessor & Jessor, 1977; Kandel, Kessler, & Margulies, 1978a, 1978b; Kellam, Brown, Rubin, & Ensminger, 1983; Kellam, Simon, & Ensminger, 1980; Needle et al., 1986; Newcomb & Bentler, 1988;

Pandina & Schuele, 1983; Simcha-Fagan, Gersten, & Langner, 1986; Vicary & Lerner, 1986; Zucker & Noll, 1987).

Sample and Data: Continuous Drug Histories

Our analyses take advantage of detailed drug histories obtained for the New York State Follow-Up Cohort. The cohort comprises 1,222 young adults who have been followed for 13 years and have been contacted three times: in adolescence at age 15 to 16 (in 1971) and in young adulthood at ages 24 to 25 (in 1980) and 28 to 29 (in 1984).

The cohort is representative of high school students formerly enrolled in Grades 10 and 11 in public secondary high schools in New York State in 1971–1972. The original high school sample was a random sample of the adolescent population attending public secondary schools in New York State in the fall of 1971, with students selected from a stratified sample of 18 high schools throughout the state. The target population for the follow-up was drawn from the enrollment list of half of the homerooms from Grades 10 and 11, with high-marijuana-using homerooms sampled at twice the rate of the others. Students who had not participated in either the fall or the spring waves of the initial 1971 study, and who were more likely to be chronic absentees, were also selected for inclusion (and sampled at a lower rate) to permit unbiased estimates of the former student population at the time of the adult follow up. The 1,222 persons reinterviewed in 1984 represented an overall completion rate of 75% of the initial high school sample of former regular students and absentees enrolled in the 10th and 11th grades. Twelve and a half percent of the sample had dropped out of high school; 84% were White and 16% non-White. As will be discussed later, different components of the sample were used in the analyses.

Structured personal interviews took an average of two hours to administer. The interview schedule included almost exclusively structured items with closed-end response alternatives. An unusual component of the schedule consisted of two charts designed to reconstruct on a monthly basis the respondents' life and drug histories. At each wave, information was collected on the histories of use of 12 drugs or drug classes since the last data collection: two legal drugs (cigarettes and alcohol), four illegal drugs (marijuana, psychedelics, cocaine, and heroin), and six classes of psychotrophic drugs (methadone, minor and major tranquilizers, sedatives, stimulants, antidepressants, and opiates other than heroin), for which medical and nonmedical use was ascertained. Colored pill charts developed for use in the general population by the National Household Survey (Miller et al., 1983) were presented to respondents to increase the accuracy of their reports about their use of minor tranquilizers, sedatives, and stimulants. Respondents were asked in what months and years they had used any of these drugs, when they had used them at the highest intensity, and how frequently and how much they had used each drug during the period of highest use. In 1980, respondents were asked to reconstruct their drug histories since 1971. In 1984, they were asked to reconstruct their histories since 1980. Chronological time lines with differentiations in years and months allowed for the timing of the use of the different drugs. To eliminate drug experimenters, histories were ascertained from those who had used each drug class at least 10 times in their lives; this criterion eliminated half of those who had ever used illicit drugs other than marijuana.

The data on which the analyses are based clearly have at least two limitations: The data (a) come from a single cohort and cannot effectively distinguish age effects from period effects, and (b) are based on retrospective reports and are subject to various distortions, such as telescoping of recall. These limitations must be kept in mind in the interpretations of the results.

Analytical Strategies

We propose that a two-step strategy is necessary to answer the question of interest: What are the risk factors for moving from substance use to abuse? The first step identifies risk factors for initiating drug use. The second step identifies risk factors for moving to regular use or abuse among those who have already used the drug.

Transitions to different levels of marijuana use may be governed by different conditions. Certain risk factors can be identified only for escalation of marijuana use. For example, characteristics of marijuana use itself (e.g., age of onset) would not be risk factors for initiation of use but are likely to be risk factors for escalation of marijuana use. A risk factor may or may not be important for both transitions. A risk factor that predicts onset but not escalation is a risk factor for heavy marijuana use because light marijuana use precedes heavy marijuana use.

We pursued this two-step stategy. We investigated the factors that predict initiation to marijuana use, and, subsequently, the factors that differentiate young people who go on to use marijuana on a near-daily or daily basis from those who do not. We identified the risk factors for each transition, using two logistic regression models. In the first model, we identified the risk factors for lifetime marijuana use in the entire sample. In the second model, we identified the risk factors for marijuana abuse among those who had ever used marijuana. Regression models were estimated for the total sample and for each sex. Sex differences were tested using interaction terms.

The risk factors for near-daily marijuana use that we examined in our analyses were measured in adolescence and not necessarily at the point at which the transition from use to abuse took place. The factors included in the models reflect both the theoretical framework that underlies our investigation, namely socialization theory, and domains of constructs identified in prior research (see references cited earlier) as important correlates or predictors of various forms of drug use. The models include factors expected to increase the risk of drug involvement and those expected to reduce such risk. In addition to interpersonal influences, an attempt was made to take into account other relevant aspects of an individual's psychosocial functioning, such as level of depression and familial factors, in particular familial history of pathology.

The factors, measured for the most part when respondents were 15 to 16 years old, cover seven major domains: sociodemographic, family history of psychiatric disorders and alcohol problems, parental relationships and attitudes, peer involvement, participation in delinquent activities, psychological symptoms, and drug-related variables. The specific variables included in the models are listed in Appendix A.

The analysis proceeded in two stages. Descriptive analyses were carried out to delineate the natural history of near-daily marijuana involvement. Multivariate analyses were carried out to identify the risk factors for initiation to marijuana use and for escalation to near-daily use. Different subgroups from the cohort were used in the analyses. The descriptive analyses are based on the total follow-up cohort. The multivariate analyses are based on subgroups who, as adolescents, participated in the initial high school survey and who were at risk for (a) onset of marijuana use and (b) escalation to near-daily use.

The Phenomenology of Near-Daily Marijuana Use

Little is known about the natural history of daily or near-daily use of marijuana or other illicit drugs. Limited data presented by Johnston, Bachman, and O'Malley (1988) for *Monitoring the Future* suggest that this pattern of regular involvement increases significantly after graduation from high school. Among seniors in the class of 1987, 14.7% reported lifetime prevalence of daily or near-daily use for at least a month. This compares with 24% among graduates of earlier classes who had been followed through ages 25 to 29. About two thirds of the former seniors who ever used marijuana on a "daily" basis (20 days or more in the past month) have done so for about a year or less (Johnston et al., 1988). (The observed duration of these spells is probably censored by the timing of the data collection.)

The continuous drug histories we obtained make it possible to make assessments through the late twenties, much beyond the period of risk for initiation to marijuana, which terminates prior to age 20 (Kandel & Logan, 1984; Raveis & Kandel, 1989). These analyses were carried out in the total sample, including the former school absentees who had been contacted for the first time in early adulthood.

It will be recalled that respondents were asked to indicate on a time chart the periods in their lives when they had used specific drugs and when they had used each the most. A follow-up question asked how often, during that period of highest use, they had used each substance. The eight response alternatives included *every day, 4 to 6 times a week, 2 or 3 times a week, once a week, 2 or 3 times a month, once a month, several times a year,* and *about once a year.* To make the present data comparable to those reported by Johnston et al. (1988), who defined daily use of a drug as use 20 times a month or more, the highest two response categories were combined into a single category that we labeled *near-daily use.*

The majority of men and women in the cohort have used marijuana. By age 28–29, 78.4% of the men and 70.0% of the women have done so. One quarter (26.2%) of the total sample has ever used marijuana on a near-daily basis. This represents over two fifths (43.6%) of those who have experimented with marijuana. These proportions are higher among men than women: 33.0% of men but only 20.3% of women have ever used marijuana nearly daily. Among the marijuana users themselves, 49.7% of male and 37.1% of female marijuana users have ever used the drug on a near-daily basis.

Because respondents indicated the specific months and years when they experienced periods of highest use, spells of near-daily marijuana use could be identified. The overwhelming majority of young adults who have used marijuana on a near-daily basis have experienced only one such spell. Very few have experienced more than two spells (Table 9.1). On the average, these spells began 3 years after the first experience with marijuana, after 39 months for men and 36 months for women (Table 9.2). The average duration of each spell and the mean age at the start of the spells are displayed in Table 9.3. The mean age at the start of the first spell is close to 19.5 years, although the range is wide. Some youths first started using marijuana on a near-daily basis at the age of 10.4, and very few as late as age 29. The first spell of such regular use is relatively long and longer among men than among women: More than three and a half years for men but two

TABLE 9.1

Number of Near-Daily Marijuana Spells Experienced by Men and Women by Age 28–29, Among Those Who Experienced Any Spells.

Number of Spells	Males (%)	Females (%)
One	81.3	84.2
Two	11.1	9.7
Three	4.5	1.4
Four	1.3	1.2
Five	—	—
Six	—	0.5
Seven	—	2.1
Eight	1.5	0.9
Nine or more	0.4	—
N	187	133

and a half years, or one shorter, for women. The second spell is much shorter for both sexes, although at least 18 months in duration. All succeeding spells are much shorter, averaging about 3 months in duration.

Only a minority of marijuana users (less than one third) go directly from using marijuana on a daily or near-daily basis to not using it at all (Table 9.4). The majority (close to two thirds) continue to use marijuana, but at a lower frequency. Thus, most young people who use marijuana on a regular basis do so for a relatively long period of time and do not resume use at that intensity once they have decreased their involvement.

By the age of 28–29 (the time of the most recent survey), most of those who had ever used marijuana on a near-daily basis (85.4%) were not currently in such a spell. Only 14.6% (16.3% of men and 12.1% of women) were currently in a spell. Of those, 72.6% were in their first spell and 24.7% in their second spell; one individual was in an eighth spell. By age 28–29, the average length of time elapsed since the last spell of near-daily marijuana use was slightly over 6 years (mean number of months = 72.5, SD = 39.0).

The quantities of marijuana used during near-daily marijuana spells are, as would be expected, much higher than during non-near-daily spells. For instance, almost 30% of the male users during near-daily spells smoke at least four to six joints at a sitting; this compares with only 5% of the male users during spells of non-daily use (Table 9.5). More than 60% of the men use an ounce of marijuana or more in a 30-day period during a spell

TABLE 9.2

Natural History of Near-Daily Spells of Marijuana Usage by Age 28–29 Among Males and Females

Features of marijuana-use history	Males				Females			
	Non-near-daily user	SD	Near-daily user	SD	Non-near-daily user	SD	Near-daily user	SD
M age at start of first marijuana use (yrs)	18.3	3.0	16.0	2.5	18.3	3.0	16.6	2.9
No. months until first near-daily spell	—		39.2	44.5	—		36.4	41.7
M age at start of first near-daily spell (yrs)	—		19.3	4.0	—		19.6	4.0
Proportions using daily by age 28–29 (%)	—		16.3		—		12.1	
n ≥	255		185		325		132	
No. months since last near-daily spell, among former users at age 28–29	—		68.7	39.1	—		77.5	38.6
n =			156				117	

of near-daily use, compared with only 7% during a spell of non-near-daily use.[1] During a spell of near-daily use, the majority of men and women remain high for 2 hours or less. The duration of the high is longer for near-daily spells than for non-near-daily spells, reflecting the greater quantity used during the former spells.

It is of interest that the quantities used diminish with age. The older the near-daily marijuana user, the lower the number of joints smoked on any one occasion (Table 9.6). This decline in quantities used is steeper for women than for men. (We cannot ascertain whether there have been changes in drug potency over time and whether the observed decline in the number of joints consumed was paralleled by an increase in THC concentration of the marijuana consumed in that same period.)

---

[1] In 1980 and 1984, respondents were asked questions about the quantities of marijuana used and the duration of high experienced in the last 30 days they used the drug in the last 12 months preceding the survey. The quantitites were computed for respondents according to whether they were in a spell of near-daily marijuana use at each period. If they were in a spell at both time periods, the quantities were computed for the longest spell recorded by each survey.

TABLE 9.3

Age at Start of Each Spell of Near-Daily Marijuana Use and Average Duration of Spells, for Men and Women by Age 28–29

Near-daily spell	Males					Females				
	M age at start of spell	SD	M duration (months)	SD	n	M age at start of spell	SD	M duration in months	SD	n
1	19.3	4.0	44.8	44.7	187	19.6	4.0	30.5	29.3	133
2	23.5	3.2	19.6	25.5	35	22.0	3.1	22.4	25.7	21
3	23.5	3.8	6.5	6.8	14	22.9	2.9	4.3	22.6	8
4	23.0	3.7	2.6	1.3	6	24.2	1.6	2.3	1.7	6
5	23.0	3.6	3.2	1.8	4	25.1	1.7	2.4	2.0	5
6	23.8	3.4	2.5	2.2	4	25.8	1.4	3.0	1.6	5
7	24.7	3.1	3.2	1.8	4	26.1	0.9	2.5	2.2	4
8	25.5	2.8	2.3	1.8	4	25.5	—	1.0	—	1
9	24.1	—	6.0	—	1					
10	25.1	—	6.0	—	1					
11	26.2	—	3.0	—	1					
12	27.2	—	3.0	—	1					
13	28.2	—	3.0	—	1					

TABLE 9.4

Marijuana-Use Pattern Following First Near-Daily-Use Spell, by Age 28–29 Among Males and Females

First Near-Daily Use Spell Followed By	Males (%)	Females (%)
No use	28.6	29.6
Use not near-daily: censored[a]	19.0	14.3
Use not near-daily, then no use	32.3	40.5
Use not near-daily, then resumes near-daily	8.6	6.5
First spell censored[a]	11.6	9.1
N	187	133

[a]Censored by the 1984 survey at age 28–29.

Other data document that near-daily marijuana use is an indicator of heavy drug involvement. Tables 9.7 and 9.8 illustrate the drug-use patterns of male marijuana users in their mid-twenties. Young adults were classified into five groups: those who had never used marijuana, those who had ever used but had not used in the past year, those who were using episodically less than once a month, those who were using less than four times a week, and those who were using consistently at least four to six times a week in the past year. As we noted earlier, young adults who use marijuana on a near-daily basis report much greater lifetime experience with a variety of drugs, much greater involvement in each, and much earlier ages of onset.

By age 29, those who have ever used marijuana nearly daily are also much more likely by age 29 than any other group of young adults to report having been in treatment for any form of drug abuse, to have been dependent on one or more drugs, and to have experienced problems in connection with their drug consumption, including drugs other than marijuana (Table 9.9) The most frequently mentioned problems refer to cognitive decrements (e.g., "interferes with thinking clearly"), negative effects on physical and psychological functioning (e.g., "reduces energy levels" and "increases feelings of depression"), and, for men, problems with one's spouse.

Vulnerability to Near-Daily Marijuana Use

To understand who the young people who escalate their pattern of marijuana use to near-daily consumption are, we examined, first, the risk factors for onset of marijuana use

TABLE 9.5

Quantity of Marijuana Used and Length of High During Spells of Near-Daily and Non-Near-Daily Use Among Males and Females

	Males		Females	
Quantities used	Non-near-daily spell[a] (%)	Near-daily spell (%)	Non-near-daily spell (%)	Near-daily spell (%)
Number of joints used per day during spells[a]				
Less than 1 joint	36.2	1.4	42.5	9.9
1 joint	32.2	17.5	37.2	32.2
2–3 joints	26.9	52.4	19.1	38.8
4–6 joints	4.6	21.3	0.4	12.3
7 or more	—	7.4	0.7	6.8
Total N	154	175	179	125
Ounces used last month used[b]				
Less than ½ oz.	84.8	22.2	85.5	41.8
½ oz.	8.2	15.5	9.1	17.3
1 oz.	7.0	41.5	5.4	20.3
2 oz.	—	13.6	—	18.1
3–5 oz.	—	7.2	—	2.5
Total N	90	65	77	41
Length of high when used[b]				
1–2 hr	85.9	57.8	72.6	61.2
3–6 hr	14.1	36.1	27.4	21.6
7–24 hr	—	6.1	—	17.2
Total N	92	66	85	41

[a]Information available for those who used marijuana at least 10 times.
[b]Restricted to those who used in last year either at age 25 or age 29.

and, second, the risk factors for progression to near-daily use. Because the risk factors were measured when cohort members were in high school, individuals who were absent from school on the days of the surveys but were interviewed in adulthood and included in the descriptive analyses, were perforce excluded from the predictive analyses ($n =$ 296). These individuals were slightly more involved in marijuana than were those who were already study participants at the first wave: 30% versus 25% experienced spells of near-daily marijuana use. There were 926 individuals who participated in all three waves of data collection. Initial study participants who were already using marijuana by the time

TABLE 9.6

Number of Marijuana Joints Used During Spells of Near-Daily Use by Age, for Males and Females

No. joints used per day	Age							
	<14	16	18	20	22	24	26	28
Males								
Less than 1 joint	6.8	3.0	2.0	2.4	3.9	4.5	6.3	3.7
1 joint	9.3	12.2	13.5	15.1	12.8	26.9	28.7	39.0
2–3 joints	50.2	53.3	60.1	53.5	56.8	52.0	45.8	38.3
4–6 joints	23.8	19.4	15.9	20.4	15.7	10.4	11.3	9.0
7 or more	9.9	12.1	8.6	8.7	10.9	6.2	7.8	10.0
N (at each age)	20	46	71	77	64	64	50	33
Females								
Less than 1 joint	—	2.0	5.7	9.7	7.3	20.7	14.4	5.4
1 joint	4.8	20.5	31.3	32.6	36.1	35.5	50.9	63.4
2–3 joints	55.8	47.2	42.8	41.1	47.3	27.1	28.8	31.2
4–6 joints	13.4	19.3	18.7	16.5	9.4	11.4	6.0	—
7 or more	26.0	11.1	1.4	—	—	5.3	—	—
N (at each age)	13	31	44	36	34	34	22	11

TABLE 9.7

Lifetime Frequency of Use of Licit and Illicit Drugs by Pattern of Marijuana Use Among Males at Age 24–25

Drugs ever used	Never used (%)	Used, not last 12 mo. (%)	≤1 time/mo. (%)	2–3 times/ mo. to 2–3 times/wk. (%)	≥4 times/ wk. (near-daily) (%)
Cigarettes, ≥1,000 times	21	49	44	57	77***
Hard liquor, ≥1,000 times	13	13	15	20	28*
Marijuana, ≥1,000 times	—	4	8	37	74***
Psychedelics, ≥10 times	0.5	4	12	16	39***
Cocaine, ≥10 times	0	8	6	27	55***
Heroin, ≥10 times	0	0.7	0.8	3	7**
≥2 illicit drugs other than marijuana	0.5	18	36	63	83***
N	141	151	87	147	90

Note. Data restricted to those who used substance at least 10 times ever.
$*p < .05.$ $**p < .01.$ $***p < .001.$

of the initial high school survey ($n = 209$) were also excluded from the sample at risk for onset of marijuana use. The analysis of progression to near-daily use, however, included those early marijuana users, when they had not yet reported any near-daily use ($n = 167$), as well as those who started using marijuana after the initial high school survey ($n = 479$). Thus, 717 (926 − 209) individuals were available for the onset analysis and 646 (167 + 479) were available for the progression analysis.

Logistic regression models were estimated predicting onset of marijuana use for the entire sample and near-daily marijuana use among those who had used marijuana. (The BMDP program was used to run the analyses.) The specific predictor variables included in the models are described in detail in Appendix A. As noted earlier, the factors belonged to seven domains: sociodemographic, family history of psychopathology, family relationships and attitudes, peer involvement, participation in delinquent activities, psychological symptoms, and drug-related variables. In the first step, models were estimated separately for male and females. In the second step, predictors that were significant for one sex and not for the other sex in the sex-specific models were all tested simultaneously using interaction terms with sex and added to the other predictors in a pooled

TABLE 9.8

Ages of First Use and Total Duration of Use of Marijuana, Cigarettes, and Alcohol by Pattern of Marijuana Use Among Males at Age 24–25

Age and duration of use	Marijuana use				
	Never used (%)	Used, not last 12 mo. (%)	≤1 time/mo. (%)	2–3 times/ mo. to 2–3 times/wk. (%)	≥4 times/wk. (near-daily) (%)
Marijuana					
Age first used (years)	—	17.8	17.2	16.8	15.7**
Total duration of use (months)	—	27.9	72.1	86.6	103.2**
Cigarettes					
Age first used (years)	15.2	14.8	15.5	15.1	14.7
Total duration of use (months)	29.1	63.5	48.6	68.7	85.5**
Alcohol					
Age first used (years)	14.2	13.1	12.9	13.1	12.5*
Total duration of use (months)	104.3	122.8	130.4	128.2	133.3**
N	141	151	87	147	90

Note. Data restricted to those who used substance at least 10 times ever.
*$p < .05$. **$p < .001$.

regression model. A final pooled model was run that included only the significant interaction terms, in addition to the basic set of predictors.

Adolescent Risk Factors for Onset of Marijuana Use

Young adults who started using marijuana after the first survey, when they were age 15–16, did so on average after 1.4 years for men and 2 years for women.

Detailed results of the logistic regressions for the total sample are presented in Appendix B in Table B1, and for males and females in Tables B2 and B3, respectively. The first two columns in each table present the regression estimates and the asymptotic standard errors of the estimates. The third column presents the standard deviations of the predictor variates that were used to compute the standardized effects (see Column 5). The fourth column presents the odds ratios between adjacent levels of predictor variates and dependent variates. For a dummy predictor variate, this is the classical odds ratio in

TABLE 9.9

Drug-Related Symptoms Reported by Age 28–29 by Marijuana Users Who Ever Experienced a Near-Daily Spell of Use and Those Who Did Not, Among Males and Females

Measure	Ever a near-daily user			
	Men		Women	
	No (%)	Yes (%)	No (%)	Yes (%)
Proportion who have ever				
Been in treatment for drug problem	3.8	14.2	0.2	4.9
Felt addicted to or dependent on drugs	5.4	27.1	6.3	19.1
Experienced any drug-related problems	48.2	69.9	36.6	61.8
Problems across drugs				
M	1.2	3.3	0.9	2.1
SD	2.3	4.6	2.6	4.3
Specific problems experienced				
Health problems	4.0	12.3	3.5	10.6
Performance in school or on job	5.5	18.1	2.6	10.1
Less energy	25.7	33.7	13.4	30.8
Thinking less clearly	21.6	45.0	15.9	29.3
Depression	7.1	22.7	9.1	13.8
Trouble with police	5.3	8.9	1.0	5.5
Accidents at home or work	1.4	5.2	3.2	1.9
Financial difficulties	3.6	18.0	1.0	5.6
Difficulties with parents	2.9	11.3	2.7	7.0
Difficulties with friends	2.0	7.9	2.8	5.3
Total $N \geq$	249	185	312	129
Difficulties with spouse or partner	18.4	30.4	6.5	12.4
Spouse/partner $N =$	181	139	255	98

a 2 × 2 table. The fifth column presents the standardized effects. When the predictor variate is a dummy variable, the standardized effect is the odds ratio (as in Column 4). When the predictor variate is a continuous variable, the standardized effect is the exponentiated value of the product of the regression coefficient (Column 1) and the standard deviation of the predictor variate. The standardized effect indicates the change expected in the dependent variable for a one-standard deviation change in value in the covariate. For continuous predictor variates, the standardized effect can be directly compared for magnitude.

Standardized effects for significant main and interaction effects are presented in Table 9.10.

For onset of marijuana use, several sex interactions are significant. Four factors are statistically significantly different between the sexes. Four factors are statistically significant for both males and females and not different between the two sexes. One factor reaches a low level of significance for males, but is not statistically significant between the sexes and is only marginally significant in the total sample.

For both sexes, frequency of attendance at religious services decreased the risk of marijuana initiation, whereas high educational expectations, participation in delinquent activities, and parental use of psychoactive drugs increase the risk. There appears to be a certain amount of parental role modeling because young persons who report their parents to be using medically prescribed psychotropic drugs, such as minor tranquilizers, are more likely to initiate marijuana use. Having a first-degree relative treated for any emotional problem almost reaches significance.[2]

TABLE 9.10

Significant Predictors of Onset of Marijuana Use Among Those Who Were Not Using Marijuana by Age 15–16 (Standardized Effects)

Predictors at age 15–16	Total	Men	Women	Sex difference ($p <$)
Delinquent participation	1.4***			
Frequency attends religious services	0.7***			
Education expectations	1.7****			
Parent psychoactive drug use in last 12 mo.[a]	1.2**			
Parent/sibling ever treated for emotional problems[a,b]	4.6*			
No. friends using marijuana		1.1	2.3****	.01
Degree of peer orientation		1.7***	1.1	.10
Closeness to parents		1.2	0.6***	.001
Parental education		0.7***	1.4***	.001
N	685	300	385	

[a]Dummy variable. Standardized effect = odds ratio.
[b]Assessment by age 29.
*$p < .10$. **$p < .05$. ***$p < .01$. ****$p < .001$.

[2]Comparison of results for the pooled sample with those for the sex-specific samples reveals seeming inconsistencies. Indeed,

In regard to the factors that are different between the sexes, two are significant for women but not for men. One is more significant for men than for women. And a fourth factor has opposite signs for men and for women.

Extent of marijuana use in the peer group is significant for females but not for males. The higher the number of friends reported to be using marijuana while the adolescent girl is in high school, the greater the risk of initiating marijuana use. For females, coming from a family with high education increases the risk of initiation, whereas being close to one's parents decreases the risk.

For males, in contrast with females, high level of parental education is related to a decrease in risk of initiation. Although marijuana use by the peer group is not significant for males, extent of peer orientation is. Strong peer orientation, when youngsters respect their peers' opinions over those of their parents, increases the risk of marijuana initiation.

In general, young people at risk for marijuana initiation are more deviant than their peers and come from families where the parents appear to experience some form of psychological problems. One factor, however, is inconsistent with the general greater deviancy of adolescents who are at risk for marijuana initiation: level of educational expectation. The higher the expected educational level, the greater the risk for marijuana use. We will return to this finding in the conclusion.

These findings generally confirm those previously reported in the literature: Peer influences are strong for onset of marijuana use. Conventionality is a restraining factor for involvement in marijuana, although high levels of educational aspirations increase the risk.

Adolescent Risk Factors for Progression to Near-Daily Marijuana Use

The same approach, with the addition of three variables, was tested to predict the transition into near-daily marijuana use among those who were already using marijuana, whether by the time of the initial school survey or subsequently. Two of the variables added to the model measure aspects of the respondent's drug history: the ages of first use of marijuana and of an illicit drug other than marijuana (prior to becoming a near-daily marijuana user, as determined from the drug-history chart). In addition, an interaction term between closeness to parents and peer orientation was included in the final

---

the coefficients for delinquent participation and parental psychoactive use are significant for the pooled sample and not significantly different between males and females. Yet the effects are nonsignificant for males. These statistical results indicate that they fall within the margin of error in which they could be positive and statistically significant for each sex.

model that was tested, and is presented in the tables, as is discussed later. The detailed model for the total sample is presented in Table B4 and for each sex separately in Tables B5 and B6.

Standardized effects for the significant predictors in the pooled sample are presented in Table 9.11.

In contrast with onset of marijuana use, there are no significant differences between the sexes in the significant predictors of escalation of marijuana use. A smaller and different set of factors predict progression to near-daily marijuana use than those that predict marijuana use onset. The reduction in number of significant coefficients is in part due to the smaller sample sizes.

The most important factor is the age at which the young person began to use marijuana. The earlier the age of onset, the greater the risk of escalation. Two other classes of factors are also important. One class pertains to a family history of psychopathology. Those with a first-degree relative, such as a parent or sibling, who had sought treatment for an emotional disorder, or those with a father who was a heavy drinker or an alcoholic when the respondent was growing up are more likely to progress to near-daily marijuana use. (Too few mothers were reported to have ever been problem drinkers for maternal

TABLE 9.11

Significant Predictors of Progression to a Spell of Near-Daily Marijuana Use Among Those Who Ever Used Marijuana (Standardized Effects)

Predictors at age 15–16	Total[a]
Parent or sibling ever treated for emotional disorder	1.4*
Father heavy drinker or alcoholic while respondent in high school	1.9**
Grade average last term	0.8*
Age at first marijuana use	0.5***
Peer Orientation × Closeness to Parents[b]	
Low	0.8
Average	1.0
High	1.3
N	385

[a]No sex-specific predictors were identified.
[b]Overall significance for interaction term is $p < .05$. Levels of significance for levels of parental closeness were not calculated.
*$p < .10$. **$p < .05$. ***$p < .001$.

excessive drinking to be included as a predictor in the models.) Finally, an important finding pertains to the role of academic performance. Young people who perform at a high level academically while in high school are less likely to become near-daily marijuana users than those with poor academic performance.

A puzzling result in the analyses pertains to the impact of parental closeness and peer orientation. These factors have generally been found to have predictable and opposite effects: Closeness to parents acts as a protective factor for drug involvement, whereas peer orientation acts as a risk factor (Brook, Whiteman, & Gordon, 1983; Kandel et al., 1978). Yet models run first without the interaction term indicated that both variables were positively related to an increased risk of progressing to near-daily marijuana-use spells. Cross-tabulations of joint high–low values on the variables revealed that two groups had the highest and identical proportions of near-daily marijuana users: those low on both factors and those high on both. That is, adolescents who were socially isolated from peers and parents and those who were close to both appeared to be at highest risk for regular marijuana involvement. The interaction term was included in the model to capture this result, and is positive. As is discussed later, the highest proportion of daily marijuana users is expected among those high both in closeness to parents and in peer orientation.

Interpretation of Predictors of Near-Daily Use of Marijuana

To provide a substantive interpretation of selected results from the logistic regression, the effects were translated into the proportions expected to initiate near-daily marijuana use among marijuana users with specific attributes, controlling for other significant predictors. Table 9.12 presents the statistically adjusted rates for different values of the significant independent variates, assuming that the values of the remaining covariates are fixed at their population means. When we control for other factors, men are 40% more likely than women to become near-daily users. Having a father who is a problem drinker or an alcoholic increases the risk by more than 50%, and having a first-degree relative treated for an emotional disorder increases the risk by 30%.

Almost twice as many marijuana users are expected to become near-daily or daily marijuana users among those who were failing in high school compared with those who excelled. Almost two and half times as many are expected to progress to near-daily marijuana use when they started using marijuana at age 13, compared with those who started at age 19.

TABLE 9.12
Adjusted Rates of Progression to Near-Daily Marijuana Use for Values of Significant Predictors

Covariate	Near-daily initiation expected (%)
Sex	
Male	36
Female	26
Parent/sibling ever treated for emotional disorder	
No	28
Yes	36
Father heavy drinker or alcoholic while respondent in high school	
No	28
Yes	43
Grade average last term	
A	24
C	34
F	45
Marijuana, age first use	
13	58
15	46
17	34
19	24
Closeness to parents/Degree of peer orientation	
Low/low	31
High/low	32
Low/high	28
High/high	39

Note. Rates are based on the assumption that the values of the remaining covariates are fixed at the population averages.

The effects of degree of peer orientation and closeness to parents interact. When we control for other covariates, the highest expected rate of daily marijuana use (39%) occurs among young people close both to parents and to peers. Attempts to interpret these results have been unsatisfactory. In particular, we tested the hypothesis (suggested to us by Joan McCord) that those close to both peers and parents may come from permissive families in which the children are encouraged to experiment in a variety of ways, but in which the children, even when near-daily users, would not be as heavily involved in marijuana use as the others. This does not seem to be the case. Both groups (those estranged from peers and parents, as well as those close to both peers and parents) initiated near-daily spells at the same age and experienced the same average duration of these spells. Similarly, the reasons for using marijuana stated by both groups are the same, except that those low in closeness to both peers and parents mention "to overcome depression" much more frequently than any other group. Thirty-nine percent of those low in closeness to both peers and parents give this reason versus 27% of those close to parents and peers and only 9% of those low in peer orientation and high in closeness to parents. Another potential explanation is that because of the interval between the measurement of the predictors and the occurrence of the event being predicted, the measures of peer and parental closeness experienced while a high school student may not be as strong and relevant measures of these domains at the time the young person reaches the period of risk for escalation to regular marijuana use as they were for onset of marijuana use. On the average, onset to near-daily marijuana use occurs about 4 years after the initial measurement of the predictive factors included in the models, compared with less than 2 years for onset of marijuana use.

Discussion and Conclusion

These data support the conclusion that heavy drug involvement is a phenomenon of late adolescence and early adulthood. A surprisingly high proportion of those who ever experiment with marijuana go on to regular, almost daily use. However, most such users relinquish this pattern of use and shift to more episodic consumption. Spells of near-daily marijuana use first occur between ages 19 and 20 and last an average of over 3½ years. The peak ages of involvement are consonant with epidemiological data on the age distribution of individuals in the general population who meet criteria for substance abuse disorders. The data from the ECA indicate that the rates of substance abuse that meet diagnostic criteria are highest in those in their twenties (Anthony & Helzer, 1991; Robins et al., 1984). However, the cross-sectional ECA data make it difficult to separate age-related trends from historical factors or cohort differences. Although cohort specificity still weakens the conclusions to be derived from the present sample, the longitudinal data document the reduced involvement with increasing age of those who use marijuana at the same near-daily frequency. Not only is there a drop with age in the prevalence of spells of near-daily use, but the amount of marijuana consumed at any one sitting also declines with age, especially after age 22. Near-daily marijuana users are for the most part involved in a pattern of multiple drug use in which marijuana is only one of the drugs that they experienced.

The findings that delinquent participation and high educational aspirations both predict marijuana initiation suggest that there may be two groups of young people who start experimenting with illicit drugs. One group would consist of those who experiment as part of an adolescent search for new experiences but who have sufficient stake in society not to progress to potentially harmful patterns of use. A second group, more delinquent and less committed to education and academic pursuits, would consist of those who go on to more regular and harmful patterns of use.

Important differences can be observed in the factors that predict onset and those that predict escalation to regular marijuana use. The importance of early onset of marijuana use for subsequent escalation is documented. This effect appears to result from two processes. Young people who start using marijuana at an early age are at risk for onset of spells of near-daily use for a longer period of time. In addition, the risks for converting from any use to regular and frequent use are consistently higher among adolescents who initiate marijuana at a younger age, compared with those who initiate at a later age, for those ages that are directly comparable. As illustrated in Figure 9.1, the hazards curves follow identical patterns through the middle and late teens for both groups, although the hazards for those who initiated marijuana use at age 16 or younger are consistently above those for adolescents who initiated after the age of 16. The earlier the age at which a young person starts using marijuana, the greater the risk of progressing to a regular and heavy pattern of marijuana consumption. This conclusion is consonant with the findings of Kaplan et al. (1986) in the only other investigation known to us of the predictors of near-daily marijuana use among marijuana users. We have emphasized the importance of early onset of drug use as a risk factor for progressing to higher stages of drug use, including progressing from marijuana to the use of illicit drugs other than marijuana (Yamaguchi & Kandel, 1984). The present data document that age of onset is also crucial for predicting heavy involvement within a particular stage. In addition, the importance of familial factors is indicated by the finding that a family history of treated mental disorders and a paternal history of heavy drinking occur more frequently among those youths who escalate than those who do not. These familial effects could reflect genetic or environmental influences (or both), which cannot be disaggregated in the present research.

The finding regarding the protective role of academic performance for escalation to regular use has crucial policy implications. An important theoretical perspective for explaining individual behavior, and in particular deviant behavior, has its origins in Hirschi's

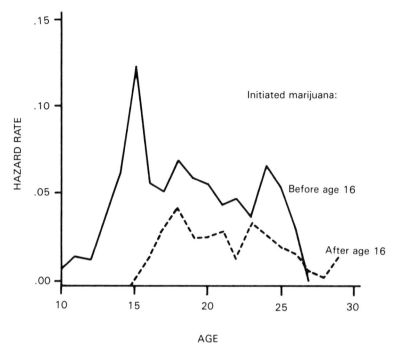

FIGURE 1.1   Hazard rate for first spell of near-daily marijuana use by age of marijuana onset.

(1969) emphasis on control and commitment. This approach stresses the importance of commitment to conventional social groups as a restraining force against participation in deviant activities. The present findings document that commitment to one's family and to religion act as restraining forces for initiating illicit drug use, because marijuana is the first drug of entry into illicit drug experimentation. Commitment to school protects against escalation to near-daily use. In contrast, attachment to peers increases the initiation of use of illicit drugs.

These findings permit a specification of the types of commitments and groups that are important at different phases of the process of drug involvement. Bonding to family appears to be especially important in the phase of initiation to marijuana.[3] Commitment to school appears to be an especially important protective and restraining factor for escalation to regular and heavy marijuana use. Young people who perform well

---

[3]In an earlier phase of this research, analyses of the risk factors for moving from one stage of drug use to another were carried out on the total high school sample of which the members of the present cohort are a subsample. Closeness to father was found

in school would have more to lose, and, correlatively, those who perform poorly would have less to lose, by becoming heavily involved in the use of illicit drugs. This finding is consonant with inferences to be drawn from the work of Hawkins (Hawkins & Catalano, 1987; Hawkins, Lishner, Catalano & Howard, 1986). Bonding to family predicts early aggressiveness among children, and improvement in school performance among preteens predicts reduced involvement in delinquent activities. We reported in prior work that drug use can lead to school failure and dropping out of school (Mensch & Kandel, 1988). Correlatively, the present data indicate that successful school performance is a protective factor mitigating against escalation to a pattern of regular marijuana use. Working toward strengthening the educational system would have many beneficial effects, including a potential reduction in the number of youngsters who go on to abusing drugs.

In closing, we would like briefly to return to the methodological issue we raised at the beginning of this chapter: How useful are existing longitudinal studies for investigating vulnerability to substance abuse, and how best can the issue be investigated?

Our opinion is that ongoing studies may not be optimally suited to answer the question of substance-abuse vulnerability, for a number of reasons. The definition of *substance abuse* itself is ambiguous. With rare exceptions, such as the ECA studies among adults (Robins et al., 1984) or Cohen and Brook's (1987) follow-up of a community sample, the studies do not include diagnostically based criteria of substance abuse that are based on current psychiatric nosology. The studies rely on quantity–frequency criteria, for which the correspondence with diagnostic criteria remains to be established. More psychometric work is required to establish such a correspondence. However, the data sets necessary to accomplish this task may not be available.

Most important, most studies do not have the closely spaced longitudinal data that are required in young adulthood to measure certain vulnerability factors at the point at which the escalation to drug involvement takes place and the factors are operative. Certain factors, such as familial ones, can be assumed to have a long time lag. The timing of their measurement is less problematic than that of factors that can be assumed to have a

---

to reduce the risk of progressing from using alcohol to using marijuana. This effect was smaller than the effect of this factor on making the transition from the use of marijuana to the use of illicit drugs other than marijuana. Differences in the two analyses must be noted. The earlier analysis was based on a sample that spanned a wider age range in adolescence, because it included 9th through 12th graders, whereas the present sample was drawn from the 10th and 11th grades. In addition, the earlier analysis was subject to right censoring (i.e., lack of knowledge for individuals who had not initiated marijuana by the date of the survey) because the analysis was limited to changes observed over a 6-month period from the fall to the spring of a school year and did not follow respondents through the completion of the major periods of risk for initiation to various classes of illicit drugs.

shorter time lag. For instance, both epidemiological and clinical data suggest that depression may be an important determinant of substance abuse (Gawin & Kleber, 1985; Kandel et al., 1978; Paton, Kessler, & Kandel, 1977). To the extent that psychological distress is important, it would need to be measured relatively closely in time preceding the transition to abuse. The difficulty is that different risk factors have different time lags. Furthermore, these lags remain to be specified.

In the absence of precise knowledge, the best way to proceed may be to carry out longitudinal assessments at annual intervals, beginning in adolescence, prior to the risk for onset of illicit drug use, and persisting through early adulthood, the period of risk for escalation to abuse. Innovative research and sampling designs need to be developed to ensure a large enough number of cases for analysis. A two-stage design, such as advocated by Shrout (Shrout & Newman, 1989) for psychiatric disorders, may be a promising option.

Such studies will require major financial commitment on the part of the funding agency and great fortitude on the part of the investigators. The payoff and excitement to be generated by such studies is well worth the effort.

References

American Psychiatric Association. (1980). *Diagnostic and statistical manual of mental disorders* (3rd ed.). Washington, DC: Author.

American Psychiatric Association. (1987). *Diagnostic and statistical manual of mental disorders* (3rd ed., rev.). Washington, DC: Author.

Anthony, J. (1983). Distribution and consequences of near-daily cannabis use. *American Journal of Epidemiology, 118,* 423.

Anthony, J. C., & Helzer, J. E. (1991). Syndromes of drug abuse and dependence. In L. N. Robins & D. A. Regier (Eds.), *Psychiatric disorders in America* (pp. 116–154). New York: Free Press.

Baumrind, D. (1985). Familial antecedents of adolescent drug use: A developmental perspective. In C. L. Jones & R. J. Battjes (Eds.), *Etiology of drug abuse: Implications for prevention* (NIDA Research Monograph 56, pp. 13–44). Rockville, MD: National Institute on Drug Abuse.

Block, J., Keyes, S., & Block, J. H. (1986, March). *Childhood personality and environmental antecedents of drug use: A prospective longitudingal study.* Paper presented at the meeting of the Society for Life History Research in Psychopathology, Palm Springs, CA.

Brook, J. S., Gordon, A. S., & Brook, D. W. (1980). Perceived paternal relationships, adolescent personality, and female marijuana use. *Journal of Psychology, 105,* 277–285.

Brook, J. S., Whiteman, M., & Gordon, A. S. (1983). Stages of drug use in adolescence: Personality, peer, and family correlates. *Developmental Psychology, 19,* 269–277.

Brook, J. S., Whiteman, M., Gordon, A. S., & Cohen, P. (1986a). Dynamics of childhood and adolescent personality traits and adolescent drug use. *Developmental Psychology, 22,* 403–414.

Brook, J. S., Whiteman, M., Gordon, A. S., & Cohen, P. (1986b). Some models and mechanisms for explaining the impact of maternal and adolescent characteristics on adolescent stages of drug use. *Developmental Psychology, 22,* 460–467.

Brook, J. S., Whiteman, M., Nomura, C., Gordon, A. S., & Cohen, P. (1988). Personality, family, and ecological influences on adolescent drug use: A developmental analysis. *Journal of Chemical Dependency Treatment, 1,* 123–162.

Clayton, R. R., & Ritter, C. (1985). The epidemiology of alcohol and drug abuse among adolescents. *Advances in Alcohol and Substance Abuse, 4,* 69–97.

Cohen, P., & Brook, J. (1987). Family factors related to the persistence of psychopathology in childhood and adolescence. *Psychiatry, 50,* 332–345.

Coombs, R. H., & Landsverk, J. (1988). Parenting styles and substance use during childhood and adolescence. *Journal of Marriage and the Family, 50,* 473–482.

Dishion, T. J., & Loeber, R. (1985). Male adolescent marijuana and alcohol use: The role of parents and peers revisited. *Journal of Alcohol and Substance Abuse, 11* (1, 2), 11–25.

Dishion, T. J., Patterson, G. R., & Reid, J. R. (1988). Parent and peer factors associated with drug sampling in early adolescence: Implications for treatment. In E. R. Rahdert & J. Grabowski (Eds.), *Adolescent drug abuse: Analyses of treatment research* (pp. 69–93). Rockville, MD: National Institute on Drug Abuse.

Dishion, T. J., Reid, J. B. & Patterson, G. R. (1987). *Empirical guidelines for a family intervention for adolescent drug use.* Eugene: Oregon Social Learning Center.

Elliott, D. S., Huizinga, D., & Ageton, S. S. (1985). *Explaining delinquency and drug use.* Beverly Hills, CA: Sage.

Gawin, F. H., and Kleber, H. D. (1985). Cocaine use in a treatment population: Patterns and diagnostic distinctions. In N. J. Kozel & E. H. Adams (Eds.), *Cocaine use in America: Epidemiologic and clinical perspectives* (NIDA Research Monograph 61, pp. 182–192). Rockville, MD: National Institute on Drug Abuse.

Hawkins, J. D., & Catalano, R. F. (1987, March). *The Seattle Social Development Project: Progress report on a longitudinal prevention study.* Paper presented at the National Institute on Drug Abuse Science Press Seminar, Washington, DC.

Hawkins, J. D., Lishner, D. M., & Catalano, R. F., Jr. (1985). Childhood predictors and the prevention of adolescent substance abuse. In C. L. Jones & R. J. Battjes (Eds.), *Etiology of drug abuse: Implications for prevention* (pp. 75–126). Washington, DC: Superintendent of Documents, U.S. Government Printing Office.

Hawkins, J. D., Lishner, D. M., Catalano, R. F., & Howard, M. O. (1986). Childhood predictors of adolescent substance abuse: Toward an empirically grounded theory. *Journal of Children in Contemporary Society, 8,* 11–48.

Hirschi, T. (1969). *Causes of delinquency.* Berkeley, CA: University of California Press.

Huba, G. J., & Bentler, P. M. (1980). The role of peer and adult models for drug taking at different stages in adolescence. *Journal of Youth and Adolescence, 9,* 449–465.

Hundleby, J. D., & Mercer, G. W. (1987). Family and friends as social environments and their relationship to young adolescents' use of alcohol, tobacco, and marijuana. *Journal of Marriage and the Family, 49,* 151–164.

Jessor, R., & Jessor, S. L. (1977). *Problem behavior and psychosocial development: A longitudinal study.* San Diego, CA: Academic Press.

Johnston, L. D. (1980, September). *The daily marijuana user.* Paper presented at the meeting of the National Alcohol and Drug Coalition, Washington, DC.

Johnston, L. D. (1981). Frequent marijuana use: Correlates, possible effects, and reasons for using and quitting. In R. deSilva, R. Dupont, & G. Russell (Eds.), *Treating the marijuana dependent person* (pp. 8–14). New York: American Council on Marijuana.

Johnston, L. D., Bachman, J. G., & O'Malley, P. M. (1979). *Highlights from Drugs and the Class of '78: Behaviors, attitudes and recent national trends.* Rockville, MD: National Institute on Drug Abuse.

Johnston, L. D., Bachman, J. G., & O'Malley, P. M. (1988). *Illicit drug use, smoking, and drinking by America's high school students, college students, and young adults 1975–1987.* Rockville, MD: National Institute on Drug Abuse.

Johnston, L. D., O'Malley, P. M., & Bachman, J. G. (1984). *Drugs and american high school students, 1975–1983.* Rockville, MD: National Institute on Drug Abuse.

Kandel, D. B. (1978). Convergences in prospective longitudinal surveys of drug use in normal populations. In D. B. Kandel (Ed.), *Longitudinal research on drug use: Empirical findings and methodological issues* (pp. 3–38). Washington, DC: Hemisphere–Wiley.

Kandel, D. B. (1980). Drug and drinking behavior among youth. *Annual Review of Sociology, 6,* 235–285.

Kandel, D. B. (1984). Marijuana users in young adulthood. *Archives of General Psychiatry, 41,* 200–209.

Kandel, D. B., Kessler, R. C., & Margulies, R. Z. (1978). Antecedents of adolescent initiation into stages of drug use: A developmental analysis. In D. B. Kandel (Ed.), *Longitudinal research on drug use: Empirical findings and methodological issues* (pp. 73–99). Washington, DC: Hemisphere–Wiley.

Kandel, D. B., & Logan, J. A. (1984). Patterns of drug use from adolescence to young adulthood: I. Periods of risk for initiation, continued use, and discontinuation. *American Journal of Public Health, 74,* 660–666.

Kaplan, H. B., Martin, S. S., Johnson, R. J., & Robbins, C. A. (1986). Escalation of marijuana use: Application of a general theory of deviant behavior. *Journal of Health and Social Behavior, 27,* 44–61.

Kellam, S. G., Brown, C. H., Rubin, B. R., & Ensminger, M. E. (1983). Paths leading to teenage psychiatric symptoms and substance use: Developmental epidemiological studies in Woodlawn. In S. B. Guze, F. J. Earls, & J. E. Barrett (Eds.), *Childhood psychopathology and development* (pp. 17–52). New York: Raven Press.

Kellam, S., Simon, M., & Ensminger, M. E. (1980). Antecedents in first grade of teenage drug use and psychological well-being: A ten-year community-wide prospective study. In D. Ricks & B. Dohrenwend (Eds.), *Origins of psychopathology: Research and public policy* (pp. 17–42). New York: Cambridge University Press.

Kleinman, P. H., Wish, E. D., Deren, S., & Rainone, G. & Morehouse, E. (1988). Daily marijuana use and problem behaviors among adolescents. *International Journal of the Addictions, 23,* 87–107.

McCord, W., and McCord, J. (1960). *Origins of alcoholism.* Stanford, CA: Stanford University Press.

Mensch, B. S., & Kandel, D. B. (1988). Dropping out of high school and drug involvement. *Sociology of Education, 61,* 95–113.

Miller, J. D., Cisin, I. H., Gardner-Keaton, H., Harrell, A. V., Wirtz, P. W., Abelson, H. I., & Fishburne, P. M. (1983). *National survey on drug abuse: Main findings 1982.* Rockville, MD: National Institute on Drug Abuse.

Needle, R., McCubbin, H., Wilson, M., Reinect, R., Lazar, A., & Mederer, H. (1986). Interpersonal influences in adolescent drug use: The role of older siblings, parents, and peers. *International Journal of the Addictions, 21,* 739–766.

Newcomb, M., & Bentler, P. M. (1988). *Consequences of adolescent drug use.* Newbury Park, CA: Sage.

Pandina, R. J., & Schuele, J. A. (1983). Psychosocial correlates of alcohol and drug use of adolescent students and adolescents in treatment. *Journal of Studies on Alcohol, 44,* 950–973.

Paton, S., Kessler, R., & Kandel, D. B. (1977). Depressive mood and illicit drug use: A longitudinal analysis. *Journal of Genetic Psychology, 131,* 267–289.

Raveis, V. H., & Kandel, D. B. (1989). Cessation of illicit drug use in young adulthood. *Archives of General Psychiatry, 46,* 109–116.

Robins, L. N., Helzer, J. E., Weissman, M. W., Orvaschel, H., Gruenberg, E., Burke, J. D., & Reiger, D. A. (1984). Lifetime prevalence of specific psychiatric disorders in three sites. *Archives of General Psychiatry, 41,* 949–958.

Shrout, P. E., & Newman, S. (1989). Design of two-phase prevalence surveys of rare disorders. *Biometrics, 45,* 549–555.

Simcha-Fagan, O., Gersten, J. C., & Langner, T. S. (1986). Early precursors and concurrent correlates of patterns of illicit drug use in adolescence. *Journal of Drug Issues, 16,* 7–28.

Single, E., Kandel, D. B., & Johnson, B. (1975). The reliability and validity of drug use responses in a large scale longitudinal survey. *Journal of Drug Issues, 5,* 426–443.

Vicary, J. R., & Lerner, J. V. (1986). Parental attributes and adolescent drug use. *Journal of Adolescence, 9,* 115–122.

Yamaguchi, K., & Kandel, D. B. (1984). Patterns of drug use from adolescence to young adulthood—III. Predictors of progression. *American Journal of Public Health, 74,* 673–681.

Zucker, R. A., & Noll, R. A. (1987). The interaction of child and environment in the early development of drug involvement: A far ranging review and a planned very early intervention. *Drugs and Society, 1,* 57–97.

Description of Predictors Entered in Multivariate Models

Missing data dummies were included for variables for which the information was missing for more than 5% of the sample.

Sociodemographic

- Sex: 1 = male, 2 = female.
- Parents' education in years: If reported for both parents, maximum was taken. The range is from 3 to 20.
- Family intactness: 1 = not living with both parents, 2 = living with both parents.

Family History of Disorders

- Parent or sibling ever teated for an emotional disorder (ascertained at ages 25 and 29): 0 = no, 1 = yes.
- Father a problem drinker or an alcoholic (ascertained at ages 25 and 29): 0 = no, 1 = yes. (No parallel variable was included for mothers because a very small proportion, 3.6%, were reported to be problem drinkers or alcoholics.)
- Missing dummy for father a problem drinker.

Parental Relationships and Attitudes at Time 1 (Age 15–16)

- Extent of parental use of prescribed psychoactive drugs in the past 12 months: 1 = not at all, 2 = a few times, 3 = once a month, 4 = several times a month, 5 = several times a week, 6 = every day.

- Extent of parental alcohol drinking in the past 12 months: 1 = *never,* 2 = *less than once a month,* 3 = *1–3 times a month,* 4 = *once a week,* 5 = *several times a week,* 6 = *1–2 drinks a day,* 7 = *3 or more drinks a day* (highest value reported by mother or father for beer, hard liquor, or both).
- Missing data dummy for parental alcohol use.
- Mother discourages marijuana use: 0 = *tolerates, prefers not use,* 1 = *positively discourages or forbids use.*
- Missing data dummy for mother discourages marijuana use.
- Parental rule against using drugs: 0 = *no,* 1 = *yes.*
- Closeness-to-parents index: Mean of closeness to mother and to father. If only one parent is in household, set to value for that parent. Mother index is average multiplied by 10 of 5 items: depending on mother for advice, feeling close to mother, wanting to be like mother, getting praise from her and talking to her about personal problems, each coded from 1 to 5 except praise, coded 1 to 6 (Cronbach's alpha = .79). Father index includes first four items (Cronbach's alpha = .77). Range of index is 10 to 52.5. (For interaction terms presented in Tables 9.11 and 9.12, the following values were defined: low closeness = 20; average closeness = 30; high closeness = 40.)

Peer Involvement at Time 1 (Age 15–16)

- Index of parent–peer orientation: whether respondent feels greater understanding from parents or friends and relies more on opinions of parents or friends (Cronbach's alpha = .70). The index is the average of the two items, each coded 1 = *parents much more* to 5 = *friends much more,* multiplied by 10. The range is from 10 to 50.
- Peer activity index: Average, multiplied by 10, of 5 items measuring frequency of getting together with friends outside of school, dating, attending parties, hanging around with a group of kids, and driving around with friends, each coded 1 to 4 (Cronbach's alpha = .69). The range is from 10 to 40.
- Number of friends using marijuana: 1 = *none,* 2 = *few,* 3 = *some,* 4 = *most,* 5 = *all.*

Commitment/Deviance at Time 1 (Age 15–16)

- Frequency of attendance at religious services: 1 = *every day,* 2 = *1–2 times per week,* 3 = *1–3 times a month,* 4 = *rarely or never.*

- Delinquency scale. Participation over the past 3 months in seven delinquent acts: theft under $2, theft $2–$50, been sent out of a classroom by a teacher, cheated on a class test, run away from home or stayed out all night without parents' permission, driven too fast, been drunk (Cronbach's alpha = .64).
- Grade average last term: $5 = A, 4 = B, 3 = C, 2 = D, 1 = F$.
- Educational expectations: $1 =$ *won't finish high school,* $2 =$ *high school only,* $3 =$ *technical or business school,* $4 =$ *some college,* $5 =$ *college,* $6 =$ *graduate or professional school.*

Psychological Symptoms at Time 1 (Age 15–16)

- Index of depressive symptoms is average score, multiplied by 10, received on how much respondent has been bothered in the past year by six symptoms: feeling unhappy, sad, or depressed; feeling hopeless about the future; feeling too tired to do things; having trouble going to sleep or staying asleep; feeling nervous or tense; worrying too much about things, each coded 1 to 3 (Cronbach's alpha = .80). The range of the index is from 10 to 30.
- Missing data dummy for depressive symptoms.

Drug-Use History

- Age of first marijuana use.
- Ever used illicit drugs other than marijuana (i.e., cocaine, psychedelics, nonprescribed sedatives, stimulants, and minor tranquilizers) prior to daily marijuana use: $0 =$ *no,* $1 =$ *yes.*

Logistic Regressions Predicting Onset of Marijuana Use
Among Nonusers and Onset of Spells of Near-Daily Use of
Marijuana Among Users
(Tables B1 to B6)

TABLE B1

Logistic Regression Predicting Onset of Marijuana Use Among Those Who Were Not Using Marijuana by Age 15–16 (*N* = 685) (Model on Total Sample With Five Significant Sex Interactions.)

Predictors[a]	b	SE	Predicted SD	Odds ratio	Standard effect
Sociodemographic					
Sex: female (vs. male)[b]	−.159	1.592	.497		
Parental education	−.397****	.114	2.912		
Parent's Education × Sex	.258****	.068			
Family intactness at age 15–16[b]	−.284	.373	.382	.75	.75
Family history of disorders					
Parent/sibling ever treated for emotional disorder[b]	1.524*	.831	.429		
Parent/Sibling Ever Treated for Emotional Disorder × Sex	−.784	.489			
Father heavy drinker/alcoholic while subject in high school[b]	.180	.340	.301	1.20	1.20
Parental characteristics at age 15–16					
Parental psychoactive use in last 12 months	.192**	.087	1.254	1.21	1.27
Parental alcohol use in last 12 months	.002	.060	1.954	1.00	1.00
Mother discourages marijuana use[b]	−.593	.418	.454	.55	.55
Parental rules against drug use	.071	.239	.415	1.07	1.07
Closeness to parents	.131***	.049	7.662		
Closeness to Parents × Sex	−.101****	.030			
Peer involvement at age 15–16					
Degree of peer orientation	.087***	.033	11.316		
Degree of Peer Orientation × Sex	−.040*	.020			
Peer activity index	.015	.017	6.230	1.02	1.10
No. friends who use marijuana	−.583*	.351	1.052		
No. Friends Who Use Marijuana × Sex	.675***	.222			
Commitment/deviance at age 15–16					
Frequency attends religious services	−.331***	.108	.908	.72	.74
Delinquent participation	.238***	.089	1.360	1.27	1.38
Grade average last term	.034	.139	.815	1.03	1.03
Educational expectations	.388****	.089	1.312	1.48	1.66
Depressive symptoms index	.007	.023	6.233	1.01	1.00
Constant	−.755	2.805			
χ^2 = 690.969					
df = 657					

[a]Dummy variables are missing for the following four variables included in the models: mother discourages marijuana use, parental alcohol use, father problem drinker, and depressive symptoms.
[b]Dummy variable.
*$p < .10$. **$p < .05$. ***$p < .01$. ****$p < .001$.

TABLE B2

Logistic Regression Predicting Onset of Marijuana Use Among Those Who Were Not Using Marijuana by Age 15–16, Males ($N = 300$)

Predictors[a]	b	SE	Predicted SD	Odds ratio	Standard effect
Sociodemographic					
Parental education	−.142**	.059	2.783	.87	.67
Family intactness at age 15–16	−1.076	.693	.382	.34	.34
Family history of disorders					
Parent/sibling ever treated for emotional disorder	.773*	.401	.415	2.17	2.17
Father heavy drinker/alcoholic while subject in high school	.134	.574	.261	1.14	1.14
Parental characteristics at age 15–16					
Parents psychoactive use in last 12 months	.062	.130	1.229	1.06	1.08
Parents alcohol use in last 12 months	.032	.092	1.856	1.03	1.06
Mother discourages marijuana use	−.405	.572	.459	.67	.67
Parental rules against drug use	.421	.346	.419	1.52	1.52
Closeness to parents	.028	.023	7.386	1.03	1.23
Peer involvement at age 15–16					
Degree of peer orientation	.046***	.016	10.878	1.05	1.65
Peer activity index	.027	.027	5.993	1.03	1.00
No. friends who use marijuana	.107	.165	1.010	1.11	1.11
Commitment/deviance at age 15–16					
Frequency attends religious services	−.341***	.164	.887	.71	.74
Delinquent participation	.158	.116	1.484	1.17	1.26
Grade average last term	.142	.214	.805	1.15	1.12
Educational expectations	.414***	.132	1.293	1.51	1.71
Depressive symptoms index	.004	.036	5.346	1.00	1.02
Constant	−.113	2.099			
$\chi^2 = $ 312.389*					
$df = $ 278					

[a]Dummy variables are missing for the following four variables included in the models: mother discourages marijuana use; parental alcohol use; father problem drinker; and depressive symptoms.

*$p < .10$. **$p < .05$. ***$p < .01$.

TABLE B3

Logistic Regression Predicting Onset of Marijuana Use Among Those Who Were Not Using Marijuana by Age 15–16, Females (N = 385)

Predictors[a]	b	SE	Predicted SD	Odds ratio	Standard effect
Sociodemographic					
Parental education	.129**	.049	3.003	1.14	1.47
Family intactness at age 15–16	.253	.492	.382	1.29	1.29
Family history of disorders					
Parent/sibling ever treated for emotional disorder	−.064	.312	.439	.94	.94
Father heavy drinker/alcoholic while subject in high school	.166	.434	.328	1.18	1.18
Parental characteristics at age 15–16					
Parental psychoactive use in last 12 months	.325**	.122	1.274	1.38	1.51
Parental alcohol use in last 12 months	−.078	.084	2.029	.92	.85
Mother discourages marijuana use	−.888	.659	.450	.41	.41
Parental rules against drug use	−.202	.338	.412	.82	.82
Closeness to parents	−.072**	.022	7.861	.93	.57
Peer involvement at age 15–16					
Degree of peer orientation	.009	.014	11.315	1.00	1.11
Peer activity index	.003	.024	6.414	1.00	1.02
No. friends who use marijuana	.755***	.167	1.084	2.13	2.27
Commitment/deviance at age 15–16					
Frequency attends religious services	−.338*	.030	.914	.71	.73
Delinquent participation	.420**	.154	1.233	1.52	1.68
Grade average last term	.006	.188	.817	1.01	1.00
Educational expectations	.354**	.123	1.304	1.42	1.59
Depressive symptoms index	.014	.030	6.739	1.01	1.10
Constant	−1.350	1.649			
χ^2 = 366.321					
df = 363					

[a]Dummy variables are missing for the following four variables included in the models: mother discourages marijuana use; parental alcohol use; father problem drinker; and depressive symptoms. *$p < .05$. **$p < .01$. ***$p < .001$.

TABLE B4

Logistic Regression Predicting Onset of a Spell of Near-Daily Marijuana Use Among Those Who Ever Used Marijuana ($N = 640$)

Predictors[a]	b	SE	Predicted SD	Odds ratio	Standard effect
Sociodemographic					
Sex: female (vs. male)	−.441	.214	.499	.64	.64
Parental education	.036	.036	2.892	1.04	1.11
Family intactness at age 15–16	−.099	.319	.383	.91	.91
Family history of disorders					
Parent/sibling ever treated for					
emotional disorder	.353*	.212	.445	1.42	1.42
Father heavy drinker/alcoholic while					
subject in high school	.659**	.317	.308	1.93	1.93
Parental characteristics at age 15–16					
Parental psychoactive use in last					
12 months	.009	.072	1.349	1.00	1.01
Parental alcohol use in last 12 months	.026	.060	1.946	1.03	1.05
Mother discourages marijuana use	−.289	.342	.454	.74	.74
Parental rules against drug use	.044	.240	.414	1.05	1.05
Closeness to parents	−.041	.039	7.844	.96	.72
Peer involvement at age 15–16					
Degree of peer orientation	−.055	.036	11.248	.95	.53
Interaction: Peer Orientation ×					
Closeness to Parents	.002**	.001			
Peer activity index	−.005	.018	6.286	.99	.97
No. friends who use marijuana	.013	.088	1.251	1.01	1.02
Commitment/deviance at age 15–16					
Frequency attends religious services	.005	.112	.887	1.00	1.00
Delinquent participation	.104	.075	1.425	1.11	1.60
Grade average last term	−.230*	.131	.826	.79	.79
Educational expectations	−.008	.086	1.273	.99	.99
Depressive symptoms index	−.017	.022	6.241	.98	.90
Marijuana, age first use	−.244****	.045	2.872	.78	.50
Used other illicit drugs prior to daily					
marijuana use	−.391	.200	.500	.68	.82
Constant	5.538***	1.916			
$\chi^2 =$ 688.993**					
$df =$ 614					

[a]Dummy variables are missing for the following four variables included in the models: mother discourages marijuana use; parental alcohol use; father problem drinker; and depressive symptoms.
*$p < .10$.   **$p < .05$.   ***$p < .01$.   ****$p < .001$.

TABLE B5

Logistic Regression Predicting Onset of a Spell of Near-Daily Marijuana Use Among Those Who Ever Used Marijuana, Males ($N = 260$)

Predictors[a]	b	SE	Predicted SD	Odds ratio	Standard effect
Sociodemographic					
Parental education	−.004	.053	2.815	1.00	.99
Family intactness at age 15–16	.246	.460	.391	1.28	1.28
Family history of disorders					
Parent/sibling ever treated for emotional disorder	.537*	.314	.440	1.71	1.71
Father heavy drinker/alcoholic while subject in high school	.660	.486	.282	1.94	1.94
Parental characteristics at age 15–16					
Parents psychoactive use in last 12 months	−.046	.115	1.261	.96	.94
Parents alcohol use in last 12 months	.072	.088	1.838	1.07	1.14
Mother discourages marijuana use	−.433	.530	.467	.65	.65
Parental rules against drug use	−.000	.347	.411	1.00	1.00
Closeness to parents	−.068	.057	7.468	.93	.60
Peer involvement at age 15–16					
Degree of peer orientation	−.083	.058	10.526	.92	.42
Interaction: Peer Orientation × Closeness to Parents	.003*	.002			
Peer activity index	−.013	.027	6.163	.99	.92
No. friends who use marijuana	.093	.130	1.189	1.10	1.12
Commitment/deviance at age 15–16					
Frequency attends religious services	−.096	.172	.838	.91	.92
Delinquent participation	.088	.107	1.512	1.09	1.14
Grade average last term	−.333*	.182	.845	.72	.75
Educational expectations	.002	.125	1.254	1.00	1.00
Depressive symptoms index	.004	.032	5.395	1.00	1.02
Marijuana, age first use	−.254****	.069	2.703	.78	.50
Used other illicit drugs prior to daily marijuana use	−.404	.293	.499	.67	.82
Constant	6.322**	2.916			
$\chi^2 =$ 339.504***					
$df =$ 273					

[a]Dummy variables are missing for the following four variables included in the models: mother discourages marijuana use; parental alcohol use; father problem drinker; and depressive symptoms.
*$p < .10$. **$p < .05$. ***$p < .01$. ****$p < .001$.

TABLE B6

Logistic Regression Predicting Onset of a Spell of Near-Daily Marijuana Use Among Those Who Ever Used Marijuana, Females ($N = 342$)

Predictors[a]	b	SE	Predicted SD	Odds ratio	Standard effect
Sociodemographic					
Parental education	.081	.052	2.959	1.08	1.27
Family intactness at age 15–16	−.276	.464	.376	.76	.76
Family history of disorders					
Parent/sibling ever treated for emotional disorder	.179	.306	.449	1.20	1.20
Father heavy drinker/alcoholic while subject in high school	.791*	.443	.329	2.21	2.21
Parental characteristics at age 15–16					
Parents psychoactive use in last 12 months	.065	.096	1.416	1.07	1.10
Parents alcohol use in last 12 months	−.012	.087	2.039	.99	.98
Mother discourages marijuana use	−.105	.475	.443	.90	.95
Parental rules against drug use	.054	.353	.416	1.06	1.06
Closeness to parents	−.020	.058	8.121	.98	.85
Peer involvement at age 15–16					
Degree of peer orientation	−.038	.052	11.422	.96	.65
Interaction: Peer Orientation × Closeness to Parents	.002	.002			
Peer activity index	.003	.026	6.397	1.00	1.02
No. friends who use marijuana	−.044	.128	1.285	.96	.95
Commitment/deviance at age 15–16					
Frequency attends religious services	.072	.157	.919	1.07	1.07
Delinquent participation	.135	.113	1.326	1.15	1.20
Grade average last term	−.177	.204	.795	.84	.87
Educational expectations	−.052	.131	1.271	.95	.94
Depressive symptoms index	−.041	.032	6.727	.96	.76
Marijuana, age first use	−.240***	.064	2.988	.79	.49
Used other illicit drugs prior to marijuana use	−.459	.289	.500	.63	.79
Constant	3.731**	2.888			
χ^2 = 336.818					
df = 317					

[a]Dummy variables are missing for the following four variables included in the models: mother discourages marijuana use; parental alcohol use; father problem drinker; and depressive symptoms.
*$p < .10$. **$p < .05$. ***$p < .001$.

CHAPTER 10

Understanding the Multidimensional Nature of Drug Use and Abuse: The Role of Consumption, Risk Factors, and Protective Factors

Michael D. Newcomb

C linical evidence, treatment experience, devastated families, and ravaged souls clearly document the existence and adversity of the condition of drug abuse and dependence. This is as true today as it was centuries ago and applies equally well to our ubiquitous involvement with cigarettes and alcohol as to our current passion with marijuana and cocaine (e.g., Siegel, 1989; Westermeyer, 1988). On the other hand, there is equally compelling evidence that many people consume these substances without suffering the severe problems of addiction, dependence, or abuse and may remain simply users of a drug without escalating their involvement, or may discontinue use entirely without intervention. In other words, for drug users, their substance involvement is somehow limited to temporary reprieves from daily stress, whereas for drug abusers, their substance involvement spills over into and interferes with major responsibilities in their lives.

This research was supported by grant DA 01070 from the National Institute on Drug Abuse. Special thanks to Julie Speckart for manuscript and figure preparation.

Although intuitively appealing and in accord with much first-hand experience, this distinction and clear demarcation between use and abuse of substances has been challenged from at least two fronts. First, epidemiological studies of community samples have failed to identify a level of involvement where users of a drug are clearly distinct from abusers of a drug. In other words, virtually all indicators of drug abuse (i.e., types of adverse consequences, dependence, dysfunction, harm, etc.) reflect continuous dimensions on which all cutoff points between use and abuse are arbitrary. This varying extent of abuse has been noted regardless of whether the drug is alcohol (Donovan, Jessor, & Jessor, 1983), marijuana (Kandel, 1984), or cocaine (Newcomb & Bentler, 1986a). These community studies revealed that drug use and abuse fall on continua of increasing drug involvement, with no clear demarcation point at which use obviously becomes abuse.

A second, more pharmacological, perspective also challenges whether a clear separation can be drawn between drug users and abusers. From this position, any drug use opens the opportunity for abuse. Drug-abuse liability reflects the biogenetic vulnerability of the user and the addictive and dependence potential of the substance. Both people and drugs range in their extent of abuse liability. For certain individuals and certain substances, even limited initial drug use often escalates (because of the psychopharmacological effects of the drug and the vulnerability of the individual), and as use or consumption increases, so does the extent of adverse consequences of use and evidence of abuse. In other words, drug use often escalates (implying no stable use patterns), and the extent of drug abuse is a direct reflection of and result from the amount of drug use. As in the epidemiological studies, drug use and abuse are not always clear and distinct phenomena, but are spread along interdependent continua of increasing drug involvement.

A Paradigm to Study Drug Use and Abuse

If this pharmacological model is accurate, the amount of drug use often constitutes the necessary and sufficient condition to explain the extent of drug abuse. Although the degree of drug use and abuse can vary, they cannot vary independently, and increasing drug use should accurately predict increasing drug abuse. This perspective is depicted in Figure 10.1, where the amount of drug consumption is the sole determinant of the extent of drug abuse.

This model is reflected in the numerous attempts throughout the years to create a single measure or index of drug involvement. For instance, Pandina, White, and Yorke

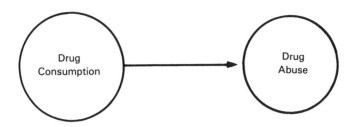

FIGURE 10.1   The pharmacological model of consumption and abuse of drugs. (This represents a simple, direct relationship between the amount of drug consumption and the extent of drug abuse. The amount of drug use is the necessary and sufficient determinant of the degree of drug abuse or dependence.)

(1981) developed the Substance Use Index, which was a single composite measure of increasing drug involvement that combined use of alcohol, marijuana, and other drugs on dimensions of frequency, quantity, and recency of use. Unfortunately, such a pursuit may be misguided and toward a fictitious goal, impossible because it oversimplifies the true multidimensional aspects of drug use and abuse while obscuring distinctions among various types of drugs.

General and Specific Patterns

Arguments from several disciplines have emphasized the multidimensional nature of drug abuse. In other words, drug abuse is a general descriptor of many different criteria of dysfunctional patterns or symptoms of drug involvement. Although a single, specific criterion may be sufficient to identify drug abuse, other criteria are equally pathogynomic and salient indicators of drug abuse. Drug abuse reflects a wide range of problems associated with drug use.

From the medical community, the third revised edition of the *Diagnostic and Statistical Manual of Mental Disorders (DSM–III–R;* American Psychiatric Association, 1987) cites up to nine possible criteria to assess for a diagnosis of psychoactive substance dependence. These cover physical, psychological, and social consequences attributable to drug use. From the psychological community, Newcomb and Bentler (1989a) identified several dimensions to consider when defining substance abuse. These dimensions reflect the classic concepts of *stimulus, organism, response,* and *consequences. Stimulus* covers the drug itself, the psychosocial environmental conditions when used, ingestion in inappropriate settings (i.e., at work; Newcomb, 1988), high frequency of use, or use in excessive amounts. Aspects of the *organism* relevant to drug abuse include developmental stage in life, genetics, biological predisposition, attitudes, motivations, maturity, and risk assessment. Components of the *response* include psychophysiological vulnerability, dependence, tolerance, and addiction. Finally, *consequences* capture any physical, psychological, interpersonal, occupational, or legal adversities related to drug use.

A close inspection of these criteria reveal that not only is drug abuse multidimensional, but so is use, ingestion, or consumption of the drug. As a result, the general model of drug use leading to drug abuse is too simple to reflect the various types of use and abuse. Thus, drug use can be characterized as a general patten of drug consumption that is reflected by several specific types of consumption (i.e., frequency, quantity, type of drug). Similarly, drug abuse can be represented as a general pattern of drug abuse that is captured by several specific types of drug abuse (i.e., at work, while driving, objective problems).

On the basis of this elaboration of the nature of drug use and abuse, the general use–abuse model of Figure 10.1 can be expanded to incorporate general and specific types of drug use and abuse. This more comprehensive model is depicted in Figure 10.2. In addition to the initial hypothesis that general drug use will predict general drug abuse, three other paths of influence can now be considered (as depicted with the dotted lines). These potential associations include (a) specific types of consumption influencing general drug abuse, (b) general drug consumption directly affecting specific types of drug abuse, and (c) specific types of drug consumption creating specific types of drug abuse.

Predictions

The pharmacological model predicts that extents of both general and specific types of drug abuse should be accounted for by levels of either general or specific drug-consumption patterns. The strength of these associations may vary according to the abuse liability of specific drugs and the biogenetic susceptibility of the individual. If this prediction is not fully supported, by finding only modest to moderate associations between amount of use and extent of abuse, then other factors must be introduced to explain the various patterns of drug abuse. In addition, this use–abuse model does not provide an adequate explanation for the varying patterns of drug use and consumption. It seems unlikely that

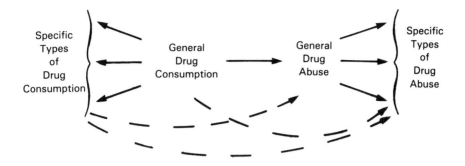

FIGURE 10.2   A multidimensional model of drug consumption and drug abuse. (This is an expansion of the pharmacological model in which both drug consumption and drug abuse are multifaceted. Each construct represents several specific types of drug consumption or drug abuse, which in turn reflect general tendencies toward each of these conditions.)

only the psychopharmacological effects of a drug are responsible for the patterns of consumption.

Personal Vulnerability and Resistance

If neither specific nor general patterns of drug use or consumption can explain fully the various patterns of drug abuse, we must expand our model further. Such a finding would suggest that the pharmacological model is incomplete and too limited to explain all facets of the drug use–abuse association. Furthermore, this model offers little to account for the variations in general and specific patterns of drug use and consumption.

For many years, researchers and theoreticians have struggled to identify the social and personal factors that are the causal influences generating initiation, escalation, and abuse of drugs. Numerous theories have been proposed from diverse perspectives that variously focus on genetic–biochemical predisposition, intrapsychic processes, interpersonal relations, and societal conditions (e.g., Lettieri, 1986). Empirical tests of these theories have typically met with modest success. However, no one factor, of the many hundreds examined, has been able to accurately predict drug-use initiation, extent of drug use, or degree of drug abuse.

Risk-Factor Model

Rather than viewing this result as a failure of science, many investigators are now seeing this conclusion as a true feature of the phenomenon (Bry, 1983). Neither drug use nor drug abuse is caused by one specific or common influence. Drug involvement is now being understood as generated by numerous factors that increase the risk of using or abusing drugs. This has led to a greater appreciation of interactional models (e.g., Sadava, 1987; Stein, Newcomb, & Bentler, 1987), to a biopsychosocial perspective (e.g., Zucker & Gomberg, 1986), and a diverse approach to understanding and preventing drug use (e.g., Segal, 1986). Instead of searching for the one most important factor that predicts drug use and abuse, attention has shifted toward a consideration of how many risk factors or conditions are present with which a person must cope.

This multiple-risk-factor model has been operationalized by creating risk-factor indices that reflect the number of psychosicial etiological influences for drug use on which a person reports extreme risk. This type of index has been tested and confirmed with both cross-sectional data (Bry, McKeon, & Pandina, 1982) and panel data (Newcomb, Maddahian, & Bentler, 1986) as a powerful predictor of drug use, frequency of drug ingestion, and heavy drug use. These results were obtained for a measure of general drug involvement (Bry et al., 1982) and for specific use of cigarettes, alcohol, marijuana, and hard drugs (Newcomb, Maddahian, & Bentler, 1986; Newcomb, Maddahian, Skager, & Bentler, 1987). Thus, it seems likely that exposure to increasing numbers of risk factors would increase the amount of drugs consumed (drug use) and the extent of abuse associated with this ingestion (drug abuse).

Protective-Factor Model

Although exposure to various numbers of risk conditions or factor affects the vulnerability to use or abuse drugs, exposure to other factors may be protective and reduce the likelihood of use or abuse of drugs. In a recent study, Newcomb and Felix-Ortiz (1991) extended the multiple-risk-factor methodology to include an index of multiple protective factors. We argued that each psychosocial factor that is associated with drug involvement can be seen as bipolar if the specific measure or scale captures the full range of the construct. One end of the scale reflects high risk for drug involvement; the other end captures high protection from drug use and abuse. Most people fall in the middle portion of the scales and are neither at heightened risk nor protected from drug involvement. For instance, a very low degree of law abidance can be considered a risk factor for drug involvement, whereas a very high degree of law abidance may be seen as protecting a person from involvement with drugs.

Risk and protective indices can be constructed in at least two ways. One approach is to assign each factor to either the risk or protective index on the basis of which of its extremes is more strongly related to levels of drug involvement. The resultant indices are composed of mutually exclusive factors that use only one endpoint of influence (risk or protection) of each bipolar factor. This approach was followed by Newcomb and Felix-Ortiz (1991) to assure empirical independence between the two indices. These indices of risk and protection were moderately correlated negatively and contributed unique influences on both concurrent and future drug use. The protective index was more strongly related to reducing involvement with use of gateway drugs (i.e., alcohol), and the risk index exerted a stronger influence on increasing illicit and problem drug use.

A second approach captures both the risk and protective endpoints of each factor in the respective multiple-factor indices. Both the risk and protective endpoints of bipolar factors are considered in constructing the two indices. This approach captures both the protective and risk potentials of each factor, but introduces an amount of empirical dependence between the indices. This more realistic approach is used in the present study.

Protective conditions may influence or limit drug use in two general ways: (a) as a direct, inhibiting force on the likelihood of drug involvement and (b) as an interactive, buffering influence that can reduce or neutralize the association between risk conditions and drug involvement. In the direct or additive model, risk and protective forces are opposed and compete as in a tug-of-war to influence a person's degree of involvement with drugs. For instance, high law abidance (a protective factor) directly limits the likelihood of drug involvement, whereas having many friends who use drugs (a risk factor) directly heightens the probability of drug involvement. On the other hand, in the interactive, moderating, or buffering model, protective forces insulate or inoculate against vulnerability and susceptibility when exposed to risk (e.g., Brook, Whiteman, Gordon, & Cohen, 1986, 1989). For instance, high law abidance reduces (protects from) the influence of drug-using friends, whereas low law abidance may enhance susceptibility to drug-using peers. Although both of these mechanisms may be important processes, the present analyses are restricted to tests of the direct or additive model, because it can be more readily operationalized and incorporated in the present methodology.

A general construct of extreme psychosocial vulnerability to drug use and abuse can be hypothesized to underlie these two indices. This is a bipolar construct, in which the upper end reflects a very high degree of risk and a very low amount of protection for use and abuse of drugs, whereas the low end represents strong protection and minimal risk for these same drug patterns. The unique aspects of risk and protection that are not captured by the general construct of vulnerability can be studied as the unique or residual variance of these indices after control for the shared or common construct (via the latent factor; see Newcomb & Bentler, 1988a, 1988b). Thus, the general and specific aspects of psychosocial vulnerability may have an effect on both drug use (consumption) and drug abuse, as depicted in Figure 10.3. Each of the three constructs are depicted as general, although it is assumed that each one also reflects more specific types of psychosocial vulnerability (risk and protection), drug consumption (frequency, quantity, and type of substance), and drug abuse (at work, while driving, when experiencing problems).

Type of Drug Substance

In addition to confounding or obscuring important dimensions of drug use and abuse, the search for a general index of drug involvement must somehow combine the use of different drug substances. All drugs are not the same. They differ in likelihood of use and potential for abuse and dependence. These differences are attributable to the varying pharmacological action of different drugs, as well as the various social–psychological statuses, values, and expectations attached to specific drugs. For instance, the association between the use and abuse of wine may be quite different than between

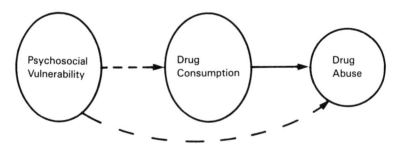

FIGURE 10.3   The clinical model of drug consumption and abuse. (This expands the pharmacological model by proposing that drug abuse may be influenced by psychosocial vulnerability both indirectly, by means of an impact on drug consumption, and directly.)

the use and abuse of cocaine. Thus, it seem essential to retain some distinctions among types of drugs in order to capture any unique patterns for predicting use and abuse.

On the other hand, it is important to recognize that at least among teenagers, use of one drug often implies use of some other drugs as well and that polydrug use is more the norm than the exception (Newcomb & Bentler, 1986b). As a result, focus on specific substances ignores the associations with other drugs, whereas reliance on a general drug-use index precludes discovery of any specific drug effects.

Operationalization of the Paradigm

In this study, patterns of use and abuse were examined for three types of drug substances: alcohol, marijuana, and cocaine. Analyses were based on both cross-sectional and longitudinal data obtained from a community sample.

First, to establish a categorical baseline for this sample, the *DSM–III–R* criteria for dependence were used to establish the prevalence of abstinence, use, and abuse (dependence) for alcohol, marijuana, and cocaine. The prevalence and likelihood of dependence on multiple drugs was also tested. According to the *DSM–III–R*, criteria for substance abuse are a less severe subset of those for substance dependence. Miller and Gold (1989) pointed out that drug abuse is not necessarily a milder expression of drug dependence and that each syndrome has similar and unique symptoms. In the present chapter *dependence* is used in accord with the *DSM–III–R* definition, whereas *abuse* is used to refer to the cumulative scale of drug problems constructed from my measures in this project. These measures of abuse range from mild to severe, and the more adverse events may be rare for this relatively young sample; their age limits the length of their drug-use careers and their opportunities to experience extensive drug problems.

Second, the association between Drug Consumption and Drug Abuse was examined for each of the three drugs in separate latent-variable structural-equation models (e.g., Bentler & Newcomb, 1986). Drug Consumption was captured as a general latent factor or construct reflected in specific measures of frequency and quantity of use. Drug Abuse was also captured by a latent construct that is reflected by several specific types of drug abuse, including objective problems with use, use at work, subjective problems with use, and driving while intoxicated. These analyses were conducted on cross-sectional data from a sample of adults in their mid-twenties.

Following these analyses, each model was expanded to include a longitudinal assessment of drug use and psychosocial vulnerability eight years earlier, when these participants were in late adolescence. Extreme psychosocial vulnerability was included as a latent construct that is reflected in specific indices of risk and protection. Frequency and/or quantity measures of the three drug substances were also included from late adolescence and served to meet several of the important criteria for making a causal inference (e.g., Newcomb, 1987). This general model is depicted in Figure 10.4. The broken lines represent only a few of the possible direct associations that may be found among general and specific aspects of psychosocial vulnerability, drug consumption, and drug abuse.

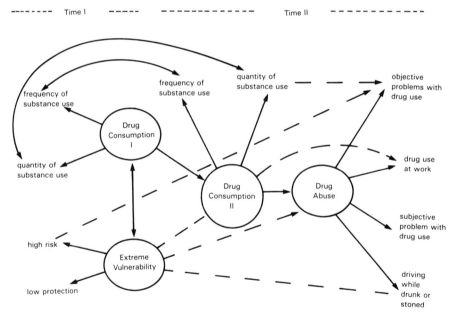

FIGURE 10.4   General operationalization of the clinical model for the current study. (Circles are latent factors, single-headed arrows are factor loadings or regression paths, two-headed arrows are correlations, and dotted lines are hypothetical examples of standard and nonstandard regression paths.)

Method

Subjects

Data were obtained from participants in a 12-year prospective study of adolescent and adult drug use and development (see Newcomb & Bentler, 1988a, 1988b). The study began in 1976 with a sample of 1,634 seventh, eighth, and ninth grade students. An excessively large student pool was chosen in order to obtain about 1,000 complete sets of students, close-friend, and parent triads that could be linked. Informed consent was obtained from both the teenagers and their parents, and best friends if possible, after approval had been obtained for participation in the study from the school district, the school principal, and the teacher, who permitted informed consent forms to be taken home. Each participant was informed that his or her responses were protected legally by a grant of confidentiality from the U.S. Department of Justice. Unfortunately, we do not have detailed information regarding the total sampling frame (or universe of subjects) from which our initial sample was drawn. All students were located at 11 Los Angeles schools in five school districts and were roughly representative of schools in the county in terms of socioeconomic status and ethnicity. This comparability was achieved by slightly oversampling lower-socioeconomic-status schools, with three high- and three medium-socioeconomic-status schools, but five lower-socioeconomic-status schools, participating. The oversampling at the school level was done to offset an expected lowered level of voluntary participation among students and parents from the lower-socioeconomic-status schools. Our subjects did not seem unusual (except for a larger percentage of girls than boys) in any critical ways, revealed a high degree of heterogeneity and variance on most variables, and appeared quite similar to other samples of that age. At this initial testing with self-administered questionnaires, students provided information regarding their drug use, personality, attitudes toward drugs, peer-interaction patterns, and perceived drug use of others.

Data were collected at five other occasions from these same participants over a period of 12 years. These retestings occurred at Years 2, 4, 5, 9, and 13 of the study. At each testing, the questionnaire was expanded and refined so that in Years, 5, 9, and 13 a rather extensive assessment of many life areas was obtained.

The cross-sectional data for this study are from the last wave (Year 13) that was collected, in 1988, when the participants were in their mid-twenties. Complete data were gathered at that time from 614 individuals from the original panel. A description of these subjects as adults is provided in Table 10.1. Obviously, a larger proportion of the sample was female, which has been an unfortunate feature of the sample from Year 1 and does not solely reflect differential attrition by sex.

The longitudinal analyses are based on data from subjects in Year 5 (late adolescence) and eight years later in Year 13 (adults). The total sample size for these analyses is 536. Although I would have preferred to use data from the earlier waves in these longitudinal analyses, these assessments contained insufficient information on important psychosocial variables to construct the risk and protective indices.

A series of analyses were run to determine whether the attrition in sample size from 1980 to 1988 was due to any systematic influence. Of the 614 subjects at Year 13, 536 had provided data in 1980, representing a 60% recapture rate over an 8-year period past high school. We compared those who we were able to locate and who provided complete questionnaires in 1988 with those we failed to assess in 1988 in terms of data obtained in 1980. We contrasted these groups in terms of 26 different drug substances and 23 personality, emotional-distress, and social-support scales from the 1980 data set. Using the Bonferroni procedure to adjust for multiple simultaneous comparisons, not one of these 49 variables was able to significantly differentiate the new sample from those lost at the .05 level of significance. The average (absolute) point-biserial correlation for these 49 tests was .02, whereas the average squared correlation was less than .002. The largest difference accounted for only 1% of the variance between groups and was not significant when using the Bonferroni method to correct for capitalizing on chance. These analyses indicate that very little of the attrition rate between 1980 and 1988 was due to self-selection on the basis of drug use or personality traits. To tease out any remaining differences, a stepwise multiple regression analysis was run using the forty-nine 1980 drug-use and personality variables as the predictor pool and retention in 1988 as the criterion variable. Using this procedure, only two variables were selected to differentiate the groups. Although significant, this equation choosing all of the best predictors was able to account for only 1% of the variance between groups. This trivial (in terms of magnitude) result indicates that those who continued in the study reported a better relationship with their family and greater use of nonprescription cold medicine in 1980 than did those who did not continue in the study. Thus, only one of the 26 drug-use measures was selected to predict attrition, and this was not an illicit drug. These extensive analyses indicate that the loss of subjects between 1980 and 1988 was not largely due to systematic self-selection or other influences on the basis of personality, emotional distress, social support, or

TABLE 10.1

Description of Sample

Variable	Male ($N = 176$)	Female ($N = 438$)	Total ($N = 614$)
Age (years)			
M	26.95	26.95	26.95
Range	26–29	25–29	25–29
Ethnicity (%)			
Black	10	16	14
Hispanic	12	10	11
White	70	62	64
Asian	8	10	10
High school graduate (%)			
Yes	96	95	95
No	4	5	5
Number of children (%)			
None	75	61	65
One	15	22	20
Two	7	13	11
Three	2	5	4
Income for past year (%)			
Under $5,001	6	21	17
$5,001 to $15,000	27	26	26
$15,001 to $30,000	44	45	44
Over $30,000	23	8	12
Living situation (%)			
Alone	8	8	8
Parents	19	19	19
Spouse	43	41	42
Cohabitation	7	8	7
Dormitory	2	0	1
Roommates	13	13	13
Other	8	11	10
Current life activity (%)			
Military	6	1	2
Junior college	2	2	2
Four-year college	7	4	5
Part-time job	5	7	6
Full-time job	73	66	68
Child rearing/homemaker	1	17	12
Other	5	3	4

drug use. Thus, the data are of sufficiently high quality to permit structural modeling to answer important theoretical and policy questions.

Measures

Each of the variables used in this study reflects one of three general domains: drug consumption, drug abuse, and risk–protection factors. Drug-consumption variables are taken from both the Year 5 (late adolescence) and Year 13 (adult) assessments, whereas the drug-abuse measures are only from the Year 13 data (to reflect outcome or consequence conditions), and the risk–protection factors are solely from the Year 5 data (to represent etiological or predictive influences). We will briefly describe each variable in its respective domains.

Drug Consumption

Drug consumption was measured by frequency (during the past 6 months) and quantity (amount typically ingested per occasion) of use for alcohol, marijuana, and cocaine. In both Years 5 and 13, alcohol frequency was a composite scale of how often beer, wine, and liquor had been consumed, and for both waves alcohol quantity was a single measure of the amount of alcohol consumed (in ounces). In both Years 5 and 13, marijuana frequency was a composite scale of how often marijuana and hashish were used, and in both years marijuana quantity was a single measure of the amount of marijuana personally consumed (in number of joints). Finally, in Year 13, cocaine frequency was a composite scale of cocaine and crack use, and in Year 5, cocaine frequency was a single general item. Cocaine quantity was not assessed in Year 5, whereas in Year 13, it assessed the number of lines or grams consumed per occasion.

Drug Abuse

Four specific types of drug abuse were used to reflect a general, latent construct of drug abuse for alcohol, marijuana, and cocaine. These specific types of drug abuse include objective problems, use at work, subjective problems, and driving while intoxicated.

Objective problems with drug use were assessed by the frequency of occurrence (during the past year) of 29 various adverse consequences attributable to drug use. These items are listed in Table 10.2. All 29 items were rated separately for the use of alcohol, marijuana, and cocaine. Of the 29 problem items, 14 were created to reflect the *DSM–III–R* criteria for drug dependence, and the remaining items tapped adverse effects not included in the diagnostic criteria. These items reflect a wide range of physical, psychological, interpersonal, and occupational functions that may have been disrupted by drug use.

TABLE 10.2

Factor Loadings on First Unrelated Factors

		Loadings on first unrelated factor		
Objective problem item		**Alcohol**	**Marijuana**	**Cocaine**
1.	Had a hangover.	.53	.43	.71
2.	Gotten nauseated and vomited.	.55	.49	.55
3.	Behaved in ways you regretted.	.65	.53	.78
4.	"Blacked out" or been unable to remember your behavior.	.61	.38	.24
5.	Used more of the alcohol or drug than you had intended.	.55	.62	.77
6.	Used the alcohol or drug over a longer period of time than you intended.	.66	.64	.79
7.	Made unsuccessful attempts to quit, cut down, or control your use.	.70	.49	.81
8.	Interfered with your work, family, or other obligations.	.74	.70	.75
9.	Important social, occupational, or recreational activities given up or reduced because of use.	.71	.56	.61
10.	Continued use of alcohol or drugs despite recurrent social, psychological, or physical problems associated with use.	.72	.68	.68
11.	Need for increased amounts of the drug in order to achieve the desired effects.	.72	.53	.76
12.	A great deal of time spent obtaining, using, and recovering from the drug.	.77	.73	.77
13.	Persistent desire or craving for the drug.	.67	.69	.78
14.	Feel emotionally or physically bad after stopping use.	.63	.71	.70
15.	Hurt your relationship with your friends or family.	.76	.75	.74
16.	Hurt your performance on the job.	.75	.67	.53
17.	Been less interested in other activities than before.	.74	.77	.76

(continued)

TABLE 10.2 *(Continued)*

	Loadings on first unrelated factor		
Objective problem item	Alcohol	Marijuana	Cocaine
18. Gotten into trouble with your boss or supervisor.	.58	.65	.45
19. Missed work.	.49	.67	.58
20. Had less energy.	.47	.69	.66
21. Felt guilty or remorseful about using alcohol/drugs.	.55	.66	.71
22. Gotten into trouble with the police.	.35	.52	.39
23. Had problems with physical health.	.45	.61	.70
24. Been physically injured.	.29	.61	.41
25. Caused physical injury to others.	.41	.38	.33
26. Engaged in sexual behavior you would have not otherwise engaged in.	.48	.52	.07
27. Been criticized or had concern expressed about your drug/ alcohol use.	.58	.54	.71
28. Gotten into a fight.	.53	.40	.58
29. Damaged property.	.49	.30	.47

Exploratory factor analyses were conducted on the three separate sets of 29 items (one each for alcohol, marijuana, and cocaine). A scree plot of the eigenvalues for these three analyses is presented in Figure 10.5. As evident in the figure, the eigenvalues for each of the first factors were quite large in relation to the others. This suggests that one general factor may underlie the separate sets of items.

An inspection of the factor loadings on each of the first unrotated factors confirmed the presence of this general factor for each of the three drugs. All 29 items and the loadings for each on the first factor for the three drugs are presented in Table 10.2. With only a few exceptions, all of these factor loadings were sizable, with only two being less than .30.

On the basis of these analyses, all 29 items for each substance were summed into a composite index of objective problems with drugs. This resulted in three separate scales; one each for objective problems with alcohol, marijuana, and cocaine. These are continuous, addictive scales representing an increasing number of problems experienced with

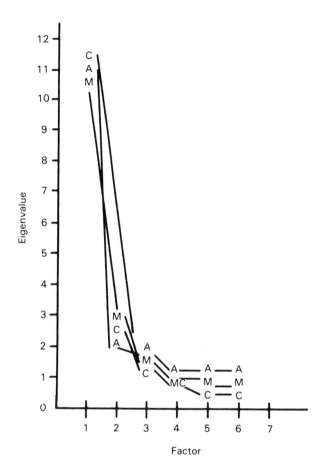

FIGURE 10.5 Scree plots for the objective problem items for alcohol, marijuana, and cocaine. (The first six eigenvalues associated with the 29 items for each substance are depicted. Item loadings on the first unrotated factor for each substance are presented in Table 10.2. A = alcohol; M = marijuana; C = cocaine.)

each drug during the past year. For some preliminary, descriptive analyses, the 14 items associated with the *DSM–III–R* diagnostic criteria were used to establish prevalence in this sample for alcohol, marijuana, and cocaine dependence.

Drug use at work was measured by asking how often the subject had been high, drunk, or stoned at work or school during the past 6 months for a variety of drugs (Newcomb, 1988). Alcohol at work was a composite of the beer, wine, and liquor items.

Marijuana at work was a composite of the marijuana and hashish items, and cocaine at work was a single item.

Three separate items captured types of subjective problems with drugs, which reflected specific aspects of drug abuse. The respondent indicated the amount of difficulty or trouble he or she had experienced with alcohol, cocaine, and other drugs during the past 3 months. The "other drugs" item was used for the marijuana analyses because a specific marijuana item of this type was not included in the survey and because marijuana is the most likely (prevalent) substance to be captured in this more general category.

Two items were used to reflect the driving-while-drunk-or-stoned domain of specific drug abuse. Both items assessed the frequency of driving while drunk or stoned during the past 6 months. The alcohol item assessed how often the respondent had driven a car drunk. The second item asked respondents to indicate how often they had driven a car while high or stoned on drugs (other than alcohol). Because the type of drug was not specified for this item, it was used in the analyses for both marijuana and cocaine.

Risk–Protection Factors

In a previous study (Newcomb & Felix-Ortiz, 1991), the theoretical bases, conceptual framework, operationalization, and empirical derivation and tests of multiple risk- and protective-factor indices were elucidated. Only a brief summary of the construction of the two indices will be presented here.

On the basis of a review of the theoretical and empirical literature on the etiological factors associated with drug use and abuse and the available data in our Year 5 survey, 14 variables were selected as potential risk or protective factors. These 14 variables do not reflect a complete or even representative list of all potential factors noted in the literature, they were limited to ones available in my data set. Nevertheless, these 14 variables reflected several psychosocial aspects of the teenagers' life, including the home environment, academic orientation, attitudes, emotional distress, deviant behavior, access to drugs, and perceived attitudes and drug usage in their peer–social–community milieu. Most risk variables are multi-item scales.

In a series of multiple regression analyses, all 14 variables were used as predictors of five different drugs (cigarettes, alcohol, cannabis, cocaine, and hard drugs). Two variables were deleted because they did not significantly contribute (low Beta weights) to predicting the use of any one of the five drugs. The 12 remaining variables tapped a wide range of each construct, and, by so doing, captured the extreme ends of each one in a bipolar manner. Thus, for each scale, one end of the distribution identifies those at increased risk for drug involvement, whereas the opposite end of the distribution reflects those with increased protection from or vulnerability to drug involvement. Both of these extremes are in relation to the middle portion of the scale, where most respondents fall who do not have any special vulnerability or resistance to drug involvement because of the particular aspect of their life measured by the variable.

Because both high protection and high risk should be relatively rare among a community sample of teenagers, cut-off points for risk and protection were arbitrarily set at about the extreme 20% for each factor. The following procedure was used to create separate risk and protective indices from these 12 variables. Initially, these two indices were set at 0 for all subjects. For each of the 12 variables, all of those who scored within 20% of the vulnerable end of a variable had 1 added to their risk index and nothing was done to their protective index. Similarly, all of those who scored within the extreme 20% of the distribution associated with little drug involvement had 1 added to their protection-factor index and nothing was done to their risk index for this variable. Thus, each of the 12 variables could contribute to only one of the two indices. Each index is an additive scale reflecting increased risk or protection with higher scores.

For each variable, its range, risk and protective cut-off point, and percent of sample at risk or protected are given in Table 10.3. Although the potential range of each index was from 0 to 12, very few people had 8 or more, and because of these outliers, this end of each of the indices was collapsed to 8 or more. Table 10.4 presents the distributions for both of these indices for the total sample and separately for men and women.

Because both factor indices were based on the same set of 12 variables, they cannot be considered independent for statistical reasons. In fact, the two scales were significantly correlated in a negative direction, as expected. This inverse association between the two factor indices reflects in part the statistical confound in the way they were created and the expectation that high risk should be associated with low protection (and vice versa). Because of the multiple factors in the indices, the statistical confound is reduced. Figure 10.6 graphically depicts this negative association between indices.

Results

The results are presented in three separate sets of analyses. The first analyses explore the prevalence in this sample of drug use and dependence for alcohol, cocaine, and marijuana according to *DSM–III–R* diagnostic criteria. The second set of analyses uses latent-variable models to examine the cross-sectional association between drug use and abuse by constructing separate models for alcohol, marijuana, and cocaine. Finally, these three

TABLE 10.3

Cut-off Points for the 12 Retained Protective and Risk Factors from Year 5 (Late Adolescence)

Factor	Variable range	Cut-off point for factor Protective	Risk	Percent of sample Protective	Risk
1. Grade point average	1–4	A	D	11.8[a]	2.8[a]
2. Educational aspiration	1–6	>4	<3	26.2[a]	15.1
3. Deviance	0–42	<2	>6	19.2	20.8
4. Law abidance	4–20	>16	<10	21.1	20.4
5. Religiosity	4–20	>19	<12	18.3	16.7
6. Depression	4–20	4	>9	18.9	19.3
7. Home relationships	8–40	>36	<25	21.0	21.1
8. Important people/ community support of use	12–53	12	>27	27.3[a]	21.1
9. Sanctions against use	6–30	>23	<11	21.9	22.2
10. Perceived adult use	9–34	<12	>19	18.6	20.5
11. Perceived peer use	9–35	<12	>20	23.5	18.5
12. Availability of drugs	6–30	<20	>28	19.9	21.0

[a]Given the characteristics of the distribution, these were the cutoffs closest to 20%.

TABLE 10.4

Sample Distribution for Protective Factors and Risk Factors

	Protective factors Percent of sample				Risk factors Percent of sample		
Number	Total	Male	Female	Number	Total	Male	Female
0	19.6	21.1	19.0	0	24.8	19.6	27.3
1	21.0	22.3	20.3	1	21.5	19.9	22.3
2	17.0	16.5	17.2	2	16.5	18.9	15.5
3	15.1	16.2	14.5	3	13.4	14.1	13.1
4	9.5	9.3	9.6	4	9.0	10.3	8.4
5	7.3	6.9	7.4	5	6.5	7.2	6.1
6	4.8	4.1	5.1	6	3.6	4.1	3.3
7	2.9	2.7	3.0	7	2.7	3.4	2.3
8 or more	2.9	1.0	3.8	8 or more	1.8	2.4	1.7

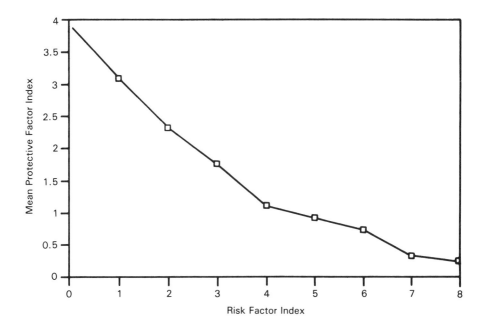

FIGURE 10.6   Bivariate plot of the mean number of protective factors associated with each number of risk factors.

cross-sectional models are expanded to include measures of risk, protection, and drug use assessed 9 years earlier.

Prevalence of Abstinence, Use, and Dependence

The prevalence rates of substance dependence in this sample of mid-twenty-year-old adults were determined according to the diagnostic criteria from the *DSM–III–R*. Fourteen items from the 29 objective drug-problems scales were designed to assess the *DSM–III–R* criteria for dependence and were used to establish the percentage of the sample that was dependent on alcohol, marijuana, and cocaine. From one to four items were used to reflect each of eight diagnostic criteria (one criterion was not used: using the drug to relieve withdrawal symptoms). The items used to reflect each of the eight criteria are listed in Table 10.5.

The *DSM–III–R* specifies that for a diagnosis of psychoactive substance dependence, at least three of these criteria must be met. For my analyses, a person qualified as meeting a criterion if they reported using the drug and any occurrence of the negative consequence on any of the items pertaining to the criterion. These diagnoses are

TABLE 10.5

Operationalization of Eight *DSM–III–R* Criteria for Psychoactive Substance Dependence

DSM–III–R criteria	Survey items (within past year)
1. Often use more or longer than intended	• Used more of the alcohol or drug than you had intended • Used the alcohol or drug over a longer period of time than you intended
2. Persistent desire or failed attempt to reduce or control	• Made unsuccessful attempts to quit, cut down, or control your use • Persistent desire or craving for the drug
3. Great deal of time obtaining, using, or recovering from use	• A great deal of time spent obtaining, using, and recovering from the drug
4. Interfere with role responsibility or physical health	• Interfered with your work, family, or other obligations • Hurt your performance on the job • Gotten into trouble with your boss or supervisor • Missed work • Hurt your relationship with your friends or family
5. Important social, job, or recreational activities reduced or given-up	• Important social, occupational, or recreational activities given up or reduced because of use
6. Continued use despite adverse effects	• Continued use of alcohol or drugs despite recurrent social, psychological, or physical problems associated with use
7. Marked tolerance	• Need for increased amounts of the drug in order to achieve the desired effects
8. Withdrawal symptoms	• Feel emotionally or physically bad after stopping use

dichotomous (present vs. absent) and are created in a different manner than the continuous, objective problem drug abuse variables. Table 10.6 presents the percentage of users of the drug for the total sample and for men and women who met each of the eight diagnostic criteria for use of alcohol, marijuana, and cocaine. In other words, the prevalence rates for these criteria in this table are only for those who reported using the drug.

TABLE 10.6
Prevalence of Eight *DSM III–R* Criteria for Psychoactive Substance Dependence

Abuse criterion	Alcohol			Marijuana			Cocaine		
	Total	Male	Female	Total	Male	Female	Total	Male	Female
N	543	157	386	188	51	137	122	42	88
1. Often use more or longer than intended	56.4	62.4	53.9	22.3	31.4	19.0	43.4	54.8	37.5
2. Persistent desire or failed attempt to reduce or control	14.0	19.1	11.9*	28.7	35.3	26.3	31.1	31.0	31.3
3. Great deal of time obtaining, using, or recovering from use	7.4	10.8	6.0	18.1	19.6	17.5	21.3	23.8	20.0
4. Interfere with role responsibility or physical health	19.9	26.8	17.1**	22.9	25.5	21.9	32.8	35.7	31.3
5. Important social, job, or recreational activities reduced or given up	5.5	7.0	4.9	7.4	7.8	7.3	26.2	19.0	30.0
6. Continued use despite adverse effects	6.6	10.2	5.2*	11.7	13.7	10.9	25.4	26.2	25.0
7. Marked tolerance	8.8	12.7	7.3*	10.6	7.8	11.7	20.5	23.8	18.8
8. Withdrawal symptoms	6.3	7.0	6.0	13.3	13.7	13.1	20.5	23.8	18.8

*$p < .05$.   **$p < .01$.

For both alcohol and cocaine, the most prevalent negative consequence was using more of the drug or using it over a longer period of time than intended. For marijuana, the most prevalent criterion was having a persistent desire for the drug or failed attempts to reduce or cut-down use. Sex differences were tested on the prevalence of each of the eight criteria on all three substances, and only four significant differences emerged. All of these significant sex differences were on the alcohol-dependence criteria. More male than female alcohol users reported persistent desire or failed attempts to reduce or control their alcohol use, alcohol's interference with their role responsibilities or physical health, continued use of alcohol despite adverse effects, and marked tolerance to alcohol. No sex differences were found on any of the dependence criteria for users of marijuana or cocaine.

Table 10.7 presents the percentage of abstainers, users, and abusers/dependents of alcohol, marijuana, and cocaine for all subjects and separately by sex. Nearly 90% of the sample were alcohol users, although only 13% were dependent on alcohol. Significantly more men were dependent on alcohol than were women. About one third of the sample used marijuana, with 8% being dependent on the drug. No sex difference was

TABLE 10.7

Prevalence of Abstinence, Use, and Dependence on the Basis of *DSM–III–R* Criteria

Substance	Abstainer	User	Dependent	Sex difference χ^2 (2)	Dependent users
Alcohol					
All subjects	11.4	75.4	13.2		14.9
Men	10.2	70.5	19.3	8.12*	21.5
Women	11.9	77.4	10.7		12.1
Marijuana					
All subjects	68.1	23.8	8.1		25.4
Men	68.2	21.0	10.8	2.92	34.0
Women	68.0	24.9	7.1		22.2
Cocaine					
All subjects	79.6	12.9	7.5		36.8
Men	75.6	14.8	9.7	2.76	39.8
Women	81.3	12.1	6.6		35.3

*$p < .05$.

found for patterns of marijuana use. Slightly more than 20% of the sample were co-caine users, whereas 7.5% were dependent on cocaine. Again, no significant sex differ-ence was noted for patterns of cocaine use. More men than women were dependent on each of the three drugs, although the only significant sex difference emerged for alcohol.

A comparison of the percent of drug users who were dependent on a given drug among the three substances can provide an indication of which drug (for whatever personal, social, or pharmacological reasons) is more likely to result in abuse or de-pendence. These rates are given in the fifth column of Table 10.7. Among the total sample, 15% of the alcohol users were dependent on alcohol, 25% of the marijuana users were dependent on marijuana, and 37% of the cocaine users were dependent on cocaine. For men only, the analogous rates were 22% for alcohol, 34% for marijuana, and 40% for cocaine. For women only, the prevalences of dependence among users were 12% for alcohol, 22% for marijuana, and 35% for cocaine. These figures indicate that cocaine has the greatest likelihood of dependence/abuse, followed by marijuana and then alcohol. This pattern holds for the total sample, as well as for men and women separately. Men appear to be at substantially greater risk for dependence on alcohol and marijuana compared with women, but for cocaine the sex differences are sharply reduced.

Two final issues that were addressed by analyses of these dependence rates were the prevalence of simultaneous dependence on two drugs and the likelihood of being de-pendent on a second drug given being dependent on another drug. Results of these anal-yses are summarized in Table 10.8. The most prevalent dual dependence was on alcohol and cocaine (4.9%), followed closely by alcohol and marijuana (4.2%), with dependence on both marijuana and cocaine the least prevalent (2.9%). These figures are based on the total sample of men and women, including users and nonusers, and may vary by sex or when only users are considered (that would adjust for the wide variation in prevalences of use for the three substances).

The likelihood of being dependent on a particular second drug is substantially higher than the overall rate of dependence on that drug. Vulnerability to dual dependence is most likely for cocaine: of those dependent on cocaine, 65% are also dependent on alcohol and 39% are dependent on marijuana. Among those dependent on marijuana, 52% are also dependent on alcohol (reflecting the second most vulnerable combination) and 36% are dependent on cocaine. Compared with dependence on marijuana and cocaine,

TABLE 10.8

Prevalence of Multiple Dependencies

Dependency	Alcohol	Marijuana	Cocaine
Dependent on			
Alcohol	13.2	—	—
Marijuana	4.2	8.1	—
Cocaine	4.9	2.9	7.5
Conditional prevalence of dependence			
Alcohol	—	52.0	65.2
Marijuana	32.1	—	39.1
Cocaine	17.0	36.0	—

Note. All χ^2 tests are significant.

alcohol dependence is least likely to co-occur with other drugs: 32% are also dependent on marijuana and 17% are dependent on cocaine.

Cross-Sectional Drug Consumption and Abuse Analyses

Three separate latent-variable structural equation models (SEMs: Bentler, 1980, 1989; Newcomb, 1990) were developed to determine the amount of association between general and specific types of drug consumption and general and specific types of drug abuse for alcohol, marijuana, and cocaine. The general patterns of drug involvement were captured in latent constructs, whereas the specific patterns were represented by the measured or observed variables used as indicators of each construct. In each of the three models, Drug Consumption was a latent factor that reflected the frequency and quantity measures of each substance, and Drug Abuse was a latent construct assumed to generate the four specific types of drug abuse for each substance (objective problems with use, use at work, subjective problems with use, and driving while intoxicated).

In all models, the various assessments of drug consumption were used to predict the various measures of drug abuse. In addition to estimating the predictive influences of Drug Consumption on Drug Abuse (as latent constructs), we also added nonstandard paths or effects to the models, as suggested by selected modification indices (Bentler, 1989). These nonstandard effects may include predicting either the Drug Abuse latent construct or its related specific drug-abuse variables from either the Drug Consumption latent construct or the residual (unique variance) of the specific drug-consumption indicators. Elaboration of this richer, more detailed, and fuller use of structural-equation modeling procedures can be found elsewhere (e.g., Newcomb, 1988, 1990; Newcomb & Bentler, 1988a, 1988b, 1989b). Following the advice of MacCallum (1986), all models were overfit by adding needed paths and then trimmed by removing nonsignificant paths to arrive at the final models.

Measures of drug consumption and abuse are not typically distributed normally and, when feasible, should be analyzed with statistical procedures that are not violated by nonnormality. For all of the SEM analyses to follow, the arbitrary generalized least-square estimation method with iterations is used (Bentler, 1989), which should produce reliable and unbiased parameter estimates, standard errors, and fit statistics regardless of normality violations.

For each of the cross-sectional analyses of the three substances, separate models were generated based on different groups of subjects. One set of models was based on the total sample of subjects. It could be argued that these models might be distorted because they include those who do not use the particular drug. Although most of the participants drank alcohol, only about one third smoked marijuana, and even fewer used cocaine. A second set of models was generated based only on those who used the particular drug. Interestingly, very similar final models were produced for both samples for each substance; only the magnitude of the parameter estimates differed in a few comparisons. The results of the cross-sectional analyses of the users groups will now be presented.

To conserve space, only the final models are presented. All final models for the cross-sectional and longitudinal data for the three substances fit the data well. Several fit indices for these final six models are summarized in Table 10.9, including the significance value associated with the chi-square-to-degrees-of-freedom ratio, the normed fit index (Bentler & Bonett, 1980), and the comparative fit index (Bentler, 1989). Standardized estimates for the parameters in all six models are graphically depicted in Figures 10.7 through 10.12.

Alcohol

The estimates for the final cross-sectional alcohol model are presented in Figure 10.7. Here it can be seen that Alcohol Consumption accounted for 45% of the variance in Alcohol Abuse $(1.00 - .55$ [factor disturbance term]) and also had a specific impact on driving while drunk. In addition, there was a specific effect of alcohol frequency on increasing objective problems with alcohol.

TABLE 10.9
Summary of Model Fit Indices

Final structural models	N	χ^2	df	p	Normed fit index	Comparative fit index
			Cross-sectional models: users only			
Alcohol	543	0.74	4	.94	.99	1.00
Marijuana	188	4.07	5	.54	.96	1.00
Cocaine	122	4.65	7	.70	.93	1.00
			Longitudinal models: all subjects			
Alcohol	536	9.56	25	.99	.99	1.00
Marijuana	536	9.20	21	.99	.98	1.00
Cocaine	536	6.48	16	.98	.98	1.00

Marijuana

The final cross-sectional marijuana model is depicted in Figure 10.8. Marijuana Consumption accounted for 65% of the variance in Marijuana Abuse, and marijuana quantity had specific influences on increasing marijuana use at work and subjective problems with drugs.

Cocaine

Results from the final cocaine model on cross-sectional data are given in Figure 10.9. In this case, Cocaine Consumption perfectly predicted Cocaine Abuse, and no nonstandard paths were necessary.

Nevertheless, in the cocaine model, as in the other two models, substantial variance was not accounted for in several of the measures assessing specific types of drug abuse. Thus, even in the cocaine model, where all of the variance of Cocaine Abuse was accounted for as a general factor, from 12% to 71% of the variance in the specific types of cocaine abuse could not be explained by the drug-consumption variables. Clearly, other factors must be considered to explain more fully these various patterns of abuse. Furthermore, no variables have been included in any of these models to account for the drug-consumption patterns.

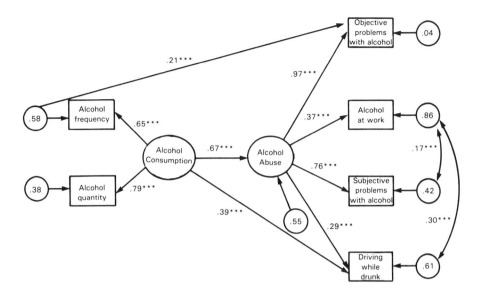

FIGURE 10.7   Final cross-sectional model for alcohol use and abuse based solely on alcohol users. (Large circles are latent constructs, rectangles are measured variables, and small circles are residual variables—as variances. Single-headed arrows are factor loadings or regression paths, two-headed arrows are correlations, and all parameter estimates are standardized. ***$p < .001$.)

Longitudinal Models of Drug Consumption Abuse and Vulnerability

The limitations noted in the cross-sectional models are addressed in three expanded models that include data from 8 years earlier. Previous assessments of alcohol, marijuana, and cocaine consumption from late adolescence were added to the appropriate cross-sectional model. In addition, the risk- and protective-factor indices from late adolescence (Year 5) were used to reflect a latent construct of Extreme Vulnerability in each of the three elaborated models. The constructs of Extreme Vulnerability and Drug Consumption in Year 5 were allowed to correlate freely (and are depicted in the figures), as were the residual variables of the repeatedly assessed drug-consumption variables (which are not depicted in the figures). The three final models resulting from these analyses are depicted in Figures 10.10 through 10.12.

In all models, Year 5 drug consumption significantly predicted Year 13 drug consumption (although much more strongly for alcohol and marijuana than for cocaine) and reflects the behavioral or life-style stability of drug involvement. Furthermore, Year 5

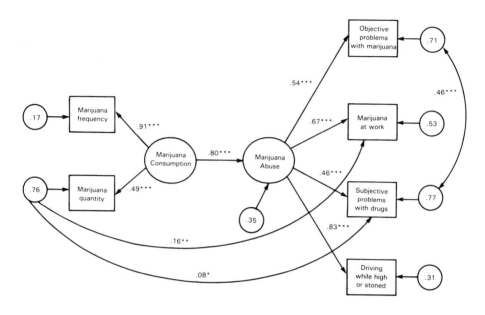

FIGURE 10.8 Final cross-sectional model for marijuana use and abuse based solely on marijuana users. (Large circles are latent constructs, rectangles are measured variables, and small circles are residual variables—as variances. Single-headed arrows are factors loadings or regression paths, two-headed arrows are correlations, and all parameter estimates are standardized. *$p < .05$. **$p < .01$. ***$p < .001$.)

Drug Consumption was significantly correlated with Extreme Vulnerability, ranging from a low of .57 for cocaine to a high of .87 for alcohol. The causal direction of these associations, of course, cannot be determined; however, the magnitude of the relations indicates that the selection of psychosocial risk and protective factors was valid.

Alcohol

The final longitudinal model for the alcohol data is presented in Figure 10.10. In addition to the findings previously mentioned, Extreme Vulnerability increased later Alcohol Abuse, and the residual of the risk factor index increased later alcohol quantity.

Marijuana

Figure 10.11 depicts the results from the final model on the longitudinal marijuana data. The residual of marijuana quantity (Year 5) increased later Marijuana Consumption. Extreme Vulnerability increased later use of marijuana at work. The residual of the risk-factor index increased later marijuana quantity and use of marijuana on the job, and had

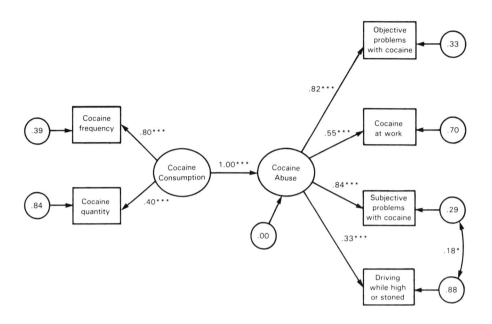

FIGURE 10.9   Final cross-sectional model for cocaine use and abuse based solely on cocaine users. (Large circles are latent constructs, rectangles are measured variables, and small circles are residual variables—as variances. Single-headed arrows are factor loadings or regression paths, two-headed arrows are correlations, and all parameter estimates are standardized. $*p < .05.$ $***p < .001.$)

direct effects on increasing later marijuana quantity and driving while stoned. Finally, the residual of the protective-factor index reduced later objective problems with marijuana and subjective problems with drugs.

Cocaine

The final model on the longitudinal cocaine data is presented in Figure 10.12. Year 5 cocaine frequency increased later cocaine quantity. Extreme Vulnerability increased later driving while high or stoned. Year 13 Cocaine Consumption was significantly predicted from the residual of the risk-factor index (positively) and the residual from the protective-factor index (negatively). Finally, the residual of the protective-factor index also had direct effects on reducing later cocaine quantity and decreasing objective problems with cocaine.

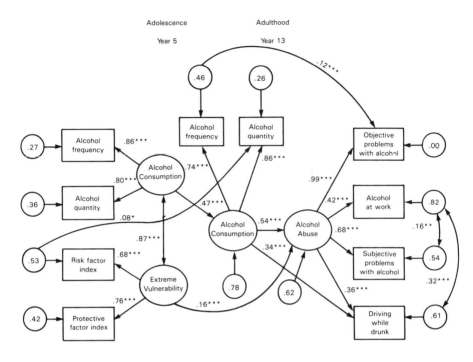

FIGURE 10.10 Final longitudinal model for alcohol use and abuse and psychosocial vulnerability. (Large circles are latent constructs, rectangles are measured variables, and small circles are residual variables—as variances. Single-headed arrows are factor loadings or regression paths, two-headed arrows are correlations, and all parameter estimates are standardized. *$p < .05$. **$p < .01$. ***$p < .001$.)

Discussion

What do these findings reveal about the usefulness of the suggested paradigm, and how do they contribute to our understanding of use and abuse of drugs? The numerous and varied analyses that I have presented can provide information and evidence for many directions of interest and discussion. I will briefly elaborate on several of these that bear on the focus of this investigation, but I must bypass others of equal merit. I encourage the reader to interpret and integrate these other implications of the findings.

The proposed paradigm provided a useful perspective within which to operationalize and test whether amount of drug use (or consumption) is a necessary and sufficient

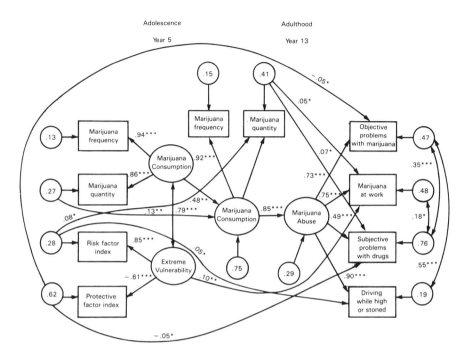

FIGURE 10.11   Final longitudinal model for marijuana use and abuse and psychosocial vulnerability. (Large circles are latent constructs, rectangles are measured variables, and small circles are residual variables—as variances. Single-headed arrows are factor loadings or regression paths, two-headed arrows are correlations, and all parameter estimates are standardized. ($p < .05$. $**p < .01$. $***p < .001$.)

condition to predict the extent of drug abuse (the pharmacological model). Or alternatively, whether other influences must be considered to understand this transition from use to abuse.

All of the findings indicate that the pharmacological model is an incomplete explanation to account for the association between use and abuse of drugs. It is critical to realize that the present, very general operationalization of the pharmacological model is inadequate, because I have not considered the biogenetic abuse liability of the individual. As a result, the distinction between models is primarily heuristic and does not represent any critical test between them.

However, consumption and abuse of three different drugs were examined, which allows for some variation in the abuse liability of specific psychoactive substances. The

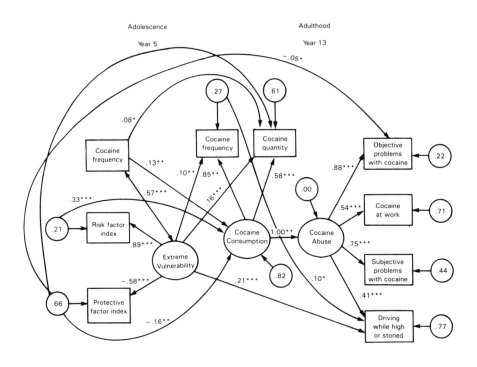

FIGURE 10.12   Final longitudinal model for cocaine use and abuse and psychosocial vulnerability. (Large circles are latent constructs, rectangles are measured variables, and small circles are residual variables—as variances. Single-headed arrows are factor loadings or regression paths, two-headed arrows are correlations, and all parameter estimates are standardized. $*p < .05.$ $**p < .01.$ $***p < .001.$)

pharmacological model would predict that drugs can vary in regard to their abuse potential because of differences in their chemical structures and in the brain sites, mechanisms, and effects of their actions. Interestingly, the pharmacological model had greater explanatory power for some drugs than for others. For instance, the general Cocaine Abuse construct was perfectly predicted by the Cocaine Consumption factor (although far from all of the variance was explained in the specific cocaine-abuse measures). On the other hand, only about 45% of the variance in Alcohol Abuse could be explained solely by Alcohol Consumption. The pattern for Marijuana Consumption and Abuse fell between these two extremes. The present findings on alcohol corroborate those of Sadava (1985), who noted a distinction between alcohol consumption and problem drinking.

Apparently, however, this degree of distinction between use and abuse does not generalize to other drugs, such as marijuana and cocaine.

The findings from the prevalence estimates corroborate this difference among drugs regarding their abuse potential due to use. Over one third of all cocaine users were dependent on the drug, whereas only 15% of alcohol users were dependent on alcohol. In other words, the nature of the substance plays a critical role in regard to the likelihood of abuse, given use of the drug. These differences may arise from the varying psychopharmacological aspects of the drugs, as well as the different personal, legal, and social statuses and expectations attached to specific substances.

This apparent distinctiveness among substances is tempered by the evidence of multiple dependencies. Abusing one substance substantially increased the likelihood of also abusing a different drug. Over half of those who were dependent on marijuana or cocaine were also dependent on alcohol. Thus, the role of multiple dependencies must be considered when examining the processes of drug use and abuse. Future research must address more directly this interdependence of substance abuses while retaining an appreciation of specific substances. Use of latent-variable models to control for common and specific types of drug dependence may be particularly useful in subsequent research to depict and examine these more complex, comprehensive, and multifaceted patterns of behavior (e.g., Newcomb & Bentler, 1988a, 1988b). Recent evidence from young adults verifies a common pattern not only of polydrug consumption (frequency and quantity), but also of using various drugs in inappropriate settings (e.g., on the job; Newcomb, 1988) and of experiencing both subjective and objective adverse consequences simultaneously with several different substances (Stein, Newcomb, & Bentler, 1988).

Another important conclusion from the present analyses is that drug use and drug abuse each reflect numerous distinct but related aspects of drug involvement and consequences. These multidimensional components must be studied in terms both of their underlying, general condition and of their separate constituents to gain a complete understanding of the phenomena. If such distinctions were not made in the present analyses, quite different conclusions could have been reached. Again, use of latent-variable models to separate the general from specific aspects of drug use and abuse seems an ideal approach to this problem.

In the attempt to study such complex behaviors as the use and abuse of drugs, careful attention must be given to the definition and operationalization of key constructs or phenomena. Drug abuse has been defined in many different ways (e.g., Siegel, 1989; Westermeyer, 1988). One typical aspect of many definitions of drug abuse is evidence of negative or adverse consequences. Experiences of negative consequences attributable to drug ingestion form the basis of most of the criteria for diagnoses of substance abuse and dependence in the *DSM–III–R*. Reports of such experiences were used to create the objective-problems-with-drugs items in this study.

At least two problems are associated with using adverse consequences as the primary indicators of drug abuse. First, observable negative effects of drug use may reflect only the extreme endpoint of a drug-abuse continuum and thereby overlook more subtle or incipient symptoms of drug abuse that occur at earlier, less severe points along the continuum. Second, this focus on the most severe symptoms of drug abuse may be inappropriate or too insensitive for certain populations of drug users. Youthful samples of drug users, such as teenagers and young adults, may have had insufficient time in their drug-use careers to suffer major adversities because of their drug use. Drug abuse is a progressive and evolving problem that may take years to reach the point of obvious impairment and dysfunction. For instance, physical deterioration because of excessive drug use may be rare for those under 30 years old (e.g., Newcomb & Bentler, 1987) and is thus probably a poor indicator of drug abuse for this population. On the other hand, adverse events that are due to drugs are quite frequent among clinic and treatment samples but are less prevalent in general community samples and are probably too severe to capture the range of drug abuse in these less-selected groups. Thus, because the present study is based on data from a community sample of young adults, the estimates of drug dependence and the objective drug-problem scales may under-assess the extent of drug abuse in these subjects.

However, numerous other criteria besides negative consequences can also reflect drug abuse (e.g., Newcomb & Bentler, 1989a). In the present study, three additional sets of measures were included to reflect specific aspects of drug abuse that were not contingent on evidence of negative consequences. Two of these were assessments of the frequency of using drugs in the inappropriate, disruptive, or dangerous situations of driving a car (even though no accidents or injuries may have yet occurred) and while at school or work (creating some degree of impaired functioning, although perhaps yet unnoticed by teachers or supervisors). The third specific measure of drug abuse used in this study that was not based on adverse effects was subjective appraisals of the extent of perceived difficulty associated with use of drugs. Although adverse consequences may contribute to these judgments of difficulty, they capture a much larger synthesis and holistic inner evaluation of one's general problems with specific drugs. These three other indicators of drug abuse may be more sensitive and appropriate for this relatively young sample and may complement the objective-problem assessments.

In the present study, drug use was conceptualized as variations in drug consumption that were reflected in measures of frequency and quantity of use. The pharmacological model has little to say regarding the initial use of drugs; these explanations must be found elsewhere. The consumption assessments of drug use did not fully explain the variations in specific and general patterns of drug abuse for any of the substances.

Because drug consumption was not fully adequate to explain all of the significant variation in the general and specific types of drug abuse, factors associated with psychosocial risk and protection were added to the models from data obtained 8 years earlier. These were represented by indices of multiple risk and protective factors that were used as indicators of a latent construct of Extreme Vulnerability. Measures of prior drug consumption from this earlier time period were also integrated in the models. Earlier drug consumption had significant effects only on later drug consumption and did not influence any type of later drug abuse. Thus, earlier drug involvement did not place an individual at greater risk for later drug abuse beyond that accounted for by concurrent patterns of drug consumption. However, psychosocial vulnerability had direct effects on both later drug consumption and drug abuse. Extreme Vulnerability significantly increased later Alcohol Abuse, use of marijuana at work, cocaine frequency, cocaine quantity, and driving while high or stoned. The specific or unique aspect of the risk-factor index (not explained by the Extreme Vulnerability construct) significantly increased later alcohol quantity, marijuana quantity, driving while high or stoned, and general cocaine consumption. The unique portion of the protective-factor index significantly reduced both objective and subjective problems with marijuana, general cocaine consumption, cocaine quantity, and objective problems with cocaine. Given the lengthy period of time between these two data points, it is surprising to find so many direct effects of earlier vulnerability and protection (although several are quite small), particularly when these effects were over and above the influence of earlier drug use.

It seems clear from these analyses that drug use is a necessary but not sufficient condition to explain drug abuse. Psychosocial vulnerability as a general factor, as well as the separate measures of risk and protection, were important etiological contributors to both later use and abuse of drugs.

These are important findings from both theoretical and practical perspectives. Theoretically, those factors or conditions that are associated with drug use and abuse must now be viewed as bipolar. The vulnerable extreme of their range certainly places an individual at risk for drug involvement. Likewise, the more of these risk conditions that are present in a person's life, the higher the likelihood of increased drug involvement and abuse; this much we have learned from previous research (e.g., Bry et al., 1982; Newcomb, Huba, & Bentler,

1986). From the present investigation, we now know at least two other possibilities related to the other extremes of these risk factors. First, the ends of these constructs opposite from risk actually reduce drug involvement, and the more of these present in a person's life, the more protected he or she is from drug use and abuse. Second, these risk and protective factors exert some degree of independent influence and can compete with each other to create the extent of drug use and abuse liability for each person. From a practical or applied perspective, these results emphasize the importance of both reducing risk conditions and enhancing protective influences to prevent or reduce drug use and abuse.

A substantive interpretation of the current results is that drug use and abuse are more likely with poor academic achievement and low academic aspirations, many deviant behaviors, little respect for the law, little belief in religion, high emotional distress, poor parent and family relations, perceived encouragement for and actual drug use among friends and community, easy access to drugs, and low likelihood of punishment for use of drugs. On the other hand, use and abuse of drugs is less likely with high academic performance and interest, avoidance of delinquency and adherence to the laws, strong religious beliefs, emotional well-being, good relations with parents and family, few models of drug use, peer and community disapproval of drug use, low availability of drugs, and fear of being caught and punished for using drugs.

Although I have shown that both risk and protective factors are associated with inhibiting or accelerating the transition from drug use to drug abuse, these factors may be differentially related to stages of drug involvement. Preliminary work on this notion was presented by Scheier and Newcomb (1991), who found that risk factors of a social nature were most related to drug-use initiation, whereas risk factors related to emotional distress were most related to exacerbation or illicit drug involvement. It is possible that different types of protective factors may be similarly related to stages in drug involvement; this speculation needs to be tested in future research.

Admittedly, the present effort is an encouraging, but crude and limited, attempt to integrate and extend current theory and empirical findings on the transition from use to abuse of drugs. Several strands of research are combined and expanded in the present study, and the resulting initial, awkward integration demands improvement and refinement in future research.

Although the current investigation cannot be faulted for examining the dynamics of using one specific drug (and thereby restricting our understanding of the abuse process to one chemical), because the use and abuse of alcohol, marijuana, and cocaine were examined, the present study is limited in this regard in at least two ways. First, these three substances do not reflect all of the drugs that are commonly used and abused in contemporary society. In particular, tobacco, amphetamines, caffeine, over-the-counter medications, and prescribed psychotropic drugs are widely used and abused. These should be included in future studies. Second, polydrug use is quite common (e.g., Clayton & Ritter, 1985; Stein et al., 1988) and was only briefly considered in the present analyses. It is questionable whether the processes associated with the use and abuse of specific drugs can also describe polydrug use and abuse.

Several improvements or variations should be made in future research in regard to the risk- and protective-factor indices. First, the range of potential influences should be expanded to include biogenetic predispositions, other personal and social characteristics, and larger socioculture forces. Second, the risk- and protective-factor indices could be constructed on sets of mutually exclusive variables. Although this alternate method would eliminate the statistical dependence introduced in the current procedure, it fails to capture the conceptual importance of both extremes of bipolar constraints related to drug involvement. There are trade-offs for each of these approaches. Finally, the present analyses were limited to the direct or additive effects of protective conditions. More attention should also be given to the buffering effect of protective forces. Brook et al. (1986, 1989) have made encouraging but limited tests of this notion by testing the interactive effect of separate protective variables. This line of research should be expanded to capture the synergistic power of multiple protective conditions, within a multivariate framework. Combing this approach with an additive model of protection, the importance of protection as a direct versus buffering process can be compared directly.

To test the buffering effect of protection, an interaction model must be used. Different degrees of association between risk and drug use and abuse are expected on the basis of the extent of protection: The higher the protection, the lower the association between risk and drug use and abuse. Interactions can be operationalized as product terms or by creating multiple-group models (e.g., Newcomb, 1990). Baron and Kenny (1986) described the conceptual and statistical meaning behind mediating and moderator effects and provided multivariate tests for these models. Using these methods, it is possible to determine the relative influence of the direct and buffering effects.

Finally, the present investigation was limited to the use and abuse of drugs at one developmental period as influenced by conditions many years earlier. Other research should examine different developmental periods in life and incorporate various lags in the prospective design. It is probable that the use and abuse of drugs may be defined differently and be associated in distinct ways depending on the specific life-span stage being studied (e.g., Newcomb & Bentler, 1989a).

In an earlier analysis of my 8-year data set, we found that increasing drug involvement as a teenager interfered with or disrupted successful completion of developmental tasks necessary for young adults (Newcomb & Bentler, 1988a, 1988b). In fact, heavy drug involvement as a teenager seemed to accelerate acquisition of adult roles and to create a pseudomaturity. I have termed this process *precocious development* (Newcomb, 1987). For instance, drug abuse as a teenager predicted early marriage and family involvement, but also much higher likelihood of divorce. Similarly, drug abuse as an adolescent was associated with disinterest in college and early entry into the workforce, but also with greater job instability. Thus, manifestations of drug abuse may affect most strongly those critical tasks faced at a particular life stage. Different areas of life may be adversely disrupted by drug abuse at younger or older ages.

The specific, substantive nature of risk and protective conditions may also vary across different life stages. One way in which these may differ is perhaps captured in the unique developmental tasks or challenges associated with each life period (Havighurst, 1972). These new responsibilities, expectations, and demands often require new adaptation and coping skills and may become either vulnerable or protective forces toward drug involvement depending on the extent and satisfaction of their acqusition and mastery.

The power of these risk and protective forces may also differ in potency and range over time; potency may be related to duration of exposure, and range may be short-term or long-term. For instance, exposure to certain risks may be precipitous and constitute an immediate vulnerability to use drugs (with a limited duration of exposure) that operates over a very short time period. A simple example of this would be at a party if a valued and respected friend passed you a bottle of whisky after she or he had just drank from it. On the other hand, certain protective forces may be enduring and stable personal dispositions or environmental conditions (with an extensive duration of exposure) that operate over long time periods. A simple instance of this might be if a strong belief in and commitment to obeying the laws of the state were acquired as a child, and later became the motivating force as an adult to refuse an invitation to a party where marijuana would be smoked. This conceptualization would predict that protective factors would be more stable over time than risk factors.

These are simply off-the-cuff examples of how risk and protective factors may differ in potency and salience, reflecting the duration of exposure to the condition, and may also vary in the length of time over which they exert their influences. These examples are used to point out the conceptual dimensions of exposure duration and a critical temporal period of influence for various risk and protective conditions. Empirical shortcomings associated with these potential variations in predictive salience reflect the necessary reliance on a fixed point of measurement and on a time lag between assessments in prospective studies (e.g., Gollob & Reichardt, 1987). Although no one study can address adequately all of these concerns, these issues suggest a need for multiple prospective studies that follow participants at several stages in life and vary in the length of time between waves of data collection from very short to quite lengthy.

These represent only a few of the directions and issues that can be followed from the present investigation. It seems that our conceptual integration and empirical demonstrations pose more questions than they answer. However, many of the issues and needed refinements seem more distinct and clear in the present context and will hopefully inform future research.

References

American Psychiatric Association. (1987). *Diagnostic and statistical manual of mental disorders* (3rd ed., rev.). Washington, DC: Author.

Baron, R. M., & Kenny, D. A. (1986). The moderator–mediator variable distinction in social psychological research: Conceptual, strategic, and statistical considerations. *Journal of Personality and Social Psychology, 51,* 1173–1182.

Bentler, P. M. (1980). Multivariate analysis with latent variables: Causal modeling. *Annual Review of Psychology, 31,* 419–456.

Bentler, P. M. (1989). *EQS structural equations program manual.* Los Angeles: BMDP Statistical Software.

Bentler, P. M., & Bonett, D. G. (1980). Significance tests and goodness of fit in the analysis of covariance structures. *Psychological Bulletin, 88,* 588–606.

Bentler, P. M., & Newcomb, M. D. (1986). Personality, sexual behavior, and drug use revealed through latent variable methods. *Clinical Psychology Review, 6,* 363–385.

Brook, J. S., Whiteman, M., Gordon, A. S., & Cohen, P. (1986). Dynamics of childhood and adolescent personality traits and adolescent drug use. *Developmental Psychology, 22,* 403–414.

Brook, J. S., Whiteman, M., Gordon, A. S., & Cohen, P. (1989). Changes in drug involvement: A longitudinal study of childhood and adolescent determinants. *Psychological Reports, 65,* 707–726.

Bry, B. H. (1983). Predicting drug abuse: Review and reformulation. *International Journal of the Addictions, 18,* 223–233.

Bry, B. H., McKeon, P., & Pandina, R. J. (1982). Extent of drug use as a function of number of risk factors. *Journal of Abnormal Psychology, 91,* 273–279.

Clayton, R. R., & Ritter, C. (1985). The epidemiology of alcohol and drug abuse among adolescents. *Advances in Alcohol and Substance Abuse, 4,* 69–97.

Donovan, J. E., Jessor, R., & Jessor, L. (1983). Problem drinking in adolescence and young adulthood: A follow-up study. *Journal of Studies on Alcohol, 44,* 109–137.

Gollob, H. F., & Reichardt, C. S. (1987). Taking account of time lags in causal models. *Child Development, 58,* 80–92.

Havighurst, R. J. (1972). *Developmental tasks and education* (3rd ed.), New York: McKay.

Kandel, D. B. (1984). Marijuana users in young adulthood. *Archives of General Psychiatry, 41,* 200–209.

Lettieri, D. J. (1986). Drug abuse: A review of explanations and models of explanations. *Advances in Alcohol and Substance Abuse, 4,* 9–40.

MacCallum, R. (1986). Specification searches in covariance structure analyses. *Psychological Bulletin, 100,* 107–120.

Miller, N. S., & Gold, M. S. (1989). Suggestions for changes in *DSM–III–R* criteria for substance use disorders. *American Journal of Drug and Alcohol Abuse, 15,* 223–230.

Newcomb, M. D. (1987). Consequences of teenage drug use: The transition from adolescence to young adulthood. *Drugs and Society, 1*(4), 25–60.

Newcomb, M. D. (1988). *Drug use in the workplace: Risk factors for disruptive substance use among young adults.* Dover, MA: Auburn House.

Newcomb, M. D. (1990). What structural modeling techniques can tell us about social support. In I. G. Sarason, B. R. Sarason, & G. R. Pierce (Eds.), *Social support: An international view* (pp. 26–63), New York: Wiley.

Newcomb, M. D., & Bentler, P. M. (1986a). Cocaine use among young adults. *Advances in Alcohol and Substance Abuse, 6,* 73–96.

Newcomb, M. D., & Bentler, P. M. (1986b). Frequency and sequence of drug use: A longitudinal study from early adolescence to young adulthood. *Journal of Drug Education, 16,* 101–120.

Newcomb, M. D., & Bentler, P. M. (1987). The impact of late adolescent substance use on young adult health status and health services: A structural equation model over four years. *Social Science and Medicine, 24,* 71–82.

Newcomb, M. D., & Bentler, P. M. (1988a). *Consequences of adolescent drug use: Impact on the lives of young adults.* Beverly Hills, CA: Sage.

Newcomb, M. D., & Bentler, P. M. (1988b). Impact of adolescent drug use and social support on problems of young adults: A longitudinal study. *Journal of Abnormal Psychology, 97,* 64–75.

Newcomb, M. D., & Bentler, P. M. (1989a). Substance use and abuse among children and teenagers. *American Psychologist, 44,* 242–248.

Newcomb, M. D., & Bentler, P. M. (1989b, September). *Effects of specific drug use and cross-time dynamics: A structural equations approach.* Paper presented at the NIDA Technical Review Meeting on Longitudinal Studies of Drug Abuse, Rockville, MD.

Newcomb, M. D., & Felix-Ortiz, M. (1991). *Multiple risk and protective factors for substance use and abuse: Derivation and cross-sectional and longitudinal tests.* Manuscript submitted for publication.

Newcomb, M. D., Huba, G. J., & Bentler, P. M. (1986). Life change events among adolescents: An empirical consideration of some methodological issues. *Journal of Nervous and Mental Disease, 174,* 280–289.

Newcomb, M. D., Maddahian, E., & Bentler, P. M. (1986). Risk factors for drug use among adolescents: Concurrent and longitudinal analyses. *American Journal of Public Health, 76,* 525–531.

Newcomb, M. D., Maddahian, E., Skager, R., & Bentler, P. M. (1987). Substance abuse and psychosocial risk factors among teenagers: Associations with sex, age, ethnicity, and type of school. *American Journal of Drug and Alcohol Abuse, 13,* 413–433.

Pandina, R. J., White, H. R., & Yorke, J. (1981). Estimation of substance use involvement: Theoretical considerations and empirical findings. *International Journal of the Addictions, 16,* 1–24.

Sadava, S. W. (1985). Problem behavior theory and consumption and consequences of alcohol use. *Journal of Studies on Alcohol, 46,* 392–397.

Sadava, S. W. (1987). Interactional theories. In H. T. Blane & K. E. Leonard (Eds.), *Psychological theories of drinking and alcoholism* (pp. 90–130). New York: Guilford.

Scheier, L. M., & Newcomb, M. D. (1991). Psychosocial predictors of drug use initiation and escalation: An expansion of the multiple risk factors hypothesis using longitudinal data. *Contemporary Drug Problems, 18,* 31–73.

Segal, B. (1986). Intervention and prevention of drug-taking behavior: A need for divergent approaches. *International Journal of the Addictions, 21,* 165–173.

Siegel, R. K. (1989). *Intoxication: Life in pursuit of artificial paradise.* New York: Dutton.

Stein, J. A., Newcomb, M. D., & Bentler, P. M. (1987). An eight-year study of multiple influences on drug use and drug use consequences. *Journal of Personality and Social Psychology, 53,* 1094–1105.

Stein, J. A., Necomb, M. D., & Bentler, P. M. (1988). Structure of drug use behaviors and consequences among young adults: Multitrait–multimethod assessment of frequency, quantity, work site, and problem substance use. *Journal of Applied Psychology, 73,* 595–605.

Westermeyer, J. (1988). The pursuit of intoxication: Our 100 century-old romance with psychoactive substances. *American Journal of Drug and Alcohol Abuse, 14,* 175–187.

Zucker, R. A., & Gomberg, E. S. L. (1986). Etiology of alcoholism reconsidered: The case of a biopsychosocial approach. *American Psychologist, 41,* 783–793.

CHAPTER 11

Relationships Between Circumstances Surrounding Initial Illicit Drug Use and Escalation of Drug Use: Moderating Effects of Gender and Early Adolescent Experiences

Howard B. Kaplan and Robert J. Johnson

We examined circumstances surrounding initial illicit drug use for their effects on escalation of use. We conducted separate multivariate analyses for men and women and, within each of these groupings, for subgroups differentiated by experiences in early adolescence. The analyses reflect changes in substantive concerns and methods that characterize the recent history of research on psychosocial influences on drug use.

This work was supported by research grants R01 DA 04310 and R01 DA 02497 and a Research Scientist Award (K05 DA 00136) to Howard B. Kaplan from the National Institute on Drug Abuse.

Research on Psychosocial Influences on Drug Use

Recent research on psychosocial factors in the etiology of substance abuse is characterized by evolution along a number of dimensions. We will focus on three trends in this evolutionary process. First, psychosocial research on substance abuse proceeds by identifying psychosocial correlates of substance abuse and then by estimating multivariate models in which the components were specified as having direct or indirect influences on substance abuse. Second, this research evolves from investigations that are concerned only with the onset of substance abuse, or from research that fails to distinguish between stages of substance abuse. Current research recognizes the different stages of substance abuse and is open to the suggestion that each stage of substance abuse may be preceded by unique psychosocial circumstances. Third, this research evolves from projects solely concerned with the linear (direct and indirect) influences of psychosocial factors on substance abuse to those that recognize the moderating effects of psychosocial variables. Research now contends that the direct or indirect relationship between a psychosocial variable and substance abuse may depend on the value of a third variable. We will document these three trends in turn and identify the current state of the evolutionary process.

Multivariate Models

Early research on substance use identified a variety of sociodemographic variables, interpersonal factors, and personality variables as correlates of substance abuse (Braucht, 1982; Bry, 1983). Correlates of initial involvement in substance use (as opposed to substance abuse) have with some reliability been identified as including peer influences on modeling of drug use, availability of substances, social support for substance use, disadvantaged socioeconomic status, familial disruption, adult drug-use models, lack of religious commitment, poor school performance, low self-esteem, tolerance for deviance, deviant behavior, lack of law abidance, need for excitement, stressful life events, and depression and anxiety (Newcomb & Bentler, 1989). Numerous longitudinal studies, more particularly, have identified a number of correlates of initial drug use. Summarizing this literature, Smith (1980) concludes as follows:

> The longitudinal evidence now available indicates that nonusing adolescents who are most likely to use marijuana and/or hard drugs during later adolescence tend to be more rebellious and deviance prone; more alienated from parents; more critical of society; more impulsive; more emotional; more pessimistic and sad; more adventuresome and

thrill seeking; more sociable and extroverted; less traditional and conservative regarding values; less oriented toward religion; less orderly, diligent, and effective in work and study habits; less intellectually curious and interested; less determined, persistent, and motivated toward achievement; less likely to feel valued and accepted by others; less trustworthy and responsible; less tender and considerate of others; and less self-controlled. (p.53)

Many research projects incorporate variously a number of these variables in their explanatory models. More often than not, the models are derived simply from the observed correlates of substance abuse. The multivariate research is in other cases guided by one of the numerous available theories of drug use (Lettieri, Sayers, & Pearson, 1980). The present program of research is guided, in contrast, by a general theory that incorporates several more specific theoretical orientations.

Our general theory views the onset of illicit drug use as a function of motivational disposition, expectations of positive consequences of acting on these dispositions, and opportunities for use. The disposition to use illicit drugs is congruent with the shared values of membership/reference group(s). The person with a history of self-enhancing experiences in the membership/reference group(s) that endorses or uses illicit drugs associates the motivation to use drugs and the norms of endorsing drug use with acceptance by the group members. Given a history of self-devaluing experiences, the individual is less disposed to conform to the shared values of the group (including perhaps illicit drug use). In the more usual case, in which the group norms proscribe illicit use of drugs and drug use is incompatible with the group values, the person is not disposed to use drugs, particularly when past conformity is rewarded with acceptance by the group members. When the experiences are essentially self-devaluing, however, the person is more disposed to use drugs and is attracted to values that contradict those of the group.

A person becomes disposed or motivated to use drugs in three ways: (a) socialization in groups that endorse drug use, (b) attraction to groups that endorse illicit drug use, or (c) loss of motivation to conform, and becoming motivated to deviate from conventional group values because of past self-devaluing experiences in such groups. The acting out of such motives or dispositions depends on opportunities to use drugs and expectations of rewarding (self-enhancing) consequences. If one is disposed to use drugs, opportunities (a supply of drugs is available and there is an occasion for use) increase the likelihood for use of drugs. Similarly, if disposed to use drugs, one is more likely to do so if one anticipates relatively few self-devaluing outcomes and relatively greater self-enhancing outcomes. The outcomes might relate to material rewards, attitudes of others, physical or psychological distress, or any of a number of valued outcomes. Whether particular outcomes are interpreted positively or negatively depends on such variables as the person's history of self-enhancing/self-devaluing experiences in the group. Less directly, the onset of illicit drug use is the outcome of determinants of disposition to use drugs, opportunities to act out dispositions, and anticipation of the consequences of drug use.

Escalation of Illicit Drug Use

Earlier research on drug use either focused on initiation of drug use or failed to distinguish between different degrees of involvement in illicit drugs (e.g, initiation as abuse). Although the correlates of initial involvement with substance use are established with some reliability (as risk factors or in terms of the interrelationships among these variables), it remains to be determined whether such variables are associated with heavy use. Furthermore, research needs to determine what additional variables are associated with progression to heavier use.

Many previous theories are differentially applicable to various stages of the progression of substance abuse, including initiation, continuation, transition from use to abuse, cessation, and relapse (Lettieri et al., 1980). Increasingly, investigators cease to

> assume that initial drug use and drug addiction have the same causes. Admittedly, some theories do take a single-stage, "take it once and hooked for life" approach. However, we found the evidence strong that many who do have an initial experience with a particular drug do not become continual users, and that many who become continual users do not become addicts. Hence, the causes for each stage may be different, and a set of stages is necessary (Gorsuch, 1980, p. 20).

It is argued, for example, that use of drugs occurs as a result of social influences, whereas abuse of drugs is more closely tied to internal psychological processes such as self-medication against emotional distress (Long & Scherl, 1984; Newcomb & Bentler, 1989). A review of drug-prevention programs supports the conclusion that the processes causing initiation of drug use differ from those that cause the abuse of drugs (Newcomb & Bentler, 1989; Tobler, 1986). Peer programs, which focus on enhancement of social skills and assertiveness, reduce the use of drugs but have less impact on the abuse of drugs. Those programs, however, aimed at promoting alternative activities, building confidence and social competence, and providing broadening experiences, do reduce the abuse of drugs:

> These results support the etiological findings that benign or nonproblem use of drugs occurs in social or peer settings (addressed in the peer program models) but that the abuse or problem use of drugs is generated by internal distress, limited life opportunities, and unhappiness (not ameliorated by the peer programs, but addressed somewhat by the alternative programs). (Newcomb & Bentler, 1989, p. 246)

In a similar vein, Simons, Conger, and Whitbeck (1988) have offered a model that distinguishes initiation from heavy use. They suggest that inconsistent findings result from the failure to distinguish experimentation from regular use, arguing that

> kids whose values emphasize immediate gratification and whose parents use substances and exercise little supervision and control, are likely to experiment with substances at an early age. However, the vast majority of kids who experiment with drugs do not go on to become regular users. The model suggests four factors which increase the probability that experimentation will escalate to heavy usage of alcohol and/or illicit drugs. The four factors are the substance use pattern of parents, type of peer group, psychopathology, and coping skills .... By operating to increase the reinforcement associated with drugs, these factors serve to escalate the degree to which substances are used. (p. 303)

In our theoretical statement that guides these analyses, escalation is a function of the circumstances surrounding initial use. These circumstances include the variables that influence initiation, that result from initial drug use, and that reflect changes in the person's psychosocial situation. Certain of these circumstances (alone or in combination) will increase drug use, whereas other circumstances will decrease illicit drug use.

Illicit drug use generally increases given three conditions: first, if the person associates need satisfaction with the illicit drug use; second, if the subject experiences a weakening of the motives that ordinarily act to constrain illicit drug use; and third, if the opportunities remain for illicit drug use.

Need satisfaction depends on the self-evaluative significance of perceived traits, behaviors, and experiences (particularly the responses of highly valued others). Illicit drug use satisfies the person's need for positive self-evaluation in a number of ways: It permits the youth to avoid conventional standards that measure his or her failure, it allows the youth to conform to the expectations of a positive reference group (e.g., drug-using peers), and it validates earlier drug use or the resulting deviant identity.

The motives that ordinarily constrain deviant impulses are reflected in the self-evaluative significance of internal and external social controls. These controls are weakened if accomplished by an absence of visible adverse consequences of earlier illicit drug use and by a decreased attraction to conventional values. These characteristics result from (a) the ongoing processes that influence the disposition to use illicit drugs and (b) the rejecting responses of conventional groups following initial drug use. The reciprocal rejection between the youth and conventional society increases the attraction to and interaction with peers who use drugs, thus providing ongoing occasions and opportunities for drug use.

Conversely, illicit drug use is less likely to increase (a) if the drug used does not appear to satisfy the needs that stimulated the initial response, (b) if the delinquent behavior stimulates threats to the satisfaction of other needs (such as those associated with continuing emotional commitment to conventional morality or fear of formal sanctions), and (c) if changes in the person's needs or in the available conventional opportunities to satisfy those needs render illicit drug use superfluous. This general statement is specified in greater detail later in the models to be estimated.

Moderating Variables

Differing from earlier concerns with the direct and indirect effects of predictors of drug use, newly evolved research concentrates on the variables that moderate psychosocial causes of substance abuse. As Baron and Kenny (1986) define the term,

> a moderator is a qualitative (e.g., sex, race, class) or quantitative (e.g., level of reward) variable that affects the direction and/or strength of the relation between an independent or predictor variable and a dependent or criterion variable. (p. 1174)

Researchers are increasingly interested in moderating effects in numerous areas of behavioral science. For example, Lefcourt (1989) reported on a number of variables that moderate the relationship between stress and mood disturbances. Among these variables are beliefs about control or effectiveness, social intimacy and interpersonal relationships, availability of social support, curiosity, and sense of humor.

The significance of such moderating effects for psychosocial causes of substance abuse is readily apparent in the area of the evaluation of drug-abuse prevention programs (MacKinnon, Weber, & Pentz, 1988). For example, urbanization can moderate prevention programming; stronger effects are observed in more urban areas (MacKinnon et al., 1988; Tobler, 1986). Race and age can moderate the success of the programs. For example,

Hansen, Malotte, and Fielding (1988) report the largest effects of drug-abuse prevention programs for Whites. Some researchers have found that drug-use prevention programs work best for younger students (Botvin, Eng, & Williams, 1980; Tell, Klepp, Vellar, & Mc-Alister, 1984), although others report no differences in effect size for junior high school and high school students (Tobler, 1986).

Apart from moderating sociodemographic variables, the literature is replete with examples of personal experiences and characteristics that moderate specified psychosocial causes of substance-abuse behavior (MacKinnon et al., 1988). For example, the effects of a cigarette smoking prevention program increase for those exposed to peer or family smokers (Best et al., 1984). These investigators also found that the program effects are greater for subjects with more smoking experience. At a later follow-up, however, the effect for experienced smokers reverses. The greatest program effects were obtained for subjects who at pretest had never smoked.

Pentz (1983) reported that highly assertive and aggressive students tended to be most affected by a social-competence program. Consistent with this, Tobler (1986) reported the greatest effects of drug-prevention programs for delinquents, abusers, and students with school problems; Evans et al. (1981) reported that a social-influences intervention affects most the subjects who are above the median in knowledge. In another study, larger reductions in drug use, as well as in the need for group acceptance were observed in the lower grades (Botvin et al., 1980).

Moderating influences have important implications for understanding causal processes. The reasons for the moderating effects of particular variables may vary. For example, the stronger effects of drug-prevention programs that were observed for higher-socioeconomic-status schools in some studies (Hansen et al., 1988; Hurd et al., 1980) could result from greater motivation on the part of educators. Teachers in higher-socio-economic-status circumstances anticipate receptivity on the part of the students, or they may anticipate the greater difficulty of lower-socioeconomic-status subjects in comprehending the messages of the program (MacKinnon et al., 1988). We will now consider the implications of the moderating effects relevant to the present analyses, in conjunction with their descriptions as conditional variables.

The Problem

The present research builds on our own previous work (Kaplan, Martin, Johnson, & Robbins, 1986; Kaplan, Martin, & Robbins, 1985) and extends the advances of other investigations of substance abuse. The present work estimates theoretically informed multivariate models that specify putative causes of substance abuse, it recognizes different stages of involvement in substance abuse, and it examines moderating effects in linear models. First, the analyses estimate the independent effects of nine variables that reflect antecedents, concomitants, or consequences of initial drug use. The dependent variable is escalation of drug use. The independent variables were selected on the basis of both theoretical and empirical considerations. Second, although most people who try illicit drugs do not proceed beyond the occasional use of small amounts, others increase the frequency and amounts of illicit drug use. The present study reports analyses formulated to explain why, among subjects who use illicit drugs at least once, some people progress to relatively frequent use (daily or near-daily use). Third, this research considers the moderating effects of variables on circumstances surrounding initial illicit drug use as causes of subsequent escalation of drug use. Gender, on theoretical and empirical grounds, is a primary contender among variables expected to exercise moderating influences. Variables other than gender are also expected to moderate the effects of the circumstances surrounding initial drug use on escalation of drug use. These moderating variables also are conditioned by gender; their effects depend on whether the subjects are men or women. The nature of the effects may be different for men and women. High values on a variable may be a contingency for the observation of an effect for male subjects, and low values may be a contingency for observation of the relationship among female subjects.

In short, we examined the effects of nine circumstances, at initial drug use, on escalation of drug use. The analyses were carried out separately for men and women. Within male and female subpopulations, we examined the conditional effects of high and low values of each of seven variables on the nine causal variables preceding escalation of drug use.

Method

The data were drawn from an ongoing longitudinal study of adolescents and young adults. The initial sample included all of the seventh grade students in a random half of the junior high schools in the Houston Independent School District as of March 1971. Students responded to a self-administered questionnaire (Time 1 data). Of the 9,335 students 7,618 (81.6%) returned questionnaires that were usable in the longitudinal study. Students also completed questionnaires in 1972 and 1973. We did not use these waves, however, in the present analyses. In late 1980, we began to trace and reinterview all of the target respondents from the 1971 study, including the 1,717 for whom baseline data were not available. Of the 7,618 Time 1 subjects, approximately 49% ($n = 3,733$) were boys and 51% ($n = 3,885$) were girls. For the present study group 5,064 subjects with Time 1 data were matched with the 6,074 subjects interviewed at Time 4. These 5,064 subjects constitute 66% of the subjects interviewed at Time 1 and 54% of the members of the original cohort. The analyses were carried out on a subset of the subjects for whom Time 1 and Time 4 data were available, namely, those who at Time 4 admitted to illicit drug use at some time in their life; this strategy was adopted because the model to be tested purports to explain why persons who experimented with illicit use of drugs (other than marijuana) at some time in their lives increase their level of drug use. Of the male subjects for whom both Time 1 and Time 4 data were available, 940 indicated that they had ever used illicit drugs (approximately 40%). Of the female subjects for whom both Time 1 and Time 4 data were available, 767 indicated that they had ever used illicit drugs (approximately 28%).

Considering attrition by gender, the male subjects for whom both early adolescent (Time 1) and young adult (Time 4) data were available constituted 62% of the male subjects who provided Time 1 data and 50% of the male subjects in the original cohort (assuming equal distributions of male and female subjects). The female subjects for whom Time 1 and Time 4 data were available constituted 70% of the female subjects for whom Time 1 data were available and 58% of the female subjects in the original cohort (again, assuming an equal number of male and female subjects).

We looked at the effects of sample attrition between Time 1 and Time 4 in a number of ways. We first examined the structure of relationships among explanatory variables at Time 1 for the subjects present at Time 1 only and for those present at Time 1–Time 4. Previous analyses have generally suggested that the correlations for the Time 1 only and for the Time 1–Time 4 groups are remarkably similar. This suggests that the structure of interrelationships observed for the subjects in the present analysis can be generalized to the cohort with some degree of confidence. However, we cannot know if there would be differences between those who were and were not reinterviewed in the structure of relationships between Time 1 and Time 4 variables. Furthermore, an examination of Time 4 subjects who were not present at Time 1 suggests that those who were lost to the sample were not unlike those who remained in the sample throughout the multiple waves. That is, they tend for the most part to have graduated from junior high school and to have come from relatively stable households. In any case, we remain cautious in generalizing the results observed to the entire cohort.

The possible effects of date of interview (and hence time at risk) were examined by correlating date of interview with the variables of interest, because the young-adult interviews were conducted over a period of several years. Time of interview did not have an appreciable effect on deviant behavior in general or on escalation of substance abuse in particular for either men or women. The correlation between date of interview and escalation of drug use was .03 for men and .02 for women.

Stepwise regression procedures were used to estimate the effects of nine independent variables (reflecting circumstances surrounding initial illicit drug use) on escalation of drug use. The regressions were accomplished separately for male and female subjects because gender was expected to influence the moderating effects of the other psychosocial variables. Within the male and female groupings, we also ran regressions separately for subgroups that were above and below the group mean on each of seven psychosocial variables, characteristics of preexisting personal and interpersonal circumstances that were expected to moderate the effects of the independent variables.

Variables

We will present the rationalization for the selection, in turn, of the dependent, independent, and moderating variables; each variable will be described in terms of its operationalization for the analyses.

Dependent Variables

The analyses attempt to account for the increased involvement in illicit drug use by subjects who used illicit drugs. Increased involvement in illicit drug use (ESCDRUG) was indicated by affirmation at Time 4 (as a young adult) that the subject had used drugs (other than marijuana) illegally or had used any illegal drugs (other than marijuana) "daily or almost daily for two weeks." Specifically, the defining question asked the following:

> Have you ever used drugs other than marijuana illegally or used any illegal drugs (other than marijuana) including LSD or other hallucinogens (for example, Mescaline, Angel Dust, PCP), amphetamines (Uppers, Speed), barbiturates (Downers, Goofballs), tranquilizers

(Librium, Valium), inhalants (glue or gasoline used to get high), heroin (Horse, Smack) or other opiates (Methadone, Opium, Morphine), Cocaine (Coke, Snow), Quaaludes (Soapers, Quads), and freebase daily or almost daily for at least two weeks?

Affirmation of the heavy use pattern generally indicates an increase in level of involvement beyond the initial use pattern because this question was only asked of people who had already indicated that they had ever used drugs illegally. The initial occasion of use was rarely a pattern of daily or almost-daily use for a period of at least 2 weeks; in this case, the item indicates initial high use rather than escalation of use. It is generally true, however, that a high level of use of drugs is preceded by a lesser level: "One rarely (if ever) becomes a compulsive user without a considerable amount of previous noncompulsive use" (Smith, 1980, p. 52). The dependent variable does not indicate a pattern of current heavy drug use; it does indicate that at some time the subject had progressed to daily or near-daily use for a period of 2 weeks.

Of the 940 men who had ever used drugs, approximately 24% ($n = 224$) indicated that they had escalated drug use. Of the 767 women who indicated they had ever used drugs, an identical 24% indicated that they had escalated ($n = 182$). Thus, although men were more likely than women to initiate illicit drug use, among those who initiated illicit drug use, women were as likely as men to escalate use.

Independent Variables

The selection of independent variables is based on both theoretical and empirical considerations. The theoretical framework for the study was outlined earlier. The empirical literature indicates that initial use of drugs is associated with a wide variety of circumstances. Some of these circumstances reflect the needs of the individuals and the expectation that drugs will satisfy those needs. For example, some individuals experience high degrees of subjective distress and anticipate that the use of drugs will reduce the experience of subjective distress. In fact, among those who initiate drug use out of these motives, some will experience a gratifying reduction in distressful self-feelings. Some individuals may initiate drug use because they feel worthless and anticipate that the drug use will, or find that the use of drugs actually does, reduce feelings of worthlessness. Other individuals initiate drug use out of a need to enhance one's sense of power, and find that drug use does increase one's sense of power. Others initiate drug use following unhappy experiences with significant others, or for expressing anger, or for dealing with the unwelcome experience of anger. Again, individuals achieve varied satisfaction of these motives following drug use. Satisfaction of needs for power or the reduction of distress, for example, might positively reinforce the initial drug use and lead to higher levels of use.

Some circumstances motivate drug use; other circumstances influence expectations of the consequences of drug use; and still others are the actual short-term consequences of initial drug use. Independent of these, other circumstances surrounding initial use are consequences that have long-term implications for escalation of drug use. The initial drug user can be the object of punitive responses or otherwise experience adverse physical and psychological sequelae. These adverse consequences might discourage higher levels of use. On the other hand, some adverse circumstances might preclude alternative response patterns and fix the individual in drug use as a dominant mode of adaptation. Circumstances surrounding initial drug use also include the person's evaluative definitions. For example, the person could define the initial drug use as a deviant activity; the definition of drug use as deviant would thus militate against increased drug involvement.

On the basis of theoretical and empirical considerations, we selected 10 variables to reflect the circumstances surrounding initial use; we expect that these variables influence the escalation of drug use. The data for these variables were taken from the responses of subjects during their young adult years (Time 4). Each subject who indicated that he or she ever used illicit drugs was asked a series of questions about the circumstances surrounding his or her initial use. These items are reported in Appendix A. The alphas, means, and standard deviations for these independent variables are presented in Appendix C.

The subjects' responses regarding circumstances surrounding initial drug use are interpreted as causal because they refer to a point in time (initial drug use) that is presumably prior to escalation of drug use. We recognize, however, that these retrospective responses can be influenced by later or heavier use; this distortion perhaps results from a need to explain or justify the escalation in terms that do not truly reflect the earlier circumstances. Some of the items (such as those relating to arrest or imprisonment) are less amenable to retrospective distortion than are others. Explaining the patterns of results in terms of retrospective distortion rather than in terms of valid indicators of earlier-occuring events requires more assumptions than we can make.

We will describe the 10 independent variables in turn and provide the rationale for their influence on drug use.

Adverse Physical and Psychological Effects (ADVERPP) is a four-item scale of unwelcome effects (e.g., guilt, feeling sick) associated with initial illicit drug use. We hypothesize that bad psychological or physical experiences at initial drug use inhibit escalation of use. We also recognize, however, that the need to avoid withdrawal or to assuage the distress associated with initial drug use can evoke further drug use (Smith, 1980). Furthermore, adverse effects can be counterbalanced by positive gains that are not immediately apparent. For example, as Smith (1980) observes,

> During the relatively early phases of escalation toward compulsive use, it is possible for consciously recognized dangers that are associated with substance use to facilitate rather than inhibit use if those dangers are experienced as more exhilarating than anxiety-provoking; if the self-initiated risk brings status and social approval to the user; or if the user pits any perceived dangers against his or her competence and self-control, and then treats the matter as a contest which he or she is sure to win. (p. 55)

Thus, in some cases, the forces favoring and those inhibiting escalation could cancel the effects of initial adverse experiences on escalation of use.

Negative Social Sanctions (NEGSANC) is scored on three items. A high score indicates that initial drug use evoked negative social sanctions (arrest, jail sentence, loss of job). Primarily on the basis of labeling theory (see below), we anticipate that being the object of negative social sanctions for initial drug use leads to escalation of use. More particularly, the labeling of individuals who experiment with drugs may lead to quite destructive consequences (Peele, 1986), which include escalation of drug use.

Attenuation of Interpersonal Ties (ATTENTI) is a two-item measure of rejection by significant others (boyfriend/girlfriend, parents, friends) and/or of causing grief to significant others (both effects resulting from initial drug use). High scores on this measure also are expected to cause escalation of drug use. Insofar as changed relationships with others result from the person's own actions (that is, using drugs), the person should experience an increased sense of self-efficacy. Insofar as the person's psychological distress is caused by his membership groups, the weakening of ties with groups should result in the perceived reduction of dysphoric affect. Insofar as the subject experiences a need to punish a significant other, such an effect of initial substance use should be gratifying. In each of these situations, the use of drugs is reinforcing. In addition, the attenuation of ties should increase opportunities for engaging in illicit activities by facilitating attraction to other membership groups that provide the means and occasions for illicit drug use. Under conditions where the individual was initially closely tied to his primary groups, the attenuation of ties would increase the experience of distress and escalation of illicit drug use as a means of reducing the distress.

Much of this reasoning is compatible with a number of arguments that appear in the literature on substance abuse. Thus, the assertion that escalation of drug use occurs in response to mounting conflicts resulting from initial substance abuse is congruent with Hendin's (1980) theoretical position. From this theoretical perspective, the experience of interpersonal strain in response to initial use should anticipate escalation of drug use as functional in dealing with distressful circumstances. Smith (1980) suggests that interpersonal conflict in response to initial drug use may be positively reinforcing insofar as the adolescent has a strong need to punish the self, a parent, or some other significant person. The expectation that social conflict in response to initial drug use would lead to escalation of drug use is also consistent with observations by van Dijk (1980) in his description of the "social vicious circle":

> The circular process is based on the fact that drug addiction has social consequences, which in their turn reinforce the use of the drug. The social sequelae may be described as dysfunction, and, finally, a disintegration within the groups the addict is (or was) functioning in. This process has harmful effects on the addict. We may only mention the reproaches of the spouse or other members of the family, the quarrels, the disdain and withdrawal of friends and acquaintances, the tensions and conflicts in the occupational sphere, and, finally, the dropping out from society. This isolation and rejection engender in the subject negative feelings, which foster an attitude of letting oneself go into the state of being an addict. This means a fixation of the role behavior that goes with it and a reinforcement of the identification with a drug-using subculture. (p. 171)

Deviant Definition of Drug Use (DEVDEFD) is a two-item scale indicating that initial drug use occurred secretly (rather than in public where others could see it) and with the expectation that there was a chance of getting into trouble because of it. The expectation of punishment implies that the subject defines the act as deviant. The deviant definition of the act is expected to be inversely related to the escalation of drug use. The fact that some individuals who define illicit drug use as deviant engaged in it nevertheless may simply suggest that the initial use was performed out of curiosity with no expectation of continuing the behavior.

Reduction of Negative Affect (REDNEGA) is scored on five items indicating that initial drug use occurred during feelings of negative affect and that it reduced those feelings. High scores increase drug use because this variable is reinforcing and because use for such purposes suggests that alternative mechanisms are not available. People expect that drug use reduces negative affect, and this leads to escalation of use. Observations in the literature support the notion that drug use is one of several alternative activities that reduce the sense of dis-ease and despair stemming from failure to satisfy basic needs and self-enhancing aspirations (Duncan, 1977; Greaves, 1980; Khantzian, 1980; Mellinger, 1978). Wurmser (1980) observed that stimulants are used against depression and weakness, psychedelics are used to counteract boredom and disillusionment, and alcohol is used to assuage feelings of guilt, loneliness, and related anxiety. Furthermore, Anhalt and Klein (1976) reported that the use of tranquilizers, amphetamines, and sedatives by junior high school students was self-medication intended to reduce painful feelings. The use of drugs to assuage distress (Fitzgibbons, Berry, & Shearn, 1973), leading to escalation of use, is supported by both theoretical statements and empirical findings. Drug use intended to erase consciousness of pain, problems, and anxieties will be addictive (Peele, 1980). L. Stein and Bowman (1977) reported that drinking to relax, to forget, to cheer up, or when tense and nervous increases the amount of alcohol consumed and decreases social functioning among men with a primary diagnosis of alcoholism.

With regard to the effect of drugs on inhibition of the development of more effective coping mechanisms, Peele (1980) observed that

> any drug which serves an analgesic function can be used addictively. It is, in fact, the experience of having pain relieved to which the individual becomes addicted. ... Persons who are faced with persistent difficulties and anxieties in their lives and who are not prepared to cope with them realistically resort to analgesic drugs for comfort. While enabling them to forget their problems and stress, the pain-killing experience engendered by the drugs actually *decreases* the ability to cope. This is because such drugs depress the central nervous system and the individual's responsive capability. Along with this, people do not focus on their problems while intoxicated with a drug, and so the sources of the stress that led them to take the drug are likely to worsen as a result of having been ignored. (p. 143)

Distress as a motivator for initial use of drugs, then, leads to escalation of drug use for a number of reasons. First, drug use is reinforced in the reduction of distress. Drug use also precludes learning more effective coping mechanisms. Therefore, reliance on drug use increases the person's inability to deal with stressful life circumstances and, in the long run, increases the experience of distress (R. J. Johnson & Kaplan, 1990). The increased distress, in turn, motivates the individual to use the only coping mechanisms that exist in his or her repertoire, namely, ongoing substance abuse.

Reduction of Self-Rejection (REDSREJ) is a four-item scale indicating that initial drug use was occasioned by self-devaluing feelings, and resulted in the reduction of such feelings. The negative feelings that are associated with self-rejection are conceptually distinguished from other negative feelings such as depression, boredom, and nervousness, which are reflected in the previous variable. Even so, Reduction of Negative Affect and Reduction of Self-Rejection are highly correlated ($r = .51$ for men; $r = .59$ for women). It is problematic, therefore, whether these affects have independent predictive effects. Initial use of drugs to reduce self-rejection is, however, expected to cause escalation of drug use because this variable implies positive reinforcement of drug use and the absence of alternative self-enhancing mechanisms. Furthermore, the use of drugs as a disvalued pattern increases the person's feelings of self-rejection and paradoxically increases the need for drugs to reduce the self-rejecting feelings.

The theoretical basis for this predication is found in such statements as that of Misra's (1980) achievement anxiety theory. In that theory, drug abuse serves as a protection from a sense of failure; the drug induces a feeling of relaxed carelessness. Hoffman (1964) asserted that the drug addict, having been unable to maintain an acceptable level of self-esteem through such symbolic modes of functioning as gratifying interpersonal experiences or vocational achievements, returns to a physiological mode of self-esteem maintenance. Wurmser (1980) further notes that the shame and sense of failure associated with drug use intensify the preexisting narcissistic conflict and exacerbate the need for new pharmacological denial of the shame and failure. Others also have noted that substance abuse may be a way of coping with personal frustrations and anticipated failure (Jessor, Jessor, & Finney, 1973).

Numerous studies have reported associations between drug use and indices of insecurity, dissatisfaction with self, a desire to change oneself, defensiveness, low self-esteem, and low self-confidence (Davis & Brehm, 1971; Segal, Rhenberg, & Sterling, 1975; Stokes, 1974). With regard to alcohol abuse, Tahka (1966) reported that among the premorbid personality characteristics of alcoholics were tendencies toward feelings of guilt or inferiority.

Increased Potency (INCRPOT) was reflected in a score based on two items. A high score indicated that initial use of the drug was perceived by the person as making him or her feel more important or powerful. High scores on this variable were expected to be associated with escalation of drug use, on the premise that feelings of increased potency are positively reinforcing, particularly for those individuals whose self-image is bound up with feelings of power. It might be expected, for example, that the relationship would be stronger for, or unique to, male subjects.

Compatible with these expectations, Simons et al. (1988) asserted that enhancement of a sense of mastery contributes to the reinforcing value of substance use; Feldman (1968) argued that drug use provides an opportunity for slum youth to enhance status and prestige in a system where those persons who demonstrate attributes of toughness, daring, and adventure are most valued. With regard to alcohol abuse, McClelland (1972) noted that alcohol use, depending on the amount consumed, the setting, and personal characteristics, has been said to increase thoughts of personalized power, that is, of winning personal victories over threatening adversaries; McGuire, Stein, and Mendelson (1966) suggested that intoxication might be sought "to facilitate fantasy fulfillment, to enhance arbitrary interpretations of reality and to eliminate sober realizations" (p. 22). The expectation that experiences of enhanced potency associated with initial drug use would be positively reinforcing and lead to escalation of drug use is consistent with data from a cross-cultural study in which it was observed that for American youth there was a relationship between the personality attributes of powerlessness, dissatisfaction, and frustration, on the one hand, and frequency of drunkenness and alcohol intake, on the other (Jessor, Young, Young, & Tesi, 1970).

Expression of Anger (EXPRANG) is reflected on a three-item scale. High scores indicate that initial drug use was occasioned by anger at significant others. We expect that high scores will escalate drug use. Positive reinforcement might come from any of a number of sources, but it usually comes from the drug-related reduction of stressful emotions. The use of drugs is reinforcing for individuals who are most loath to express anger and under conditions in which the expression of anger is costly. For example, individuals who had close relationships with their parents are most loath to feel and express anger. In addition, the use of illicit drugs occasioned by anger at significant others might function to express contempt for those who were the objects of the person's anger, by contravening their normative expectations.

Thus, drugs might be positively reinforcing because they serve either or both of two functions. The effect of drug use in response to feelings of anger on escalation of drug use is consistent with the literature on the use of certain drugs to deal with aggressive impulses:

> In repeated life histories obtained from addicts, I was impressed with how dysphoric feelings associated with anger, rage, and restlessness were relieved in the short term by heroin and other opiates. This was even more apparent when observing addicts in treatment as they became stabilized on methadone and their aggression and restlessness subsided. I began

to suspect that heroin addicts might be using opiates specifically as an antiaggression drug. (Khantzian, 1980, p. 30)

Wurmser (1980) also noted that narcotics and hypnotics are used against rage, shame, jealousy, and related anxiety; Tahka (1966) reported that among the premorbid personality characteristics of alcoholics were inhibitions of aggressive (and sexual) impulses.

Jessor et al. (1973) also suggested that such behaviors as marijuana use may serve as an expression of opposition to or rejection of conventional society (including the norms that define the behavior as a problem). The use of drugs as an expression of anger is also consistent with Chein's (1980, p. 82) observation that for individuals who are deeply alienated from society but who have sufficient resources left to want to hit back, drugs are attractive insofar as their use if frowned upon and condemned by the representatives of conventional society.

Motivation for Peer Acceptance (MOTPEER) is reflected in a seven-item measure indicating that initial drug use was motivated or occasioned by peer expectations and had positive consequences for peer associations. A high score was expected to be associated with escalation of drug use either because the peer involvement was intrinsically satisfying or because involvement with drug-using peers provided increased opportunities and occasions for illicit drug use, as well as expectations about benign effects (Kaplan, Johnson, and Bailey, 1987; Simons et al., 1988). Others have made similar observations relating to the functions of peer involvement in drug use. Thus, Schoolar, White and Cohen (1972) argued that individuals seek in the drug culture the closeness and sharing experiences they were lacking in their earlier home lives. Jessor et al. (1973) suggested that such activities as marijuana use may serve to demonstrate solidarity with peers or membership in a subculture. Furthermore, in view of observations that low expectations of peer affection are associated with drinking-related complications (Jessor, Carman, & Grossman, 1970), it would not be unexpected to find that gratifications from drug-using peers would be positively reinforcing and related to escalation of drug use. Finally, Chein's (1980) comments on the functions of drug use illustrate the range of benefits to be obtained from the involvement of peers in initial drug use:

> There are three interrelated benefits the addict acquires from his involvement from narcotics: He gains an identity, one posing little to live up to. He gains a place in a subsociety where he is unequivocally accepted as a peer, a not-too-demanding place among his fellow man. He acquires a career, at which he is reasonably competent, devoted to maintaining his supply, avoiding the police, and rituals of taking the drug. (p. 82)

Moderating Variables

We expect that the influences of the independent variables on escalation of drug use are moderated by gender (reflecting the influence of psychosocial correlates of gender differentiation) and by a number of psychosocial variables prior to escalation for drug use. We expect, further, that the moderating influence of earlier psychosocial variables are conditional on gender. Hence, the stepwise regression analyses of the independent variables' effects on escalation of drug use are carried out separately for male and female subjects, and separately for subgroups of high and low scores on each of seven variables measuring psychosocial characteristics in the seventh grade. The latter analyses were executed separately for male and female subjects. We now discuss the rationale for using gender as a moderating variable and for the expectation that gender would interact with seventh grade psychosocial characteristics to moderate the effects of the circumstances surrounding initial use of drugs on escalation of drug use. We then discuss the measurement of the seventh grade psychosocial variables and the rationale for their selection as moderating variables.

Gender

Social identities determine expectations for attributes and behaviors. If the person displays the attributes and behaviors that are appropriate to his or her various social identities (particularly to the more salient identities), the group will respond in ways that satisfy the youth's needs or that permit him or her to gain satisfaction of the needs. Among the salient identities that define the person's position in society are those based on gender.

Gender is expected to moderate relationships among putative antecedents or consequences of substance abuse and to interact with other moderating influences, in part because each gender is socialized to value different outcomes. The degree to which each gender approximates or fails to approximate gender-specific values will influence adaptive responses. For women, for example, feelings of bodily attractiveness are associated with a more positive self-concept, whereas feelings of physical effectiveness are more closely tied to men's self-concept (Attie & Brooks-Gunn, 1987). It has been argued that normative expectations regarding appropriate male behavior emphasize self-reliance and the inhibition of emotional expressiveness, self-disclosure, and help-seeking. Women, in contrast, are taught to value close relationships and to define themselves in terms of those relationships (Belle, 1987). Individuals may restrain themselves from acting out deviant activities if this activity is defined as being contrary to the proper behavior associated with a valued identity. A woman might restrain herself from committing an illegal violent act, for example, not only because it is illegal or because of any consequences that might occur if she was apprehended, but also because she is a woman and because deviant acts in general and violent acts in particular are unwomanly. That is, violent acts are inappropriate behaviors for women. If a particular act violates the normative expectations associated with social identities that are important to the person, that person will restrain himself or herself from committing that act, even if the opportunity and motivation to commit the act are present.

The literature is replete with examples of reports (a) showing the association of gender with patterns of deviant responses (including substance abuse), (b) demonstrating correlations of gender with a variety of psychosocial characteristics, (c) reporting the moderating influence of gender on relationships involving normative psychosocial patterns, deviant response patterns in general, and substance-abuse patterns in particular, and (d) suggesting the interaction of gender with other moderating variables in affecting drug-abuse patterns or their outcomes.

Regarding the association of gender with deviant activity, although self-report studies show extensive and generalized involvement in illegal behaviors for both sexes and also observe similar patterns of offenses for both sexes (R. E. Johnson, 1979), men participate more in common forms of delinquency in part because (it is believed) they are freer to deviate than women, particularly in the higher classes (Hagan, Gillis, & Simpson, 1985); men, more than women, define risk-taking and delinquency positively (Hagan, Simpson, & Gillis, 1979). Regarding the association of gender with patterns of substance abuse, Smart and Whitehead (1974) observed that men are consistently more frequent users of alcohol, tobacco, marijuana, and hallucinogens, whereas tranquilizer use is more characteristic of women. Biener (1987) observed that men are more likely to use alcohol and women are more likely to use prescription drugs. These differences result from social norms affecting exposure to each of the substances, as well as from the expectations of appropriateness.

Concerning psychosocial correlates of gender, men and women have different standards for self-evaluation (Douvan & Adelson, 1966; A. Stein, 1971) and differ in modes of adaptive responses to failure. Girls are reported to display a greater need for affiliation than are boys (Exline, 1962; Lansky, Crandall, Kagan, & Baker, 1961; Spangler & Thomas, 1962). Furthermore, girls are more likely to show greater interest in, and positive feelings for others (Maccoby, 1966). Maccoby and Jacklin (1974) reported that men tend to score higher on lie and defensiveness scales. Men are more likely to be stimulated to respond to aggression, and women are more likely to avoid problems. Boys tend to initiate more conflicts than do girls, and girls are more likely to change the activity in which they were engaged following conflict (McCandless, Bilous, & Bennett, 1961). S. P. Moore (1964) reported that boys, following frustration, are more likely to display direct aggression with less displacement of aggression. T. Moore and Ucko (1961) reported that anxious boys are more likely to give aggressive responses, whereas anxious girls are more likely to give passive responses or to avoid the problem (that is, give no response). Men are more likely to manifest, turning against object defenses or projection defenses, whereas women are more likely to show "turning against self-defenses" (Bogo, Winget, Gleser, 1970; De Fundia, Dragunas, & Phillips, 1971; Gleser and Ihilevich, 1969). Boys are more likely to manifest hyperaggression among children brought to a clinic, whereas girls are reported to have more problems related to overdependence and emotional overcontrol (Beller & Neubauer, 1963).

The following findings are illustrative of the moderating influences of gender on relationships among various normative psychosocial patterns, deviant patterns in general, and substance-abuse patterns in particular. Conditional relationships among normative psychosocial variables are observed when boys' casual involvement with many adults increases their social perspective-taking skill, internal locus of control, and empathy. For girls, however, casual involvement with many adults is inversely related to social perspective-taking skill and internal locus of control. Intimate involvement with adults increases socioemotional development for girls only (Bryant, 1985). Belle (1987) also cites findings (Waldrop & Halverson, 1975) that social maturity and facility with peers have different correlates for boys and girls. Boys with greater social facility have more friendships, however, girls who had greater social facility differed from girls who had less social facility primarily in terms of the intensity and intimacy of the friendships that they possessed.

Gender modifies the relationships between deviant patterns and their putative antecedents and consequences; this effect is illustrated by the different process of becoming involved in delinquent behavior for boys compared with girls (Schoenberg, 1975). R. E. Johnson (1979) reported that school performance, perceived parental love, attachment to parents, susceptibility to peer influence, delinquent associates, and perceived risk of apprehension influence boys' delinquent behavior more than that of girls. In contrast, attachment to school and delinquent values are more salient for female delinquency. Tittle and Rowe (1973) observed that girls are influenced far more by sanction threats than are boys. Furthermore, girls are more likely to show emotional upset when they believe they have deviated from adult expectations (Sears, Ray, & Alpert, 1965). Earlier findings from our laboratory (Kaplan, 1980) showed that self-enhancing effects of deviant behavior were more likely to be observed for males than for female subjects, consistent with the conclusion of other researchers (M. Gold & Mann, 1972) to the effect that delinquency is predominantly a masculine defense and does not function as well to raise girls' self-esteem.

Gender also modifies the relationships between substance-abuse patterns and their putative antecedants and consequences; this is illustrated by observations that correlates of heavy drug use differ for men and women and frequently appear to reflect traits that are contrary to the cultural stereotypes associated with gender roles among nonusers. Thus, Holroyd and Kahn (1974) observed that heavy users (men with their impulsiveness and curiosity, and women with their achievement needs) seem to have rejected the cultural stereotypes that are characteristic of male and female nonusers. Furthermore, prior drug use is reported to be a better predictor of future drug use among boys than is involvement with delinquent peers, whereas for girls the influence of the two predictors is approximately equal (Elliott, Huizinga, & Ageton 1985). Gender also moderates the effects of drug-prevention programs, although the nature of the effect is not consistent (MacKinnon et al., 1988). The moderating effect of gender on psychosocial causes of substance abuse is also exemplified by the observations of Jessor et al. (1973): Marijuana use among women is associated with alienation (i.e., a sense of isolation from others and a concern about identity), but among men use of marijuana is associated with social criticism. The moderating effects of gender on relationships between more serious substance-abuse patterns and psychosocial antecedents was noted by Mogar, Wilson, and Helm (1970): Alcoholism is related to personal meanings and motives depending on sex and personality types.

Newcomb (1988) reported gender-specific correlates of disruptive drug use among men and women who used illicit drugs. For men, greater disruptive drug use is predicted by low self-acceptance, as well as by such variables as low trust in physicians, low illness sensitivity, having a full-time job, and heavy use of cigarettes For women, greater disruptive drug use is predicted by low law abidance, more extroversion, less depression, more psychosomatic symptoms, and feeling powerless, among other variables. Moderating effects of gender on the relationship between substance-abuse patterns and psychosocial consequences have also been reported. Robbins (1989) observed that substance abuse is related to intrapsychic problems for women and to problems in social functioning for men. Women are vulnerable to depression, feeling suspicious or distressful, and feeling upset. Men are vulnerable, however, to social-functioning problems, including trouble at school or on the job, financial difficulties, and trouble with the law. Covington (1986) reported that White men have higher self-esteem with exposure to deviant others and with involvement in the drug dealing. In contrast, White females exposed to the street drug market report lower self-esteem.

Finally, we consider the literature dealing with the joint moderating influences of gender and other psychosocial variables on relationships between substance-abuse patterns and their antecedents or consequences. Studies that examine separately how gender or other psychosocial variables moderate the relationship between psychosocial characteristics and substance-use-related outcomes have one limitation: They fail to look at higher order interactions. A variable can influence escalation of drug use for women but not for men. That effect, however, depends on certain characteristics of the female population. The effect in question can be observed for women who are high on self-derogation but not for those low on self-derogation. The opposite effects might be observed for men. That is, the relationship in question may be observed for low-self-derogating men but not for high-self-derogating men. R. E. Johnson (1979) pointed out that although theorists may attribute certain causal factors to one gender, for example, the putative role of parental factors in female delinquency, empirical studies often point to contradictory evidence. Nye (1958) concluded, for example, that parental control is more salient for girls than for boys, whereas Schoenberg (1975) reported that girls' affective ties to parents have less impact on their delinquent associations and behavior. It is possible that such contradictory findings are a consequence of failing to specify factors that interact with gender to moderate these relationships.

The significance of gender as a conditional variable and the differential moderation of relationships for men and women can be observed in many quarters. For example, Gove and Crutchfield (1982) reported that in single-parent families, poor parent–child relationships were more closely associated with female delinquency than with male delinquency, in intact families, these relationships for male and female adolescents were almost identical. The interactions between gender and other psychosocial variables on deviant behavior is further illustrated by the observation that differences between the sexes in deviant behavior are far less among those who grew up in households without a father and where the women's independence was equal to or greater than men's. Presumably, the presence of an independent male head of household is more likely to permit the female spouse to conform to traditional female role expectations and thereby to serve as a conforming role model for the female children (Tittle, 1980).

Clearly, we must take into account the moderating effects of gender, whether alone or in interaction with other psychosocial variables, if the effects of initial drug-use circumstances on escalation are to be explained. We now turn to a consideration of the rationale for the selection of other psychosocial variables as moderating factors.

Psychosocial Characteristics in Early Adolescence

The literature on substance abuse provides ample support for the general proposition that numerous psychosocial variables moderate the relationships between patterns of substance abuse and their putative antecedents or consequences. The conditional nature of the effects of alcohol use was suggested by McClelland (1972), who argued that alcohol use increases thoughts of social power and personalized power (that is, of winning personal victories over threatening adversaries) depending on the amount consumed, the setting, and personal characteristics of the subjects. More specifically, the effect of drugs on self-perceived ability and self-confidence reinforces drug-use particularly for persons lacking social skills and who are low in self-esteem and self-efficacy. Simons et al. (1988) argued that

> based upon learned expectancies and experience with some drug, individuals lacking social skills may find that use of the substance makes them feel less self-conscious and more socially capable. Similarly, persons low in self-esteem and self-efficacy might discover that certain drugs make them feel more able and confident. In such instances, the use of the substance takes on a reinforcing value because it establishes the conditions (i.e., it becomes a discriminative stimulus) for experiencing other reinforcers. (p. 304)

S. R. Gold (1980) argued, in a similar vein, that as drug users rely more and more on drugs for feeling good and in control, they reaffirm their belief that they are powerless to cope without drugs. Thus, they continue or escalate their illicit drug use. Implicit in this argument is the expectation that individuals who are more dependent on drugs as coping mechanisms to begin with, that is, individuals who do not see their fate as within their own control or who do not believe that they are of intrinsic worth, increasingly use drugs as a coping mechanism. Furthermore, Ausubel (1980) noted that different classes of drugs are adjustive (and therefore lead to escalation), depending on their fit with personality traits. Thus, the euphoric effects of drugs are highly adjustive for *inadequate personalities* that is, motivationally immature individuals

> lacking in such criteria of ego maturity as long-range goals, a sense of responsibility, self-reliance and initiative, volitional and executive independence, frustration tolerance, and the ability to defer the gratification of immediate hedonistic needs for the sake of achieving long-term goals. (pp. 4–5)

Initial depression, anxiety, or both prior to initial drug use has been implied to moderate the effect of distress on escalation of use. Thus, Simons et al. (1988) argued that "substance use may act as a negative reinforcer for individuals undergoing emotional distress. This is particularly likely to be the case for adolescents manifesting psychopathology in the form of depression and/or anxiety" (p. 304).

Chein (1980) suggested that severity of personality disturbance conditions the likelihood of becoming addicted. Greaves (1980) also argued that severity of personality disturbance may condition the relationship between use of drugs to assuage distress and escalation of illicit drug use. Individuals characterized by disturbed personality patterns have not learned to satisfy their emotional needs in less destructive ways.

Other variables hypothesized to moderate the association between patterns of substance abuse and their antecedents or consequences include risk taking, social support, and social modeling of drug use. Frederick (1980) suggested that risk taking is a conditional factor in the progression from experimentation to substance abuse. If motivation and habits remain relatively constant, a change in risk-taking behavior could tip the scales toward drug abuse. Chein (1980) argued that the lack of a cohesive and supportive family affects the transition from use to addiction; Frederick (1980) offered the degree to which drug-using social supports are available; and Simons et al. (1988) predicted that "adolescents are more apt to use substances to relax or to cope with stress, and are more likely to imbibe frequently and in large quantities, if such behaviors are modeled by their parents" (p. 303).

On the basis of such observations and the theoretical considerations discussed earlier, a number of variables were selected as hypothetical moderators of the effects of initial drug experiments on escalation. These variables characterize the personal and interpersonal situations of the subjects in the seventh grade, at the time of the initial test administration. Many of these variables have been hypothesized and observed to be associated with initiation of drug use but have not been observed to have linear effects on escalation of use. Nevertheless, these variables are hypothesized to moderate (independently or in interaction with gender) the relationships between circumstances surrounding initial illicit drug use and escalation.

The means for each of the variables were computed separately for male and female subjects. The moderating conditions on each variable are defined as being above or below the gender-specific variable means.

The conditional variables, with few exceptions, occur before escalation of use. The data for the moderating variables were collected in 1971. Only 19 of the subjects reported escalation of drug use before 1972. Of these, 10 increased drug use during 1971 and may well have done so subsequent to the Time 1 test administration, which occurred early in the year.

The high and low values for each variable, alone or in combination with gender, are expected to moderate the effects of initial drug-use circumstances on escalation. The items making up each of the conditional variables are presented in Appendix B. The alphas, means, and standard deviations for each of the values appear in Appendix C. We consider in turn the measures and rationales for selection of each of the variables that we expected to have moderating effects.

Deviant Behavior (DEVIANCE) is measured by responses to five items indicating involvement in various forms of deviance (theft, carrying weapons, vandalism). This variable, reflecting early involvement in deviance, is expected to moderate the effect of circumstances of initial use of drugs on escalation of drugs, because individuals who had low scores at Time 1 were less likely to have alternative ways of dealing with distress, other than substance abuse. For most of the predictors of escalation of drug use, we expect unique or stronger effects for individuals with lower Time 1 deviance scores.

Perceived Rejection by Teachers (RJTT) was reflected on a four-item scale. This variable reflects, among other things, the extent to which individuals perceive themselves to be part of the conventional order and, therefore, the extent to which they are subject to conventional sanctions. It might be expected, for example, that high scores on this variable would be a condition for escalation of drug use following severe social sanctions for initial drug use. Where individuals had already perceived themselves as being rejected by teachers at the time of the first test administration, it is to be expected that the experience of negative social sanctions in response to initial drug use would lead to escalation of use, because these individuals would be less motivated to conform to the normative expectations of the conventional value system and would be less subject to its sanctions against escalated use of drugs.

Drug-Using Peers (PEERSUP) was reflected in a four-item scale indicating that friends and the kids at school used illicit drugs at the time of the initial test administration. Particularly for individuals who were more dependent on interpersonal gratifications (that is, female subjects), it was to be expected that for individuals whose close associates had already been using drugs, the adverse effects of initial drug use on interpersonal relationships would increase involvement with deviant peers and, hence, escalation of drug use.

Perceived Rejection by Parents (RJTP) is reflected in a three-item score. The high score indicates perceptions of being a failure according to the standards of parents and of being rejected by parents. This variable is expected to moderate the effects of circumstances surrounding initial drug use on escalation of use, because it reflects both the experience of needs on the part of individuals and the presence or absence of social sanctions. Thus, high rejection by parents might indicate feelings of impotency. For individuals who are high in experiences of rejection by parents at Time 1, it is to be expected that experiences of increased potency, in association with initial drug use, would be positively reinforcing. For individuals who are low in perceived rejection by parents, however, experiences of increased potency might not be as reinforcing. On the other hand, individuals who are low in perceived rejection by parents at Time 1 would be more likely to be distressed by the consequences of initial drug use for disrupting interpersonal relationships and for the experiences of anger at significant others. In response to these distressful experiences, the individual would be more likely to require escalated use of drugs to assuage these feelings. Furthermore, the increased use of drugs would be facilitated by the attenuation of ties with the significant others that was reflected in the disrupted interpersonal relationships. For individuals who have already perceived themselves as rejected by their parents, these experiences would not exacerbate their need for use of drugs.

Perceived Rejection by Peers (PEERREJ) is reflected in a four-item scale indicating perceptions of being a failure according to the standards of, and being rejected by, the kids at school. This variable is expected to moderate the effects of circumstances surrounding initial drug use on escalation of drug use primarily because it indicates prior involvement in the conventional order and the salience of particular personal values. Thus, individuals who had not earlier been rejected by peers would be most likely to be distressed by the adverse effects of initial drug use on interpersonal relationships. Accompanying the increased distress would be an increased need to assuage the distress through escalated use of drugs.

Self-Derogation (SDRG) was measured by a seven-item score. High scores indicated self-derogation ("at times I think I am no good at all," "I certainly feel useless at times"). Self-derogation measured during the seventh grade was expected to moderate relationships between circumstances surrounding initial use of drugs and escalation of drug use, because self-derogation reflects unfulfilled needs and expectations of more or less negative outcomes. Thus, it might be anticipated that for individuals who are high in self-derogation, but not for individuals who are low in self-derogation, the experiences of increased potency in association with initial drug use would reinforce drug use. Increased feelings of potency would not only be intrinsically gratifying for individuals who perceive themselves as lacking in feelings of power or importance, but would also facilitate the belief that one could escalate drug use with impunity. High self-derogating individuals would also be more likely than low self-derogating individuals to be inhibited from escalating use if they defined initial drug use as deviant behavior.

Sensitivity to Attitudes of Conventional Adults (SENCON) is reflected in a five-item scale indicating the importance to the subject of what parents and teachers think of him or her. As in the case of the preceding variable, the significance of others' attitudes may reflect any of a number of circumstances, including deterrents against engaging in deviant behavior. Thus, it might be expected that high levels of sensitivity to the attitudes of conventional others might be a precondition for deviant definitions of drug use to be inversely related to escalation of drug use.

Results

We conducted stepwise regression analyses of the data, which also produced the correlation matrices found in Table 11.1. This table includes the intercorrelations among the 9 independent variables and the dependent variable, and the means and standard deviations for the 10 variables. The data are presented separately for the male subjects (above the diagonal) and the female subjects (below the diagonal). We do not present the correlation matrices for the subgroups of men and women formed by grouping them according to high and low values on each of seven moderating variables.

The results of the regression analyses are presented in Table 11.2 (men) and Table 11.3 (women). The final column in each table presents the unstandardized regression coefficients and standard errors for all of the men or women, respectively. The other 14 columns present the unstandardized regression coefficients and standard errors for subgroups of male (Table 11.2) and female (Table 11.3) subjects differentiated according to whether they were high or low (above or below the mean) on each of seven moderating variables. Thus, the results of 15 regression equations for male subjects and 15 regression equations for female subjects are reported.

The variables reflecting circumstances surrounding initial drug use collectively accounted for 17% of the variance among male subjects and 19% of the variance among female subjects in escalation of drug use. For certain subgroups (men who are low on Self-Derogation and high on Perceived Rejection by Parents, women who are high on

TABLE 11.1

Correlation Matrix for Predictors of Escalated Drug Use (Men Above the Diagonal, Females Below the Diagonal)

Predictor	1	2	3	4	5	6	7	8	9	10	M	SD
1 ADVERPP	—	.272	.311	.194	.104	.349	.140	.304	.282	.106	.197	.252
2 NEGSANC	.210	—	.365	.112	.231	.309	.117	.306	.216	.325	.079	.186
3 ATTENTI	.357	.376	—	.122	.256	.376	.137	.361	.239	.231	.172	.319
4 DEVDEFD	.178	.149	.146	—	.185	.170	.148	.106	.292	.014	.685	.359
5 REDNEGA	.112	.264	.351	.161	—	.513	.317	.343	.376	.264	.325	.241
6 REDSREJ	.379	.280	.490	.110	.593	—	.300	.409	.352	.205	.123	.207
7 INCRPOT	.160	.244	.288	.107	.304	.335	—	.179	.426	.188	.228	.356
8 EXPRANG	.289	.291	.412	.076	.351	.538	.228	—	.284	.289	.056	.157
9 MOTPEER	.359	.344	.407	.284	.332	.376	.448	.332	—	.202	.367	.248
10 ESCDRUG	.128	.337	.294	.013	.321	.299	.191	.221	.201	—	.240	.426
M	.258	.091	.238	.673	.355	.184	.241	.113	.412	.237	—	—
SD	.290	.183	.367	.357	.267	.257	.370	.230	.266	.426	—	—

Note. Scale scores were computed for subjects available at Time 1 and Time 4 on the basis of the average of the nonmissing items if the nonmissing items constituted at least two thirds of the items in the scale (see R. J. Johnson & Kaplan, 1987).

TABLE 11.2

Significant Stepwise Regression Coefficients of Predictors of Drug Use and Time 1 Moderating Variables (Men)

Predictor	DEVIANCE		RJTT		PEERSUP		RJTP		PEERREJ		SDRG		SENCON		
	High	Low	High	Low	High	Low	High	Low	High	Low	High	Low	High	Low	Total
ADVERPP	—	—	—	—	—	—	—	—	—	—	—	—	—	—	—
	—	—	—	—	—	—	—	—	—	—	—	—	—	—	—
NEGSANC	.563	.580	.612	.513	.620	.590	.697	.476	.349	.770	.390	.975	.542	.542	.553
	.149	.100	.108	.131	.122	.116	.156	.100	.156	.100	.107	.126	.114	.130	.072
ATTENTI	—	—	—	—	—	—	—	.116	—	.134	—	—	.151	—	—
	—	—	—	—	—	—	—	.056	—	.059	—	—	.066	—	—
DEVDEFD	—	—	—	—	—	—	—	—	-.20	—	-.12	—	—	—	-.08
	—	—	—	—	—	—	—	—	.075	—	.053	—	—	—	.038
REDNEGA	.350	.179	.315	—	.272	—	.327	.165	.296	—	.272	—	—	.277	.240
	.124	.074	.092	—	.100	—	.132	.073	.109	—	.088	—	—	.102	.050
REDSREJ	—	—	—	—	—	—	—	—	—	—	—	—	—	—	—
	—	—	—	—	—	—	—	—	—	—	—	—	—	—	—
INCRPOT	—	—	—	.208	—	.129	.245	—	—	.154	.164	—	.107	.138	.119
	—	—	—	.055	—	.055	.090	—	—	.049	.055	—	.054	.064	.038
EXPRANG	—	.422	.400	.394	.366	.388	—	.462	.429	.363	.376	.548	.375	.338	.430
	—	.117	.132	.147	.144	.134	—	.116	.156	.130	.120	.171	.154	.135	.089
MOTPEER	—	.211	—	—	—	.196	—	—	—	—	—	—	—	—	—
	—	.070	—	—	—	.080	—	—	—	—	—	—	—	—	—
R^2	.13	.17	.21	.12	.19	.16	.24	.15	.14	.23	.16	.24	.16	.18	.17

TABLE 11.3

Significant Stepwise Regression Coefficients of Predictors of Drug Use and Time 1 Moderating Variables (Women)

Predictor	DEVIANCE High	DEVIANCE Low	RJTT High	RJTT Low	PEERSUP High	PEERSUP Low	RJTP High	RJTP Low	PEERREJ High	PEERREJ Low	SDRG High	SDRG Low	SENCON High	SENCON Low	Total
ADVERPP	—	—	—	—	—	—	—	—	—	—	—	—	—	—	—
	—	—	—	—	—	—	—	—	—	—	—	—	—	—	—
NEGSANC	—	.532	.593	—	.521	.439	.481	.571	.537	.495	.571	—	.553	.483	.551
	—	.103	.116	—	.118	.151	.205	.098	.140	.119	.113	—	.110	.158	.083
ATTENTI	—	.136	.147	.160	.151	—	—	—	—	.139	—	.269	—	.173	.160
	—	.050	.064	.065	.065	—	—	—	—	.059	—	.065	—	.075	.042
DEVDEFD	—	—	—	-.15	-.17	—	—	—	—	—	—	—	-.13	—	-.09
	—	—	—	.058	.062	—	—	—	—	—	—	—	.055	—	.040
REDNEGA	—	.306	.345	.373	.247	.350	—	.314	.302	.385	.297	.338	.427	.274	.355
	—	.066	.089	.087	.090	.088	—	.079	.095	.081	.098	.089	.072	.109	.056
REDSREJ	.688	—	—	—	—	—	—	.210	—	—	—	—	—	—	—
	.159	—	—	—	—	—	—	.084	—	—	—	—	—	—	—
INCRPOT	—	—	—	—	.143	—	.207	—	—	—	.127	—	—	—	—
	—	—	—	—	.057	—	.098	—	—	—	.062	—	—	—	—
EXPRANG	—	—	—	—	—	.311	—	—	—	—	—	—	—	—	—
	—	—	—	—	—	.120	—	—	—	—	—	—	—	—	—
MOTPEER	—	—	—	—	—	—	—	—	—	—	—	—	—	—	—
	—	—	—	—	—	—	—	—	—	—	—	—	—	—	—
R^2	.18	.16	.21	.10	.19	.16	.08	.18	.14	.17	.17	.15	.16	.15	.19

Perceived Rejection by Teachers), the percentage of the explained variance in escalation of drug use increased to 24% for men and 21% for women.

Three variables are significant predictors of escalation of drug use for both male and female subjects. Negative Social Sanctions as a consequence of initial drug use increases later drug use. Deviant Definition of Drug Use at the time of initial drug use prevents escalation. Reduction of Negative Affect encourages later escalation of drug use.

Three of the independent variables have gender-specific effects on escalation of drug use. For men, but not for women. Increased Potency and Expression of Anger at the time of initial drug use causes escalation of drug use. For female subjects, but not for male subjects, Attenuation of Interpersonal Ties causes escalation of drug use.

Three of the independent variables have no significant effects on escalation of drug use for either men or women. These variables are Adverse Physical and Psychological Effects, Reduction of Self-Rejection, and Motivation for Peer Acceptance. However, for the last two of these variables, the effects on escalation of use are significant for specific subgroups of men, women, or both.

Different moderating influences depend on the particular predictor of escalation of drug use. In many instances, as expected, the moderating effects are influenced by the subject's gender. Peer influences are stronger for men than for women: Either high or low Perceived Rejection by Peers moderates the effects of initial use circumstances on escalation of drug use for five of the independent variables among the male subjects. Among the female subjects, this variable moderates only one relationship.

We will discuss the specific results concerning each of the independent variables. For each of these variables, we will consider in turn (a) the presence or absence of significant effects on escalation of drug use for both men and women versus gender-specific effects and (b) conditional effects that are observed for both men and women versus moderating gender-specific effects on the relationship between the independent variable and escalation of drug use.

Adverse Physical and Psychological Effects (ADVERPP)

For neither men nor women and under no conditions examined were adverse consequences of initial substance abuse related to escalation of drug use. The adverse consequences reflected in this measure (finding it an unpleasant experience and having adverse physical effects) do not inhibit escalation of use. Nor does the experience of adverse consequences have a significant positive reinforcing effect, as might have been argued on the basis of findings in the literature that continuity or escalation of substance abuse may be attributed to motivation to forestall the distressing consequences of withdrawal from drug use. Either this variable truly has neither positive nor negative effects on escalation of use or it has countervailing positive and negative effects.

Negative Social Sanctions (NEGSANC)

Negative Social Sanctions, resulting from initial drug use, increased substance abuse significantly for both men and women. For men, the relationship was significant under all of the conditions examined. For female subjects, the relationship was significant for all but 3 of the 14 conditions. The overall effect was approximately the same for men and women.

The effects of negative social sanctions, leading to escalation of drug use, are explained by labeling theory. The escalation of drug use is secondary deviation, that is, "deviant behavior or social roles based upon it, which becomes a means of defense, attack, or adaptation to the overt and covert problems created by the societal reaction to primary deviation" (Lemert, 1967, p. 17).

According to the guiding theory that incorporates effects of labeling, these negative social sanctions lead to escalation of drug use via three paths (Kaplan, Johnson, & Bailey, 1988). First, negative social sanctions threaten the sanctioned individuals' self-acceptance. Positive evaluation and acceptance of the label of drug user is a defense against negative self-feelings. The deviant identity becomes the basis for positive self-evaluation rather than a stigma. Continuing deviant behavior validates the new deviant identity. The valued identity motivates conformity to normative expectations that prescribe drug use. Insofar as he or she successfully conforms to those normative expectations and validates the identity, the person is able to evaluate himself or herself positively.

Second, the stigma of sanctions increases negative self-feelings, and the correlated loss of social rewards and experience of social cost alienate the individual from the conventional order. The individual loses motivation to conform to the conventional society; indeed, he or she develops a motivation to deviate from the normative expectations of the conventional society.

Third, these sanctions increase drug use by first fostering association with drug-using peers. Sanctions preclude opportunities to interact with conventional others in ways that easily provide resources for gratification of needs. In the absence of such resources, the person is unable to approximate self-values. This leads to involvement in drug-using groups as a way of gaining the resources to satisfy self-values. Drug-using groups also offer values that the person may more easily approximate than conventional values. Adherence to deviant values symbolizes rejection of the conventional standards according to which the person has devalued himself or herself and has been devalued by others. Once the person is part of a drug-using group, he is provided with increased occasions and opportunities to escalate drug use.

The pattern of conditional effects suggests that different mechanisms are operating for men and women to account for the effect of Negative Social Sanctions on escalation of use. For men, the effect of negative social sanctions is stronger under two conditions: The effect is stronger for individuals below the mean on Perceived Rejection by Peers, and for subjects below the mean on Self-Derogation, than for subjects in the mutually exclusive categories (although the effect was significant for all conditions among male subjects). For women, the effect of Negative Social Sanctions on escalation of drug use is significant under conditions of low early Deviant Behavior, high Perceived Rejection by Teachers, and high Self-Derogation. Thus, for Self-Derogation, the conditional effects are in the opposite direction for men and women. For men, Negative Social Sanctions' influence on escalation of drug use is more pronounced for well-defended (as indicated by low Self-Derogation) and interpersonally competent (as indicated by low Perceived Rejection by Peers) subjects. For such individuals, the escalation of drug use may reflect the transformation of a deviant identity into a positively valued one, identification with that now-positively valued identity, and conformity to the role prescriptions for that identity (including, of course, use of drugs). The transformation of the value structure in a way that permits continued self-acceptance is indicative of a well-defended person.

The conditions under which negative sanctioning of men leads to escalation of use are compatible with Smith's (1980) observation that consciously recognized dangers increase, rather than inhibit, use if the self-initiated risks bring status and social approval or if the user pits the perceived dangers against his competence and self-control and then treats the matter as a contest that he or she is sure to win. Individuals with high self-confidence might regard sanctions as a challenge rather than a circumstance that inhibits substance abuse.

Our findings indicate that women increase drug use in response to negative social sanctions because the pharmacologic properties reduce associated distressful self-feelings. For example, we found that Sanctions increase drug use for women high in Self-Derogation but not for those low in Self-Derogation. This relationship was also observed under conditions of high Perceived Rejection by Teachers and low Deviant Behavior. This suggests that the relationship holds when the undefended person is the object of rejecting experiences but still part of the conventional order (indicating that the experience of being rejected was likely to be emotionally meaningful). The distressful effects of negative sanctions may be far greater for the women because such sanctions are uncommon. The mean score on Negative Social Sanctions at Time 1 for male subjects was more than twice the score of female subjects (Hagan et al., 1979). Sanctioning women creates more stigma than for men, possibly because of the greater degree of deviance required to evoke formal negative sanctions for women than for men.

Attenuation of Interpersonal Ties (ATTENTI)

Attenuation of Interpersonal Ties resulting from initial drug use causes women, but not men, to increase drug use. Thus, women (but not men) use drugs to cope with the disruption of ties, because their dependence on primary relationships is so great. The notion that girls are more likely than boys to have a general interest in affective relationships with family members and to have boyfriends as focal points has a long-standing tradition in criminological treatments (Covington, 1988; Naffine, 1987).

The female-specific escalation of drug use in response to interpersonal strain associated with initial use is congruent with the observation of Jessor et al. (1973) that female marijuana use is associated with increases in alienation (a sense of isolation from others) and a concern about identity. Attenuation of interpersonal ties also implies the weakening of social controls that would ordinarily inhibit escalation of drug use. Covington (1985) reported that control-theory predictors of delinquency explained a substantial amount of variance for women but very little for men. Presumably, women experience more supervision during adolescence and are more affected when ties to supervision are broken.

Apparently, both male and female subjects increased drug use in response to Attenuation of Interpersonal Ties following initial drug use if they were part of the normative peer network as reflected in low scores on a measure of Perceived Rejection by Peers.

The effects of disruption of interpersonal relationships on escalation of drug use suggest that different mechanisms are operating for men and women. For men, escalation of drug use in response to Attenuation of Interpersonal Ties depends on internalization of conventional adult values. When the male subjects perceive themselves as violating these norms, the experience of distress in conjunction with a disposition to use certain kinds of defense mechanisms leads to escalation of use. The moderating influence of internalization of adult norms is suggested by the relationship being conditional upon high scores on Sensitivity to Attitudes of Conventional Adults. For the disruption of interpersonal relationships to stimulate escalation of drug use, the individuals would have had to be integrated within a normative interpersonal nexus prior to the disruption of the relationships.

Consistent with this, the relationship between disruption of interpersonal relationships consequent to initial drug use and escalation of drug use was contingent upon being low on Perceived Rejection by Parents.

In short, men will escalate drug use when initial drug use disrupts the interpersonal nexus on which they depend. The distress that results motivates the person to increase drug use.

For women, different mechanisms are observed for the conditions under which interpersonal strain associated with initial drug use leads to escalation. For women, escalation of use depends on three conditions: (a) the absence of internal constraints, (b) opportunities to adopt substance abuse-related responses, and (c) the absence of alternative externalizing responses. The absence of internalized social controls is reflected in low Self-Derogation scores and in low sensitivities to the attitudes of conventional adults. Opportunities to engage in substance abuse is reflected in high scores on a measure of association with drug-using peers. The absence of alternative deviant response patterns is reflected in low scores on early participation in deviant activities.

Women ordinarily are inhibited from acting out deviant coping responses and are less likely to have opportunities to engage in drug use than men; under other conditions, women lose inhibitions and have the opportunity to engage in substance abuse. Both situations allow the disruption of interpersonal ties to cause escalation of drug use. Conversely, men are less likely than women to depend on primary relationships; under such conditions, however, men increase drug use.

Deviant Definition of Drug Use (DEVDEFD)

Consistent with expectations for both men and women, Deviant Definition of Drug Use disinhibits escalation of substance abuse. For men, the relationship was particularly strong where the individual did not have strong coping skills that would permit him to sustain positive self-attitudes in the face of the performance of deviant behavior. Thus, for men, deviant definition of drug use decreases escalation of use for individuals who are high on Self-Derogation and Perceived Rejection by Peers. For women, unlike men, the controls against escalation of use reside with interpersonal social controls rather than with personal inability to justify increased use. Deviant Definition of Drug Use inhibits escalation of use for women with low scores on Perceived Rejection by Teachers and for those with high scores on Sensitivity to Attitudes of Conventional Adults; we picture women who are immersed in a conventional network and who are dependent on this network for satisfaction of needs.

The negative effect of deviant definitions on escalation of drug use among women under conditions of prior association with drug-using peers is puzzling. This may suggest that the effects of Deviant Definition of Drug Use is tied to observation of adverse interpersonal consequences of drug use for the drug-using peers.

Reduction of Negative Affect (REDNEGA)

For all subjects, the Reduction of Negative Affect implicated in initial drug use increased escalation. Our findings are consistent with the observation of other researchers (e.g., Simons et al., 1988) that regular users of drugs are motivated by a concern for reducing negative affect. Khantzian (1980) also noted that the central problem for most people who have become addicted to opiates is that they have failed to develop effective solutions for emotional pain. Their response has been to revert to the use of opiates as an all-powerful device.

The effect of Reduction of Negative Affect on escalation of drug use is stronger for women. The greater strength of the effect for women than for men is consistent with earlier notions that women use drugs to contain distress.

The results indicate many gender-specific effects. Alienation from conventional society, for men, moderates the effect of intent to reduce negative affect on escalation of drug use. Thus, the effects of such intent on escalation of drug use are stronger under, or unique to, conditions indicating higher levels of early involvement in deviance (DEVIANCE), of perceived rejection by teachers (RJTT), of perceived rejection by parents (RJTP), of perceived rejection by peers (PEERREJ), and of low sensitivity to the evaluations of conventional adults (SENCON). These conditional variables may reflect the source of the male subjects' distress, that is, inhering to experiences in the conventional social system. These conditions may also reflect the absence of effective social sanctions that might forestall escalation of drug use. That is, alienation from the conventional system signifies the absence of restraints that might be meaningful to the alienated subjects.

For men, peer support is also a condition under which drug use intended to reduce distress causes escalation of drug use. Men using drugs for this purpose require peer support. Furthermore, initial-drug-use motives to reduce stress have an effect on escalation of drug use only in the absence of ego strength; high ego strength permits the male subject to deal with subjective distress in more conventional ways. Ego weakness is reflected in high self-derogation (SDRG). Under this condition, but not under mutually exclusive conditions, initial drug use intended to reduce distress increases subsequent drug use. For male subjects at least, our findings are consistent with those of Pearlin and

Radabaugh (1976), who concluded that "intense anxiety is especially likely to result in the use of alcohol as a tranquilizer if a sense of personal efficacy is lacking and self-esteem is low" (p. 661).

For women, escalation of drug use represents a way of dealing with distress at initial use when they are part of the conventional world and are sensitive to the attitudes of conventional others. Ties to the conventional world are reflected in low scores on self-reports of deviant activities (DEVIANCE). Conditions of dependency on the attitudes of conventional others is reflected in conditions of greater sensitivity to the attitudes of conventional adults (SENCON) and in lower scores on perceived rejection by parents (PJTP).

Reduction of Self-Rejection (REDSREJ)

Reduction of Self-Rejection as motivation for, and a consequence of, initial drug use had no significant effects on escalation of drug use among either male or female subjects. Nor was a significant effect observed for any subgroups of men differentiated according to high and low values on the moderating variables.

However, for female subjects, initial drug use out of a motivation to reduce feelings of worthlessness was related to subsequent escalation of drug use among those who reported higher levels of early Deviant Behavior and who reported low levels of Perceived Rejection by Parents. These conditions may reflect early contravention of internalized parental norms. Under these circumstances, in which women internalize parental norms or are motivated to conform to parental norms (as indicated by low levels of perceived parental rejection) and in which women violate these norms (as indicated by relatively high levels of early involvement in deviant behavior), those who are initially motivated to use drugs to assuage feelings of guilt and worthlessness escalate use.

Increased Potency (INCRPOT)

Increased Potency from initial drug use causes escalation of drug use for men but not women. This male-specific effect is consistent with the notion "that males have a greater need to be daring and to prove themselves to their friends in their search for masculine identity than do females in their search for female indentity" (R. E. Johnson, 1979, p. 128). Because men are more concerned with threats to their sense of power, actions (using illicit drugs) that enhance their sense of potency reinforce subsequent use. The male-specific concern with power is suggested by the greater tendency of men than women to use alcohol (Jessor, Carman, & Grossman, 1970; Smart & Whitehead, 1974), a pattern that has been said to increase power fantasies (McClelland, 1972).

However, for both men and women, certain common conditions were identified under which Increased Potency had significant effects on escalation of drug use. A number of these moderating variables suggest the presence of low self-evaluation and the need for self-enhancement. Thus, for both men and women, experiences of enhanced power following initial drug use had significant effects on escalation of drug use under conditions where the subjects in the seventh grade had higher levels of Self-Derogation and tended to perceive themselves as rejected by their parents (RJTP), but not under mutually exclusive conditions. For such individuals, the experience of increased potency related to initial drug use would increase the likelihood of escalation of drug use as the same life circumstances that led to initial self-devaluing experiences continued to exert their influences on the subjects' lives.

Other theorists share the expectation that potency effects of initial drug use cause escalation only under certain conditions. When people's experiences are such that they learn that their behavior has no effect on the environment, the result is "learned helplessness" (Maier & Seligman, 1976; Seligman, 1975). As this applies to drug abuse, subjects who resort to drugs are unable to effectively control outcomes (including self-acceptance). Drugs supply the person with a sense of personal control over his or her own feelings; this reduces distress and reinforces the value of drug use. S. R. Gold (1980) cited empirical studies that suggest that experimentally induced false beliefs of control over aversive stimuli reduce the experience of distress associated with those stimuli:

> Underlying the anxiety of drug abusers is a belief that they cannot alter or control the situation; that they are powerless to affect their environment and decrease or eliminate the sources of stress. The belief that they are powerless to cope with stress is the major cognitive distortion of drug abusers. One consequence of this is the intense feeling of low self-esteem that is a well-known clinical entity among drug abusers.... Under the influence of the drug the individual temporarily experiences an increased sense of power, control, and well-being. The sense of powerlessness is replaced by an exaggerated sense of being all powerful—no task too great and no feat impossible while "high." Thus, drugs can do for abusers what they believe they cannot do for themselves: get rid of anxiety, lead to good feeling about themselves, and make them believe they are competent, in control, and able to master their environment. (pp. 8–9)

Similarly, according to Steffenhagen (1980), individuals with low self-esteem, given a situation of perceived social stress, are more likely to abuse drugs to free themselves from social responsibility and to allay feelings of inferiority. Consistent with this position, individuals characterized by high levels of self-derogation and perceived rejection by parents would be most likely to escalate drug use after perceiving that drug use was associated with increased feelings of importance or power, as we in fact observed.

A number of gender-specific moderating influences on the relationship between Increased Potency and escalation of drug use were also observed. For men, a significant effect of Increased Potency was observed for subjects who scored low on Perceived Rejection by Teachers, low on Drug-Using Peers, and low on Perceived Rejection by Peers, but not for mutually exclusive categories of men. For women, a significant effect of Increased Potency was observed for subjects who scored high, but not for those who scored low, on Drug-Using Peers.

For male subjects, the use of drugs as a self-enhancing mechanism may be considered unusual. Ordinarily, the masculine role permits a variety of aggressive response mechanisms. Under conditions in which such responses are precluded by preexisting circumstances, escalation of drug use is more likely to be positively reinforced by experiences of self-enhancement associated with initial drug use. Such circumstances are likely to be reflected in the conventional world, as reflected in low Perceived Rejection by Teachers and Peers and low scores on a measure of association with Drug-Using Peers. Unlike the men, female subjects were likely to escalate drug use in response to experiences of self-enhancement associated with initial drug use only when peer support was high. The female subject, ordinarily not highly motivated by the need for enhancement of power, finds the experience gratifying but only under conditions where peer support is present. For men, the absence of peer support represents an absence of opportunities for alternative deviant adaptations and for a medium in which opportunities are provided to affirm potency.

Expression of Anger (EXPRANG)

The association of initial drug use with Expression of Anger at significant others increased escalation of drug use only for men. This association is significant for virtually all conditions. In only 2 of the 14 conditions did the relationship fail to reach significance. For women, anger associated with initial drug use is not significantly associated with escalation of use. Furthermore, in only one of the conditions is the relationship observed.

This gender-specific effect may reflect the male-specific need to externalize one's anger. The escalation of drug use in response to that anger may reflect any of several circumstances. First, the illicit use of drugs may reflect a symbolic rejection of the standards of others (work and school authorities, parents, other significant individuals).

Escalation of illicit drug use is a way of getting even with these others. Consistent with this conjecture, Jessor et al. (1973) reported that the use of marijuana among women is associated with a relative increase in alienation (e.g., a sense of isolation from others, concern about identity), but among men marijuana use was associated with social criticism (a conviction about the inadequacy of policies, mores, and institutions of the larger American society). Second, drugs serve as a way of assuaging distressful feelings of anger. It might be expected that men who are more likely to experience and express angry emotions would benefit most from the reduction of these distressful feelings through the use of drugs. That is, drug use to assuage angry emotions might be most reinforcing for men. As S. R. Gold (1980) observed,

> The drug user now knows that anxiety does not have to be tolerated, as drug taking has been successful in the past in removing tension and producing good feelings. It is therefore expected that drug use will increase both in frequency and in the number of different situations in which it was employed. For example, arguments with parents may be a primary source of conflict and anxiety for the adolescent drug abuser. Drug taking will frequently follow such an argument. (p. 9)

Third, the experience of anger may have other distressful consequences that increase motivation to use drugs for their analgesic properties. Finally, the experience of anger may serve to attenuate the person's conventional relationships. These relationships previously served as social controls against the acting out of deviant impulses. The weakening of these relationships reflects the weakening of the same social controls that previously inhibited acting out of any dispositions to increase substance abuse. At the same time, certain of the pharmacologic effects might serve as a disinhibiting function, permitting the expression of the angry impulses.

A number of gender-specific moderating influences on the relationship between Expression of Anger and escalation of drug use were noted. For men, EXPRANG had a significant positive effect on escalation of drug use among subjects who had low scores on Deviant Behavior and those who had low scores on Perceived Rejection by Parents. For female subjects, EXPRANG had a significant effect on escalation of drug use for individuals who were low on Drug-Using Peers. These gender-specific effects appear to be related to differential socialization to gender-related social roles.

Generally, aggression is more likely to be compatible with a male role than a female role. Thus, aggression tends to evoke greater anxiety or guilt among women (Buss & Brock, 1963; Rothaus & Worchel, 1964; Sears, 1961; Wyer, Weatherley, &

Terrell, 1965), perhaps in part because of a tendency for boys' mothers to be more permissive of aggression toward parents and peers (Sears, Maccoby, & Levin, 1957) and a tendency for teachers to express a greater liking for dependent girls than for aggressive girls (Levitin & Chananie, 1972). Thus, it is to be expected that boys will be more disposed to respond to anger in kind, except under conditions where they are inhibited from doing so. Under those conditions, the individual might respond in ways that would assuage his anger and that might express his resentment without exposing him to risks. Thus, individuals who are part of the conventional structure, as reflected in being low on Perceived Rejection by Parents and low on scores of early engagement in Deviant Behavior, are more likely to eschew expression of anger in favor of drug-use responses that would assuage the anger. This is precisely the pattern that we found for men.

Given the association between maleness and the expression of aggression, it is conceivable that in circumstances that do not otherwise inhibit escalation of drug use, this pattern would function for men as an expression of aggressiveness toward the normative structure of which they were a part but in which they fail to find gratification. For women, it is less likely that they would express aggression toward society overtly by the adoption of deviant patterns unless they (less characteristically for their gender) were not inhibited from expressing such resentment, as indicated by engaging in this behavior in the absence of social support (that is, under the condition of low scores on PEERSUP).

Motivation for Peer Acceptance (MOTPEER)

Motivation for Peer Acceptance as a stimulus for initial drug use does not have a significant effect on escalation of drug use for either male or female subjects. This may be surprising in the light of the numerous studies reporting strong relationships between association with drug-using peers and personal use. This apparent contradiction may be accounted for by several circumstances. First, Motivation for Peer Acceptance may be influential only for initiation but not for escalation of drug use. Second, earlier studies may have failed to control for correlates of peer influences. That is, peer influences may have no independent effects on escalation of drug use. Third, the effect of peer influences was conditional on certain factors that were present in studies in which the influence was observed.

In the present study, for female subjects, no conditions were noted under which peer involvement in the initial drug-use process led to escalation of drug use. For male subjects, two conditions were noted under which significant effects of MOTPEER on escalation of drug use were observed. Consistent with the observation of male-specific (but not female-specific) conditional relationships for the association between peer involvement in initial drug use and subsequent escalation of drug use, Covington (1985) reported that cultural-deviance predictors were important in explaining male crime but were unimportant in explaining female crime. The subcultural image presumably reinforces male criminal acts but not female criminal acts. Men reinforce each other's acts and reject their female counterparts. Images promoted by the deviant subculture tend to be masculine, and therefore men receive more positive reinforcement for these images (Covington, 1988).

An examination of the male-specific moderators of the relationship between peer factors surrounding initial drug use and escalation of use lends some insight into the dynamics of this relationship. In particular, it is apparent that whatever effect Motivation for Peer Acceptance has on escalation of illicit drug use must be considered independently of preexisting involvement with deviant peers. If the individual had already been involved in deviant behavior by the time of initial drug use, motivation to initiate drug use to gain peer approval would have no independent effect on escalation. For such individuals, no new gratifications would be gained from involvement with deviant peers. However, for individuals who had not already gained such gratifications, that is, for individuals who had reported low levels of Deviant Behavior in the seventh grade and who were not already involved in networks of drug-using peers (PEERSUP) by the seventh grade, initiation of use in conjunction with the need for peer approval or with opportunities for modeling of drug-use patterns did increase the likelihood of escalation of drug use. In short, peer influences on initial drug use were important for escalation only for individuals who were not already involved in these patterns.

Summary

We estimated 30 multivariate regression equations predicting escalation of drug use. All equations represent the causal effect of nine variables representing the circumstances associated with the initial use of drugs. The 30 equations are estimated under 14 conditions for both men and women, then unconditionally for both. The effects are discussed in terms of strong and pervasive major effects, explanations congruent with gender-role dispositions for gender effects, and personal vulnerability or social conditions that contribute to conditional effects. Both theoretical and methodological implications are drawn from these findings.

The substantive findings are summarized in Table 11.4. These findings are arranged in order of major effects, gender-specific effects, and conditional effects. The "major effects" are significant for both men and women under a majority of the conditions. Men and women are both vulnerable to the effects of specific labeling: Getting into trouble because of initial drug use increases drug use. The labeling effect is strong and present for nearly all of the psychosocial conditions. Initial drug use intended to remedy negative affect also increases drug use for both men and women. These two variables, as discussed below, are also notable for the conditions under which they do not exert their effect. These two effects predominate in nearly all of the models and routinely account for 13% to 14% of the variance of escalated drug use.

The "gender-specific effects" are significant for either men or women under a majority of conditions. Use of drugs to express anger or to increase a sense of potency are male-specific causes for increased drug use. These effects represent male congruent role dispositions for the expression of aggressive behavior. When dependence on interpersonal ties is disrupted, only women routinely increase drug use. This female-specific

TABLE 11.4
Summary of Major, Gender-Specific, and Conditional Effects

Major effects	Gender-specific effects	Conditional effects
Labeling Negative Affect		
	Men: Express Anger Increase Potency	Men: Attenuated Ties (3) Deviant Definition (2) Peer Motivation (2)
	Women: Attenuated Ties	Women: Deviant Definition (3) Reduced Self-rejection (2) Increase Potency (3) Express Anger (1)

Note. The major effects are significant for both men and women under a majority of the conditions. The gender-specific effects are significant for either men or women under a majority of conditions. The conditional effects are significant in unique cases, indicated by the number of conditions in parentheses. The gender-specific and conditional effects are both considered congruent with gender-role dispositions. Theoretical discussions of these effects appear in the text.

effect also reflects the greater importance and centrality of interpersonal relationships in the conventional socialization of adolescent girls. These gender specific variables can increase the explained variance in escalated drug use from 2% to 10%.

The "conditional effects" are significant in unique cases, indicated by the number of conditions in parentheses. These variables usually appear as additional effects under conditions that make the individual more vulnerable. For example, in addition to major effects and gender-specific effects, men low in rejection by peers or highly sensitive to conventional standards are also sensitive to attenuation of ties with significant others. Conditional effects can also appear in models in which major effects or gender-specific effects are weakened. For example, fractured interpersonal ties increase male drug use under conditions of low perceived parental rejection, a condition when intent to increase potency is not significant.

These findings enhance our understanding of both theoretical and methodological problems that can plague research in areas such as drug abuse and addiction. Many times, such problems produce conflicting research results or results that fail to support previous findings.

We argue that a number of these contradictions or inconsistencies and failures to empirically confirm theoretical statements might be resolved if future research were to attend to four kinds of issues. First, the time has arrived when greater attention must be paid to the moderating influences of psychosocial variables. We have observed that the relationships between circumstances surrounding initial drug use and escalation of drug use vary according to the gender of the subject and vary within each gender according to any of a variety of psychosocial circumstances that characterized the individual prior to the escalation of substance abuse. We suspect that a number of apparent contradictions might be resolved if the conditions under which the relationships were observed were better delineated.

The theoretical position of this chapter is that different persons (e.g., men and women) with different personalities and behavioral experiences of social circumstances have different levels of vulnerability to causes of drug abuse and addiction. Some conditions increase vulnerability; others reduce vulnerability. The two genders often have typical ways of responding to the causes of addictive behaviors; these responses represent gender-specific vulnerability. Women, for example, are often more vulnerable to the effects of reduced socioemotional ties than are men. Men, more than women, respond with addictive or abusive drug use because of the need to express anger. Both of these generalizations, however, are mitigated by circumstances of personalities. For women, above-average values on measures of deviant behavior or emotional character (sensitivity to conventional standards) can obviate the influence of broken social ties. In the case of deviance, the ties are not relevant to begin with; in the case of sensitivity, the internal sense of social control negates the consequences of lost ties. Among men, similarly, above-average scores on deviance and rejection by parents inhibit the intent to satisfy aggressive needs through drug abuse. When these conditional personality or behavioral traits in question are rare, the effects of this independent variable are observed. When these extremes of behavior or personal characteristics are prevalent in the study sample, however, the dominant influences disappear.

Second, greater attention must be paid to the discrimination among explanations of different stages of substance abuse. Although models explaining the onset of substance abuse may not vary between men and women, it is quite possible that gender either operates as a moderating variable in conjunction with other moderator variables or is sufficient by itself to moderate relationship between independent variables and escalation (as opposed to onset) of substance abuse.

Third, future research must take into account, to a greater degree than has occurred heretofore, variability in patterns of substance abuse. The variable effects of circumstances surrounding initial use of illicit drugs, as well as the variability by gender and other moderating influences for men and women respectively, may be accounted for in part by preferences for different substances. A number of observations in the literature have suggested that dispositions toward and effects of particular substances vary. For example, Spotts and Shontz (1980) noted that chronic amphetamine users are "achievement oriented men who are strongly reactive against threats of weakness or impotence," whereas narcotics abusers "seek a tranquil, serene existence through ego constriction; they would rather withdraw from the problems of life than conquer them." For others, barbiturates permit getting away from a sense of failure for a period of time or else "set the conditions which allow the user to release his tensions and arguments, brawls, and accidents, with no subsequent sense of guilt, responsibility, or even awareness of what happened" (pp. 64–65). In our study, the data surrounding circumstances of initial use were not available for individual substances. Future research, however, should run parallel analyses for individual substances to see if the observed conditional relationships and the differential predictors anticipated escalation of use of particular substances.

Finally, the specification of independent, mediating, and moderating variables must be guided by a well-developed theoretical framework. A number of the conditional relationships were predicted by the guiding theoretical model. Our findings confirm expectations that certain mechanisms were operative and conditioned the reinforcing influences of circumstances surrounding initial use on escalation of use. Certain other expectations, however, were not rewarded, and some significant relationships that were observed were not predicted; these circumstances challenge the specificity and flexibility of the theoretical framework. Thus, the theory is challenged to accommodate serendipitous findings. If it can do so successfully, the theoretical approach may still be viable. In case of confirmation of expectations, the theory is challenged to further specify the conditions under which hypothesized relationships will be observed or to otherwise reformulate and to submit the revised theory to empirical testing. Only by such a process will the orderly accumulation of knowledge, and the rational design of interventions based on such knowledge, occur.

Independent of their substantive and theoretical significance, these findings have important methodological implications. Research in the area of drug addiction often centers around samples that may exaggerate extremes in behavior or personality characteristics. Sample selection bias introduces methodological problems that contribute to the contradictions or inconsistencies in the literature.

Consider the exceptions to the effects of labeling. Labeling is effective for men under all circumstances and ineffective only among women and then under only three conditions: (a) women already labeled by other deviant acts are not vulnerable to further labeling; (b) those low on self-derogation resist the specific labeling effect; and (c) women who avoid rejection by teachers also avoid the effects of labeling. However, in special circumstances, failure to attribute cause to this variable may occur. Researchers ought to be wary about accepting negative findings when studying school-based samples of women or samples of only delinquent adolescent females. Either condition could dampen the effect of specific labeling.

Another example of highly likely selection bias that can obscure causal effects may be seen in the case of negative affect. Intended reduction of negative affects fails to increase later drug use under seven conditions—five specific to men and two to women. The intent of women to reduce distress does not escalate drug use if the woman perceives rejection by parents or is already delinquent. Thus, the study of a sample of delinquent or troubled girls (i.e., runaways) would not reveal this effect that so dominates the other conditions. The risks of misattributed cause are high because the study of drug abuse is likely among these special samples. The intent of men to reduce distress fails to escalate drug use when they are self-confident but isolated from peers (either rejecting or supportive networks) or sensitive to conventional attitudes. Those who similarly feel support from teachers avoid the lure of continual drug use to reduce distress.

Some effects are very circumstantial, that is, their influence is moderated by gender and by psychosocial vulnerability. These conditions of vulnerability permit some addictive influences to operate when, under generalized conditions, they would not promote abuse or addiction. These effects, although significant under some conditions, are thus not detected in research among undifferentiated samples. Among these effects are those of peer influence on conventional (nondeviant) men or those of self-enhancement among deviant women. In such cases, specialized samples enable the researcher to discover unique or idiosyncratic causes of drug abuse and addiction, some of which could be relevant for specialized groups seeking treatment, groups unable to afford treatment, and other clinical groups. These idiosyncratic differences can explain how research using clinical samples can produce findings contrary to general surveys.

In sum, if a full understanding of escalation of drug use is to be obtained, the investigator must routinely take into account the theoretically and methodologically indicated moderating influences of psychosocial characteristics such as gender and early adolescent experiences.

References

Anhalt, H. S., & Klein, M. (1976). Drug abuse in junior high school populations. *American Journal of Drug and Alcohol Abuse, 3,* 589–603.

Attie, I., & Brooks-Gunn, J. (1987). Weight concerns as chronic stressors in women. In R. C. Barnett, L. Biener, & G. K. Baruch (Eds.), *Gender and stress* (pp. 218–254). New York: Free Press.

Ausubel, D. P. (1980). An interactional approach to narcotic addiction. In D. J. Lettieri, M. Sayers, & H. W. Pearson (Eds.), *Theories on drug abuse: Selected contemporary perspectives* (NIDA Research Monograph 30, DHHS Publication No. ADM 80-967, pp. 4–7). Washington, DC: U.S. Government Printing Office.

Baron, R. M., & Kenny, D. A. (1986). The moderator–mediator variable distinction in social psychological research: Conceptual, strategic, and statistical considerations. *Journal of Personality and Social Psychology, 51,* 1173–1182.

Belle, D. (1987). Gender differences in the social moderators of stress. In R. C. Barnett, L. Biener, & G. K. Baruch (Eds.), *Gender and stress* (pp. 257–277). New York: Free Press.

Beller, E. K., & Neubauer, P. B. (1963). Sex differences and symptom patterns in early childhood. *Journal of the American Academy of Child Psychiatry, 2,* 414–433.

Best, J. A., Flay, B. R., Towson, S. M. J., Ryan, K. B., Perry, C. L., Brown, K. S., Kersell, M. W., & d'Avernas, J. R. (1984). Smoking prevention and the concept of risk. *Journal of Applied Social Psychology, 14,* 257–273.

Biener, L. (1987). Gender differences in the use of substances for coping. In R. C. Barnett, L. Biener, & G. K. Baruch (Eds.), *Gender and stress* (pp. 330–349). New York: Free Press.

Bogo, N., Winget, C., & Gleser, G. (1970). Ego defenses and perceptual styles. *Perceptual and Motor Skills, 30,* 599–604.

Botvin, G. J., Eng, A., & Williams, C. L. (1980). Preventing the onset of cigarette smoking through life skills training. *Preventive Medicine, 9,* 135–143.

Braucht, G. (1982). Problem drinking among adolescents: A review and analysis of psychosocial research. In *Special population issues.* (NIAAA Alcohol and Health Monograph 4, DHHS Publication No. ADM 82-1193, pp. 143–164). Washington, DC: U.S. Government Printing Office.

Bry, B. H. (1983). Predicting drug abuse: Review and reformulation. *International Journal of the Addictions, 18,* 223–233.

Bryant, B. (1985). The neighborhood walk: Sources of support in middle childhood. *Monographs of the Society for Research in Child Development, 50* (3, Serial No. 210).

Buss, A. H., & Brock, T. C. (1963). Repression and guilt in relation to aggression. *Journal of Abnormal and Social Psychology, 66,* 345–350.

Chein, I. (1980). Psychological, social, and epidemiological factors in juvenile drug use. In D. J. Lettieri, M. Sayers, & H. W. Pearson (Eds.), *Theories on drug abuse: Selected contemporary perspectives* (NIDA Research Monograph 30, DHHS Publication No. ADM 80-967, pp. 76–82). Washington, DC: U.S. Government Printing Office.

Covington, J. (1985). Gender differences in criminality among heroin users. *Journal of Research in Crime and Delinquency, 22,* 329–354.

Covington, J. (1986). Self-esteem and deviance: The effects of race and gender. *Criminology, 24,* 105–138.

Covington, J. (1988). Crime and heroin: The effects of race and gender. *Journal of Black Studies, 18,* 486–506.

Davis, G. C., & Brehm, M. L. (1971). Juvenile prisoners: Motivational factors in drug use. *Proceedings of the American Psychological Association, 6,* 333–334.

De Fundia, T. A., Dragunas, J. G., & Phillips, L. (1971). Culture and psychiatric symptomatology: A comparison of Argentine and United States patients. *Social Psychiatry, 6,* 11–20.

Douvan, E., & Adelson J. (1966). *The adolescent experience.* New York: Wiley.

Duncan, D. F. (1977). Life stress as a precursor to adolescent drug dependence. *International Journal of the Addictions, 12,* 1047–1056.

Elliott, D. S., Huizinga, D., & Ageton, S. S. (1985). *Explaining delinquency and drug use.* Beverly Hills: Sage.

Evans, R. I., Rozelle, R. M., Maxwell, S. E., Raines, B. E., Dill, C. A., Guthrie, T. J., Henderson, A. H., & Hill, P. C. (1981). Social modeling films to deter smoking in adolescents: Results of a three-year field investigation. *Journal of Applied Psychology, 66,* 399–414.

Exline, R. V. (1962). Effects of need for affiliation, sex, and the sight of others upon initial communications in problem-solving groups. *Journal of Personality, 30,* 541–556.

Feldman, H. W. (1968). Ideological supports to becoming and remaining a heroin addict. *Journal of Health and Social Behavior, 9,* 131–139.

Fitzgibbons, D. J., Berry, D. F., & Shearn, C. R. (1973). MMPI and diagnosis among hospitalized drug abusers. *Journal of Community Psychology, 1,* 79–81.

Frederick, C. J. (1980). Drug abuse as learned behavior. In D. J. Lettieri, M. Sayers, & H. W. Pearson (Eds.), *Theories on drug abuse: Selected contemporary perspectives* (NIDA Research Monograph 30, DHHS Publication No. ADM 80-967, pp. 191–194). Washington, DC: U.S. Government Printing Office.

Gleser, G. C., & Ihilevich, D. (1969). An objective instrument for measuring defense mechanisms. *Journal of Consulting and Clinical Psychology, 33,* 51–60.

Gold, M., & Mann, D. (1972). Delinquency as defense. *American Journal of Orthopsychiatry, 42,* 463–479.

Gold, S. R. (1980). The CAP control theory of drug abuse. In D. J. Lettieri, M. Sayers, & H. W. Pearson (Eds.), *Theories on drug abuse: Selected contemporary perspectives* (NIDA Research Monograph 30, DHHS Publication No. ADM 80-967, pp. 8–11). Washington, DC: U.S. Government Printing Office.

Gorsuch, R. L. (1980). Interactive models of nonmedical drug use. In D. J. Lettieri, M. Sayers, & H. W. Pearson (Eds.), *Theories on drug abuse: Selected contemporary perspectives* (NIDA Research Monograph 30, DHHS Publication No. ADM 80-967, pp. 18–23). Washington, DC: U.S. Government Printing Office.

Gove, W. R., & Crutchfield, R. D. (1982). The family and juvenile delinquency. *Sociological Quarterly, 23,* 301–319.

Greaves, G. B. (1980). An existential theory of drug dependence. In D. J. Lettieri, M. Sayers, & H. W. Pearson (Eds.), *Theories on drug abuse: Selected contemporary perspectives* (NIDA Research Monograph 30, DHHS Publication No. ADM 80-967, pp. 24–33). Washington, DC: U.S. Government Printing Office.

Hagan, J., Gillis, A. R., & Simpson, J. H. (1985). The class structure of gender and delinquency: Toward a power-control theory of common delinquent behavior. *American Journal of Sociology, 90,* 1151–1178.

Hagan, J., Simpson, J. H., & Gillis, A. R. (1979). The sexual stratification of social control: A gender-based perspective on crime and delinquency. *British Journal of Sociology, 30,* 25–38.

Hansen, W. B., Malotte, C. K., & Fielding, J. (1988). Evaluation of a tobacco and alcohol abuse prevention curriculum for adolescents. *Health Education Quarterly, 15,* 93–114.

Hendin, H. (1980). Psychosocial theory of drug abuse: A psychodynamic approach. In D. J. Lettieri, M. Sayers, & H. W. Pearson (Eds.), *Theories on drug abuse: Selected contemporary perspectives* (NIDA Research Monograph 30, DHHS Publication No. ADM 80-967, pp. 195–200). Washington, DC: U.S. Government Printing Office.

Hoffman, M. (1964). Drug addiction and "hypersexuality": Related modes of mastery. *Comprehensive Psychiatry, 5,* 262–270.

Holroyd, K., & Kahn, M. (1974). Personality factors in student drug use. *Journal of Consulting and Clinical Psychology, 42,* 236–243.

Hurd, P. D., Johnson, C. A., Pechacek, T., Bast, L. P., Jacobs, D. R., & Leupker, R. V. (1980). Prevention of cigarette smoking in seventh grade students. *Journal of Behavioral Medicine, 3,* 15–28.

Jessor, R., Carman, R. S., & Grossman, P. H. (1970). Expectations for need satisfaction and patterns of alcohol use in college. In G. Maddox (Ed.), *The domesticated drug: Drinking among collegians* (pp. 321–342). New Haven, CT: New Haven College and University Press.

Jessor, R., Jessor, S. L., & Finney, J. (1973). A social psychology of marijuana use: Longitudinal studies of high school and college youth. *Journal of Personality and Social Psychology, 26,* 1–15.

Jessor, R., Young, H. B., Young, E. B., & Tesi, G. (1970). Perceived opportunity, alienation, and drinking behavior among Italian and American youth. *Journal of Personality and Social Psychology, 15,* 215–222.

Johnson, R. E. (1979). *Juvenile delinquency and its origins.* Cambridge, England: Cambridge University Press.

Johnson, R. J., & Kaplan, H. B. (1987). Corrigendum: Methodology, technology and serendipity. *Social Psychology Quarterly, 50,* 352–354.

Johnson, R. J., & Kaplan, H. B. (1990). Stability of psychological symptoms: Drug use consequences and intervening processes. *Journal of Health and Social Behavior, 31,* 277–291.

Kaplan, H. B. (1980). *Deviant behavior in defense of self.* San Diego, CA: Academic Press.

Kaplan, H. B., Johnson, R. J., & Bailey, C. A. (1987). Deviant peers and deviant behavior: Further elaboration of a model. *Social Psychology Quarterly, 50,* 277–284.

Kaplan, H. B., Johnson, R. J., & Bailey, C. A. (1988). Explaining adolescent drug use: An elaboration strategy for structural equations modeling. *Psychiatry, 51,* 142–163.

Kaplan, H. B., Martin, S. S., Johnson, R. J., & Robbins, C. (1986). Escalation of marijuana use: Application of a general theory of deviant behavior. *Journal of Health and Social Behavior, 27,* 44–61.

Kaplan, H. B., Martin, S., & Robbins, C. (1985). Toward an explanation of increased involvement in illicit drug use: Application of a general theory of deviant behavior. In J. R. Greenley (Ed.), *Research in community and mental health* (Vol. 5, pp. 205–252). Greenwich, CT: JAI Press.

Khantzian, E. J. (1980). An ego/self theory of substance dependence: A contemporary psychoanalytic perspective. In D. J. Lettieri, M. Sayers, & H. W. Pearson (Eds.), *Theories on drug abuse: Selected contemporary perspectives* (NIDA Research Monograph 30, DHHS Publication No. ADM 80-967, pp. 29–33). Washington, DC: U.S. Government Printing Office.

Lansky, L. M., Crandall, V. J., Kagan, J., & Baker, C. T. (1961). Sex differences in aggression and its correlates in middle-class adolescents. *Child Development, 32,* 45–58.

Lefcourt, H. M. (1989). Personal and social characteristics that alter the impact of stressors. In J. H. Humphrey (Ed.), *Human stress: Current selected research* (Vol. 3, pp. 1–13). New York: AMS Press.

Lemert, E. M. (1967). *Human deviance, social problems, and social control.* Englewood Cliffs, NJ: Prentice-Hall.

Lettieri, D. J., Sayers, M., & Pearson, H. W. (Eds.). (1980). *Theories on drug abuse: Selected contemporary perspectives* (NIDA Research Monograph Series No. 30, DHHS Publication No. ADM 80-967). Washington, DC: U.S. Government Printing Office.

Levitin, T. A., & Chananie, J. D. (1972). Responses of female primary school teachers to sex-typed behaviors in male and female children. *Child Development, 43,* 1309–1316.

Long, J. V. F., & Scherl, D. J. (1984). Developmental antecedents of compulsive drug use: A report on the literature. *Journal of Psychoactive Drugs, 16,* 169–182.

Maccoby, E. E. (Ed.). (1966). *The development of sex differences.* Stanford, CA: Stanford University Press.

Maccoby, E. E., & Jacklin, C. N. (1974). *The psychology of sex differences.* Stanford, CA: Stanford University Press.

MacKinnon, D. P., Weber, M. D., & Pentz, M. A. (1988). How do school-based drug prevention programs work and for whom? *Drugs and Society, 3,* 125–143.

Maier, S. F., & Seligman, M. E. P. (1976). Learned helplessness: Theory and evidence. *Journal of Experimental Psychology: General, 105,* 3–46.

McCandless, B. R., Bilous, C. B., & Bennett, H. L. (1961). Peer popularity and dependence on adults in preschool age socialization. *Child Development, 32,* 511–518.

McClelland, D. C. (1972). Examining the research basis for alternative explanations of alcoholism. In D. C. McClelland, W. N. Davis, R. Kalin, & E. Wanner (Eds.), *The drinking man* (pp. 276–315). New York: Free Press.

McGuire, M. T., Stein, S., & Mendelson, J. H. (1966). Comparative psychosocial studies of alcoholic and nonalcoholic subjects undergoing experimentally induced ethanol intoxication. *Psychosomatic Medicine, 28,* 13–26.

Mellinger, G. D. (1978). Use of illicit drugs and other coping alternatives: Some personal observations on the hazards of living. In D. J. Lettieri (Ed.), *Drugs and suicide: When other coping strategies fail* (pp. 249–278). Beverly Hills, CA: Sage.

Misra, R. K. (1980). Achievement, anxiety, and addiction. In D. J. Lettieri, M. Sayers, & H. W. Pearson (Eds.), *Theories on drug abuse: Selected contemporary perspectives* (NIDA Research Monograph 30, DHHS Publication No. ADM 80-967, pp. 212–214). Washington, DC: U.S. Government Printing Office.

Mogar, R. E., Wilson, W. M., & Helm, S. T. (1970). Personality subtypes of male and female alcoholic patients. *International Journal of the Addictions, 5,* 99–113.

Moore, S. P. (1964). Displaced aggression in relation to different frustrations. *Journal of Abnormal Psychology, 68,* 200–204.

Moore, T., & Ucko, L. E. (1961). Four-to-six: Constructiveness and conflict in meeting doll play problems. *Journal of Child Psychology and Psychiatry and Allied Disciplines, 2,* 21–47.

Naffine, N. (1987). *Female crime: The Construction of women in criminology.* Winchester, MA: Allen & Unwin.

Newcomb, M. D. (1988). *Drug use in the workplace: Risk factors for disruptive substance use among young adults.* Dover, MA: Auburn House.

Newcomb, M. D., & Bentler, P. M. (1989). Substance use and abuse among children and teenagers. *American Psychologist, 44,* 242–248.

Nye, F. I. (1958). *Family relationships and delinquent behavior.* New York: Wiley.

Pearlin, L. I., & Radabaugh, C. W. (1976). Economic strains and the coping functions of alcohol. *American Journal of Sociology, 82,* 652–663.

Peele, S. (1980). Addiction to an experience: A social–psychological–pharmacological theory of addiction. In D. J. Lettieri, M. Sayers, & H. W. Pearson (Eds.), *Theories on drug abuse: Selected contemporary perspectives* (NIDA Research Monograph 30, DHHS Publication No. ADM 80-967, pp. 142–146). Washington, DC: U.S. Government Printing Office.

Peele, S. (1986). The "cure" for adolescent drug abuse: Worse than the problem? *Journal of Counseling and Development, 65,* 23–24.

Pentz, M. A. (1983). Prevention of adolescent substance abuse through social skill development. In T. Glynn, L. Leukfeld, & J. Ludford (Eds.), *Preventing adolescent drug abuse: Intervention strategies* (NIDA Research Monograph 47, DHHS Publication No. ADM 83-1280, pp. 195–232). Washington, DC: U.S. Government Printing Office.

Robbins, C. (1989). Sex differences in psychosocial consequences of alcohol and drug abuse. *Journal of Health and Social Behavior, 30,* 117–130.

Rothaus, P., & Worchel, P. (1964). Ego-support, communication, catharsis, and hostility. *Journal of Personality, 32,* 296–312.

Schoenberg, R. J. (1975). *A structural model of delinquency.* Unpublished doctoral dissertation, University of Washington, Seattle.

Schoolar, J. C., White, E. H., & Cohen, C. P. (1972). Drug abusers and their clinic-patient counterparts: A comparison of personality dimensions. *Journal of Consulting and Clinical Psychology, 39,* 9–15.

Sears, R. R. (1961). Relation of early socialization experiences to aggression in middle childhood. *Journal of Abnormal and Social Psychology, 63,* 466–492.

Sears, R. R., Maccoby, E. E., & Levin, H. (1957). *Patterns of child rearing.* Evanston, IL: Row, Peterson.

Sears, R. R., Ray, L., & Alpert, R. (1965). *Identification and child rearing.* Stanford, CA: Stanford University Press.

Segal, B., Rhenberg, G., & Sterling, S. (1975). Self-concept and drug and alcohol use in female college students. *Journal of Alcohol and Drug Education, 20,* 17–22.

Seligman, M. E. P. (1975). *Helplessness: On depression, development and death.* San Francisco: Freeman.

Simons, R. L., Conger, R. D., & Whitbeck, L. B. (1988). A multistage social learning model of the influences of family and peers upon adolescent substance abuse. *Journal of Drug Issues, 18,* 293–315.

Smart, R. G., & Whitehead, P. C. (1974). The uses of an epidemiology of drug use: The Canadian scene. *International Journal of the Addictions, 9,* 373–388.

Smith, G. M. (1980). Perceived effects of substance use: A general theory. In D. J. Lettieri, M. Sayers, & H. W. Pearson (Eds.), *Theories on drug abuse: Selected contemporary perspectives* (NIDA Research Monograph 30, DHHS Publication No. ADM 80-967, pp. 50–58). Washington, DC: U.S. Government Printing Office.

Spangler, D. P., & Thomas, C. W. (1962). The effects of age, sex, and physical disability upon manifest needs. *Journal of Counseling Psychology, 9,* 313–319.

Spotts, J. V., & Shontz, F. C. (1980). A life-time theory of chronic drug abuse. In D. J. Lettieri, M. Sayers, & H. W. Pearson (Eds.), *Theories on drug abuse: Selected contemporary perspectives* (NIDA Research Monograph 30, DHHS Publication No. ADM 80-967, pp. 59–70). Washington, DC: U.S. Government Printing Office.

Steffenhagen, R. A. (1980). Self-esteem theory of drug abuse. In D. J. Lettieri, M. Sayers, & H. W. Pearson (Eds.), *Theories on drug abuse: Selected contemporary perspectives* (NIDA Research Monograph 30, DHHS Publication No. ADM 80-967, pp. 157–163). Washington, DC: U.S. Government Printing Office.

Stein, A. (1971). The effects of sex-role standards for achievement and sex-role preference on three determinants of achievement motivation. *Developmental Psychology, 4,* 219–231.

Stein, L., & Bowman, R. S. (1977). Reasons for drinking: Relationship to social functioning and drinking behavior. In F. A. Seixas (Ed.), *Currents in alcoholism* (Vol. 2, pp. 479–485). New York: Grune & Stratton.

Stokes, J. P. (1974). Personality traits and attitudes and their relationship to student drug using behavior. *International Journal of the Addictions, 9,* 267–287.

Tahka, V. (1966). *The alcoholic personality* (Report No. 13). Helsinki: Finnish Foundation for Alcohol Studies.

Tell, G. S., Klepp, K., Vellar, O. D., & McAlister, A. (1984). Preventing the onset of cigarette smoking in Norwegian adolescents. The Oslo Youth Study. *Preventive Medicine, 13,* 256–275.

Tittle, C. R. (1980). *Sanctions and social deviance: The question of deterrence.* New York: Praeger.

Tittle, C. R., & Rowe, A. R. (1973). Moral appeal, sanction threat, and deviance: An experimental test. *Social Problems, 20,* 488–498.

Tobler, N. S. (1986). Meta-analysis of 143 adolescent drug prevention programs: Quantitative outcome results of program participants compared to a control or comparison group. *Journal of Drug Issues, 16,* 537–567.

van Dijk, W. K. (1980). Biological, psychogenic, and sociogenic factors in drug dependence. In D. J. Lettieri, M. Sayers, & H. W. Pearson (Eds.), *Theories on drug abuse: Selected contemporary perspectives* (NIDA Research Monograph 30, DHHS Publication No. ADM 80-967, pp. 164–173). Washington, DC: U.S. Government Printing Office.

Waldrop, M., & Halverson, C. (1975). Intensive and extensive peer behavior: Longitudinal and cross-sectional analysis. *Child Development, 46,* 19–26.

Wurmser, L. (1980). Drug use as a protective system. In D. J. Lettieri, M. Sayers, & H. W. Pearson (Eds.), *Theories on drug abuse: Selected contemporary perspectives* (NIDA Research Monograph 30, DHHS Publication No. ADM 80-967, pp. 71–74). Washington, DC: U.S. Government Printing Office.

Wyer, R. S., Weatherley, D. A., & Terrell, G. (1965). Social role, aggression, and academic achievement. *Journal of Personality and Social Psychology, 1,* 645–649.

Independent Variables

ADVERPP   Adverse Physical and Psychological Effects

1. Thinking of the first time you ever used illegal drugs, did you feel guilty or ashamed either while doing it or afterwards?
2. Thinking of the first time you ever used illegal drugs, did you get physically injured or sick because of it?
3. Thinking of the first time you ever used illegal drugs, did you experience bad psychological effects?
4. Thinking of the first time you ever used illegal drugs, did you feel that generally it was an unpleasant experience?

NEGSANC   Negative Social Sanctions

1. Thinking of the first time you ever used illegal drugs, did you either have a close call with the police or get arrested because of it?
2. Thinking of the first time you ever used illegal drugs, did you serve time in jail or prison, etc. because of it?
3. Thinking of the first time you ever used illegal drugs, did you lose your job or have trouble on the job because of doing it, or have trouble with teachers or school authorities because of it?

ATTENTI   Attenuation of Interpersonal Ties

1. Thinking of the first time you ever used illegal drugs, did you feel rejected by your boy/girlfriend, parents, friends or others who were important to you because of doing it?

2. Thinking of the first time you ever used illegal drugs, did you cause grief to someone you loved by doing it?

DEVDEFD   Deviant Definition of Drug Use

1. Thinking of the first time you ever used illegal drugs, did you before doing it, think there was a chance of getting into trouble because of it?
2. Thinking of the first time you ever used illegal drugs, did you do it where no one else could see it (rather than in public where others could see it)?

REDNEGA   Reduction of Negative Affect

1. Thinking of the first time you ever used illegal drugs, did you feel less depressed either while doing it or after doing it?
2. During the week before you used illegal drugs for the first time, did you feel down (emotionally) much of the time?
3. During the week before you used illegal drugs for the first time, did you feel bored much of the time?
4. Thinking of the first time you ever used illegal drugs, did you feel less bored either while doing it or after having done it?
5. Thinking of the first time you ever used illegal drugs, did you feel that generally it was a pleasant experience?
6. During the week before you used illegal drugs for the first time, did you feel particularly nervous or tense much of the time?

REDSREJ   Reduction of Self-Rejection

1. Thinking of the first time you ever used illegal drugs, did you do it to get away from your troubles?
2. Thinking of the first time you ever used illegal drugs, did you feel less guilty or ashamed either while doing it or after having done it?
3. Thinking of the first time you ever used illegal drugs, did you feel less worthless or less like a failure either while doing it or after having done it?
4. During the week before you used illegal drugs for the first time, did you feel like a failure or worthless much of the time?

INCRPOT   Increased Potency

1. Thinking of the first time you ever used illegal drugs, did you feel more important while doing it or for having done it?

2. Thinking of the first time you ever used illegal drugs, did you feel more powerful either while doing it or because you had done it?

EXPRANG   Expression of Anger

1. Thinking of the first time you ever used illegal drugs, did you do it because you were angry at someone or something?
2. During the week before you used illegal drugs for the first time, did you get suspended or expelled from a school or have trouble with teachers or other school authorities, or have trouble at work (fired, argument with boss)?
3. During the week before you used illegal drugs for the first time, did you have a serious argument with one or both of your parents or someone else who was very important to you?

MOTPEER   Motivation for Peer Acceptance

1. Thinking of the first time you ever used illegal drugs, did you get accepted by a new group of friends because of doing it?
2. Thinking of the first time you ever used illegal drugs, did you do it to show you weren't afraid?
3. Thinking of the first time you ever used illegal drugs, did you do it because your friends were doing it?
4. Thinking of the first time you ever used illegal drugs, did you start running around with people who got into trouble a lot?
5. Thinking of the first time you ever used illegal drugs, did you see a close friend do it first?
6. During the week before you used illegal drugs for the first time, did you run around with people who got into trouble a lot?
7. During the week before you used illegal drugs for the first time, did you feel like you didn't have any close friends?

Moderating Variables

DEVIANCE   Deviant Behavior

1. Within the last month did you take things worth between $2 and $50 that didn't belong to you?
2. Within the last month did you carry a razor, switch blade or gun as a weapon?
3. Within the last month did you break into and enter a home, store or building?
4. Within the last month did you damage or destroy public or private property on purpose that didn't belong to you?
5. Within the last month did you take things worth $50 or more that didn't belong to you?

RJTT   Perceived Rejection by Teachers

1. My teachers are usually not very interested in what I say or do.
2. By my teachers' standards I am a failure.
3. My teachers do not like me very much.
4. My teachers usually put me down.

PEERSUP   Drug-Using Peers

1. Do many of the kids at school take narcotic drugs?
2. Do many of your good friends smoke marijuana (grass)?
3. Do many of your good friends take narcotic drugs to get high?
4. Do many of the kids at school smoke marijuana (grass)?

RJTP   Perceived Rejection by Parents

1. As long as I can remember my parents have put me down.

2. My parents are usually not very interested in what I say or do.
3. My parents do not like me very much.

PEERREJ   Perceived Rejection by Peers

1. More often than not I feel put down by the kids at school.
2. I am not very good at the kinds of things the kids at school think are important.
3. The kids at school are usually not very interested in what I say or do.
4. Most of the kids at school do not like me very much.

SDRG   Self-Derogation

1. I wish I could have more respect for myself.
2. On the whole, I am satisfied with myself.
3. I feel I do not have much to be proud of.
4. All in all, I am inclined to feel that I am a failure.
5. I take a positive attitude toward myself?
6. At times I think I am no good at all.
7. I certainly feel useless at times.

SENCON   Sensitivity to Attitudes of Conventional Adults

1. It is very important to me what my parents think of me.
2. It is very important to me what my teachers think of me.
3. When my parents dislike something I do it bothers me very much.
4. I think it is important to obey the teachers.
5. When my teachers dislike something I do it bothers me very much.

Means and Standard Deviations for Independent and Moderating Variables by Gender

	Men			Women		
Variable	*M*	*SD*	alpha	*M*	*SD*	alpha
Independent variables[a]						
ADVERPP	7.27	1.66	.83	7.04	1.88	.84
NEGSANC	5.80	1.13	.87	5.78	1.21	.86
ATTENTI	3.68	.919	.81	3.56	1.04	.83
DEVDEFD	2.66	1.01	.66	2.69	1.06	.67
REDNEGA	10.1	2.48	.85	9.98	2.76	.87
REDSREJ	7.57	1.55	.86	7.34	1.79	.87
INCRPOT	3.58	.971	.79	3.56	1.04	.83
EXPRANG	5.88	1.08	.89	5.72	1.28	.84
MOTPEER	11.5	2.93	.88	11.3	3.23	.90
Moderating variables[b]						
DEVIANCE	.341	.770	.59	.109	.405	.44
RJTT	.951	1.23	.71	.718	1.11	.71
PEERSUP	1.12	1.30	.75	1.22	1.33	.76
RJTP	.318	.682	.59	.269	.646	.62
PEERREJ	1.30	1.28	.63	1.23	1.29	.68
SDRG	2.26	1.71	.61	2.43	1.78	.64
SENCON	3.60	1.30	.58	3.87	1.28	.64

[a] The means, standard deviations, and alphas were computed from raw scores for all respondents at Time 4.

[b] The means, standard deviations, and alphas were computed from raw scores for all respondents at Time 1.

CHAPTER 12

Psychosocial Risk Factors in the Transition From Moderate to Heavy Use or Abuse of Drugs

Judith S. Brook, Patricia Cohen, Martin Whiteman, and Ann S. Gordon

A question of great importance is why some adolescents progress to higher stages of drug use, multiple drug use, or abusive intake of substances, whereas others do not. Although some investigations have examined the predictors of different degrees of alcohol and marijuana use, as yet, there have been few systematic studies of the predictors of abuse of these substances in adolescents. The need for further research on frequent use or abuse of drugs and alcohol during adolescence is widely acknowledged (Jones & Battjes, 1985). The literature, extensive and varied as it is, still leaves unresolved many questions regarding the antecedents, correlates, and consequences of heavy use or abuse of drugs by adolescents. A major goal of this study is thus to explore the personality, family, and peer factors that increase the risk of alcohol abuse and heavy marijuana use. Building on recent research

This study was supported by Research Grant DA03188 and in part by Research Scientist Development Award DA00094 from the National Institute on Drug Abuse to Judith S. Brook.

Appreciation is expressed to Coryl Jones for her advice. In addition, the authors are extremely grateful to Meyer Glantz for his helpful suggestions and comments. We thank Sandy Stillman for assistance with the analysis and Susan Karaban for help with preparation of the manuscript. The original study from which the childhood data were obtained was conducted by Leonard Kogan.

findings, we further propose to study the interplay of these personal and interpersonal factors as they relate to different degrees of drug involvement.

Until the 1970s, research designed to investigate the etiology of adolescent alcohol or drug use usually focused on those factors that were associated with use compared with nonuse. This emphasis was appropriate in the America of the 1950s and 1960s, when drug use was relatively rare among adolescents and problem use was limited to a small, although worrisome, subgroup. Even during the turbulent period of social upheaval that began in the mid-1960s, illicit drug use and consumption of hard liquor remained, in percentage terms, a relatively minor activity in the secondary school population nationwide (Jersild, Brook, & Brook, 1978). (Marijuana use became relatively common on college campuses and elsewhere among college graduates and other young people. Drinking, traditionally popular in this age group, continued to be commonplace.) However, as substance use became more and more common at lower age–grade levels and some experience with marijuana and other illicit drugs became more normative among high school students, the simplistic use–nonuse approach to research became unrealistic and a change in focus was necessary.

Concerning the question of why some adolescents become heavily involved in drugs, by the early 1970s, studies had begun to reveal the etiologic complexity of adolescent drug use. Investigations into the differential patterns of alcohol and drug use among adolescents were undertaken (Adler & Lotecka, 1973; Blumenfield, Riester, Serrano, & Adams, 1972; Hamburg, Kraemer, & Jahnke, 1975; Jessor & Jessor, 1977; Pandina & White, 1981). A number of investigators (Huba, Wingard, & Bentler, 1980; Jessor & Jessor, 1977) began to study the etiology of drug use from an interactional perspective, which views individuals as psychological and biological beings in constant interaction with their environment. As noted by Hamburg et al. (1975), what was needed in the study of drug use among adolescents was a differentiated approach from both a descriptive and an etiologic perspective. Another proponent of this interactional perspective is Magnusson (1988), who noted that individuals develop as integrated organisms in reciprocal interaction with their environment. Their development is influenced by and affects the reciprocal process of interaction among psychological and biological factors. Magnusson focused on the interrelations of interpersonal and intrapersonal variables as they affected development, including deviant behavior. In a related vein, Jessor and Jessor (1977) maintained that adolescent problem behavior was the result of prior personality constellations (the intrapersonal aspect, such as attitude to deviance) and the environmental system, which includes both parents and peers. Another interactive framework that has received a great deal of attention is that of Bentler and Newcomb, who have studied intrapersonal factors (such as disposition to social conformity) and environmental influences (such as peer drug use and broader sociocultural factors; Newcomb & Bentler, 1988). Other major investigators who have used an interactional approach include, but are not limited to, Kandel, Kessler, and Margulies (1978), Labouvie and McGee (1986), and Pandina and Schuele (1983).

In this study, we have attempted to apply an interactional approach to the study of the transition from lower to higher levels of drug use by selecting variables from three separate domains: personality, family, and peer. In the personality area, we have included three subsets: attitudinal unconventionality, emotional distress, and aggressive/acting-out. These factors have been previously implicated in drug use and abuse. Adolescents who reject dominant social norms are likely to initiate and sustain drug use. Such adolescents have an orientation to sensation seeking and are tolerant of deviance (J. S. Brook, Whiteman, Gordon, & Cohen, 1986a, 1986b; Jessor, Chase, & Donovan, 1980; Kay, Lyons, Newman, Mankin, & Loeb, 1978; Wingard, Huba, & Bentler, 1980). We have included measures of emotional distress because of their importance in the clinical literature, even though there is some inconsistency in the research literature (Alterman, 1985; Jersild et al., 1978; Khantzian, 1985; Stein, Newcomb, & Bentler, 1987; Swaim, Oetting, Edwards, & Beauvais, 1989). In fact, some researchers found that in certain adolescent populations, experimental users of marijuana and other illicit drugs were in better psychological health than either heavy users or a subgroup of abstinent nonusers (Baumrind & Moselle, 1985; J. Block, personal communication, June 1989). The third subset, aggression/acting-out behavior, is characterized by aggression, impulsivity, rebelliousness, and deviancy, all of which have been found to be strongly related to drug use (Kandel, 1978; Penning & Barnes, 1982).

Socialization within the family as it concerns drug use centers on two aspects of interpersonal influences: (a) modeling and (b) child-rearing practices. The modeling effects of parental drug-use behavior on adolescent drug use are well documented, although such effects vary depending on the drug in question (for reviews, see J. S. Brook, Whiteman, Gordon, & Brook, 1983; Penning & Barnes, 1982).

Child-rearing practices also constitute a principal means by which parents affect the potential for drug use in their offspring, with each of the two major parenting dimensions of warmth and control exerting a distinct influence on the overall quality of the parent–child relationship. In our own research (J. S. Brook, Brook, Gordon, Whiteman, & Cohen, 1990) we have focused on the warmth aspect, that is, the attachment relationship between the parent and child, as it affects the child's drug use. The nature of mutual attachment has been explored through such variables as parental support, communication, responsiveness, affection, and the child's identification with the parent. Many of these variables are potent in their association with drug use, particularly when adolescents have formed an attachment to conventional or traditional parents (J. S. Brook, Whiteman, Gordon, & Brook, 1984). Our work (J. S. Brook et al., 1990) has suggested that mutual attachment serves as a deterrent to drug use for several reasons. First, it fosters the development of cognitions of act consequence, leading to attitudes that drugs are harmful. Second, attachment is associated with the development of a sense of inner security, which results in a decreased need for drugs. Third, a closer attachment relationship leads to greater parental identification and the resulting internalization of traditional societal values. Finally, mutual attachment leads to an increased sense of mastery of the environment, which appears to reduce the risk of drug use.

The control dimension of parenting has also been found to be of importance in the etiology of drug use by adolescents (Hawkins, Lishner, & Catalano, 1985). Overall, it appears that parents of drug users do not use reasonable reinforcements contingent on the child's behavior. In our own research (J. S. Brook et al., 1990), we have found that the attachment relationship is consistently more important than the control dimension in insulating the adolescent from drug use.

Aside from the family, the peer group commonly serves as a major socialization influence on the adolescent's drug use. The strong association between friends' drug use (modeling) and self drug use is well documented (for a review, see Kandel, 1980). A dual process of selective association and socialization by peers appears to best explain how peers influence adolescent drug use (Kandel, 1985). There is also evidence that normative initiation to drug use, movement to recreational use (light or moderate), and progression to abuse seem to be influenced most directly by peer factors (Kandel, 1978; Swaim et al., 1989).

In addition to focusing on the multiple influences involved in adolescent drug use, recent research has also centered on factors related to specific categories or patterns of use, that is, the use of different drugs and/or the degree of use (e.g., Barnes, Farrell, & Cairns, 1986; Baumrind, 1985; Kaplan, Martin, Johnson, & Robbins, 1986; Newcomb, Maddahian, & Bentler, 1986; Pandina & Schuele, 1983). In the present study, we were able to build on these investigations and add to our understanding of different degrees of substance involvement by studying the interplay of personality, family, and peer factors. Sets of personality, family, and peer factors may have independent lines of associations with different degrees of drug use. On the other hand, either the personality or the peer characteristics may serve to mediate family influences.

Assuming that there are diverse pathways to drug use, Bry, McKeon, and Pandina (1982) and Newcomb et al. (1986) tested the notion that the number of different risk factors was related linearly to heavy drug use. We attempted to replicate their findings with heavy marijuana use and to extend their work by examining the association of a number of different risk factors with alcohol abuse.

Finally, complementary to this risk approach, we were interested in examining statistically interactive combinations of protective factors that might deter adolescents from heavy marijuana use or alcohol abuse. For example, in previous research, we found that the effects of low childhood anger (a protective factor) were synergistically enhanced by later low adolescent aggression to peers (another protective factor), resulting in the least amount of adolescent drug use (J. S. Brook et al., 1986a).

In sum, the present study examined the interplay of personality, family, and peer influences with different levels of drug involvement: light use versus moderate use versus abuse of alcohol; and light use versus moderate use versus heavy use of marijuana. In addition, the association between the number of risk factors and drug use (alcohol abuse and heavy marijuana use) was tested. Finally, we attempted to determine whether the efficacy of a protective factor can be enhanced by another protective factor to decrease the risk of substance use.

Method

Sample and Procedure

This research is based on data from a longitudinal study of a random sample of youngsters residing in two upstate New York communities (Albany and Saratoga). The families were first sampled in 1975 (T1). At that time, the children were between the ages of 1 and 10. (A description of the original sampling plan and study procedures appears in Kogan, Smith, & Jenkins, 1977.) The families were contacted for a second interview (T2) in 1983 when the children were between the ages of 9 and 18. A third interview (T3) was conducted 2½ years later, when the children were between the ages of 11 and 20. In the present study, we looked at those children who were between the ages of 5 and 10 at the time of the original interview (T1) and between the ages of 16 and 21 at the time of the third follow-up (T3). The higher age range was selected to allow for the development of alcohol abuse and heavy drug use. Eighty percent of the original sample of children age 5 to 10 ($n = 583$) were assessed in follow-up interviews. Of these, 417 had complete drug and alcohol data at T3 and comprised the subjects for this study. On the basis of census data, the original sample was generally representative of families with children of comparable ages residing in the northeast United States, with respect to socioeconomic status and family composition. However, because of the areas selected for sampling, there was an underrepresentation of minority-group families and an overrepresentation of Catholics and rural residents. A description of the sample appears in Table 12.1.

All interviews were conducted in the respondents' homes by pairs of trained lay interviewers. At T1, only the mothers were seen, whereas at the two follow-ups both mothers and adolescents were simultaneously, but separately, interviewed. Each interview took about an hour and contained a wide range of scales assessing the youngster's personality, family relations, and peer attributes. As noted earlier, we have limited our analyses for this study to the T3 data collection to maximize the possibility of obtaining heavy drug use and abuse by the adolescents, now ages 16 to 21. For theoretical interest,

TABLE 12.1
Demographic Characteristics of the Sample

Age of adolescents	
M	18 years
Range	15 to 21 years
Sex of adolescents	
% Female	51
% Male	49
Race of adolescents	
% White	91
% Black	4
% Other	5
Religion of adolescents	
% Catholic	55
% Protestant	36
% Other	9
Intact families (biological father in the household)	
% Intact	71
% Not intact	29
Family income	
Mdn range	$25,000–29,000
Overall range	≤$4,000–≥$75,000

Note. N = 518.

we have also included an assessment of childhood aggression obtained when the children were ages 5 to 10. (Please note that because of the young age of the adolescents at T2, there was not enough heavy drug involvement to allow us to make comparisons of drug use over time, T2 to T3. Because we plan to do a follow-up of our subjects in the future, we will then be in a position to do such an evaluation.)

Measures

The scales used in this investigation cover three basic domains: personality attributes, family relations, and peer attributes. The scales, for the most part, are adaptations of existing scales with adequate psychometric properties. Table 12.2 lists the scales (grouped into domains), their sources, their reliabilities (Cronbach's alphas), and a sample item. It should be noted that some of the scales were grouped to form composite measures. These composite measures include childhood aggression, acting-out behavior, incompetence, and pathology in the personality domain, and maternal and paternal attachment in the family domain.

Dependent Variables

Alcohol and marijuana use were each classified into three categories on the basis of frequency of use over the previous 2 years. The alcohol (beer, wine, or hard liquor) categories were nonuse or light use (those who used a few times a year or less), moderate use (subjects who were neither light users nor abusers), and abusers. Alcohol abuse was defined by criteria of the third revised edition of the *Diagnostic and Statistical Manual of Mental Disorders* (American Psychiatric Association, 1987) as being present when alcohol use continued despite the presence of a recurrent social, educational, occupational, psychological, or physical problem attributable to or exacerbated by its use, or a physical hazard associated with drunken driving. The presence of these problems was determined by interviews with both the youth and the mother, and at least two positive indications were required to meet the criterion for alcohol abuse. Among the abusers, 78% reported drinking at least once a week and 22% reported drinking on a daily basis.

The marijuana categories were nonuse or light use (those who used once or twice a year or less), moderate use (those who used more than experimentally but less than once a week), and heavy users (those who used once a week or more). Other illegal drugs were omitted because we did not have a sufficient number of heavy users or abusers for analytic purposes.

TABLE 12.2
Psychosocial Measures

Measures/scale	Source	α	No. of items	Sample item
Personality domain				
Childhood aggression[a]				
Anger	Cohen & Velez (1983)	.55	(3)	How often does your child scream when he/she is angry?
Aggression to Siblings	Cohen & Velez (1983)	.66	(4)	How often does child pick on siblings?
Noncompliance	Cohen & Velez (1983)	.57	(6)	When child is asked to do something, does he or she usually do it or not?
Temper	Cohen & Velez (1983)	.50	(3)	When child gets angry, does he or she kick things?
Nonconforming Behavior	Cohen & Velez (1983)	.50	(6)	How often do you think child takes things that don't belong to him or her?
Acting out[a]				
Rebelliousness	Smith & Fogg (1979)	.80	(8)	When rules and regulations get in my way, I sometimes ignore them.
Low Responsibility	Gough (1957)	.46	(6)	It's all right to get around the law, if you don't actually break it.
Impulsivity	Gough (1957) Jackson (1974)	.49	(6)	I am often said to be hotheaded or bad-tempered.
Deviancy	Gold (1966)	.68	(5)	How often have you taken something not belonging to you worth $5 or more?
Incompetence[a]				
Noncompliance	Cohen & Velez (1983)	.51	(2)	When you are asked or told to do something, do you usually do it?
Low Task Persistence	Cohen & Velez (1983)	.44	(9)	When you do something, how important is it to you to do it exactly right?
Sensation Seeking	Zuckerman, Eysenck, & Eysenck (1978)	.56	(7)	I like "wild" uninhibited parties vs. I prefer quiet parties with good conversation.
Ego Integration	J. S. Brook, Whiteman, Brook, & Gordon (1981)	.61	(7)	I feel like losing my temper at people.

(continued)

TABLE 12.2 *(Continued)*

Measures/scale	Source	α	No. of items	Sample item
Pathology[a]				
Depression	Derogatis, Lipman, Rickels, Uhlenhuth, & Covi (1974)	.69	(5)	Over the last few years, on the average how much have you been bothered by feeling blue?
Anxiety	Derogatis et al. (1974)	.58	(4)	Over the last few years, on the average how much have you been bothered by feeling nervous or shaky inside?
Obsessiveness	Derogatis et al. (1974)	.63	(4)	Over the last few years, on the average how much have you been bothered by difficulty in making decisions?
Family domain				
Maternal attachment[a]				
Identification	J. S. Brook, Whiteman, & Gordon (1982)	.92	(14)	How much do you want to be like your mother in your role as a parent?
Affection	Schaefer (1965)	.71	(4)	My mother frequently shows her love for me.
Time Spent	J. S. Brook, Brook, Gordon, Whiteman, & Cohen (1990)	.58	(3)	Overall, how much time do you spend just talking with your mother?
Nonconflictual Environment	Schaefer & Finkelstein (1975)	.88	(5)	Your child does what he or she wants to instead of what you tell him or her to do.
Paternal attachment[a]				
Identification	(See Maternal attachment scales)	.93	(14)	(See Maternal attachment scales)

(continued)

TABLE 12.2 *(Continued)*

Measures/scale	Source	α	No. of items	Sample item
Affection	(See Maternal attachment scales)	.73	(4)	(See Maternal attachment scales)
Time Spent	(See Maternal attachment scales)	.65	(3)	(See Maternal attachment scales)
Nonconflictual Environment	(See Maternal attachment scales)	.90	(5)	(See Maternal attachment scales)
Maternal Permissiveness	Schaefer (1965)	.67	(4)	She allows me to go out as often as I please.
Paternal Permissiveness	Schaefer (1965)	.57	(4)	(See Maternal attachment scales)
Parental Legal Drug Use	—	—	—	How often do you (your husband) drink beer or wine?
Parental Illegal Drug Use	—	—	—	How often have you (your husband) ever smoked marijuana?

Peer domain				
Friend Legal Drug Use	—	—	—	How many of your friends smoke cigarettes on a regular basis?
Friend Illegal Drug Use	—	—	—	How many of your friends use marijuana at least once a month on the average?
Friend Deviancy	Gold (1966)	.81	(5)	How many of your friends have gotten into a serious fight at school or at work?
No. Achieving Friends	J. S. Brook, Whiteman, & Gordon (1983)	.59	(2)	How many of your friends get all A and B grades?
Time Spent With Friends	J. S. Brook, Whiteman, & Gordon (1983)	.66	(7)	How often do you hang out with other kids?

Note. All scales are based on the adolescent's report except for the following, which are based on maternal report: Anger, Aggression to Siblings, Noncompliance, Temper, Nonconforming Behavior, Maternal/Paternal Nonconflictual Environment, and Parental Legal and Illegal Drug Use. With the exception of the childhood aggression scales (which were measured when the children were 5 to 10 years of age), all scales were assessed when the adolescents were 16 to 21 years old.

[a]Composite measure.

Analytic Strategy

Three domains of predictor variables were examined. All these variables were found in previous research to be associated with legal or illegal drug use. Two series of logistic regression analyses were run, one for alcohol and one for marijuana. The effects of each domain were examined in separate regressions: One series of regressions compared nonusers and light users with moderate users, and the other series compared moderate users with heavy users and abusers. We controlled for both sex and age in all analyses. In addition to examining the main effects of the predictor variables, we also ran selected logistic regressions examining the interactive effects of these variables.

The major purpose of these analyses was to see which variables placed the adolescent at greatest risk for being in a higher as opposed to a lower drug-involvement group. Therefore, we transformed the logistic regression coefficients into odds ratios that compared the odds of being in the higher involvement group for those who were one standard deviation above the mean with those who were one standard deviation below the mean on each predictor variable.

Results

The percentages in each of the alcohol groups were as follows: nonuse or light use $= 29$; moderate use $= 59$; and abuse $= 11$. The percentages in the marijuana groups were as follows: nonuse or light $= 51$; moderate $= 40$; and heavy $= 9$.

Alcohol Findings

Logistic Regressions To Determine Unique Predictors of Alcohol Involvement

As previously described, to determine more precisely the unique and relative importance of various psychosocial factors associated with increased levels of alcohol use, six multivariate logistic regressions were carried out. In the first three regressions, personality, family, and peer factors served as the independent variables and nonuse or light use versus moderate use of alcohol served as the dependent variable. In the next series of three regressions, the same personality, family, and peer factors were examined to contrast moderate users of alcohol with alcohol abusers. The results of these regressions appear in Table 12.3, which presents the odds ratios for each significant predictor. We will discuss first those factors that increased the odds of being in a moderate as opposed to a nonuse or light alcohol-use group (see Column 1 of Table 12.3). Of the control variables, age, but not sex, was associated with greater involvement.

TABLE 12.3

Personality, Family, and Peer Risks Within Domains of Higher Levels of Alcohol Use/Abuse

Risk	Nonuse or light use vs. moderate use: Odds ratio	Moderate use vs. abuse: Odds ratio
Personality domain		
Aggression during childhood	0.62	3.13**
Acting out	1.55	2.83*
Incompetence	1.15	1.13
Tolerance of deviance	3.97**	1.78
Low ego integration	1.97	0.84
Sensation seeking	2.51**	2.22
Pathology	1.10	1.38
Family domain		
Maternal low attachment	2.10**	2.51**
Paternal low attachment	1.20	0.54
Parent legal drug use	1.20	1.49
Parent illegal drug use	1.15	1.65
Maternal permissiveness	1.06	1.75
Paternal permissiveness	1.72*	0.59
Peer domain		
Peer legal drug use	3.97**	2.36
Peer illegal drug use	1.58	2.94**
Peer deviancy	2.66**	2.14
Nonachieving friends	0.38	1.94
Time spent with friends	2.05**	1.20

Note. Age and sex were entered as controls. Each domain was examined separately. The odds ratios are for one standard deviation above the mean compared with one standard deviation below the mean.
*$p < .07$. **$p < .05$.

In the personality area, controlling for the other personality variables (plus sex and age), tolerance of deviance was the most important correlate distinguishing light from moderate alcohol use. Adolescents who were more tolerant of deviance were almost four times as likely to be moderate users than to be nonusers or light users. Adolescents who were more sensation seeking also increased their chances of being in the moderate alcohol-use group. In the family area, adolescents with low maternal attachment were twice as likely to be moderate users as were those with good attachment to mother. Similarly, paternal permissiveness was associated with greater alcohol involvement. There were three peer variables that increased the odds of being in the moderate rather than the non-user or light group: more friend legal drug use, more friend deviancy, and more time spent with friends. In general, variables within each of the domains of personality, family, and peers contribute to the pool of significant risk factors involved in moderate alcohol use. Furthermore, unconventional behavior, as expressed in tolerance of deviance and sensation seeking and greater acceptance of deviance (e.g., permissiveness) on the part of the parent, is expressed in the adolescent's moderate use of alcohol.

Regarding the results comparing moderate alcohol users with abusers in the personality domain, it is particularly striking that childhood aggression increased the odds of adolescent alcohol abuse threefold despite control on the acting-out variable measured during adolescence. As shown in Table 12.3, for those adolescents who engaged in more acting-out behavior, the risk of being in the alcohol-abuse group was almost tripled. The delayed effect of lack of behavioral control, as measured by the childhood aggression and adolescent acting-out measures, as well as peer modeling of illegal drug use, increased the odds of alcohol abuse. Low maternal attachment also increased the odds of being an abuser rather than a moderate user of alcohol. Both age and sex (being male) were associated with greater involvement and were controlled in the analyses discussed above.

Overall, more factors separated the nonusers and light users from the moderate users than separated the moderates from the abusers. It may be that when adolescents become moderate users, moderate use becomes the most important predictor of abuse and other factors assume less importance. It should be noted, however, that factors from all three domains predicted both moderate use and abuse.

Having identified the unique predictors in each of the domains, we then combined the significant predictors across domains in additional logistic regressions. As shown in Table 12.4, moderate alcohol use was related to an internal attitudinal characteristic, whereas alcohol abuse was associated with the more overt expression of aggression and acting-out behavior. In a related vein, moderate alcohol use was related to less serious forms of peer drug use, whereas alcohol abuse was associated with more serious forms of peer drug use.

Composite Risk Index and Its Impact on Moderate Use Versus Abuse of Alcohol

A composite risk index was developed to examine the effect of cumulative risks from all of the domains on increased involvement in alcohol—from moderate use to abuse (see Figure 12.1). As shown previously in Table 12.3, Column 2, there were four significant psychosocial predictors differentiating between these two groups: childhood aggression, acting-out behavior, maternal low attachment, and peer illegal drug use. For each of these

TABLE 12.4

Personality, Family, and Peer Risks Across Domains of Higher Levels of Alcohol Use/ Abuse

Risk	Odds ratio
Nonuse or light use vs. moderate alcohol use	
Tolerance of deviance	3.60*
Sensation seeking	1.65
Maternal low attachment	1.38
Paternal permissiveness	1.25
Peer legal drug use	3.67*
Peer deviancy	1.58
Time spent with friends	2.05*
Moderate alcohol use vs. alcohol abuse	
Aggression during childhood	2.61*
Acting out	2.61*
Maternal low attachment	0.98
Peer illegal drug use	3.52*

Note. Age and sex were entered as controls. The variables (risks) included were those that were significant ($p < .05$) when each domain was examined separately as shown in Table 12.3. *$p < .05$.

risk predictors, a score of *1* (risk) was assigned to the subjects in the top 25% of the distribution and a score of zero (nonrisk) was assigned to those in the bottom 75%. A cumulative score (ranging from *0* to *4* was then given to each subject on the basis of his or her total number of risks. This was the composite risk index, which was then examined in cross-tabular analysis with the two groups: moderate users and abusers. The results are depicted in Figure 12.1 and indicate clearly that as the total number of risks increased, so did the likelihood of being in the abuse rather than the moderate-use group. For example, for people with no risks, only 8% were in the abuser group, whereas, among those with four risks, 43% were abusers.

Marijuana Findings

Logistic Regressions to Determine Unique Predictors of Marijuana Involvement

As with the alcohol analyses, six logistic regressions were run. The first three examined separately the effects of variables in each domain on nonuse or light use compared with

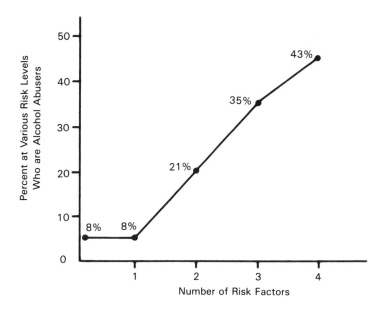

FIGURE 12.1   The effect of cumulative risk on moderate use versus abuse of alcohol. (For no risks, n = 96; one risk, n = 89; two risks, n = 53; three risks, n = 49; four risks, n = 7. N = 294.)

moderate marijuana use. The next three examined these variable effects on moderate compared with heavy marijuana use. Again, sex and age were entered as controls.

The factors associated with nonuse or light use compared with moderate use appear in the first column of Table 12.5, which shows that the personality factors associated with moderate involvement in marijuana use were similar to those that increased the risk for moderate alcohol use (see Table 12.3). Thus, the odds of being in the moderate as opposed to the nonuse or light use marijuana group were increased five times for those adolescents who were more tolerant of deviance and three times for those who were more oriented to sensation seeking. In addition, acting-out behavior also increased the likelihood of greater marijuana involvement. Three types of family mechanisms increased the odds of moderate marijuana use: attachment, control, and drug modeling. In the peer area, all of the variables except one (peer legal drug use) increased the risk of moderate versus nonuse or light marijuana use. Thus, the risks of moderate marijuana use in adolescents who were in drug-using peer groups and those who spent a great deal of time with their friends were 7.3 and 3.4 times higher, respectively, than for adolescents who were not in drug-using peer groups and who did not spend a great deal of time with

TABLE 12.5

Personality, Family, and Peer Risks Within Domains of Higher Levels of Marijuana Use/Abuse

Risk	Nonuse or light use vs. moderate use: Odds ratio	Moderate vs. heavy use: Odds ratio
Personality domain		
Aggression during childhood	1.49	1.65
Acting out	2.72**	3.13**
Incompetence	1.02	1.30
Tolerance of deviance	5.15**	0.82
Poor ego integration	0.79	1.97
Sensation seeking	3.00**	1.37
Pathology	1.08	0.43
Family domain		
Maternal low attachment	3.06**	0.98
Paternal low attachment	0.63	3.00**
Parent legal drug use	2.22**	0.71
Parent illegal drug use	0.92	1.46
Maternal permissiveness	0.99	1.75
Paternal permissiveness	1.72*	0.57
Peer domain		
Peer legal drug use	1.06	1.52
Peer illegal drug use	7.24**	2.77**
Peer deviancy	2.45**	1.10
Nonachieving friends	1.75**	1.68
Time spent with friends	3.39**	1.52

Note. Age and sex were entered as controls. Each domain was examined separately. The odds ratios are for one standard deviation above the mean as compared with one standard deviation below the mean.
*$p < .06$. **$p < .05$.

friends. Having deviant and nonachieving friends also added to the risks. Finally, age, but not sex, was related to being in the higher marijuana-use group.

The second column of Table 12.5 presents the results involving the predictors of moderate versus heavy marijuana use. There was only one significant predictor from each domain that increased the odds of being in the heavy-use group: Heavy use was 3.1 times likelier in adolescents who acted out, 3.0 times likelier in adolescents who reported paternal nonattachment, and 2.8 times likelier in adolescents who were involved with illegal-drug-using peers. For these groups, sex, but not age, was a significant predictor. Being male increased the risk of heavy use.

As with the alcohol-use comparisons, it appears that more factors differentiate non-users or light users from moderate users than differentiate moderate from heavy users. It should also be noted that adolescent acting-out and friend illegal drug use were particularly potent because they predicted risks for both comparative groups.

When comparing the marijuana-use groups with the alcohol-use groups, great similarity emerged in terms of both individual and domain predictors. However, there were some notable exceptions. Peer-group factors were more important for moderate use of marijuana than for alcohol, particularly in view of the odds ratio of 7.24 for friend illegal drug use, no doubt because of the different legal status of alcohol and marijuana. Whereas lack of maternal attachment significantly increased the odds for alcohol abuse, lack of paternal attachment was implicated in heavy marijuana use.

Having identified the unique psychosocial factors that are related to moderate and heavy marijuana use, we then combined significant predictors across the three psychosocial domains in two additional regressions. The results of these analyses appear in Table 12.6. Friend illegal drug use increased the odds of moderate use versus nonuse or light use almost five times and heavy marijuana use versus moderate use almost seven times. The attitudinal predictors were confined to moderate use.

The unique predictors of nonuse or light use versus moderate marijuana use are similar to those for nonuse or light use versus moderate alcohol use (see Table 12.4), with friend illicit drug use replacing friend licit drug use for the marijuana groups. Movement from moderate to heavy use, however, was different. Aggression during childhood and acting-out behavior were particularly potent in predicting alcohol abuse, whereas peer illegal use was the strongest predictor of heavy marijuana use.

Composite Risk Index and its Impact on Moderate vs. Heavy Marijuana Use
The basic strategy for the development of the composite risk index was described earlier. There were three risk predictors for discriminating between moderate and heavy marijuana users: acting-out behavior, friend illegal drug use, and low paternal attachment. Thus, the composite risk index ranged from scores of zero to 3. Using cross-tabular analysis, an examination was made of the composite risk index by the number of subjects who were heavy users compared with those who were moderate users. The results are illustrated in Figure 12.2. As shown in Figure 12.2, as the number of risks increased, so did the percentage of those who were heavy users. For example, of the people with no risks, only 5% were heavy users. Of those with three risks, 40% were in that group.

TABLE 12.6

Personality, Family, and Peer Risks Across Domains of Higher Levels of Marijuana Use/Abuse

Risk	Odds ratio
Moderate vs. nonuser or light user	
Acting out	1.08
Tolerance of deviance	4.22*
Sensation seeking	1.82
Maternal low attachment	1.43
Parental legal drug use	1.62
Paternal permissiveness	1.25
Peer illegal drug use	4.67*
Peer deviancy	1.62
Nonachieving friends	1.55
Time spent with friends	3.13*
Heavy vs. moderate user	
Acting out	2.05
Paternal low attachment	2.14
Peer illegal drug use	6.82*

Note. Age and sex were entered as controls. The variables (risks) included were those that were significant ($p < .05$) when each domain was examined separately as shown in Table 12.5.
*$p < .05$.

Interactive Effects on Moderate Use Versus Alcohol Abuse and Moderate Versus Heavy Marijuana Use

We now present only those interactive analyses that deal with movement into alcohol abuse or heavy marijuana use. The dependent variables in the following interactional analyses are moderate use versus abuse in the case of alcohol and moderate versus heavy use in the case of marijuana.

Because childhood aggression is an important early predictor, we first examined its interaction with both family and peer dimensions in the transition from moderate alcohol use to abuse. The findings indicated that only one interaction was significant, probably because of chance. Low childhood aggression interacted with low peer deviancy, decreasing the odds of alcohol abuse. The same analyses were done with moderate versus heavy marijuana use as the dependent variable. Two interactions were significant: Peer Illegal Drug Use × Childhood Aggression and Peer Deviancy × Childhood Aggression (see

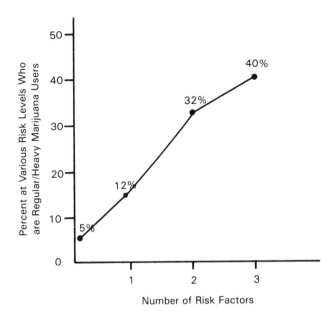

FIGURE 12.2   The effect of cumulative risk on moderate versus regular or heavy use of marijuana. (For no risks, n = 56; one risk, n = 68; two risks, n = 62; three risks, n = 20. N = 206.)

Figures 12.3 and 12.4). As shown in Figures 12.3 and 12.4, a protective personality trait such as low childhood aggression can be enhanced by protective peer factors (low peer illegal drug use and low peer deviancy), decreasing the odds of heavy marijuana use. In other words, low aggression serves as a protective factor unless the youngster is in a drug-using or deviant peer group.

Discussion

These findings lend some support to the interactional approach as espoused by Magnusson (1988), in that factors from all three domains predict both moderate and heavy drug involvement (alcohol abuse and heavy marijuana use; Jessor & Jessor, 1977; Sadava, 1987; Stein et al., 1987). Not all of the factors from all of the domains emerged as significant, which suggests that some selectivity is required for those investigators who take an interactional approach. For instance, we find that only specific psychosocial variables pose risks for alcohol abuse. Such variables include those related to personality (acting-out), familial attachment (maternal attachment), and peer modeling (friend illegal drug use). This suggests that the

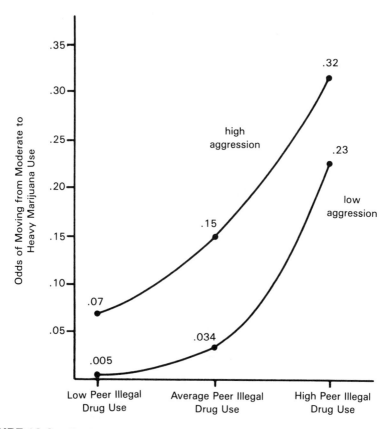

FIGURE 12.3   The interaction of peer illegal drug use and childhood aggression.

pathways to alcohol abuse may stem from personality factors and lack of familial attachment, as well as from the influence of peer models and the availability of drugs from peers. The importance of selected contributions from the various domains was also found for moderate alcohol use and moderate and heavy marijuana use.

A second delimitation to a generalized interactional approach is that many more factors are associated with transition to moderate than with transition to heavy use of drugs. One possible explanation is that because the number of adolescents involved in the latter transition is smaller, the statistical power for this group is not as great. Beyond this methodological point, it should be noted that the effects of psychosocial variables become less important once the effects of moderate drug use as a precondition for more severe drug abuse have had a chance to operate.

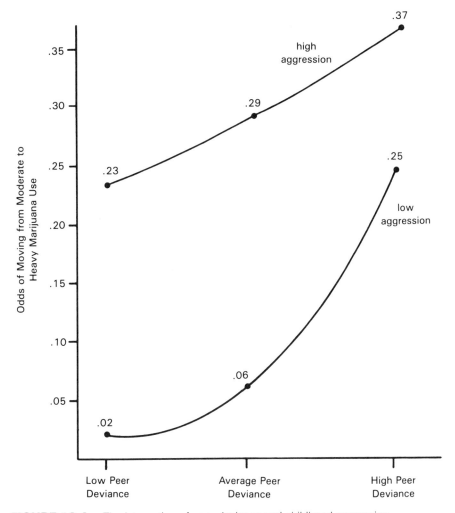

FIGURE 12.4 The interaction of peer deviance and childhood aggression.

Personality

The personality domain examined in this investigation is a complex one consisting of three subsets: (a) emotional distress, (b) aggression/acting-out, and (c) attitudinal unconventionality. Contrary to our expectation, the emotional-distress subset and its relation to alcohol and marijuana use was not significant in this study. Differences in reported intrapsychic distress were not related to either moderate or heavy use or abuse of alcohol or marijuana. Several possible interpretations for these findings are possible. First, the clinical literature suggests that heavy marijuana users and alcohol abusers may fail to report affective distress as a result of conscious or unconscious denial. Second, our measure of internal distress was based only on an assessment of psychological symptoms. Had we examined the relationship between psychopathology and drug use, it is possible that a significant relationship would have emerged.

In contrast with findings regarding more internal emotional distress, the aggressive/ acting-out syndrome was related to alcohol abuse and moderate and heavy use of marijuana. One might suggest several explanations for these results. First, acting-out adolescents, characterized by aggression, low responsibility, rebelliousness, and impulsivity, may find drugs attractive because they are a means of immediate gratification. Alcohol abuse and different degrees of marijuana use may be a consequence of the presence of both internal (difficulty in self-regulation of impulses) and external (the availability of drugs that are easily obtained) factors. Second, among aggressive and acting-out adolescents, alcohol abuse and marijuana use may be a manifestation of rebellion against familial and extrafamilial demands. These findings with regard to marijuana involvement are in accord with several recent investigations (D. W. Brook & Brook, in press; Newcomb & Bentler, 1988). However, with respect to alcohol abuse, previous studies have not demonstrated systematically the importance of the acting-out syndrome.

The third subset consists of adolescent unconventionality, which is expressed as tolerance of deviance and sensation seeking. This was related to moderate use of alcohol and marijuana, which supports previous findings in the literature (J. S. Brook, Whiteman, Nomura, Gordon, & Cohen, 1988; Jessor & Jessor, 1977; Newcomb & Bentler, 1988). However, these unconventional traits did not appear to be related to greater involvement in marijuana or alcohol abuse. It may be that unconventionality serves to move adolescents into moderate use but that a more basic and enduring personality constellation, characterized by impulsivity and aggression, is necessary for movement into abuse. Moreover, when adolescents become moderate users, moderate use becomes the most important predictor of abuse, and other factors assume less or no importance.

One particularly striking finding was that childhood aggression increased the odds of alcohol abuse threefold despite control on the acting-out variable measured during adolescence. Moreover, low childhood aggression in the context of low friend deviance and drug use tended to insulate the adolescent from heavy marijuana involvement. Aggression is important because it taps both emotional and behavioral undercontrol. Aggression takes on added importance because it is a stable trait and, thus, can have an impact on alcohol abuse despite intervening protective conditions. These findings are a special case of the more general formulations of Block and Kellam regarding the long-term significance of childhood aggression (Block, Block, & Keyes, 1988; Kellam, Brown, Rubin, & Ensminger, 1983). In the present study, we focused on childhood aggression as a unitary trait. What needs to be explored further is the complex relationship between aggression and the child's social surrounding. The child's aggression may either provoke the adverse reactions of others or predispose the child to identify with the aggressive behavior of others.

Family and Peer

Less mutual maternal attachment was an especially important predictor because it decreased the odds of moderate alcohol and marijuana use and alcohol abuse. These findings are in accord with our family interactional framework, which highlights the importance of an affectionate parent–child mutual attachment in which the youngster identifies with the parent (J. S. Brook et al., 1990). The results also add to earlier findings and further indicate that attachment is of importance as it relates to abuse, as well as to light and moderate use. Paternal permissiveness was also of importance, but in terms of moderate use, not alcohol abuse or heavy marijuana use. Dishion and Loeber (1985) reported that permissiveness was associated with greater use. However, it appears from our research that once adolescents become involved in moderate drug use, parental attempts at control are ineffective in preventing more serious drug use. Nor is there any evidence in the present study that drug abuse has an impact on the control techniques used by the parent.

We also found, as have other researchers, that friend drug use, deviance, and a great deal of time spent with friends are associated with moderate alcohol and marijuana use (D. W. Brook & Brook, in press; Kandel et al., 1978). Friend legal drug use probably increases the odds of an adolescent's drug use for two reasons: (a) It reflects the modeling of friends who are moderate users, and (b) it reflects the availability of drugs from those role models. Friend illegal use is especially potent because it increases the odds of alcohol abuse, as well as moderate and heavy marijuana use. It should also be noted that previous research has suggested that there is a bidirectional relationship between friend and self substance use or abuse (e.g., J. S. Brook et al., 1990; Kandel, 1985).

Multiple Risks

The findings of the present study indicate that alcohol abuse and heavy marijuana use are not only a function of specific individual risk factors, but are also related to the cumulated number of psychosocial risk factors. These findings support the coping model of

Pandina and his associates (e.g., Bry et al., 1982), which posits that adolescent drug involvement increases as the total number of risks the adolescent must cope with in his or her life increases. Additionally, our work supports their conclusion that examining risks from diverse areas of the adolescent's life increases the prediction of drug involvement. Multiple-risk models for drug use have also been used successfully to explain mental illness (Dohrenwend, 1973).

We have also demonstrated that a multiple-risk model is effective in predicting abuse, as well as heavy use. Although we have included a number of major psychosocial risk factors, our analysis, needless to say, has not been all-inclusive. It would be of interest in future investigations to add other psychosocial risk factors in order to determine whether their inclusion increases the adolescent's risk for alcohol abuse and heavy marijuana use.

Interactions

Our findings indicate that low childhood aggression interacts with low peer deviance and low peer illegal drug use, insulating the adolescent from heavy marijuana use. As shown previously, low aggression serves as a protective factor for later heavy marijuana use if the adolescent is not involved in later deviant and illicit drug-using peer groups. These findings therefore support a "Protective/Protective" mechanism: The least amount of drug use occurs among adolescents who are low on aggression during childhood and low on peer deviance and drug use during adolescence. The findings further support the importance of childhood aggression. Childhood resiliency, as assessed by low aggression, serves as a main effect for insulating the adolescent from alcohol abuse. In other situations, low childhood aggression acts as a moderating influence in its impact on heavy drug use. An inquiry that lies ahead for research on heavy drug use and abuse involves childhood aggression and how its potential influences conjoin with a variety of psychosocial factors in affecting drug use behavior in adolescents.

Conclusions and Implications for Prevention

On the basis of the variables that have been found significant for moderate and/or heavy ·drug use, one can put together a more general substance use/abuse pathway and more specific pathways to either alcohol or marijuana use/abuse. Figure 12.5 presents these alternative pathways. It can be seen from the General Pathway in Figure 12.5 that lack of attachment predisposes an adolescent to tolerance of deviance and to greater time spent with friends, which, in turn, are related to moderate substance use (alcohol and

GENERAL PATHWAY

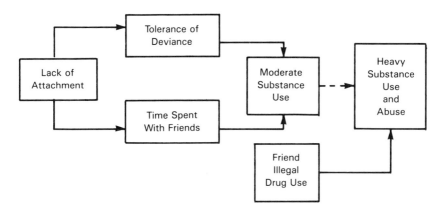

ALCOHOL PATHWAY

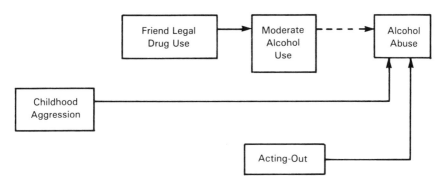

MARIJUANA PATHWAY

FIGURE 12.5 Pathways for general substance, alcohol, and marijuana use. (The broken arrows represent relationships not explored in this cross-sectional analysis, but based on consistent relations reported in the literature.)

marijuana). Moderate substance use is a usual condition for the progression to heavy substance use or abuse. In addition, friend illegal drug use is related to more serious substance involvement.

The pathways diverge somewhat when we deal with moderate alcohol use as compared with moderate marijuana use (see the Alcohol and Marijuana Pathways in Figure 12.5). In the former case, friend legal drug use emerges as important. In the latter case, friend illegal drug use comes to the fore. These results are understandable in light of the different legal status of alcohol and marijuana. When we turn to the comparison of alcohol abuse and heavy marijuana use, we note that the aggressive, acting-out syndrome is related to alcohol abuse but not to heavy marijuana use. The overall picture that emerges for substance abuse suggests a sequence of distancing from parents, resulting in both unconventional attitudes and greater involvement with peers, which in turn generates moderate use. Moderate substance use in the context of friend illegal drug use results in more severe substance use or abuse. In the case of more serious alcohol use or abuse, childhood aggression and adolescent acting-out emerge as more compelling factors for alcohol abuse than for heavy marijuana use. In the case of alcohol abuse, there is the possibility of reciprocal causation in the sense that childhood aggression predisposes to adolescent acting-out and alcohol abuse, and an instance of alcohol abuse may further exacerbate the existing tendency to abuse alcohol.

As noted above, friend legal drug use is a more significant factor in the case of moderate alcohol use, whereas friend illegal drug use becomes more potent in the case of moderate marijuana use. Therefore, given the relatively large amount of time spent with friends, the nature of the models the friends present (whether they are using legal or illegal drugs) will differentially affect whether the adolescent will use alcohol or marijuana. Friend illegal drug use increases the probability of heavy drug involvement, for both marijuana and alcohol.

Heavy substance use is influenced by two kinds of drug-imbued factors that tend to be proximal. These proximal variables include moderate substance use and friend illegal drug use. More general factors, such as tolerance of deviance, a great deal of time spent with friends, and lack of attachment, tend to be more distal. An exception to this general conclusion is childhood aggression, which, although distal, has a powerful impact on later alcohol abuse. This relationship might partially explain the association of alcohol abuse and violence.

To sum up, in addressing the issue of the prevention of heavy substance use and abuse, one can think of four sets of contributors, each of which contains variables that are either distal or proximal to problem drug use. The first set consists of personality variables, among which early childhood aggression would be a more distal factor, whereas adolescent tolerance of deviance or acting-out behavior would be more proximal. The second set of factors deals with lack of parent–child mutual attachment (distal), with an attendant turning to the peer group to satisfy developmental needs not met in the parent–child relationship (a more proximal factor). The third set of factors, which is relatively proximal in nature, centers on association with a drug-using culture, that is, friends who use legal and illegal drugs. The final link in the chain (and the one that is the most proximal to heavy use and abuse) is one's own moderate use of drugs along with having friends who use illegal drugs.

Intervention, then, can be viewed either from the developmental perspective (factors that are distal or proximal) or in an intervention mode (the particular set of factors to address). In thinking of a more distal intervention, one might focus on areas such as childhood aggression or lack of attachment, whereas a more proximal approach would deal with the adolescent's acting-out behavior (including moderate use of drugs) or contact with friends who use legal or illegal drugs. From the viewpoint of the interventional mode, one would try to focus on all domains where the child is at risk, but if this is not possible, addressing risks in any one area should reduce the chances of the adolescent's following the remaining pathways to drug use. For example, improvements in parent–child attachment should assist in preventing the adolescent from turning to deviant peers for support. In general, any intervention needs to incorporate not only the developmental stage, but also the mode of intervention: personality disposition, family alienation, or peer-group impact.

In conclusion, it is clear that the analysis of mediating and moderating effects on different degrees of drug involvement deserves more attention. The interactional perspective seems to be especially helpful in the conceptualization of adequate strategies for research on factors in the development of drug-use behavior.

References

Adler, P. T., & Lotecka, L. (1973). Drug use among high school students: Patterns and correlates. *International Journal of the Addictions, 8,* 537–548.

Alterman, A. I. (Ed.). (1985). *Substance abuse and psychopathology.* New York: Plenum Press.

American Psychiatric Association. (1987). *Diagnostic and statistical manual of mental disorders* (3rd ed., rev.). Washington, DC: Author.

Barnes, G. M., Farrell, M. P., & Cairns, A. (1986). Parental socialization factors and adolescent drinking behaviors. *Journal of Marriage and the Family, 48*, 27–36.

Baumrind, D. (1985). Familial antecedents of adolescent drug use: A developmental perspective. In C. L. Jones & R. J. Battjes (Eds.), *Etiology of drug abuse: Implications for prevention* (Research Monograph No. 56, pp. 13–44). Rockville, MD: National Institute on Drug Abuse.

Baumrind, D., & Moselle, K. A. (1985). A developmental perspective on adolescent drug use. *Advances in Alcohol and Substance Use, 5*, 41–67.

Block, J., Block, J. H., & Keyes, S. (1988). Longitudinally foretelling drug usage in adolescence: Early childhood personality and environmental precursors. *Child Development, 59*, 336–355.

Blumenfield, M., Riester, A. E., Serrano, A. C., & Adams, R. L. (1972). Marijuana use in high school students. *Diseases of the Nervous System, 33*, 603–610.

Brook, D. W., & Brook, J. S. (in press). Family processes associated with alcohol and drug use and abuse. In E. Kaufman & P. Kaufmann (Eds.), *Family therapy of drug and alcohol abuse: Ten years later.* New York: Gardner Press.

Brook, J. S., Brook, D. W., Gordon, A. S., Whiteman, M., & Cohen, P. (1990). The psychosocial etiology of adolescent drug use: A family interactional approach. *Genetic, Social, and General Psychology Monographs, 116*(2).

Brook, J. S., Whiteman, M., Brook, D. W., & Gordon A. S. (1981). Paternal determinants of male adolescent marijuana use. *Developmental Psychology, 17*, 841–847.

Brook, J. S., Whiteman, M., & Gordon, A. S. (1982). Qualitative and quantitative aspects of adolescent drug use: Interplay of personality, family, and peer correlates. *Psychological Reports, 51*, 1151–1163.

Brook, J. S., Whiteman, M., & Gordon, A. S. (1983). Stages of drug use in adolescence: Personality, peer, and family correlates. *Developmental Psychology, 19*, 269–277.

Brook, J. S., Whiteman, M., Gordon, A. S., & Brook, D. W. (1983). Paternal correlates of adolescent marijuana use in the context of the mother–son and parental dyads. *Genetic Psychology Monographs, 108*, 197–213.

Brook, J. S., Whiteman, M., Gordon, A. S., & Brook, D. W. (1984). Identification with paternal attributes and its relationship to the son's personality and drug use. *Developmental Psychology, 20*, 1111–1119.

Brook, J. S., Whiteman, M., Gordon, A. S., & Cohen, P. (1986a). Dynamics of childhood and adolescent personality traits and adolescent drug use. *Developmental Psychology, 22*, 403–414.

Brook, J. S., Whiteman, M., Gordon, A. S., & Cohen, P. (1986b). Some models and mechanisms for explaining the impact of maternal and adolescent characteristics on adolescent stage of drug use. *Developmental Psychology, 22*, 460–467.

Brook, J. S., Whiteman, M., Nomura, C., Gordon, A. S., & Cohen, P. (1988). Personality, family, and ecological influences on adolescent drug use: A developmental analysis. *Journal of Chemical Dependency Treatment, 1*, 123–162.

Bry, B. H., McKeon, P., & Pandina, R. J. (1982). Extent of drug use as a function of number of risk factors. *Journal of Abnormal Psychology, 91*, 273–279.

Cohen, P., & Velez, C. N. (1983). *Measures of psychopathology in a community sample of children* (Children in the Community project). Unpublished manuscript.

Derogatis, L. R., Lipman, R. S., Rickels, K., Uhlenhuth, E. H., & Covi, L. (1974). The Hopkins symptom checklist (HSCL): A self-report symptom inventory. *Behavioral Science, 19,* 1–15.

Dishion, T. J., & Loeber, R. (1985). Adolescent marijuana and alcohol use: The role of parents and peers revisited. *American Journal of Drug and Alcohol Abuse, 11,* 11–25.

Dohrenwend, B. S. (1973). Life events as stressors: A methodological inquiry. *Journal of Health and Social Behavior, 14,* 167–175.

Gold, M. (1966). Undetected delinquent behavior. *Journal of Research in Crime and Delinquency, 3,* 27–46.

Gough, H. G. (1957). *The California Psychological Inventory.* Palo Alto, CA: Consulting Psychologists Press.

Hamburg, B. A., Kraemer, H., & Jahnke, W. (1975). A hierarchy of drug use in adolescence: Behavioral and attitudinal correlates of substantial drug use. *American Journal of Psychiatry, 132,* 1155–1163.

Hawkins, J. D., Lishner, D., & Catalano, R. F. (1985). Childhood predictors and the prevention of adolescent substance use. In C. L. Jones & R. J. Battjes (Eds.), *Etiology of drug abuse: Implications for prevention* (Research Monograph No. 56, pp. 75–126). Rockville, MD: National Institute on Drug Abuse.

Huba, G. J., Wingard, J. A., & Bentler, P. M. (1980). Longitudinal analysis of the role of peer support, adult models, and peer subcultures in beginning adolescent substance use: An application of setwise canonical correlation methods. *Multivariate Behavioral Research, 15,* 259–279.

Jackson, D. N. (1974). *Personality Research Form.* Goshen, NY: Research Psychologists Press.

Jersild, A. T., Brook, J. S., & Brook, D. W. (1978). *The psychology of adolescence.* New York: Macmillan.

Jessor, R., Chase, J. A., & Donovan, J. E. (1980). Psychosocial correlates of marijuana use and problem drinking in a national sample of adolescents. *American Journal of Public Health, 70,* 604–613.

Jessor, R., & Jessor, S. L. (1977). *Problem behavior and psychosocial development.* San Diego, CA: Academic Press.

Jones, C. L., & Battjes, R. J. (Eds.). (1985). *Etiology of drug abuse: Implications for prevention* (Research Monograph No. 56; DHHS Publication No. ADM 85-1335). Rockville, MD: National Institute on Drug Abuse.

Kandel, D. B. (1978). *Longitudinal research on drug use.* Washington, DC: Hemisphere.

Kandel, D. B. (1980). Drug and drinking behavior among youth. *Annual Review of Sociology, 6,* 235–285.

Kandel, D. B. (1985). On processes of peer influences in adolescent drug use: A developmental perspective. *Advances in Alcohol and Substance Abuse, 4,* 139–163.

Kandel, D. B., Kessler, R. C., & Margulies, R. Z. (1978). Antecedents of adolescent initiation into stages of drug use: A developmental analysis. *Journal of Youth and Adolescence, 7,* 13–40.

Kaplan, H. B., Martin, S. S., Johnson, R. J., & Robbins, C. A. (1986). Escalation of marijuana use: Application of a general theory of deviant behavior. *Journal of Health and Social Behavior, 27,* 44–61.

Kay, E. J., Lyons, A., Newman, W., Mankin, D., & Loeb, R. C. (1978). A longitudinal study of the personality correlates of marijuana use. *Journal of Consulting and Clinical Psychology, 46,* 470–477.

Kellam, S. G., Brown, C. H., Rubin, B. R., & Ensminger, M. E. (1983). Paths leading to teenage psychiatric symptoms and substance use: Developmental epidemiological studies in Woodlawn. In S. B. Guge, F. J. Earls, & J. E. Barrett (Eds.), *Childhood psychopathology and development* (pp. 17–47). New York: Raven Press.

Khantzian, E. J. (1985). The self-medication hypothesis of addictive disorders: Focus on heroin and cocaine dependence. *The American Journal of Psychiatry, 142,* 1259–1264.

Kogan, L. S., Smith, J., & Jenkins, S. (1977). Ecological validity of indicator data as predictors of survey findings. *Journal of Social Service Research, 1,* 117–132.

Labouvie, E. W., & McGee, C. R. (1986). Relation of personality to alcohol and drug use in adolescence. *Journal of Consulting and Clinical Psychology, 54,* 289–293.

Magnusson, D. (1988). *Individual development from an interactional perspective: A longitudinal study.* Hillsdale, NJ: Erlbaum.

Newcomb, M. D., & Bentler, P. M. (1988). *Consequences of adolescent drug use: Impact on the lives of young adults.* Newbury Park, CA: Sage.

Newcomb, M. D., Maddahian, E., & Bentler, P. M. (1986). Risk factors for drug use among adolescents: Concurrent and longitudinal analyses. *American Journal of Public Health, 76,* 525–531.

Pandina, R. J., & Schuele, J. A. (1983). Psychosocial correlates of alcohol and drug use of adolescent students and adolescents in treatment. *Journal of Studies on Alcohol, 44,* 950–973.

Pandina, R. J., & White, H. R. (1981). Estimation of substance use involvement: Theoretical considerations and empirical findings. *International Journal of the Addictions, 16,* 1–24.

Penning, M., & Barnes, G. E. (1982). Adolescent marijuana use: A review. *International Journal of the Addictions, 17,* 749–791.

Sadava, S. W. (1987). Interactionist theories. In H. T. Blane & K. E. Leonard (Eds.), *Psychological theories of drinking and alcoholism* (pp. 90–130). New York: Guilford Press.

Schaefer, E. S. (1965). Children's report of parental behavior: An inventory. *Child Development, 36,* 413–424.

Schaefer, E. S., & Finkelstein, N. W. (1975, August). *Child behavior toward parent: An inventory and factor analysis.* Paper presented at the 83rd Annual Convention of the American Psychological Association, Chicago.

Smith, G. J., & Fogg, C. P. (1979). Psychological antecedents of teenage drug use. In R. Simmons (Ed.), *Research in community and mental health: An annual compilation of research* (Vol. 1, pp. 87–102). Greenwich, CT: JAI Press.

Stein, J. A., Newcomb, M. D., & Bentler, P. M. (1987). An eight-year study of multiple influences on drug and drug use consequences. *Journal of Personality and Social Psychology, 53,* 1094–1105.

Swaim, R. C., Oetting, E. W., Edwards, R. W., & Beauvais, F. (1989). Links from emotional distress to adolescent drug use: A path model. *Journal of Consulting and Clinical Psychology, 57,* 227–231.

Wingard, J. A., Huba, G. J., & Bentler, P. M. (1980). A longitudinal analysis of personality structure and adolescent substance use. *Personality and Individual Differences, 1,* 259–272.

Zuckerman, M., Eysenck, S., & Eysenck, H. J. (1978). Sensation-seeking in England and America: Cross-cultural, age, and sex comparisons. *Journal of Consulting and Clinical Psychology, 46,* 139–149.

CHAPTER 13

A Developmental Psychopathology Model of Drug Abuse Vulnerability

Meyer D. Glantz

I nvestigation into the etiology of drug abuse is more than just curiosity about the origin of this destructive pathological behavior. An understanding of the causal patterns and factors leading to drug abuse is crucial for effective prevention and treatment.

The term *abuse* is not used here to refer to the entire range of involvement with illegal drugs. Although there is no clear demarcation indicating the transition from use to abuse, the two terms do, at least toward the extremes, connote qualitatively different phenomena. *Use* implies, at least at the lower end of its connotative range, controlled, quantity- and frequency-limited consummation of the drug without necessarily (i.e., definitionally) having significant adverse consequences; this level of use typically does not play a major role in the psychological function of the user. This use of the term is not meant to imply that use is benign or that there is any level of drug involvement that is not potentially problematic and dangerous. Rather, the distinction of the terms *use* and *abuse* is intended to acknowledge that there are gradations of involvement with drugs and that different characteristics and etiologies are associated with individuals involved at these

The author would like to thank Ralph Tarter, Roy Pickens, Zili Amsel, and Linda Gerson for their comments on earlier versions of this chapter.

The views expressed in this chapter are those of the author and do not necessarily represent the opinions or policies of the National Institute on Drug Abuse or the Federal Government.

different gradations. The term *abuse* refers to the higher levels of drug involvement. Abuse implies that the individual has lost easy voluntary control over drug use and the ready ability to terminate repetition of the behavior. Abuse indicates that the use of the drug has become a goal in itself; severe abusers function as if they literally "need" the drug. Abuse invariably leads to serious adverse consequences, probably including impairment in at least one important area of function. The abuser continues the drug use despite problems caused by it. *Drug abuse* denotes that the behavior has taken on the characteristics of a psychopathological behavior. Typically, the abuser is physiologically and/or psychologically dependent on the drug, and its use has become a major coping mechanism in the individual's repertoire.

In research and clinical settings, abuse is commonly defined according to a consequences-oriented problem-based classification system such as the *Diagnostic and Statistical Manual of Mental Disorders* (American Psychiatric Association, 1987) or the generally comparable *International Classification of Diseases* (World Health Organization, 1980) or through the use of a quantity–frequency measure of drug use. These standard definitions and criteria for drug abuse are accepted and implied in the chapter. As usually employed, the term *drug abuse* does not include the abuse of alcohol or other legal substances. Although there is probably heuristic value in considering alcohol abuse and alcoholism to be a subset of drug abuse, the term will be used here to refer only to illegal psychoactive substances, and this paper will focus on the abuse of illegal drugs.

Drug abuse etiology has been largely unexplored until recently. The majority of etiological research either has focused on the etiology of use or has failed to discriminate between use and abuse. Because at least some level of experience with alcohol and/or illicit drugs is highly prevalent in our society, and because the majority of users do not make the transition to abuse, it is clear that the etiology of abuse, as distinct from the etiology of use, is a critical issue. This is reinforced by the observation that the determinants of use are not necessarily the determinants of abuse. Part of the reason that so much of the previous etiological research did not focus on abuse was that the general models and underlying assumptions being made about drug abuse did not direct researchers to make the distinction.

Successful determination of the etiology of drug abuse depends, in part, on accurately structured conceptual models and valid basic assumptions to guide research. The basic drug-abuse conceptualization or model that is employed has considerable impact on the ways in which research is planned, related data are evaluated, and intervention decisions are made. For the most part, two general, often contrasting models have dominated the construal of drug abuse in the research and intervention communities and, to some extent, in the general public. These models are presented here in the form of polarized, extreme statements of these perspectives. This use of "strawman" characterizations is intended to emphasize the respective natures of these conceptions and to contrast their differences. The first of these models, in large part a reflection of the societally dominant perspective, views drug abuse primarily as a product of social and pharmacological forces.

The Social–Pharmacogenic Model

The social–pharmacogenic model asserts that virtually any use of an illegal drug by any person carries risks of significant detrimental consequences and strongly facilitates subsequent use, possibly to the point of abuse and dependence. Therefore, any use of illegal drugs is extremely dangerous and unsanctionable. This perspective, in combination with certain pragmatic and other factors, has led to a policy and research orientation for much of the concerned community in which any but the most nominal levels of drug use are construed as undifferentiated abuse perpetrated by a (largely) undiscriminated class of abusers. Tacitly incorporated into this model is the notion that drug abuse is a linear extension of drug use, differentiated only as a matter of degree on a single continuum, and the idea that initial and early-stage use, perhaps in combination with certain other contributive factors, is the virtual "cause" of drug abuse. For some, allied inferences suggest that the risk for drug abuse is only moderately individualized once exposure has occurred and that the drugs themselves are such powerful neuropharmacological influences that it is their characteristics that are the virtual "cause" of drug abuse (as opposed to the characteristics of the abusers themselves). Escalation is strongly mitigated by exposure-related variables. In general, escalation is seen as being caused by a combination of drug related effects and continued social pressures. Protective factors are primarily those that insulate individuals from the influences of deviant drug abusing peers who support both initiation and escalation.

This social–pharmacogenic model logically leads to a number of conclusions, including the following: The appropriate goal of a drug abuse prevention intervention is the prevention of absolutely any illicit drug or alcohol use. Drug abuse presentation programs can follow a generic model basically applicable to most populations, and most populations should be targeted to an approximately comparable degree. A zero-tolerance prevention goal is feasible. Risk prior to any initial drug involvement is generally low, and involvement with drugs is readily resistible if the appropriate attitudes and beliefs have been instilled. The social–pharmacogenic model asserts that illicit drug involvement, particularly drug initiation, is the product of exogenous influences. It is almost as if most individuals are "naturally" disinclined to use psychoactive substances, to which they may succumb because of external coercive forces. Preventive interventions should therefore educate about the problems of drug abuse and strengthen resistance skills: "No use guarantees no abuse."

According to this perspective, once an individual is abusing or is dependent on a given drug, the characteristics and consequences of the drug itself (in combination with continued peer pressure) are primarily responsible for the individual's resistance to cessation of use of the drug despite the obvious detrimental consequences of using the drug. Additionally, if a given drug (such as cocaine) is a powerfully seductive and addictive drug being abused by a large number of people, successful interdiction of the supply of that drug will, to a large extent, resolve the abuse problem. Treatment, to be successful, need only deal with the pharmacologically created physiological dependence and with removing the abuser from the influence of drug-using peers. This general type of model has been most commonly subscribed to by those involved with drug-abuse prevention programs.

In contrast with the social–pharmacogenic model is an alternative, more clinical model that most associated with nonpharmacologically oriented treatment programs and research.

The Clinical–Psychiatric Model

Although this alternative perspective acknowledges some contributive influences of particular drug effects and external social pressures, the endogenous characteristics of the individual are assumed to be primarily determinative of that individual's vulnerability to drug abuse. Drug abuse diathesis is assumed to be determined by intraindividual conditions existing prior to initial drug exposure; individuals are seen as differentially at risk for drug abuse or dependence both prior to and after drug use. Individuals may have a heightened susceptibility to a particular drug or type of drug; this increased vulnerability may be biologically based. However, according to this model, many, if not most, abusers are vulnerable to abuse (and perhaps, though not necessarily, to initial use) because of influences typically designated as psychological or psychiatric. Although acknowledging the potency of characteristics of abused drugs related to physical dependence and abuse liability, this model emphasizes psychological vulnerability and dependence. Environmental factors are assumed to play a minor role at most.

According to the clinical–psychiatric model, if high-risk individuals do not become involved with a given illicit drug, they will probably become involved with an alternative substance; if they somehow never became involved with the unsanctioned, inappropriate use of any drugs or alcohol, they will probably still manifest considerable dysfunctional or maladaptive behavior. Abusers are presumed to be looking for an effect rather than for a drug, and if an abuser's current drug of choice is not readily available, he or she will substitute an alternative, even one with significantly different pharmacologic effects, or will even engage in an alternative nondrug behavior intended to produce the desired effect. The particular drug of abuse is seen as almost incidental. Abusers may be drawn to a general type of drug, but their abuse is a dependence on an effect more than on the drug; drugs will be used in different fashions to produce different effects. According to this model, most drug abusers are polydrug abusers.

As viewed by the clinical–psychiatric model, drug abuse is not just a greater magnitude of use with the added complications of drug-use consequences, but is also a distinct psychopathological state. It is assumed that the psychiatric consequences of drug abuse only compound the preexisting preabuse psychiatric dysfunctions. It is implied by this model that high-risk individuals are not likely to respond to informational or resistance-strengthening prevention efforts. Initiation of low-level involvement with drugs may be a largely social phenomenon (at least for the general population), but escalation to and maintenance of higher levels of use is likely to be a more clinical–psychiatric phenomenon. This may be particularly true where the prevalence of adolescent drug or alcohol use is so high as to approach a virtual social norm. (An alternate view suggests that perhaps even the initial introductory use of psychoactive substances by future abusers is a distinct prodromal behavior.)

According to this model, although general population substance use prevention efforts are desirable, a second major prevention effort aimed specifically at individuals vulnerable to the transition from use to abuse is critical. Vulnerable potential abusers must be identified early and receive psychiatric treatment that targets the primary vulnerability-enhancing characteristics and their consequences. Impaired areas of function, premonitory or early stage psychopathologies, and dysfunctional social–familial environments will commonly be the appropriate targets of effective preventive interventions. Further complicating this, the influences that are determinative of an individual's initiating drug use may not be the same as those involved in escalating and maintaining the abuse, and even these factors may change over time and circumstances. In terms of this perspective, treatment must resolve the underlying psychiatric difficulties for it to be effective and lastingly successful. Protective factors will primarily be those related to or supportive of emotional and psychological well-being and controlled functioning. Treatment and prevention must be individualized to resolve the particular psychopathology of the individual.

Within the clinical–psychiatric model are hypotheses about the nature of the contributory psychopathologies; most fall into two general categories. The first, usually referred to as the "self-medication" hypothesis, assumes that the abuser is drawn to the use of drugs as a means of coping with (i.e., "treating") emotional distress and/or cognitive (often regulatory) dysfunctions. A more neurologically oriented version of the self-medication hypothesis proposes either that some individuals are "treating" a neurochemical-system impairment or that they have a heightened susceptibility to a drug or drugs because of their biologically determined responsiveness. The second general category of hypotheses about the nature of the contributing psychopathologies is based on the assumption that drug abuse is part of a cluster of psychopathological, deviant, antisocial behaviors and is etiologically related to antisocial personality disorder, sociopathy, and other severe conduct disorder pathologies.

There is, unarguably, considerable validity to both the social–pharmacogenic and the clinical–psychiatric models. However, both perspectives have serious limitations that impair their ability to provide the most useful directions for research and interventions. A first step in developing more accurate and heuristic models is a consideration of what is currently known about the etiology of drug abuse.

Research has identified a number of risk factors associated with the etiology of drug abuse; as used here, *risk factors* refers to those characteristics that are assumed to have causal influence. Although no single etiological pattern is likely to involve all of these factors, and although distinct patterns cannot be incontrovertibly described, the findings clearly point in certain directions and offer useful and substantiated implications. The following is a summary of the research-based data on those identified etiological influences that exacerbate an individual's vulnerability to abuse level involvement with drugs and that may serve early in the individual's life as potential identifiers and risk indicators of future drug abuse.

Drug-Abuse Risk Factors

Drug abusers are a heterogeneous group, and there are multiple patterns of abuse, each having numerous potential etiologies. There are many diverse pathways that may lead to substance abuse, and individuals are differentially at risk for engaging in drug use and for making the transition from drug use to drug abuse and dependence. The factors that are determinative of drug use are at least partly different from those leading to abuse (see Kandel, 1981). Drug abuse is a multiply determined behavior; it is not "caused" by a single antecedent factor. In fact, the greater the number and severity of any of the precursory risk factors, the greater the risk for drug abuse (Bry, 1983, 1989; Bry, McKeon, & Pandina, 1982; Maddahian, Newcomb, & Bentler, 1988). Protective factors (frequently the bipolar opposites of risk factors) may counterbalance or nullify risk factors (e.g., Brook, Whiteman, Gordon & Cohen, 1986; Labouvie and McGee, 1986). Even the simplest of etiological pathways are likely to involve a complex set of interacting factors. The contributing, predisposing, and protective factors may be genetic–physiological, psychological–psychopathological, familial–social, or environmental–cultural.

Family–Genetic and Neurological Factors

Substance abuse, antisocial personality disorder, certain affective psychopathologies, and criminal or delinquent behavior tend to cluster in families (e.g., Hesselbrock, 1986; Kosten, Rounsaville, & Kleber, 1985; Mirin, Weiss, & Michael, 1986). There appears to be a familial–genetic component to substance abuse (at least in some cases). Monozygotic twins are approximately twice as likely to be concordant for alcoholism as dizygotic twins, and this effect to be considerably greater for males than for females. It is estimated that approximately 30% of the variance of the (familial) transmission of alcoholism is attributable to genetic factors (Merikangas, 1990; Pickens et al., 1991). The genetic transmissibility of drug abuse (as a specific behavior) is not as clear, perhaps because of its highly heterogeneous nature. According to the only twin study of drug abuse, the drug-abuse concordance rate for monozygotic twins was significantly greater than for dizygotic twins for males but not for females (Pickens et al., 1991). Multigenerational (familial) and/or sibling psychopathology, as well as delinquent or criminal behavior or drug abuse, is a significant vulnerability factor (Kumpfer & DeMarsh, 1986). Males, who are generally at greater risk for drug abuse, appear to be particularly vulnerable to familial–genetic risk factors.

It is commonly known that drugs differ in their abuse liability, that individuals are differentially susceptible to various psychoactive substances, and that at least some drugs seem to be compatible with neurotransmitter receptor sites in the brain in such a way as to create a reinforcing effect on the user. The presumptive case for a neurobiological component to drug-abuse etiology is fairly strong. The heritable contribution to substance-abuse etiology also further supports arguments for a neurobiological component to the etiology of substance abuse. At least in some cases, neurological (particularly neurochemical) pathologies appear to play a role in susceptibility to drug abuse (e.g., King, Jones, Scheuer, Curtis, & Zarcone, 1990; Tarter, Alterman, & Edwards, 1985, 1989). Despite the probable neurochemical pathology involved in at least some patterns of drug abuse, risk for drug abuse does not generally appear to be highly specific for a particular substance. Rather, the risk seems to be for a class of drugs or a type of effect (e.g., Maddux & Desmond, 1989; Solomon & Corbit, 1974; Steele & Josephs, 1990; Wise, 1988; Wise & Bozarth, 1987), with the particular substance being abused determined by social and availability factors. Additionally, it is a common observation that, with the exception of some marijuana abusers, most drug abusers are polydrug abusers even though they typically have a drug of choice.

Deviance and Delinquency

Jessor and Jessor (1977) and Robins (1978) have proposed the notions of (respectively) a "problem behavior proneness" or a "deviance (antisocial) syndrome." These concepts refer to the observation that many types of adult deviant–antisocial behavior patterns are preceded during late childhood and early adolescence by a self-reinforcing cluster or cycle of "problem" behaviors. These behaviors typically include rejection of societal rules, goals, and values; uninvolvement with or rejection of traditional (e.g., religious) beliefs and structured, supervised organizations; some degree of alienation; resistance to authority; rebellious behavior; "problem" or illegal behaviors; and a high tolerance for deviance. This moderate level deviance and involvement with delinquent behaviors and peers facilitates and predisposes the individual toward an escalation of antisocial and deviant behaviors. Coupled with increasing life stresses, these aberrations in turn lead to still greater behavioral divergence, including the possibility of some form of substance abuse. The majority of problem-behavior children, and even of conduct disorder problem children and adolescents, do not develop into antisocial or drug abusing adults. However, early antisocial behaviors and deviance are strong risk factors for drug abuse (Donovan, Jessor, & Jessor, 1983; Elliott, Huizinga, & Ageton, 1985; Elliott, Huizinga, & Menard, 1989; Huizinga, Menard, & Elliot, 1989; Kaplan, Martin, Johnson, & Robbins, 1986; Kellam,

Brown, Rubin, & Ensminger, 1983; Loeber, 1985, 1988; Magnusson & Bergman, 1990; W. McCord & McCord, 1960; Robins, 1966; Robins & McEvoy, 1990; Robins & Wish, 1977; Rutter & Giller, 1983).

Gateway or Stepping-Stone Hypothesis

As described by Kandel's gateway or stepping-stone hypothesis (Kandel & Faust, 1975; Kandel, Kessler & Margulies, 1978), drug-involved adolescents typically progress through developmental stages of drug-use initiation, with each stage facilitating escalation to increasingly deviant and illegal substances. Initial research identified four sequential stages of involvement with drugs: (a) beer or wine, (b) cigarettes or hard liquor, (c) marijuana, and (d) other illicit drugs (having a higher abuse liability). Although subsequent research did not substantiate an inevitable fixed sequence for all populations, the basic stage concept has been verified as a common etiological pattern (Donovan & Jessor, 1983; Elliott et al., 1989; Greene, 1980; Huizinga et al., 1989; Newcomb & Bentler, 1986, 1990; Voss & Clayton, 1987).

Use and the characteristics of that use are clearly risk factors for abuse. Initiation of the use of an illegal substance is typically preceded by having or developing values supportive of that behavior; use of previous stepping stone stage substances may facilitate the acceptance of such values. Involvement with more socially and legally allowable psychoactive substances does appear to be a significant diathetic factor for, and facilitator of, subsequent use of illicit substances and possible dependence-level involvement with those substances. The research clearly shows that the earlier the drug involvement, the higher the drug use frequency, the faster the escalation of use, and the greater the abuse liability of the substances being used, the greater the risk of drug abuse being attained and maintained (Kandel, 1984; Kandel, Murphy, & Karus, 1985; Kaplan et al., 1986; Mills & Noyes, 1984; Robins & McEvoy, 1990; Robins & Przybeck, 1985; Welte & Barnes, 1985; Yamaguchi & Kandel, 1984).

Psychopathology and Psychological Factors

Psychopathology, sometimes in an early or premorbid stage, is a risk factor for drug abuse. Although a number of psychopathologies may have etiological impact, depression and antisocial–sociopathic personality disorder or characteristics have been most clearly and repeatedly identified in research (Alterman, Tarter, Baughman, Bober, & Fabian, 1985; Block, Block, & Keyes, 1988; Cadoret, Cain, & Grove, 1980; Cadoret, Troughton, O'Gorman, & Heywood, 1986; Christie et al., 1989; Deykin, Levy, & Wells, 1987; Grove et al.,

1990; Hesselbrock, Hesselbrock, & Stabenau, 1985; Muntaner et al., 1989; Newcomb & Bentler, 1990; Paton, Kessler, & Kandel, 1977; Ross, Glaser, & Germanson, 1988; Turnbull & Gomberg, 1988). The role of aggressiveness in the etiology of drug abuse is not clear (Loeber, 1988); some of the inconsistency in reports may relate to the ways in which aggressiveness is construed by those labeling the individuals' behavior. Aggressiveness probably has some role in at least some etiologic patterns (e.g., Stattin & Magnusson, 1989). Posttraumatic stress disorders, as well as the sequelae of childhood physical and sexual abuse, are also predisposing factors (Hendin & Pollinger-Haas, 1984; Robinowitz, Robers, Patterson, Dolan, & Alkins, 1981; Rohsenow, Corbett, & Devine, 1988).

Several aspects of impaired psychological function have been implicated in the etiology of drug abuse. One such contributive psychological dysfunction is a difficulty in emotional regulation (Block, 1971; Block et al., 1988; Brook, Whiteman, Gordon, & Cohen, 1989; Labouvie, Pandina, White, & Johnson, 1990; Lerner & Vicary, 1984; Marlatt, 1987; Tarter et al., 1985). A high behavior activity level in childhood, impulse control problems, hyperactivity (particularly in combination with aggression), and impaired behavioral self-regulation are also predisposing factors (Block et al., 1988; Cloninger, Sigvardsson, & Bohman, 1988; Gittelman, Mannuzza, Shenker, & Bonagura, 1985; Hechtman, Weiss, & Perlman, 1984; Kramer & Loney, 1982; Loney, 1988; Shedler & Block, 1990; Tarter & Edwards, 1988; Tarter, Laird, Kabene, Bukstein, & Kaminer, 1990).

Emotional distress, difficulties in coping, and psychological maladjustment are contributing antecedents to drug abuse (Gomberg, 1982; Huba, Newcomb, & Bentler, 1986; Kandel & Raveis, 1989; Kaplan et al., 1986; Labouvie, 1987; Newcomb & Bentler, 1990; Pandina & Schuele, 1983; Shedler & Block, 1990). Personal and social maladjustment, difficulties in forming healthy relationships, lower levels of social support, social integration and connectedness, and impaired interpersonal problem-solving facilities are also risk factors (Carman, 1979; Jones, 1968; Kaplan et al., 1986; W. McCord & McCord, 1960; Newcomb & Bentler, 1990; Shedler & Block, 1990). Findings on low self-esteem as an etiological factor are inconsistent. This may be due in part to measurement and construct conceptualization problems, to the failure to distinguish use from abuse in the research, or to other issues related to drug abusers' defenses of their self-image. However, as some studies have reported, it seems likely that low (or perhaps fragile) self-esteem is involved in some etiological patterns (Kaplan, 1977; Newcomb & Bentler, 1990; Shedler & Block, 1990). Dropping out of school is a risk factor (e.g., Holmberg, 1985; National Institute on Drug Abuse, 1990). This factor, although not necessarily an antecedent to drug involvement, may be related to low self-esteem, low involvement in traditional social institutions and values, poor relationship with parents, environmental stress, and/or, possibly, psychological dysfunctions as etiological factors.

There appears to be considerable credibility to the supposition that drug *use* is more a product of social, situational, and environmental determinants, whereas drug *abuse* is, to a much greater extent, the consequence of biological, psychological, and psychiatric determinants. The social–pharmacogenic model is probably not descriptive of a common drug-abuse etiology pattern because of its underestimation of endogenous factors. Nevertheless, social factors exert major contributive influences on drug abuse. The failure to consider the important role of these influences is a major weakness of the clinical–psychiatric model.

Social and Environmental Factors

Family Factors

A number of family-related factors facilitate the development of both drug use and abuse. These include poor quality of the parent–child relationship and of the parent–child attachment, severe family disruptions including divorce and psychiatric disturbance, poor quality of parenting, and parental and sibling drug use and attitudes supportive of drug use and deviance (Brook, Brook, Gordon, Whiteman, & Cohen, 1990; Brook, Whiteman, & Gordon, 1983; Brook, Whiteman, Nomura, Gordon, & Cohen, 1988; Cadoret, Troughton, Merchant, & Whitters, 1990; Cadoret et al., 1986; Cohen, Brook, Cohen, Velez, & Garcia, 1990; Hechtman et al., 1984; Hirschi, 1969; Jessor & Jessor, 1977; Johnson, Schoutz, & Locke, 1984; Jurich, Polson, Jurich, & Bates, 1985; Kandel et al., 1978; Kaplan et al., 1986; Kumpfer, 1987; Kumpfer & DeMarsh, 1986; W. McCord & McCord, 1959; Rhodes & Jason, 1990; Shedler & Block, 1990; Thorne & DeBlassie, 1985; Vaillant & Milofsky, 1982).

Peer Factors

Association with drug-using peers is a powerful predictor of drug use. Peer influences are important in influencing initiation of, and lower levels of, illicit drug use (e.g., Bank et al., 1985; Elliott et al., 1985; Kandel, 1985; Needle et al., 1986; Swaim, Oetting, Edwards, & Beauvais, 1989). Additionally, drug users maintain drug-using peer networks (e.g., Kandel, 1984), and there appears to be considerable similarity between the drug use of an individual and the drug use of that individual's peers (e.g., Kandel, Davies, & Baydar, 1990). However, a clear contributive effect of association with drug-using peers to the transition from drug use to abuse has not been demonstrated (e.g., Kaplan et el., 1986). There is, however, some evidence of peer influence on greater levels of use in the earlier stages of drug involvement (Brook, Whiteman, & Gordon, 1982; Kandel & Yamaguchi, 1985). It remains possible that future research on involvement with drug-using peers will identify stronger drug abuse etiological effects. It is important to note that the contributive effects of peer and family influences are likely to be different during different stages and periods of the individual's life.

Environmental Factors

Socioeconomic status has not been shown to have a strong direct impact on drug abuse etiology (see Brook et al., 1988). However, certain associated factors do seem to play a contributive role. Growing up in a high crime neighborhood, living in a community with a ready availability of drugs and an accepting attitude toward their use, and association with delinquent peers are contributive influences on drug-abuse etiology (Brook et al., 1988; Clayton & Voss, 1981; Cohen et al., 1990; Elliott et al., 1985; Robins & McEvoy, 1990; Westermeyer, 1979). Severe environmental stress and other related environmental factors can also facilitate drug abuse (e.g., Hampton & Vogel, 1973; Robinowitz et al., 1981; Robins, 1974; Westermeyer, 1976). Some of the ethnic and other group differences in drug use and abuse that have been reported may be attributable to differences in environmental influences.

Enhancing Drug-Abuse Etiology Models

It is highly unlikely that all of the etiological influences that have been identified are involved in any single etiological pattern. There may be some etiological paths that are more genetically and biologically determined and others that are more socially influenced. Some may be largely psychiatric in nature; one common pattern may involve the conduct disorder – antisocial personality disorder cluster that has been observed, and another may be primarily a function of impaired affect or behavior regulation. The social–pharmacogenic and clinical–psychiatric models may both be valid in the sense that they each represent different paths that different subgroups of abusers have followed. However, most etiologic patterns probably do not involve only one primary type of factor. Rather, the most valid models of drug abuse are likely to be systemic ones in which drug abuse is understood to result from a complex of endogenous and exogenous factors that interact developmentally over time. Therefore, a synthesis of the social–pharmacogenic and clinical–psychiatric models is likely to be more accurate and more useful than either of these models applied individually. Incorporating a developmental orientation into the synthesis is likely to enhance it even further.

A developmentally oriented drug abuse etiology model emphasizes the origin of the risk for drug abuse as evolving, particularly during the maturational period of the individual. The factors constituting the risk are not constant but develop through the interactions of the individual with his or her environment and in the context of that individual's progression through the stages and maturational tasks of growing up. Vulnerability develops, and in this sense it is not just a set of static, predisposing antecedent factors, but rather a dynamic process. No single vulnerability factor is the "cause" of drug abuse by itself; instead, it is a contributive component in an interactive system that leads to emergent factors that in turn interact and evolve. Any single risk factor must be understood as having its etiological influence in the context of many other factors with which it interacts over time, probably developing through a number of transformations, eventually leading to heightened vulnerability to drug abuse. Thus, a given factor may have a different contributive effect at different developmental periods. Similarly, a factor's contribution will vary in the context of the particular other factors with which it interacts. Particular combinations of characteristics and circumstances interacting over time will differentially predispose an individual to, or protect him or her from, vulnerability to drug abuse.

A developmental psychopathology model of drug abuse emphasizes both the psychopathological nature of drug abuse and its etiology, as well as the developmental character of the etiology. Many forms of psychopathology have identifiable prodromal manifestations during childhood. It is hypothesized that certain patterns of drug (and alcohol) abuse have etiologies that begin in early childhood with detectable and predictable deviations from normal behavior. The particular model proposed here is not assumed to be relevant to all possible patterns and forms of drug abuse, but is hypothesized to be relevant to a sizable group of abusers. The particular drug or drugs that are used will not discriminate those to whom the model applies; the distinguishing characteristic is the pattern of abuse, a pattern in which the lives of the abusers and their psychological functioning are characterized by the integral role that drug use plays. These are individuals whose abuse is strongly founded in psychological and psychopathological dysfunctions, the origins of which begin early in childhood. In general, these precursory characteristics do not typically manifest themselves as severe, blatant, highly dysfunctional childhood psychopathology, but rather as moderate deviations and deficits in functioning that are exacerbated rather than compensated for by the environment.

I assumed here that maturation includes a sequence of developmental transitions and that infants have temperament characteristics. Some of these characteristics have at least some degree of enduring continuity subject to endogenously and exogenously influenced transformations. The behavioral expression of temperament characteristics is directed by age- and stage-related factors, as well as by environmental context. For example, a high behavior-activity level in an infant and in that same child at 7 years of age may be assumed to demonstrate some continuity, although its manifestation will be very different at the different ages. It is also assumed that an important determination of the course of a child's development is the compatibility between the child's characteristics and the characteristics of the parents and caretakers. These interactions will in turn be strongly influenced by environmental circumstances. For example, a difficult-to-soothe infant being raised by intolerant, frustrated parents living under stressful circumstances will almost certainly develop differently than an "easy" baby being cared for by affectionate, attentive parents living in a supportive, high-resource environment.

The application of a developmental perspective to the etiology of drug abuse is certainly not a new idea. For example, both the gateway hypothesis and the problem-behavior-proneness model are essentially developmental concepts. Many researchers have incorporated some developmental orientation into their research on and depictions of drug use and abuse etiology (e.g., Baumrind & Mosell, 1985; Brook et al., 1990; Greenspan, 1985; Hawkins, Lishner, Catalano, & Howard, 1985; Huba & Bentler, 1982; Huizinga et al., 1989; Jessor & Jessor, 1977; Kellam et al., 1983; Kumpfer & DeMarsh, 1986; Loeber, 1990; McCord, 1988; Robins, 1984; Vaillant, 1983). Most conceptualizations of drug-abuse etiology that do include some developmental concepts are limited by both the range of factors and dimensions and the time spans of the periods and stages that they encompass.

A Developmental Psychopathology Model of Drug Abuse Etiology

One possible developmental psychopathology model of drug-abuse etiology will be presented here. It is based on a synthesis of the research as reviewed above and on basic principles of development and developmental psychopathology. It differs from most etiological models in terms of its developmental psychopathology orientation and its inclusion of early-infancy antecedents. Hopefully, this model is useful and accurately describes a prevalent pathway leading to drug-abuse vulnerability. However it is not expected that this would be the only possible etiological pathway involving developmental psychopathology characteristics. The proposal is primarily intended to be illustrative and to focus attention on certain types of patterns and processes hypothesized to play an important determinative role in the etiology of some severe forms of drug abuse. Given the research findings on which this model is based, it is probable that it is more relevant to males than to females.

Neonatal Period (0–3 Months)

The high-risk child hypothesized here begins infancy with many of the temperament characteristics associated with the "difficult child," a pattern described in the temperament-characteristics classification formulated by Chess and Thomas (1984). It is postulated that at this stage, the high risk child has the following characteristics:

- A higher than average lability and intensity of affect; both the frequently expressed negative affect and the less frequently expressed positive affect are intensely (and loudly) expressed;
- a lower (than normal) capacity to habituate to new stimuli or to adapt to change; negative affect expression or withdrawal would be the more common response; lower ability to self-calm or self-organize;
- greater than average persistence of response to discomfort;
- early stage development of state control or self-regulation is lower than average;
- lower than average orientation to people;
- lower than average response to calming by caregivers; lower than average positive response to cuddling and other presumably positive contact with people; and
- lower than average regularity of biological cycles, for example, difficult sleeping or feeding patterns.

Given that there is some degree of instability of temperament characteristics until at least the third month of life (see Green, Bax, & Tsitsikas, 1989), a purely temperament-based model would probably describe hypothesized antecedents beginning with age 3 months. The model proposed here incorporates the earlier period to emphasize that temperament alone does not account for the developing vulnerability. Vulnerability is viewed here as the product of the interaction of the characteristics of the child with the individuals and experiences of the environment. In terms of the infancy period, a "difficult" temperament alone is not a sufficient condition for subsequent drug abuse. Whatever heightened risk a "difficult" infant might have because of this temperament factor might readily be compensated for or nullified by numerous other influences, particularly by the parents during infancy. However, instead of having parents who could adjust to and compensate for their infant's difficult characteristics, the high risk child's parents respond with frustration, intolerance, and possibly detachment. The problems of the child and the developing vulnerability are exacerbated. It is this incompatibility between the characteristics of the parents and the child, or the "poorness of fit" (see Chess & Thomas, 1984), that is the crucial condition during this early developmental period. Given a sufficient level of parental intolerance and of lack of affectionate interaction, even an "easier" baby might begin to develop a more high risk pattern. Because the primary caregiver is commonly the mother, the quality of her response is particularly influential. The parents' style of dealing with their child may be exacerbated by environmental stresses and insufficient social and functional resources.

It is reasonable for the proposed model to consider hypotheses about the possible contribution of parental substance abuse to the temperament or other difficulties of the high risk child. Even independent of the potential genetic implications and teratogenic effects of maternal–paternal drug and/or alcohol abuse, the possible negative consequences of parental substance abuse for the offspring are considerable. If nothing else, it would certainly not be expected that alcoholics and drug abusers would be good parents or good role models. Of relevance to drug abuse etiology, the possible genetic, teratogenic, behavioral, neglect, and abuse consequences of parental alcohol and/or drug abuse may lead to effects for the offspring that not only are harmful, but that in some cases, particularly predispose the offspring to developing his or her own subsequent substance abuse. Although the proposed model does not attempt to parcel out or make specific predictions of these effects, it is expected that parental substance abuse would, probably through several different means, exacerbate vulnerability to substance abuse in the offspring. Therefore, it is expected that the hypothesized high risk child is more likely to have a parent or parents who have been or currently are involved in substance abuse.

Infancy (3–10 Months)

The characteristics of the high risk-child during this period are a direct extension of the hypothesized neonatal-period regulatory difficulties and early infant–parent relationship difficulties. During this period, the infant's difficult temperament continues (or perhaps begins), the infant–parent incompatibility grows, and because of the problematic parental response, the infant's difficulties probably worsen. The high-risk child manifests the following characteristics during infancy:

- Lower than average attachment to primary caregivers; an impaired capacity to form strong affective relationships and attachments; behavior less social and interactive than average;

- a higher insistence on attention from and proximal contact with caregivers despite lack of attachment and general sociability; greater than average separation anxiety; the child is likely to be viewed as being demanding while providing little reinforcement for those attempting to meet the child's needs;
- impairment in other early stage social skills such as the ability to discriminate the moods of the caregiver;
- difficulty in appropriately integrating, differentiating, and self-regulating emotional states; behavior more a function of internal stimuli and states; poorer than average "turntaking";
- difficulty in organizing experiences in an interactive (i.e., cause and effect) pattern; combined with the parents' difficulties in meeting the child's needs and their lowered responsiveness, this exacerbates the infant's experience of environmental noncontingency and minimizes the infant's sense of security (i.e., that the world has structure and will meet his or her needs);
- lower than average formation of contingency relationships with interpersonal and external world; lower than average differentiation of self and other; and
- lower adaptability and flexibility and deficit in the foundation of coping style.

Two of the most important tasks for the first 6 to 8 months are the formation of a primary attachment to the parents and the preliminary organization of sensory motor function, including rudimentary self-regulation. For the high risk child, by the end of the infancy period, a poor attachment to the caregiver is established and the skills that form the foundation for later coping mechanisms, self-regulation, and social relationships are somewhat compromised. These deficits are the foundations of serious developing dysfunctions.

Toddler Period (1–2 Years)

A critical developmental issue for this age period is the child's beginning exploration, experimentation, and mastery of the environment. The high risk child does not have a successful attachment to the parents, and they are therefore not able to serve as a secure base from which to explore and begin to have an effect on the environment. As the 1-year-old high risk child develops more skills and autonomy, the nascent dysfunctions become more evident and continue to develop. The high-risk child manifests the following characteristics at this stage:

- Continued poor attachment to parents; difficulty with affiliative behavior with others;

- frequent negative affect and complaint;
- lower than average behavior self-control, higher overall activity level, shorter attention span, greater distractibility;
- greater than average level of general insecurity;
- higher than average occurrence of both aggressive behavior and temper outbursts;
- polarized behaviors and highly dichotomized (i.e., "black–white") conceptualizations; and
- lower than average capacity to conceptualize and predict causes and effects and lower than average ability to organize behavior in such a manner as to have desired effects on aspects of the environment and on other people.

Parental style is likely to be more unresponsive, inflexible, unaffectionate, and non-supportive, and perhaps even more hostile than average. The high risk toddler is likely to have a lower than average social orientation and to have made less progress in developing a sense of security with others and a sense of effectiveness in the environment. The parents are unlikely to foster the development of successful autonomy, and this may contribute to enduring dependency problems or conflicts for the child. The high risk child is less likely than average to have some of the typical supportive underpinnings of this period, such as comforting parent–child games, routines, and rituals. Other individuals in the environment, such as siblings, extended family, and other child care providers, do not compensate for the problems of the high risk child and therefore have a lowered level of involvement with him or her.

Preschool Period (3–4 Years)

Opportunities and capacity for children to interact with peers typically increase for children of this age. However, the high risk child does not function well in this arena, and his or her interpersonal difficulties continue to develop during this period. Regulatory and mastery difficulties also continue. As with the interpersonal difficulties, these problems become more evident as they become more relevant to age appropriate demands and behaviors, and the normal social and other mastery successes and reinforcements are missed. During this stage, the high risk child demonstrates the following:

- Lower than average affective investment in interpersonal contacts and relationships and other external objects and events; compared with their peers, the high risk child has made less progress in developing social skills and peerrelationships;

- deficit in foundations of ego functioning, including lower than average reality testing, organization of thoughts, and ability to delay gratification; symbolic conceptualizations may be more primitive than average;
- higher than average negative affect, affective lability, intensity expression, and orientation;
- lower than average capacity to regulate impulses and higher activity level;
- more frequent than average aggressive "preantisocial" behavior; and
- less developed than average problem solving strategies, more rigid and stereotyped concepts and conceptualizations; less effective and valid world view.

Findings from the longitudinal Berkeley, California study (Block et al., 1988) lend support for most of these early preschool period hypotheses. In addition to the predictions about high risk children at this age, the present model predicts that the parents' child rearing practices are more manifestly problematic. The parent–child problems foster a lack of autonomy, poor problem solving, and low self-esteem. The parents of these hypothesized high risk children typically employ performance contingent approval and affection; the children are more likely than average to have a developing self-image of being a "bad boy (or girl)."

Early School Period (5–7 Years)

Children commonly enter some type of school setting around age 5. The high risk child is less able than his or her peers to adapt and respond to the achievement, performance, and behavior control demands of this new environment. In relation to the social deficits of the high risk child, it is likely that he or she is not affiliated with the dominant "normal" peer group cluster; the high risk child is likely to be associated with a subgroup that is mildly deviant or not to have a strong peer group affiliation at all. The sense of "not being liked" or not being worth liking will probably continue or worsen.

The following characteristics are hypothesized for the high risk child at this stage:

- A compromised bond and relationship with parents that is not compensated for by relationships with other family members, teachers, or others in *loco parentis*; lack of any close, affectionate noncontingent relationships;
- poor peer relationships and impaired social skills; less than average integration into social system; lower capacity for empathy;
- greater than average negative affect, which is probably denied;
- lower capacity to organize, regulate, and control emotions and impulses;

- impulsivity possibly manifested as conduct problems and/or aggressiveness;
- predominantly low self-image and lower than average sense of competence, probably denied; lower than average self-reliance;
- lower than average internalization of the concepts of *fairness* and *right and wrong*;
- lower than average conceptualizing and problem solving ability;
- vulnerability to stress, including distortions in reality testing when stressed;
- poor or inconsistent school achievement; and
- difficulty in balancing and satisfying own needs in the context of practical considerations and the needs of others.

Several longitudinal research studies have related observations of subjects at this age period to subsequently greater involvement with drug use or abuse. Considerable consensus is evident. Drawing on data from the New York Longitudinal Study, Lerner and Vicary (1984), using Chess and Thomas's (1984) temperament classification, found that "difficult" temperament at age 5 was predictive of more severe tobacco, alcohol, and marijuana use in adulthood. Kellam et al. (1983) reported that the Woodlawn, Chicago studies found that aggressiveness, and to a greater extent aggressiveness plus shyness, in males measured in the first grade (age 6–7 years) was a strong predictor of increased teenage cigarette, alcohol, and marijuana use as measured at age 16–17 years. The Berkeley study (Shedler & Block, 1990) reported that the following characteristics at age 7 years were associated with frequent drug use at age 18 years: poor peer relations, little concern with reciprocity and fairness, stress symptoms, indecisiveness, lack of planfulness or forethought, lack of trustworthiness and dependability, lower self-confidence and self-reliance, and an inability to admit to negative feelings. Other related characteristics were associated at a lower statistical significance level. To summarize the Berkeley study findings, at age 7, the future frequent users were "unable to form good relationships," were "insecure" with evidence of low self-esteem, manifested "numerous signs of emotional distress," which they denied, and had poor coping, adapting, and interpersonal problem solving skills. Although the limitations of these studies make their findings more suggestive than conclusive, the findings do support the hypothesized developmental psychopathology model.

The Berkeley study also reported observations of the parents of the children in the study, made when the children were 5 years old (Shedler & Block, 1990). Mothers of future frequent users were "relatively cold, unresponsive, and underprotective," as well as being performance oriented without being supportive. In contrast, fathers of the future frequent users did not differ significantly from fathers of children in the comparison group. It is hypothesized here that although the parents of some high risk children may have other parent–child interaction styles than those identified by the Berkeley study, the negative interpersonal, competency, and self-image consequences for the high risk child are basically the same.

Middle and Late Childhood (8–11 Years)

The Berkeley study additionally reported observations of the future frequent users at age 11 years (Shedler & Block, 1990). They were described as being "visibly deviant from their peers, emotionally labile, inattentive and unable to concentrate, not involved in what they do, [and] stubborn" (p. 618). Other observed characteristics were related to coping, problem solving, and interpersonal difficulties. Again, these findings support the proposed developmental psychopathology model.

The characteristics of the high risk child at this stage are likely to be a direct extension or exacerbation of the previous stage characteristics. However, some of the manifestations of these further developed impaired characteristics become more evident and have greater consequences in terms of interpersonal and environmental interactions. The demands of school achievement and peer group integration are areas in which the high risk child performs poorly. Therefore, many of the supports and rewards available to low-risk children are defeats and deprivations for high risk children. The high risk child has already begun to develop maladaptive problem solving and coping mechanisms. Importantly, he or she is also relatively unsuccessful at developing adaptive skills and strategies, which are therefore generally less available in his or her repertoire even if the maladaptive ones are successfully discouraged from use.

The high risk child is likely to be affiliated at this stage with more deviant peer groups, and his or her social role identification and self-image are strongly based in this group. He or she is likely to be engaged in at least some deviant behaviors and/or to be identified as having some conduct or behavior problems; these are early aspects of *problem behavior proneness.* Parents of high risk children are not likely to be positive role models for successful emotional control or coping with stress. The high risk child may have parent or sibling role models of drug use; at this stage, these role models take on increased salience. Supported by the peer group, the child may have used cigarettes or alcohol, beginning the "stepping-stone" path. The high risk child is unlikely to be strongly influenced by any protective factors. For example, he or she is unlikely to be seriously involved in any group that reinforces traditional values, such as a religious organization. Family problems and stresses will exacerbate the high risk child's problems. For most high risk children, vulnerability to drug abuse is established by the end of this stage or the beginning of the next.

Adolescence

For the hypothesized high risk adolescent, detachment from parents, school, and traditional organizations and values escalates during this stage. An antagonistic relationship with the parents is likely. Affective bonds that continue with the parents are likely to be maladaptive, involving hostility, dependency conflicts, and/or emotional alienation to a much greater extent than is expected with typical adolescent "rebellion" and development of young adult independence. The impairments and problems of the previous stage remain stable or increase. Deviance and unsanctioned behavior are also likely to increase. The high risk teenager is likely to be strongly integrated into a deviant or delinquent peer group; this further supports more open and active deviant and antisocial activities. In a cyclical fashion, each deviant or delinquent behavior fosters further antisocial behavior, and each progressive step of involvement with alcohol or drugs facilitates greater reliance on substance use and lesser development of and reliance on more adaptive function. Fathers, who may have a particularly positive effect during this age period (see Brook et al., 1990), fail to exert this protective influence. The high risk teenager is unlikely to have a prosocial role model. Other protective influences, compensating factors, or effective interventions are absent or insufficiently effective.

Positive affect, self-esteem, and defense mechanisms may rally for some part of this period, but, if so, the gains are fragile and soon lost. Anger, defensive negativism, and blaming and rejection of others maybe more in evidence during this stage. There may be an increase in social activity for the high risk teenager, but it is likely to be superficial and lacking in any genuine affectionate attachment. Some tangential accomplishments, such as success in athletics or dating, are possible, but their benefits are likely to be transitory. The risk of dropping out of school is greater than normal. Adolescents are characteristically concrete and egocentric in their thinking, and the development of more abstract and self-decentered conceptual skills is part of the normal development during adolescence; the high risk adolescent is less successful than his peers in developing these adult conceptual abilities. The high risk adolescent is also less successful in developing mature problem solving and affective coping skills.

Drug and/or alcohol involvement is likely to escalate. This is facilitated by increased peer support and practical resources and opportunity for increased use; availability is an important contributive factor. The high risk adolescent may be characterized at this stage as having affect- and behavior-regulation dysfunctions; a deficit in social skills and relationships; impaired ego functions and impaired problem solving and conceptualizing skills; negative affect and low self esteem, which are denied; established deviant behaviors and relationships; and possibly some personality disorder or other developing psychopathology. Reliance on substance use as a coping mechanism is developing or has been established. The high risk child has become a high risk adolescent whose most likely prognosis involves drug abuse.

Conclusion

The future for the hypothesized high risk child described by this illustrative developmental psychopathology model of drug abuse etiology is pessimistic, but the implications of this type of model are not. Vulnerability is not destiny. There are individuals who are apparently subject to multiple risk factors yet whose protective factors and resiliency permit them to avoid substance abuse. Furthermore, there is the clear implication in this model that effective preventive and early treatment intervention is possible. Although considerable further research is needed, the possibility of creating descriptive profiles and methodology for the early identification of high risk children seems feasible. Similarly, the development of effective family and clinically oriented early interventions also seems feasible.

References

Alterman, A., Tarter, R., Baughman, T., Bober, R., & Fabian, S. (1985). Differentiation of alcoholics high and low in childhood hyperactivity. *Drug and Alcohol Dependence, 15,* 111–121.

American Psychiatric Association. (1987). *Diagnostic and statistical manual of mental disorders* (3rd ed., rev.). Washington, DC: Author.

Bank, B., Biddle, B., Anderson, D., Hauge, R., Keats, D., Keats, J., Marlin, M., & Valantin, S. (1985). Comparative research on the social determinants of adolescent drinking. *Social Psychology Quarterly, 48,* 164–177.

Baumrind, D., & Mosell, K. (1985). A developmental perspective on adolescent drug abuse. *Advances in Alcohol and Substance Abuse, 4,* 41–67.

Block, J. (1971). *Lives through time.* Berkeley, CA: Bancroft.

Block, J., Block, J., & Keyes, S. (1988). Longitudinally foretelling drug usage in adolescence: Early childhood personality and environmental precursors. *Child Development, 59,* 336–355.

Brook, J., Brook, D., Gordon, A., Whiteman, M., & Cohen, P. (1990). The psychosocial etiology of adolescent drug use: A family interactional approach. *Genetic, Social, and General Psychology Monographs, 116,* (2, Whole No. 2) 111–267.

Brook, J., Whiteman, M., & Gordon, A. S. (1982). Qualitative and quantitative aspects of adolescent drug use: Interplay of personality, family, and peer correlates. *Psychological Reports, 51,* 1151–1163.

Brook, J., Whiteman, M., & Gordon, A. S. (1983). Stages of drug use in adolescence: Personality, peer, and family correlates. *Developmental Psychology, 19,* 269–277.

Brook, J., Whiteman, M., Gordon, A S., & Cohen, P. (1986). Dynamics of childhood and adolescent personality traits and adolescent drug use. *Developmental Psychology, 22,* 403–414.

Brook, J., Whiteman, M., Gordon, A. S., & Cohen, P. (1989). Changes in drug involvement: A longitudinal study of childhood and adolescent determinants. *Psychological Reports, 65,* 707–726.

Brook, J., Whiteman, M., Nomura, C., Gordon, A. S., & Cohen, P. (1988). Personality, family, and ecological influences on adolescent drug use: A developmental analysis. *Journal of Chemical Dependency Treatment, 1,* 123–161.

Bry, B. (1983). Predicting drug abuse: Review and reformulation. *International Journal of the Addictions, 18,* 223–233.

Bry, B. (1989). The multiple risk factor hypothesis: An integrating concept of the etiology of drug abuse. In S. Einstein (Ed.), *Drug and alcohol use: Issues and factors.* New York: Plenum Press.

Bry, B., McKeon, P., & Pandina, R. (1982). Extent of drug use as a function of number of risk factors. *Journal of Abnormal Psychology, 91,* 273–279.

Cadoret, R., Cain, C., & Grove, W. (1980). Development of alcoholism in adoptees raised apart from alcoholic biologic relations. *Archives of General Psychiatry, 37,* 561–563.

Cadoret, R., Troughton, E., Merchant, L., & Whitters, A. (1990). Early life psychosocial events and adult affective symptoms. In L. Robins & M. Rutter (Eds.), *Straight and devious pathways from childhood to adulthood* (pp. 300–313). Cambridge, England: Cambridge University Press.

Cadoret, R., Troughton, E., O'Gorman, M., & Heywood, E. (1986). An adoption study of genetic and environmental factors in drug abuse. *Archives of General Psychiatry, 43,* 1131–1136.

Carman, R. (1979). Motivations for drug use and problematic outcomes among rural junior high school students. *Addictive Behaviors, 4,* 91–93.

Chess, S., & Thomas, A. (1984). *Origins and evolution of behavioral disorders: From infancy to early adult life.* Cambridge, MA: Harvard University Press.

Christie, K., Burke, J., Regier, D., Rae, D., Boyd, J., & Locke, B. (1989). Epidemiologic evidence for early onset of mental disorders and higher risk of drug abuse in young adults. *American Journal of Psychiatry, 145,* 971–975.

Clayton, R., & Voss, H. (1981). *Young men and drugs in Manhattan: A causal analysis.* Rockville, MD: National Institute on Drug Abuse.

Cloninger, C. R., Sigvardsson, S., & Bohman, M. (1988). Childhood personality predicts alcohol abuse in young adults. *Alcoholism: Clinical and Experimental Research, 12,* 494–505.

Cohen, P., Brook, J., Cohen, J., Velez, C., & Garcia, M. (1990). Common and uncommon pathways to adolescent psychopathology and problem behavior. In L. Robins & M. Rutter (Eds.), *Straight and devious pathways from childhood to adulthood* (pp. 242–258). Cambridge, England: Cambridge University Press.

Deykin, E., Levy, J., & Wells, V. (1987). Adolescent depression, alcohol and drug abuse. *American Journal of Public Health, 77,* 178–182.

Donovan, J., & Jessor, R. (1983). Problem drinking and the dimension of involvement with drugs: A Guttman scalogram analysis of adolescent drug use. *American Journal of Public Health, 73,* 543–551.

Donovan, J., Jessor, R., & Jessor, L. (1983). Problem drinking in adolescence and young adulthood: A follow-up study. *Journal of Studies on Alcohol, 44,* 109–137.

Elliott, D., Huizinga, D., & Ageton, S. (1985). *Explaining delinquency and drug use.* Beverly Hills, CA: Sage.

Elliott, D., Huizinga, D., & Menard, S. (1989). *Multiple problem youth: Delinquency, substance use, and mental health problems.* New York: Springer-Verlag.

Gittelman, R., Mannuzza, S., Shenker, R., & Bonagura, N. (1985). Hyperactive boys almost grown up: I. Psychiatric status. *Archives of General Psychiatry, 42,* 937–947.

Gomberg, E. (1982). The young male alcoholic: A pilot study. *Journal of Studies on Alcohol, 43,* 683–700.

Green, J., Bax, M., & Tsitsikas, H. (1989). Neonatal behavior and early temperament: A longitudinal study of the first six months of life. *American Journal of Orthopsychiatry, 59,* 82–93.

Greene, B. (1980). Sequential use of drugs and alcohol: A reexamination of the stepping-stone hypothesis. *The American Journal of Drug and Alcohol Abuse, 7,* 83–99.

Greenspan, S. (1985). Research strategies to identify developmental vulnerabilities for drug abuse. In C. L. Jones & R. Battjes (Eds.), *Etiology of drug abuse: Implications for prevention* (pp. 136–154). Rockville, MD: National Institute on Drug Abuse.

Grove, W., Eckert, E., Heston, L., Bouchard, T., Segal, N., & Lykken, D. (1990). Heritability of substance abuse and antisocial behavior: A study of monozygotic twins reared apart. *Biological Psychiatry, 27,* 1293–1304.

Hampton, P., & Vogel, D. (1973). Personality characteristics of servicemen returned from Vietnam identified as heroin abusers. *American Journal of Psychiatry, 130,* 1031–1032.

Hawkins, J. D., Lishner, D., Catalano, R., & Howard, M. (1985). Childhood predictors of adolescent substance abuse: Toward an empirically grounded theory. *Journal of Children in Contemporary Society, 18,* 11–48.

Hechtman, L., Weiss, G., & Perlman, T. (1984). Hyperactives as young adults: Past and current substance abuse and antisocial behavior. *American Journal of Orthopsychiatry, 54,* 415–425.

Hendin, H., & Pollinger-Haas, A. (1984). *Wounds of war: The psychological aftermath of combat in Vietnam.* New York: Basic Books.

Hesselbrock, V. (1986). Family history of psychopathology in alcoholics: A review and issues. In R. Meyer (Ed.), *Psychopathology and addictive disorders.* New York: Guilford Press.

Hesselbrock, V., Hesselbrock, M., & Stabenau, J. (1985). Alcoholism in men patients subtyped by family history and antisocial personality. *Journal of Studies on Alcohol, 46,* 59–64.

Hirschi, T. (1969). *Causes of delinquency.* Berkeley: University of California Press.

Holmberg, M. B. (1985). Longitudinal studies of drug abuse in a fifteen-year-old population: 1. Drug career. *Acta Psychiatrica Scandinavia, 71,* 67–79.

Huba, G., & Bentler, P. (1982). A developmental theory of drug use: Derivation and assessment of a causal modeling approach. In P. Baltes & O. Brim (Eds.), *Life-span development and behavior* (Vol. 4, pp. 147–203). San Diego, CA: Academic Press.

Huba, G., Newcomb, M., & Bentler, P. (1986). Adverse drug experiences and drug use behaviors: A one-year longitudinal study of adolescents. *Journal of Pediatric Psychology, 40,* 180–193.

Huizinga, D., & Menard, S., & Elliot, D. (1989). Delinquency and drug use: Temporal and developmental patterns. *Justice Quarterly, 6,* 419–455.

Jessor, R., & Jessor, S. (1977). *Problem behavior and psychosocial development: A longitudinal study of youth.* San Diego, CA: Academic Press.

Johnson, G., Schoutz, F., & Locke, T. (1984). Relationships between adolescent drug use and parental drug behaviors. *Adolescence, 19,* 295–299.

Jones, M. (1968). Personality correlates and antecedents of drinking patterns in adult males. *Journal of Consulting and Clinical Psychology, 32,* 2–12.

Jurich, A., Polson, C., Jurich, J., & Bates, R. (1985). Family factors in the lives of drug users and drug abusers. *Adolescence, 20,* 143–159.

Kandel, D. (1981). Drug use by youth: An overview. In D. Lettieri & J. Ludford (Eds.), *Drug abuse and the American adolescent* (pp. 1–24). Rockville, MD.: National Institute on Drug Abuse.

Kandel, D. (1984). Marijuana uses in young adulthood. *Advances in Adolescent Mental Health, 3,* 127–143.

Kandel, D. (1985). On processes of peer influences in adolescent drug use: A developmental perspective. *Advances in Alcohol and Substance Abuse, 4,* 139–163.

Kandel, D., Davies, M., & Baydar, N. (1990). The creation of interpersonal contexts: Homophily in dyadic relationships in adolescence and young adulthood. In L. Robins & M. Rutter (Eds.), *Straight and devious pathways from childhood to adulthood* (pp. 221–241). Cambridge, England: Cambridge University Press.

Kandel, D., & Faust, R. (1975). Sequences and stages in patterns of adolescent drug use. *Archives of General Psychiatry, 32,* 923–932.

Kandel, D., Kessler, R., & Margulies, R. (1978). Antecedents of adolescent initiation into stages of drug use: A developmental analysis. In D. B. Kandel (Ed.), *Longitudinal research on drug use: Empirical findings and methodological issues* (pp. 73–99). Washington, DC: Hemisphere–Wiley.

Kandel, D., Murphy, D., & Karus, D. (1985). Cocaine use in young adulthood: Patterns of use and psychosocial correlates. In N. Kozel & E. Adams (Eds.), *Cocaine use in America: Epidemiologic and clinical perspectives* (pp. 76–110). Rockville, MD: National Institute on Drug Abuse.

Kandel, D., & Raveis, V. (1989). Cessation of illicit drug use in young adulthood. *Archives of General Psychiatry, 46,* 109–116.

Kandel, D., & Yamaguchi, K. (1985). Developmental patterns of the use of legal, illegal, and medically prescribed psychotropic drugs from adolescence to young adulthood. In C. L. Jones & R. Battjes (Eds.), *Etiology of drug abuse: Implications for prevention* (pp. 193–235). Rockville, MD: National Institute on Drug Abuse.

Kaplan, H. (1977). Antecedents of deviant responses: Predicting from a general theory of deviant behavior. *Journal of Youth and Adolescence, 6,* 86–101.

Kaplan, H. B., Martin, S. S., Johnson, R. J., & Robbins, C. A. (1986). Escalation of marijuana use: Application of a general theory of deviant behavior. *Journal of Health and Social Behavior, 27,* 44–61.

Kellam, S., Brown, C., Rubin, B., Ensminger, M. (1983). Paths leading to teenage psychiatric symptoms and substance use: Developmental epidemiological studies in Woodlawn. In S. Guze, F. Earls, & J. Barrett (Eds.), *Childhood psychopathology and development* (pp. 17–51). New York: Raven Press.

King, R., Jones, J., Scheuer, J., Curtis, D., & Zarcone, V. (1990). Plasma cortisol correlates of impulsivity and substance abuse. *Personality and Individual Differences, 2,* 287–291.

Kosten, T., Rounsaville, B., & Kleber, H. (1985). Parental alcoholism in opioid addicts. *Journal of Nervous and Mental Disease, 173,* 461–469.

Kramer, J., & Loney, J. (1982). Childhood hyperactivity and substance abuse: A review of the literature. *Advances in Learning and Behavioral Disabilities, 1,* 225–259.

Kumpfer, K. (1987). Special populations: Etiology and prevention of vulnerability to chemical dependency in children of substance abusers. In B. Brown & A. Mills (Eds.), *Youth at high risk for substance abuse* (pp. 1–72). Rockville, MD: National Institute on Drug Abuse.

Kumpfer, K., & DeMarsh, J. (1986). Family environmental and genetic influences on children's future chemical dependency. *Journal of Children in Contemporary Society, 18,* 49–91.

Labouvie, E. (1987). Relation of personality to adolescent alcohol and drug use: A coping perspective. *Pediatrician, 14,* 19–24.

Labouvie, E., & McGee, C. (1986). Relation of personality to alcohol and drug use in adolescence. *Journal of Consulting and Clinical Psychology, 54,* 289–293.

Labouvie, E., Pandina, R., White, H., & Johnson, V. (1990). Risk factors of adolescent drug use: An affect-based interpretation. *Journal of Substance Abuse, 2,* 265–285.

Lerner, J., & Vicary, J. (1984). Difficult temperament and drug use: Analyses from the New York Longitudinal Study. *Journal of Drug Education, 14,* 1–8.

Loeber, R. (1985). Patterns of development of antisocial child behavior. *Annals of Child Development, 2,* 77–115.

Loeber, R. (1988). Natural histories of juvenile conduct problems, delinquency, and associated substance use: Evidence for developmental progressions. In B. Lahey & A. Kazden (Eds.), *Advances in Clinical Child Psychology* (Vol. 11, pp. 73–124). New York: Plenum Press.

Loeber, R. (1990). Development and risk factors of juvenile antisocial behavior and delinquency. *Clinical Psychology Review, 10,* 1–41.

Loney, J. (1988). Substance abuse in adolescents: Diagnostic issues derived from studies of attention deficit disorder with hyperactivity. In E. Rahdert & J. Grabowski (Eds.), *Adolescent drug abuse: Analyses of treatment research* (pp. 19–26). Rockville, MD: National Institute on Drug Abuse.

Maddahian, E., Newcomb, M., & Bentler, P. (1988). Risk factors for substance use: Ethnic differences among adolescents. *Journal of Substance Abuse, 1,* 11–23.

Maddux, J., & Desmond, D. (1989). Family and environment in choice of opioid dependence or alcoholism. *American Journal of Drug and Alcohol Abuse, 15,* 117–134.

Magnusson, D., & Bergman, L. (1990). A pattern approach to the study of pathways from childhood to adulthood. In L. Robins & M. Rutter (Eds.), *Straight and devious pathways from childhood to adulthood* (pp. 101–115). Cambridge, England: Cambridge University Press.

Marlatt, G. A. (1987). Alcohol, the magic elixir: Stress, expectancy, and the transformation of emotional states. In E. Gottheil, K. Druley, S. Pashdo, & S. Weinstein (Eds.), *Stress and addiction* (pp. 302–322). New York: Brunner/Mazel.

McCord, J. (1988) Identifying developmental paradigms leading to alcoholism. *Journal of Studies on Alcohol, 49,* 357–362.

McCord, W., & McCord, J. (1959). *Origins of crime: A new evaluation of the Cambridge–Somerville study.* New York: Columbia University Press.

McCord, W., & McCord, J. (1960). *Origins of alcoholism.* Stanford, CA.: Stanford University Press.

Merikangas, K. R. (1990). The genetic epidemiology of alcoholism. *Psychological Medicine, 20,* 11–22.

Mills, C., & Noyes, H. (1984). Patterns and correlates of initial and subsequent drug use among adolescents. *Journal of Consulting and Clinical Psychology, 52,* 231–243.

Mirin, S., Weiss, R., & Michael, J. (1986). Family pedigree of psychopathology in substance abusers. In R. Meyer (Ed.), *Psychopathology and addictive disorders* (pp. 57–77). New York: Guilford Press.

Muntaner, C., Nagoshi, C., Jaffe, J., Walte, D., Haertzen, C., & Fishbein, D. (1989). Correlates of self-reported early childhood aggression in subjects volunteering for drug studies. *American Journal of Drug and Alcohol Abuse, 15,* 383–402.

National Institute on Drug Abuse. (1990). *National Household Survey on Drug Abuse, 1990.* Rockville, MD: National Institute on Drug Abuse, Division of Epidemiology and Prevention Research.

Needle, R., McCubin, H., Wilson, M., Reineck, R., Lazar, A., & Mederer, H. (1986). Interpersonal influences in adolescent drug use: The role of older siblings, parents, and peers. *International Journal of the Addictions, 21,* 739–766.

Newcomb, M., & Bentler, P. (1986). Frequency and sequence of drug use: A longitudinal study from early adolescence to young adulthood. *Journal of Drug Education, 16,* 101–120.

Newcomb, M., & Bentler, P. (1990). Antecedents and consequences of cocaine use: An eight-year study from early adolescence to young adulthood. In L. Robins & M. Rutter (Eds.), *Straight and devious pathways from childhood to adulthood* (pp. 158–181). Cambridge, England: Cambridge University Press.

Pandina, R., & Schuele, J. (1983). Psychosocial correlates of alcohol and drug use of adolescent students and adolescents in treatment. *Journal of Studies on Alcohol, 44,* 950–973.

Paton, S., Kessler, R., & Kandel, D. (1977). Depressive mood and adolescent illicit drug use: A longitudinal analysis. *Journal of Genetic Psychology, 131,* 267–289.

Pickens, R., Svikis, D., McGue, M., Lykken, D., Heston, L., & Clayton, P. (1991). Heterogeneity in the inheritance of alcoholism. *Archives of General Psychiatry, 48,* 19–28.

Rhodes, J., & Jason, L. (1990). A social stress model of substance abuse. *Journal of Consulting and Clinical Psychology, 58,* 395–401.

Robinowitz, R., Robers, W., Patterson, E., Dolan, M., & Alkins, H. (1981). Adjustment differences among male substance abusers varying in degree of combat experiences in Vietnam. *Journal of Consulting and Clinical Psychology, 19,* 426–437.

Robins, L. (1966). *Deviant children grown up: A sociological and psychiatric study of sociopathic personality.* Baltimore: Williams & Wilkins.

Robins, L. (1974). *The Vietnam drug user returns.* Washington, DC: Special Action Office Monograph.

Robins, L. (1978). Sturdy childhood predictors of adult antisocial behavior: Replications from longitudinal studies. *Psychological Medicine, 8,* 611–622.

Robins, L. (1984). The natural history of adolescent drug use. *American Journal of Public Health, 74,* 656–657.

Robins, L., & McEvoy, L. (1990). Conduct problems as predictors of substance abuse. In L. Robins & M. Rutter (Eds.), *Straight and devious pathways from childhood to adulthood.* (pp. 182–204). Cambridge, England: Cambridge University Press.

Robins, L., & Przybeck, T. (1985). Age of onset of drug use as a factor in drug use and other disorders. In. C. L. Jones & R. Battjes (Eds.), *Etiology of drug abuse: Implications for prevention* (pp. 178–192). Rockville, MD: National Institute on Drug Abuse.

Robins, L., & Wish, E. (1977). Childhood deviance as a developmental process: A study of 223 urban Black men from birth to 18. *Social Forces, 56,* 448–473.

Rohsenow, D., Corbett, R., & Devine, D. (1988). Molested as children: A hidden contribution to substance abuse? *Journal of Substance Abuse Treatment, 5,* 13–18.

Ross, H., Glaser, F., & Germanson, T. (1988). The prevalence of psychiatric disorders in patients with alcohol and other drug problems. *Archives of General Psychiatry, 45,* 1023–1032.

Rutter, M., & Giller, H. (1983). *Juvenile delinquency: Trends and perspectives.* New York: Guilford Press.

Shedler, J., & Block, J. (1990). Adolescent drug use and psychological health: A longitudinal inquiry. *American Psychologist, 45,* 612–630.

Solomon, R., & Corbit, J. (1974). An opponent-process theory of motivation: I. Temporal dynamics of affect. *Psychological Review, 81,* 119–145.

Stattin, H., & Magnusson, D. (1989). The role of early aggressive behavior in the frequency, seriousness, and types of later crime. *Journal of Consulting and Clinical Psychology, 57,* 710–718.

Steele, C., & Josephs, R. (1990). Alcohol myopia: Its prized and dangerous effects. *American Psychologist, 45,* 921–933.

Swaim, R. C., Oetting, E., Edwards, R., & Beauvais, F. (1989). Links from emotional distress to adolescent drug use: A path model. *Journal of Consulting and Clinical Psychology, 57,* 227–231.

Tarter, R., Alterman, A., & Edwards, K. (1985). Vulnerability to alcoholism in men: A behavioral–genetic perspective. *Journal of Studies on Alcohol, 46,* 329–356.

Tarter, R., Alterman, A., & Edwards, K. (1989). Neurobehavioral theory of alcoholism etiology. In C. Chaudron & D. Wilkinson (Eds.), *Theories of alcoholism.* Toronto: Addiction Research Foundation.

Tarter, R., & Edwards, K. (1988). Psychological factors associated with the risk for alcoholism. *Alcoholism: Clinical and Experimental Research, 12,* 471–480.

Tarter, R., Laird, S., Kabene, M., Bukstein, O., & Kaminer, Y. (1990). Drug abuse severity in adolescents is associated with magnitude of deviation in temperament traits. *British Journal of the Addictions, 85,* 1501–1504.

Thorne, C., & DeBlassie, K. (1985). Adolescent substance abuse. *Adolescence, 20,* 335–347.

Turnbull, J., & Gomberg, E. (1988). Impact of depressive symptomatology and alcohol problems in women. *Alcoholism: Clinical and Experimental Research, 12,* 374–381.

Vaillant, G. (1983). *The natural history of alcoholism: Causes, patterns, and paths to recovery.* Cambridge, MA: Harvard University Press.

Vaillant, G., & Milofsky, E. (1982). The etiology of alcoholism: A prospective viewpoint. *American Psychologist, 37,* 494–503.

Voss, H., & Clayton, R. (1987). Stages in involvement with drugs. *Pediatrician, 14,* 25–31.

Welte, J., & Barnes, G. (1985). Alcohol: The gateway to other drug use among secondary-school students. *Journal of Youth and Adolescence, 14,* 487–498.

Westermeyer, J. (1976). The pro-heroin effects of anti-opium laws in Asia. *Archives of General Psychiatry, 33,* 1135–1139.

Westermeyer, J. (1979). Influence of opium availability on addiction rates in Laos. *American Journal of Epidemiology, 109,* 550–562.

Wise, R. (1988). The neurobiology of craving: Implications for understanding and treatment of addiction. *Journal of Abnormal Psychology, 97,* 118–132.

Wise, R., & Bozarth, M. (1987). A psychomotor stimulant theory of addiction. *Psychological Review, 94,* 469–492.

World Health Organization. (1980). *International classification of diseases* (9th ed.). Geneva: Author.

Yamaguchi, K., & Kandel, D. (1984). Patterns of drug use from adolescence to young adulthood: III. Predictors of progression. *American Journal of Public Health, 74,* 673–681.

CHAPTER 14

Predictive Factors in Adult Substance Abuse: A Prospective Study of African American Adolescents

Ann F. Brunswick, Peter A. Messeri, and Stephen P. Titus

D rug abuse is known to be a behavior with multiple determinants. Its etiology lies in areas as diverse as anatomy, chemistry, age, gender, socioeconomic status, culture, and historical period; it is a product of complex interactions that might well be described as a "web of causation" (Mausner & Kramer, 1985). The research of which the present study is a part started from the premises (a) that the pattern of these interactions will vary according to position in the social structure and (b) that increased vulnerability derives from a disadvantaged social position that brings with it limited access to the opportunity structure. Examining etiological factors in a disadvantaged minority group thus provides a different perspective on conditions that affect the trajectory to drug abuse than that of largely White and middle-class samples. This divergence derives from differences in life histories, in experience with social institutions, and in responses and responsiveness to social policy.

The authors gratefully acknowledge the assistance of John L. P. Thompson, (associate research scientist, Public Health, Sociomedical Sciences, Columbia University) in helping with computer analyses.

Our research is rooted in an ongoing study of urban African Americans. The research follows a developmental ecological model, (Bronfenbrenner 1979; Brunswick, 1979, 1980a, 1985; Brunswick, Merzel, & Messeri, 1985, Brunswick & Messeri, 1984a, 1986; Kurdek, 1981) that taps domains of behavior influences proceeding from (a) aggregate macrosocial factors relating to culture, historical time, and so on, which make up ascriptive social position, (b) achieved social roles (marriage and family, occupation), (c) institutional (formal) and interpersonal (informal) affiliations (social bonds), and, finally, (d) selected intraindividual factors. The developmental perspective is operationalized by testing, for the same individuals, indicators from two sequential life stages—the adolescent and the early adult transition (term adopted from Levinson, 1986)—for their contributions to the likelihood of continuing illicit drug use in adulthood—specifically, continuing at heavy levels defined as near-daily, if not daily, use. Those with continuing careers of heavy drug use are compared with others of similar gender, ethnicity, age, socioeconomic status, and geographic area who also had a history of regular drug use that they terminated before adulthood (former users). A secondary comparison of former users is made to those who continued use as adults but at controlled or moderate levels. This protects against confounding the influences on continuing regular drug use, regardless of level, with those influences specific to continuing at heavy, and what can be termed abusive, levels.

Research that has investigated long-term consequences of adolescent drug use (Brunswick, Lewis, & Messeri, 1991b; Kandel, Davies, Karus, & Yamaguchi, 1986; Newcomb & Bentler, 1988) suggests that the adverse consequences of drug use largely befall those who continue use into adulthood. Individuals who do not continue heavy drug use after the adolescent or early adult years appear, for the most part, to experience little if any long-term ill effects. Thus, heavy drug use continued into adulthood was selected as the definition of abuse in this study.

Context for This Research

The thesis that the "web of causation" will operate differently with respect to a disadvantaged minority group, African Americans in particular, involves a hypothesized sequence of influences on drug use that emphasizes socioeconomic and contextual factors over intrapersonal ones (Brunswick, 1979, 1980a; Brunswick & Boyle, 1979; Cordes, 1985). Furthermore, drug abuse may be symptomatic of the social isolation increasingly experienced by a significant segment of African American youth. This isolation derives from a broader social problem that encompasses "global economic shifts, limited local job opportunities, and the cumulative effects of years of deprivation and exclusion" (Brunswick & Rier, in press). It is symptomatic, too, of an increasing polarization within African American society between those who are "making it" and those who are not (Massey & Eggers, 1990; Swinton, 1989; Wilson, 1987). Specifically, as predicted by Merton's half-century-old theory of social strain (Farnsworth & Lieber 1989; Merton, 1957)— that is, the strain between socially accepted goals and the inability to attain them through accepted channels—excluded persons are prompted to seek success through "innovative" (i.e., nonnormative or socially disapproved) means. To give more emphasis to this segment of the causal link to drug abuse, the term *structural strain* has been adopted as an appropriate explanatory perspective on African Americans' drug abuse. (Brunswick & Rier, in press).

Social learning theory (Rotter, Chance, & Phares, 1972) also provides an important perspective on African Americans' drug abuse and polydrug abuse, in which abuse is viewed as contingency reinforcement for unmet social expectancies (i.e., for role deprivation vis-à-vis conventional economic and occupational attainment or stable family and interpersonal ties.

Social control theory adds a critical explanatory dimension. To the extent that individuals occupy marginal social positions that reduce if not completely deny them access to the opportunity structure, they are less bound by and responsive to dominant social norms and behavioral proscriptions (Thompson, Smith-DiJulio, & Matthews, 1982). This detachment from conventional norms is expressed in what we refer to as asynchrony or unconventionality in life-stage roles (e.g., incomplete education, absence of regular employment, being an unmarried adult). Simultaneously an expression of reduced social access, lack of age-appropriate role attainments adds further to weakened bonds to the normative social institutions through which societal values are transmitted.

In predominantly White samples, the role-conflict hypothesis has satisfactorily explained the termination of youthful drug use by ages in the mid-twenties, when adult roles of employment and marriage are assumed (Bachman, O'Malley, & Johnston, 1984; Kandel, Simcha-Fagan, & Davies, 1986; Miller et al., 1983; Yamaguchi & Kandel, 1985). It is not inconsistent, then, to expect continued drug abuse in circumstances where, for reasons of access or availability, conventional adult roles are not assumed (i.e., the aging effects that appear in White populations may not occur with the same frequency or necessarily with the same results in an African American population). For example, note the distribution of the present sample on selected adult role attainments (Table 14.1),

TABLE 14.1

Selected Life Attainments at Ages 26–31

Variable	% Males (*n* = 211)	% Females (*n* = 215)
Years of schooling completed		
Incomplete high school	33	28
High school completed	19	16
Post-high school: Vocational/technical	12	15
Any college	35	41
AA degree	4	4
BA or higher	7	11
Marital/Cohabiting Status		
Currently married	23	21
Currently living with partner (cohabit)	16	14
Living without spouse or partner	61	65
Fertility		
Baby by age 17	16	31
No. children at ages 26–31		
0	49	29
1–2	39	53
3+	12	18
Major activity		
Employed (work)	55	49
Attending school	6	6
Both work and school	3	9
Armed forces	2	—
Jail	6	—
Unemployed/not occupied	28	37
Looking for work	21	12
Not looking for work[a]	7	25

Note. Full Wave 3 sample. Because of rounding, percentages may not equal exactly 100.
[a] Includes women who are housewives, plus men and women in poor health (4% and 3%, respectively).

especially the number unemployed and unmarried and without a mate. The sample also consistently experienced less of a decline in adult substance use than research on other samples would suggest (see Table 14.2). This is consistent with Yamaguchi and Kandel (1985), who found that African American women in their New York State sample were more likely than White women to continue marijuana use. Recent demographic analyses confirm that marriage rates among low-income African American women are significantly

TABLE 14.2

Continuation of Drug Use at Age 26

Substance	Percentage of lifetime users continuing use at age 26	
	% Women	% Men
Cigarettes	83 (139/168)[a]	85 (124/146)
Heavy alcohol	60 (34/57)[b]	77 (65/84)
Marijuana	63 (100/160)	75 (137/182)
Cocaine	82 (69/84)	77 (83/108)
PCP	63 (5/8)	68 (19/28)
Inhalants	— (0/3)	31 (4/13)
Heroin	46 (13/28)	30 (10/33)

Note. From Brunswick, Messeri, & Aidala (1990). Reprinted with permission.
[a] Percentage of nonexperimental users by Wave 3 who were currently using at age 26.
[b] Heavy alcohol was percentaged on regular monthly or more frequent users of five or more drinks per day.

lower than among comparable White women and that they are continuing to decline (Bennett, Bloom, & Craig, 1989).

Furthermore, young Black men have nearly double the unemployment rate of Whites (U.S. Bureau of the Census, 1988). The rate of joblessness for young inner-city Black men, in particular, approaches 50% (Bradbury & Brown, 1986; Swinton, 1989). The drug economy and its associated substance use may satisfy economic and occupational needs for some whose employment options are severely constrained (Brunswick, 1988a). These demographic data provide a context for viewing our research and its results.

Research Model

The selection of predictor variables for analysis was guided for the most part by the theoretical considerations outlined above, plus attention to intraindividual factors and prior drug-use experiences taken from the following pattern of domains: (I) structural influences on ascriptive social position, (II) role asynchrony or unconventional roles, (III) social bonds to traditional sources of authority, formal or informal, (IV) perceived opportunity (social expectancy), (V) demoralization and ontogenic strain (domain of "personality" factors), and (VI) a microtheory pertaining to drug use, marijuana gateway theory (i.e., early onset predicts longer terms and heavier patterns of use). Early marijuana use, with respect to social control theory, can be viewed as a problem behavior (Jessor & Jessor, 1977) resulting from weakened bonds to conventional norms. It is tested here as its own construct, for its independent role in predicting adult drug abuse.

These six domains of influences were measured at two prior life stages—adolescence and the early adult transition—to test proximal compared with distal influences, as well as developmental vulnerabilities, in the transition to adult drug abuse.

Figure 14.1 shows the hypothesized direction of effects and major causal linkages between adolescent and early adult predictors. Postadolescent variables are hypothesized to exert direct causal effects on continued drug use into adulthood. Both direct and indirect effects are theoretically plausible for variables measured during the adolescent life stage. Adolescent predictors may indirectly affect adult use as antecedents of later life situations or personal attributes that directly increase the risk of continued adult use. We hypothesize that adolescent variables that directly affect the adult drug-use outcome

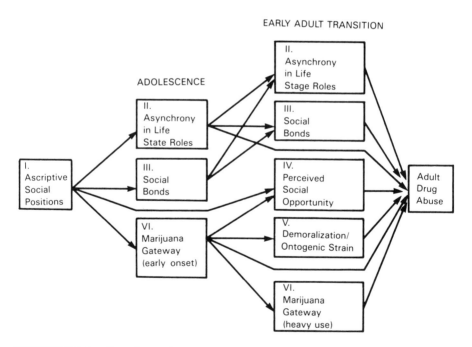

FIGURE 14.1 Hypothesized developmental model testing risk factors in the transition to adult drug abuse in an African American sample.

capture early socialization experiences that foreclose influence from subsequent conditions or changes in outlooks and expectancies.

For the most part, the same domains of variables, although not necessarily identical indicators, were modeled for both life stages. Chief exceptions were as follows: (a) Ascriptive social position (social structural factors, Domain I) was obviously an antecedent to both life stages; (b) perceptions of the opportunity structure (social expectancies), as attitudinal measures, were modeled only for the temporally more proximal life stage (early adult transition); and (c) demoralization and ontogenic strain, for the same reason, were modeled only for the early adult transition. (Life-stage-specific models are discussed further under Method, below.)

Prior Research

The most frequent conceptual approach to explaining the etiology of drug use is that of the interaction of individual characteristics with a matrix of social influences (e.g., problem-behavior proneness theory, Jessor, 1979; Jessor & Jessor 1977; and deviance syndrome, Robins & Wish, 1977). The theoretical perspective guiding this research, as noted above, was formulated to identify processes leading to drug abuse among African Americans, with appropriate emphasis on various domains of social and contextual influences.

Our review of the literature is organized around the major domains tested in the research model. Table 14.3 summarizes these domains and their indicators, the major theoretical systems from which they derive, and investigators who have contributed findings to that domain.

It must be noted at the outset that little research has yet been conducted modeling the four issues critical to this study of the transition to adult drug use, namely (a) causal, not correlational, factors; (b) causal factors in abuse rather than drug use per se; (c) causal factors specific to African American abuse; and (d) an epidemiologic or population-representative perspective. Most of the reported studies pertained to adolescent onset or to marijuana onset only, because of insufficient rates of harder drug use in school and national household samples.

Beginning with the most "macro" and distal factors, which are experienced indirectly in the form of subgroup differentiated norms and values stemming from ascribed background factors (family, socioeconomic status, gender, cohort or historical period, culture, race, and even geography of residence—e.g., urban vs. rural), research has demonstrated the link between substance-use onset, on the one hand, and lower socioeconomic

TABLE 14.3
Prediction of Drug Abuse

Domain	Indicators[a]	Theory	Investigators
I. Social structure (normative macro influences)	Race Gender Birth cohort Family on welfare Father absent Urbanicity	Structural strain Cohort and period effects	Boyle & Brunswick (1980) Brunswick & Boyle (1979) Clayton & Voss (1981) Fishburne, Abelson, & Cisin (1980) Helzer, Robins, & Davis (1975–1976) Kleinman (1978) Kleinman & Lukoff (1978) O'Donnell, Voss, Clayton, Slatin, & Room (1976) O'Malley, Johnston, & Bachman (1984) Robins, Darvish, & Murphy (1970)
II. Asynchrony in life-stage roles (age-inappropriate school, work, or family roles)	*Adolescence:* Parent by age 17 High school dropout *Postadolescence:* Marriage at ages 23–25 Months idle No. children Cohabit at ages 23–25	Precocious development Role conflict (Manifestation of) structural strain	Bachman, O'Malley, & Johnston (1984) Jessor & Jessor (1977) Johnston (1973) Kandel, Kessler, & Margulies (1978) Kandel, Simcha-Fagan, & Davies (1986) Kleinman & Lukoff (1978) Miller, Cisin, Gardner-Keaton, Wirtz, Abelson, & Fishburne (1983) O'Donnell, Voss, Clayton, Slatin, & Room (1976) Robins, Darvish, & Murphy (1970) Robbins (1989) Smith & Fogg (1978) Yamaguchi & Kandel (1985)

III. Social bonds	*Primary groups:* Peer influence Spare time with family Recreational index No. close friends Hrs./day radio *Formal organizations:* Religion No. organizations Yrs. education	Social Control Differential association Problem-behavior proneness	Akers (1977) Brook, Lukoff, & Whiteman (1977) Brunswick (1988a, 1988b) Brunswick & Messeri (1984a, 1984b) Clayton & Voss (1981) Elliott, Huizinga, & Ageton (1982) Hirschi (1969) Huba, Wingard, & Bentler (1979) Jessor (1979) Jessor, Chase, & Donovan (1980) Jessor & Jessor (1977) Kandel (1978, 1982) Kandel & Adler (1982) Kandel, Single, & Kessler (1976) Kaplan, Martin, & Robbins (1982) Kleinman (1978) Kleinman & Lukoff (1978) O'Donnell & Clayton (1979) O'Donnell, Voss, Clayton, Slatin, & Room (1976) Thompson, Smith-DiJulio, & Matthews (1982)[a]
IV. Perceived social opportunity	Achievement orientation Job goals	Social control Social learning (Manifestation of) structural strain	Elliott & Voss (1974) Hirschi (1969) Jessor & Jessor (1978) Johnston, Bachman, & O'Malley (1981) Kaplan (1980) Rotter, Chance, & Phares (1972) Smith & Fogg (1978) Thompson, Smith-DiJulio, & Matthews (1982)

TABLE 14.3 (*Continued*)

Domain	Indicators[a]	Theory	Investigators
V. Demoralization/onto-genic strain	Things gone past 5 years. Problem that upsets you Amount worry Things want to change about self Self-esteem Personal efficacy	Locus of control Self-derogation Stress-coping	Bandura (1977) Baumrind (1985) Dohrenwend, Dohrenwend, Oksenberg, Cook, & Shrout (1981) Frank (1972) Hawkins, Lishner, & Catalano (1985) Jessor, Chase, & Donovan (1980) Kandel (1978) Kandel, Simcha-Fagan, & Davies (1986) Robbins (1989) Rotter, Chance, & Phares (1972) Simcha-Fagan, Gersten, & Langner (1986) Smith & Fogg (1978)
VI. Early drug use	Use of marijuana by age 14 Frequency of marijuana use as young adult	Marijuana gateway	Brunswick (1979) Brunswick & Boyle (1979) Clayton & Voss (1981) Kandel (1978) Kandel, Simcha-Fagan, & Davies (1986) Kandel & Yamaguchi (1985) Kleinman & Lukoff (1978) O'Donnell, Voss, Clayton, Slatin, & Room (1976) Rachal et al. (1982) Robins & Murphy (1967) Robins & Pryzbeck (1985)

[a] Indicators refer to variables in the Longitudinal Harlem Health Study (Brunswick, 1980b). Race and urbanicity are homogeneous and were not tested.

background (e.g., Kleinman, 1978) and migration status (Brunswick & Messeri, 1984a; Kleinman & Lukoff, 1978), on the other. Within this ascriptive domain, race has been the single most frequently analyzed variable, and, notwithstanding contradictory findings from national household drug surveys (for a discussion, see Brunswick & Rier, in press), most investigators have observed higher rates among Black than White individuals in their samples (Clayton & Voss, 1981; Helzer, Robins, & Davis, 1975–1976; O'Donnell, Voss, Clayton, Slatin, & Room, 1976).

In the present study, adolescent indicators of role asynchrony were precocious parenting (parent by age 17) and school drop-out.[1] The latter variable has been widely studied and uniformly acknowledged to be a significant correlate of drug-use initiation, although not a predictor in the temporal sense (drug onset usually antecedes dropping out). Although drop-out is often only the culmination of a history of school failure, this latter variable (poor academic attainment) is a well-documented predictor of substance-use onset (Brunswick & Messeri, 1984a, 1984b; Clayton & Voss, 1981; Jessor & Jessor, 1977; Johnston, 1973; Kandel, 1978; Robins, Darvish, & Murphy, 1970; Robins & Wish, 1977; Smith & Fogg, 1978). The postadolescent indicators of role asynchrony in this study have been used by other investigators to test the role conflict hypothesis: These indicators are being unmarried, cohabiting, and parenting (see Bachman et al., 1984; Yamaguchi & Kandel, 1985), as well as unemployment (O'Donnell et. al, 1976). The results of these researchers confirmed that attaining the adult statuses reflected in these variables led to termination of drug-use careers.

The role of peer influence in drug-use initiation has received considerable empirical attention (e.g., Akers, 1977; Elliott, Huizinga, & Ageton, 1982; Hirschi, 1969; Simcha-Fagan, Gersten, & Langner, 1986). Kleinman (1978) noted that peer influence was less powerful as a predictor of drug use among Black than White individuals. Investigators have identified other primary group characteristics as links to drug use in predominantly White samples, for example, a cold or rejecting, inconsistent, distant parent–child relationship (Baumrind, 1985; Brook, Lukoff, & Whiteman, 1977, Jessor & Jessor, 1977, Kandel, 1974; Kandel, Kessler, & Margulies, 1978; Simcha-Fagan et al., 1986). In the present study, measures of the effect of peer and parent relations are subsumed in Domain III, social bonds. This domain also includes a component of formal ties or bonds

---

[1] *Phrased in life-stage terms, adolescents and young adults who occupy statuses that would be regarded as inappropriate for their age according to conventional values would be at greatest risk for drug abuse and, therefore, for continued adult use. Implicit in this perspective is that drug abuse is deviant behavior and that adolescent experimentation and casual use is normatively more acceptable than such use as an adult.*

to conventional institutions, represented by religious orientation and church attendance (Kandel, 1982; Kleinman & Lukoff, 1978) and by years of schooling, which represent exposure to normative and conventional values.[2]

Closely linked, theoretically, to formal, conventional bonds are attitudes and beliefs regarding the conventional opportunity structure, represented by Domain IV in the present study (Jessor & Jessor, 1978; Kandel et al., 1978; Smith & Fogg, 1978). Like Domain III, this is an intrinsic component of social control theory (Hirschi, 1969; Thompson, Smith-DiJulio, & Matthews, 1982). In the present study, these variables were measured at the early adult transition by level of aspiration and expectancy regarding education and by beliefs that occupational aspirations would be met. The process of effects (i.e., the relationship between these measures and drug abuse, as is also the case in Domain III) can also be explained by social learning theory (i.e., when positive reinforcements or opportunities for pursuing socially desirable achievements are absent, alternative goals and behaviors will be pursued; Brunswick, 1980a, 1988a; Hawkins, Lishner, & Catalano, 1985; Smith & Fogg, 1978).

In terms of numbers of studies, the area of causal factors that has received the most research attention is Domain V of the present study, which refers to intraindividual or psychogenic factors that sometimes appear as antecedent personality traits (e.g., rebelliousness, hostility, aggression–withdrawal; Baumrind, 1985; Shedler & Block, 1990; Simcha-Fagan et al., 1986; Smith & Fogg, 1978). This was true of one of the few causal (i.e., longitudinal) studies of African American marijuana onset, conducted by Kellam and his colleagues (Kellam, Ensminger, Branch, Brown, Fleming, 1984). In a 10-year follow up of their Chicago sample of first graders, a combination of shyness and aggression significantly predicted boys' adolescent marijuana use.

Apathy, pessimism, and depression have also been linked to drug-use and drug-abuse onset (Powers, 1987; Smith & Fogg, 1978; Wills & Shiffman, 1985). Jessor, Chase, & Donovan (1980), however, reported that perceived environmental factors accounted for twice as much variance as personality factors in drug initiation. Newcomb and Bentler (1989) pointed to the possibility that abuse of drugs may be more strongly tied to

---

[2]*Social control theory, in combination with theories of differential association, further suggests that in addition to attainment of conventional statuses, attachment to groups and organizations with conventional values operates as a second component of social bonds that deters adult drug use. For example, length of schooling, church attendance, and participation in clubs and other formal activities are indicative of bonds to conventional society and therefore exert social pressures against continued drug use.*

The consequences of strong attachment to primary or informal groups are less clear-cut, in part because they depend on the value orientation of the informal group. Thus, strong ties to the family (especially a well-functioning family that does not include models for drug use) may generally be regarded as a deterrent to drug use, but the influence of a peer group in which countervailing norms exist may reinforce drug use.

"internal psychological processes" (p. 24) than is use. Bachman et al. (1984) found that depression and anxiety did not predict drug use. Thus, there is conflicting evidence as to the predictive power of personality "traits," if not "states," in the onset of drug use. This may be partially explained by inconsistency across investigations in the use of broad multidomain models compared with those more narrowly focused on intraindividual states. Furthermore, causal direction has frequently been inferred from cross-sectional data (i.e., the reverse causal processes may actually be at work).

Self-esteem and sense of efficacy represent more socially directed components of intragenic factors. When combined with other aspects of affective distress, such as depression and anxiety, they constitute a measure of demoralization (Brunswick, 1988b; Dohrenwend, Dohrenwend, Oksenberg, Cook, & Shrout, 1981; Frank, 1972). Diminution in self-esteem has been linked to drug-use onset by Kaplan (1978, 1980; Kaplan, Martin, & Robbins, 1982), who formulated self-derogation theory to explain marijuana-use onset. This theory explicitly models change in self-esteem as an interactive outcome of negative social reinforcement experiences (i.e., it is context bound).

In sum, although the intraindividual or personality–psychogenic area has generated considerable research interest, it has also generated inconsistent findings and conclusions.

Domain VI in our study tests the consistently observed link between early onset of substance use (modeled here as marijuana-use onset by age 14) and longer terms of use and heavier use of all drugs (e.g., Brunswick, 1979, Brunswick & Boyle, 1979; Clayton & Voss, 1981; Kandel, 1978; Kandel, Simcha-Fagan, & Davies, 1986; Kleinman & Lukoff, 1978; O'Donnell et al., 1976; Rachal et al., 1982; Robins & Murphy, 1967; Robins & Przybeck, 1985).

Study Questions

On the basis of a representative sample of urban African Americans, our longitudinal analysis addressed the following questions:

1. What pattern of developmental precursors significantly predicts (i.e., increases the likelihood of) drug abuse in adulthood?
2. How do developmental trajectories leading to heavy adult use differ from those predicting any continuing adult use (i.e., use at moderate or controlled levels)?

3. Are patterns of effects contingent on gender (i.e., are African American men and women responsive to different patterns of predictive factors in their transitions to heavy drug use in adulthood)?

Method

Source of Data

The data for this study came from the first, second, and third waves of an ongoing prospective health study of African Americans begun when they were adolescents in the late 1960s. The study panel, about equally divided between men and women, numbered when first studied 668 and included ages 12 through 17. Subjects were drawn over two consecutive years (1967 and 1968) from an area probability sample of housing units in Central Harlem (New York City), using a sampling ratio of 1 in 25 households each year. All age-appropriate adolescents residing in these households were drawn into study. The study panel was thus drawn, for the most part, before the ages of greatest loss from households and provides a diversity of status attainments, life-styles, and drug-use behavior that is more representative of urban African Americans than samples appearing in most adult (or school) cross-sections.

In subsequent follow-up studies, the sample was restricted to individuals remaining in the metropolitan New York City area. This decision was based on both theoretical and methodological considerations. First, the theoretical model emphasizes situational and contextual determinants, and unequivalent geographic dispersion would attenuate the results in this respect. Second, practical considerations rendered as inefficient the cost of obtaining widely dispersed interviews, considering the uncontrolled sampling heterogeneity that it would introduce.

The first restudy extended over two years, 1975–1976, 6 to 8 years after initial study and when the panel members were 18 through 23 years old. In that first restudy, 94% of the initial sample was located. Completed interviews numbered 536, representing an 89% response rate among the surviving New York City sample (with similar rates of completion for men and women) and an 80% completion rate based on the entire initial sample regardless of whether the individual had died or had been identified with an address outside of the metropolitan New York City area (see Table 14.4).

The second restudy (Wave 3) was conducted in 1983–1984 (7 to 8 years after the prior wave of interviews), when panel members were 26 through 31 years old and

TABLE 14.4
Sample Completion

Measure	Wave 2[a]			Wave 3[b]		
	% Total	% Male	% Female	% Total	% Male	% Female
Response rate (eligible sample only, including nonlocated)						
Interview completed	89	90	88	86	83	88
Refused	2	1	4	4	3	5
Not located	7	6	7	10	13	6
Never at home/nomadic	2	3	1	*	—	1
N	601	308	293	479	239	240
Sample completion (including dead & moved out of area)						
Located and interview completed	80	79	82	77	72	82
Refused	2	1	3	4	3	5
Never home/nomadic	2	2	1	*	—	1
Dead	2	3	1	2	4	—
Armed Forces	3	5	*	1	2	—
Other out of area/ institutionalized	6	5	7	8	8	7
Not located	6	6	6	9	12	5
N	668	351	317	536	277	259

Note. Because of rounding, percentages may not total exactly 100.
* Less than one half of one percent.
[a] Response and completion rates were calculated on the basis of the initial Wave 1 sample.
[b] Response and completion rates were calculated on the basis of the Wave 2 sample only. In addition, 15 respondents were interviewed at Wave 3 who had not been available for the second interview (12 men and 3 women, 7 "never home" and 8 "out of area," chiefly military), for a total Wave 3 interviewed sample of 426. Through the third wave, a total of 12% of the initial sample had moved out of the area, 4% were dead, 5% had refused the reinterview, and 13% had not been located.

approximately 15 years had elapsed since the study began. This time, 91% of the prior wave's sample was located, and the response rate based on the Wave 2 surviving New York City sample was 86%, somewhat higher than that for women and lower for men (Table 14.4). Combined with 15 respondents who had not been available for their second interviews, a total of 426 interviews were completed at Wave 3.

The analysis for this chapter is based on 411 respondents who were interviewed at all three study waves. This constitutes about 77% of the sample interviewed at the second wave, when drug-use information was asked for the first time. The retained sample and those lost in follow-up were generally similar on a wide range of Wave 2 variables. A somewhat greater proportion of men (17%) than women (12%) were lost in follow-up. Higher male loss was attributable to their death rate (6% of men compared with 1% of women up to the third wave) and to greater difficulty in location (e.g., fewer men than women could be located through welfare rolls and Medicaid). The male loss, furthermore, came disproportionately from older cohorts and from heroin users (see the discussion in Brunswick et al., 1985).

At all study times, data were collected through individual interviews conducted in respondents' homes by ethnic- and gender-matched interviewers following a structured interview schedule with mainly closed-end questions.[3]

Measures

Drug Use (Dependent Variable)

Life histories of drug use were obtained at both the second and third interviews. Respondents were asked at both waves about their use of marijuana, hallucinogens ("acid" and other psychedelics), cocaine, heroin, methadone, amphetamines ("uppers"), depressants ("downers"), glue and other inhalants, alcohol, and cigarettes. The list of substances was expanded at the third-wave interview to specify PCP ("dust," "angel dust"). Multiple measures of onset were obtained as checks in establishing reliability of reports on the timing of initiation to the use of each drug (i.e., how old respondent was, how long ago it was, and what his or her major activity was at time of first use). Usual frequency and recency of last use were among other items of information obtained about each drug.

An operational measure of drug abuse was constructed for this analysis by combining the self-reported information about the two most prevalent of the illicit substances: marijuana and cocaine. Use of each of these substances was commonplace among members of the Harlem panel (see the discussion in Brunswick et al., 1985, and Brunswick, Messeri, & Aidala, 1990). Through the third wave of interviews, about three quarters of the women respondents and nearly 90% of the men reported that they had used marijuana on more than a trial basis. Just over half of the men and 40% of the women reported use of cocaine on three or more occasions.

Not all of this use occurred with enough frequency or over sufficiently long periods of time that it necessarily constituted abusive use in the sense that it impaired social,

---

[3]At the request of respondents, a small number of interviews were conducted in study offices or other locations outside of the home. Approximately 10 interviews were conducted in prison at both Waves 2 and 3.

psychological, or physical functioning (Newcomb & Bentler, 1989). A reliable direct measure of problem use of drugs, however, was not available.[4] Instead, a group of users was distinguished who were likely to be at elevated risk of impaired performance of adult roles, on the basis of continued regular multiweekly or daily use of one or both of these substances beyond their young adult years. An adult-use status typology was constructed separately for each drug, dividing respondents into four categories: (a) heavy regular adult users, (b) moderate regular adult users, (c) former regular users, and (d) no lifetime history of regular use.

The classification of respondents involved successive differentiation of the sample according to frequency and age at most recent use. First, individuals were distinguished who at some time had used cocaine and/or marijuana regularly (Categories 1, 2, or 3). Regular use was operationally defined to be of at least monthly frequency for one or more years. Nonregular users (Category 4) grouped together respondents (a) who may have used these substances for extended periods of time, but not more than a few times a year, with those (b) who never used or (c) who only experimented once or twice.

Next, continued regular use as an adult (Categories 1 and 2) necessitated an age determination. Individuals were classified as adult users if they reported use occurring in or after the calendar year of their 26th birthday. Age 26 was selected as the cutoff for adult use because it was the minimum age that all panel members had attained at the time of the third wave of interviews (the age range at the third interview was between 26 and 31 years). Moreover, age 26 coincides with the lower limit of the adult age group (distinguished from "young adult") in the national surveys of drug abuse (e.g., sponsored by the National Institute on Drug Abuse, 1988). Finally, adult regular heavy users (Category 1), who used daily or, at a minimum, multiple times a week, were distinguished from an adult moderate regular use group, whose frequency of use was between once a week and once a month (Category 2).

Preliminary analysis for differences among the 4-group adult drug-use typology was performed separately for cocaine and marijuana users. Subsequently, and in the results reported below, a composite "adult drug use" variable was derived by cross-classification of the four categories of marijuana and cocaine use. Table 14.5 shows the results of this cross-classification and the composition of the adult drug-status groups. The groups are as follows:

---

[4] When asked directly about problems from drug use, some individuals who reported no problems still had been in treatment, and some for extended periods. We thus were not satisfied that this approach yielded a valid measure of conditions that might satisfy objective criteria of problem use.

TABLE 14.5

Composition of Adult Drug-User Groups

Group	Total		Men		Women	
	n	%	*n*	%	*n*	%
Heavy use group						
Adult heavy cocaine						
and adult heavy marijuana	28	39	14	35	14	44
and adult moderate marijuana	1	1	1	3	0	0
and former regular marijuana	5	7	2	5	3	9
and never regular marijuana	2	3	0	0	2	6
Adult moderate cocaine						
and adult heavy marijuana	36	50	23	58	13	41
N		72		40		32
Moderate use group						
Adult moderate cocaine						
and adult moderate marijuana	16	12	7	9	9	16
and former adult marijuana	9	7	5	6	4	7
and never adult marijuana	3	2	0	0	3	5
Former regular cocaine						
and adult heavy marijuana	12	9	10	13	2	4
and adult moderate marijuana	7	5	7	9	0	0
Never regular cocaine						
and adult heavy marijuana	47	35	31	39	16	28
and adult moderate marijuana	42	31	19	24	23	40
N		136		79		57
Former use group						
Former regular cocaine						
and former regular marijuana	14	13	7	14	7	13
and never regular marijuana	1	1	1	2	0	0
Never regular cocaine						
and former regular marijuana	90	86	41	84	49	88
N		105		49		56

Note. Because of rounding, percentages may not total exactly 100.

- Heavy regular adult users: All adult heavy users of cocaine, plus moderate users of cocaine only if they were also adult heavy users of marijuana ($n = 72$; men $= 40$; women $= 32$).

- Moderate regular adult users: All other adult regular cocaine users, plus former adult cocaine users if they were adult regular heavy or moderate marijuana users, and all other heavy or moderate adult marijuana users. ($n = 136$; men $= 79$; women $= 57$)

- Former regular users: Regular users of either marijuana or cocaine (or both) who did not continue using either substance regularly past age 25. ($n = 105$; men $= 49$; women $= 56$)

- Nonregular users: No lifetime history of regular monthly use of either marijuana or cocaine. This group was used in preliminary screening analyses only and was dropped from the final logistic regression analyses. ($n = 98$; men $= 30$; women $= 68$)

This classification assumes that cocaine use indicates greater substance-use involvement and hence greater risk of abuse than does marijuana use alone. The bivariate distribution in Table 14.5 is consistent with such a hierarchical relationship between cocaine and marijuana use. Regular use of cocaine is almost always associated with marijuana use, whereas sizable numbers of marijuana users have not ventured into cocaine use. Note particularly that all but eight adult heavy cocaine users were adult heavy marijuana users as well. Only two individuals in the adult heavy-use group had never used marijuana regularly. The heavy, moderate, and former-user groups defined above constituted the outcome variable in the analysis.

Predictor Variates

As reported above, independent variables were grouped into six domains measured at one or both life stages. The domains grouped variables measuring (I) social structure, (II) asynchrony or nonconventionality in life-stage roles, (III) social bonds, (IV) perceived social opportunity, (V) demoralization or ontogenic strain, and (VI) early marijuana use.

Life stage was assigned either by the wave from which the measures were obtained or by the age of occurrence. The latter refers to role-attainment variables that were constructed from event-history data to permit dating the time of a change in a discrete state, such as age when first child was born, or the status prevailing at ages immediately preceding the "choice" of adult drug abuse (e.g., marital status, cohabiting, unemployment ["months idle"] at ages 23–25). Adolescent life-stage variables were obtained from the first-wave interview (when the sample ranged in age from 12 to 17) or from retrospective questions asked at the next study wave that permitted dating the occurrence of a specified change in status before age 18 (e.g., first child born before age 18, or marijuana use begun by age 14). The latter cutoff (i.e., age 14) for "early" marijuana use was selected because it was the age by which 20% of users had started using. Early adult transition variables, referred to as postadolescent (PA), were obtained primarily from the second-wave interviews (when the sample ranged in age from 18 to 23) or from event-history data collected at the third wave that could be used to establish an individual's status with respect to an event at ages 23–25.

Covariates

Cohort was entered as a control in all multidomain models, within and across life stages. The six birth years represented in the sample were collapsed into older (birth years 1952 through 1954) and younger (birth years 1955 through 1957) cohorts to control both for developmental variability and for varying temporal distance in the timing of data collections relative to drug-use status measured at age 26. (Appendix A presents, for all independent variables entered in the logistic analysis, their coding, range of values, means, and standard deviations, as well as the components and reliability of indices and scales.)

Analytical Procedure

The predictive power of a large pool of independent variables for adult drug use was explored in several phases. In the initial stage, stepwise discriminant analyses were performed to eliminate variables that clearly did not differentiate respondents when classified into the marijuana and cocaine adult drug-use typologies. Independent variables were grouped into five domains (omitting parameters of marijuana use in this screening phase for obvious reasons) at the adolescent and the early-adult-transition life stages. Gender-specific stepwise discriminant analysis was performed separately on each of the 10 groups of independent variables. Thus, each independent variable was eligible for inclusion in four possible discriminant functions (i.e., for each drug and each gender). A variable was retained for subsequent analysis if it entered at least one of the discriminant functions at the .1 significance level. Variables dropped from the analysis for failing to meet this relatively liberal criterion are noted in Appendix B.

Having eliminated a substantial group of noninformative variables, we turned our attention to a focused analysis of the causal effects of the remaining variables on the likelihood of a transition from adolescent and/or postadolescent regular use to either moderate or heavy adult regular use. To model these transitions, we first restricted the study sample to those at risk of continued adult drug use, as indicated by any "regular use" of either marijuana or cocaine prior to age 26. Dropping the group with no history of regular monthly use reduced the sample for analysis from 411 to 313. Two dichotomous variables were then constructed on the basis of the composite adult drug-use typology described earlier, one matching former regular users with adult heavy users, and the other comparing former regular users with adult moderate users.

Logistic regression analysis was applied to measure the simple and multivariate effects of the independent variables on each of the transitions (i.e., heavy drug use in adulthood versus terminating use, and continuing drug use at moderate levels in adulthood versus terminating use. Logit regression coefficients were estimated on a personal computer using the unordered multilogit option of the maximum-likelihood procedure LOGIT in Statistical Software Tools, Version 1.1 (Dubin and Rivers, 1986). The unordered logit option simultaneously fit data to two logistic regression equations that contrasted, respectively, the moderate and heavy adult user groups with former regular users.

The logistic regression analysis proceeded in three stages: (a) estimation of simple effects and possible gender interactions, (b) estimation of multivariate life-stage-specific models constructed from the full variable set at each life stage, retaining significant gender interactions from the first stage, and (c) estimation of trimmed models that combined the more statistically and/or theoretically significant variables from both life stages to yield the final cross-life-stage model. Separate gender models were subsequently run to confirm the findings from this pooled cross-life-stage model.

In the first stage, logit coefficients for the effect of each predictor variable were estimated, adjusted only for gender and interaction with gender. The purpose here was to screen, one at a time, for variables that exerted gender-specific effects on one or both transitions. When gender-conditioned effects were present, the interaction term was retained into the next stage of analysis.

Next, multidomain, life-stage-specific models were estimated. Perceived opportunity and psychogenic factors were entered only for the more proximal early adult transition (PA) life stage. Note that self-esteem did not even enter the logistic analysis because it had failed to pass the discriminant analysis screen (see Appendix B). The dichotomous cohort variable ($1 =$ younger cohort; $0 =$ older cohort) and the gender variable ($1 =$ male, $0 =$ female) were included as controls in all equations. As indicated above, gender-interaction terms were also included for variables when results of the previous analysis suggested the presence of qualitatively distinct gender effects for one or both transitions.

The coefficients have a relative risk interpretation. If a coefficient is positive, it indicates that the variable adds to the logit or log odds of the outcome transition (i.e., increases its likelihood). Negative coefficients indicate a restraining effect of that variable on the transition being fitted. The significance and sign (direction) of the modeled effects are interpreted without proceeding to more precise odds calculations (i.e., odds ratios).

The final phase of the analysis estimated parsimonious or trimmed cross-life-stage models for both moderate and heavy transitions. To pare down the number of variables while avoiding the loss of those whose effects might strengthen as we improved the overall fit of the model, relatively liberal selection criteria were again applied. Thus, only variables that were well below levels of conventional statistical significance were removed, leaving in the equation several whose substantive impact was problematic even in the single-life-stage models. As a further step in improving the parsimony of the models, different sets of independent variables were culled for the two transitions. To corroborate the gender-specific effects identified in this final cross-life-model, gender-specific models were also fitted with the cross-life-stage variables as a check on the appropriate interpretation of gender-conditioned effects.

Results

In the introduction of the findings, it is useful to note the distribution of men and women into the four adult drug-status groups (see Table 14.6). The simple proportion of all men who became adult heavy drug users (20%) was not significantly greater than that for all women (15%). Proportions for those who had used these drugs regularly but terminated use by age 26 were nearly identical for the two genders. Differences resided primarily in

TABLE 14.6

Sample Distribution on Adult Regular Use Typology

Use	Total		Men		Women	
	n	%	*n*	%	*n*	%
Heavy	72	18	40	20	32	15
Moderate	136	33	79	40	57	27
Former	105	26	49	25	56	26
Never used regularly	98	24	30	15	68	32

the proportions who never initiated use of either of these drugs, where the rate for women (32%) was double that for men (15%), and in the proportions who maintained adult drug use at moderate levels, which was done by considerably more men (40%) than women (27%).

Results of the logistic analysis are summarized in Tables 14.7, 14.8 and 14.9, which present logit coefficients and standard errors from the life-stage equations and the cross-life-stage models predicting heavy use and moderate use, respectively.

Considering first the life-stage-specific equations, Table 14.7 presents estimates from equations predicting heavy and moderate adult use, using adolescent variables only, and Table 14.8 presents those from equations with variables from the early adult transition only. For purposes of comparison, the "univariate" effects of these variables are shown in the first column, adjusted for gender and, when prior analyses so indicated, interaction with gender but no other variables.

In the adolescent multidomain equation (Table 14.7), the only social-structure variable that had a direct effect on adult drug abuse was living in a family on welfare (borderline significance). Asynchronous life-stage role effects were expressed in the significance of fathering a child by age 17 (note that the adolescent-parenting variable was conditional: significant for men only). Two social-bond variables were significant: Participating in a greater number of recreational activities outside of the home enhanced the likelihood of drug abuse as an adult, and religiosity, which had the reverse effect, restrained or reduced the likelihood that an adolescent or early adult drug user would continue to use drugs heavily as an adult.

The equation predicting moderate adult use (Table 14.7) identified different adolescent influences: a significant gender effect (which has already been noted in the descriptive sample distribution shown in Table 14.6), dropping out of high school, and two ambiguous social-bond effects for women only: marginal restraining effects of peer influence and, similarly, of increased radio listening.

As for influences on the transition to adult heavy use modeled from the early adult variables only (Table 14.8), even fewer variables were significant than in the adolescent model. (This is a suggestive finding in and of itself.) Being in the older cohort and, for women only, not being married increased risk. Heavier marijuana use in early adulthood increased the likelihood of men's adult drug abuse, with no effect on women's transition to heavy use. However, more frequent marijuana use in early adulthood decreased the likelihood of women's moderate drug use as adults.

TABLE 14.7
Life-Stage-Specific Logistic Regression Models (Transitions to Adult Moderate and Heavy Drug Use)

Adolescent stage variable	Risk of heavy adult use				Risk of moderate adult use			
	Simple gender adjusted		Adolescent life stage		Simple gender adjusted		Adolescent life stage	
	b	*SE*	*b*	*SE*	*b*	*SE*	*b*	*SE*
Domain I: Social structure								
Gender	—	—	.445	.617	—	—	.987**	.447
Birth cohort	-.578*	.312	-.534	.368	-.163	.270	-.274	.308
Family on welfare	.519*	.310	.577*	.346	.125	.263	.075	.286
Domain II: Role asynchrony								
Parent by 17	.135	.544	-.290	.620	.379	.451	-.273	.426
Parent by 17 × Sex	-1.359	.891	2.050**	.972	-.576	.907	—	—
High school dropout	.242	.333	.353	.400	.634	.280	.707**	.317

Domain III: Social bonds							
Peer influence	−.198	.257	−.077	.274	−.542	.273	−.552*	.297
Peer influence × Sex	.293	.318	.162	.340	.413	.325	.331	.347
Spare time/family	−.657**	.328	−.487	.373	−.259	.268	−.387	.299
Religiosity	−.256***	.097	−.221**	.108	−.007	.083	.050	.091
Recreation index	.078***	.029	.072**	.032	.021	.024	.029	.027
No. close friends	.018	.022	.017	.024	−.016	.020	−.023	.021
Hrs./day radio	.139	.118	.109	.132	.187*	.102	.158	.108
Hrs./day radio × Sex	−.297*	.165	−.270	.179	−.341**	.139	−.339**	.145
Domain VI: Marijuana gateway							
Use of marijuana by age 14	.863	.527	.843	.571	.222	.495	.230	.316
Use of marijuana by age 14 × Sex	−.663	.696	−.861	.759	.105	.628	—	—
Constant	—	—	−1.537*	.611	—	—	−.149	.480

Note. Cohort: younger = 1, older = 0. Gender: male = 1, female = 0; when an indicator is shown with its gender interaction, the main term identifies the female value, the interaction term the male.

* $p \leq .1$. ** $p \leq .05$. *** $p \leq .01$.

TABLE 14.8
Full Life-Stage Logistic Regression Model (Transitions to Adult Moderate and Heavy Drug Use)

| | Risk of heavy adult use | | | | Risk of moderate adult use | | | |
| | Simple gender adjusted | | Early adult life stage | | Simple gender adjusted | | Early adult life stage | |
Early adult transition variable	b	SE	b	SE	b	SE	b	SE
Domain I: Social structure								
Gender	—	—	-.050	1.820	—	—	-.685	1.561
Birth Cohort	—	—	-.891**	.352	—	—	-.264	.295
Domain II: Role asynchrony								
Unmarried 23–25	1.352**	.675	1.42*	.740	.406	.439	.067	.362
Unmarried 23–25 × Sex	1.092	.850	-1.659*	.930	.004	.625		
Months idle	.029**	.011	.021	.014	.021**	.010	.006	.012
No. children	.130	.158	-.109	.202	.134	.136	-.179	.169
Cohabit 23–25	.880*	.510	.462	.512	.204	.477	.102	.521
Cohabit 23–25 × Sex	.464	.878	.929	.962	1.574**	.803	1.768**	.857

Domain III: Social bonds								
No. organizations	-.094	.343	-.171	.353	-.364	.327	-.104	.353
No. organizations × Sex	-1.189	.89	-.107	.112	.929*	.535	.923	.575
Yrs. education	-.134*	.076	-.113	.098	-.211***	.067	-.216**	.096
Religiosity	-.148*	.086			-.178**	.073	-.202**	.082
Domain IV: Perceived opportunity								
Achievement orientation	-.071	.083	.048	.111	-.155**	.070	-.036	.095
Domain V: Demoralization/ontogenic								
General strain	-.189	.156	-.139	.168	.086	.130[a]		
Personal efficacy	.177	.199	-.132	.138	-.175*	.102	-.050	.115
Personal efficacy × Sex	.124	.173	.144	.193	.242	.150	.153	.166
Domain VI: Marijuana gateway								
Frequency of marijuana use	-.025	.131	-.002	.116	-.172	.109	-.184**	.092
Frequency of Marijuana × Sex	.648***	.234	.472**	.213	.284*	.162	.229	.142
Constant	—	—	1.456	1.426	—	—	.932	1.192

Note. Cohort: younger = 1, older = 0. Gender: male = 1, female = 0.

[a] Given trivial effect size, variable omitted from multidomain model.

* $p \leq .1$, ** $p \leq .05$, *** $p \leq .01$.

TABLE 14.9

Trimmed Cross-Life-Stage Logistic Model (Risk of Heavy Adult Use)

Variable	Life-stage		Cross-life-stage (all)		Cross-life-stage (female)		Cross-life-stage (male)	
				Adolescence				
	b	SE	b	SE	b	SE	b	SE
Domain I: Social structure								
Birth cohort	-.533	.354	-.865**	.387	-1.415**	.568	-.318	.555
Gender	.818	.533	2.756***	.893				
Family on welfare	.586*	.331	.326	.363	.695	.552	.152	.505
Domain II: Role asynchrony								
Parent by 17	-.094	.588	-.479	.649	-.272	.695	1.431*	.797
Parent by 17 × Sex	1.783*	.952	1.892*	.995				
Domain III: Social bonds								
Religiosity	-.230**	.105	-.270**	.117	-.182	.171	-.372**	.167
Recreation index	.074**	.031	.073**	.003	.055	.050	.091**	.047
Hrs./day radio	.101	.129	.288	.139	.220	.145	-.225*	.137
Hrs./day Radio × Sex	-.294*	.176	-.477**	.191				

	Early adult							
Domain VI: Marijuana gateway								
Use of marijuana by 14	.882	.554	1.329**	.625	1.405**	.640	−.436	.546
Use of Marijuana by 14 × Sex	−.859	.735	−1.859**	.821			.197	.599
Domain II: Role asynchrony								
Unmarried 23–25	−1.502**	.665	1.784**	.757	1.965**	.788	.197	.599
Unmarried 23–25 × Sex	−1.743***	.836	−1.690*	.959				
Months idle (23–25)	.022**	.010	.029**	.015	.045**	.021	.011	.022
Domain III: Social bonds								
Yrs. education	−.051	.057	−.100	.099	.027	.158	−.175	.131
Religiosity	−.112	.087	−.039	.102	.018	.134	−.125	.166
Domain VI: Marijuana gateway								
Frequency of marijuana use	.086	.090	−.061	.122	.011	.130	.582***	.214
Frequency of Marijuana × Sex	.125	.111	.621***	.239				
Constant	1.656***	.541	−1.501*	.902	−1.845	1.207	1.342	1.159

Note. Gender: male = 1, female = 0. Cohort: younger = 1, older = 0.
*p ≤ .1. **p ≤ .05. ***p ≤ .01.

Table 14.9 presents results of the cross-life-stage model (i.e., with significant predictors from both life-stages in a single equation) predicting the transition to heavy use, and Table 14.10 presents the same information for the transition to moderate use. The first pair of columns in each table present, for comparison, the estimated logit coefficients and associated standard errors obtained for each variable in a pruned (reduced) life-stage-specific equation. The next columns present estimated logit coefficients and standard errors for the gender-pooled cross-life-stage models, then for gender-specific female and male cross-life-stage replication models.

Cross-life-stage results will be discussed by domains of influence, focusing on the transition to heavy use Table 14.9. Because almost all variates exerted gender-distinct effects (confirmed in the gender-specific models, Table 14.9, Columns 5–8), results will be discussed separately by gender. Figure 14.2 illustrates the gender-distinct developmental processes of influence on the transition to adult heavy use that the findings identified.

Women
Social Structure
Being in the younger cohort (i.e., having been born in the late 1950s) exerted a strong effect on reducing the likelihood of a woman's heavy drug use compared with that of a woman born earlier in the 1950s.

No other background social-structure variate sustained a significant effect throughout the cross-life-stage model. Whereas, in the adolescent model, living in a household receiving welfare support appeared to have a marginal and not gender-conditioned influence on heavy use, when early adult variables of role asynchrony and other factors were controlled, the earlier welfare effect was no longer of consequence. (Different results might have been observed had the sample included a contrasting White or middle-class component.)

Early Adult Asynchrony
Not being married between ages 23 and 25 exerted a strong effect on increasing women's, but not men's, odds of adult heavy use. The effect was unique to women and to their heavy use.

Unemployment also increased the likelihood of a woman's adult heavy drug use. This effect, too, was unique to women and to their heavy use.

Having begun using marijuana early (by age 14) added to a young woman's chances of adult heavy drug use. Like the variables above, the effect of early use was limited to

TABLE 14.10

Trimmed Cross-Life-Stage Logistic Model (Risk of Moderate Adult Use)

Variable	Life-stage		Cross-life-stage (all)		Cross-life-stage (female)		Cross-life-stage (male)	
	b	SE	b	SE	b	SE	b	SE
			Adolescence					
Domain I: Social structure								
Birth cohort	−.291	.286	−.320	.304	−.179	.421	−.494	.453
Gender	1.059**	.423	1.469**	.671				
Domain III: Social bonds								
Peer influence index	−.471*	.279	−.446	.279	−.463*	.281	−.150	.207
Peer Influence × Sex	.270	.333	.302	.343				
Hrs/day radio	.159	.103	.208*	.109	.204*	.108	−.175	.108
Hrs/day Radio × Sex	−.341**	.141	−.367**	.149				
Domain VI: Marijuana gateway								
Marijuana use by age 14	.279	.308	.231	.345	.334	.558	.122	.454

TABLE 14.10 *(Continued)*

Variable	Life-stage		Cross-life-stage (all)		Cross-life-stage (female)		Cross-life-stage (male)	
	b	*SE*	*b*	*SE*	*b*	*SE*	*b*	*SE*
			Early adult					
Domain II: Role asynchrony								
Cohabit age 23–25	.174	.492	.203	.518	.269	.513	1.768**	.691
Cohabit × Sex	1.796**	.812	1.517*	.853				
Domain III: Social Bonds								
No. organizations	−.128	.342	−.177	.361	−.269	.368	.903*	.495
No. Organizations × Sex	1.153**	.559	1.012*	.586				
Yrs. education	−.158***	.052	−.234***	.073	−.131	.099	−.349***	.108
Religosity	−.222***	.080	−.195**	.084	−.177	.111	−.212	.130
Domain VI: Marijuana gateway								
Frequency of marijuana use	−.173***	.067	−.213**	.095	−.214**	.095	.039	.117
Frequency of Marijuana × Sex	.041	.087	.252*	.144				
Constant	−.041	.371	.037	.603	−.452	.697	2.081***	.788

Note. Cohort: younger = 1, older = 0. Gender: male = 1, female = 0.
*$p \leq .1$. **$p \leq .05$. ***$p \leq .01$.

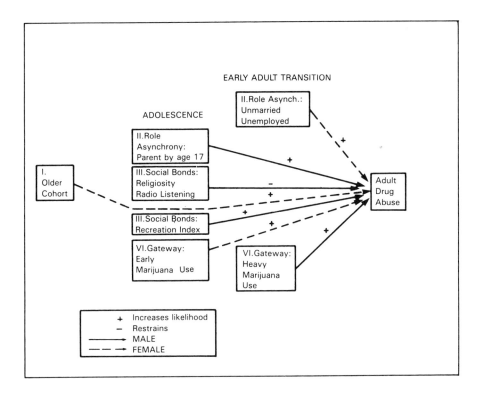

FIGURE 14.2 Observed domain relationships predicting heavy adult drug use.

women and to their heavy drug use. Neither men's adult heavy use nor adult moderate use on the part of either gender registered an effect from early marijuana onset.

Neither earlier (adolescent) role asynchrony, nor social-bond variables, nor perceived opportunity (in early adulthood), nor ontogenic strain showed a significant influence on women's transition to adult heavy drug use.

Men

Social Structure

When other variables in the model were controlled, being a man significantly increased the odds of adult substance abuse relative to women's chances. Unlike women, the odds of heavy drug use were not significantly different for the older versus younger cohorts of men. As for women, the family of orientation's welfare status no longer exerted an influence when early adult transition variables were included in the model.

Adolescent Role Asynchrony

Parenting a child by age 17 increased the likelihood of a man's adult heavy drug use. No later role variable showed an effect.

Social Bonds

Similarly, adolescent social bonds, but not those in early adulthood, increased the odds of a man's becoming an adult drug abuser. Specifically, adolescent religiosity had a restraining effect. So too, to a weaker extent, did hours of radio listening as an adolescent. The power of men's adolescent religious commitment was not an artifact of its correlation with later religiosity, the overtime autocorrelation being a modest .25. Note that identical indicators of religiosity were taken at both life stages, then modeled simultaneously in the cross-life-stage equation.

Participation in recreational activities outside of the home had an enhancing effect on the odds of male adult drug abuse. Significant adolescent social-bond effects were gender specific and showed an impact for men only.

The effect of time spent listening to the radio (in adolescence) is one of the enigmatic findings that has appeared in other analyses of this longitudinal study (Brunswick, 1980b). More time radio listening as an adolescent reduced men's odds of adult heavy use. No information is available as to the processes surrounding this effect, but it persists more often than can justly be attributed to random error. Radio time, furthermore, was the only variable that showed a significant impact in both moderate and heavy adult use models, consistently reducing men's likelihood of both transitions and increasing women's likelihood of moderate use.

Marijuana Gateway

Early age of marijuana onset did not affect men's likelihood of continuing heavy drug use as adults. More frequent marijuana use in postadolescence, not early use, added to the odds of men's adult heavy drug use.

As found for women, neither perceived opportunity nor ontogenic strain or demoralization in early adulthood influenced men's risk of adult drug use, moderate or heavy.

Conditions Without Influence on the Transition to Adult Heavy Use

Conditions that did not have an effect but that were predicted to, on the basis of prior research dealing with role-status effects and continuing marijuana use (cf. Bachman,

O'Malley, & Johnston, 1984; Kandel & Logan, 1984; Yamaguchi & Kandel, 1985), included the following:

- Family welfare or its correlated factor, women-headed household;
- adolescent childbearing (women);
- dropping out of high school; the limited effects of this variable in the multivariate models and of the correlated variable, years of education completed, were noted above and held true even after removing one or another of the variables to offset any dilution of effect arising from redundancy (collinearity);
- unemployment (men); and
- cohabitation, which appeared in univariate analysis to increase the odds of women's heavy use; in the multivariate model, this effect was attenuated and limited to men's transition to adult moderate use.

Demoralization or ontogenic strain, the psychogenic factors that were tested, included personal efficacy, self-esteem, sense of alienation, and general strain (composite scale of worries and dissatisfaction). Of these, efficacy alone, even in the simple effects model Appendix A, showed as much as a suggestive or weak restraining effect, which was limited to women.

Similarities and Differences in Transitions to Heavy and Moderate (Controlled) Drug Use in Adulthood

When we controlled for relationships among the other modeled variables, men had a significantly greater likelihood of continuing drug use into adulthood, at both use levels, compared with women, a finding that reflects the more stringent sanctions against drug use for women. It also reflects the powerful role of both implicit and enforced norms governing drug use.

Cohort, an indicator of changing norms, had an impact on heavy drug use (but not on moderate use) that was restricted to women. For reasons discussed at the close of this chapter, we interpret this to reflect the responsiveness of heavy drug use (but not less socially deviant moderate use) to changing social policies. To date, these policies have had a greater effect on women in the African American community than on men.

Similarly, the lesser norm-violating character of adult moderate drug use is reflected in its reduced predictability from asynchrony–nonconventionality in social roles. Role asynchrony, which had been influential in women's transition to heavy use, showed no effect in the transition to moderate use. For men, for whom early parenting had been an influence on adult heavy use, cohabiting (a considerably less norm-violating behavior) captured the significant role influence on moderate use.

No social-bond indicator gave evidence of an independent effect on women's transition to heavy use. Two not-easily-interpretable effects on moderate use were observed: a restraining effect from reported greater adolescent peer influence and an enhancing effect from increased hours of radio listening in adolescence. Whereas adolescent social-bond influences had predominated in men's transition to heavy use, adolescent bonds played no significant role in predicting men's moderate use. Instead, bond variables from the early adult transition were operating: More education restrained men's moderate drug use as adults, and belonging to a greater number of organizations increased the likelihood of men's controlled adult use.

Finally, joining in ambiguity the observation of a restraining effect of adolescent peer influence on women's transition to moderate adult use, heavier marijuana use in early adulthood had a restraining effect on women's chances of continuing to use marijuana at controlled levels as adults. Neither indicator of marijuana gateway influence operated on men's choice of adult moderate use, but heavy use in early adulthood significantly increased men's odds of being an adult heavy drug user.

Summary and Discussion

We test a developmental ecological model of behavioral influences that proceeded, first, with life-stage-specific logistic regressions, using predictors drawn from six postulated domains of influences, and then estimated a cross-life-stage model that included all significant variables from the stage-specific regressions, along with their gender interactions when indicated. This revealed distinct processes leading to heavy versus moderate or controlled adult use. For both drug-use outcomes, furthermore, strikingly different gender processes were observed within this African American sample:

1. Macrosocial or structural processes linked to normative variations in life histories, generally, and drug use, specifically, were seen first in the simple distribution of male and female samples on the adult drug-use typology and then in the multiplicative effects of cohort and gender. Although simple logit coefficients did not reveal significant differences between men and women or between older (born 1952–1954) and younger (born 1955–1957) cohorts, being a woman in the older cohort significantly increased the likelihood of adult heavy use compared with women born later in the same decade.

Meanwhile, although in life-stage-specific models gender had not shown a significant independent effect over and above the observed conditioning of specified variables, once variables from both life stages were simultaneously controlled, men were shown to be at greater risk.

2. Other than early onset of marijuana use (by age 14) and the social structural influence of cohort, women's earlier influences were all processed through adult role attainment. Being unmarried and unemployed independently added to the likelihood of women's adult drug abuse.

3. Years of education, which might have been expected to have a significant independent influence given its import as a link to conventional values, for the most part did not show an effect. The single model in which education did operate demonstrated that it restrained men's adult moderate use (i.e., with increasing years of education, men were more likely to cease using illicit drugs than to maintain use at a controlled level). The absence of an effect of educational attainment in the other modeled transitions probably reflects the existence of other modi operandi for adapting to educational disadvantage in this population.

4. Even in the model predicting moderate adult use, years of education (a measure of traditional bonds) had no predictive value for women's adult drug abuse. More generally, and perhaps contrary to expectation, variables that were classified as predictors of social bonds (to conventional values) did not distinguish whether women continued to use illicit drugs in adulthood.[5] Measures of adult role attainment–asynchrony alone showed an independent impact on the transition to women's drug abuse.

5. The male developmental trajectory was notably different and, at first glance, contradictory to expectations based on general gender stratification theory (cf. Barnett, Beiner, & Baruch, 1987; Levinson, Darrow, Klein, Levinson, & McKee, 1978). Adult role attainment (employment) showed no influence on male transitions to either heavy or moderate use. Instead, adolescent role asynchrony, represented by the measure of early fathering (i.e., by age 17), had a marginally significant effect. A marginal effect on the transition to moderate use was also observed for cohabiting in the years immediately prior to the age 26 choice point. Generally, social-bond influences predominated over role-attainment ones in men's predictive models, and they were

---

[5] Two exceptions to this generalization appeared in the model predicting transition to moderate use where greater peer influence in adolescence had a restraining effect in the transition to moderate adult use and increased radio listening in adolescence predicted a greater likelihood of moderate drug use in adulthood. However, because age-appropriate conventional roles did deter women's adult drug abuse, we assume that significant social bonding to traditional values took place before adolescence, the first life stage captured in this study.

carried forward from the adolescent life stage. No indicators modeled from the early adult transition (except heaviness of marijuana use) influenced men's transition to heavy use. Thus, men's effects, in contrast with women's, were in place in the adolescent life stage. Even when early adult indicators were tested alone without the adolescent measures, they showed little predictive impact on men's transition to adult substance abuse. The predictive value of early (adolescent) religiosity for the transition to adult heavy use is a particularly seminal finding, and it is discussed further below. In general, what these findings say is that, in contrast with the African American woman, the man's trajectory is set by adolescence and, furthermore, that by early adulthood this course may be beyond the reach of conventional social controls, to which women show greater responsiveness.

6. Marijuana gateway theory, with respect to the traditional predictiveness of early age of onset, was supported when modeling the female trajectory, but it lacked support in the predictive model for men. This might be explained by the normativeness of early marijuana use among African American males and its pervasiveness (87% lifetime prevalence of nonexperimental marijuana use among men, Brunswick et al., 1990). This is further evidence of the probable removal, noted above, of a subset of African American men, identified in the adult heavy drug-abuse group, from dominant societal norms and controls that guide developmental processes of drug onset and termination among White populations and, it would appear, among African American women as well.

This seems to say that, for men, drug use, even early use, is not the issue. It is, rather, to have social bonds—formal and informal social supports—to assist in maturing out of use. This process may be akin to what was observed in the same male study sample's heroin use: Substantial proportions of men who used heroin stopped spontaneously within a 4-year period of use (Boyle & Brunswick, 1980).

7. On the basis of the absence of effect from the demoralization or ontogenic strain measures, these data provided no support for a coping theory of adult drug abuse. This absence of predictive power is not surprising when adult drug abuse is viewed not as a manifestation of individual deviance, but rather as a result of social processes that influence a behavior practiced by 20% of the men and 15% of the women in this community-representative sale. Our findings agree with a recently completed test of the coping function of drug use, modeled with the same longitudinal sample (Brunswick, Lewis, & Messeri, 1991b). The results of that study showed that unemployment and drug use had direct additive stress effects for women. Stress

effects for men were multiplicative: Neither drug use nor unemployment alone, but each conditioned on the other, produced stress. No stress-reduction effects from drug use were in evidence for either gender.

8. The absence of effect from the perceived-opportunity and ontogenic domains cannot be taken as a refutation of the structural strain or social learning – reinforcement theories of drug use. The timing of measurement may be at issue—that is, the early adult transition from which these measures were drawn was likely too late, developmentally, to capture expectancy effects. Support for this interpretation comes from an earlier analysis of adolescent predictors of cigarette smoking (Brunswick & Messeri, 1984a), which showed that lower educational expectancy increased the likelihood of men's smoking on-set, as did a greater sense of alienation.

Then, too, drug abuse is only one among several possible responses to a pervasive condition of social exclusion (e.g., "quiet resignation," somaticization, are other alterna-tives). The latter would more likely be responses among individuals with stronger bonds to, or identification with, conventional authority. Note, that only marijuana and cocaine were included in the drug typology; heavy alcohol use not accompanied by adult use of illicit drugs was not tested in this analysis.

Generally, the observed patterns of predictors of adult drug abuse support the use-fulness of a structural-strain explanation in combination with social control and social learning models in explaining drug abuse among adult African Americans. Asynchrony or reduced levels of role attainment and the absence of affiliations with institutions of tradi-tional social control are manifestations of structural strain at the same time that they shut off individuals from channels of conventional authority and from the opportunity for positive reinforcement of socially desirable or prosocial behavior.

The negative consequences of the absence, in adolescence, of bonds to social insti-tutions that are the customary purveyors of traditional norms and values are perhaps the most salient etiological finding in the male transition to adult drug abuse. This finding takes on particular importance in light of the historical role of the church in African American culture. This study thus confirmed the powerful social-control influence of reli-giosity. Even though the analysis specifically omitted all individuals who had never used drugs with at least monthly regularity (a group we can rightly assume would be drawn from the more heavily religiously committed), religiosity in adolescence was still the most powerful deterrent of men's adult heavy drug use among those who did use drugs. Al-though in the same direction, its influence was weak in the female model. This, we sur-mise, was because adolescent religiosity was more likely to have screened women out of regular drug use in the first place. But once one was engaged in use, it served to constrain the period and intensity of use for men. This was in contrast with the effects of early adult religiosity, which, for both men and women, reduced the risk of continuing drug use at even moderate or controlled levels.

What are we to make of the repeated observations of divergent male and female responses to influences across almost every domain: social roles including marriage and employment, cohort effects, and even early marijuana use? And what are the implications for directions of future policy to deter drug abuse among urban African Americans? The findings show that social-role deprivation and absence of bonding (and opportunities for bonding) to dominant societal norms are more pervasive and severe for inner-city African American men than women. Even so, female adult drug abuse appeared more responsive to dominant social norms. Take, for example, the unexpected and striking cohort effects on women's risk for adult abuse, which did not appear for men. Cohort, as indicated earlier, was both a substantive indicator and a methodological control for the variable timing of adolescent and early-adult measures relative to the outcome at age 26. The fact that cohort variation was not observed for both genders suggests that substantive rather than methodological factors are at work.

These gender differences could stem from secular changes in alternatives and opportunities that affected African American women and not men and that affected younger and older female cohorts differently. The early 1970s, saw in New York City, the legalization of abortion and the introduction of open municipal college enrollment to any high school graduate seeking it. Women in the sample had a small educational advantage over men, with 41% ever entering a 2- or 4-year college and 11% earning a bachelor's degree. This was in comparison with 35% of the men entering college and 7% earning a bachelor's. In this sample, 55% of women who had ever been pregnant reported at least one abortion. Because the individuals in the older cohort were nearly 20 years old, on average, when these social policy changes were introduced, compared with members of the younger cohort still in their teens, these social changes appear to be at least a partial explanation for women's significantly changed cohort risk of heavy drug use as adults. These gender differences also signify that social innovations in the 1970s have affected women more than men. Taken one step further, these differences suggest that African American women can or will respond to straightforward improvements in social programs and opportunities; their rates of retention in drug treatment programs also support such a conclusion (Brunswick & Messeri, 1985, 1986; Brunswick, Messeri, & Aidala, 1990).

However, the absence of a similar cohort differentiation among men, together with other differences in the patterning of effects on the transition to adult drug abuse, described above, demonstrates that, by early adulthood, African American men are less readily affected by social innovations and social institutions than are women. A system needs to be modeled for men that will provide the bonding to conventional values that the church formerly provided and that at present no social agency is providing, and that will also satisfy needs for (interpersonal) affiliation and appropriate adult male role models—an institution that can reward socially sanctioned values, beliefs, and behavior. Such a social agency need not necessarily be along conventional church and religious lines, but it needs to engage young males, beginning in childhood, in activities that have meaning for their affective, valuative, and cognitive development. Simultaneously, structural changes are essential for increasing access to the opportunity structure even while social agencies improve the skills African American males need for successful maneuvering in this structure (see Massey & Eggers, 1990; Swinton, 1988; Wilson, 1987). In the absence of population-appropriate interventions for African American men, we are unlikely to see among them the downturn in marijuana and cocaine use observed in the recent National Household Drug Surveys (U.S. Department of Health and Human Services, 1989) and in surveys of high school seniors (Johnston, O'Malley, & Bachman, 1989). If such downturns are the result of increased perceptions of risk and social disapproval for drug-use behavior, as Bachman, Johnston, & O'Malley (1990) report, these are not issues to which socially disengaged African American populations can respond.

Hawkins et al. (1985) earlier stressed the importance of a developmental perspective in planning interventions and the need for intervening well before the anticipated age of initiation of drug use (i.e., recognizing that the conditions predisposing to drug use are already in place in childhood). Our findings are in full accord with this theoretical stance and underscore the need for early childhood intervention, as suggested above, in the processes that are currently leading to isolation from dominant values and norms.

The analogy to a "web of causation" (introduced at the start of this chapter as necessary to understanding causal factors in African American drug abuse) has implications for an appropriate theoretical stance as well. These findings support a theory of drug-abuse vulnerability that overlays social learning and social control theories with a structural-strain perspective, a perspective that is essential to understanding factors influencing African American youth's trajectory to substance abuse.

References

Akers, R. (1977). *Deviant behavior: A social learning approach* (2nd ed.). Belmont, MA: Wadsworth Press.

Bachman, J. G., Johnston, L. D., & O'Malley, P. M. (1990). Explaining the recent decline in cocaine use among young adults: Further evidence that perceived risks and disapproval lead to reduced drug use. *Journal of Health and Social Behavior, 31,* 173–184.

Bachman, J. G., O'Malley, P., & Johnston, L. (1984). Drug use among young adults: The impacts of role status and social environment. *Journal of Personality and Social Psychology, 47,* 629–645.

Bandura, A. (1977). Self-efficacy: Toward a unifying theory of behavioral change. *Psychological Review, 84,* 191–215.

Barnett, R. C., Beiner, L., & Baruch, G. K. (1987). *Gender and stress.* New York: Free Press.

Baumrind, D. (1985). Familial antecedents of adolescent drug use: A developmental perspective. In C. Jones & R. Battjes (Eds.), *Etiology of drug abuse* (NIDA Drug Research Monograph No. 56, pp. 13–44). Rockville, MD: National Institute on Drug Abuse.

Bennett, N. G., Bloom, D. E., & Craig, P. H. (1989). The divergence of Black and White marriage patterns. *American Journal of Sociology, 95,* 692–722.

Boyle, J., & Brunswick, A. (1980, Winter). What happened in Harlem? Analysis of a decline in heroin use among a generation unit of urban black youth. *Journal of Drug Issues,* pp. 109—130.

Bradbury, K., & Brown, L. (1986, March–April). Black men in the labor market. *New England Economic Review,* 32–42.

Bronfenbrenner, U. (1979). *The ecology of human development.* Cambridge, MA: Harvard University Press.

Brook, L. S., Lukoff, I. F., & Whiteman, M. (1977). Peer, family, and personality domains as related to adolescents' drug behavior. *Psychological Reports 41,* 1095–1102.

Brunswick, A. (1979). Black youths and drug-use behavior. In G. Beschner & A. Friedman (Eds.), *Youth and drug abuse: Problems, issues, and treatment* (pp. 443–490). Lexington, MA: Lexington Books.

Brunswick, A. (1980a). Social meanings and developmental needs: Perspectives on Black youths drug use. *Youth & Society, 11,* 449–473.

Brunswick, A. (1980b). *Health and drug use among urban Black youths: Predictors, concomitants and consequences: Final report* (Research Grant R01 DA 00852). Rockville, MD: National Institute on Drug Abuse.

Brunswick, A. (1985). Health services for adolescents with impairment, disability, and/or handicap: An ecological paradigm. *Journal of Adolescent Health Care, 6,* 141–151.

Brunswick, A. (1988a). Young Black males and substance use. In J. T. Gibbs (Ed.), *Young, Black, and male in America: An endangered species* (pp. 166–187). Dover, MA: Auburn House.

Brunswick, A. (1988b). Drug use and affective distress: A longitudinal study of urban Black youth. In R. A. Feldman & A. R. Stiffman (Eds.), *Advances in adolescent mental health* (Vol. 3, pp. 101–125). JAI Press.

Brunswick, A., & Boyle, J. (1979). Patterns of drug involvement: Developmental and secular influences on age at initiation. *Youth & Society, 11,* 139–162.

Brunswick, A., Lewis, C., & Messeri, P. (1991a). *Drug use and stress: Testing a coping model in an urban African American sample.* Unpublished manuscript.

Brunswick, A., Lewis, C., & Messeri, P. (1991b). A life span perspective on drug use and affective distress in an urban African American population. *Journal of Community Psychology, 19,* 123–135.

Brunswick, A., Merzel, C., & Messeri, P. (1985). Drug use initiation among urban Black youth: A seven-year follow-up of developmental and secular influences. *Youth & Society, 17,* 189–216.

Brunswick, A., & Messeri, P. (1984a). Causal factors in onset of adolescents' cigarette smoking: A prospective study of urban Black youth. *Advances in Alcohol and Substance Abuse, 3,* 35–52.

Brunswick, A., & Messeri, P. (1984b). Gender differences in processes of smoking initiation. *Journal of Psychosocial Oncology, 2,* 49–69.

Brunswick, A., & Messeri, P. (1985). Timing of first drug treatment: A longitudinal study of urban Black youth. *Contemporary Drug Problems, 2,* 401–418.

Brunswick, A., & Messeri, P. (1986). Pathways to heroin abstinence: A longitudinal study of urban Black youth. *Advances in Alcohol and Substance Abuse, 5,* 103–122.

Brunswick, A., Messeri, P., & Aidala, A. (1990). Changing drug use patterns and treatment behavior: A longitudinal study of urban Black youth. In R. R. Watson (Ed.), *Prevention and treatment of drug and alcohol abuse* (pp. 263–311). Clifton, NJ: Humana Press.

Brunswick, A., & Rier, D. (in press). Structural strain: Drug use among African American youth. In R. L. Taylor (Ed.), *Black youth: Perspectives on their social and economic status.* Newbury Park, CA: Sage.

Clayton, R., & Voss, H. (1981). *Young men and drugs in Manhattan: A causal analysis* (NIDA Research Monograph Series 39). Rockville, MD: Department of Health and Human Services.

Cordes, C. (1985). At risk in America. *APA Monitor, 16(1),* 9–11, 27.

Dohrenwend, B., Dohrenwend, B., Oksenberg, L., Cook, D., & Shrout, P. (1981). What brief psychiatric screening scales measure. In *Health survey research methods* (NCHSR Research Proceedings Series, DHHS Publication No. PHS 81-3268, pp. 188–198).

Dubin, J., & Rivers, R. (1986). *Statistical software tools, Version 1.0.* Pasadena, CA: Dubin/Rivers Research.

Elliott, D., Huizinga, D., & Ageton, S. (1982). *Explaining delinquency and drug use* (Report No. 21). Boulder, CO: Behavioral Research Institute.

Elliott, D., & Voss, H. (1974). *Delinquency and dropout.* Lexington, MA: Heath.

Farnsworth, M., & Lieber, M. J. (1989). Strain theory revisited. *American Sociological Review, 54,* 263–274.

Fishburne, P., Abelson, H., & Cisin, I. (1980). *National survey on drug abuse: Main findings 1979.* Rockville, MD: Department of Health and Human Services.

Frank, J. D. (1972). The bewildering world of psychotherapy. *Journal of Social Issues, 28,* 27–43.

Hawkins, J., Lishner, D., & Catalano, R., Jr. (1985). Childhood predictors and the prevention of adolescent substance abuse. In C. Jones & R. Battjes (Eds.), *Etiology of drug abuse* (NIDA Drug Research Monograph No. 56, pp. 13–44). Rockville, MD: National Institute on Drug Abuse.

Helzer, J., Robins, L., & Davis, D. (1975–1976). Antecedents of narcotic use and addiction. *Drug and Alcohol Dependence, 1,* 183–190.

Hirschi, T. (1969). *Causes of delinquency.* Berkeley: University of California Press.

Huba, G., Wingard, J., & Bentler, P. (1979). Beginning adolescent drug use and peer and adult interactions. *Journal of Consulting and Clinical Psychology, 47,* 265–276.

Jessor, R. (1979). Marihuana: A review of recent psychosocial research. In R. Dupont, A. Goldstein, & J. O'Donnell (Eds.), *Handbook on drug abuse* (pp. 337–355). Rockville, MD: National Institute on Drug Abuse.

Jessor, R., Chase, J., & Donovan, J. (1980). Psychosocial correlates of marijuana use and problem drinking in a national sample of adolescents. *American Journal of Public Health, 70,* 604–613.

Jessor, R., & Jessor, S. L. (1977). *Problem behavior and psychosocial development: A longitudinal study of youth.* San Diego, CA: Academic Press.

Jessor, R., & Jessor, S. L. (1978). Theory testing in longitudinal research on marihuana use. In D. B. Kandel (Ed.), *Longitudinal research on drug use: Empirical findings and methodological issues* (pp. 41–71). Washington, D.C.: Hemisphere-Wiley.

Johnston, L. (1973). *Drugs and American youth.* Ann Arbor, MI: Institute for Social Research.

Johnston, L., Bachman, J., & O'Malley, P. (1981). *Highlights from student drug use in America, 1975–1981.* Washington, DC: National Institute on Drug Abuse.

Johnston, L., O'Malley, P., & Bachman, J. (1989). *Drug use, drinking, and smoking: National survey results from high school, college, and young adult populations 1975–88* (DHHS Publication No. ADM 89-1638). Rockville, MD: National Institute on Drug Abuse.

Kandel, D. (1978). Convergences in prospective longitudinal surveys of drug use in normal populations. In D. B. Kandel (Ed.), *Longitudinal research on drug use: Empirical findings and methodological issues* (pp. 3–38). Washington, D.C.: Hemisphere-Wiley.

Kandel, D. (1982). Epidemiological and psychosocial perspectives on adolescent drug use. *Journal of American Academic Clinical Psychiatry, 21,* 328–347.

Kandel, D., & Adler, D. (1982). Socialization into marijuana use among French adolescents: A cross-cultural comparison with the United States. *Journal of Health and Social Behavior, 23,* 295–309.

Kandel, D., Davies, M., Karus, D., & Yamaguchi, K. (1986). The consequences in young adulthood of adolescent drug involvement. *Archives of General Psychiatry, 43,* 746–754.

Kandel, D., Kessler, R., & Margulies, R. (1978). Antecedents of adolescent initiation into stages of drug use: A developmental analysis. In D. Kandel (Ed.), *Longitudinal research in drug use: Empirical findings and methodological issues* (pp. 73–99). Washington, DC: Hemisphere-Wiley.

Kandel, D., & Logan, J. (1984). Patterns of drug use from adolescence to young adulthood: I. Periods of risk for initiation, continued use, and discontinuation. *American Journal of Public Health, 74,* 660–666.

Kandel, D., Simcha-Fagan, O., & Davies, M. (1986). Risk factors for delinquency and illicit drug use from adolescence to young adulthood. *Journal of Drug Issues, 16* (1), 67–90.

Kandel, D., Single, E., & Kessler, R. (1976). The epidemiology of drug use among New York State high school students: Distribution, trends, and change in rates of use. *American Journal of Public Health, 66,* 43–53.

Kandel, D., & Yamaguchi, K. (1985). Developmental patterns of the use of legal, illegal, and medically prescribed psychotropic drugs from adolescence to young adulthood. In C. Jones & R. Battjes (Eds.), *Etiology of drug abuse* (NIDA Drug Research Monograph No. 56, pp. 13–44). Rockville, MD: National Institute on Drug Abuse.

Kaplan, H. (1978). Social class, self-derogation and deviant response. *Social Psychiatry, 13,* 19–28.

Kaplan, H. (1980). Self-esteem and self-derogation theory of drug abuse. In D. Lettieri, M. Sayers, & H. Pearson (Eds.), *Theories of drug abuse: Selected contemporary perspectives* (National Institute on Drug Abuse Research Monograph No. 30, DHHS Publication No. ADM 83-967, pp. 128–131). Washington, DC: U.S. Government Printing Office.

Kaplan, H., Martin, S., & Robbins, C. (1982). Applications of a general theory of deviant behavior: Self-derogation and adolescent drug use. *Journal of health and Social Behavior, 23,* 274–294.

Kellam, S. G., Ensminger, M. E., Branch, J., Brown, F. M., & Fleming, P. (1984). The Woodlawn Mental Health Longitudinal Community Epidemiological Project. In S. A. Rednick, M. Harway, & K. M. Finello (Eds.), *Handbook of longitudinal research* (Vol. 2). New York: Praeger.

Kleinman, P. (1978). Onset of addition: A first attempt at prediction. *International Journal of the Addictions, 13,* 1217–1235.

Kleinman, P., & Lukoff, I. (1978). Ethnic differences in factors related to drug use. *Journal of Health and Social Behavior,* 19, 190–199.

Kurdek, L. (1981). An integrative perspective on children's divorce adjustment. *American Psychologist, 36,* 856–866.

Levinson, D. J., Darrow, C., Klein, E., Levinson, M., & McKee, B. (1978). *The seasons of a man's life.* New York: Ballantine.

Levinson, D. J. (1986). A conception of adult development. *American Psychologist, 41,* 3–13.

Massey, D. S., & Eggers, M. L. (1990). The ecology of inequality: Minorities and the concentration of poverty, 1970–80. *American Journal of Sociology, 95,* 1153–1188.

Mausner, S., & Kramer, S. (1985). *Epidemiology: An introductory text.* Philadelphia: Saunders.

Merton, R. (1957). *Social theory and social structure.* New York: Free Press.

Miller, J., Cisin, I., Gardner-Keaton, H., Wirtz, P., Abelson, H., & Fishburne, P. (1983). *National survey on drug abuse: Main findings 1982.* Rockville, MD: National Institute on Drug Abuse.

National Institute on Drug Abuse. (1988). *National Household Survey on Drug Abuse: Main findings 1985.* (DHHS Publication No. ADM 88-1586). Rockville, MD: National Institute on Drug Abuse.

Newcomb, M. D., & Bentler, P. M. (1988). *Consequences of adolescent drug use: Impact on the lives of young adults.* Newbury Park, CA: Sage.

Newcomb, M. D., & Bentler, P. M. (1989). Substance use and abuse among children and teenagers. *American Psychologist, 44,* 242–248.

O'Donnell, J., & Clayton, R. (1979). Determinants of early marijuana use. In G. Beschner & A. Friedman (Eds.), *Youth drug abuse: Problems, issues, and treatment* (pp. 63–110). Lexington, MA: Lexington Books.

O'Donnell, J., Voss, H., Clayton, R., Slatin, G., & Room, R. (1976). *Young men and drugs: A nationwide survey* (NIDA Research Monograph Series 5). Rockville, MD: Department of Health and Human Services.

O'Malley, P., Johnston, L., & Bachman, J. (1984). Period, age, and cohort effects on substance use among American youth, 1976–82. *American Journal of Public Health, 74,* 682–688.

Powers, R. J. (1987). Stress as a factor in alcohol use and abuse. In E. Gottheil, K. A. Druly, S. P. Pashko, & S. Weinstein (Eds.), *Stress and addiction* (pp. 248–260). New York: Brunner/Mazel.

Rachal, J., Guess, L., Hubbard, R., Maisto, S., Cavanaugh, E., Waddell, R., & Benrud, C. (1982, Spring). Facts for planning No. 4: Alcohol misuse by adolescents. *Alcohol, Health and Research World.*

Robbins, C. (1989). Sex differences in psychosocial consequences of alcohol and drug abuse. *Journal of Health and Social Behavior, 30,* 117–130.

Robins, L., Darvish, H., & Murphy, G. (1970). The long-term outcome for adolescent drug users: A follow-up study of 76 users and 146 nonusers. In J. Zubin & A. Freedman, (Eds.), *The psychopathology of adolescence* (pp. 159–178). New York: Grune & Stratton.

Robins, L., & Murphy, G. (1967). Drug use in a normal population of young Negro men. *American Journal of Public Health, 57,* 1580–1596.

Robins, L., & Przybeck, T. (1985). Age of onset of drug use as a factor in drug and other disorders. In C. Jones & R. Battjes (Eds.), *Etiology of drug abuse* (NIDA Drug Research Mongraph No. 56, pp. 178–192). Rockville, MD: National Institute on Drug Abuse.

Robins, L., & Wish, E. (1977). Childhood deviance as a developmental process: A study of 223 urban Black men from birth to 18. *Social Forces, 56,* 448–471.

Rotter, J., Chance, J., & Phares, E. (1972). *Applications of social learning theory of personality.* New York: Holt, Rinehart & Winston.

Shedler, J., & Block, J. (1990). Adolescent drug use and psychological health. *American Psycologist, 45,* 612–630.

Simcha-Fagan, O., Gersten, J., & Langner, T. (1986). Early precursors and concurrent correlates of patterns of illicit drug use in adolescence. *Journal of Drug Issues, 16,* 7–28.

Smith, G., & Fogg, C. (1978). Psychological predictors of early use, late use and non-use of marijuana among teenage students. In D. Kandel (Ed.), *Longitudinal research on drug use: Empirical findings and methodological issues* (pp. 101–113). Washington, DC: Hemisphere-Wiley.

Swinton, D. H. (1989). Economic status of Blacks 1987. In J. Dewart (Ed.), *The state of Black America 1988.* New York: National Urban League.

Thompson, E. A., Smith-DiJulio, K., & Matthews, T. (1982). Social control theory: Evaluating a model for the study of adolescent alcohol and drug use. *Youth & Society, 13,* 303–326.

U.S. Bureau of the Census. (1988). *Statistical abstract of the United States* (109th ed.). Washington, DC: U.S. Government Printing Office.

U.S. Department of Health and Human Services (1989). *National Household Survey on Drug Abuse: Population estimates 1988* (DHHS Publication No. ADM 89-1636). Rockville, MD: National Institute on Drug Abuse.

Wills, T., & Shiffman, S. (1985). Coping and substance use: A conceptual framework. In S. Shiffman & T. Will, (Eds.) *Coping and substance use* (pp. 1–24). San Diego, CA: Academic Press.

Wilson, W. J. (1987). *The truly disadvantaged.* Chicago: University of Chicago Press.

Yamaguchi, K., & Kandel, B. (1985). Dynamic relationships between premarital cohabitation and illicit drug use: A life event history analysis of role selection and role socialization. *American Sociological Review, 50,* 530–546.

Logistic Regression (Risk of Moderate and Heavy Adult Drug Use, Adjusting for Sex Only)

Variable	Risk of heavy adult use		Risk of moderate adult use	
	b	SE	b	SE
Adolescence				
Domain I: Social structure				
Birth cohort	−0.835*	0.452	−0.196	0.388
Birth Cohort × Sex	0.489	0.627	0.088	0.540
Father present	−0.722	0.472	0.037	0.379
Father Present × Sex	0.588	0.639	−0.121	0.527
Family on welfare	−0.650	0.453	−0.103	0.378
Family on Welfare × Sex	−0.210	0.624	0.419	0.527
Domain II: Role asynchrony				
Parent by 17	0.135	0.544	0.379	0.451
Parent by 17 × Sex	1.359	0.891	−0.576	0.907
High school dropout	0.357	0.479	0.312	0.412
High School Dropout × Sex	−0.173	0.666	0.578	0.566
Domain III: Social bonds				
Peer influence index	−0.198	0.257	−0.542	0.273
Peer Influence Index × Sex	0.293	0.318	0.413	0.325
Spare time with family	−0.436	0.462	0.033	0.381
Spare Time With Family × Sex	−0.464	0.656	−0.581	0.535
Religiosity	−0.222	0.139	0.024	0.122
Religiosity × Sex	−0.067	0.194	−0.060	0.168
Recreation Index	0.072*	0.042	−0.019	0.037
Recreation Index × Sex	0.017	0.058	0.071	0.050
No. close friends	0.041	0.040	−0.019	0.040
No. Close Friends × Sex	−0.033	0.048	0.003	0.047
Hrs./day radio	0.139	0.118	0.187*	0.102
Hrs./Day Radio × Sex	−0.297*	0.165	−0.341**	0.139

APPENDIX A *(Continued)*

Variable	Risk of heavy adult use		Risk of moderate adult use	
	b	*SE*	*b*	SE
Domain VI: Marijuana gateway				
Early use of marijuana (by age 14)	0.863	0.527	0.222	0.495
Early Use × Sex	−0.663	0.696	0.105	0.628
	Early adult transition			
Domain II: Role asynchrony				
Job goals	−0.019	0.320	−0.148	0.272
Job Goals × Sex	0.315	0.453	0.302	0.386
Unmarried 23–25	−1.352**	0.675	−0.406	0.439
Unmarried 23–25 × Sex	1.092	0.850	−0.004	0.625
Months idle	0.032**	0.016	0.017	0.013
Months Idle × Sex	−0.007	0.023	0.008	0.020
No. children	0.085	0.216	0.033	0.185
No. Children × Sex	0.123	0.322	0.221	0.279
Cohabit 23–25	0.880*	0.510	0.204	0.477
Cohabit 23–25 × Sex	0.464	0.878	1.574**	0.803
Domain III: Social bonds				
No. organizations	−0.094	0.343	−0.364	0.327
No. Organizations × Sex	−1.189	0.887	0.929*	0.535
Yrs. education	−0.092	0.107	−0.131	0.092
Yrs. Education × Sex	−0.094	0.152	−0.167	0.134
Religiosity	−0.090	0.109	−0.170*	0.097
Religiosity × Sex	−0.144	0.175	−0.030	0.149
No. close friends	−0.015	0.074	−0.020	0.063
No. Close Friends × Sex	0.014	0.078	0.018	0.066
Hrs./day radio	0.026	0.039	−0.010	0.036
Hrs./Day Radio × Sex	−0.040	0.057	−0.014	0.051
Domain IV: Perceived social opportunity				
Achievement orientation	−0.134	0.121	−0.128	0.104
Achievement Orientation × Sex	0.112	0.121	−0.043	0.104
Domain V: Demoralization/ontogenic strain				
Personal efficacy	−0.177	0.119	−0.175*	0.102
Personal Efficacy × Sex	0.124	0.173	0.242	0.150
Alienation	−0.147	0.177	−0.080	0.152
Alienation × Sex	0.088	0.230	0.002	0.197

Variable	Risk of heavy adult use		Risk of moderate adult use	
	b	*SE*	*b*	SE
General strain	−0.023	0.220	0.018	0.187
General Strain × Sex	−0.314	0.314	0.115	0.262
Domain VI: Marijuana gateway				
Frequency of marijuana	0.025	0.131	0.172	0.109
Frequency of Marijuana × Sex	−0.648***	0.234	−0.284*	0.162

Note. Significant variables were identified through the discriminant function screening. These results provided the basis for retaining gender interaction terms in the multivariate logistic models. Cohort: younger = 1, older = 0. Gender: male = 1, female = 0.
*$p ≤ .1$. **$p ≤ .05$. ***$p ≤ .01$.

Variables: Descriptive Data

Variable[a]	Total		Men		Women	
	M	SD	M	SD	M	SD
Adolescence						
Domain I: Social structure						
Birth cohort (d) (younger = 1)	.59	.49	.60	.49	.58	.50
Father present (d)	.44	.50	.45	.50	.43	.50
Family on welfare (d)	.49	.50	.49	.50	.49	.50
Domain II: Role asynchrony						
Parent by age 17 (d)	.16	.36	.10	.29	.23	.42
High school dropout (d)	.35	.48	.39	.49	.31	.46
Domain III: Social bonds						
Peer influence (i) (Count of 8 items scored 1 if follows ideas of friends, 0 otherwise: spending money, dress, hair style, time home at night, when see doctor, where see doctor, future work, school effort. Range = 0 to 5.[b] Reliability: male = .72, female = .65.[c])	.50	.96	.62	1.06	.37	.82
Spare time with family (d)	.38	.48	.34	.47	.43	.49
Religious commitment (i) (Sum of two items: no. times/month attend church; importance of religion in life [scored 1 = not important, 4 = very important]. Range = −3.6 to 2. Reliability: male = .55, female = .54.)	7.03	1.61	.09	1.63	−.03	1.59

Variable[a]	Total		Men		Women	
	M	**SD**	**M**	**SD**	**M**	**SD**
Recreational activities (i) (Sum of number of times a month: go to movies, library, community center, participate in sports, go dancing. Range = 0 to 23. Reliability: male = .53, female = .52.)	9.18	5.54	9.81	5.67	8.46	5.32
Number of close friends (c)	7.87	7.21	10.15	7.96	5.22	5.09
Listen to radio, hrs./day (c)	1.94	1.96	1.71	1.88	2.21	2.02
Domain VI: Marijuana gateway						
Use of marijuana by age 14 (d)	.28	.45	.35	.48	.21	.41
	Early adult transition					
Domain II: Role asynchrony						
Married at age 23–25 (d)	.21	.41	.20	.40	.21	.41
Months idle age 23–25 (c)	12.37	14.20	9.99	13.46	15.14	14.58
No. children by age 25 (c)	.84	1.01	.65	.95	1.07	1.03
Cohabiting age 23–25 (d)	.21	.41	.20	.40	.23	.42
Domain III: Social bonds						
Religious commitment (i) (Sum of two items: no. times/month attend church; importance of religion in life [scored 1 = not important, 4 = very important]. Range = −2.9 to 4.9. Reliability: male = .54, female = .50.)	−.19	1.80	−.11	1.59	−.28	2.03
Listen to radio, hrs./day (c)	6.23	5.24	6.28	5.06	6.17	5.46
Number of organizations (c)	.23	.53	.19	.44	.26	.61
Years of education (c)	3.76	2.04	3.49	1.96	4.06	2.10

APPENDIX B (Continued)

Variable[a]	Total		Men		Women	
	M	*SD*	*M*	*SD*	*M*	*SD*
Domain IV: Perceived opportunity						
Achievement orientation (i) (Sum of two standardized items: educational goals; expected educational attainment. Range = −4.48 to 2.54. Reliability: male = .90, female = .92.)	−.06	1.92	−.18	1.98	.09	1.85
Domain V: Demoralization/ ontogenic strain						
Personal efficacy (i) (Sum of responses on three items scored 1 = strongly agree . . . 4 = strongly disagree: Every time I try to get ahead someone or something stops me; people like me don't have a chance to be successful in life; for success, good luck is more important than hard work. Range = 3 to 12. Reliability: male = .44, female = .54.)	8.79	1.80	8.83	1.69	8.74	1.92
Alienation (i) (Sum of responses on three items scored 1–4 [code for 4 in brackets]: There is not much chance that people will really do anything to make this a better world [strongly agree]; people would sooner help others than look for their own good [strongly disagree]; most public officials . . . are not really interested in the problems of the average person [strongly agree]. Range = 2 to 8. Reliability: male = .56, female = .59.[c])	5.32	1.37	5.34	1.46	5.29	1.26

Variable[a]	Total		Men		Women	
	M	**SD**	**M**	**SD**	**M**	**SD**
General strain (s) (Factor analysis of four items: All in all how have things gone for you in the past 5 years [1 = very badly . . . 5 = very well];[d] about how often do you have a problem that upsets you [1 = hardly ever, 2 = sometimes, 3 = very often]; would you say you worry [1 = not at all, 2 = a little, 3 = a lot]; how much of yourself would you like to change [1 = not anything, 2 = a few things, 3 = a lot of things]. Range = −2.06 to 2.76. Reliability: male = .47, female = .50.)	0.0	1.0	0.0	1.0	− .05	1.01
Domain VI: Marijuana gateway Frequency of marijuana use (c) (Reverse coding: daily low.)	2.19	.942	2.22	.991	2.47	1.05

[a]Variable names indicate high pole unless otherwide stated. d = dummy variable; c = continuous; i = index; s = scale.

[b]Ranges for indices and scales are for men and women combined.

[c]Reliabilities are for full samples (351 men and 317 women for adolescents, 277 men and 259 women for postadolescents).

[d]Scoring reversed for uniform directionality.

[e]Reliabilities scored on Wave 3 data.

Variables Lacking Significance in Preliminary Screening

Domain I: Social structure

Mother's education
Mother's birthplace
Own birthplace
Mobility Index
Housing Quality Index
Household size
Living in poverty census tract

Domain II: Asynchrony in life-stage roles

Left home before age 18
Behind in school
Wants paying job
Single parent

Domain III: Social bonds

Parental influence scale
Hours watch TV
Number of friends outside of
    neighborhood

Domain V: Demoralization/ontogenic strain

Time orientation
Self-esteem
Psychological Well-Being Scale

Note. Screening performed by discriminant function analysis against marijuana and cocaine adult use typologies.

CHAPTER 15

Another Time, Another Drug

Joan McCord

R ecent research has suggested that drinking alcohol is almost a necessary precursor for using illegal drugs and that abusing the legal drug alcohol sets the stage for abusing illegal drugs (Kandel, 1980; Mills & Noyes, 1984; Osgood, Johnston, O'Malley, & Bachman, 1988; Welte & Barnes, 1985). Understanding the etiology of alcohol abuse is therefore a preliminary step toward understanding the transition to other forms of drug abuse. Understanding alcohol abuse is important also because its consequences, like those of illegal drugs, are known to be harmful both physically and socially. In the case of both alcohol abuse and the abuse of illegal substances, the "addict" appears knowingly to choose self-inflicted damage. If we can learn why such choices occur in the one case, we will have information relevant to comprehending the other. And finally, a focus on alcohol is important because the history of its widespread use and condemnation gives a perspective to contemporary problems of substance abuse.

The parallel between alcohol and opium abuse was drawn in 1921 by Edward A. Ross, who noted that what opium was to China, alcohol was to the United States: "Even

This study was partially supported by U.S. Public Health Service Research Grant MH26779, National Institute of Mental Health (Center for Studies of Crime and Delinquency). I wish to express appreciation to the Department of Probation of the Commonwealth of Massachusetts, to the Division of Criminal Justice Services of the State of New York, to the Maine State Bureau of Identification, and to the states of California, Florida, Michigan, New Jersey, Pennsylvania, Virginia, and Washington for supplemental data about the men. I thank Richard Parente, Robert Staib, Ellen Myers, and Ann Cronin for their work in tracing the men and their records; Joan Immel, Tom Smedile, Harriet Sayre, Mary Duell, Elise Goldman, Abby Brodkin, and Laura Otten for their careful coding; and Daniel Glaser for his helpful comments on an earlier version of the manuscript. The author is responsible for statistical analyses and for the conclusions drawn from this research.

in small quantities alcohol is an upsetter and deranger of the functions of the mind as well as of the body" (p.187). Citing industrial accidents, as well as physical and mental problems, putatively caused by alcohol, he argued that unless Prohibition were success-ful, the country would go through a period of self-destruction in which people susceptible to alcohol would annihilate one another or themselves. A geneticist, Ross predicted that "by the year 2100 A.D. our descendents might be as constitutionally resistant to alcohol beguilement as are the Portuguese today" (p. 189).

Earlier commentators had noted relationships between drinking and criminal be-havior. Enrico Ferri (1897), for example, remarked on the relationship between the "abun-dance of vintage" and crimes of violence in France between 1850 and 1880. Ferri believed that alcohol was clearly a cause of crime, and he urged an international effort to reduce the use of alcohol. Some estimates of the link between alcohol and crime were gained by surveys of convicts. In one study in the United States, Koren attributed 50% of the crimes of more that 13,000 convicts to drinking alcohol (cited in Howard, 1918). Lombroso (1912/ 1968) made similar claims in England, with even higher estimates of the relationship be-tween alcohol and crime. Other studies presented figures close to 100%. In summarizing the evidence, the sociologist George Elliott Howard (1918) indicated the dimensions of the problem: "To master the crime-producing environment which consists in alcohol and the organized alcohol traffic may cost more courage, wisdom, and toil than it cost to abolish human slavery ..." (p. 63).

Movement toward Prohibition had gained momentum during World War I as social workers, joined by industrialists, backed Prohibition as patriotic. Servicemen were not al-lowed to drink, and dry zones were created surrounding military bases. Around the same time, according to Timberlake (1966), scientific evidence had been adduced to show that "inebriety in parents was a cause of physical, mental, and moral degeneracy in children ..." (p. 44).

Local elections revealed resistance to the temperance movement. In 1916, Boston voters rejected almost two to one a bill that would have prohibited the licensing of sa-loons. Yet by 1917, 26 states had outlawed the sale of liquor. That year, a surprise federal move prohibited interstate shipment of liquor into the dry states, and on April 4, 1917, a resolution was introduced in congress to prohibit the "manufacture, sale, or transporta-tion of intoxicating liquors within, the importation thereof into, or the exportation thereof from the United States and all territory subject to the jurisdiction thereof for beverage purposes."

Timberlake (1966) traced the success of the movement to enforce Prohibition to a conjuction of scientific discoveries and social changes brought about through the Progressive movement. The Eighteenth Amendment did not take effect until January 16, 1920, although the War Prohibition Act, enacted on November 21, 1918, and enforced after July 1, 1919, was the effective beginning of national Prohibition in the United States. Restricted liquor sales had been in place since 1917, and by 1919, the voting public seemed overwhelmingly to favor Prohibition. Referring to passage of national Prohibition, the 14th edition of the Encyclopedia Britannica, published in 1929, described the process as follows: "It was adopted after full and free public discussion, in the face of determined and powerful opposition, by larger majorities and greater unanimity in Congress and in the forty-six States (out of a total of 48 States) which ratified it than any other amendment" (Lindsay, 1929, p. 566).

Nonetheless, enforcement remained a problem (Catlin, 1932; Gebhart, 1932). Between 1920 and 1930, enforcement was the responsibility of the Treasury Department. Jurisdiction switched to the Department of Justice with passage of the Williamson Act in 1930. In 1929, the Jones Law had increased penalties for violation to a maximum of $10,000 or up to 5 years imprisonment. This was modified in 1931 to reduce penalties for offenders who sold or transported less than a gallon of liquor. That year, too, the Supreme Court handed down a unanimous opinion to overturn a year-old District Court decision by Judge William Clark that had raised questions about the constitutionality of the Eighteenth Amendment.

Perception that drinking was a common practice throughout Prohibition, coupled with repeal of the Eighteenth Amendment in 1933, has led some observers to cite Prohibition as a failed policy of drug control. Nevertheless, there is some evidence that crime decreased during the period (Ferdinand, 1967) and that the incidence of alcohol psychoses may have also decreased (Burnham, 1968; Emerson, 1932). Sinclair (1962) argued that a change in drinking patterns created the mistaken impression that alcohol consumption had increased. During the early years of the 20th century, saloons were the social clubs for immigrants, but the middle classes drank little. Sinclair suggested that Prohibition made drinking stylish, becoming fashionable for the middle classes, while making it more difficult for the working classes to find a drink.

A variety of attempts have been made to identify the effects of Prohibition. Hospital admissions for cirrhosis of the liver and deaths from alcoholism fluctuated slightly throughout the years of Prohibition (Brown, 1932). Crime rates in New York City decreased during this period (Willbach, 1938). Yet in Chicago, "the ratios of the population arrested for crimes against the person showed an almost continuous increase up to 1927 which was followed by an almost uninterrupted decrease through 1939" (Willbach, 1941).

Studies of the effects of Prohibition have not examined the impact of changing populations caused by immigration and urbanization. Yet dramatic changes in the population took place between 1920 and 1930 (Lyman, 1932). Without a control for social class, it would be premature to judge whether the prohibition of alcohol had an impact on drinking or on other socially relevant problems. The purpose of the present study was to take a new look at the effects of Prohibition by comparing two cohorts of people whose exposure to the propaganda and to the legal changes would have affected them differently.

Method

Subjects for the study came from a generation of men born between 1872 and 1913. They were selected because their sons were part of a youth study active between 1935 and 1945. Descriptions of the fathers' behavior became available through their participation in the latter study. Of the original 232 families, information was available about the drinking habits of 183 fathers.

All subjects lived in overcrowded, run-down neighborhoods of Cambridge and Somerville, Massachusetts. High crime rates, poverty, and obvious property deterioration were grounds for selecting neighborhoods, and the subjects were selected because of the neighborhood in which they lived and because of the ages of their sons.[1]

Data were gathered between 1939 and 1945 when, approximately twice a month, counselors visited the homes of boys to try to help them and their families. The counselors appeared at various times of the day and throughout the week. After each encounter, the counselors filed a detailed report that included conversations and described behavior. Covering a span of more than 5 years, these running records provided the information used in the present study. In 1957, coders who had access to no information other than that in the case records transcribed the information into categorical scales describing the parents, the boys, and family interactions.

---

[1] An additional criterion for selection was that the son could be matched to a boy with a similar character and background. See Powers and Witmer (1951) for details.

In terms of occupation,[2] 60% ($n = 108$) of the fathers were unskilled workers. Most of the remaining fathers, 32% ($n = 58$), were skilled workers. Only 8% held white-collar positions, including one professional. The sample included nine Blacks; the remaining subjects were Whites. Almost half had completed the eighth grade, although only 20 had graduated from high school, and 3 had graduated from college.[3] About half ($n = 96$) were born in the United States. Italy ($n = 33$), Canada ($n = 22$), and Portugal ($n = 15$) were the birth places of most of the rest.[4]

Information from criminal records, gathered for the fathers in 1948 and for their sons in 1976, was added to the information gained through the case records. Some additional information about the lives of the subjects was collected through interviews with the adult sons between 1975 and 1980. Questionnaires, interviews, and records of treatment for alcoholism, also collected between 1975 and 1980, added data about the sons.

To justify considering each family as independent, 16 brothers were dropped from the analyses. If one brother had been interviewed and the other had not ($n = 7$), the interviewed brother was included. If both or neither had been interviewed ($n = 9$), the one whose given name came first alphabetically was selected.

Subjects were divided into two groups according to their dates of birth. Those born between 1896 and 1913 (inclusive) would have been exposed to the antiliquor campaign and to Prohibition during their minority; they were less than age 21 in 1917. Those born between 1872 and 1895 had reached majority by 1917. The impact of legal and social changes can be expected to differ for the adolescents, whose average age was 16 in 1917, and the adults, whose average age was 29 in 1917; therefore, these groups provide the basis for assessing effects of Prohibition. Dates of birth were missing for 2 of the 183 subjects for whom drinking problems could be coded; they were dropped from the study.

Ratings analyzed for the present study focus on problems related to alcohol and crime. Paternal behavior was evaluated in terms of drinking problems reported in the case records; these were coded in 1957. At that time, two raters independently read a 10% random sample of the cases in order to estimate the reliability of the coding.

One of the codes identified fathers as habitual, excessive drinkers. For this identification, the ratings of the two coders were in agreement on 92% of the fathers. A second rating noted whether fathers had lost jobs or had family problems because of their current or prior drinking; ratings indicated 96% agreement on this code. Fathers were

---

[2] *The occupations of three fathers were unknown.*

[3] *The education of 24 fathers was unknown.*

[4] *The birth places of two fathers were unknown. No other country was the birth place for as many as 5 of the subjects.*

considered to have problems with alcohol if they were so rated or if they had been ar-rested at least three times for driving under the influence of alcohol or for public drunk-enness. Additional evidence for drinking problems was gathered through interviews. Sons were asked to describe their fathers' attitudes toward drinking; coded for reliability, two raters agreed on 91% of the ratings. A father was also considered to have problems with drinking if his son described him as regularly drunk or making trouble when he drank. According to these criteria, among the 181 men in the study, 94 (52%) had drinking problems.

Among the 181 men whose drinking problems, dates of birth, and drinking habits could be rated, 17 were teetotalers, including 9% of the 75 men born before 1896 and 9% of the 106 men born after 1895. Only 10 fathers had been convicted for the illegal sale of alcohol.

Information about the sons of the subjects was collected between 1975 and 1980, when they ranged in age from 45 to 53 years. Records from courts, clinics for treatment of alcoholism, and mental hospitals were searched for each of the men. Voting records, visits to old home neighborhoods, and a variety of tracing techniques led to the retrieval of addressess for 98% of the sons. Once found, they were asked to respond to question-naires and to participate in interviews. Both the questionnaires and the interviews used the CAGE test (Ewing & Rouse, 1970) to identify alcoholics. In this test, respondents are asked if they have ever taken a morning eye-opener, felt the need to cut down on drink-ing, felt annoyed by criticism of their drinking, or felt guilty about drinking. A man was considered an alcoholic if he responded affirmatively, as do alcoholics (Mayfield, McLeod, & Hall, 1974), to at least three of these questions. A son was also considered to be alco-holic if he had received treatment for alcoholism, if he had been arrested at least three times for public drunkenness or driving while intoxicated, or if he described himself as an alcoholic. Additionally, a son was considered an alcoholic if he had been arrested twice for alcoholism and answered affirmatively to two of the CAGE questions. By these criteria, the sons of 57 of the subjects were classified as alcoholics.

Criminal records of the fathers had been searched in 1948, and those of the sons were checked in 1975. These records showed the age of conviction as well as the charge for each of the men who had appeared in court. Ninety-six of the fathers and 134 of the sons had been convicted for at least one nontraffic crime. Street crimes that appear on the Federal Bureau of Investigation Index are considered "serious"; 46 fathers and 59 sons had been convicted for crimes in the Federal Bureau of Investigation Index.

Results

Men exposed to Prohibition as adolescents had a higher probability of manifesting problems with alcohol than did those men who were already adults in 1917. Whereas 41% of the men who were over 21 in 1917 had problems with alcohol, 58% of those between 17 and 21 in 1917 had problems with alcohol ($\chi^2_{(1)} = 5.176, p < .023$).

Age at exposure to Prohibition appeared to have little direct impact on whether a person became a criminal. Comparisons of the proportions convicted for nontraffic crimes and for serious crimes revealed no significant difference in relation to age at exposure. In both cohorts, however, criminal behavior was strongly related to having problems with alcohol (Table 15.1).

Although there was little difference in the proportions who committed at least one nontraffic crime, men who were exposed to Prohibition during adolescence differed from those who were already adults by 1917 in terms of the number of crimes they committed, with the younger cohort more actively criminal. The 75 men who were over 21 in 1917 committed an average of 2.15 nontraffic crimes (SD = 5.8); the 106 who were under 21 in 1917 committed an average of 5.24 crimes (SD = 11.93), $t_{(161.6)} = 2.306, p < .022$. In terms of the probability of committing at least one more crime, those exposed to Prohibition as adolescents were more likely to be recidivists. For the men exposed to Prohibiton as adolescents, the probability of recidivism was higher following the first through the fifth crime, and convicted men who had been older during Prohibition were more likely

TABLE 15.1

Exposure to Prohibition, Alcohol Problems, and Criminal Behavior

| | Father's age at exposure to prohibition | | | |
| | 17–21 | | Over 21 | |
Criminal activity	Drinking problem (%)	No problem (%)	Drinking problem (%)	No problem (%)
Not convicted	21	80	26	66
Minor crimes	37	11	39	23
Serious crimes	42	9	35	11
N	62	44	31	44

Note. $\chi^2_{(6)} = 49.10, p = .000$.

to be recidivists after convictions for at least seven crimes. Figure 15.1 shows the probability for recidivism after each crime number to the ninth crime.

The older men also committed fewer serious crimes. Those exposed to Prohibition as adolescents committed an average of 0.73 (SD = 1.54) serious crimes, compared with an average of 0.28 (SD = 0.61) for the older men, $t_{(145.7)}$ = 2.69, $p < .007$.

The group exposed to Prohibition as adolescents began committing crimes at younger ages. The mean age for the 57 convicted men who were under 21 in 1917 was 27.2 (SD = 7.8), whereas the mean age for the 38 convicted men who were at least 21 in 1917 was 39.7 (SD = 9.8), $t_{(93)}$ = 6.913, $p < .0001$. For serious crimes, the average age at first conviction among the 30 men exposed to Prohibition as adolescents was 26.33 years (SD = 8.17), whereas the mean age for the 15 convicted men who were at least 21 in 1917 was 38.73 years (SD = 6.66), $t_{(43)}$ = 5.09, $p < .0001$.

Figure 15.2 shows hazard rates for ages at first convictions, both for all nontraffic crimes and for only serious crimes (SAS Institute, 1985). The distributions indicate peak hazard rates in the early twenties for those exposed to Prohibition as adolescents and in the mid-forties for those exposed to Prohibition as adults. For nontraffic crimes, the Wilcoxon test for differences had a chi-square value of 9.612, $p < .0019$. For serious crimes, the Wilcoxon test for differences had a chi-square value of 4.206, $p < .0403$.

Age differences between those exposed to Prohibition as adolescents and those exposed as adults are evidenced among both the men who had problems with alcohol and those who did not. Figure 15.3 shows the distribution for the ages at first conviction for all nontraffic crimes. As can be seen, in both groups, men who had problems with alcohol were also at greater risk for being convicted—well into their mid-fifties. The Wilcoxon test of equality over strata had a chi-square value of 8.587, $p < .0034$.

Figure 15.4 shows age-related hazard rates for the first serious crime. Within both the younger and the older cohorts, men who had problems with alcohol were at greater risk for committing a first serious crime. The Wilcoxon test of equality over strata had a chi-square value of 26.267, $p < .0001$.

Hazard rates for age at first conviction, adjusted for year of birth, show similar patterns for the two cohorts. Among both the older and the younger men, hazard rates rose between 1915 and 1935, falling therafter (Figure 15.5).

The evidence suggests that men exposed to Prohibition as adolescents were more likely than older cohorts to have problems with alcohol and to commit crimes. If biological or cultural differences between cohorts accounted for the observed differences in patterns of crime, one would expect that sons as well as fathers in the two cohorts would

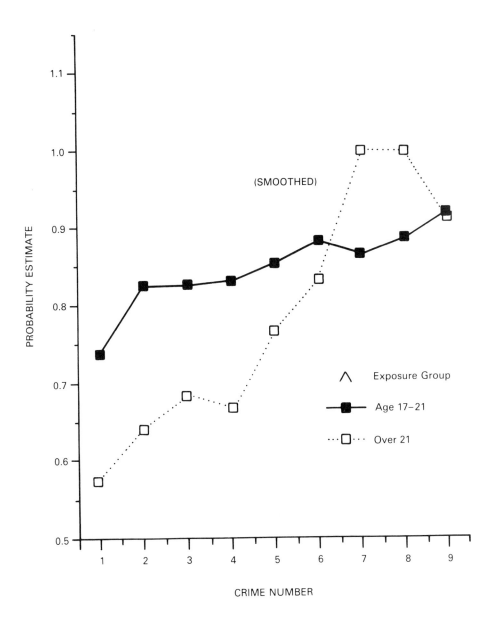

FIGURE 15.1   Age at exposure to prohibition: conditional probability for committing at least one more nontraffic crime.

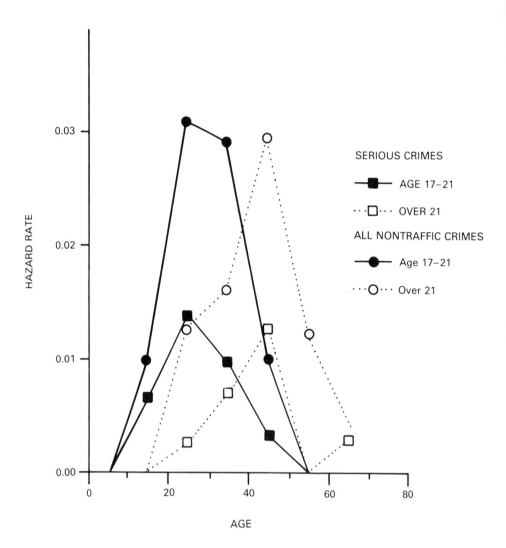

FIGURE 15.2   Age at exposure to prohibition: age at first conviction.

differ in their crime rates. This was not the case. Sons of the two cohorts differed little in their ages at first conviction for nontraffic crimes or for serious crimes. Nor did they differ reliably in terms of the number of nontraffic crimes or serious crimes for which they were convicted (Table 15.2).

Almost equal proportions of the sons of the two cohorts were alcoholic: 31%of the younger men and 32% of the older ones. For both cohorts, sons of alcoholics

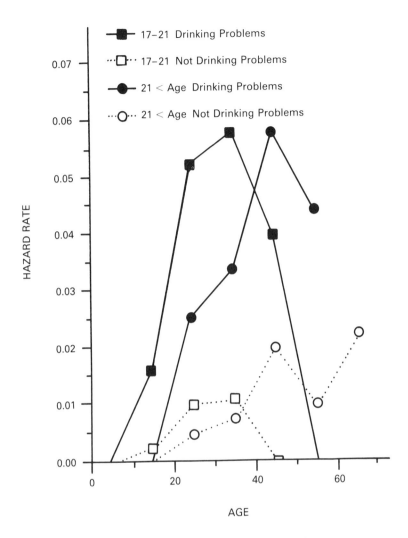

FIGURE 15.3 Prohibition exposure and drinking problems: age of conviction for nontraffic crimes.

were more likely to be alcoholics, with the stronger relationship among older men (Table 15.3).

Summary and Discussion

This chapter has compared two cohorts of men exposed to Prohibition at different periods in their lives. Members of the younger cohort were adolescents as the issues

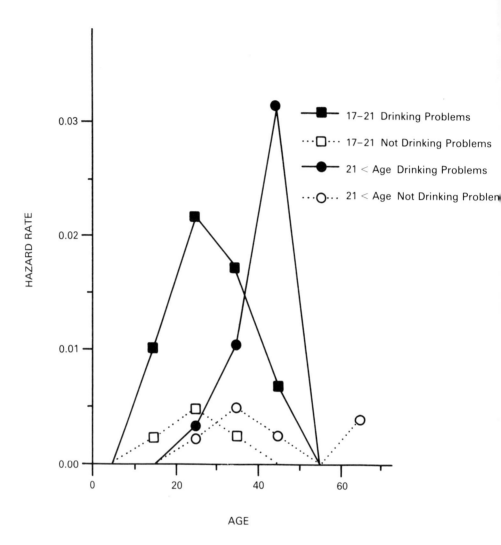

FIGURE 15.4   Prohibition exposure and drinking problems: age of first conviction for serious crimes.

were argued and the legislation passed to make the sale and purchase of liquor an offense. Members of the older cohort had already reached majority when the Eighteenth Amendment became law. The first group was expected to be more responsive to the changes. They might have shown responsiveness by exhibiting greater control over drinking; such was the optimistic perception of those who have argued the case for

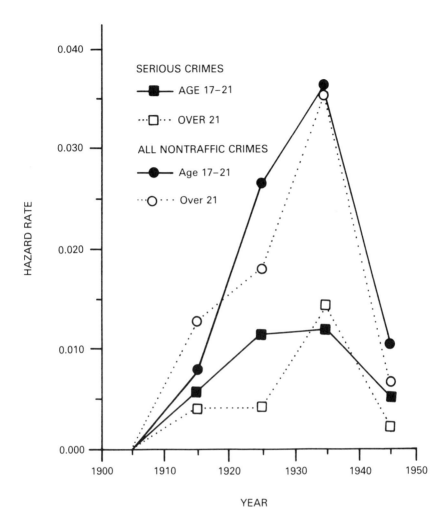

FIGURE 15.5 Age at exposure to prohibition: year of first conviction.

Prohibition. They might have shown a greater disrespect for the law; such was the pessimistic perception of those who consider Prohibition to have been a failure. This study suggests that the pessimists were more nearly correct than the optimists. At least for these men, Prohibition seems to have introduced factors that increased criminal behavior. The data also suggest that age at first crime, a variable known to predict subsequent

TABLE 15.2

Exposure to Prohibition and Son's Criminal Behavior

| Son's criminal behavior | Father's age at exposure to prohibition | | | |
| | 17–21 | | Over 21 | |
	M	SD	M	SD
Age at first conviction				
Nontraffic crime	20.90	8.09	21.53	8.63
Serious crime	16.97	7.13	18.67	9.45
Number of crimes				
Minor	2.58	4.89	2.09	3.56
Serious	0.78	1.64	0.63	1.54

TABLE 15.3

Father's Exposure to Prohibition and Alcohol Problems, and Percent of Sons With Alcoholism

| Father's experience | Father's age at exposure to prohibition | | | |
| | 17–21 | | Over 21 | |
	N	Alcoholic sons (%)	N	Alcoholic sons (%)
Drinking problems	62	40	31	45
No drinking problems	44	18	44	23

Note. $\chi^2_{(3)} = 10.11$, $p = .018$.

criminality (Blumstein, Cohen, Roth, & Visher, 1986; Farrington, 1983; McCord, 1981), was influenced by Prohibition.

Crime rates can change because a population base shifts (Greenberg, 1979), as well as because of increases in criminal behavior. Increases in criminal behavior occur either when more people become criminals or when criminals commit more crimes (Barnett, Blumstein, & Farrington, 1989; Blumstein et al., 1986; Willbach, 1938). The data presented here indicate that Prohibition influenced criminal behavior by increasing the amount of crime committed by criminals rather than by increasing the number of criminals.

There are several ways to interpret a relationship between Prohibition and increased crime. One argument would rest on the view that Prohibition was an illegitimate attempt to legislate morality that might have created resistance to broad range of legal restrictions. A variant of psychological reactance theory (J.W. Brehm, 1966; S.S. Brehm & Brehm, 1981), this argument maintains that the attempt to enforce too much weakened social control. A more sociological argument would note that Prohibition affected primarily the lower classes. Prohibition would thus be perceived as unfair, as legislation serving the interests of the powerful. Affected populations could thus have reduced their beliefs in the legitimacy of all laws. A third alternative would emphasize the fact that in Boston, anti-Prohibition sentiment had been strong prior to endorsement of the Eighteenth Amendment. If resistance to Prohibition was perceived in a favorable light, teenagers may have judged that obedience to the law was of dubious value. Another possibility, of course, is that the results are due to unmeasured or unanalyzed conditions.

On balance, it seems to me that Prohibition increased alcohol abuse and antisocial behavior among some groups. This conclusion rests on the following summary of the present results: (a) Men exposed to Prohibition as adolescents were more likely than older cohorts to have problems with drinking. (b) Criminal activity, which was linked to drinking problems, was higher among those who had been exposed to Prohibition as adolescents. (c) The cohorts were apparently similar in terms of variables affecting their sons' criminal behavior and alcoholism. (d) Across age groups, rates for first offenses rose sharply at the beginning of Prohibition.

Recognizing that any set of data is subject to multiple interpretations, a plausible conclusion seems to be that Prohibition may be counterproductive. Those least attached to social consensus about the legitimacy of drug use may perceive failed attempts at enforcement as evidence that the law more broadly interpreted can be ignored. If this conclusion is correct, then a government that seeks to change behavior would be wise to do so by persuasion rather than through Prohibition.

References

Barnett, A., Blumstein, A., & Farrington, D. P. (1989). A prospective test of a criminal career model. *Criminology, 27*(2), 373–388.

Blumstein, A., Cohen, J., Roth, J. A., & Visher, C. A. (Eds.). (1986). *Criminal careers and "career criminals"* Washington, DC: National Academy Press.

Brehm, J. W. (1966). *A theory of psychological reactance.* San Diego, CA: Academic Press.

Brehm, S. S., & Brehm, J. W. (1981). *Psychological reactance: A theory of freedom and control*. San Diego, CA: Academic Press.

Brown, F. W. (1932). Prohibition and mental hygiene: Effects on mental health-specific disorders. *Annals of the American Academy of Political and Social Science, 163*, 61–68.

Burnham, J. C. (1968). New perspectives on the prohibition "experiment" of the 1920's. *Journal of Social History, 2*(1), 51–68.

Catlin, G. E. G. (1932). Alternatives to prohibition. *Annals of the American Academy of Political and Social Science, 163*, 181–187.

Emerson, H. (1932). Prohibition and mortality and morbidity. *Annals of the American Academy of Political and Social Science, 163*, 53–60.

Ewing, J., & Rouse, B. A.. (1970, February). *Identifying the hidden alcoholic*. Paper presented at the 29th International Congress on Alcohol and Drug Dependence, Sydney, Australia.

Farrington, D. P. (1983). Offending from 10 to 25 years of age. In K. T. Van Dusen & S. A. Mednick (Eds.), *Prospective studies of crime and delinquency* (pp. 73–97). Boston: Kluwer-Nijhoff.

Ferdinand, T. N. (1967). The criminal patterns of Boston since 1848. *American Journal of Sociology, 78*(1), 84–99.

Ferri, E. (1897). *Criminal sociology*. New York: Appleton.

Gebhart, J. C. (1932). Movement against Prohibition. *Annals of the American Academy of Political and Social Science, 163*, 172–180.

Greenberg, D. (1979). Delinquency and the age structure. In S. Messinger & E. Bittner (Eds.), *Criminology review yearbook* (pp. 586–620). Beverly Hills, CA: Sage.

Howard, G. E. (1918). Alcohol and crime: A study in social causation. *American Journal of Sociology, 24*, 61–80.

Kandel, D. B. (1980). Drug and drinking behavior among youth. *Annual Review of Sociology, 6*, 235–285.

Lindsay, S. M. (1929). Prohibition. In *Encyclopedia Britannica* (14th ed., Vol. 18, pp. 566–572). New York: Encyclopedia Britannica.

Lombroso, C. (1968). *Crime: Its causes and remedies*. Montclair, NJ: Patterson Smith. (Original work published 1912)

Lyman, R. H. (1932). *The world almanac and book of facts for 1932*. New York: New York World-Telegram.

Mayfield, D., McLeod, G., & Hall, P. (1974). The CAGE questionnaire: Validation of a new alcoholism screening instrument. *American Journal of Psychiatry, 131*, 1121–1123.

McCord, J. (1981). A longitudinal perspective on patterns of crime. *Criminology, 19*(2), 211–218.

Mills, C. J., & Noyes, H. L. (1984). Patterns and correlates of initial and subsequent drug use among adolescents. *Journal of Consulting and Clinical Psychology, 52*, 231–243.

Osgood, D. W., Johnston, L. D., O'Malley, P. M., & Bachman, J. G. (1988). The generality of deviance in late adolescence and early adulthood. *American Sociological Review, 53*(1), 81–93.

Powers, E., & Witmer, H. (1951). *An experiment in the prevention of delinquency: The Cambridge-Somerville Youth Study*. New York: Columbia University Press.

Ross, E. A. (1921, January). Prohibition as the sociologist sees it. *Harper's Magazine*, pp. 186–192.

SAS Institute. (1985). *SAS user's guide: Statistics.* (rev. ed.). Cary, NC: Author.

Sinclair, A. (1962). *Prohibition, the era of excess.* Boston: Little, Brown.

Timberlake, J. H. (1966). *Prohibition and the progressive movement, 1900–1920.* Cambridge, MA: Harvard University Press.

Welte, J. W., & Barnes, G. M. (1985). Alcohol: The gateway to other drug use among secondary-school students. *Journal of Youth and Adolescence, 14,* 487–498.

Willbach, H. (1938). The trend of crime in New York City. *Journal of Criminal Law, Criminology, and Police Science, 29,* 62–75.

Willbach, H. (1941). The trend of crime in Chicago. *Journal of Criminal Law, Criminology, and Police Science, 31,* 720–727.

CHAPTER 16

The Many Paths to Drug Dependence

George E. Woody, Harold C. Urschel III, and Arthur Alterman

A ddiction and dependence are often used synonymously by clinicians, although dependence is the term of the third revised edition of the *Diagnostic and Statistical Manual of Mental Disorders* (*DSM–III–R*; American Psychiatric Association, 1987) condition in which individuals become involved in compulsive, nonprescribed self-administration of high doses of certain classes of psychoactive agents. Those who treat addicts usually do not observe the transition from initial drug use to dependence because they see the patient only after dependence has occurred. However, in the normal course of treating patients, therapists hear many versions about how dependence begins, and they also have the opportunity to interview and observe patients who have relapsed after extended drug-free periods. When seen from a clinical perspective, these retrospective accounts indicate that there are many paths to drug dependence. This paper will illustrate some of these paths, using clinical examples, and will discuss their importance for designing prevention efforts.

Diagnosing Drug Dependence: Strength and Persistence of Drug-Seeking Behavior

Many of the criteria for diagnosing dependence are clinical observations that document the strength of drug-seeking behavior, the loss of control over drug consumption, and its persistence. The *DSM–III–R* criteria for dependence are as follows:

A. At least three of the following:

(1) substance often taken in larger amounts or over a longer period than the person intended.

(2) persistent desire or one or more unsuccessful efforts to cut down or control substance use.

(3) a great deal of time spent in activities necessary to get the substance (e.g., theft), taking the substance (e.g., chain smoking), or recovering from its effects.

(4) frequent intoxication or withdrawal symptoms when expected to fulfill major role obligations at work, school, or home (e.g., does not go to work because hung over, goes to school or work "high," intoxicated while taking care of his or her children), or when substance use is physically hazardous (e.g., drives when intoxicated).

(5) important social, occupational, or recreational activities given up or reduced because of substance use.

(6) continued substance use despite knowledge of having a persistent or recurrent social, psychological, or physical problem that is caused or exacerbated by the use of the substance (e.g., keeps using heroin despite family arguments about it, cocaine induced depression, or having an ulcer made worse by drinking).

(7) marked tolerance: need for markedly increased amounts of the substance (i.e., at least a 50% increase) in order to achieve intoxication or desired effect, or markedly diminished effect with continued use of the same amount.

Note: The following items may not apply to cannabis, hallucinogens, or phencyclidine (PCP):

(8) characteristic withdrawal symptoms (see specific withdrawal syndromes under Psychoactive Substance-induced Organic Mental Disorders).

(9) substance often taken to relieve or avoid withdrawal symptoms.

B. Some symptoms of the disturbance have persisted for at least one month, or have occurred repeatedly over a longer period of time. (*DSM–III–R*, pp. 167–168. Reprinted by permission.)

As seen by these criteria, a person who is dependent on an abusable substance demonstrates an overwhelming involvement with that psychoactive agent. Some of the most dramatic examples of this involvement are those involving medical problems. These include continuing to inject drugs into extremities whose veins are sclerosed and riddled with abscesses from earlier contaminated injections; injecting drugs into intravenous tubing on the medical ward while being treated for bacterial endocarditis; or impulsively sharing "works" with a person who is known to be infected by human immunodeficiency virus. Another example of the strength of dependence is the addict's preoccupation with obtaining and using drugs. The dependent individual's life centers around drug acquisition, drug use, and recovery from the effects of drugs. Opiate addicts often describe how they organize every day around getting drugs, how they fear being without drugs, and how they plan the next day's drug purchases before going to bed at night.

The loss of control over drug use is perhaps best seen clinically by the addict's tendency to use all of the drug that is available at any one time (Wesson & Smith, 1985). Often, when addicts are asked how much they use, the answer is "as much as I can get." This loss of control is similar to processes that are seen in other mental disorders such as psychosis or depression, and it supports the disease concept of addiction (Minkoff, 1989).

The persistence of the drug-seeking behavior that characterizes dependence is perhaps best seen by the tendency to relapse. Relapse can occur even after long periods of abstinence; it is a particularly impressive aspect of addiction, especially when seen in spite of repeated treatments or after having suffered many adverse consequences from the dependence. Examples are professional athletes or physicians who lose substantial income, or even their entire career, yet who return to drugs after extended (and expensive) treatments.

Of these three qualities, the strength of the involvement with drugs is perhaps the most impressive. Clinicians never stop being amazed by the work that addicts will perform, the creative deceptions that they will use, and the violations of moral codes that occur in their efforts to obtain drugs. Any clinician with experience in treating addicts has hundreds of stories to illustrate this point.

One such story is that of a physician who worked 9- to 10-hour days but then added even more time to this long schedule by performing minor surgical procedures that required narcotic analgesia in the evening, after the hospital staff had left. This was done so that he could divert narcotics with little risk of being observed. After seeking treatment and while being maintained on naltrexone (a narcotic antagonist that prevents one from feeling narcotic effects or developing physiological dependence), he confessed to attempting to deactivate the naltrexone by placing the tablets in a microwave oven, a procedure that he claimed was partially successful.

Another more common example is that of addicts who steal personal items from family members to sell for drugs. Upon applying for treatment, these patients not uncommonly describe this behavior with a genuine sense of guilt over doing something that is totally against their basic feelings and values but that reflects how badly they needed opiates.

Treatment as a Means to Reduce or Manage the Strength and Persistence of Drug-Seeking Behavior

Much of what goes on in addiction treatment can be interpreted as an attempt to suppress or redirect drug seeking behavior. One example is the therapeutic community. This type of program usually has a phenomenal amount of structure and support aimed at discouraging a wide range of behaviors that are associated with drug use. Another example is relapse prevention training. Here, the dependent person is taught to identify situations that stimulate the urge to use drugs and is encouraged to avoid those situations or to develop alternative behaviors when exposed to them (Childress, McLellan, Ehrman, & O'Brien, 1988). A third example is drug counseling. This is provided by most treatment programs. Counseling provides encouragement and support to become abstinent by directly confronting drug use and by encouraging people to become involved in drug free and socially productive activities.

In a different yet related manner, treatment with high doses of methadone almost always suppresses heroin use. This probably occurs in several ways. First, methadone reduces or eliminates narcotic withdrawal symptoms for 24–36 hours if taken in sufficient doses. Second, when taken in high doses, methadone produces tolerance to the effects of narcotics. This means that people on high doses of methadone usually have difficulty experiencing euphoria from heroin unless it is also taken in very high doses, a situation that rarely occurs. Addicts who inject heroin while on high doses of methadone usually experience few narcotic effects, and as a result they discontinue or markedly reduce heroin consumption. This tolerance to narcotic effects produced by high doses of methadone is known as *narcotic blockade.*

The success of methadone in reducing heroin use points to the potential importance of biological therapies for drug dependence. Almost all drugs that produce dependence also cause either tolerance or both tolerance and physiological dependence when used repetitively and in high doses (Jaffe & Martin, 1985). The best examples of drugs that produce tolerance and dependence are opiates, sedatives, and alcohol. There has been a question about the ability of stimulants such as cocaine to produce physiological dependence, but few disagree that tolerance to its subjective effects results when used repetitively and in high doses (Gawin & Ellinwood, 1989; Gawin & Kleber, 1988).

Recent studies have indicated that dependence on alcohol and opiates is associated with alterations in the hypothalamic–pituitary–adrenal axis even long after abstinence has been maintained (Adinoff et al., 1990). Although not proof that addiction is a biological disorder, these studies support the idea that biological alterations may be important contributors to the strong and persistent drug-seeking behavior that characterizes dependence (Wise, 1988). Furthermore, these studies are consistent with Dole's theory, which views opiate addiction as a self-induced metabolic disease. In Dole's view, methadone reduces opiate use by "normalizing" physiological alterations that have been caused by long-term heroin self-administration (Dole, Nyswander, & Kreek, 1966).

Clinical Vignettes

Cited below are seven brief clinical vignettes that illustrate how multiple paths can lead from initial drug use to dependence. Each vignette is preceded by a brief summary of its main clinical features.

Vignette 1

No psychiatric symptoms; no family history of drug or alcohol problems; alcohol dependence during teens; used heroin, liked how he felt, and wanted to get high more often; good work history.

A 44-year-old man with no family history of alcoholism or drug abuse. He began drinking at age 14 and met criteria for alcoholism by 18–19. He stopped alcoholic drinking while in the service, and shortly after discharge he injected heroin when it was offered by a friend. He denies having psychiatric problems at the time, although he has experienced three episodes of major depressive disorder since age 28. He liked the way heroin made him feel, and continued to inject it once or twice a week for about 10 years.

He increased his intake to daily use during his early 30s because he wanted to experience the good feeling more often. He realized he was addicted when his "whole body felt bad" after he did not take heroin for 1–2 days. He continued with his addiction, and now took heroin to feel "normal," as well as to feel "high." During this time he worked regularly as a steelworker. He first sought treatment only two weeks ago because he remained depressed after the death of his wife and because he has become increasingly concerned about his addiction since needing a partial amputation of two fingers after damaging them by attempting to inject drugs into their small veins.

Vignette 2

Late onset of abuse and addiction; no family history of drug or alcohol problems; no psychiatric, drug, or alcohol problems, but was having arguments with wife; liked the way cocaine made him feel.

A 68-year-old man, married for 46 years, works for the post office. Normal record of military service. No drug history; drinks one fifth of gin a month; never drunk and no blackouts.

First crack use was one and a half years ago. Had been having arguments with his wife. She had been accusing him of spending too much time away from home and using drugs. He denies this, says he was playing cards with friends.

One day after work, young women (19–20 years of age) offered him sex in return for money to purchase crack. He tried crack, enjoyed it and would use $20 a weekend approximately once every two months. Two weeks ago he used $200 in one night, felt dizzy and out of control, and wanted help.

Vignette 3

Cocaine dependence with onset at age 40; psychiatric problems.

A 42-year-old man, separated for 14 years, with a good work history. Grandfather was alcoholic, but no other family problems with drugs or alcohol. Normal childhood with good parental relationships.

Social use of alcohol. Although doing well economically, felt depressed and isolated and claims to have always been an angry person. Easily agitated, frustrated, and impatient.

Snorted cocaine in 1984 and used it 1 to 2 times a month for 4 months. Says it did not cause a "high" but made him feel numb, passive, and more compassionate. In 1986, his schizophrenic brother killed himself, and shortly afterward he found his girlfriend in bed with another man. At the same time, he was having problems at work. Smoked crack after being offered it by a friend who said it would make him feel better.

Used cocaine once a week, increasing to daily use over one year, at which time he felt he had lost control. Says that he became addicted because the quick high from smoking crack was so good and that changing the route of administration really made a difference.

Vignette 4

Cocaine dependence; no family history of alcohol or drug problems; arguments with wife associated with anxiety and depression; had used alcohol and marijuana to self-medicate but found that cocaine worked better.

A 35-year-old man, currently separated. History of using alcohol and marijuana to relieve dysphoria. At age 28 was offered cocaine when depressed. Snorted 3 to 4 lines and had a "totally relaxed feeling, separated from any problems that I had ... felt macho, like a stud, like I could take on a whole roomful of women at one time."

The next time there was an argument with his wife, he went straight to cocaine; began using 4 to 6 "lines" on weekends. He continued sporadic use until leaving the service at age 29. He had increasing arguments with his wife, had access to more money, and increased the cocaine use. Cocaine made him feel good all the time, and he did not want to argue when under its influence.

Vignette 5

Negative family history for alcohol and drug problems; hyperactive as a child; multiple drug abuse as an adolescent; addicted to narcotics and benzodiazepines to counteract paranoia and anxiety caused by hallucinogens.

A 37-year-old single man who was hyperactive while in grade school. Used alcohol to intoxication about once a week beginning at age 14. Sporadic use of LSD, mescaline, amphetamines, and marijuana beginning at age 18. Marijuana slowed him down and made him feel in control. Occasional use of intravenous heroin at age 20.

While in the service, he found that LSD, marijuana, mescaline, and amphetamines produced paranoia and panic/anxiety. He drank alcohol and used heroin to calm down. When not using heroin, the paranoia and panic became worse, and while he was on heroin these feelings disappeared. He increased heroin use to daily and became addicted. Began work at the Navy yard when age 26, earned more money, and heroin use increased. When addicted for 3–6 months, he found that the antianxiety effect of heroin diminished and he began using Valium (up to 100 mg a day) and Xanax (4 to 5 mg a day).

Vignette 6

Antisocial personality disorder; addicted to intravenous amphetamines and narcotics; developed regular and problematic use immediately after drug exposure.

A 32-year-old man with all of the childhood behaviors typical of antisocial personality disorder. Used many drugs, including Dexedrine tablets and "snorting" methamphetamine. At age 14, he used amphetamine intravenously and became "hooked," using it every day almost immediately after first use. Increased intake of alcohol when his girlfriend became pregnant at about the same time.

At about age 15, he used intravenous heroin and "fell in love" with it, immediately using it daily. He continued to use mainly heroin, but also many other drugs, including amphetamines and benzodiazepines. He has had several mostly unsuccessful trials on methadone. Currently recovering from injuries he sustained when struck by a bus while high on Xanax and Valium.

He is well known to all clinic staff and has been "high" on the premises so many times that he has been banned from the methadone program. We are hoping he will accept treatment in a therapeutic community, but he has not done so as of this writing. He says that he has an "addictive personality" and that if he were offered a box of chocolates, he would eat the whole thing even though he knew it would make him sick. States that he always has to have an abundance of everything.

Vignette 7

Mother alcoholic, father drug dependent; probable antisocial personality disorder; used many drugs including intravenous heroin, but did not like them, except intravenous amphetamine, which felt terrific; increased use at time of stress and became addicted to amphetamines and cocaine.

A 37-year-old man who grew up in an alcoholic and drug-dependent family in a disadvantaged area. Was defiant as a child and participated in street gangs and racial riots during the 1960s.

Tried alcohol, barbiturates, Darvon, marijuana, heroin, and LSD, but was not attracted to any of these drugs. Tried intravenous amphetamine and had a "fantastic rush"; thought everything was positive, felt strong with increased energy. No drug had ever made him feel this way. He began using only on weekends, but increased to daily use when he felt depressed and bogged down with the responsibility of raising three children after he married. Began selling heroin and became addicted to that as well. Switched his addiction to cocaine when it became available.

Factors That Contribute to the Development of Addiction

These cases illustrate several factors that are regularly associated with drug use among addicts. It is important to keep in mind that the reasons people cite for initially using drugs often differ from those they give for continuing to use after addiction develops (Fialkon, 1985). This observation implies that something changes within an individual during the course of drug use among those who become addicted. It also implies that different prevention strategies may be needed, not only according to individual factors such as social group, psychopathology, and so on, but also according to where the individual is along the path from use to dependence. These clinical vignettes illustrate reasons for initial as well as current use. Some of the common factors that are associated with drug use, both initially and regularly, as demonstrated by these vignettes, are as follows.

Seeking Euphoria

All addicting drugs share the ability to produce feelings that are described as a "high" or "euphoria" (Wise, 1988). Drugs of abuse and addiction differ in the degree to which they produce these effects, and this difference is an important factor in determining abuse liability (Zuckerman, 1987). Addicts relate primarily to the euphoric properties of the drug, and in this way they differ markedly from the person who takes an addicting drug in an appropriate way for a legitimate medical condition. For example, people with chronic pain who need long-term narcotics become physically dependent, but they usually do not become addicts. They may comment that the drug made them "high," but they do not seek out this aspect of the drug. They take it as recommended, gradually discontinue it if the pain disappears, and do not develop drug-seeking behavior unless the pain recurs.

Each of the vignettes above points to euphoria (feeling "high") as playing a strong role in the development and maintenance of dependence, especially Vignettes 1, 2, 6, and 7. The vignettes also demonstrate how euphoria can operate alone or can be combined with other factors. For example, euphoria seems to have been the primary motivator for initial and continuing drug use in Vignettes 1, 2, and 6, but it was combined with a reduction of psychiatric symptoms in other cases.

This way of seeking out the euphoric properties of drugs is a common bond shared by almost all addicts, and it is very impressive to clinicians. Addicts congregate to get "high," they talk about getting high, they experiment with drug combinations in attempts to get high in new ways, they talk about their early experiences with drugs and how the first high was often the best, they talk about how the dope is "great" or "garbage," and they fondly reminisce about times when they were high.

However, the wish to get high is not limited to addicts; it is seen commonly in individuals who self-administer controlled substances. The feature that distinguishes people who become dependent from those who do not is the persistence and intensity of the drug consumption. It is as if the addicts develop, very rapidly in some cases, a very strong internal "force" that pushes them to repeat the drug experience. Use or abuse of drugs does not necessarily imply that this "force" that is associated with addiction is present, nor that it will develop.

Inherent Biological Vulnerability

Most future addicts use drugs intermittently over an extended period of time before they become addicted, but some claim to have felt "addicted" after only one or a few exposures. This usually seems to occur when the individual uses drugs with a high abuse liability, such as amphetamines, cocaine, or narcotics, and uses them in a way that provides a rapid onset of drug effects. Examples are the injection of heroin or the inhalation of cocaine via "free-base" or "crack." The phenomenon of rapid addiction suggests that some people are especially vulnerable, perhaps because of their biology. Among these people, it is as if the biological substrate associated with addiction is present even before the drug is used. A predisposition to addiction has been shown in family studies of alcoholism, where it appears that there are genetic factors that contribute to the development of alcohol dependence (Buydens-Branchey, Branchey, & Noumain, 1989).

Vignette 6 probably demonstrates this predisposition best, but it is also seen in Vignette 7. Patient 6 became intensely involved with both amphetamines and opiates very shortly after taking these drugs intravenously. He is well known to the clinic staff, all of whom have been impressed with the degree to which he "loves to get high" and continues to use drugs in spite of very adverse consequences. He also has antisocial personality disorder, which may be related to his rapid development of dependence. Patient 7 seems to have had the same immediate response to amphetamines, but not to other controlled substances. It is as if this person was predisposed to become addicted to a drug of only one class, but not to others.

Cases such as Vignettes 6 and 7 may be important to study in depth. These individuals may have biological vulnerabilities or other characteristics that are similar to those that develop in others only after prolonged self-administration of an abusable substance (Irwin, Schuckit, & Smith, 1990). A better understanding of the factors that predispose such individuals to develop dependence may provide new information about the changes that occur in those who are not predisposed and who become dependent only after extended periods of drug use (McCord, 1988; Vaillant, 1986).

Reducing Negative Affects and Psychiatric Symptoms

This is another common reason given for drug use in many circumstances. It is given as a reason for initial use, for repetitive use, for use during treatment, and as a cause for relapse. Most drugs of abuse also have psychotropic effects that are perceived as desirable but that are separate from their ability to produce euphoria. An example is the reduction of anxiety by sedatives, alcohol, and narcotics. Another example is mood elevation produced by stimulants (Pittel & Hofer, 1972). These positive psychotropic effects can make specific classes of drugs especially appealing to individuals who are suffering from psychiatric symptoms that are relieved, even if only temporarily, by certain types of addictive drugs (Khantzian, 1985).

This interface between psychiatric symptoms and drug dependence is very complicated. Some drugs of abuse cause psychiatric symptoms, some psychiatric symptoms predate involvement with drugs, some symptoms occur in the course of dependence and are related to social and psychological problems that are a consequence of the dependence, other problems occur during dependence and have nothing to do with the drug problem, and still others are produced by long-term drug use (the so-called "residual" or "persistent" drug effects).

Self medication of psychiatric symptoms as a significant contributor to drug use and eventual dependence is best seen in Vignettes 2, 3, 4, and 7. In each case, psychiatric symptoms were reduced by the drug of abuse, and this symptom reduction led to repetitive use and eventual dependence. Patients commonly identify the time at which their addiction developed, or a relapse after an extended drug-free period, with a situation in which they felt distressed and turned to regular drug use for relief. Reduction in psychiatric symptoms is probably one of the most common reasons given by patients for relapse after achieving abstinence.

Vignette 5 demonstrates an unusual and complex association between psychopathology and dependence. Here, the dependence resulted when the patient continued to consume narcotics and benzodiazepines after learning that these drugs relieved the anxiety and paranoia that developed after ingestion of hallucinogens. In this case, the drugs of dependence were taken to counteract adverse effects of other abusable drugs on which the patient had never become dependent.

The association between psychopathology and addiction has received considerable attention because it has treatment implications (Kadden, Getter, Cooney, & Litt, 1989; Woody et al., 1984). Patients with high levels of psychopathology are very difficult to treat and generally have a poorer prognosis than do those with few psychiatric symptoms (McLellan, Luborsky, Woody, Druley, & O'Brien, 1983). Such patients usually have a range of problems, including more severe drug use. If psychiatric symptoms are caused by the drug use itself, abstinence treatment alone will usually work. If symptoms are less closely drug-related, then a focused psychiatric treatment may be needed. If psychiatric symptoms can be reduced by a standard treatment, then the addiction may be controlled more easily.

Frequency and Intensity of Use

The development of addiction is usually associated with a period during which the intensity and frequency of drug use increase (Gawin & Ellinwood, 1989; Gawin & Kleber, 1988). This often occurs when the method of self-administration becomes more efficient. The best example is the explosion of cocaine abuse and addiction when "free-base" and "crack" became available. Prior to that time, when cocaine was taken by the much less efficient method of insufflating the powder through the nose ("snorting," "doing lines"), fewer patients presented for cocaine treatment. Perhaps the best example of this phenomenon has been observed in the Bahamas, which experienced a hundredfold increase in emergency-room visits for cocaine treatment after free-base and crack were introduced (Jekel et al., 1986). This is seen in Vignette 2, where the switch from intranasal cocaine to crack appears to have contributed significantly to the dependence.

A second way that contributes to an increase in the intensity and frequency of use is when the supply of drugs suddenly becomes more available. This occurs when large amounts of drugs become available for purchase, such as was seen when cocaine importation increased. It can also occur when the individual becomes able to purchase more drugs, such as happens after receiving a large sum of money from a lawsuit or an inheritance.

Poor Coping Skills

Vignettes 2, 3, 4, and 7 all demonstrate poor coping skills associated with psychopathology and dependence. If these patients had found a nonpharmacological means to cope with their psychiatric symptoms, they may not have become dependent. This area has significant implications for prevention because it implies that the chances for developing dependence may be reduced by strategies that improve coping skills among a vulnerable population.

Overwhelming Trauma

Vignette 3 demonstrates extreme trauma producing psychiatric symptoms that contribute to dependence. This case is similar to that of some military veterans who became dependent on opiates after experiencing psychiatric symptoms associated with overwhelming trauma. Such cases may be fairly common among poor inner-city neighborhoods, where people are exposed to violence and many forms of social disruption, including persistent feelings of hopelessness and helplessness.

Discussion

The preceding vignettes provide some examples of the variety and complexity of the paths that can lead to drug dependence. It is very important to keep these multiple paths in mind when thinking about prevention strategies. A strategy that works for one group may be ineffective with another. The end result is the same, but the paths can vary tremendously. The vignettes also show that dependence can develop well beyond adolescence and can occur in people with a good work history and a record of productive achievement (Giordano & Beckman, 1985; Scaturo, 1987).

Whatever the contributing factors, the clinician must deal with the addiction itself, which in many ways resembles a drive state (Bejerot, 1972). This sequence of self-induced exposure followed by addiction has been described by Bejerot (1987) as follows:

> It is characteristic of both drug addiction and analogous drug-free conditions that they are very little affected by rational thought. It is as difficult to talk an alcoholic into abstinence as to get a love-sick person to give up an unsuitable partner.
>
> Drug dependence may therefore be described clinically as a deep, chronic love relationship to the pleasant effects of the drug. More theoretically it could be said that drug addiction is a dependence acquired through unconscious conditioning, where the craving for the drug effects has taken on the character and strength of natural drives. It is plausible to assume that in regard to neurophysiology the condition goes back to some extent to the same key structures as sexuality and may be considered as equivalent to this. (p. 178)

This description emphasizes the possible biological contributors to addiction, and it omits the psychosocial components, which are clearly described in the preceding vignettes. The possibility that long-lasting biological alterations are produced by repeated drug self-administration and then become significant contributors to addiction underscores the importance of developing effective prevention techniques.

In an effort to further characterize the variety of risks for the development of substance use disorders, we interviewed the personnel of our methadone maintenance program for their opinions on the main factors that lead from drug use to dependence. The following list summarizes the answers of these experienced treatment providers:

1. Regularity of use.
2. Increased availability through a cheaper form of a drug (i.e., crack) or through "dealing" a drug.
3. Increased euphoria of a drug through changing the route of its administration into the body (i.e., switching from snorting cocaine to intravenous use).
4. Emotional trauma or abuse.
5. Negative feeling states (i.e., depression).
6. Poor coping skills.
7. Anhedonia.
8. Broken families.
9. Genetic predisposition; biological vulnerability.
10. Escape from social pressures.
11. Inadequate level of having been loved while growing up.

This list could also be used to characterize the factors that contribute to relapse. Similarly, the total number of salient risks for an individual could potentially serve as a measure of relapse risk, after treatment has ended. Assessment of these risks could also prove useful in developing relapse prevention treatments. For example, someone with poor coping skills and psychiatric symptoms could be given psychotherapy plus coping skills therapy. Someone who is relatively normal but involved with a group of people who enjoy getting "high" might be moved by a social intervention that effectively places negative values on this behavior throughout the group.

Many patients who have relapsed after long periods of sobriety have said that during a relapse, after that first use, they feel like they had never quit (even after 20 years of sobriety). They feel like a switch was "clicked right back on" with that initial reuse of the drug, and therefore the initial reuse usually ends with an extended binge. Clinically, we see this irreversible change expressed in the Alcoholics Anonymous philosophy of "once an addict, always an addict." Thus, despite prolonged abstinence and treatment, most people who have been dependent can never return to social use without relapsing.

For a few of the patients described in the vignettes, the first use was the most vulnerable point in the entire transition from use to dependence. For these individuals, any strategy that inhibits drug experimentation becomes an extremely worthy undertaking. For the other, larger group, which is not so predisposed and which becomes addicted only after prolonged use and often in association with psychiatric symptoms, or with trauma or social pressure, many prevention strategies can be applied even after drug use has occurred. Interventions include better coping skills, developing attitudes that value abstinence and health rather than drug use and getting "high," improving the quality of life by social projects and employment opportunities, and providing effective psychiatric and medical treatment.

Although the case histories described here can provide guidelines for developing prevention strategies, the processes that differentiate those who use drugs and become addicted from those who do not are poorly understood. Perhaps we can better understand why individuals make the transition from use to dependence through prevention studies that are carefully designed and evaluated. Because the pathways to addiction are so diverse, a wide range of strategies will probably need to be tested, and each should be tailored to cultural and individual factors.

References

Adinoff, B., Martin, P. R., Bone, G. H., Eckardt, M. J., Roehrich, L., George, D. T., Moss, H. B., Eskay, R., Linnoila, M., & Gold, P. W. (1990). Hypothalmic–pituitary–adrenal axis functioning and cerebrospinal fluid corticotropin releasing hormone and corticotropin levels in alcoholics after recent and long-term abstinence. *Archives of General Psychiatry, 47,* 325–330.

American Psychiatric Association. (1987). *Diagnostic and statistical manual of mental disorders* (3rd ed., rev.). Washington, DC: Author.

Bejerot, N. (1972). A theory of addiction as an artificially induced drive. *American Journal of Psychiatry, 128,* 842–846.

Bejerot, N. (1987). Addiction: Clinical and theoretical considerations. In J. Engel & L. Oreland (Eds.), *Brain reward systems and abuse* (pp. 177–180). New York: Raven Press.

Buydens-Branchey, L., Branchey, M., & Noumain, D. (1989). Age of alcoholism onset. *Archives of General Psychiatry, 46,* 225–230.

Childress, A. R., McLellan, A. T., Ehrman, R., & O'Brien, C. P. (1988). Classically conditioned responses in opiod and cocaine dependence: A role in relapse? In B. A. Ray (Ed.), *Learning factors in substance abuse* (NIDA Research Monograph No. 84, pp. 25–43). Washington, DC: Department of Health and Human Services.

Dole, V. P., Nyswander, M., & Kreek, M. J. (1966). Narcotic blockade. *Archives of Internal Medicine, 118,* 304–309.

Fialkon, M. J. (1985). Biologic and psychosocial determinants in the etiology of alcoholism. In R. E. Tarter & D. H. VanThiel (Eds.), *Alcohol and the brain: Chronic effects* (pp. 245–263). New York: Plenum Medical.

Gawin, F. H., & Ellinwood, E. H. (1989). Cocaine dependence. *Annual Review of Medicine, 40,* 149–161.

Gawin, F. H., & Kleber, H. D. (1988). Evolving conceptualizations of cocaine dependence. *Yale Journal of Biology and Medicine, 61,* 123–136.

Giordano, J. A., & Beckman, K. (1985). Alcohol use and abuse in old age: An examination of Type II alcoholism. *Journal of Gerontological Social Work, 9,* 65–83.

Irwin, M., Schuckit, M., & Smith, T. L. (1990). Clinical importance of age at onset in Type 1 and Type 2 primary alcoholics. *Archives of General Psychiatry, 47,* 320–324.

Jaffe, J. H., & Martin, W. R. (1985). Opioid analgesics and antagonists. In A. G. Gilman, L. S. Goodman, T. W. Rall, & F. Murad (Eds.), *The pharmacological basis of therapeutics* (pp. 491–531). New York: Macmillan.

Jekel, J. F., Podlewski, H., Patterson, S. D., Allen, D. F., Clarke, N., & Cartwright, P. (1986). Epidemic free-base cocaine abuse. *Lancet, 1,* 459–462.

Kadden, R. M., Getter, H., Cooney, N. L., & Litt, M. D. (1989). Matching alcoholics to coping skills or interactional therapies: Posttreatment results. *Journal of Consulting and Clinical Psychology, 57,* 698–704.

Khantzian, E. J. (1985). The self-medication hypothesis of addictive disorders: Focus on heroin and cocaine dependence. *American Journal of Psychiatry, 142,* 1259–1264.

McCord, J. (1988). Identifying developmental paradigms leading to alcoholism. *Journal of Studies on Alcohol, 49,* 357–362.

McLellan, A. T., Luborsky, L., Woody, G. E., Druley, K., & O'Brien, C. P. (1983). Predicting response to alcohol and drug abuse treatments: Role of psychiatric severity. *Archives of General Psychiatry, 40,* 620–625.

Minkoff, K. (1989). An integrated treatment model for dual diagnosis of psychosis and addiction. *Hospital and Community Psychiatry, 40,* 1031–1036.

Pittel, S., & Hofer, R. (1972). The transition to amphetamine abuse. In *Current concepts on amphetamine abuse* (pp. 169–176). Rockville, MD: National Institute of Mental Health.

Scaturo, D. J. (1987). Toward an adult developmental conceptualization of alcohol abuse: A review of the literature. *British Journal of Addiction, 82,* 857–870.

Vaillant, G. (1986). Cultural factors in the etiology of alcoholism: A prospective study. *Annals of the New York Academy of Sciences, 472,* 142–148.

Wesson, D. R., & Smith, D. E. (1985). Cocaine treatment perspectives. In N. J. Kozel & E. H. Adams (Eds.), *Cocaine use in America: Epidemiologic and clinical perspectives* (NIDA Research Monograph No. 61, pp. 193–203). Washington, DC: U.S. Government Printing Office.

Wise, R. A. (1988). The neurobiology of craving: Implications for the understanding and treatment of addiction. *Journal of Abnormal Psychology, 97,* 118–132.

Woody, G. E., McLellan, A. T., Luborsky, L., O'Brien, C. P., Blaine, J., Fox, S., Herman, I., & Beck, A. T. (1984). Psychiatric severity as a predictor of benefits from psychotherapy: The Penn–VA Study. *American Journal of Psychiatry, 141*, 1172–1177.

Zuckerman, M. (1987). Biological connection between sensation seeking and drug abuse. In J. Engel & L. Oreland (Eds.), *Brain reward systems and abuse* (pp. 165–176). New York: Raven Press.

Name Index

Subject Index